# AMERICAN POLITICAL BEHAVIOR

**REVISED EDITION**

**Howard D. Mehlinger**
**John J. Patrick**

**GINN AND COMPANY** A Xerox Education Company

# About the Authors

HOWARD D. MEHLINGER is a Professor of History and Education and Director of the Social Studies Development Center at Indiana University. He holds both M.S. in Ed. and Ph.D. degrees from the University of Kansas. He has eleven years of experience as a world history and American government teacher in Kansas and Pennsylvania high schools. In addition to numerous articles on teaching social studies, he is the co-author of a book on the 1905 Russian Revolution and a book on social studies instruction. He is a member of many professional associations, including the American Political Science Association and a member of the APSA Committee on Pre-Collegiate Education. In 1975 he was Vice-President of the National Council for the Social Studies. In 1976 he was President-Elect of the Council, and in 1977 he became President of NCSS.

JOHN J. PATRICK is Associate Professor of Education and Co-Director of the High School Political Science Curriculum Project at Indiana University. He received his Bachelor of Arts from Dartmouth College and the Master and Doctoral degrees from Indiana University. He taught history and civics in two Chicago-area high schools for seven years. He is the author or co-author of the following books: *Political Socialization of American Youth*, a research bulletin of the National Council for the Social Studies; *The Young Voter; The Progress of the Afro-American;* and *Toward Effective Instruction in Secondary Social Studies.* In addition, he has written more than twenty published articles about instruction and curriculum development in the social studies. He is a member of several professional associations, including the National Council for the Social Studies, the American Political Science Association, and the Social Science Education Consortium.

GINN AND COMPANY
Home Office: Lexington, Massachusetts 02173
0-663-33717-8

# Contents

# Preface
# to Teachers

Knowledge of politics is an essential ingredient of an adequate education. Through the study of politics important lessons can be learned about the management of conflict, the resolution of issues, the distribution of rewards and punishments, the mechanisms of social change, and the maintenance of order.

Knowledge of politics can contribute to the attainment of individual or group goals. Those who understand the political behavior of their society possess a foundation from which to devise fruitful political strategies. For example, understanding the conduct of elections, the activities of political parties, and the factors which influence voter choices can contribute to wiser and more rewarding voter behavior. Comprehension of the ways that public officials make decisions can contribute to the development of effective techniques for influencing the conduct of government.

A major purpose of this book is to increase political knowledge and sophistication. During the past thirty years social scientists have greatly expanded our knowledge of political affairs. This book is an attempt to present to high school students up-to-date findings of social scientists about political behavior. In line with this purpose, this edition of our book has been revised extensively to include current case studies and new knowledge of patterns of political behavior.

The process of acquiring knowledge of politics ought to be lively and exciting, since the subject is concerned essentially with public controversy, social problems, the articulation of human needs, and the decisions of authorities about who gets what, when, and how. In this book we have tried to capture the vitality and drama of politics through the use of cases which describe the political activities of typical citizens and political leaders. These cases are brief stories about various aspects of political behavior such as voting, demonstrating, bargaining, decision-making, and the like. Simulations, games, political attitude surveys, and data-processing activities are other instructional activities designed to enliven the course.

As a safeguard against biased presentation of information and propaganda, students of political behavior must learn skills of critical thinking and social scientific inquiry. One characteristic of the well-educated person is the ability to make sound judgments about the worth of ideas. Thus, we have tried to design lessons aimed at teaching the skills of using evidence and logic to substantiate factual claims and to consider value claims rationally.

We hope that vastly increased ability to extract meaning from politically relevant experiences and to cope with political demands and challenges is an outcome of studying this book. Certainly this hope is consistent with the traditional American ideal that an informed and politically efficacious citizenry is an essential condition of democracy.

*Howard D. Mehlinger*
*John J. Patrick*

# Acknowledgments

American Political Behavior is a product of the Social Studies Development Center at Indiana University. Development of the initial product, which began in 1966, was supported by a grant from the U.S. Office of Education in the Department of Health, Education and Welfare. From 1966-1972, the authors directed the development of American Political Behavior, which involved extensive field trials and revisions of the product prior to publication.

Since the publication of American Political Behavior in 1972, the authors have continued systematically to gather evidence about the strengths and weaknesses of this course. They have solicited critical responses about the course from high school teachers, students, political scientists, and social studies educators. From this evidence, the authors have revised this edition of the course extensively.

Since 1966, a great many people have contributed to the development of this program. In the space available it is possible to acknowledge only a small portion of those who have helped.

At Indiana University Professor Shirley Engle launched the project and chaired an Advisory Committee. Its other members were Professors Frederick Smith, Alfred Diament, and William Siffin.

Mrs. Judy Gillespie, a colleague in the Development Center, developed the simulations and games. Help in writing various chapters came from Professor Lee Anderson of Northwestern University, Mr. Robert Hanvey, and Professor Fred Coombs of the University of Illinois.

Professor Leroy Rieselbach, Indiana University, helped throughout the development of the course and wrote a paper about political behavior for teachers. Professor Harold Barger, Trinity University, and Professor F. Chris Garcia, University of New Mexico, offered many helpful suggestions for the revision. Professor Gerald Marker at Indiana University provided valued counsel and assistance with the original project, especially in dissemination activities.

Approximately 100 teachers used this course at one time or another during its experimental trials. Their role was invaluable in the initial development and the evaluation of the course. Since the program's publication in 1972 we received many tips from teachers by letter, personal conversation, and a survey of users. Many of their ideas have been incorporated. The authors are deeply indebted to each of them.

We are also grateful to many graduate student assistants who have helped us, especially Mr. Russell Cassity, Mr. Edward Poole, Mr. James Lewellen, Mr. Michael Cabat, and Mr. Eugene Michaels who aided us in the initial development of the course. Mrs. Beate Kukainis, Assistant Professor of Political Science at Texas A&M University, was particularly important in gathering information for Unit Five of this second edition. Mr. Richard Kraft, an APB teacher in Hacienda Heights, California, made a number of contributions that appear in the revised teacher's guide and worksheets. We also wish to acknowledge the able support of Mrs. Eve Russell and Mrs. Jean Brown.

Finally, the authors wish to thank publishers and copyright holders for permission to reproduce copyrighted material. Specific acknowledgments appear throughout the text.

# UNIT ONE

# Introduction to the Study of Political Behavior

# 1 What Is Political Behavior?

Political behavior occurs among all human groups. People can't do without it.

Learning more about political behavior is a main objective of this course. The first step is to think about these two questions:

**1.** What is political behavior?
**2.** Why do people behave politically?

## Two Cases of Political Behavior

The following two cases can help you begin to answer the two questions. The cases show different kinds of political behavior and give some clues about why people behave politically.

**Case 1. What Is a Park Worth?**

Herbert Henson rose slowly from his chair and looked around the council chamber nervously. The room was crowded with angry people. Some supported him, but he knew that many were against his ideas. Still, he felt strongly that he must try once again to influence the Lakeville City Council. Henson said:

> Citizens of Lakeville, members of the city council, Mayor Harding, I beg you to follow my advice and build a new park in West Side. The young people of this area have no place to play. The neighborhood is run-down. Our children deserve something more from the city than they have been receiving. Others in this city get what they want. Why are we always left out? We may be poor, but we're part of this city too.

Henson sat down amid shouts and handclaps. The head of the council gaveled the meeting back to order. He then pointed to a tall, well-dressed man. "Mr. Randolph, you have the floor." Robert Randolph spoke:

> I agree that a park is needed in West Side. But this project can wait until another year. What we need right now is an overpass between the Sunnyside neighborhood and the Kennedy Elementary School. Let me remind you that the children of Sunnyside must cross Highway 62 to get to school. It's a very busy highway. And Amy Wright would be alive today if we had had an overpass across this busy street. How many more children must die before we build an overpass?

The room was quiet as Randolph sat down. Others spoke in favor of the proposed overpass and the park.

The head of the city council thanked the citizens for their ideas and reminded them that the city budget would not allow both an overpass and a park this year. Henson and his friends left.

"I know which project will be postponed," said Henson. "First of all, the city council will take care of those rich people in Sunnyside. Some big-shot lawyer like Robert Randolph speaks, and the city council listens. When a poor man like me speaks, no one cares."

"Yeah," said José Arroyo, a leader of the Mexican Americans in West Side. "It makes a difference who you are in this town. Those people in Sunnyside always get more from the government than we do. Their streets are smooth. Their garbage is always picked up on time. If the police pick up one of their kids, they get him off quietly."

"It's different in old West Side," said Louise Hunter. "Sometimes two weeks go by before they pick up the garbage. The streets are full of holes. And the cops are always around busting our kids' heads."

**City Council Votes for Overpass.** At their next meeting the city council voted funds to build an overpass across Highway 62 to connect the Sunnyside neighborhood with the Kennedy Elementary School. The council also passed a resolution pledging to start a park project as soon as funds would permit.

Henson, Arroyo, Hunter, and their followers were angered. They phoned council members, the mayor, and other public officials to complain. They threatened to withdraw all political support from the mayor if he approved the council's decisions. They reminded the mayor that votes from West Side gave him victory in the last election.

Mayor Harding did not want to offend the West Side voters. But he also felt that the overpass had to be built. He decided to seek a compromise, to reach a settlement that would satisfy both sides. He called Henson, Hunter, and Arroyo and asked them to come to his office. He also asked the head of the city council to be there.

**The Mayor's Compromise.** At this meeting the mayor suggested that land for the West Side park be bought at once. Funds were on hand for this, but not for park development. He said that the park work could begin next year. He pledged that he would see the park project completed before his term in office was over. The head of the city council agreed to support this plan. Henson, Hunter, and Arroyo, though not fully satisfied, felt that the mayor really cared about their park project and would complete it. They promised to continue supporting the mayor.

At their next meeting the city council set aside funds to buy park land. The mayor pledged to see this project completed within the next two years.

West Side people were pleased because finally they could count on having a public park in their community. The Sunnyside residents were satisfied that an overpass would be built to protect their children. And the mayor was pleased to keep the political support he needed to stay in office.

**1.** What does this case reveal about (a) what political behavior is? (b) why people behave politically?
**2.** Do you like or dislike the outcome of the case? Why?

**Case 2. The Klan Comes to Town**
Robert Swanson, mayor of Bloomingdale, paced the floor of his office nervously. He had to make a quick decision, and he didn't know what to do.

Last week, officers of the Ku Klux Klan in nearby Bedrock had said that they would come to Bloomingdale to march and hand out leaflets about the Klan. There was a public outcry against the march in Bloomingdale. Petitions were handed out against the Klan parade. Over 5000 people had signed one petition that was printed in the *Bloomingdale Evening Star.* It read:

> We, the undersigned, deplore the Ku Klux Klan. It spreads hatred among people. It would deprive blacks and Jews of their rights. Therefore, we believe the Ku Klux Klan should have no right to parade and speak in Bloomingdale. We demand that Mayor Swanson and the city council prevent the Klan from holding a demonstration in our city.

The petition started a fierce debate that was carried on in the newspapers, in meetings of organizations in Bloomingdale, and on the streets. An editorial in the *Bloomingdale Evening Star* said:

> We oppose the Ku Klux Klan and everything it stands for. However, we also support the cause of free speech. And we oppose any effort to deprive any group, no matter how unworthy, of this basic democratic right. If the right of free speech is denied to the Klan today, it may be denied to others tomorrow. Once we

lower the barriers that guard the basic right of free speech, we threaten the very foundation of democratic government.

Thus, even though we are against what the Ku Klux Klan represents, we defend the Klan's right to free speech. We advise Mayor Swanson to permit the Klan to have its public rally.

Letters to the newspaper both supported and opposed the editorial. Some letters had threats of violence.

As talk of violence kept up, the mayor and his advisers became alarmed. People from various groups spoke to the mayor. Most of these men and women asked the mayor to stop the Klan from coming to Bloomingdale. They were afraid of trouble that could lead to property damage and human injury. Some of the city's leaders were opposed to free speech for the Klan on principle. They said that such an undemocratic group should have no right to freedom of speech.

The mayor tended to agree with these arguments. He wanted to avoid trouble. Yet the arguments of the newspaper editorial kept going through his mind: *Once we lower the barriers that guard the basic right of free speech, we threaten the very foundation of democratic government.*

The Bloomingdale Civil Liberties Union supported the newspaper's position. Like the newspaper editors, the Civil Liberties Union members opposed the Klan. But they supported the right of free speech, even for groups like the Klan. They advised the mayor to allow members of the Klan to hold the public rally.

For a week the mayor heard arguments for and against the right of the Klan to demonstrate publicly in Bloomingdale. Civic leaders

5

and ordinary citizens tried to influence him. His decision would have the force of law. What should he do?

**1.** What does this case reveal about (a) what political behavior is? (b) why people behave politically?
**2.** What decision do you think the mayor should make? Why?

## Aspects of Political Behavior

Political behavior is complex. Several kinds of activities of ordinary citizens and public officials can be called political behavior. Political behavior is mixed with other kinds of behavior. Eating a meal is not often political behavior. But going to a Jefferson-Jackson Day banquet, or lunching with the mayor to influence city policy, involves political behavior. It is difficult in some cases, therefore, to distinguish exactly political behavior from other kinds of human behavior.

Since political behavior is complex, it is hard to define exactly. However, main aspects of political behavior can be identified.

### Political Behavior Involves Conflict over Values

A *conflict* is a sharp disagreement or struggle about what ought to be done in some situation. A conflict results when different individuals want a situation to be settled in opposite ways. For example, there is conflict when two or more persons seek election to the same public office, like that of mayor, governor, or President. There is conflict when people argue about how best to use a limited supply of wealth. Perhaps some want to use funds to clear slums and to build houses for poor people. Perhaps others want to use the same money to build roads.

#### Conflicts Arise over Issues and Values

*An issue is a disagreement about what is worth doing and what is not.* The following questions could become issues that divide a group of people, that cause conflict among a group. Should the group accept one religious practice rather than another, or should all religions be tolerated? Should the group start a war to conquer another group of people, or should peace be kept at any cost? What should be the limits of free speech? Should medical care be made available to all

Identify the political issue in each of these headlines.

# March on Broad Street Protests Day-Care Cuts

## E.P.A. Head Opposes a Plan To Share Pesticide Control

## N.A.A.C.P. TO APPEAL ON DETROIT SCHOOLS

# 'Open Ed' questioned at Miff meeting

members of a society regardless of ability to pay? Should public housing be provided for poor people?

Issues generate conflicts about values. *Values are strong beliefs about what is right or wrong, about what is good or bad.* People living together may clash about which goals to value. For example, different people may wish to use the same resources to achieve different goals. Some may believe that available wealth should be spent to improve the armed forces of the country. These people value security from attack more than other goals. Other people may believe that available wealth should be spent to improve the standard of living of poor people. They value opportunity for poor people more than other goals.

### Conflict about Methods

In some cases, the conflict is over the best way to reach a goal. For example, two candidates for governor may both want poor people in their state to have better housing. Both value the goal of helping the poor. But they may clash over the issue of how best to reach this goal. One candidate may believe that the state should enter the business of home building in order to provide poor people with low-cost housing. The other may think that laws should be passed to make it more profitable for private business to build low-cost housing. The two persons disagree about the method of getting more housing.

To show that you understand the meaning of conflict as an aspect of political behavior, refer to the two cases on pages 2–6 and answer these questions.
1. What are the issues in the two cases?
2. What are the value conflicts in the cases?

**IRRESISTIBLE FORCE MEETS. . . . . .IMMOVABLE OBJECT**

What is the issue in conflict here? What are some values held by people (a) who favor strict gun controls and (b) who oppose such controls?

Editorial cartoon by Pat Oliphant. Copyright *Washington Star.*
Reprinted with permission *Los Angeles Times* Syndicate

7

## Political Behavior Involves the Use of Influence

*Influence is ability to control, or direct, the behavior of others.* A mayor can influence many people who work in city government. Candidates for public office try to influence voters. Voters try to influence candidates and public officials to make decisions that will favor the voters in some way.

People use influence to try to gain things that they value. One group of citizens may try to get their state officials to pass laws to raise taxes on tobacco and to prevent smoking in public places. These people *value* restricting smoking as much as possible. In contrast, other people may try to influence their state government *not* to pass laws that penalize smokers. These people *value* the right of persons to decide for themselves (without government interference) when, where, and how often to smoke.

People use many different *political techniques* to try to influence a person or group. They take part in demonstrations, write letters to newspapers, and make phone calls to public officials. They give money, sponsor fund-raising dinners, and go door to door asking for votes for the candidate they favor. Americans use such techniques as negotiation, petition, personal contact, and many other methods to influence the behavior of others.

### Influence Requires Political Resources

The power to influence the behavior of others stems from ability to use political resources. A *political resource* is the means one person has to influence the behavior of another. Examples of political resources are time, money, votes, control over jobs or information, prestige in a group, popularity, intelligence, skill as a negotiator, skill as a leader, and the power of public office.

This listing is not complete. In different situations, different assets become political resources. For example, a wealthy woman who can help to pay for the television appearances of her favorite political candidate may find that one political resource, money, enables her to exert influence if her candidate wins. In another situation the ability to make rousing speeches can be an equally valuable resource.

A group of people with the same goal usually can wield more power than any one person. A petition with 10,000 names calling for a new school is likely to be more influential than calls to the local school board from two or three concerned parents. As a member of a group with a common goal, a person with few resources may be able to combine his or her assets with others to compete successfully against a person with greater political resources. For example, a group of tenants might organize an effective protest to get repairs made to an apartment building, while as individuals their complaints were not taken very seriously.

Through the use of influence, people try to gain valued objectives. For example, a woman wins a seat on the city council. She may feel that she should listen to the opinions of people who helped her. Their resources—such as time, money, knowledge, and skills—may help them to influence her.

**Resources Alone Do Not Spell Influence**

Some persons with many resources have little political influence. They lack *motivation* to use their resources for political purposes. For example, some wealthy people with leadership skills may not care about politics. They may choose to use their wealth and leadership to support the arts.

Some people who might take an interest in politics lack *opportunities* to use political resources in some situations. For example, laws keep noncitizens from voting. Social pressures and tradition have kept many able women from trying to become political leaders. In some parts of America it has been customary to limit the political opportunities of black people and Native Americans (Indians).

1. Find at least one example of political influence in each case on pages 2–6.
2. What techniques are used to try to influence the behavior of others in the cases?
3. What are political resources of these persons or groups?
   a. The editor of the *Bloomingdale Evening Star*
   b. Robert Randolph
   c. Herbert Henson
   d. Mayor Harding
4. How are political resources related to political techniques in the cases?
5. How are resources related to the outcome of Case 1?

Identify political techniques and resources in the illustration.

## Political Decisions May Resolve Conflicts

A *political decision* is a choice about whether to give or withhold things which people value. At times everyone in a group can agree easily about who should get what, when they should get it, and how they should get it. But often people disagree sharply about what they should or should not do. Political decisions may settle these value conflicts.

Legislators, mayors, governors, and the President of the United States are important officials who make decisions daily about who should get what, when, and how. For example, in a recent meeting the city council of Bakerville was faced with the issue of whether or not to allow low-cost, prefabricated homes to be built in the city. Following is an excerpt from the official record of this meeting.

*Chairperson:* This meeting of the city council will now come to order. This evening we will hear testimony on a proposed city ordinance that would revise the housing codes for this city, thereby making possible the construction of low-cost, prefabricated homes. Mr. Wilson will speak for those who wish to change the building codes. Mr. Ward will present arguments for keeping the existing codes.

*Mr. Wilson:* I speak for the American Housing Company. We have built houses in many cities like your own. We provide a chance for low-income families to buy modern homes. A survey of your city reveals that many low-income families cannot afford houses in the city and are forced to find space in run-down apartments. By making the houses in sections in our plant, we are able to build good homes at a big saving to the buyers. We want the city council to pass the new ordinance so that we can build homes the poor can afford.

*Mr. Ward:* I speak for the home builders, bankers, and realtors of this community. We think that factory-made homes aren't needed in this town. There are many houses for sale. Also it is not fair to local builders and workers for the American Housing Company to begin building cheap houses in this town and deprive our skilled workers of their income. Moreover, such homes look cheap; they'll spoil the beauty of the town as they quickly fall apart. For these reasons we're against the proposed ordinance.

During the next three weeks many people in Bakerville tried to influence the decision of the city council about the housing law. After much talk and bargaining, the council passed the ordinance, or law, to allow the low-cost homes. This new law is a decision that settles a conflict.

Political decisions may make winners and losers of people in conflict. The decision of the Bakerville City Council helps some people and hurts others. It is a decision about who gets what, when, and how. The housing company won the chance to make profits, and poor families won the chance to buy low-cost housing. The people represented by Mr. Ward were the losers in this conflict.

**Many Political Decisions Are Compromises**

Bargaining that results in compromise is the way many conflicts are settled. A compromise occurs when each party to a conflict agrees to give up *part* of what is wanted in order to gain *some* of what is wanted. Following is an example of the use of bargaining and compromising to settle a conflict.

The garbage collectors in Bakerville said that they would strike unless they received a $20 per week wage increase. The mayor and city council did not want to increase the wages more than $5 per week. But they also wanted to avoid a strike. Thus, they offered a $12 a week raise. The workers very much wanted a $20 pay raise. But they also did not want to strike, as they would lose money if they stayed away from work in protest. Thus they took the $12 a week pay raise. The conflict was settled through a compromise. The parties reached a bargain that required each party *to give up a little* of what was wanted *in order to get a little.*

Often the alternative to compromise is total victory or total defeat, after a long, costly struggle. To avoid severe struggles or the chance of total defeat, parties to a conflict often decide to settle their differences through compromise.

1. What political decisions were made in the cases on pages 2–6?
2. Who made the decisions in each case?
3. Can you find an example of compromise in these cases?

**Political Behavior Occurs within a System of Government and Rules**

Journalist Frank Kent some years ago wrote a book called *The Great Game of Politics,* and every student has heard the expression "playing politics." If indeed political activity is something of a game, it cannot be played without a set of rules. *Rules are standards for human behavior.* For example, the rules of baseball are the standards for behavior in a baseball game. These rules control, or direct, the behavior of players. No game would be possible without the rules.

Organized baseball could hardly be played without one or more umpires to interpret and enforce the rules. If a dispute or conflict arises, the umpire must make a decision to settle the issue. Umpires are a part of the governmental structure of organized baseball. At the head of this "government" is a Commissioner. He holds a post created many years ago to save the game from collapse. The "government" of organized baseball includes a group with power to revise the rules of the game from time to time.

Rules likewise control, or direct, American political behavior. Rules for political behavior are set down in the Constitution of the

Identify the issues and policy decisions in the headlines.

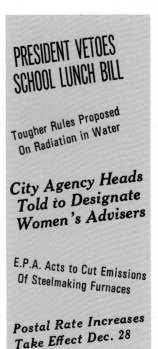

PRESIDENT VETOES SCHOOL LUNCH BILL

Tougher Rules Proposed On Radiation in Water

City Agency Heads Told to Designate Women's Advisers

E.P.A. Acts to Cut Emissions Of Steelmaking Furnaces

Postal Rate Increases Take Effect Dec. 28

11

Carmack in *The Christian Science Monitor.* © 1968 TCSPS

**The umpire speaks.**

United States, in the constitutions of the fifty states, and in various laws passed by Congress and the state legislatures. The American government—federal, state, and local—makes and revises the rules and serves as umpire to enforce the rules and settle disputes.

**Rules May Be Written or Unwritten**

Very many of the rules which control political behavior appear in our written law codes. The Constitution names some things which Congress and the President may do, and it also stops officials from engaging in other types of political behavior. Our laws tell when elections are to be held, how they are to be held, which Americans may vote, who shall pay taxes, and so on.

Americans, however, are also guided in their political behavior by many unwritten rules, or *customs.* It is customary, for example, for the loser of an election to send formal congratulations to the winner. Not every loser will do this, but most of them will observe the custom. Most of the methods used by citizens to influence public officials are simply customary ways of behaving politically.

**Most Rules Are Obeyed Willingly**

Many persons and groups in the community have some power to enforce rules—parents, teachers, employers, baseball umpires, and the like. But the agency with the most power to enforce rules is the government.

12

Although a government must be able to enforce rules, it depends upon the willingness of people to follow the rules. For example, it would not be possible for the police to enforce traffic laws if most people were unwilling to obey the laws. But we don't need a police officer present to make most people stop for a red light or to drive on the right side of the highway. Most people in our country readily accept and obey basic traffic rules.

Because most people in our country believe that they should obey the law, the government can keep order. Since most Americans accept the government's right and duty to make and enforce laws, the government continues to make and enforce laws successfully. Willingness to obey the laws appears to be related to several conditions in a community or nation. Laws are most likely to be obeyed under these conditions: (a) People feel that the laws are just and needed. (b) Officials who make and enforce the laws are respected by the people. (c) Violations of the law are reasonably certain of being detected and punished.

**Rules and Government Prevent Anarchy**

*Anarchy is behavior without rules.* For example, if there were no traffic laws to control the behavior of auto drivers, there would be anarchy on the highways. Drivers would "do their own thing." Wrecks would happen all the time. People driving tanks, armored cars, or huge trucks could perhaps push their way around. But others would not have the freedom to travel easily or safely.

Anarchy is like trying to play a game of baseball without rules. Without rules, confusion would destroy the baseball game.

Anarchy means that people are "free" to do as they please so long as they have the strength and power to have their way. Anarchy

How does the cartoon illustrate anarchy? What does the cartoonist seem to think about protest as a political technique?

**"Wait a minute! Who's in charge here?"**

means that there is no security, no order, no peace, and no real freedom to come and go in safety. Anarchy is the opposite of behavior according to rules.

If people can't settle conflicts through orderly political behavior, anarchy may destroy the group. Since people fear anarchy, they try to settle conflicts according to rules.

To show that you understand the meaning of rules and government as aspects of political behavior, refer to the two cases on pages 2–6 and answer these questions.
**1.** Find at least one example of a rule which controlled, or directed, behavior in each of the cases.
**2.** Why did individuals behave politically according to rules?

### Political Behavior Is an Important Part of Life

Through political behavior, conflict is managed and things which people value are given or withheld.

The stakes of political behavior are very high. Through political behavior, people seek rewards for themselves and for those whom they represent. Political decisions determine which people gain rewards and which people are denied rewards.

Through political behavior, issues of war or peace, of life or death, and of freedom or oppression are decided. Political behavior produces decisions which determine the quantity and quality of many services basic to modern human life, such as water supplies, transportation facilities, postal services, education, health care, and so on.

Political behavior is necessary to life within human groups. So long as people disagree and compete, they will need to behave politically to settle conflicts and to maintain order and cooperation.

## The Shoreline Airport Case

The following case study illustrates several aspects of political behavior discussed on pages 6–14. (1) There is an issue that leads to value conflict. (2) The parties to the conflict use their political resources to try to influence a favorable resolution of the conflict. (3) A political decision will be made to settle the conflict. (4) The conflict will be settled in an orderly way, according to rules accepted by everyone involved in the conflict. (5) Some people in the case will gain something they value from the settlement of the conflict.

**Does Shoreline Need New Airport Facilities?** Walter Simko, president of the Shoreline Chamber of Commerce, picked up his copy of the *Shoreline Evening Herald* and turned to the editorial page. He began to read "Culp's Column," a daily feature written by Lester Culp. As he read, Walter Simko became more and more annoyed.

"Martha," he shouted to Mrs. Simko, "listen to what this fool Culp says about the airport issue."

For nearly one year, the City Council has been discussing whether or not to build new city airport facilities. Conflicting opinions about this issue have been presented to the City Council.

The Council meets tomorrow to discuss the airport issue. Responsible citizens of Shoreline must contact their council members and urge them to oppose airport expansion.

Our present airport is large enough to serve a city like Shoreline. Money for airport expansion can be put to better use building new schools and parks. While only a few higher-income people would benefit from enlarging the city airport, all of Shoreline citizens would benefit from new educational and recreational facilities. The people of South Side need a new elementary school. Our city needs a larger library and civic center.

In addition, expanding the city airport would greatly increase air traffic to our city. This would cause discomfort to the people of Shoreline, since more and bigger jets landing here mean more noise and air pollution. Therefore, we must urge the City Council to reject the proposals to build new airport facilities.

After reading "Culp's Column" to Martha, Walter phoned Roger Rand, the city council member for his district.

"Hello, Roger, this is Walter. Did you read 'Culp's Column' in the *Evening Herald?*"

"Yes, Walter, I did," said Roger Rand. "Culp's arguments are sure to cause trouble for us at the city council tomorrow night."

"Why don't you contact Maxine Douglas and arrange for her to testify before the Council," said Simko. "Maxine can present a convincing argument in support of airport expansion."

"I agree, Walter, and I'll see that Maxine is there," replied Rand.

"Fine," said Simko. "I'll see you tomorrow."

**The "Expansionists" State Their Case.** The next evening George Geddes, president of the Shoreline City Council, called the meeting to order. After disposing of other business, Geddes called on Maxine Douglas to testify about the need for new airport facilities. Following are excerpts from a transcript of this portion of the Council meeting:

*Geddes:* Ms. Maxine Douglas is here tonight as a representative of the Branis Corporation, the engineering-consultant firm hired by the airport authority to do a study of Shoreline's future airport needs. Ms. Douglas, we're pleased that you're able to be here to help us this evening.

*Douglas:* I'm pleased to be of service to you.

*Geddes:* What are your opinions about the airport issue, Ms. Douglas?

*Douglas:* First of all, Mr. Geddes, we of Branis do not propose an entirely new airport. The present site has too much invested in it with the new terminal just finished last year and the two million dollars you are now spending for runway expansion. Nevertheless, my company believes that Shoreline, with its rapid growth rate, must plan now for the year 2000, before it's too late to take advantage of its current airport investment. By then Shoreline will need a major airport capable of handling international carriers.

We base our position on facts. The number of air passengers from Shoreline is growing rapidly. In 1952 only 9 percent of this area's air passengers came from Shoreline. By last year over 40 percent did. This, in round numbers, meant that 750,000 Shore-liners flew somewhere last year. Many had to drive forty-five miles to Freetown to get a flight because they could not get reservations at the Shoreline Municipal Airport. The simple fact is that the present airport can't handle the needs of Shoreline's own population. And this is not counting the needs of the rest of the metropolitan area.

*Geddes:* Ms. Douglas, some critics of your proposal have said that the extra noise and air pollution caused by more jet aircraft traffic would outweigh any advantages connected with expansion of our airport. What do you think?

*Douglas:* As aeronautical engineers, naturally we keep up on the latest scientific information on noise and pollutant control. I predict that given the time and effort being expended, we will have jet noise licked soon. As for air pollution, this is a harder problem. But I predict that science will solve it too in the near future. And about jet noise, our readings one mile from the runways show that the noise has never gone over 50 decibels, and this level is not harmful.

*Geddes:* I agree, Ms. Douglas, that you may in time control some of the problems of jet flights. But what about the decline in the value of properties near airports? How do you assure people who live in houses near the airport that they are safe?

*Douglas:* Statistics on deaths caused by planes show that most deaths result during landings. But these deaths, statistics also tell us, occur in areas within a quarter of a mile of the landing strip. The expansion plans we suggest take this factor into account. Land within the danger zone would be bought and cleared.

*Geddes:* Thank you for your help, Ms. Douglas.

After the city council meeting, Walter Simko went to a nearby restaurant where he met Councilman Rand. The two men ordered sandwiches and coffee and discussed the meeting.

"Maxine did a fine job tonight," said Simko. "I'm sure her testimony will convince many doubtful citizens of the need to expand airport facilities."

"Her testimony also seemed to make a good impression on the three council members who are still undecided on this issue," said Rand.

"By the way, I've decided to answer Culp in the *Evening Herald*," said Simko. "I've written a letter to the editor, and it should appear in the paper tomorrow. Look for it, Roger."

Walter Simko's letter appeared in the next edition of the *Evening Herald*. It pointed out that a larger airport would mean more money and more jobs for Shoreline residents. The letter also argued that problems of air pollution and noise would probably be solved by scientists in the near future and concluded with the following statement:

We should not lose sight of our great chances because of a few problems. The chance for Shoreline must be seized now, or it may soon be lost to a more aggressive community in our area.

**Simko Meets Resistance.** Marshall Levy, director of the Safe and Sane Airport Committee (SSAC), read Simko's letter in the *Herald*. He smashed his fist down hard on his kitchen table. "Simko thinks he's won his battle for an expanded airport, but we'll make waves when we hold our anti-airport demonstration."

"Right! We'll shake up old man Simko tomorrow," replied Carol Elliot, the associate director of SSAC. "When Simko and his friends on the city council realize that the people are against their airport plans, they'll have to change their minds and see things our way."

On the following day Marshall Levy and Carol Elliot led a march of more than 5000 demonstrators. They chanted slogans and carried signs protesting the airport expansion and denouncing the Branis Corporation, Walter Simko, and the Chamber of Commerce. The marchers halted in front of City Hall.

**The Opposition Presents Its Petition.** Marshall Levy walked up the steps of City Hall and spoke through a bull horn:

Attention, Mayor Curtis and members of the City Council. You had better listen to us if you want to keep your jobs. We represent people power, and we are against spending city funds to expand the airport for the benefit of Walter Simko and a few other local big shots.

For six months we've been meeting in local schools, clubrooms, and churches to study the problem of air transportation and its effect on our environment. Over 10,000 citizens have signed our petition against expansion of airport facilities in any part of the Shoreline metropolitan area. We're here today to deliver this petition to you, Mayor Curtis.

Here are just a few of our reasons for opposing increased air traffic in Shoreline:

1. Jet planes pollute the air with carbon monoxide and nitrogen oxides which produce smog, lung diseases, and hurt our local truck-garden industry.

2. Jet landings and takeoffs produce noise levels of up to 110 decibels. Medical experts have told us that an 85 decibel level, if continuous, is enough to create serious emotional disturbances in people.

3. Two invaluable public facilities—the Sands Wildlife Refuge and the Placer State Hospital for the mentally ill—will be made useless by an expansion of the present airport.

I could go on, but let me close by urging all of you to make your opinions known to your city council. United we can preserve our environment. Otherwise our city council may approve this monstrous plan that threatens the pleasant environment we all share in Shoreline. Mr. Simko and others of his kind must stop thinking only in terms of dollar bills. We must not ruin our environment in order to increase the profits of a few business firms.

Levy's speech ended with a roar of approval from the crowd.

The following day the *Shoreline Evening Herald* reported the demonstration at City Hall. The paper also announced that the council members planned to vote on the airport issue at their next meeting. Would the editorial by Lester Culp and the demonstration of the Safe and Sane Airport Committee influence their decision? Or would the testimony of Maxine Douglas and the arguments of Walter Simko sway their votes?

To demonstrate what you have learned about aspects of political behavior, answer these questions about the airport case.
1. What is the main issue?
2. Why did this issue develop?
3. What are the political resources of the parties to the conflict?
4. How did the parties to the conflict try to influence the outcome of the case?
5. What political decisions might be made in this case?
6. What is the relationship of rules to the political behavior in this case?
7. What does this case indicate about what is political behavior and why people behave politically?
8. In your opinion, what political decision should be made in this case? Why?

# 2 Political Participants

Political behavior, we have seen, involves the use of influence to determine who gets what, when, and how. Through political behavior, value conflicts are resolved and social order is maintained.

The main objectives of this chapter are (1) to increase your knowledge of political participants and (2) to develop your ability to make wise judgments about when and how to take political action.

## Who Participates?

On pages 22–23 are pictures of different types of people. Try to figure out which of these types of people are very likely and which are not very likely to be involved in political activity.

### Public Officials

Who are the political participants in American life? The most obvious ones are public officials—people who hold jobs in government. Mayors, governors, legislators, bureaucrats, judges, and the like are involved daily in politics.

Units Four and Five, pages 258–572, are about various types of public officials.

The top officials in national, state, and local government act as leaders in making and carrying out political decisions. Lower-ranking officials may have influence on the decisions of the leaders and also play a key role in the enforcement of decisions.

### Unofficial Political Specialists

Many participants do not hold public office but still play a big part in influencing the day-to-day decisions of public officials. Newspaper editors, labor union leaders, leaders of civic organizations such as the Chamber of Commerce, and TV news commentators take a regular part in political activities. We shall call these people *unofficial political specialists,* since they do not hold public office. However, they spend far more time taking part in politics than do typical citizens.

Most unofficial political specialists have access to political resources not available to most of us. Among these resources are the leadership of a large organization, access to the communications media, possession of important knowledge that public officials need, and access to money to finance political campaigns and other activities.

The head of the AFL-CIO is an unofficial political specialist. While much of his activity deals with the economic goals of union members, the AFL-CIO president is a major political force in this country. He tries to help elect public officials who favor the labor point of view, and then tries to influence them to make decisions that favor labor.

Dr. Martin Luther King was an important unofficial political specialist. He was a leader of many black people who were demanding civil rights reform. He was able to influence public officials to gain many reforms. Yet Dr. King held no post in the government.

The publisher of *The New York Times* can influence the opinions of many citizens and government leaders by the choice of articles to print or not print and by the editorial columns.

Unofficial political specialists believe that government policy, at least in their own area of interest, is important. They care about issues, election outcomes, and the decisions of public officials. These specialists are also likely to know more than the casual spectator does about issues, the way government works, and politics in general.

**Typical Citizens as Political Participants**

Most people are neither public officials nor unofficial political specialists. And most tend to be much less involved in influencing the day-to-day decisions of public officials. Most factory workers, teachers, students, housekeepers, secretaries, and salespeople usually limit their participation to voting and observing the political activity around them. Many don't bother to vote. From time to time, when an issue is very important to them, they may take part in a political campaign or a public demonstration. When the issue has been settled, they tend to withdraw from political life.

Many people who are *not* very involved in public political affairs are more involved in *private political activities*. For example, high school students who are too young to vote in public elections may be very active in the political life of their school. They may be candidates for offices in school clubs. They may organize groups to influence the decisions of school officials. Helping elect officers of a church group or voting on an issue in a club are other examples.

While this book contains examples of private political behavior, the focus is on the public arena where officials, unofficial political specialists, and other citizens interact to resolve value conflicts.

1. Identify who you think are *unofficial political specialists* below.
   a. Legislative Director for the Rifle and Revolver Association
   b. Governor of Illinois
   c. Republican grocer who votes in every public election but does nothing else "political"
   d. Editor of local newspaper who writes political editorials
   e. Doctor who testifies before a committee of the state legislature on the effects of marijuana
   f. State legislator who hears testimony
   g. Democratic party leader who influences the position the Democratic candidate takes on labor legislation
   h. Wealthy business person who never dabbles in politics.

Left: Tennis Champion Chris Evert
Below: Mayor Tom Bradley of Los Angeles

Right: workers in an industrial plant
Below: TV newscaster Walter Cronkhite

*Left:* Washington Post publisher, Katharine Graham
*Below:* Congresswoman Bella Abzug

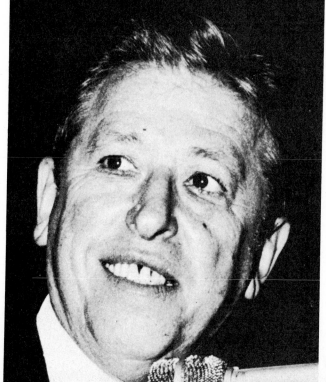

*Left:* Al Barkan, head of AFL-CIO's
Committee on Political Education.
*Below:* G. M. Davis, Los Angeles city official

**TAKING PART IN POLITICS**

1. Campaigning for office

**2.** Turn to the Shoreline Airport Case on pages 14–19 and answer these questions.

    **a.** Which persons in the Shoreline Airport Case are public officials?

    **b.** Which persons in the case are unofficial political specialists?

    **c.** Why do people become unofficial political specialists?

## How Do People Take Part in Politics?

    By taking part in politics, people try to influence decisions of public officials in order to get things that they value. Some of the ways that Americans take part are shown in the following pictures.

2. Giving money to a campaign

3. Getting names on a petition

4. Working for a candidate

5. Joining an interest group

6. Voting in a public election

7. Testifying before a legislative committee

8. Making a speech on television

9. Writing to a legislator

10. Reading an interest group's political advertisement

11. Attending a meeting of the Voters League

12. Taking part in a protest

## Taking Part through Organizations

Several of the people in the drawing are part of some organized political group. This would likely be the case in pictures 1, 3, 4, 5, 11, and 12. The other pictures show people who might be acting as "lone wolf" participants. However, it is possible that these people too are acting in behalf of an organization. The person in picture 2 could be making a campaign gift as a member of a political group. The voter in picture 6 could be one of a large bloc of voters who have decided to support the same candidates. The persons in pictures 7 and 8 could be speaking as representatives of some political group. The letter writer in picture 9 could be part of a big letter-writing campaign put on by a group wanting to influence the outcome of an issue in Congress.

Taking part in politics through organizations is very important in the United States. Americans tend to be joiners. When faced with a social problem, they usually join forces to try to solve it. A few people prefer to deal with social problems as loners, but most think that they can do more through group activity. They prefer to combine their resources with those of others who have similar values and goals.

Organized group activity is most suitable to the public political arena in the United States. This behavior is supported both by custom and law. The First Amendment to the Constitution guarantees the right to express opinions through political organizations.

> Congress shall make no law . . . abridging the freedom of speech, or of the press, or the right of the people peacefully to assemble and to petition the government for a redress of grievances.

The Supreme Court has said that this article protects the rights of Americans to organize for the purpose of presenting requests and demands to their government.

### Interest Groups

Organizations which try to influence the decisions of public officials in order to achieve goals that members value are called *interest groups.* There are hundreds of interest groups which represent the values and goals, or interests, of different Americans.

Some of these organizations represent the interests of *occupational groups* such as teachers, farmers, lawyers, doctors, factory workers, retail merchants, and others. Following are three examples. (1) The Committee on Political Education (COPE) of the AFL-CIO represents the interests of many workers, especially blue-collar workers. (2) The American Political Action Committee of the American Medical Association (AMPAC) represents the political interests of medical doctors. (3) The American Farm Bureau Federation represents the interests of farmers.

Some interest groups are formed to promote the interests of *ethnic or religious groups,* such as Jews, Catholics, blacks, Chicanos, and Native Americans. For example, the Anti-Defamation League of B'Nai

B'rith is a Jewish interest group. The National Urban League was organized to promote the interests of black people.

Other interest groups are organized around the *shared experiences* of members. For example, armed forces veterans belong to the American Legion, the Veterans of Foreign Wars, or some other associations. Many hunters and other gun users belong to the National Rifle Association.

Other interest groups are based on the *political ideologies* of members. For example, the Americans for Democratic Action (ADA) is an organization of political liberals. In contrast, the Americans for Constitutional Action (ACA) attracts people who hold conservative beliefs.

Common Cause is a new and very unusual kind of interest group. Founded by John Gardner in 1970, Common Cause claims to represent the public interest rather than the needs of special groups. In describing the purposes of his more than 300,000-member organization, Gardner said: "We will uphold the public interest against all comers—special interests, self-seeking politicians, self-perpetuating bureaucrats, industry, professional groups."[1] In recent years, Common Cause has been a strong force in getting several laws to reform government.

We could go on and on giving examples, but clearly interest groups are a major feature of the American political scene.

Much of the conflict in American politics is between interest groups with clashing values and goals. The National Association of Manufacturers (NAM) takes the side of factory owners and managers. The NAM often clashes with the AFL-CIO, which speaks up for the interests of factory workers. In recent years the interests of environmental groups, such as the Sierra Club and the National Audubon Society, have conflicted with the interests of energy producers, such as the National Coal Association and the American Petroleum Institute.

Interest-group leaders, and those who work for them, often act as lobbyists. A *lobbyist* is a person who tries to influence lawmakers, such as members of Congress, state legislatures, and city councils, to pass or reject particular laws. The term "lobbyist" stems from the fact that persons who try to influence lawmaking are often seen in the halls, or lobbies, of buildings that house lawmakers.

There are more than 2000 registered lobbyists in Washington, D.C., who work full time to influence members of Congress. A sign of the importance of lobbyists is that interest groups spend millions of dollars each year to support them.

**Political Parties**

Another main type of political organization interacts with interest groups. It is the political party. In the United States the Democrats and Republicans are rival political parties. Both political parties and

1. Reprinted from *In Common Cause* by John W. Gardner. By permission of W. W. Norton & Company, Inc. Copyright © 1972 by W. W. Norton & Company, Inc.

HOW LOBBYISTS
INFLUENCE
DECISION-MAKERS

LOBBYING HEADQUARTERS

Legislative Representative

Coordinator of Political Affairs

Direct Influence on Decision-Makers

Public Relations Department

Influence on Public Opinion

RADIO AND TV

NEWSPAPERS AND MAGAZINES

PUBLIC SPEECHES

BOOKS AND PAMPHLETS

ORGANIZED DEMONSTRATIONS

HOORAY! BOO HISS!

5

GOVERNMENT
DECISION MAKERS

Congress
Testifying before legislative committees; contacting key legislators and committee chairmen

Executive Agencies
Working for the appointment of favorable administrators; meeting with bureaucratic officials; conducting write-in campaigns to executive departments

Political Parties
Working for the election of favorable candidates; influencing political party platforms

interest groups organize people to make requests and demands upon the government. However, in contrast to interest groups, the primary purpose of a political party is to elect candidates to public office. The party thereby permits its members to exercise influence in government. An interest group like the National Rifle Association tries hard to influence public officials. But it does not really try to control government decision-making by electing its own people to public office. It is left to the political parties to recruit, select, and support candidates for public office.

Membership in a political party is voluntary, but any eligible voter can join merely by registering to vote. No dues are paid. A member does not have to agree strongly with the ideas of the party that she or he joins. And members may even switch now and then to vote for candidates of the other party.

Many interest groups maintain lobby headquarters in Washington. Some lobbyists will make direct contacts with members of Congress. Others will engage more directly in public-opinion activities aimed at putting public pressure on government officials.

27

Besides their role in elections, parties play another key role in the political process. We have seen how issues arise in politics and how groups form on all sides of any issue. How can all of these interests be expressed in public policy? Parties provide an important key. To win an election, a political party must appeal to as many interests as possible without turning away others that already support it. So it must find candidates that will be attractive to a wide range of interests. It must also draw up a platform and get its candidates and officeholders to take stands on issues which will gain support for the party. As a result, both major parties in America have to find ways to smooth over the differences between conflicting interest groups where possible and combine these various interest groups into a majority. By narrowing the choice of the voter down to one of two candidates—Republican or Democrat, the American two-party system helps reduce the conflict that might arise in a society which embraces many strong and diverse interests.

The kind of party that competes for public office through elections differs very much from the kind that wants to overthrow a government by force and abolish real elections. Such a group is sometimes called a "party." But it differs from the political parties we are talking about.

Nor are we talking about small minor parties which run candidates but with no real hope of victory. The Federalists and the Whigs, once major parties, failed to survive for long after they stopped winning elections. Some minor parties, such as the Socialist party, do survive year after year. But they use elections as a way to advertise their programs or ideology rather than as a real attempt to gain control of the government.

For the party in a competitive system (such as the American political system) the crucial goal is winning public offices. In the process the party must make concessions on programs and candidates to voters or interest groups that might be tempted to support the other party.

### Keys to Effective Participation
Suppose you are a leader of an interest group which is trying to make some changes through political action. What are some things you might do to enable the group to succeed? Consider the following six keys to effective participation.

**Organizing Skillfully**
Those who know how to organize people and their resources skillfully hold one main key to getting results. When people take part alone or as a poorly organized group, they often are not very effective.

Skillful organization is needed to combine the resources of various persons and groups. A result of pooling resources skillfully is *group solidarity,* which is a chief means to political strength and influence.

Good organization is basic to the political success of mass movements. From time to time, masses of Americans who don't belong

to interest groups will be driven to action by some issue or event that affects them deeply. In the 1960s, for example, issues linked with the Vietnam war got millions of people to take part in public demonstrations. The black civil rights movement and the women's liberation movement have also led to mass political action in recent years. The success of these and other mass movements has been based on skill in organizing people not much involved in politics.

### Focusing Participation

Many interest groups fail because they try to do too much all at once. They spread limited resources across too many activities and goals. In trying to do too much, they achieve little or nothing.

Sometimes interest groups fail because they are not clear about what they want to achieve. Successful participants are able to focus their time, energy, skills, and money on a few clear goals that everyone in the group wants to achieve. If the group has few resources, it may fix on only one or two goals at a time.

### Sustaining Participation

It often takes much time and effort to reach political goals. Thus, to succeed in politics one must be willing to *sustain* political activity, to stay with it for a long time in spite of problems. For example, Common Cause worked for almost four years to influence the passing of a law to reform the financing of election campaigns. The Sierra Club has worked for more than ten years to get stricter controls on strip mining. For more than thirty years the American Medical Association has worked to persuade Congress to defeat bills that would provide compulsory national health insurance.

Many people give up too quickly. They are roused to action by an issue or event that concerns them. If they don't win quickly, they quit. They don't see that gaining a political goal can be slow and difficult, especially if it is very controversial and the opposing groups are strong.

Winning a political battle from time to time, even if the victory is small, helps sustain a group. Interest groups which lose all their political battles are not likely to stay alive. Members who never see a return on time, money, energy, and skills will stop making these investments.

### Fitting Activities to Resources

The best way for an interest group to avoid early political death is to learn how to fit political activities and goals to available resources. Ability to influence political decisions is tied to resources. For example, interest groups use time, money, knowledge, and skills to help friendly candidates and to try to defeat others. In 1974 the American Medical Association's political action committee gave $792,697 to support the election of public officials who cooperated with AMA's lobbyists. The AFL-CIO donated $1.4 million to help friendly candidates and to defeat others.

See pages 8–9 in chapter 1 for more commentary about political resources.

An interest group with little money can't afford to hire lobbyists. It may have to get free publicity by creating "newsworthy" events. It might stage a series of *public demonstrations* in order to get public attention in newspapers and on TV and radio. The most common demonstrations are boycotts, picketing, sit-ins, rent strikes, and parades. Notice in the pictures that there are three main types of demonstrations.

Groups with few resources have often used public demonstrations to present their grievances. In recent years, however, more privileged groups who thought they could gain access to public officials in no other way have at times used demonstrations.

There are three main forms of demonstrations. (1) *Nonviolent* ones are legal and peaceful, such as the one showing mothers protesting the diversion of heavy traffic through their neighborhood when a nearby highway was closed for repairs. (2) But if the mothers tried to block the traffic, it would be an *obstructionist* type of protest. One picture below shows students and workers blocking a street in Paris during a strike. (3) The *violent* protest involves fighting, rock throwing, shooting, or other attempts to cause injury or property damage. Another picture shows youthful protesters attacking the U.S. Embassy in Cyprus.

### Trading Favors

Successful politicians, it has been said, have mastered the art of making others feel obligated. Such politicians know how to trade favors. Those who get something of value are expected to give something in return.

Patronage is a clear example of the trading of favors in politics. *Patronage is the granting of a governmental favor in exchange for political support.* For instance, a candidate for mayor promises certain people that they will get city jobs or other favors if they help the candidate win the election. When the candidate wins, he or she fulfills the promise. Some may get city jobs for themselves and/or their friends. Others may get the mayor's help in getting a desired ordinance passed by the city council. Some mayors can influence the granting of contracts and liquor licenses to their supporters.

In order to trade favors, one has to control resources. Those with many things of value to trade are in the best bargaining position. However, to be a good trader one needs *skill in bargaining* as well as an ample supply of resources.

Successful interest groups are skillful traders of favors. In return for help in passing a law it favors, an interest group will help friendly legislators win reelection. The group will give money and the time, energy, and skill of its members to the election campaigns.

Lobbyists who work for interest groups often trade their expert knowledge for cooperation from legislators. Lobbyists are supposed to be experts about special topics that are related to their group's special interest. For example, lobbyists for the Sierra Club are experts about such matters as strip mining and air pollution. Sierra Club lobbyists often provide facts to members of Congress and to state legislators about environmental issues and problems. In return, they hope to win support from these lawmakers for the goals of their group.

### Building Coalitions

An important strategy for trading favors to win political advantages is *coalition-building*. A *coalition* is an alliance of groups who decide to join forces in support of some common goal. For example, the black civil rights movement has been an alliance of several interest groups. This coalition has included labor unions, business and professional groups, and white ethnic groups as well as several civil rights organizations made up mainly, or entirely, of blacks.

Most conflicts over big issues like civil rights have involved opposing coalitions. Pollution is another example. Business and labor groups have joined forces to oppose alliances of environmental groups.

In order to build a coalition, interest group leaders usually have to bargain. They have to be willing to trade favors for their *mutual benefit.* Each group of the coalition usually has to give up some of what it wants in order to win the support of others. Those who are too rigid to make compromises tend to work alone.

The women's rights coalition consists of a number of separate organizations, some of whose emblems are shown here.

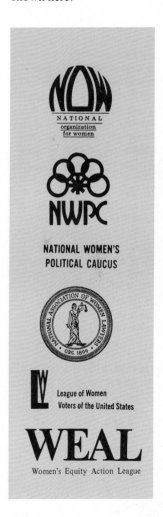

31

### Six Cases of Political Participation

We have looked at six keys to effective participation. Apply these keys to the following six brief cases.

#### Case 1. A Class Election

Roy is running for president of his senior class. Abe is president of the Lettermen's Club, made up of all boys who have earned athletic letters. Abe would like for the senior class to set aside a portion of the class dues to sponsor a senior-class float in the annual Homecoming parade. He tells Roy that if Roy will advocate using some of the class treasury for this purpose, the Lettermen's Club will support him for class president.

#### Case 2. Fighting City Hall for Services

The leaders of the Action for Community Improvement (ACI), a group of poor, inner-city residents, had tried to get an appointment with the mayor for two months. However, they were told day after day that he was too busy to see them. The ACI leaders wanted improvements in street repair, garbage pick-up, and other services in their neighborhood. The ACI leaders claimed that the city tended to neglect them while unfairly giving most of the city's services to other areas. Finally, ACI leaders decided to force the mayor and others in the city to hear their complaints. They arranged a public demonstration in front of City Hall. Reporters from the daily papers and the local TV stations covered the event. The leaders of ACI vowed to keep up their protests until the mayor promised to help them.

#### Case 3. Downtown Parking Garage

The Downtown Businessmen's Association (DBA) had tried for years to get the city to build two high-rise parking garages in the downtown shopping area. The mayor and city council kept saying that there were too many other needed projects. Meanwhile the downtown merchants kept losing business to a new shopping center with its huge parking lot at the edge of the city. But the DBA leaders kept trying to reach their goal. A chance for success finally came when several other groups in the city agreed to join with the DBA to put pressure on the mayor and city council. Three local labor unions, a consumer protection group, and the Chamber of Commerce stood together to influence the city government to build the new garage.

#### Case 4. A State Lottery

The headline in the local paper said: "Gilbert Proposes State Lottery to Raise Money for Schools." Richard Witte read the article with disgust. He opposed gambling. A state lottery to raise money was more than he could take. He sat down to write a letter of complaint to Georgia Gilbert, his state legislator. He also wrote a letter to the local paper declaring his strong opposition to a state lottery. He tried to arrange a meeting with Georgia Gilbert, but her aide said that Ms. Gilbert was too busy. He assured Witte that Representative Gilbert would carefully consider his arguments against the state lottery. Many other people in the state opposed the lottery bill. However, lobbying for it were several well-organized interest groups including the state teachers' association and three labor unions. These groups pooled their resources to get the lottery bill passed.

### Case 5. Consumer Protection

The local Consumer Protection Association (CPA) was set up last year with fanfare and high hopes. The CPA leaders had pledged to achieve five main goals at once. They promised to influence local businesses (1) to lower prices, (2) to improve services, (3) to provide higher quality products, (4) to follow fair hiring and promotion practices, and (5) to give more funds to improve the downtown business area. The group tried to work toward each of these goals during its first year. The result was very sad. They spent most of their money while reaching none of their goals. Many members dropped out. After one year the CPA seems doomed.

### Case 6. Ousting "the Machine"

After twelve years of persistent effort, the Citizens for Better Government (CBG) was able to defeat the local political "machine" which seemed to have the resources to roll over all opposition. During its first five years, the CBG almost gave up in the face of few "wins" and vast opposition. However, they believed strongly in their single goal: Win control of the city government from "the machine." The CBG leaders learned from their mistakes and gradually developed resources and popular support. Eventually they sponsored candidates for the city council who defeated "the machine's" candidates.

**1.** What are the political objectives of the individuals or groups in each case?
**2.** How are the persons or groups trying to achieve their objectives in each case?
**3.** Which persons or groups are using one or more of the six "keys" to effective participation discussed in this chapter? Which are not?
**4.** What is your opinion of the political actions of the persons and groups in these cases? Who is taking part more or less wisely?

The following three chapter sections are case studies of political participation. Try to apply what you have read in chapters 1 and 2 to the analysis of these cases.

## A Tightly Knit Organization

The following case study is about the activities of an interest group, the Connecticut State Rifle and Revolver Association, and its lobbyists. As you read, try to identify the unofficial political specialists, their goals, and their techniques of influencing public officials.

**A New Firearms Bill Arouses an Interest Group.** Dan Juliani was the first to hear about the bill. In his former post as president of the Connecticut State Rifle and Revolver Association, and then as its legislative director, he had come to know many Connecticut legislators and their staff members. He had a reputation as a discrete, trustworthy man. Legislators drawing up bills on firearms would often come to him for information and advice and to sound out his organization's position on their proposals. This time the sponsor of the bill did not check with him, but Juliani heard about it quickly enough anyway. And he did not like what he heard.

Cartoon by Lou Grant. Copyright 1968, *Los Angeles Times* Syndicate

The leaders of the Connecticut State Rifle and Revolver Association were prepared for such a bill. They had watched as similar bills for gun registration and owner licensing had come up in other states in the wake of President John Kennedy's assassination. As representatives of the gunowners and firearms dealers in Connecticut, the Association's leaders strongly opposed such restrictions.

34

Control of firearms would, they reasoned, hurt their members in several ways: (1) Sportsmen might find it harder to buy guns and could be required to obtain licenses or to register their weapons. (2) Carrying guns across state lines or even within the state might be restricted. (3) Gun control would make it hard to interest new members in gun sports. (4) Sales of weapons might decline, hurting gun dealers and the state's large firearms industry.

The leaders were committed to fight any bill which threatened to restrict the sale, ownership, or transportation of guns. And the bill Juliani had spotted looked like their first big fight.

Juliani reported his findings to James E. Murray, III, the current legislative director of the Connecticut State Rifle and Revolver Association. They agreed at once that the bill was not at all acceptable to the Association. Its leaders wanted to keep Connecticut as free of gun-control laws as possible. Their organization's effectiveness would surely be tested now. As Murray wrote later in *The American Rifleman*, "Time was against us. If certain news media had learned of the pending bill, and had made it a major issue, the battle might have been lost before it had even begun." But this was the kind of challenge their tightly knit organization had been preparing for.

**The Gun Lobbyists Provide a New Bill.** Juliani and Murray first went to Dr. John Blake, the legislator who was sponsoring the proposed bill. Blake listened to their views. He admitted that he had little knowledge of firearms legislation. The chief of police in his home district had merely described a local gun problem and suggested that the legislature do something about it.

Murray carefully picked a committee from all segments of the shooting sports to cooperate with Dr. Blake in getting a new law. Dr. Blake further agreed to give the Association time to draft its own. In just three days the Association had prepared its own "model" bill. The revised bill was quite different from the original and in every way more favorable to the "gun" interests in Connecticut.

Dr. Blake quickly agreed to substitute the Association's draft for his own much stronger bill, which had called for the registration of all guns and the licensing of owners. The new bill had easier registration conditions. And it called for setting up a Board of Permit Examiners to review complaints of people who had been denied handgun permits. Thus the leaders of the Association had been able to turn a "bad" proposal into a bill which was, in fact, more favorable to their interests than existing laws.

To make the bill more attractive to legislators worried about the rise in street crimes, penalties for use of weapons in violent crimes were increased. But instead of having to renew pistol permits every year, sportsmen under the revised bill would be granted permits for a five-year period. And, best of all for the Association, no registration of firearms or additional licensing would be required of its members.

**Gun Lobby Uses Other Resources.** Round One had gone to the Association before most legislators or the press were even aware of the issues. Still, much work lay ahead for the Association before its own substitute bill could become law. It went to the Joint Committee on the Judiciary. The Association quickly rounded up speakers to testify for the bill. Years of experience led the gun lobbyists to pick speakers who sounded reasonable and to screen out witnesses who might appear as crackpots or extremists.

The first real objection to the bill came from the state police. They wanted a broader definition of weapons considered "deadly and dangerous" than was in the present bill. They also objected to the Association's draft on several other grounds. Once again the Association swung into action. Right after the hearing, Murray contacted people from the Connecticut State Police and other opposition groups. Through informal talks with these people, Murray was able to pinpoint objections to the Association's bill and to make some technical changes in its language. The end of the legislative session was drawing near, however, and basic differences of opinion still had not been resolved. Until some agreement could be reached, the bill stood little chance of passage.

With only days to spare, a subcommittee of the Judiciary Committee was set up to meet with interested parties to work out a compromise. The talks led the Association to agree (a) to return to the old definition of dangerous and deadly weapons and (b) to allow the local authorities (rather than the state police) to issue handgun permits. In return, it was agreed to establish a Board of Permit Examiners (which was to include representatives from the Rifle and Revolver Association and Ye Connecticut Gun Guild) with the power to take evidence; to issue, revoke, or reinstate permits; and to force local issuing authorities to follow the orders of the Board.

All interested parties seemed satisfied with the result. The amended bill passed the legislature without major opposition. And the new law actually benefited the members of the Rifle and Revolver Association. How did they do it? Murray attributed the Association's success to tight organization and able leadership which enabled them to influence the legislators successfully.

1. What was the main issue or value conflict in this case?
2. What participation techniques were used by the Connecticut State Rifle and Revolver Association?
3. Why was the Association successful?
4. What is your opinion of the participation techniques used?

### The Squeaky Wheel

The political techniques of interest-group leaders vary. Some interest groups, such as the Connecticut State Rifle and Revolver Association, have vast political resources. They have ample money, good organizational skills, and many contacts with important public officials. They can use and support one or more full-time lobbyists to influence political decisions.

Other interest groups have few political resources. They are unable to pay for a lobbyist. The Navajo Indians of the southwestern United States can be viewed as an interest group with few political resources.

Following is a case study about a Navajo Indian who plays the role of unofficial political specialist for her tribe.

**Problems of the Navajo Tribe.** The Navajo are a proud tribe who call themselves Dineh, which means "the people." The pride has remained in the face of widespread poverty. In a recent year seven out of every ten adults could not read or write the English language. Over half of those able and willing to work were unemployed. Most families lived in hogans made of logs and adobe. Few had running water or electricity.

For many years Congress promised more money to correct these conditions. But the promises meant little to most Navajo. They had heard such promises all their lives. Only in recent years has the federal government made a real effort to raise the tribe's living standard. Health care is a prime concern. Governmental health services have been spread too thin to control trachoma, an eye disease which leads to blindness. Tuberculosis, infant mortality, and malnutrition are other critical health problems on the Navajo reservation.

Over $50 million is now spent each year, primarily on health and education. Around 90 percent of Navajo children are now in school, compared with about 50 percent in 1952. Recent programs help the Navajo live in modern American society without loss of the rich Navajo cultural heritage. Furthermore, mineral deposits—coal, gas, oil, uranium, helium—have provided an income of several million dollars a year to the tribe. A few large industries have built plants near the reservation to take advantage of the labor supply. Still, the job is far from done.

Faced with economic difficulties and uncertainty in government policy, the Navajo have taken steps to help themselves. At Window Rock the tribal council meets four times a year to wrestle with the affairs of the tribe. Representatives elected in hard-fought campaigns assemble at the new hogan-shaped building in their boots, plaid shirts, and Western hats. The women council members wear the colorful long skirts and handwoven shawls of Navajo tradition.

Aside from managing the internal affairs of the tribe, the council must give attention to the tribe's ties to the federal government. The government has, at times, been cruel or negligent, and at other times tried to do for the Navajo what they could do for themselves. One council member, whom we shall call Maria Begay, has devoted many years to improving health conditions for the Navajo. Her work brings her into contact with a variety of government agencies.

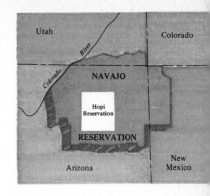

The Reservation of the nation's largest Indian tribe covers over 15 million acres in the area shown here.

**Maria Confers with a Bureaucrat.** Maria Begay sat impatiently in the easy chair in the hall outside an office in the Health, Education, and Welfare building in Washington, D.C. It had been a long trip from Window Rock, Arizona, but she had made it many times before. Her appointment was for 10 o'clock this morning. As usual, the Public Health official was running behind schedule. Slowly, Maria smoothed the folds in her colorful Navajo dress. She knew what to expect when the door finally opened. There would be no surprises this morning—no instant victories, no quick defeats. She would return to Window Rock with little new to report, but with the hope that her presence in Washington would have some effect in the long run.

"Come in, Maria, it's good to see you again," said the balding middle-aged man approaching her with hand outstretched. "Hello, Mr. Drew," responded Maria, "why are you so jovial—you must know why I'm here?" Drew showed her into his inner office and poured them both a cup of coffee. "I can guess," he smiled.

"What happened?" Maria was reserved, polite, but direct. She had never really understood why government officials smiled when they had trouble, but put on long faces when things went well.

"We got caught, Maria. It's as simple as that. When we told you last spring that funds for the new hospital in Tuba City would be in this year's budget, there wasn't a doubt in my mind about it. But take a look at this." He handed her a memo from the budget office stating that all agencies must trim their proposed budgets for the next fiscal year by 20 percent, by order of the President. "You know the reasons as well as I. The energy crisis. Inflation. Trying to save something of the poverty program. The election this fall."

"Mr. Drew," Maria began slowly, "you talk of poverty. You have seen the Navajo Reservation. Where is federal money needed more than in our area? You have published the statistics yourself. In our land two babies die at birth for every one of yours. In our land five times as many people have tuberculosis. I have worked for the last six years for this hospital. The Tribal Council has given it top priority on our list of public health improvements. Now you tell me it will have to wait because it is in the 20 percent that must be cut. Do you expect me to tell my people that?"

Maria was restrained but firm. She had not come to Washington to hear why the grant was not included this year. She had come to try to get it put back in the budget, if possible, or at least make certain it would be in next year.

**Maria Becomes a Squeaky Wheel.** There is an old saying that "it is the squeaky wheel that gets the grease." Bureaucrats and other government officials have a pretty good idea of which wheels are going to squeak and cause them trouble. This is just another way of saying that they usually know who will complain loudly about their decisions and who will accept them without too much protest. If Drew had cut another part of his budget, Maria Begay would be happy. But someone else would complain. He expected to get less pressure from Maria and the Navajo than from the others.

Maria was there today to show him that he was wrong. And whether or not she could change his mind about this year's funding, she certainly could make it clear that the needs of the Navajo could not be shoved aside without getting a reaction from her.

Maria operates without large financial resources. She does not have the legal skill to draft legislation. She could probably not launch a campaign to bring in 500 letters to members of Congress, let alone 500,000. She cannot rely on having members of her tribe scattered through the committees of Congress, although she has found some lawmakers who are more sympathetic to her demands than others. But she has developed tactics which stretch her thin resources as far as they will go in influencing government policy.

**How Maria Uses Her Resources.** First, she appeals to the consciences of public officials. Most Americans have a deep sense of guilt about the treatment of Native Americans. Maria points to promises made but not kept through the years. She compares Navajo living standards with those in the nation at large and appeals to an official's sense of fair play. And Maria is well suited for this job because she is a full-blood Navajo, the granddaughter of a tribal chieftain, and a life-long resident of the reservation.

Maria is persistent, year after year, in pushing for her cause. Bureaucrats cannot ignore her demands, although they may try to put her off. As she works, she develops experience and understanding of the ways of government. It may be easy for a public official to tell her "no" the first time, but it is not so easy the second time, for she then has answers.

Finally, although Maria does not have vast resources, she does have one the federal government needs. Federal agencies want facts about the needs of the Navajo and what the priorities should be. They need to know what Navajo leaders are thinking and doing. Maria provides such information. She also stirs up her members or calms them down. If her demands are not granted, she manages to get enough publicity and get the ear of enough members of Congress to make

Many Navajo families make a meager living from the land.

life miserable for the Public Health Service and the Bureau of Indian Affairs. If, on the other hand, she gets support from these agencies, she tells her people of the progress being made through cooperation with the federal government. Which way would you rather have it if you were an official in the Public Health Service? Maria Begay has few resources, but she uses them skillfully.

1. What are Maria Begay's political objectives?
2. What political techniques does Maria Begay use?
3. How are political techniques related to political resources? (Consider both "A Tightly Knit Organization" and "The Squeaky Wheel" as sources of information for answering this question.)
4. What is your opinion of the techniques in this case?

## The Activists

Some interest-group leaders do not have direct access to public officials as the gun lobbyists or Maria Begay did. They try to influence government through public opinion. Following is a case study about leaders who tried to influence public opinion.

**Background of the Case.** In the fall of 1967, Gail Lewis was a 20-year-old sociology major at a midwestern state university. Gail felt strongly that the United States should not have troops fighting in Southeast Asia. Many of her fellow students shared her views on the Vietnam conflict. However, they felt powerless to influence the government's policy. They could not afford to pay for a lobbyist to plead their cause. They had no experience in political organizing.

One of Gail's closest friends was Ron Abernathy, a 23-year-old graduate student at the university. Ron also opposed the nation's role in Vietnam. He was well informed on the history of Southeast Asia. He was angry at the large-scale bombing of North Vietnam by American planes. He thought President Johnson was making a big mistake in sending more and more troops. Ron would be losing his student deferment at the end of next year. He hadn't yet decided whether or not he would resist induction to the army.

One day Gail and Ron were drinking coffee in the Student Union. "You know, Gail," said Ron, "I think the public has begun to have serious doubts about this war. If those of us who feel strongly about it can organize to dramatize what is happening, it could really shake things up. No administration can continue to carry out a military policy that has strong public opinion against it. If we could just convince people to speak out against the war, it might just make the government change its policy. There's no group on campus set up to protest our involvement in Vietnam. We should organize one."

"Well," replied Gail, "I'm not sure it will do much good. I can't see how a few students with no money, no votes, and no connections are going to be listened to on this campus, much less in Washington.

All the people in government care about is their popularity ratings with the voters.''

"But don't you see," Ron argued, "if we can show the President that the war is unpopular with the American people, then we may have some effect on foreign policy. We've got to get people reading and hearing about the war and talking about it among themselves.''

"It's worth a try," Gail agreed, "but I have my doubts.''

**Formation of the "People's Lobby."** For the next two months Ron and Gail talked with friends about setting up an antiwar protest organization. They contacted the National Mobilization Committee to End the War in Vietnam, the coordinator for many antiwar groups throughout the country. They found that the "Mobe" welcomed a campus chapter. They formed a small group called the "People's Lobby" with Abernathy as chairman. But time had been short and not much was accomplished before final exams and summer vacation.

When school began again in the fall, Ron called a strategy planning session. About sixty students showed up. Ron began by saying, "If you are opposed to the war, and want its immediate end, then join us in finding ways to reach this goal. The People's Lobby wants peace now. If that's what you want, you've come to the right place. Our job tonight is to make plans for the coming year. I'd like to hear some ideas.''

A heated debate followed. Some wanted the People's Lobby to pick peace candidates and take part in campaigns to elect them. Others felt that members should go door to door talking to people about the group's opposition to the war. But the majority wanted protest activities on the campus. This group wanted to sponsor "teach-ins" on the war, hold peace rallies, and try to interest faculty members in joining the protest.

**The People's Lobby Goes into Action.** Throughout the year the People's Lobby became more and more active. They sponsored speakers and folksingers who came to campus to take part in a teach-in on Vietnam. They picketed army recruiters when they came to the school to try to enlist students. When a leading chemical company sent agents to the college to interview students for jobs, People's Lobby staged a sit-down strike in the building to publicize the fact that the company was making napalm, a substance used in firebombs in Vietnam.

In moments of depression, Ron wondered how effective they really were. It seemed far-fetched that their activity in one college could have any effect at all on the nation's foreign policy. They certainly were not well-organized. There was not even an up-to-date list of members. The group had very little money. Meetings and rallies were announced by word of mouth or on mimeographed sheets because newspaper advertising was too much. But the results of their sit-ins were always reported in next morning's paper, and the group quickly became known on the campus and in the community. On one occasion, when two members had been arrested for blocking a doorway during a sit-in, the local television station had run a half-hour special on the People's Lobby, including interviews with Ron and the college president.

**The American Public Reconsiders Vietnam.** Public opinion was changing. Opinion surveys that showed the American people strongly supporting President Johnson's handling of the war only a few years back indicated, by late 1967, that only 28 percent of the people still approved. Mass demonstrations, such as those waged by the People's Lobby, were surely not the only reason for declining support of an unpopular war. During 1967 alone, 9353 American servicemen had been killed—more than in the six previous years of the war combined. The nation had been spending over $2 billion a month on the conflict and had lost more than 3000 planes and helicopters. The price of trying to bring democracy to a shaky regime on the other side of the world was beginning to be felt by all.

The People's Lobby and other protest groups around the country did everything they could to stir up reaction against the war. In October 1967 the National Mobilization Committee organized a demonstration in Washington. It drew thousands of protestors to the Lincoln Memorial from all over the country.

As new protest groups formed through the nation, it became clear that a small but very committed minority was so strongly opposed to the war that they were willing to face arrest, if necessary, to make their point. Lacking the resources to change government policy from the inside, they chose instead to try to influence the opinion of people everywhere. And, at least in part, they succeeded. In November 1967, President Johnson complained that the "bullying" tactics of some of

Antiwar activists tended to reject conventional modes of influencing public opinion against the war in Vietnam.

his Vietnam critics amounted to "irresponsible dissent" and called them "extremely dangerous to our national interest." But early in the next year he made the first major move to reduce the level of fighting by ordering a halt to the bombing by American planes of most of the territory in North Vietnam. At the same time he declined to run for another term as President and stepped up the search for a negotiated settlement of the war. The protest movements and demonstrations around the country had helped to change public opinion. In turn, public opinion certainly played a major part in President Johnson's decision.

Vietnam was a hot issue in the 1968 presidential campaign between Democrat Hubert Humphrey and Republican Richard Nixon. Antiwar "activists" across the country worked hard to keep the issue alive.

**Nixon and the Vietnam Issue.** When Nixon became President in 1969, the antiwar activists waited anxiously to see if he would fulfill his campaign pledge to withdraw American soldiers from Vietnam. When he decided to continue fighting in Southeast Asia, the antiwar activists decided to keep up their protests.

The new wave of protest was based on a rising public feeling against the war. By 1971 more than 60 percent of the respondents in several nationwide polls wanted the withdrawal of all United States forces from Vietnam. Also a strong coalition of interest groups was forming to pressure Nixon to stop the war. Common Cause was a primary member of the growing coalition. On February 23, 1971, the chairman of Common Cause, John Gardner, announced a national lobbying campaign to persuade Congress to "legislate an end to the war." A group called the National Council for an Indochina Deadline was set up in 1971 to pressure the government to withdraw from Vietnam by the end of 1971. It included such public figures as Arthur Goldberg, Stewart Udall, Clark Clifford, and Nicholas Katzenbach. They had served under Kennedy and Johnson in high-ranking jobs.

During 1971–1972 the United States was still involved in Vietnam, and the war remained a hot issue. The 1972 presidential campaign included much debate about the war, and once more President Nixon pledged to end it. This time he did so in the face of vast antiwar pressure from both public opinion and a large coalition of interest groups. The noisy, but seemingly weak, voices of a few antiwar activists in 1967 had grown to an enormous roar by 1973.

1. What were the political objectives of the antiwar activists?
2. What political techniques did they use?
3. Compare the techniques of the antiwar activists with those of Maria Begay and the Connecticut State Rifle and Revolver Association. How can you explain differences in their techniques?
4. What is your opinion of the political participation techniques in this case?

# 3 Making Judgments about Political Behavior

Political participants make *judgments* regularly. They make judgments in the halls of Congress, in meeting rooms of interest groups, in courtrooms, city halls, and voting booths.

One important objective of this course is to increase your ability to analyze judgments of people who take part in politics. Another goal is to increase your skill to make reasoned judgments about political behavior.

## Types of Judgments

What kinds of judgments are made by people who take part in politics? Why do they make these judgments? Speculate about answers to these questions on the basis of these four examples.

*Example 1.* In 1973 the leaders of the Sierra Club used many of their political resources to try to get Congress to pass a law to regulate the strip mining of coal. These leaders made the *judgment* that the strip-mining industry has been doing too much damage to the land.

*Example 2.* In December 1974 Congress passed a bill to regulate the strip mining of coal. The bill brought forth lengthy arguments. However, in the *judgment* of a majority in Congress, the bill had more good points than bad ones. Thus it was passed.

*Example 3.* In December 1974 President Ford vetoed the strip-mining bill. He said that in his *judgment* the bill would cut coal output severely, raise unemployment of miners and factory workers, and inflate costs and prices. Thus he concluded that he must not approve the bill.

*Example 4.* On January 3, 1975, an editorial writer for the *Louisville Courier-Journal* criticized President Ford for vetoing the strip-mining bill. In the *judgment* of the writer, the veto was a big mistake. "The strip-mine bill wasn't perfect legislation, but it was a much-needed step toward acknowledging that the full cost of energy consumption entails more than the most economical way to extract fuel from the ground." The editorial urged the new, 94th Congress to "move speedily to repass the bill and bring some long overdue sanity to the surface-mining industry."[1]

*A judgment is an opinion or conclusion.* In each of the four examples people made judgments about a bill to regulate the strip mining of coal.

After Congress passes a bill, it is sent to the President for his signature. The President may veto, or reject, the bill by refusing to sign it. The Congress can override a presidential veto with a two-thirds vote in each house.

---

1. *The Louisville Courier-Journal,* January 3, 1975. Used by permission.

All public officials and unofficial political specialists regularly make judgments about various aspects of political behavior. On election day the voters make judgments about whom their public officials should be.

### Factual and Value Judgments

Political participants make *factual judgments* about the way things are. *These are beliefs that describe or explain reality.* For example, the leaders of the Sierra Club made this factual judgment: The strip mining of coal has eroded thousands of acres of land and has added to the pollution of streams and to the decline of wildlife.

People in politics also make *value judgments* about the way things should be. *These are beliefs about what is good or bad, better or worse.* For example, the Sierra Club leaders made this value judgment: The environment should be protected from damage by strip mining.

President Ford made a different set of factual and value judgments about strip mining at the end of 1974. He concluded that a bill passed by Congress to regulate strip mining should not become a law. This was a value judgment. He based his decisions on two other judgments, one a factual judgment and the other a value judgment. His factual judgment was that the proposed strip-mining law would reduce coal output severely, raise unemployment greatly, and boost the costs and

Bills to regulate strip mining often seek to require the strip miner to restore the land to its original contour rather than leave unsightly gashes and piles of debris.

prices of many goods and services. His value judgment was that it would be very bad for the country to suffer a drop in coal output and rises in unemployment and in costs and prices. As of December 1974 he valued prevention of damage to the economy more than prevention of damage to the environment. In contrast, the Sierra Club valued prevention of environmental damage the most.

These examples show that making judgments about political affairs is often not easy. Reasonable people may interpret the same evidence about reality in different ways and make conflicting value judgments.

To test your ability to distinguish statements of fact and value, decide which of the following speakers are stating factual judgments and which are stating value judgments.

The first speaker is making a factual judgment. We do not know whether she prefers, or values, a federal system of government.

The second speaker is making a value judgment. He says that he prefers the government of the United States to all other governments. He does not tell why he prefers it. Perhaps this government, more than other ones, satisfies the things he values. Someone who holds different values than Speaker 2 might not believe that the American system is best. A person who values dictatorship would not consider the government of the United States to be the best in the world.

The third speaker is stating a value judgment. He also tells something about why he holds this value judgment. He reveals that he prefers a weak government to a strong one.

Identify the value judgments and the factual judgments in the following list of statements.
1. Rich people are more likely than poor people to become political leaders.
2. Everyone ought to have an equal chance to become a political leader.

**3.** Republicans are more likely than Democrats to be very active in political affairs.

**4.** Republicans are better citizens than Democrats.

**5.** It would be in the best interests of manual laborers to vote regularly for Democratic candidates.

**6.** In the last mayoral election in our city, manual laborers tended to vote for the Democratic candidate.

**7.** It's a good thing for the country that older adults take a bigger part than younger adults in election campaigns.

**8.** Older adults are more likely than younger adults to take part in election campaigns.

## Gathering Evidence to Make Factual Judgments

We use our senses—the ability to see, touch, hear, taste, and smell —to make judgments about what is a fact. Something that all people, or nearly all, can agree that they experience with their senses is considered a fact. For example, it is a fact that Richard Nixon got more votes than George McGovern in the 1972 election. This fact was established by counting the votes cast for President and seeing who won.

Of course, it is impossible using only our own senses to gather all the facts we need to make a judgment. No one person saw all the votes for President being counted in 1972. We have to assume that the few thousand persons who took part in the counting gave out fairly accurate reports. Also on many matters we tend to accept the word of experts as to what are the facts. For example, most of us accept the word of experts who conduct experiments in physics about what are the facts of modern physical science.

Moreover, many of the beliefs that we accept as facts are *inferences.* We sense, for example, that it is raining in our town today. Then we hear on the weather report that it is raining in other places in our region. We therefore infer that it is raining throughout the region. We don't have to jump in our car and ride around in order to establish the fact that it is raining in the region.

Political scientists often make inferences about a large group of people on the basis of facts gathered about a smaller group. For example, they reported that older adults were more likely than younger adults to have voted in the 1972 presidential election. To find evidence, the political scientists might have tried to ask all eligible voters in the United States whether or not they took part in the 1972 election. But they really could not do this. Instead they studied a sample, or small group, of voters. The sample was representative of all voters in the United States. Here is what they found: 52 percent in the 18–24 age group voted, and 67 percent of those older than 25 voted. The highest rate—over 70 percent—was by those in the 45–64 age group.

On the basis of their study of a small group of voters (supposedly representative of all voters in the United States) the political scientists inferred this factual judgment: Older adults were more likely than younger adults to have voted in the 1972 presidential election.

Following are two cases of social scientists making factual judgments about political behavior. Read the cases and try to answer the questions which follow.

### Case 1. Who Runs Agri-city?

Agri-city is a small rural town in the midwest that serves as a trade center for farmers. The population is about 11,500.[2]

Three social scientists wanted to find out who has most political influence in Agri-city. They interviewed two groups of people, asking both the same question: Who has the most political influence in Agri-city? The first group included 268 people who were thought to be representative of the town's population. In the second group were those who were named as town influentials by the first group of 268.

On the basis of the evidence gathered from these interviews, the research team made these factual judgments.

• The most influential people in Agri-city do not hold public office. They are the vice-president of the bank, the owner of a real-estate business, an auto dealer, a department store owner, and a jewelry store owner.

• The mayor is seen as the most influential public official in Agri-city. However, he was the only public official to be listed among the ten most influential people in the town.

### Case 2. Political Decision-Making in Levittown

In June 1958, Levittown, New Jersey, was ready for settlers. The firm of Levitt and Sons, Inc., had planned and built this new suburb. Herbert Gans, one of the first residents, came there to conduct a study of human behavior. Some of his questions were about the behavior of public officials and of those who try to influence political decisions.

To answer his questions, Gans became a participant-observer. He lived in Levittown for two years and took an active part in the life there. He joined organizations, went to public meetings, and took part in political activities. All the while, he observed the behavior of people in Levittown. He talked to many people who seemed to be representative of the town. He took notes about the things he saw and heard. Gans also read newspapers and public documents containing information about life in Levittown. In short, Gans gathered and organized evidence. Then he used it to make factual judgments about political behavior in Levittown. Following are some of them.[3]

2. Agri-city is a fictitious name used to disguise the identities of people involved in this study. The full report can be found in Mary Zey Ferrell, O. C. Ferrell, and Quentin Jenkins, "Social Power in a Rural Community," *Growth and Change* (Vol. 4, No. 2) April 1973, pp. 3–6.

3. Herbert J. Gans, *The Levittowners* (New York: Pantheon Books, A Division of Random House, Inc. © Copyright, 1967, by Herbert J. Gans). Used by permission of Random House, Inc.

• Government officials tended to make decisions that would satisfy large groups of voters who could apply pressure on the decision-makers through their leaders. For example, there were many Catholics in Levittown with able leaders in direct contact with town officials. The officials tended to make decisions that pleased this group.

• Small groups having important political resources were able to influence decisions of public officials to a great extent. For example, people who were developing new stores and shopping centers had much influence on decisions that concerned their business interests. And representatives of Levitt and Sons, the developer, had a good deal of influence on the decisions of government officials.

• Government officials tended to ignore the demands of groups with few political resources.

• Minority groups with few political resources, however, were able to increase their influence by focusing attention on certain issues, stirring up public conflict about these issues, and organizing group action, such as passing around petitions and speaking in public meetings.

**1.** What factual judgments were made in each of the studies?

**2.** The factual judgments were based on evidence. How was the evidence gathered?

**3.** What examples of inferences can you find in each study?

**4.** Can you think of any political participants who might be interested in the conclusions made in these two studies? Why? What use could they make of the conclusions?

## Techniques for Gathering Evidence

Those who study political behavior gather evidence in three main ways:

• They ask questions of people about political beliefs or behavior.

• They observe political behavior directly.

• They examine products of political behavior.

### Asking Questions

In the Agri-city study, questions were asked of townspeople in order to gather evidence about political influence in the town. From this evidence factual judgments were made about who has more or less influence in Agri-city.

A person studying political behavior asks questions of various kinds to gather evidence. For example, a person might ask, "For whom do you intend to vote in the next election?" Or the person might ask people their opinions about various issues.

### Observing Behavior Directly

The study in Levittown is an example of direct observation as a way to gather evidence. For two years Herbert Gans observed public policy-makers and those who tried to influence political decisions. He took notes on what he saw and heard. These recorded observations

A political scientist gathers data to make factual judgments. She is interviewing with a tape recorder.

are the facts, or data, that Gans used as evidence to support his judgments about political behavior in Levittown.

**Examining Behavior Products**

Herbert Gans read documents about political behavior in Levittown. He examined behavior products. *A product of behavior is a record of some type that has resulted from human activity.* For example, the artifacts found in Egyptian pyramids or in Indian mounds in North America are products of human behavior in the distant past. Social scientists examine these artifacts as a way to gather facts about the way certain people lived many years ago. Copies of constitutions, newspapers, laws, and speeches are also products of human behavior. Political scientists examine these records to obtain data about past political behavior.

The three main ways of gathering evidence—asking questions, observing behavior directly, and examining behavior products—are often used together by a political scientist trying to answer a question and/or support factual judgments. For example, Herbert Gans used each of these techniques, although he depended most on direct observation.

**Using Information Gathered by Experts**

Instead of making personal observations, one may use evidence from experts who have used one of the three methods cited above. For example, social scientists use information gathered and organized by the Gallup Poll, the Survey Research Center of the University of Michigan, the United States Census Bureau, and other reliable data-gathering organizations.

1. Following is a factual judgment: Nonwhites tended to vote for the Democratic candidate in presidential elections during the period 1952–1972. Does the evidence in *Table 1* support or reject this factual judgment?

2. Following is a factual judgment: Catholics are more likely than Protestants to vote for the Republican candidate in presidential elections. Does the evidence in *Table 2* support or reject this factual judgment?

3. What technique was used to gather the evidence in *Tables 1 and 2?* Is this a good technique to use in order to infer factual judgments such as those in exercises 1 and 2 above? Why?

**Table 1.** Percentage of Nonwhite Voters Who Voted for the Democratic Presidential Candidate, 1952–1972

| Year | Percent |
|------|---------|
| 1952 | 79% |
| 1956 | 61 |
| 1960 | 68 |
| 1964 | 94 |
| 1968 | 85 |
| 1972 | 87 |

**Table 2.** Percentage of Catholic and Protestant Voters Who Voted for the Republican Presidential Candidate, 1952–1972

| Year | Catholic | Protestant |
|------|----------|------------|
| 1952 | 49% | 63% |
| 1956 | 49 | 63 |
| 1960 | 22 | 62 |
| 1964 | 24 | 45 |
| 1968 | 33 | 49 |
| 1972 | 52 | 70 |

## Making Value Judgments

Value judgments express preferences. Consider this value judgment: *Poor people ought to take an active part in politics.* As a value judgment, this statement can't be supported or rejected with facts. Rather, we may judge this belief to be right or wrong on the basis of how we prefer that people would behave. We learn our preferences about what people should believe and how they should behave from those with whom we live—our parents, teachers, friends, etc. In contrast, consider this factual judgment: *Poor people are much less likely than rich people to take an active part in politics.* This belief can be judged right or wrong on the basis of factual evidence about how people take part in politics. One can observe what rich and poor people do in order to decide whether a belief about their political behavior is true or false.

*Tables 1–2:* American Institute of Public Opinion, THE GALLUP POLL, Princeton, New Jersey.

## Value Judgments of Newspaper Editors

See chapters 5 and 6 for a discussion of American political values, how people learn these values, and how these values influence political behavior.

Newspaper editors make and express value judgments about political behavior daily. They decide which of the many stories coming from the wire services will be run and where they should go in the paper. Even *The New York Times,* which is one of the largest American papers, can publish only part of the news that comes in each day. The decision whether or not to print a story about a public official charged with income-tax evasion can have a big impact on politics. And if it is printed, it will make a difference whether it appears on page one or page five. When stories are too long for the space allotted, an editor will delete the paragraphs that are least essential. Or if a reporter files a story that the editor believes is unbalanced, or not clearly written, the editor may rewrite a portion of it. Letters to the editor may flood the newspaper office, making some selection necessary to decide which of these to print.

Another job of the editor is writing editorials. A news story is supposed to give a factual, unbiased account of an event. An editorial expresses the value judgments of the paper on the issues of the day. By reading the editorials the reader can tell just where the paper stands and what the arguments for the position are.

The endorsement of *The New York Times* in its editorials is eagerly sought by presidential candidates and may be a big factor in the election. But the endorsement of the *Danville News* may be just as important to a person running for district attorney in a county. While most readers do not pay a great deal of attention to editorials and the arguments they present, some do—and these few may have a great deal of influence.

Editors are not entirely free to express their own opinions in an editorial. There are several competing pressures on editors. They are employees of the publisher or owner of the paper. The editor also needs to think about the economic well-being of the paper—both in terms of its circulation and its advertising income. Any position the editor takes may offend the publisher, readers, or advertisers.

The position often taken in editorials is that of "watchdog" of the rights of the public. For example, when a politician has taken part in illegal or unfair dealings, an editor may write an unfavorable editorial about the person without offending readers or employer. Editorial writers strongly endorse prosperity, good government, and projects that promise to help the business community and most readers.

However, when there is a sharp split in a community on an issue like school desegregation, editorial stands are likely to be more cautious. Likewise, the writer who launches an anti-smoking campaign may run the risk of offending cigarette advertisers. Thus, editorials are often about issues of "morality," that is, issues with which most of the public can easily identify and agree on who is right and who is wrong.

## Value Judgments of Political Cartoonists

Political cartoonists express value judgments on the editorial pages of newspapers. To convey their judgments, cartoonists use symbols to represent political opinions, values, nations, interest groups, etc. For example, Uncle Sam or an eagle is used to represent the United States. An elephant is the symbol of the Republican party and the donkey symbolizes the Democratic party. An olive branch or dove is a symbol for peace. An arrow or hawk is used to symbolize war.

Following is an example of the use of symbols in a political cartoon. The eagle is a symbol of the United States. The bear is a symbol of Russia. The hammer and sickle on the bear's back is a Communist symbol. The "gulch" that separates the eagle and the bear is a symbol for the differences in political values and attitudes that have made the governments of the Soviet Union and the United States oppose one another. The caption "Time to Bridge That Gulch" means that the cartoonist believed that Russians and Americans should be more friendly toward one another.

**"Time to Bridge that Gulch."**

Why would most Americans react differently from most Russians to the symbols shown in this cartoon?

Bruce Russell. Copyright, 1946, *Los Angeles Times*. Reprinted by permission.

53

A political cartoon usually consists of three main parts: (1) One or more main characters appear in a cartoon. The character may represent a real person or stand for a group of people, an organization, a nation, etc. (2) Other symbols are added to convey the cartoonist's mood or opinion. (3) Captions or labels are added to enable the reader to choose, among the variety of meanings a symbol can convey, the one the cartoonist intended. The caption, usually brief, often summarizes the cartoonist's point of view.

Often the cartoon of the day will be tied to an issue discussed in one of the editorials. The link between a written editorial and a political cartoon is shown on the next page. Both the cartoon by Burck and the editorial, "Clean Air and Water Is a Right," appeared on the editorial page of the *Chicago Sun-Times* in 1970. Both present value judgments about the topic of pollution.

Examine the political cartoon below and those on page 56. Then answer these questions.

**1.** What value judgments are expressed in the cartoons?
**2.** How do the cartoonists convey their value judgments?
**3.** Do you agree with the value judgments expressed? Why?

*PRIMROSE PATH*

Editorial cartoon by Don Hesse. Copyright © St. Louis Globe-Democrat. Reprinted with permission of Los Angeles Times Syndicate.

"BYAAACH!"

*Chicago Sun-Times* editorial cartoon by Jacob Burck. Reprinted with permission.

Often the cartoonist and editorial writer make a joint attack on a particular problem as shown on this page.

### Clean Air and Water Is a Right

The new Pollution Control Board has its work cut out for it. As *The Sun-Times* has pointed out in its news columns and on this page, Illinois does not have one stream or lake where the water is clean enough to drink, to swim in or to fish in. The air we breathe is filthy and getting worse.

As we noted on this page on Friday, more and more communities are faced with the problem of what is the more important, a clean environment or jobs in industries that foul the air and water?

Illinois is faced with that problem today. We expect the new Pollution Control Board to come down on the side of a clean environment as the right of every citizen.[4]

4. From an editorial in the *Chicago Sun-Times*, July 13, 1970. Reprinted by permission.

" HURRY... THERE'S NO TIME TO LOSE..."

Gene Basset for Scripps-Howard Newspapers

"THERE'S SOMETHING I'VE BEEN MEANING TO SPEAK TO YOU ABOUT"

Bob Taylor, *Dallas Times Herald*

## Factual and Value Judgments in Political Affairs

Political decisions involving clear choices between good and bad are easy to make. However, many judgments involve conflict between two or more things that most people think are good. For example, look at these two statements: (1) Freedom of speech is good. (2) Protection of people and property is good. Most of us value both of these ideals. But how do we make a choice when these two ideals seem to be in conflict?

The difficulty shows up in the case study, "The Klan Comes to Town," on pages 4–6. You recall that the mayor had to decide whether or not to prevent the Ku Klux Klan from holding a rally in his city. He valued freedom of speech, but he also valued public safety, security, and order. To stop the Klan from holding a rally would violate the American tradition of free speech, but public safety would be protected. To allow the Klan to hold a rally would support the tradition of free speech, but raise the risks of public disorder.

To resolve a conflict, public officials often must choose something they value at the expense of something else they value. They try to make factual judgments about what will likely happen if they make one decision or another. Then they decide which of the possible outcomes they prefer. This involves value judgment. The preferred *outcome* becomes a *rule* to guide decisions about what ought to be done.

In Case 1 on pages 2–4, the mayor of Lakeville and the city council made this value judgment: We need to build an overpass across a busy highway. This was a tough decision because it was made at the expense of people living in the west end of town. Building the overpass meant that a park could not be built for the West Side.

The city officials supported their decision with this factual judgment: If we build an overpass on Highway 62, we will cut down the risk of Sunnyside children being hit by cars. The outcome of safety for children seemed to be valued more than the outcome of more park space for West Side.

However, the mayor and the city council also wanted to avoid the outcome of unrest in the West Side. They valued the continued political support of West Side. Thus they promised to have a park built as soon as possible. In this way they were able to achieve another outcome that they valued, the continued political backing of the West Side people.

Many recent decisions about environmental issues have required hard choices between two or more "good" things. For example, we all agree that preventing air pollution is good. We also agree that preventing unemployment, poverty, and high prices is good. Unfortunately, these different "good" things can easily come into conflict as shown in the next case study. As you read it, find examples (a) of factual and value judgments and (b) of people using factual judgments to support their value judgments.

57

A reddish brown haze has been a common sight over the steel mills in Gary.

### Shutting Down the Open Hearth

Steel is the major product of Gary, Indiana, a city of 175,000 on Lake Michigan. Since 1909, the open-hearth furnaces of the United States Steel Company in Gary have lit the midnight sky with an eerie orange glow and have dimmed the midday sun with thick clouds of dark smoke. These furnaces have poured out several million tons of steel—and several thousand tons of pollutants—each year.

Despite the dirty air, most residents of Gary have been pleased over the years to see smoke rising from the steel mill. Smoke meant production. Production meant jobs. Jobs meant bread. Whenever the furnaces have shut down—due to strikes or bad times—the people of Gary have suffered.

During the 1960s many Americans became alarmed about pollution. They started to pressure the owners of factories to stop harming the environment. Strict laws were passed to regulate pollution.

### Value Conflicts in Pollution Control

The strong pressures to regulate pollution have led to difficult value conflicts for factory owners, workers, and public officials. Most people agree that pollution by factories is bad. And most people agree that unemployment and a big drop in factory output are bad. The problem has been to find out how to limit pollution enough to protect health and at the same time to protect output and jobs.

This thorny conflict in values posed a tough problem for people in Gary at the end of 1974. The federal government's Environmental Protection Agency (EPA) had ordered the steel company to shut down its ten open-hearth furnaces on or before December 31, 1974. In the judgment of EPA officials, the ten furnaces were making Gary's air a serious health hazard.

Company officials replied by asking the EPA to allow the operation of the furnaces until June 1, 1975. By this time, the company promised to replace the dirty furnaces with a cleaner way of making steel, the "basic oxygen process" (BOP).

The EPA officials didn't want to extend the time limit. They argued that the company was told to close its ten open-hearths on or before December 31, 1973, and had already been granted a one-year extension.

An open-hearth furnace is being loaded, or "charged," with molten pig iron. Flames sweep across the dish-shaped hearth, melting the charge and refining the steel.

The company officials reminded the EPA that they had been replacing their open-hearths with the cleaner BOP shops over the past nine years. In 1965 the plant had over fifty open-hearth furnaces. As of 1974, only ten remained.

The company claimed that it had to keep on using the last ten open-hearths for a short time because it was 240,000 tons a month behind in filling orders. Furthermore, some of the new BOP shops were not producing to capacity due to technical snags. A shutdown of the ten open-hearths, which produced 80,000 tons of steel per month, would mean a severe drop in earnings. Company officials also stressed that 2500 workers would lose their jobs if the furnaces were shut down.

### Gary Officials React to the Issue

Government officials in Gary were torn by the open-hearth issue. Since the early 1960s, they had pressured United States Steel to clean up its operation. But they had always been cautious to try to protect the economic well-being of Gary too. Thus, despite their interest in shutting down the open-hearths, Gary public officials decided to support the company's request. Mayor Richard Hatcher said that he was torn between protecting Gary's public health and protecting its economic welfare. However, Hatcher proclaimed: "To prevent great economic harm at a time of grave economic strain locally and nationally, I am hereby instructing Gary's corporation counsel to contact the appropriate state and federal agencies and inform them of our willingness to support a new six months' variance for the operation of the open-hearths. By granting this extension, an economic catastrophe involving thousands of families and threatening the economic fabric of the entire Gary community is averted."[5]

EPA officials turned aside Mayor Hatcher's plea. They wanted to enforce the "shut down" order. They decided that the company could operate the open-hearths only by paying a $5000 per day fine as an incentive to phase out the furnaces.

### The Case Goes to Court

In the face of EPA resistance, the company took its case to court. In court, EPA officials claimed that Gary had the dirtiest steel plant in the country. John Wilks, United States Attorney for Northern Indiana, urged a shutdown unless a fine was paid.

United States District Judge Alan Sharp agreed with Wilks. He ruled that the company could operate the furnaces until March 31 only if they paid a $2300 a day fine to begin on January 1, 1975. Judge Sharp said: "I am not at all impressed with the good faith with which U.S. Steel comes into this court today. I do not want it on my conscience that I have been a party to the extended pollution of the air in . . . Gary. Neither do I want it on my conscience that

---

5. *Chicago Tribune,* December 20, 1974. Reprinted, courtesy of the *Chicago Tribune.*

some action I have taken or not taken increased the already difficult economic situation that faces the city of Gary."[6]

The company chose to shut down the open-hearths rather than to "pay a daily tribute to the government." More than 2500 workers lost their jobs.

Thousands of workers in related industries were laid off as a result of the shutdown. For example, the International Harvester Company in Chicago dismissed 2200 workers because of the need for steel products which would not be coming from Gary.

**Reactions to the Shutdown.** Steelworkers in the Gary area reacted bitterly. Some condemned Judge Sharp's decision and defended the company's action: "I think it's stupid," said Larry Stone. "Why shut the shop down? One time we had more furnaces than this open and it didn't kill nobody."

Hector Cruz said, "It's going to put a lot of people out of work. Pollution's been here ever since we've been here, but I wouldn't pay $2300 a day to keep this plant open either."

Other steelworkers blamed the company for their trouble. "The onus is on U.S. Steel," said Edward Sadlowski, a union leader. "You can make steel and have clean air at the same time."[7]

Francis Mayo, an EPA official, said that Judge Sharp's decision to let the company operate while paying a fine was fair to all parties.

A company official said, "It is difficult to understand how the public interest is served by forcing the closing . . . at this time with the inevitable losses of production and unemployment."[8]

City officials in Gary were dismayed. Robert Miertschin, Gary city attorney, said, "U.S. Steel agreed in 1965 to have their open hearths shut down in 1973. Now U.S. Steel is attacking environmentalists and refusing to take any blame for what is happening. That is their disaster. Their good faith is in serious question."[9]

Mayor Hatcher summed up the situation by saying it was "a classic confrontation between ecology and the economy." In such a conflict of values, there is no clear right or wrong.

1. What is the main value conflict in this case?
2. Why did the value conflict occur in this case?
3. Identify at least one value judgment made by each of these types of participants in this case
   a. official of the U.S. Steel Company
   b. Gary public official
   c. steelworker
   d. public official in the federal government

---

6-8. Quoted in *The Louisville Courier-Journal,* December 30, 1974, and January 1975. Used by permission.
9. *Chicago Tribune,* December 31, 1974. Reprinted, courtesy of the *Chicago Tribune.*

**4.** Identify at least one factual judgment made by (a) an official of U.S. Steel, (b) an official of the EPA.

**5.** What arguments did officials of U.S. Steel and the EPA use to defend their value judgments? How did they use facts to defend their value judgments?

**6.** What is your value judgment about the outcome? Why?

## Using Polls to Make Judgments about Political Behavior

Public opinion is an important part of American politics. At times, political leaders try to mold public opinion. Sometimes they merely try to follow it. At all times, successful American politicians consider public opinion when making judgments about political behavior.

Today's political leaders have a big advantage over those of earlier times in gauging the public mood. This advantage stems from the *public opinion poll.* A poll is a way to gather information from a group of people by asking questions of them. For example, pollsters ask people about their voting behavior, their opinions about issues, their ratings of candidates, their beliefs about various interest groups, etc. In this way, they have gathered much information that can be used to support or reject factual judgments about political behavior.

Fifty to sixty years ago there were no pollsters to record public opinion reliably and accurately. Politicians of earlier times had to rely entirely on their personal experience and intuition—or on the experience and intuition of their advisers—for estimating public opinion. By contrast, today's politicians can draw upon a large fund of accurate data.

The Gallup Poll and the Harris Survey are the best known of the several polls now published in leading papers and magazines. Numerous private polls are used by some people in politics. People at the Survey Research Center of the University of Michigan—and other such centers—conduct polls as part of their continuing studies of political behavior.

The growing number of politicians who use polls shows the importance of this tool. In both the 1968 and 1972 presidential election campaigns, the Republican party spent more than $400,000 on polls. More than 80 percent of recent candidates for the United States Senate used polls during their campaigns. Recent Presidents have been avid poll watchers. According to Joseph Napolitan, a pollster who has helped manage several campaigns, "Running a campaign without a poll is like trying to find your way through a strange country without a road map. Very often what politicians think people are thinking is quite different from what the people are actually thinking."[10]

---

10. Joseph Napolitan, *The Election Game and How to Win It* (Garden City, N.Y.: Doubleday & Company, Inc., 1972), p. 123.

"One more response like that, sir, and I'll be forced
to put you down as a hostile respondent."

### How Politicians Use Polls

Polling has become a big feature of political life. Polls help political leaders and their followers to make wise, informed decisions. But they also have been used to manipulate and mislead. The cases that follow can help you think about the use and misuse of polling in politics.

### Case 1. To Run or Not to Run?

In 1970 the Democratic party in New York picked Richard Ottinger as its candidate for the United States Senate. The Republicans nominated the incumbent, Charles Goodell.

James Buckley disagreed strongly with the ideas of both major party candidates and was tempted to enter the race as an independent. His friends urged him to run. But still he waited. He did not want to waste time and money trying for an office that might be beyond his reach.

Buckley had big doubts about the mood of New York voters. Did enough of them agree with his ideas to give him a fighting chance?

Buckley and his advisers decided that only a public opinion poll could answer this question. As it turned out, more voters seemed to agree witth Buckley's ideas than with those of Goodell or Ottinger. Buckley decided to run for senator—and he won.

### Case 2. The Winning Message

Frank Licht, the Democratic governor of Rhode Island in 1970, was worried about reelection. A private poll of Rhode Island voters, taken for Licht by Joseph Napolitan, showed the governor running far behind Herbert DeSimone, his Republican challenger. According to Licht's pollster, 48 percent of the voters endorsed DeSimone, 19 percent were for Licht, and 33 percent were undecided.

Although the poll showed Licht far behind DeSimone, the governor's position was not hopeless. It was still early in the campaign. DeSimone could not yet count on a majority.

More important, one-third of the voters had not decided. Licht needed to find out what appeal he could make to this undecided group without losing the small base of support he already had.

Napolitan advised Licht to poll a small sample of the Rhode Island voters. The poll's purpose was to find out what issues were most important to the voters and what their opinions were on these issues.

Napolitan's poll showed that the chief issue was state taxes. A large majority were angry about some recent tax laws and proposals for new taxes.

In response to these polling results, Licht focused on the tax issue for the rest of the campaign. His opponent did not. Governor Licht was able to convince Rhode Island voters that he would deal with the tax issue more effectively than DeSimone. Licht's emphasis on the tax issue was the winning message in the 1970 campaign for governor of Rhode Island.

### Case 3. The Bandwagon Effect

The 1971 mayoral primary election in Philadelphia was a hot, three-way contest. Congressman William J. Green, State Representative Hardy Williams, and former Police Commissioner Frank J. Rizzo were competing to be the Democratic candidate.

At a crucial point in the campaign, one week before the balloting, a poll of registered Democratic voters was reported on the front page of the *Philadelphia Daily News.* The poll showed Rizzo way out in front, Hardy a poor second, and Green a very distant third with only 12 percent of the vote.

Congressman Green immediately protested to the *Daily News* editors. He claimed that the poll did not show his true voting strength. He also argued that the poll's publication might convince voters that Rizzo was a certain winner and that a vote for Green or Hardy would be wasted on the loser.

After looking into Green's protest, the newspaper concluded that the mayoral poll was not taken properly and likely was not valid.

Shortly afterward, the paper reported this conclusion in a front-page story.

The story came too late to help William Green. Frank Rizzo won the primary, but Green ran second with 35 percent of the vote. This tally in the election held up his claim that the 12 percent forecast was a sham.

Green complained that the poll helped to launch Rizzo's bandwagon. Many undecided voters, according to Green, voted for Rizzo only because they thought he could not lose.

**1.** What factual judgments were made by (a) James Buckley, (b) Frank Licht, (c) William J. Green?

**2.** What value judgments were made by (a) James Buckley, (b) Frank Licht, (c) the editor of the *Philadelphia Daily News?*

**3.** How did these people use factual judgments to support their value judgments: (a) James Buckley, (b) Frank Licht?

**4.** What are your value judgments about the uses of polls as described in Cases 1-3? Why?

### Can You Trust the Polls?

During the 1968 presidential election, candidate George C. Wallace probably spoke for many people when he said: "They lie when they poll. They are trying to rig an election."

Is this true? To borrow a phrase from 1928 presidential candidate Alfred E. Smith, "Let's look at the record."

**"No—and I don't like the Democrats either."**

Editorial cartoon by Don Hesse. Copyright © St. Louis Globe-Democrat. Reprinted with permission of Los Angeles Times Syndicate.

One way to look at the record is to compare poll predictions with the actual election results. What does the record, as shown in *Table 3* on the next page, say about one pollster's accuracy?

The Gallup Poll has been a very accurate indicator of voter behavior in recent presidential elections. Since 1952 the average error of the Gallup Poll in predicting the outcomes of national elections has been only 1.4 percent.

When done correctly, an opinion survey is very likely to yield a true picture of the public mood at the time the poll was taken. Pollster Louis Harris reports that "any national sample we construct will be accurate to within 3 percentage points on a sample of 1,500 or over in 95 out of 100 cases."[11]

But every poll is not taken correctly. And at times phony polls are taken on purpose in order to mislead the public. Since opinion surveys do play such a large role in today's election process, we need to learn how to identify defective polls.

Two main indicators of any public opinion poll's value are (1) the method of picking persons to poll and (2) the quality of the questions asked in the poll.

### Selecting Individuals to Poll

Pollsters want to gather information about very large groups of people. However, it would be almost impossible to make a study of all people in the United States, or in one of the fifty states, or even in one city. Pollsters need to be able to make accurate conclusions about a large group of people by studying a sample, or small group of people. To do this, the sample must be picked at random.

Random selection means that every person in the larger group has the same chance of getting into the sample as every one else. For example, assume that you wish to pick at random a sample of 100 students from a population of 500 seniors in one high school. You might put the 500 names in a box, mix the contents thoroughly, and select 100 names in such a way that every senior has the same chance of being picked. Studying the opinions of a randomly selected sample of 100 persons enables one to make accurate factual judgments about the opinions of the total group of 500 persons.

Wrong sampling methods can lead to the gathering of poor data. Factual judgments based on these defective data will be inaccurate.

Look over the following examples carefully. Which methods are likely, and which are not likely, to contribute to reliable and accurate public opinion polling? Why?

*Example 1.* On May 10, 1973, a question on the front page of the *Detroit Free Press* was framed: "John Dean has agreed to tell

---

11. Reprinted from *The Anguish of Change* by Louis Harris. By permission of W. W. Norton & Company, Inc. Copyright © 1973 by W. W. Norton & Company, Inc.

**Table 3. Gallup Poll Estimates and Election Results in the Presidential Elections of 1964, 1968, and 1972**

| | 1964 | | 1968 | | | 1972 | | |
| --- | --- | --- | --- | --- | --- | --- | --- | --- |
| | Dem. | Rep. | Dem. | Rep. | Third Party | Dem. | Rep. | Other |
| Election Results | 61.4% | 38.6% | 42.9% | 43.5% | 13.6% | 38% | 61% | 1% |
| Gallup Estimate | 64.0 | 36.0 | 42.0 | 43.0 | 15.0 | 38 | 62 | — |

all he knows about White House involvement in Watergate if he's granted immunity from prosecution. Should he be given immunity?''

Below the question, readers were asked to call the newspaper's editorial office to "vote" *yes* or *no* on this question.

A follow-up issue of the paper reported the percentage of people who responded *yes* or *no.*

*Example 2.* An article in *The New York Times,* March 13, 1970, reported this finding: Only 4 percent of the people in Harlem agreed with a proposal to build a large state government office building in their community.[12]

The method for picking people in this poll was to stand on a street corner and ask 6000 passersby their opinions.

*Example 3.* A student council committee in a small rural Indiana high school wanted to find out student opinion on the effectiveness of the council. Each of the school's 354 students was asked to respond to an opinion questionnaire.

*Example 4.* A social scientist at a large university (more than 20,000 students) wanted to find out student opinion about some recent Nixon foreign policy decisions. She selected a sample of 400 students to respond to her opinion questionnaire. The sample was picked as follows: (1) A list of all the students in the university was obtained. (2) The name of each student was written on a card, and the cards were placed in a large container. (3) After the cards were thoroughly mixed, 400 names were picked at random, one by one.

You should have identified as *correct* the procedures described in examples 3 and 4.

If all the students gave an honest answer, the method in example 3 would surely present a true picture. Every student in the school took part in the poll.

The method in example 4 would probably lead to a true picture of all student opinion in the university, since a representative, or random, sample of all the students was likely to have been picked for the poll.

One can have confidence in this sample from the way it was selected: Each person in the population had the same chance to be included in the sample.

---

*Table 3:* American Institute of Public Opinion, THE GALLUP POLL, Princeton, N.J.

12. © 1970 by The New York Times Company. Reprinted by permission.

Huffine in *The Wall Street Journal*

**"The odds against ever again having four flat tires in a
heavy rainstorm are 6,349,833,604,284.6 to 1"**

### Probability Theory

Using random samples to make accurate factual judgments about
larger groups is based on *probability theory.* For example, pretend
that you have a tub that holds 10,000 marbles of equal size. Half
the marbles are red and half are green. You select randomly 400 marbles from the tub. According to probability theory, you are very likely,
within a 5 percent margin of error, to select 200 green marbles and
200 red marbles. According to probability theory, you are very likely
to obtain the same results if you repeat this activity again and again.

Probability theory is a complicated subject which, for our purposes, we don't need to study in detail. Rather, for the moment you
are asked to accept the belief that probability theory gives you confidence to select a random sample of people that is a close approxi-
mation, in miniature, of the population you want to study. If, for
instance, the large university population (in example 4 above) had
been 70 percent white and 30 percent black, then an accurate sample
would have included a ratio of whites to blacks that was about 7 to
3. In the 400-person sample, there should have been around 280 whites
and 120 blacks. Within a small margin of error, this would probably
be the actual fact.

The samples in examples 1 and 2 are *not* likely to have yielded
true pictures of the larger populations from which they were drawn.
They were defective samples because some persons had a better
chance than others to be picked.

In example 1, only readers of the *Detroit Free Press* had a chance
to become part of the sample. In example 2, only people who happened

68

to walk by the interviewers on the street had a chance to be picked. Opinion polls based on such unrepresentative samples are worthless.

### How Pollsters Pick Random Samples

It is easy to pick a random sample of a small group of people, such as all the students in your school or all the people who live in your neighborhood. It is much harder to pick a random sample of a much larger population, such as all the people in your state or in the United States. Lists of every person in a state or in the nation, from which a random sample could be picked, are not available. However, lists of counties, cities, and areas within counties and cities are available. Thus, a random sample of all counties, or of smaller geographic units, in the United States can be picked. Within these smaller areas that have been randomly selected, one can obtain a list of all residents. A random sample of the residents within each geographic unit can be picked. Studying these randomly selected residents of randomly selected geographic areas in the nation provides a random sample of all residents of the United States.

The method of the Gallup Poll for getting random samples of all Americans is very similar to the method just described. For example, Gallup picks at random 300 sections of the nation and selects at random five or six residents of each section. This random sample of 1500–1800 people is representative of adults in the population of the United States.

Notice that the size of Gallup's national sample is small. The size of the sample, beyond a certain minimum size needed to avoid distortion, is less important that the method of selection. A sample may contain 50 million people, rather than 1500, and yet be unreliable because of faulty selection. According to probability theory, only a randomly selected sample has a very high chance of being an accurate representation of the group from which it was picked.

Random samples can't give absolute certainty of an accurate study. One can only claim that random samples are highly likely to yield accurate results within a small margin of error. Since there is no good alternative to accurate large-scale studies of political opinion and behavior, the random sample is a very valuable tool.

To show what you have learned about sampling, complete the following two exercises.

### Exercise A

Judge the three examples of sampling which follow. Decide which technique is most likely to produce accurate results in a political opinion study.

Three teams of researchers wanted to find out student opinions about political participation at a midwestern university. The university had 10,000 students. Each team used the same set of questions, but each used a different sampling technique.

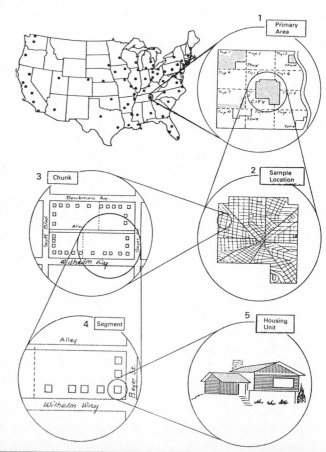

Illustration 8-1
SRC Sampling Method

| | |
|---|---|
| 1 Primary Area | |
| 2 Sample Location | |
| 3 Chunk | |
| 4 Segment | |
| 5 Housing Unit | |

SURVEY
RESEARCH
CENTER

SEGMENT LISTING SHEET

A. LISTED BY *Susan Metz* DATE 3/18/'68

B. UPDATED BY *Susan Metz* DATE 9/9/'68

_____ DATE _____

C. PSU *Fall River*

PLACE *Hampton City*

D. SEGMENT NO. *203A*

E. TYPE OF SEGMENT:

Take-all ☐

Take-part ☒

| Line No. | Description (or address) of Dwelling Unit | Project Number |
|---|---|---|
| 1. | 221 Elm St., upper right | |
| 2. | 221 Elm St., upper left | |
| 3. | 104 Fieldston Terrace | |
| 4. | 127 Fieldston Terrace | |
| 5. | 103 Fieldston Terrace | |
| 6. | 120 Sherwood St. | |
| 7. | 336 Oak St. | |
| 8. | 272 Oak St. | |
| 9. | 220 Oak St. | |
| 10. | Apartment over large garage behind 272 Oak St., entrance on west side of structure | |

*Sampling Technique of Team I.* Team I stopped the first 1000 students whom they met on a street in the middle of the campus. Each student was asked the questions about political participation.

*Sampling Technique of Team II.* Team II went to the office of the university registrar. This office listed the name of every student at the university. The researchers assigned a number to the name of each student. All the numbers were placed in a large box and mixed. Then the researchers pulled 400 student numbers out of the box. Each of these 400 students was visited by a researcher and asked to answer the questions about political participation.

*Sampling Technique of Team III.* Team III decided to use a smaller list of students from which to pick a larger sample. These researchers went to the university office where students registered their automobiles. The team obtained a list of 6000 student owners of automobiles. The researchers decided to pick every fifteenth name on this list to include in their sample. Then the researchers visited each of the 400 students in this sample and asked them to answer the questions.

**1.** Which of these three teams used the best sampling technique? Explain your choice.

**2.** How widely can the researchers generalize in making factual judgments from the data gathered in the above example? Or to say this in another way, how large is the group of students described by factual statements made from these data? Choose one or more of the following groups; (a) all university students in the United States, (b) all university students in the midwestern region of the United States, (c) all university students in the university where this particular attitude survey was made.

**3.** In order to extend the generalizability of their findings, what must the researchers do?

Polling organizations provide some training for interviewers—often by means of a handbook. On the opposite page are two portions of a handbook of the Survey Research Center of the University of Michigan. One of the circles in the inset diagram shows a polling "segment." The listing sheet identifies the dwellings in such a segment. One or more homes may be chosen for polling.

**Exercise B**

In 1936 the *Literary Digest,* a popular magazine, selected a sample of voters in the United States and asked the individuals in this sample for whom they would vote in the upcoming presidential election of 1936: the Republican candidate, Alfred Landon; or the Democratic candidate, Franklin D. Roosevelt. The *Literary Digest* selected a sample of 2,375,000 persons from lists of automobile and telephone owners in the United States. On the basis of this study the *Literary Digest* predicted that Alfred Landon would win a landslide victory. In fact, Franklin D. Roosevelt won a landslide victory.

What was wrong with the *Literary Digest* study?

---

*Opposite:* Interviewer's Manual, Revised Edition. © 1976, Institute for Social Research, The University of Michigan. Used by permission.

## Quality of the Questions

Although a public opinion poll may be based on a perfectly representative sample, it is still no better than the questions it asks. A pollster who uses faulty questions will gather unreliable answers. Factual judgments based on these defective data will be inaccurate.

### Asking Clear Questions

Good opinion poll questions are clear. They are understood easily and interpreted similarly by all those asked to answer them. Clear questions are likely to yield reliable answers because they are likely to mean about the same thing to those who answer them. Here are two questions that might be used in a public opinion study. Which question is better?

*Question A:* Do you approve of the way the President of the United States is doing his job?

*Question B:* What do you think about the President?

Question A is better because it is clearer than Question B. Question B is vague; it does not tell what the respondents are to judge about the President.

Why is Question C likely to be unclear?

*Question C:* Do you believe that candidates for mayor are blowing the voters' minds with their campaign promises?

This question includes slang words, ''blowing the voters' minds,'' which might not mean the same thing to all respondents.

What is wrong with Question D?

*Question D:* Did you take part frequently in political activities last year?

This question is unclear because of possible confusion about the meaning of ''frequently.'' Words such as ''often,'' ''usually,'' and ''frequently'' do not mean the same thing to every person. For instance, taking part six times might be ''frequent'' to one person and ''infrequent'' to another. Here is how it might be rewritten:

**SMIDGENS**

Reprinted by permission, Bob Cordray and National Newspaper Syndicate

*Did you take part in political activities last year (a) more than 10 times; (b) between 5 and 10 times; (c) less than 5 times; (d) not at all?*

In order to write clear questions, pollsters often show a list of questions to other people and ask for improvements. Pollsters often test their questions by trying them out with some people who are like those they plan to study. For example, if the pollsters are studying the opinions of college students, they might try out the questions on college students. If they find that a question is not clear, they will try to figure out why and then change it.

### Asking Unbiased Questions

Good questions also are *unbiased.* That is, the question must not suggest that one answer is better than another.

*Oscar Peterson, a suspected Communist sympathizer, is running against Jack Martin for mayor this fall. Do you prefer either candidate at this time?*

This question is "loaded" against Oscar Peterson. It uses emotional words, "Communist sympathizer," to sway respondents away from selecting Oscar Peterson.

What is wrong with this question?

*Bob Smith is running for Congress this year in our district. Who is your choice in the district congressional election?*

This question could have biased the answers of many respondents who may have named some candidate other than Smith had he, or she, been a part of the question too.

Another type of biased question uses the prestige of a person or group to suggest the "right" answer. Here is an item from a congressman's poll of voters in his district. Notice how the prestige of the Presidency was used to bias the question.

*Do you favor the President's proposal to make the federal government more efficient and responsive by consolidating seven cabinet departments into four new ones?*

In addition to the bias that creeps in by using the words "President's proposal," the answers of many respondents might have been biased by the words "efficient" and "responsive." It is not easy to be against something that could make government more efficient and responsive.

**1.** Look at the following questions which might have been used in public opinion polling. Which of them are defective? Why?

    **a.** Fewer than two-thirds of the eligible voters cast their ballots in the last city election. Were you one of those who didn't bother to vote?

    **b.** Do you believe that draft dodgers in the Vietnam War should have been given amnesty when more than 50,000 patriotic

Americans sacrificed their lives in this crusade against the evils of communism?

**c.** Do you frequently read about politics in newspapers or news magazines?

**d.** If the election were held today, which of the two candidates for mayor of Steeltown would you vote for, John Jastremski or Howard Mendelbaum?

**e.** If a person wanted to make a speech in this community against churches and religion, should he/she be allowed to speak?

**f.** Do you think the President was jiving the people in his speech last night?

**2.** Rewrite the defective items in the above list so that they would be acceptable polling questions.

### Checklist for Judging Public Opinion Polls

To help protect the public against phony polls, the National Committee on Published Polls has been set up to establish standards of quality control. The committee urges readers and users of polls to use the following kinds of questions as guides in judging any political poll. Only those polls about which you can answer "yes" to every question in the checklist should be judged as *potentially* reliable.

1. Is an exact definition given of the population sampled?
2. Is the exact sampling procedure described?
3. Is the sampling procedure very likely to yield a representative sample from which accurate conclusions can be made about the population?
4. Is the sample size revealed?
5. Is the sample large enough to yield accurate conclusions about the population?
6. Are the questions asked of respondents presented exactly as they were asked in the poll?
7. Are the questions used in the poll clear and unbiased?
8. Is the number of respondents with "no opinion" revealed, and is this statistic considered in the report of the findings?
9. Is the procedure for obtaining answers revealed (face-to-face interview, telephone interview, etc.)?
10. Is the date the poll was taken presented?
11. Are the findings of the poll stated clearly?
12. Are the reported findings consistent with the procedures used to conduct the poll?

Public opinion polls are an important part of American politics. Lack of skill in reading and judging them puts one at a disadvantage. The phony poll exploits public ignorance to achieve unfair political advantage. Constant judging of polling practices can help protect against the misuses of political polls.

# THE GALLUP POLL

## SPONSORED BY LEADING REPUBLICAN, DEMOCRATIC AND INDEPENDENT NEWSPAPERS

| | |
|---|---|
| SUGGESTED INTRODUCTION: I'm taking a GALLUP POLL. I'd like YOUR opinion on some topics of interest. | Time Interview Starts: ............................ |

1. Do you approve or disapprove of the way Ford is handling his job as President?

   1( ) Approve   2( ) Disapprove   v( ) No opin.

   COMMENT:_____

2. Do you approve or disapprove of the way President Ford is dealing with economic conditions in this country?

   1( ) Approve   2( ) Disapprove   v( ) No opin.

   COMMENT:_____

3. Do you think the economic situation in the United States during the next six months will get better or will get worse?

   1( ) Better  2 ( ) Worse  3( ) Stay about
   v ( )No opinion                      same

4. Some economists think the U.S. economy is heading toward a depression, such as the nation experienced in the 1930's. Do you agree or disagree?

   1( ) Agree   2( ) Disagree  v( ) No opinion

5. (HAND RESPONDENT CARD 1) If you had to choose one of these two plans to reduce consumption of gasoline, which would you prefer?

   1( ) Plan A  2( ) Plan B  3( ) Neither
   v( ) No opinion

6. How many drivers, if any, are there in your household?

   1( ) One  2( ) Two  3( ) Three  2( ) Four
   5( ) Five  6( ) Six or more  7( ) None

7. Would you say that you and your family are presently living <u>within</u> your means, <u>somewhat beyond</u> your means, or <u>far beyond</u> your means?

   1( ) With  2( ) Somewhat beyond
   3( ) Far beyond   v ( ) No opionion

8. How would you describe the current financial situation of you and your family—excellent, good, only fair, or poor?

   1( ) Excellent  2 ( ) Good  3( ) Only fair
   4( ) Poor  v ( ) No opinion

9. Would you say that you and your family are better off or worse off financially today than you were 12 months ago?

   1( ) Better off   2 ( ) Worse off
   3( ) About same   v ( ) Don't know

10. Looking ahead, do you think that 12 months from now you and your family will be better off financially or worse off?

    1( ) Better off   2 ( ) Worse off
    3) ) About same   v ( ) No opinion

11. Are you now employed full time, part time, or not employed?

    1 ( ) Full time  2( ) Part time
    3 ( ) Not employed

12. Thinking about the next 12 months—how likely do you think it is that you will lose your job or be laid off—very likely, fairly likely, not too likely, or not at all likely?

    1( ) Very  2( ) Fairly  3( ) Not too
    4( ) Not at all  v ( ) No opinion

13. There is a lot of discussion about how to describe the economic situation the country is in today. (HAND RESPONDENT CARD 2) Which one of these comes closest to how you, your-self, would describe the country's economic situation?

    1( ) Mild recession   2( ) Serious recession
    3( ) Mild depression 4( ) Serious depression
    5( ) None of these   v( ) No opinion

Page 1

American Institute of Public Opinion, THE GALLUP POLL, Princeton, New Jersey.

# UNIT TWO

## Similarities and Differences in Political Behavior

# 4 Comparing Political Behavior

People of different groups often behave politically in very different ways. Yet, in some very basic ways, the political behavior of all groups of people is very similar.

Increasing your knowledge of similarities and differences in the political behavior of different groups is a main objective of this book. Trying to answer these two questions will help you reach this objective.

1. What are some basic similarities and differences in the political behavior of different groups of people?
2. Why do these basic similarities and differences exist?

Following are three cases describing political behavior. They can help you begin to answer these two questions.

## Three Cases about Settling Conflict

The Ifugao, the Dinaric Serbs, and the people of the United States have tended to settle certain types of personal conflicts in different ways. The next three cases show how these three societies would try to settle a personal conflict over slander. Slander is saying something false that hurts the reputation of another person.

### Case 1. Settling Conflict through Mediation

The Ifugao (e-few'-gow) people live in rugged mountain country of northern Luzon Island in the Philippines. Disputes in cases where one person has slandered another are settled by a mediator, or go-between, known as a *monkalun*. A *monkalun* is neither an elected nor an appointed official. Rather, any adult man who is a member of a leading family in the Ifugao society can be chosen to serve as a *monkalun*. Any person who complains of being slandered chooses a member of one of the leading Ifugao families to serve as a *monkalun*. The *monkalun* tells an accused person of the charges and tries to use his influence to bring about a settlement of the conflict.

The *monkalun* is neither a judge nor a policeman. He has no power to decide which person is right or wrong, to hand down punishments, or to enforce laws. Rather, the *monkalun* tries to settle the conflict by getting the two disputing persons to make a settlement that is satisfactory to both of them. Since the two parties to the conflict will not speak to one another, the *monkalun* carries messages from one to the other.

In a case of slander, the *monkalun* is usually able to settle the conflict by getting the person who did the slandering to pay damages to the person who was harmed. This payment might be farm animals or crops. Typically the accused will try to bargain with the complainer

The Ifugao people live in a mountainous area of the Philippines.

to lower the cost of the damage payment. Of course, this bargaining by the parties is conducted through the *monkalun.*

If the *monkalun* can't arrange a settlement, then the person who was harmed may try to settle the dispute by killing the accused.

### Case 2. Settling Conflict through "Blood Vengeance"

In the Dinaric Mountain region of Yugoslavia the Serbian people still talk about the bitter acts of "blood vengeance" that once took place there. Just seventy years or so ago, "blood vengeance" was the only honorable way for a Dinaric Serb to get back at someone who had hurt or insulted him. "Blood vengeance" meant that a man who had been hurt by slander was expected to kill the man who had harmed him. In this way he could gain revenge for the harm that had been done.

The "blood vengeance" could take the form of a public fight, but often it was carried out through ambush. The only way to avoid "blood vengeance" was for the person who had caused harm to another

to beg for mercy and to pay "blood money" to the avenger. This public shame and payment of "blood money" only took place when a person was afraid to stand up to an avenger. One who paid "blood money" to save his life was despised as a weakling and a coward.

Personal conflicts were often expanded to long-term "blood feuds" among families in the Dinaric Mountains. One member of a family would try to avenge the harm done to a father, brother, or cousin. This would result in retaliation. Thus a vicious circle of conflict between families would occur.

Although these "blood" conflicts were severe, they were carried out according to rules. Those who broke the rules faced the threats of community disapproval and social isolation.

### Case 3. Settling Conflict through Judicial Decision

In the United States personal conflicts such as slander are often settled by a judge, or a judge and jury, in a court of law. For example, one person may charge another person with slander and try to gain money in return for the damages suffered. The court decides whether payment must be made and, if so, how much. Here is an example of a conflict involving slander.

Miss Clark was a cashier in a large grocery store owned by Mr. Brown. Miss Clark felt that some of Mr. Brown's employment practices were unfair, and she had complained to officials of her union about his activities. Mr. Brown was annoyed by Miss Clark's action and felt that she should have come to him with her complaints.

One day, several weeks after Miss Clark complained to the union, Mr. Brown accused her of stealing $5 worth of goods from the store. He spoke up quite loudly in front of several employees and customers.

Miss Clark denied that she had stolen anything from the store. She said that Mr. Brown was only trying to embarrass her because she had complained to her union about him. She decided to show Mr. Brown that he could not get away with spreading damaging lies about a person. She charged him with slander and sued him for damages to her reputation.

Mr. Brown protested that Miss Clark had been a dishonest and "upstart" employee. He declared that he would not pay one cent in damages. Miss Clark replied that Mr. Brown should save his protests for the judge, who would decide how to settle this case.

1. What (a) differences and (b) basic similarity about settling conflict are described in these cases?
2. Why did these differences and similarity in settling conflict exist?
3. Which of the three techniques for settling conflict is best? Explain.
4. What does your answer to question 3 reveal about your values and why you have these values?

80

## Stating Hypotheses about
## Similarities and Differences

The facts needed to answer some questions are easy to get. Thus everyone can agree about what the correct response is. For example, facts in the above three cases about conflict can be used to answer this question exactly: What differences and similarities about settling conflict are described in these cases?

In contrast, the facts needed to answer some questions are not handy. Thus one must speculate, or guess, about the correct response. For example, all the facts needed to answer the following question do not show up in the three cases about conflict: Why did these similarities and differences in settling conflict exist?

You might have some good hunches about the right answer to this question. However, to decide whether your hunch, or tentative answer, is correct, you need to gather more facts. You need to find out *why* similarities and differences in political behavior exist among different groups of people.

A preliminary, or tentative, answer to a question about political behavior can be stated as a hypothesis. A hypothesis is a guess about the way things are. It is stated precisely so that it can be checked against reality.

For example, perhaps you want an answer to this question: "Do players on varsity athletic teams make better grades than other students in my school?" You might respond to this question with this hypothesis: *Players on varsity athletic teams achieve lower grade-point averages than do students who do not play on varsity athletic teams.* As a hypothesis about differences in grade-point averages, this statement is a guess, an untested answer. To decide whether this hypothesis does, or does not, fit the facts, you must gather information about the grades of athletes and non-athletes in your school.

Notice that the preceding hypothesis focuses on a comparison between students who play on varsity teams and students who do not play on these teams. Many hypotheses about political behavior are about similarities and differences. For example, consider the alternative hypotheses which might be stated in response to this question: Are younger (18-29) or older (30 and over) adults more likely to picket or take part in a street demonstration? Below are three alternative, or conflicting, hypotheses about similarities or differences in the political behavior of younger and older people.

1. Younger adults are *more* likely than older adults to picket or take part in a street demonstration.

2. Younger adults are *less* likely than older adults to picket or take part in a street demonstration.

3. There is likely to be little or no difference in the tendencies of younger or older adults to picket or take part in a street demonstration.

As alternative hypotheses about political activity, these statements are three conflicting guesses. They are untested answers to a question about similarities or differences in political activity. Only one of these conflicting hypotheses can be correct. To find out which hypothesis is true, one must gather reliable evidence about the political behavior of younger and older adults.

Look at the evidence in *Tables 1-2,* gathered through polling of a nationwide sample by the Louis Harris organization. What do these data tell about which of the above hypotheses was correct at the time the data were gathered?

**Table 1.** Percentages of Younger and Older Adults Who Say They Have Picketed or Taken Part in a Street Demonstration

| Age Group | Percent Responding |
| --- | --- |
| 18–29 | 18% |
| 30–49 | 11 |
| Over 50 | 6 |

**Table 2.** Percentages of Younger and Older Adults Who Say They Might Take Part in a Demonstration to Change Things They Don't Like about Government

| Age Group | Percent Responding |
| --- | --- |
| 18–29 | 45% |
| 30–49 | 28 |
| Over 50 | 11 |

Some hypotheses are statements of comparison between groups *at a particular time.* Here is an example: Older adults are more likely (at the present time) than younger adults to campaign or work actively for a candidate for Congress.

Other hypotheses are statements of comparison about change from *one time to another.* Here is an example: Younger adults were more involved in campaigning or working actively for a candidate for Congress in 1976 than they were in 1972.

**1.** In response to each hypothesis below, (a) state one alternative hypothesis, (b) tell how evidence can be gathered and used to support or reject the hypotheses.

**a.** Poor people were more involved in trying to influence public officials in 1976 than they were in 1966.

**b.** Rich people are more likely than poor people to try to influence public officials.

**c.** There is little or no difference in the political activity of farmers and construction workers.

*Tables 1–2: Confidence and Concern: Citizens View American Government,* a Survey of Public Attitudes by the Subcommittee on Intergovernmental Relations of the Committee on Government Operations, United States Senate, pp. 256, 259. Survey conducted by Louis Harris and Associates in 1973. Reprinted by permission of the *Chicago Tribune.* All Rights Reserved.

**2.** In response to the following questions about political behavior, (a) state a hypothesis in response to the question, (b) tell how evidence can be gathered and used to support or reject the hypothesis.

**a.** Can you compare the political resources of lawyers and factory workers?

**b.** Is violent political activity more likely to occur in democracies or dictatorships?

**c.** Are women more involved in political leadership positions today than they were in 1976?

## Using Concepts to Make Comparisons

A concept refers to things that go together, that can be grouped on the basis of common characteristics. For example, rich people, poor people, and influence are concepts that appear in hypothesis 1b in the above exercises. *Rich people* are a group, or category, of persons with common characteristics, such as much wealth and a high standard of living. We understand the name *poor people* to mean persons who share certain characteristics, such as little wealth and a low standard of living. *Influence*, as you learned in chapter 1, is the ability to control, or direct the behavior of others. Various behaviors which fit the category "trying to use influence" have a common characteristic—they have something to do with trying to control or direct the behavior of others.

Concepts allow us to organize, describe, and compare facts. Conflict, rules, public officials, political decision, and political resources are some of the concepts that you have used to organize and compare facts about political behavior.

Mediation, adjudication, and capitulation are three concepts that can be used to compare the political behavior discussed in the three cases about settling personal conflict on pages 78–80. *Mediation* means that the parties to a conflict agree to let another person or group (a mediator) suggest a way to settle the conflict. However, the parties to the conflict are not required to accept the suggestions of the mediator. *Adjudication* means to settle a personal conflict in a court of law. The parties to the conflict are required to accept the decision of the judge, or adjudicator. *Capitulation* means that one party to a conflict forces a settlement on the other party.

*Diagram 1* illustrates the application of these concepts to the three cases. The Ifugao case is an example of mediation. The Dinaric Serbs case is an example of capitulation. The Clark-Brown slander case is an example of adjudication.

The concepts of mediation, adjudication, and capitulation direct our attention to certain details of the cases and away from other details. Using these concepts to compare political behavior is *one* way to interpret the facts in the cases in a meaningful way.

**Diagram 1. Techniques for Settling Conflicts**

| Techniques | Ifugao | Dinaric Serbs | Clark-Brown |
|---|---|---|---|
| Capitulation | | X | |
| Mediation | X | | |
| Adjudication | | | X |

**Diagram 2. Type of Rules**

| Rules | Ifugao | Dinaric Serbs | Clark-Brown |
|---|---|---|---|
| Informal | X | X | |
| Formal | | | X |

The concepts that we decide to use in a comparison determine the way we see and interpret the facts we are studying. Facts do not "speak for themselves." Facts become meaningful when they are related or organized. Concepts are used to organize and interpret facts, to give them a "voice."

Applying different concepts to the same facts results in different interpretations of the facts. For example, the concepts of formal rules and informal rules can be applied to the interpretation of the three cases about settling personal conflict on pages 78–80. A formal rule is a law that is made and enforced by a government. An informal rule is a custom or tradition that has developed gradually through repeated use. Social pressures, rather than the power of government, are used to enforce informal rules.

*Diagram 2* illustrates the application of these concepts to the three cases. Case 1—the Ifugao—is an example of informal rules. Case 2—the Dinaric Serbs—is also an example of informal rules. Case 3—Clark-Brown—is an example of formal rules.

Applying different concepts to the cases about personal conflict leads to different interpretations of the cases. The concepts of mediation, capitulation, and adjudication provide one way to interpret these cases. The concepts of formal rules and informal rules provide another way to interpret these cases.

Concepts can help us make precise comparisons. The definition of a particular concept is a rule for deciding whether certain facts are, or are not, examples of the concept. The rule, or definition, that we have used for mediation is this: The parties to a conflict agree to let another person or group suggest the way to settle the conflict. By applying this definition to the Ifugao case, we see that the facts in the case are an example of mediation. Likewise we can see that the facts in the other two cases are not examples of mediation.

Concepts can be related to make general statements of comparison. For example, the concepts of involvement in political activity and age groups can be related to make this comparative generalization: Older adults are more involved than younger adults in various kinds of political activities. *Diagram 3* illustrates this relationship.

*Diagram 3.* **Involvement in Political Activities**

| Age Group | Less | More |
|---|---|---|
| Younger (18–29) | X | |
| Older (Over 30) | | X |

The relationship shown in *Diagram 3* can be supported with evidence from *Table 3.*

As shown in *Table 3,* younger people take part less than older people in nine of ten kinds of political activities. Public demonstrations are the only type that young adults practice more than older adults.

Apply what you have learned about using concepts to make comparisons of political behavior in the following three cases.

*Table 3.* **Political Activities of Younger and Older Adults**

| Type of Activity | Age Group | | |
|---|---|---|---|
| | 18–29 | 30–49 | Over 50 |
| 1. Signed a petition | 66% | 75% | 66% |
| 2. Attended a speech or rally for a political candidate | 46 | 51 | 52 |
| 3. Written a letter to your Congressman | 31 | 37 | 30 |
| 4. Contributed financially to a political campaign | 26 | 35 | 36 |
| 5. Written a letter to your U.S. Senator | 17 | 29 | 28 |
| 6. Visited or talked in person with your Congressman | 15 | 25 | 25 |
| 7. Campaigned or worked actively for a candidate for Congress | 10 | 15 | 16 |
| 8. Visited or talked in person with your U.S. Senator | 8 | 13 | 17 |
| 9. Campaigned or worked actively for a candidate for the U.S. Senate | 8 | 11 | 13 |
| 10. Picketed or taken part in a street demonstration | 18 | 11 | 6 |

### Case 1. Government among the Iroquois

Popular opinion had much influence on the government of the Iroquois Indians in the eighteenth century. The Iroquois government was a confederacy of five main tribes: Senecas, Cayugas, Onondagas, Mohawks, and Oneidas. The Confederacy Council, the highest governing group, consisted of 50 chiefs representing the five tribes. The Mohawks and the Oneidas each had 9 representatives; the Onondagas, 14; the Cayugas, 10; and the Senecas, 8. This unequal representation on the Confederacy Council did not mean unequal power, because each tribe could cast only one vote. And no decision could be made unless all five tribes were in favor of it.

*Table 3: Confidence and Concern: Citizens View American Government,* p. 256.
Reprinted by permission of the *Chicago Tribune.* All Rights Reserved.

The tribal council continues even today to be the typical means of Indian self-government.

Members of the Council were chosen by the women of the various villages and could be removed from office if they did not do a good job of representing their people.

Each tribe in the Iroquois confederacy had its own tribal council made up of leading men chosen by the women of the tribe. And each village within a tribe had its own governing council of men picked by the women of the village.

All business of the councils—whether Confederacy Council, tribal council, or village council—was conducted publicly and openly. No decision was made without giving all members the chance to speak as much as they wanted to about an issue. Council meetings were usually watched by most of the people represented by the council.

**Case 2. Government in Saudi Arabia**

In Saudi Arabia in the 1970s a king headed the government. He got his position through hereditary right and could rule until death.

The king shared power with a council of ministers. The king chose the ministers, who in turn picked lower government officials. There were no political parties and no public elections in Saudi Arabia.

The basic law of Saudi Arabia was the divine law of the religion of Islam. Other laws were made by the king and the council of ministers.

Although the king and the council ran the government, they depended upon various local leaders to help enforce laws and administer services. Thus, the king and the council had to consider the influence and wishes of these local leaders when making public policy.

### Case 3. Government in a Small Midwestern City

Oberlin, Ohio, has a council-manager type of government. The voters of Oberlin elect a city council of seven members. The council appoints a city manager. The council has the power and duty to make laws. The city manager has the power and duty to enforce the laws and to administer the business of the city.

The members of the city council have the power to dismiss the city manager, but only by a five-vote majority or more. The voters of Oberlin have a chance to elect new council members at regular intervals.

The powers and duties of the city council and the city manager appear in the city charter, a document which describes the plan of government and serves as the basic law in Oberlin.

To practice the use of concepts to make comparisons, complete these exercises.

**1.** Use the following two concepts to answer questions about the governmental organization cases on pages 85–87.

*Popular control of government* means that (a) the people have some way of taking part in the selection and removal of important government officials and (b) the people can influence important political decisions of public officials.

*Separation of governmental power* means that independent power to make, enforce, and apply (or interpret) laws is distributed among several individuals or groups. For example, in the United States the Congress makes laws; the President and other officials enforce the laws; courts apply the laws to particular cases.

**a.** Compare the three cases in terms of *popular control of government*. Use *Diagram 4* to assist your comparison, *but do not mark the diagram.*

---

***Diagram 4. Popular Control***

| Degree of Control | Case | | |
|---|---|---|---|
| | Iroquois | Saudi Arabia | Oberlin |
| Little | A | B | C |
| Much | D | E | F |

COUNCIL-MANAGER GOVERNMENT

VOTERS

CITY COUNCIL

Board of Education

Municipal Judges

CITY MANAGER
employs officials
to administer

Planning
Civil Service
City Clerk

Law

Sanitation

Finance

Public Health

Public Safety

Public Works

Public Property,
Parks, Recreation

Public Welfare

Water Dep't.

Other Depts.

**b.** Compare the three cases in terms of *separation of governmental powers*. Use *Diagram 5* to assist your comparison, but do not mark it.

**Diagram 5. Separation of Powers**

| Degree of Separation | Iroquois | Saudi Arabia | Oberlin |
|---|---|---|---|
| Little | A | B | C |
| Much | D | E | F |

Column header note: Case

**c.** What is the relationship of *popular control of government* to *separation of governmental powers* in the three cases? Use *Diagram 6* to assist your comparison. For example, does Case 1 fit in box A, B, C, or D? In which boxes do Cases 2 and 3 fit?

**2.** Which of the three types of government organization is best? Which is worst? Explain.

**3.** What is the difference between your answers to the several parts of item 1 and the questions in item 2?

**Diagram 6. Popular Control and Separation of Powers**

| | Degree of Separation | |
|---|---|---|
| **Degree of Popular Control** | **Little** | **Much** |
| Little | A | B |
| Much | C | D |

**4.** What do your answers to the questions in item 2 reveal about your values and why you have these values?

**5.** Can you state hypotheses about why there may be important differences in the political behavior of different groups of people?

## Pitfalls in Making Comparisons

There are several pitfalls that can trap one into making false judgments about political behavior. In chapter 3 you had a chance to learn about how faulty questions and samples can lead to inaccurate factual judgments. Here we have a lesson about how to avoid false judgments when making comparisons about political behavior.

Look at the following statements, which are factual judgments about similarities and differences in political behavior. There is a fallacy, or flaw, in each of the examples. Try to identify what is wrong with the factual judgment in each example.

1. Homer Barnes knows nine people in his town who claim Polish-American ethnic identity. Eight of these Polish Americans support the Republican party. Homer also knows nine Italian Americans. Four of these people support the Republican party. Homer concludes that, in general, Polish Americans are more likely than Italian Americans to support the Republican party. *What is wrong with Homer's conclusion?*

2. Various studies have shown that older adults are more likely than younger adults to be involved in various kinds of political activities. Kathy Perkins is 20 years old and Karen Kowalski is 40 years old. Thus, without observing their political behavior, one can conclude correctly that Karen Kowalski is more involved in political activities than Kathy Perkins is. *What is wrong with this conclusion?*

3. A poll of a random sample of adults in Zenith City, taken in 1976, yielded this finding: Females are less likely than males to say that they follow political events reported in newspapers, magazines, and on television. George Wagner read this finding and concluded that the females in Zenith City would be less interested than the males in the city mayoral election to be held in 1980. *What is wrong with this conclusion?*

PITFALLS IN MAKING COMPARISONS

RELYING ON OWN EXPERIENCE

OVERLOOKING EXCEPTIONS

MAKING PREDICTIONS

OVERGENERALIZATION

BLIND FAITH IN AUTHORITY

4. Mike Schmidt read the results of the poll described in example 3 above. He concluded that the females in Chicago also are less interested than Chicago males in political news. *What is wrong with this conclusion?*

5. The leader of our group says that women in New York are more likely than men to support the Republican party. Since our leader is a wise man, one must conclude that his statements about political behavior are true. *What is wrong with this conclusion?*

## Relying on Personal Experience

The flaw in example 1 is trying to make a conclusion about a large group of people on the basis of personal experience with a very small, unrepresentative sample. For example, the nine Polish Americans in the example were not a representative sample of all Polish Americans. Thus, one cannot make an accurate generalization about all Polish Americans from the nine people in this example.

People often appeal to personal experience to justify their beliefs. For example, having known two English persons who lacked a sense of humor, one might conclude that all English people are this way. Or having known three brilliant Jews, one might decide that all Jewish people are very bright. The chief weakness here is that personal experiences are too limited. One is forced to make generalizations on the basis of a very small sample of the total population. In order to verify most beliefs, one must go beyond immediate experiences.

## Overlooking Exceptions

The mistake in example 2 above is trying to apply exactly a conclusion about a large group of people to one person in the group. The general conclusion in example 2 is correct. Data from many studies tell us that older adults are more likely than younger adults to be involved in political activities. However, Kathy Perkins and Karen Kowalski may be exceptions to the tendency.

Most of our factual judgments about similarities and differences in the political behavior of various groups are *tendency statements.* One can always find exceptions. A particular person might be one of these exceptions.

## Making Predictions from Survey Data

The flaw in example 3 is that one can't make exact predictions about political beliefs and behavior from data gathered through a survey, or poll. The fact that women in Zenith City tended to lack interest in politics in 1976 does not mean that they are certain to have a low level of interest four years later. Past performance may be a guide to the future. But there is no certainty that people *will* think and act exactly as they once thought and acted. Changing conditions often lead to differences in behavior from one time to another.

## Overgeneralization

The error in example 4 is making a conclusion that goes beyond the population which was sampled. The random sample in example 3 represents the adult population of Zenith City. Thus, one can only make conclusions from this sample about the adults in Zenith City. It is wrong to use this sample to make conclusions about the adult population of Chicago. Keep in mind that one should not overgeneralize from findings about a particular sample.

## Blind Faith in Authority

The flaw in example 5 is a "blind," or uncritical, acceptance of authority. People who too readily trust the conclusions of an authority run high risks of accepting incorrect beliefs.

Appealing to authority can be useful. If we need to decide a conflict about the correct spelling of a word, we should consult a good dictionary to settle the dispute. We often find it useful to consult books written by experts to find facts or interpretations of facts. But at the same time we need to learn how to judge whether an authority can be relied on. Do other experts agree with the authority we are using? Does "our expert" have "an axe to grind"? Does our expert use facts carefully? Keep in mind that blind faith in authority can lead one to accept false conclusions.

Can you apply what you have learned about "pitfalls" in making comparisons? Look at the data in *Table 4.* Next read the following list of conclusions about these data. Identify each wrong conclusion and tell what is wrong with it.

---

**Table 4. Income and Involvement in Various Political Activities in Zenith City, 1976**

|  | Low Yearly Income | High Yearly Income |
|---|---|---|
| Less Involvement | 88% | 25% |
| More Involvement | 12 | 75 |
| TOTAL | 100 | 100 |

(Data based on a random sample of 1500 adults in Zenith City.)

---

1. Mary Sanders, who lives in Zenith City, earns a high income. Thus, one can conclude correctly that she is very involved in various political activities.
2. In the United States those with low incomes are likely to be less involved in various political activities than are those with high incomes.
3. In 1990 those with high incomes in Zenith City are certain to be more involved in various political activities than are those with low incomes.

92

**4.** Donald Anderson knows twenty-five people with high incomes in Zenith City. Each of these people is uninvolved in political activities. Thus, Anderson rejects as false the data in *Table 4.*

**5.** In Zenith City those with low incomes are likely to be less involved than those with high incomes in various political activities.

**6.** In Zenith City those with high incomes are likely to be less involved in various political activities than are those with low incomes.

# 5 Culture and Political Behavior

Culture is a main influence on political behavior. The concept of *culture* can be used to make comparisons, to identify and interpret similarities and differences in political behavior.

## How Culture Affects Political Behavior

Culture is the name given to the typical beliefs and practices of a society. They guide the way the people of a society live. For example, in American society we believe in, and therefore practice, compulsory education of the young, monogamy (one husband or wife) in marriage, and freedom of the press. These are aspects of American culture.

Every human society has a culture. It takes in all learned behavior—from how to plant corn or build a fire to the right way of getting a marriage partner. Humans create culture to solve basic problems, to satisfy basic needs. All people must eat, sleep, and protect themselves from weather in order to survive and to live in ways that they enjoy. A culture is a society's fund of wisdom, collected over its past, that gives the members of the society ready-made solutions to basic problems. It consists of the thoughts and ideas gathered over many centuries about what is good and bad and about what is true and false. Statements such as "Do unto others as you would have them do unto you," "It is wrong to kill, steal, or lie," and "Education is the key to opportunity" reflect basic values of the American culture.

### Learning the Culture

Over a long period of time, a child slowly acquires the culture of his or her society. In contrast to other animals, human beings are not born with instincts that control how they organize a society, gather food, build shelters, or satisfy other basic needs. Humans must learn how to achieve their goals. Thus, compared to other animals, childhood helplessness is very long. From infancy onward, the child slowly acquires the skills and knowledge needed for survival.

Language is the key to the creation and continuation of culture. Through language the members of a society let one another know their needs and wants. Through a written language the ideas of people who lived long ago can be passed on to people living today. Thus, some ideas of the ancient Greeks and Romans, along with ideas of other peoples who lived long ago, are part of our culture today. Without language, every generation would have to start over again to learn solutions to basic human problems, rather than using the solutions handed down from the past and changing or adding to them.

94

The link between culture and human behavior is shown by the following story about a trader's wife in Arizona told by anthropologist Clyde Kluckhohn in *Mirror for Man.* The trader's wife often served a tasty meal of meat sandwiches to her guests. To some guests the meat tasted like tuna fish. To others it tasted like chicken. At the end of the meal the hostess would tell her guests that they had eaten neither chicken nor tuna. Rather, it was rattlesnake meat. They would become sick and vomit what they had thought was a tasty meal.[1]

The guests got sick because eating rattlesnake meat *was not* part of their culture. They had never learned that such meat is edible. While all people must eat in order to live, a culture guides what they eat and avoid eating.

### Culture and Political Behavior

Beliefs about political behavior are part of a culture. For example, in the lesson on pages 83–89 you saw that the people of Saudi Arabia thought that a king should rule and that most people should have little or nothing to say about public policy decisions. These political beliefs were a part of the culture of Saudi Arabia. In contrast, Americans believe that the people should elect representatives to rule and that the people should have the right to influence public policy decisions. These political beliefs are part of the American culture.

The typical political beliefs of a society can be called a *political culture.* As a culture is typical beliefs about how to behave, a political culture is typical beliefs about how to behave politically. A political culture is one part of a society's culture. For example, in the lesson on pages 78–80 you noted differences in political behavior of Americans, the Ifugao, and the Dinaric Serbs. These different political cultures influence people in the three societies to behave differently. The Ifugao believe that a *monkalun* ought to settle personal conflicts. This is a value judgment held by most of the Ifugao. In contrast, the Dinaric Serbs thought that conflicts should be settled through "blood vengeance" or the payment of "blood money." This was a value judgment of the past Dinaric Serbian society. Most Americans hold the value judgment that serious disputes ought to be settled in a court of law.

Political culture influences political behavior. For example, the belief that decisions should be made by majority vote is part of the American political culture. This political value has influenced Americans to make rules for the people to elect representatives by majority vote and for elected representatives to make laws by majority vote.

Another American political value is freedom of religion. This value is supported by the First Amendment of the Constitution of our nation.

1. Based on *Mirror for Man* by Clyde Kluckhohn. Copyright, 1949, by the McGraw-Hill Book Company, Inc. Used with permission of McGraw-Hill Book Company.

It provides that Americans shall have freedom to worship as they please, or not to worship at all if they prefer. Thus hundreds of different religious practices are found in American society. And many Americans follow no religion. Individuals who value religious freedom and decision-making by majority vote often disapprove of people opposed to these values.

The political culture also indicates a society's view of authority. Americans think that the police should have the authority to arrest lawbreakers. But Americans also believe that the police should not decide the guilt or innocence of an accused person. Part of the American political culture is that judges and juries should decide guilt or innocence and the punishment to be given. People who use power correctly, in line with their political culture, are seen as good citizens. Those who use power not in line with their political culture may be seen as bad citizens, or even criminal.

Culture tells people how to greet one another: with a polite bow in Japan and a handshake in America. Two men greeting each other with a kiss on the cheek is a culture trait in Chile and many other places.

When conflicts within the society are settled in a way that fits the political culture, most people will accept these decisions as just and right. Enforcing decisions that most people consider correct is a fairly easy matter. People who believe that a law is just will usually obey it automatically. The power of the government to enforce laws is used to control the behavior of those who would not otherwise obey the law.

1. Each of the following is a statement about political beliefs and behavior. Which of these statements reflect the political culture of the American society?
   a. Individuals should have the right to own property.
   b. Individuals should be equal before the law.
   c. There should be only one political party in a society.
   d. All individuals should be forced to go to church.
   e. Children should follow the directions of the police officer who directs traffic near their school.
   f. No one ought to have the right to criticize the government.
   g. The police have the right to arrest anyone they think might cause trouble.
   h. Adult Americans should vote on election day.
   i. Individuals should have freedom of speech.
   j. Laws should be made and enforced by one person.
   k. The same rights should be granted to all citizens in a society, regardless of race, creed, national ancestry, or sex.
   l. Black people should be allowed to hold positions in government.
   m. The leaders of our government should be elected by majority vote.
2. Study the previous statements again.
   a. Which statements are American political beliefs that are, for the most part, practiced in our society?
   b. Which statements are American political beliefs that are often not lived up to in our society?
3. Why might there be a gap between some political beliefs in a society and political behavior in the society?
4. Why are ideals important features of political life in a society even when there is a large gap between ideals and realities?

## Learning a Political Culture

*Socialization* is what social scientists call the process of becoming an accepted member of a society. Socialization is the learning of the society's culture. It begins at birth and continues throughout life.

A person is not born with a culture. Rather, people are born into a culture that they continue to learn as long as they are part of the society that created the culture.

Aspects of our political culture are shown here: (top left) getting voters to register; (top right) an open hearing by a city council; (bottom left) singing the National Anthem at the 1975 All-Star game; (bottom right) political campaigning.

Because a culture is learned, not inborn, it can also be changed through learning. Suppose an American girl is taken to live in a strange country at a young age and grows up under the care of people there. She will not learn to behave like other Americans. Rather, she will learn the culture of this other country. She will learn its laws, religion, customs, and language because she will have learned these ways of behavior at home, at school, at play, and at work.

This link between behavior and culture is very well described by anthropologist Clyde Kluckhohn in his book *Mirror for Man:*

> Some years ago I met in New York City a young man who did not speak a word of English and was obviously bewildered by American ways. By "blood" he was as American as you or I, for his parents had gone from Indiana to China as missionaries. Orphaned in infancy, he was reared by a Chinese family in a remote village. All who met him found him more Chinese than American. The facts of his blue eyes and light hair were less impressive than a Chinese style of gait, Chinese arm and hand movements, Chinese facial expression, and Chinese modes of thought. The biological heritage was American, but the cultural training had been Chinese. He returned to China.[2]

Through the process of socialization, a person learns what is considered right and wrong political behavior in his society. *Through socialization, an infant born in the United States learns to behave politically in the American way.* As part of the process, most American children learn to obey the commands of a traffic officer and to pledge allegiance to the flag. They learn to choose a class president by majority vote and to support freedom of speech. They learn to express many other American political behaviors and beliefs. Children learn these things at home from parents, at school from teachers, at church from the clergy, and at play and at work from friends.

The preceding discussion tells how socialization is related to similarities in behavior among members of a group. However, the process of socialization also helps to explain why different people, from the same society, may behave politically in different ways. Most people in the same society are exposed to the same political culture, but not in exactly the same way. And they do not learn exactly the same things. For example, Richard and Larry live in the same city. Richard's father is the mayor of the city, and Larry's father is a factory worker. Richard's father and mother are always talking about political affairs at home. Sometimes Richard goes to parties where he meets many of the city's political leaders. By contrast, Larry's father does not care about politics. He does not even read the papers, and he does not vote in elections. It is quite likely that Larry and Richard, although

© 1963 United Features Syndicate, Inc.

---

2. From *Mirror for Man* by Clyde Kluckhohn. Copyright, 1949, by the McGraw-Hill Book Company, Inc. Used with permission of McGraw-Hill Book Company.

living in the same society with the same political culture, learn different things about the political life of their society from their parents. Because no two people have exactly the same experiences, no two persons are socialized in exactly the same way.

To show what you have learned about the relationship of socialization to political beliefs and behavior, complete the exercise which follows.

Your teacher will show you some pictures of political symbols. You will also receive a "Five-Point Reaction Scale," such as the scale below. Indicate your reaction to each one of the political symbols on this scale.

**Five-Point Reaction Scale**

| | | | | |
|---|---|---|---|---|
| Very Bad Feeling | Bad Feeling | Little or No Feeling | Good Feeling | Very Good Feeling |

Your teacher will help you to tabulate and organize the responses of you and your classmates to the pictures of political symbols. On the basis of your tabulation and organization of these responses, answer the following questions.

1. Why do you think you and others in your class responded as you did to the pictures of political symbols?

2. Do you think most other American teen-agers would have responded to these pictures in the same way that your class responded? Explain your answer.

3. Can you think of any groups of Americans who might have responded to any of these pictures very differently from the way your class responded? Explain.

4. Do you think most Russian teen-agers would have responded to these symbols in the same way that your class responded? Which symbols would most Russian teen-agers have ranked differently from the way your class ranked them? Explain.

5. How do the ideas of culture and socialization apply to your responses to items 1-4 above?

6. What good outcomes for a society might result from the process of socialization?

7. What bad, or dangerous, outcomes for a society might result from the process of socialization?

## Differences in Political Culture

Different countries have different political cultures. And within the same country the political culture may differ a little from group to group. The concepts of democracy and autocracy provide one way to look at, or interpret, differences in political culture and political behavior.

Workers at an auto plant in the Soviet Union cast their ballots for members of the Supreme Soviet in a 1970 election. The ballot lists only one candidate for each office. Those who wish to express disapproval can put their unmarked ballot in the box. How do elections in the United States (bottom) differ from those in the USSR?

### Democratic Political Beliefs

In the United States most people think that democracy is good and that children should be taught to accept democratic political beliefs. These are important beliefs in the American political culture. What are democratic beliefs? Below are some political beliefs that most people would call democratic.

*Political decisions should be made according to majority vote.*

a. Laws should be made by a majority vote of representatives of the people.

    b. The leaders of our government should be elected by majority vote.

*The rights of individuals should be protected.*
    a. These rights include freedom of speech, religion, and assembly.
    b. Individuals should have the right to own property.
    c. Individuals should have equality of opportunity.
    d. Individuals should be equal before the law.
    e. The rights of individuals should be granted to all citizens, regardless of race, creed, national ancestry, or sex.

*There should be free competition, regulated by rules, among political groups and ideas.*
    a. Political conflicts should be decided by free and open exchange of ideas that takes place within a framework of law and order.
    b. Political parties should be free to compete with one another for control of the government.
    c. Individuals should be free to join different groups that stand for the social and political ideas they favor.

### Autocratic Political Beliefs

Autocracy is the opposite of democracy. Democracy means rule by the people with protection of individual (and minority group) rights. Autocracy means rule by one person or by a small elite group. The rights of minorities are not often protected. In some autocratic societies, such as Nazi Germany in 1933-1945, members of minority groups have been jailed or even put to death. Autocratic political systems do not allow competition among political parties. Rather one party, such as the Communist party in the Soviet Union, dominates political life. Ideas are not freely debated. Instead there is a "party line," a correct view of the world determined by political leaders. Individuals who dissent from the "party line" may go to prison or be killed.

### Diagramming Political Beliefs

*Diagram 7* shows differences between autocratic and democratic political cultures. According to this diagram, two main political beliefs are basic to democratic political culture: (1) a belief in majority rule practices; (2) a belief in protection of the rights of individuals and

*Diagram 7.* **Comparison of Democratic and Autocratic Cultures**

| Majority Rule Practices | Protection of Individual Rights | |
| --- | --- | --- |
| | Less | More |
| Less | Autocratic Culture | |
| More | | Democratic Culture |

102

minorities. The extent to which a group, or nation, believes in and practices majority rule and protection of the rights of minorities is the extent to which the group, or nation, can be called democratic. Majority rule alone does not indicate a democracy, or the enjoyment of real freedom. As the British historian Lord Acton said, "The most certain test by which we judge whether a country is really free is the amount of security enjoyed by minorities."

When trying to decide whether a political culture or government is democratic, remember that among the nations of the world there are no perfect democracies. Political cultures or governments are more or less democratic in terms of the standards of majority rule and protection of individual rights. Likewise, no political culture or government is a complete autocracy. Rather political cultures or governments may be more or less autocratic according to our standards of majority rule and protection of the rights of minorities.

**Beliefs about Majority Rule and the Rights of Minorities**

The political beliefs expressed by most people in a society are indicators of its political culture. In numerous polls[3] a vast majority of Americans have expressed strong support for the following political beliefs:

1. Public officials should be chosen by majority vote.
2. Laws should be made by a majority vote of representatives of the people.
3. Every citizen should have an equal chance to influence government policy.
4. The minority should be free to criticize majority decisions.
5. People in the minority should be free to try to win majority support for their opinions.
6. Accused persons should have the right to question witnesses against them.
7. Citizens should have the right to hold meetings on any subject about which they may want to meet.
8. Citizens should have the right to print any point of view they want to print.

Since Americans by a large majority agree with these statements, we might conclude that the people strongly support majority rule with protection of minority rights. However, before jumping to conclusions,

---

3. Robert S. Erikson and Norman R. Luttbeg, *American Public Opinion: Its Origins, Content and Impact* (New York: John Wiley & Sons, Inc., 1973). Used by permission. Items 6-8 from *The Anguish of Change,* see footnote p. 104.

**Table 5. Percent of Nationally Representative Sample Which Agreed with Statements about Rights of Individuals**

| Statement | Percent Agreeing |
|---|---|
| 1. Organizations which preach the violent overthrow of the government should be outlawed. | 67% |
| 2. FBI agents should be able to testify in criminal cases without cross-examination. | 50 |
| 3. Attendance at campus protest meetings ought to be grounds for the expulsion of a college student. | 48 |
| 4. Newspapers which preach revolution should be banned. | 52 |
| 5. Authorities should have the right to censor TV, radio, newspapers, and the theater for unpatriotic or revolutionary content. | 57 |

consider the evidence in *Table 5.* On the basis of evidence from this table, and from preceding paragraphs, try to answer the following questions.

**1.** Does this evidence support or reject these hypotheses?
**a.** Americans tend to be strongly opposed to censorship of the mass media.
**b.** Americans tend to strongly support rights of minorities under all circumstances.
**c.** A large majority of Americans believe that accused persons should always have the right to question any witnesses against them.
**2.** Can you identify conflicts, or contradictions, between the political beliefs supported by most Americans on page 103 and the evidence in *Table 5?*
**3.** What are your hypotheses about why these contradictions exist?
**4.** What do these contradictions suggest about gaps between ideals and realities in American political life?
**5.** Do you think that most Americans would agree with these words of the French philosopher Voltaire: "I disagree with what you say, but I will fight to the death for your right to say it"? Do you agree with this statement?
**6.** Do you agree with this statement: "When a government abuses the rights of its citizens, they have the right to overthrow it"?
**7.** Americans seem to pay "lip service" to democratic beliefs. They support them in general. But they are not always willing to support the rights of extremely unpopular individuals or minority groups. Do you agree or disagree with this statement?
**8.** With which of the political beliefs in the list on page 103 and in *Table 5* do you agree? Why?

*Table 5:* Reprinted from *The Anguish of Change* by Louis Harris. By permission of W. W. Norton & Company. Inc. Copyright © 1973 by W. W. Norton & Company, Inc.

## Cultural Variations within a Country

There are clear differences in the political cultures of different countries, such as between the United States and the Soviet Union. There also are important cultural differences within a country like the United States. For example, the United States includes many groups with varying beliefs and behavior. Social scientists refer to these various groups within a society as subcultures.

A *subculture* is the way of life of a smaller group within the larger society. A subculture includes all the standards of right and wrong that guide behavior in the smaller group. Childrearing practices, religious practices, food preparation and diet, language, and manner of dress also often differ from one subculture to another.

The United States has many subcultures. Within every region of the country are groups with varying beliefs and styles of behavior. The Mexican Americans of Los Angeles and southern Texas, the Puerto Ricans of New York and Chicago, the Italian Americans of Newark and Boston, the Polish Americans of Chicago and Detroit, and the mountaineers of Appalachia are merely a few of the many groups with distinct cultures that are part of the American society.

In spite of their differences, our subcultures share some basic beliefs and ways of behavior. These common beliefs and activities are what hold these peoples together in American society.

Many people see the cultural variations in the United States as a source of strength. Others express fear about the risk of conflict between groups with very different values.

### The Forces of Change and Maintenance

Conflict within and between cultures often is linked with the threat of change and efforts to resist change. Through the process of socialization, a group tries to *maintain* traditions, to keep things as they have been. However, as a group comes into contact with others, it is exposed to new ideas and ways of behavior which could *change,* more or less basically, the group's beliefs and styles of behavior.

Suppose, for example, that a business firm decides to build a factory on the outskirts of a small rural town. The company offers to transfer many of its workers from a plant that is shutting down in a city hundreds of miles away. The newcomers soon begin to take part in town affairs and in its schools, churches, and clubs. The newcomers also begin to suggest ways that the town and its institutions should do some things differently. The newcomers represent a force for *change.*

Soon many townspeople begin to fear the newcomers. People begin to say, "The ways we have been doing things here suit us fine." And many people become very upset because their children seem to be getting strange ideas from their contacts with the newcomers. The townspeople begin to take steps to hold on to, or maintain, their customs and traditions. Social scientists call this a force for *maintenance.*

Some of the newcomers, of course, also feel threatened by change. Some of their children are picking up new ways of behaving. Among the newcomers there will also be efforts to maintain *their* old traditions.

Thus when two cultures come into contact, the forces of change and maintenance may operate on both sides.

Following is a case about conflict arising out of cultural differences. In this case, there are examples of tension between the opposing forces of maintenance and change. After reading it, try to answer the questions about conflict, maintenance, and change which follow the case.

### The Plain People's Resistance

The Amish are called the "plain people" because they prefer a simple way of life. They are known for their intense resistance to changes in their traditions.

Groups of Amish people live in rural areas in twenty states—notably in Pennsylvania, Ohio, Indiana, Kentucky, Iowa, and Wisconsin. The approximately 50,000 Amish people in the United States live chiefly by farming. They are very religious and base their customs and laws upon their interpretation of the Bible. They prefer to live apart from other Americans out of fear that extended contact with the dominant culture would in time lead to a loss of their unique cultural values.

Two passages from the Bible are often quoted by the Amish to sum up their view of the world. The first is: "Be not conformed to this world, but be ye transformed by the renewing of your mind that ye may prove what is that good and acceptable and perfect will of God." To the Amish, this means that they should set themselves apart from the ways of other people. Thus the Amish dress in an old-fashioned way and resist any changes in clothing fashion. They refuse to use modern farm machinery, preferring horse-drawn plows and carts to tractors and trucks. They refuse to buy television sets and to use modern home appliances. They shun electricity, telephones, and cars.

The second Biblical quotation that gives a clue to the Amish subculture is: "Be ye not unequally yoked together with unbelievers; for what fellowship hath righteousness with unrighteousness? And what communion hath light with darkness?" To the Amish, this means that they should not mix socially or marry non-Amish persons and should not have business partnerships with "outsiders."

The Amish have kept their traditions alive by teaching their children to speak a form of German as well as English. The ancestors of the Amish came to America from German-speaking areas of Europe. At home, and within the Amish community generally, German is spoken rather than English. English is used when the Amish come into contact with the larger American society.

The Amish attempt to maintain their culture by running their own schools in which the education of Amish children is carefully supervised. Amish children may not attend public school for fear that they

106

might reject the Amish way of life in favor of more typical American ways. The Amish culture is preserved by denying Amish children exposure to other ways of life during the early childhood years.

### The Relationship of the Amish Culture to Political Behavior

The Amish culture gives rise to distinct political beliefs. In line with their religion, the Amish are pacifists. They believe wars, or any kind of fighting, is a sin against God. The Amish are law-abiding, hard working, thrifty people. They take pride in their orderliness and their readiness to submit to authority. However, they prefer to be left alone in order to protect their way of life. Thus, when the laws of state or national government conflict with the rules of the Amish society, the Amish are faced with a moral problem. Should they obey the laws of the American government, under which they live, or should they follow the values of their culture?

The Amish way of life includes political apathy. The Amish readily obey most laws. But they do not ordinarily organize for political action or take part in election campaigns. The Amish try very hard not to get involved in the political affairs of the larger American society. Once in a while, however, the Amish way of life brings them into conflict with the government. This occurs when state or national government laws conflict with Amish religious beliefs. Usually the Amish choose to disobey a law rather than to violate a religious belief. For example, in Iowa in the early 1960s, the Amish people became involved in a dispute over the education of their youngsters. Following is a case about conflict resulting from differences between the Amish subculture and the larger American culture.

109

### Showdown at the Charity Flats School

On November 22, 1965, five public officials representing the state of Iowa forced their way into the Charity Flats school near Hazleton, Iowa. They pushed aside two Amish men who were standing guard before the door of the one-room schoolhouse. Inside the school sixteen Amish children sang "Jesus Loves Me." Several mothers stood around the room and wept.

The state officials had come for a "showdown" to end a three-year dispute between the state of Iowa and several Old Order Amish families. For three years the public officials had been trying to force the Amish to improve their schools according to state law or to send their children to public schools. For three years the Amish had resisted the orders of the public officials. The officials had come to take the Amish children to a nearby public school. The children, backed by their parents, were determined to resist. One of the state officials, a truant officer, gently grasped a little girl's shoulder. He told her to move outside and get into a school bus that would take her to a nearby public school. The room was very quiet. Suddenly the girl screamed and pulled away. The other children screamed and wept.

The public officials frowned. They bowed their heads and walked out of the schoolroom. The "showdown" had failed.

Several days later the governor of Iowa, Harold Hughes, called for a halt in the efforts of state officials to force the Amish to obey state education laws. The state legislature began to consider action to resolve the school dispute. After much debate, the state legislature passed a law in 1967 that protects the right of Old Order Amish children to attend their own schools. The law provides that state laws about compulsory education of children do not apply to children of religious orders whose religious principles conflict with state education laws. Thus, the "showdown" at the Charity Flats School ended in a victory for the Amish.

### History of the Charity Flats Dispute

How did the contest between the Amish and the Iowa state government start? Why did the public officials try to force a "showdown" at the Charity Flats School? Why did the Amish win a victory in the state legislature? Let's look at the history.

The dispute started on November 8, 1961, when the Oelwein Community School District was formed by consolidating several neighboring school districts. The new Oelwein School Board had to decide how to deal with fifty-three Old Order Amish children who attended two Amish parochial schools in the new consolidated district.

The school board decided to close the Amish schools and require the Amish students to attend a nearby public school. They based their decision on a study by the Iowa State Department of Public Instruction which reported that the Amish schools did not meet the standards for schools set by Iowa state law. According to the report the Amish schools were run-down and the teachers were not competent. The school board told the Amish to improve their schools or shut them down. They ordered them to hire teachers who could qualify for teachers' licenses from the Iowa State Department of Public Instruction and to add science courses to their curriculum. The Amish teachers had no schooling beyond the eighth grade.

The Amish refused to obey the school board's orders. They argued that the orders violated their right of religious freedom. The Amish gave the following arguments in support of their position.

We must send our children to our own schools in order to teach the word of God and to maintain our way of life. If we allow our children to attend the public schools, they will learn sinful ways. They will not be able to live according to the customs of our people.

The government officials say that they have no objection to the Amish way of life. They say that we are free to live apart according to our ways. Then why don't they let us teach our children, in our own schools, how to live a good Amish life?

Our people do not harm others. We are good citizens. We work hard and mind our own business. Our children do not become juvenile delinquents and our adults do not become criminals. In our schools we teach our children to have good moral standards. Let us continue to teach them how to be righteous.

Our educational ideals do not bring harm to other Americans. Our educational system only helps us to make good Amish people out of our children. Our schools help us to protect our way of life from the perversions of other values.

## Public Officials State Their Position

While sympathizing with the Amish, the public officials believed the Amish brand of education to be inferior. They pointed to the aging facilities and outdated textbooks. They criticized the Amish for using teachers having only an eighth-grade education.

The following description of the two Amish schools by Donald Erickson appeared in *Commentary* in January 1968:

In keeping with the Plain People's philosophy, their schools are rustic, not to say primitive, and reflect little attention to aesthetics. The two buildings near Hazleton are reasonably clean and cheerful, though finished rather roughly and marred in spots by flaking paint.

Each is furnished with two outdoor privies, a coal shed, and a well with a manual pump. The North school boasts two seesaws, two swings, and some old tires as playground equipment; the South school has none at all.

In each school the only entrance to the single classroom is through a small vestibule, in which there are shelves and nails

111

for lunch buckets and coats. Each classroom has rough board floors; extra-tall windows on two sides for ventilation and light (there is no electricity); short shelves holding a collection of dog-eared books; a kitchen sink with water crock and paper towel dispenser; a large Regulator clock clucking high on the wall; bits of blackboard; five rows of ancient desks; a teacher's desk and chair; two or three sturdy work tables; cardboard boxes full of discarded textbooks; and some roll-up maps that are probably priceless antiques. In the rear of the room, there is a massive stove, which is kept stoked by boys assigned to the task. Pupils' drawings, virtually all of brightly colored rural scenes, are tacked on the walls.[4]

The government officials argued that the crude Amish schools gave the children no chance to become anything other than Amish farmers. They argued that in these schools the children could not get an education that could equip them with skills needed to live apart, if they should choose to, from their Amish subculture.

Furthermore, the officials argued that all groups should have equal treatment before the law. Thus, the Amish should not be given the right to ignore the school laws. They argued that the laws permit the Amish, or any other group, to have its own schools if these schools meet standards set by state law. But the Amish schools did not.

The Amish refused to change their schools to meet state requirements. They also refused to send their children to the public school in Hazleton. The government therefore decided to take action. The county superintendent of schools started the first legal action against the Amish on November 24, 1962. The county attorney prosecuted ten Amish men for the misdemeanor of sending their children to a school without licensed teachers. All ten were found guilty and fined. Eight refused to pay the fines, on religious principle, and served three days in jail.

### School Officials Attempt a Compromise

In January 1963 the Oelwein School Board tried to reach a compromise settlement. They offered to allow the Amish to operate their schools, under the direction of the school board, for two more years. After that time the children would go to public schools. The Amish rejected the offer.

Another compromise was tried in September 1964. The Oelwein School Board offered to provide special ungraded classrooms for Amish students within the public school on a one-year trial basis. The Amish refused this offer.

A turning point came in September 1965. Four new members were elected to the Oelwein School Board. During the election campaign,

---

4. Reprinted from *Commentary*, by permission. Copyright © 1968 by the American Jewish Committee.

112

these winning candidates had promised to deal firmly with the Amish if elected. Also the newly elected county attorney had promised to enforce all laws and to give no special treatment to the Amish. Apparently public opinion in Oelwein County was against the Amish in the school dispute.

With the backing of the county attorney, the newly elected Oelwein School Board brought charges against several Amish men for breaking the state school laws. They were found guilty. The court decided to require the men to pay a $24 fine at the end of each school day until their children enrolled in the public school in Hazleton.

The men continued to refuse to send their children to the public school, and daily their fines mounted. By the middle of November 1965, the Amish owed several thousand dollars in fines to the state for refusing to obey the school laws.

Clearly, the Amish were not to be broken through court action. The county attorney did not want to send the men to jail or to bankrupt them through the payment of fines. He said that he did not want to punish the Amish. Rather, he wanted to force them to obey the law, just as everyone else had to do.

**Plans Are Made for the Showdown**

The county attorney worked out a plan that he believed would settle the problem. He decided to use the state truancy laws. He would claim that Amish children who did not attend public schools were truant. Thus, he could legally seize them and force them to attend the Hazleton public school. He even got several Amish leaders to agree to this plan. They said that their people, who do not believe in violence, would not resist when the officials came to take the children to the public school.

The truant officer sent a school bus to pick up the Amish children. They were put on the bus and spent three hours at the public school. Next day, when the bus came to pick them up again, they ran away.

The county officials then decided to take the children out of their one-room schools. The result was the conflict at Charity Flats.

The events at Charity Flats School got nationwide attention. Public opinion in Iowa and around the country seemed to favor the Amish cause. Governor Hughes became concerned about the bad publicity for his state. He also believed that the Amish should be able to live a different kind of life if they so desired. He declared publicly, "I am determined to try to find a way, if possible, to make Iowa a place where the Amish people can live and follow their religious beliefs. Why should they be forced to leave Iowa because of a religious issue? Certainly we can find a suitable solution." The governor threw his political weight behind efforts to get a solution to the conflict that the Amish could live with.

Eventually a majority of the lawmakers in the Iowa legislature agreed with Governor Hughes on this issue. They sympathized with the plight of the Amish. They also believed that public opinion in Iowa favored the Amish on this issue. Thus, in 1967 the legislature passed a law exempting the Amish from obeying the state education laws.

### A Supreme Court Decision

Five years later, on May 15, 1972, the United States Supreme Court made a ruling about compulsory education laws that favored the Amish and supported the Iowa decision of 1967. In this case, *Wisconsin* v. *Yoder,* the issue was whether the Amish should be exempted from state laws requiring youngsters to attend school beyond the eighth grade.

The Amish schools do not go beyond the eighth grade. Most people finish the eighth grade when they are thirteen or fourteen years old. However, education laws in Wisconsin, and most other states, require school attendance until a person is sixteen.

The Amish in Wisconsin resisted the enforcement of the school attendance law among their group. They did not want to send their children to public high schools. And in line with their religious beliefs, they did not feel the need to operate their own schools beyond the eighth grade. However, Wisconsin officials tried to force the Amish people in the state to send their children to public high schools until

Hazelton's Amish children fled when officials arrived to take them to their new school.

age sixteen. The Amish resisted. Thus the United States Supreme Court was asked to resolve this conflict.

By a vote of 7 to 0, the Supreme Court ruled that the Wisconsin state law requiring Amish children to attend high school violated the "free exercise of religion" clause of the First Amendment to the Constitution. Thus the Amish were exempted from having to obey the Wisconsin law or similar laws in other states. The issue of whether or not compulsory school attendance laws apply to the Amish has been settled in favor of the Amish by the highest court in the land.

Apply your knowledge of culture, socialization, conflict, maintenance, and change to the analysis of the preceding case. Use the following questions to guide your analysis.

1. What is the issue in this case?
2. What is the value conflict in this case?
3. What do these ideas have to do with the value conflict in this case: culture, socialization, maintenance, and change?
4. What decisions were made to resolve the conflict in this case?
5. What were the consequences of these decisions for the Amish? Apply the ideas of culture, maintenance, and change to your answer.
6. What does this case suggest about how willing the majority are to protect the rights of minorities in the United States?
7. Do you like or dislike the outcome of this case? Why?

# 6 Social Status and Political Behavior

*Social status* is the position that a person holds in a group. Family members have such statuses, or positions, as mother, son, sister, and husband. People in school have such statuses as student, teacher, bus driver, and principal.

Status is linked to behavior. A person is expected to act in certain ways because of the position he or she holds in a group. In school we have one set of expectations for teachers, another for students, another for coaches, and so on. The set of expectations that go with any status is called its *role.*

When you learn a role, you know how your society expects you to behave in a certain position, or status. Some of our roles guide our political behavior.

## Status and Role

Through socialization, people learn the roles that go with their statuses. *Roles are guides to behavior.* For example, a quarterback on a football team plays a certain role. This person is expected to select plays, call signals, and throw passes. The quarterback *status* is what determines the role. A football end has a different status on the team. The role of this player is to follow the orders of the quarterback, not to give them, and to catch passes, not to throw them. The roles of quarterback and end differ because these persons hold different positions, or statuses, on the team.

The performance of roles is a society in action. Whenever people behave in agreement with their culture, they are performing roles that their society accepts. An actor in a play is expected to play a role that fits the play's script. People in a society are expected to play roles that fit their culture.

Every role in a society is related in some way to another role. The role of a parent is related to the role of a child. For example, if American parents are to behave in agreement with American culture, they are expected to provide food and shelter for their child. They are expected to send their child to school. And they are expected to give their child directions about how to behave in many kinds of social situations. The child's role includes living with parents and obeying their rules.

The role of a teacher is related to the role of students. The teacher is expected to keep order in the classroom and help students learn. The culturally acceptable role of students is to learn from the teacher and to respect and obey the teacher's rules.

116

Identify the role positions (statuses) that this young woman occupies. Give
one expectation that is part of each role shown here.

### An Individual Plays Many Roles

Each person in a society plays many roles. During the same day, a man may need to play the roles of husband, father, steelworker, spectator at a football game, and friend at a party after the game. In the same day a woman may need to play the roles of wife, mother, lawyer, and president of the local chapter of the League of Women Voters.

During a lifetime individuals must learn to play the different roles of child, teen-ager, adult, and elderly adult that are part of their culture. For example, young children are not supposed to play certain roles in American culture, such as driving cars or working to earn a living, but adults usually are. Most elderly adults are expected to retire from the task of earning a living once they pass a certain age.

### Status Determines Political Roles

Political roles are related to the positions, or statuses, that a person occupies. For example, the President is expected to play certain roles because of the position, or status, of Chief Executive. The President

**HOW THE MAYOR'S ROLE RELATES TO THOSE OF OTHER POLITICAL ACTORS**

Swearing-in an appointee

Advising city council

Asking governor for state aid

Hearing complaints of citizens

is expected to enforce laws, make treaties with foreign nations, command the nation's military forces, serve as host to visiting leaders of foreign nations, and to play many other roles that go along with the status of President. Members of the President's White House staff are expected to carry out the orders of the President. Their status on the White House staff determines their role.

Political roles are related to the laws and customs of a group of people. For example, the law that the President has the authority to command all military forces is part of the American political culture. This power is given to the President by the Constitution. When the President orders a general to send troops to an American base in Asia, the political role of commander in chief is being played. However, it is a political custom in the United States that the military should be controlled by civilian leaders. Thus, the President neither wears a military uniform nor identifies too closely with military figures when playing this role.

In line with custom, those who hold the status of adult citizen are supposed to play the political role of voter. According to law, those under eighteen years of age are not able to play the voter's

Consulting with school superintendent

Negotiating with city workers

Holding a press conference

Appealing for re-election

role in public elections. In line with custom, American men have been expected to be more interested and active in politics than are women. The United States has never had a woman President, and few women have become lawmakers or judges. However, in recent years American women have shown much more political interest and activity. This shows that a part of our political culture is changing.

## Political Roles Are Interrelated

Every political role is related in some way to another political role. The role of a political leader, such as the President, a governor, or a mayor, is related to the roles of followers. For example, a mayor is supposed to play the political role of law enforcer in the city, and the people of the city are supposed to play the political roles of law-abiding citizens.

The role of voter is related to the role of elected public official. People vote for a candidate for public office because they believe that the candidate, if elected, will do certain things to improve the government. They play the political role of voter in order to influence what the government does. Elected public officials are supposed to play their political role in a way that satisfies many, if not most, of the people who voted for them. If they fail to play this role, they face the strong risk of defeat in the next election.

Each person takes on many political roles. During the same day, the mayor may play the political roles of law enforcer, law obeyer, voter, winner of an election, and host to a visiting political leader. During the same day, an ordinary citizen of the same city may play the political roles of law obeyer, voter, participant in a political rally, and discusser of political affairs with a friend.

## Personality and Performance of Political Roles

Since no two people have exactly the same personality, no two persons behave politically in exactly the same way. These personality and political behavior differences result from the differences in socialization that exist in every society. The political culture of any society is not learned in exactly the same way by each individual.

*Personality is all the characteristics of behavior that distinguish one person from another.* It is a person's way of reacting to his or her environment. No two people have exactly the same personality because no two persons have exactly the same physical and cultural heritage or exactly the same experiences.

The link between personality, socialization, and culture is shown by the following example. James and Robert are identical twins. This means that they have the same inborn capabilities. They look almost exactly alike. A short time after birth their parents died. James was adopted by a doctor and went to live in a big city. Robert was adopted by a poor farmer. James went to college and became a high school teacher. Robert dropped out of school after the eighth grade. He became a farm laborer. James likes to read books, attend plays, and to play classical music on the piano. Robert seldom reads books and likes to play folk music on the guitar. On radio he listens to popular and country music.

Jim and Robert behave differently because they have had different experiences. Even though they are identical twins, they learned to behave differently because their cultural environments and socialization were not the same.

Let's see how a couple of personal traits might help to account for differences in the way people perform political roles. One trait is mental ability. Some people are brighter than others. Because of limited mental ability some persons are not able to learn certain political roles. No amount of teaching can fit a mentally slow person for the role of Supreme Court justice. Also people with high mental ability are more likely to become political leaders if they so choose.

Another trait is shyness. A person who hates to meet new people or talk to an audience will avoid some roles. Such a person will not want to go door to door to canvass voters. Such a person will not want the role of "candidate," or "precinct captain," or political leader of any kind.

No two people are likely to behave politically in exactly the same way. Still, people who learn the same political culture will behave in similar ways much of the time. With a knowledge of American political culture, you can predict much of the political behavior of Americans in certain typical situations. For example, take a group of American lawmakers. Whether they are members of Congress, state legislatures, or city councils, they will not make laws without a majority vote. The idea of majority rule is a basic part of our political culture.

## Predicting Political Behavior Is Risky

Keep in mind, however, that you can't predict many kinds of political behavior solely on what you know about a political culture. A political role tells what people might do in typical situations. But people do not always act in expected ways. Different personalities cause people to have different views of how they should behave politically. Often there is a difference between what a person ought to do (the role) and what he or she actually does (role behavior).

For example, Americans are taught that their citizen role requires them to vote. Yet many American citizens do not go to the polls on election day. Some of these nonvoters feel that they have little influence, so they don't take part in politics. Their role behavior departs from the citizen role, from what American citizens are expected to do. The feeling of having no power is a personality trait. This trait accounts for the gap between role and role behavior in this case—that is, between the expected behavior and the actual behavior.

121

## Two Ways of Playing Politics

The links between political roles, socialization, and political behavior are shown by this fictional account of a high school election. Use your knowledge of culture, socialization, personality, status, and role to answer the questions following this case.

Jim and Nick had campaigned hard against each other. Both boys wanted to be student government president. Both boys were school leaders and believed that becoming student government president was one of the highest honors anyone could achieve in the school.

During the campaign Jim tried to influence students to vote for him by pointing out that he had much experience as a leader in school clubs during the past three years. Nick tried to influence students to vote for him by telling everyone that he was much smarter and much nicer than Jim. Nick said that Jim was dull and lazy. He often called Jim names when he talked about the election.

Jim and Nick competed to fill the school's hallways with political signs. Jim's campaign workers had been able to finish making their signs before Nick's followers had completed their signs. So they were able to place Jim's signs in the most prominent places. Nick became angry and ripped down some of Jim's signs. He said that it was not fair for one candidate to "hog all the best places."

On election day Jim stood in front of the school. As the students passed by, he shook hands with as many as possible and asked them to please vote for him. Nick also stood out in front of the school and shook hands with as many students as possible and asked for their votes. However, several times he yelled at students who wore signs on their coats that favored Jim. He called these students stupid and said that they would be sorry if he lost the election. When all the votes were counted, Jim had won a landslide victory.

**1.** What are your hypotheses about why Nick lost this election by a landslide vote?
**2.** Why did Nick and Jim play the role of candidate so differently?

## Socioeconomic Status and Political Behavior

There are differences in the political behavior of upper and lower status groups in the United States. How do we decide who are upper or lower status people? What do these rankings have to do with political behavior?

In all societies some persons have higher status than others. In all societies people who possess more of the things the society values are thought to have a better position, or a higher rank, in the society than those who have fewer such things.

*Socioeconomic status (SES) is the label that social scientists apply to a person's rank in a society.* Those with a high rank are said to have high socioeconomic status, or high SES. Persons with a low

122

rank are said to have a low socioeconomic status, or low SES. The "economic" in this label tells us that a person's income and material possessions are among the main standards used to judge his or her social rank. However, wealth alone does not determine rank.

## Characteristics Associated with Socioeconomic Status

What are standards, or criteria, used by Americans to rank themselves and others socially? The social characteristics typically identified with social position appear in the chart on the next page.

In American society well-to-do people usually have more prestige, or a higher rank, than poor people. A person or family with a large income can afford a nice home in a high-prestige neighborhood. High income or wealth also permits the person to acquire other "badges of success"—one or more expensive cars, the best in household furnishings, perhaps a summer home, and so on. High income also opens the doors to membership in high-prestige social organizations—the Country Club, for example. High educational attainment as represented by a college degree is in itself a "badge of success" and tends to give a person high social rank. But the college education is even more important as a means of entering a high-prestige occupation, such as business executive, physician, lawyer, and the like. And high-prestige occupations *tend* to pay high incomes. In short, many of the SES characteristics are interrelated.

**Social Characteristics Associated with Upper and Lower Status Individuals in the American Society**

| Upper Status | Lower Status |
| --- | --- |
| High income | Low income |
| Many material possessions | Few material possessions |
| High-prestige occupation | Low-prestige occupation |
| High educational attainment | Low educational attainment |
| Membership in high-prestige social organizations | Membership in low-presige social organizations or no organization affiliation |
| Residence in high-prestige neighborhood | Residence in low-prestige neighborhood |
| Many outstanding accomplishments | Few or no outstanding accomplishments |

Mr. Smith has a higher SES than Mr. Brown when judged by the items on the chart. Mr. Smith is a college graduate. He is a top executive in a textile factory. He earns about $65,000 a year, lives in a fine home, and is a leader in civic and social organizations. In contrast, Mr. Brown is a high school graduate. He is a machine operator in the textile factory. He earns $11,000 a year, lives in a five-room apartment, and belongs to no high-prestige social or civic organizations in the community.

123

Occasionally a person with little wealth enjoys a high social rank. A few occupations enjoy high prestige but do not provide high incomes —the ministry, for example. Or a person's high social rank may rest chiefly on some feat which brings high honors but not very much money. And a wealthy person may fail to obtain high social rank if it is generally known that the money came through illegal activities.

## Socioeconomic Status and Influence

Those with higher SES *tend* to have more influence on public officials than those with lower SES. They *tend* to have more political resources such as money, education, and skills. If they choose, they can use these resources to influence political decisions. For example, recall the case on page 48, "Who Rules Agri-city?" The most influential people in this town are those with high SES: the president of the local bank, the owner of a real-estate business, an auto dealer, a department store owner, etc. These upper status people in Agri-city have more political resources and influence than do lower status people such as unskilled laborers, waiters, or clerks.

1. Use evidence in *Tables 6–8* to support or reject each of the following hypotheses about political resources, participation, and influence of lower and higher status people. Use this key:

    A. The data support the hypothesis.
    B. The data reject the hypothesis.
    C. The data neither support nor reject the hypothesis.

**Table 6. Responses to Question: Is there something people can do about an unjust or corrupt public official?**

| | Responses | | |
| | Can Do | Can't Do | Not |
| Group | Something | Something | Sure |
|---|---|---|---|
| 1. Income per Year | Percent | Percent | Percent |
|   Under $5000 | 46% | 42% | 12% |
|   $5000 to $9999 | 56 | 35 | 9 |
|   $10,000 to $14,999 | 59 | 35 | 6 |
|   $15,000 and over | 69 | 27 | 4 |
| 2. Education | | | |
|   Eighth grade | 35% | 51% | 14% |
|   High school | 54 | 37 | 9 |
|   College | 72 | 24 | 4 |

*Tables 6–8: Confidence and Concern: Citizens View American Government,* a Survey of Public Attitudes by the Subcommittee on Intergovernmental Relations of the Committee on Government Operations, United States Senate, pp. 241, 259, 260. Survey conducted by Louis Harris and Associates, 1973. Reprinted by permission of the *Chicago Tribune.* All Rights Reserved.

124

**a.** Lower status people are less likely than upper status people to believe that they can influence public officials.

**b.** There is little or no difference in the political knowledge of upper and lower status people.

**c.** Lower status people believe that they have less political skills than upper status people have.

**d.** Lower status people are more active in politics than upper status people are.

**e.** There is little or no relationship between having more or less money and more or less political knowledge, skill, and influence.

**f.** Margaret Petty is a lower status person; Anne Burton is an upper status person. Therefore, we can hypothesize that Anne Burton is certain to have more knowledge of politics and to be more involved in politics than Margaret Petty is.

**2.** Make an alternative hypothesis, which is supported by the data in *Tables 6–8,* to each hypothesis that you rejected in the list above.

***Table 7.*** **Kinds of Actions People Might Possibly Take to Change Things They Don't Like about Government**

| Response | Income Level | | | |
|---|---|---|---|---|
| | Under $5000 | $5000–$9999 | $10,000–$14,999 | $15,000 and over |
| | Percent | Percent | Percent | Percent |
| 1. Contact someone in local politics | 64% | 72% | 78% | 82% |
| 2. Join a local citizens group | 56 | 71 | 75 | 84 |
| 3. Join a political party and work to make changes | 52 | 62 | 66 | 80 |
| 4. Write a letter to the newspaper | 50 | 66 | 66 | 77 |
| 5. Send money to support a local citizens group to demand action | 47 | 57 | 64 | 80 |

***Table 8.*** **Percentage of People Who Rate Themselves High and Low in Knowledge of Current Political Events**

| Group | Self-Ratings of Knowledge of Politics | | |
|---|---|---|---|
| | High | Low | Not Sure |
| 1. Income per Year | Percent | Percent | Percent |
| Under $5000 | 31% | 67% | 2% |
| $5000–$9999 | 33 | 66 | 1 |
| $10,000–$14,999 | 34 | 65 | 1 |
| $15,000 and over | 47 | 53 | — |
| 2. Education | | | |
| Eighth grade | 25% | 74% | 1% |
| High school | 32 | 66 | 2 |
| College | 48 | 52 | — |

### Open and Closed Societies

Opportunities to earn a higher SES vary from society to society. In an *open society* there is much chance for people with low SES to move to a higher position. In a *closed society* there is little chance for persons with a low position to rise to a higher position. *Diagram 8* shows how open and closed societies differ.

There are no completely open or closed societies. Rather, societies can be thought of as more or less open or more or less closed according to the amount of opportunity that lower status people have to "move up the ladder." The American society has tended to be more open than many others. Through educational and job opportunities many persons have been able to move from lower to higher positions.

Notice the difference in the shapes of the open and closed societies in *Diagram 8.* A diamond shape is used to describe the open society and a pyramid shape to show the closed society. The diamond shape shows that in an open society most people occupy positions in the middle of the society. There are fewer people in positions at the very top or very bottom. By contrast, the pyramid shape shows that in a closed society most people occupy positions at the bottom. Very few people occupy positions at the higher levels.

In any society—whether open or closed—some groups will have more political resources than other groups. In the more open societies, however, people may find chances to improve their position through political action.

### Measuring Socioeconomic Status, Resources, and Potential for Influence

To show what you have learned about SES and political behavior, read these descriptions and complete the exercises that follow.

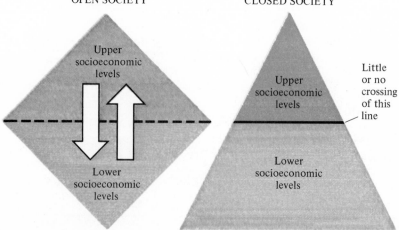

DIFFERENCES BETWEEN OPEN AND CLOSED SOCIETIES

OPEN SOCIETY

CLOSED SOCIETY

Upper socioeconomic levels

Lower socioeconomic levels

Upper socioeconomic levels

Lower socioeconomic levels

Little or no crossing of this line

*Mr. Green* is president of the First National Bank in Lynnville. He is a graduate of Harvard University. He earns over $100,000 a year. He recently moved into a new home in the city's finest residential area. His $120,000 house has four bathrooms, six bedrooms, and a big yard with a swimming pool. Mr. Green is a member of the Chamber of Commerce, the school board, and the exclusive Town Club. His four children attend a private boarding school.

*Mr. Jackson* works as janitor in the First National Bank in Lynnville. He completed the eighth grade before dropping out of school. He earns less than $7000 a year. He pays $80 monthly rent for a three-room apartment in a run-down section of town. He has never been invited to join any of the community's service clubs. He sees the inside of the Town Club only when Mr. Green pays him extra money to do some cleaning there. His three children attend the local public schools.

*Mr. Jones* is a bookkeeper in the First National Bank in Lynnville. After high school, he took a two-year course in accounting. He earns $12,000 a year. He owns a small frame home in a neat residential section. His two children attend the public school. He has never been to the Town Club. His only social contacts with Mr. Green are at social affairs related to the First National Bank.

*Mr. Thomas* is a lawyer. One of his chief clients is the First National Bank in Lynnville. He graduated from the law school at the state university. He has a successful law practice and earns over $40,000 per year. His three children attend the local public schools. Mr. Thomas belongs to several civic and social organizations, but has not yet been invited to join the Town Club.

**1.** Rank the individuals in the preceding descriptions according to the following position ranking scale.

| ? | ? | ? | ? |
|---|---|---|---|
| **Highest** | **Upper Middle** | **Lower Middle** | **Lowest** |

**2.** Tell why you ranked each person as you did in item 1.
**3.** Rank the men, from first to last, according to their possession of political resources.
**4.** Which of the four has the most potential for influencing government officials? Why?
**5.** Which of the four has the least potential for influencing government officials? Why?
**6.** From the preceding descriptions, can you make exact predictions about who will have the most influence in any political situation? Why?

## Differences in Status and Political Participation

The following story points up differences in political behavior associated with socioeconomic status. As you read the story, compare the beliefs and behavior of these three main political participants: Fred Miller, Joe Johnson, and Larry Mason.

### Case 1. Fred Miller, a Man with "Clout"

Fred Miller grew up in a comfortable home. His father was a lawyer with a high income. His parents belonged to several leading social and civic organizations.

In school Fred was an able student and a good athlete. He never doubted that he was an important member of his school and community. He learned that every citizen has both a right and a duty to take part in politics through reading, listening, forming and expressing opinions, and voting. Seeing his parents take part in politics helped to convince him of the importance of these duties.

In college Fred was further encouraged by his studies, his teachers, and his friends to succeed in being an important, responsible citizen. He also learned how to deal with people effectively. Fred became confident that goals could be achieved and changes could be made by taking part in politics.

After college, Fred went into business for himself. Through wise business deals and a few years of hard work, Fred became owner of a large restaurant chain. With this business doing well, Fred bought a row of apartment houses in a run-down section of his city.

**Fred's Political Activity.** Fred became a leader in the local organization of the Republican party. He gives money and time, and uses his influence, in support of "his" candidates. They are often elected.

In return for support, Fred Miller expects "his" candidates to do favors for him. Because Fred has been able to get candidates elected and to get policies adopted that he favors, he is known as a man with "clout," or much influence, in the local government.

Fred Miller uses his "clout" to further his business interests and to help his friends. For example, a bill that would have hurt his business was proposed in the city council. Fred and several other restaurant owners joined to oppose the bill. They spoke against the bill at meetings of business executives and clubs and in other public speeches. Most importantly, Fred contacted the mayor and three city council members, and told them that he and his friends would oppose them in the next election if they allowed the bill to pass. The bill was defeated, and Fred Miller's reputation as a "man with clout" was confirmed.

Fred Miller uses customary channels of political influence. He has not taken part in marches, sit-ins, pickets, or other types of protest. Rather, he makes political bargains through direct contact with public officials and community leaders.

**A New Problem Arises.** Fred had never had any major troubles until the summer when the people living in his apartment houses began

128

complaining loudly. Fred knew the buildings were in poor condition, but he rarely went to see that his apartments had become rat-infested, filthy, and run-down. The plumbing needed fixing, and the walls were cracked and shabby. Many of the dwellings were severe fire hazards. Fred either ignored the complaints or made only slight efforts to correct extreme problems. As long as Fred could keep the apartments rented, he thought conditions must be fairly good. Besides, Fred believed that his tenants did not take proper care of their apartments and would only damage them again if he made repairs. Moreover, Fred reasoned that he would have to raise the rents if he made improvements. Most of his tenants could not afford a rent increase. So Fred consoled himself by thinking that the present situation was best for everyone.

In response to many complaints from tenement residents, the city government devised a plan to set stricter standards for housing in the city. This housing plan was designed to please the tenants in the slum section where Miller's apartments were located. The mayor seemed anxious to please the voters in the slum secton, because they were getting more and more militant and critical of the city government. Some slum-area residents had recently formed a political action group.

**Fred Mobilizes His Political Resources.** Fred Miller thought the proposed housing plan would cost him much money. So he quickly set up a meeting of people who owned other houses in the slum. Fred opened the meeting with the following remarks: "It seems to me that we should send someone to meet with the mayor and the directors of the sanitation and housing departments. Our representative could explain our position and present all the arguments against this proposed plan. We can probably convince them not to put the plan into operation. But even if the mayor decides to carry it out, perhaps we can get him to water it down, make it less harmful to us."

Mr. Larson spoke up next: "This might work, Fred, but maybe we should also get a petition signed by the owners and present it to the mayor at the same time. The more people we have on our side, the more convincing we'll be."

"Good idea, Larson," replied Fred, and the others nodded in agreement. "I'll appoint a committee to get the petition ready. We'd better select someone tonight to represent us at a meeting with the mayor, that is, if you all think the meeting is a good idea."

"I think it would help our cause to get some of the people in town on our side," remarked Frank Hays. "Suppose I write a letter supporting our position to the editor of the paper."

"No, I don't think that's a good idea, Frank," Fred replied. "If we do that, we'll arouse more opposition than support. But why not send such a letter to other business people who would be likely to agree with us anyway?"

"I suppose that makes sense," Frank responded.

The owners decided that Fred should ask for a meeting with the mayor and speak for them at this meeting. Fred was less confident than usual. He knew that he faced a difficult challenge. While he could apply pressure to the mayor, his opposition was stronger this time than ever before. He was not sure that he had enough "clout" to win this battle.

### Case 2. Joe Johnson, an Apathetic Citizen

Joe Johnson was born in the hills of eastern Kentucky, where he lived until the age of eight. Then his family moved to the slum section of Fred Miller's city. Since his father made very little money, Joe's family could not afford luxuries and had to do without some necessities. For example, the food was mostly low-cost starches. Sometimes their clothing had patches, or did not fit well, or was not warm enough. There was no money to give the children good medical or dental care.

Joe got a poor education. In his slum area it was hard to get good teachers. The schools were poorly equipped. Most students did not think education was important, but everyone had to attend school until the age of sixteen. Joe's parents had almost no education, and they gave their children little encouragement to succeed in school.

Joe's parents lacked knowledge and interest in politics, so they never took part. If they talked about politics at all, their only comment was that it should be left to people who knew more than they did. Joe's parents tended to take things as they came. A social worker once tried to organize the people in Joe's neighborhood against merchants who seemed to be overcharging their customers. A well-organized group could have forced an end to these unfair practices, but it would have taken much time and work. The social worker could not find enough people willing to carry out the project.

Seeing no prospects for a good career by staying in school, Joe quit at sixteen and began working. He soon married and started a family, still earning low wages at whatever job he could get. The only place he could afford to live was in a slum area. Joe lived in one of Fred Miller's houses.

**Joe Knew Little about Politics and Cared Less.** He never voted, skipped news stories in papers and magazines, and almost never talked about public issues. His worries about money made him feel that he had no control over his life. He felt he would always be dependent on outside sources—a boss, a loan company, or an unemployment check to keep his family going. He felt especially inferior when trying to deal with people of higher status than himself. Joe Johnson was an *apathetic* citizen.

131

Joe's political life was also typical of many other people in his neighborhood. This became clear one summer when political action was needed. Several times during the spring and summer Joe and some of the other tenants had called Fred Miller's office and complained about bad plumbing, crumbling walls, broken windows, and rats. Each time Fred promised to do something but then didn't. The tenants grew more and more resentful. Although many felt the same as Joe, they had no formal organization and no contacts with influential people. Effective action against the owners seemed impossible.

## Case 3. Larry Mason, a Political Activist

While Joe Johnson and his friends griped about their housing problem, Larry Mason was busy trying to solve it through political action. During the past year Larry Mason, with several other young men and women, had formed the Community Organization for Underprivileged People (COUP) to help poor people deal more effectively with public officials and business people.

Larry Mason was born and raised in Joe Johnson's neighborhood. His family was poor and large, and Larry had to quit school at age sixteen to help support his younger brothers and sisters.

After two years of working at low-paying jobs, Larry became a "runner" for a local gambling syndicate. As a "runner" Larry collected bets for "numbers," "policy," and "bolito" gambling operations. He then earned a sizable income and became known as a man with "good connections." Larry sometimes used his new wealth and influence to do favors for his friends. He was becoming a neighborhood leader when the police cracked down on the local gambling operation and arrested Larry. He was sentenced to three years in prison.

**Larry Decides to Use His Political Skills.** During his term in prison, Larry passed the time by reading. He read articles about the problems of poor people in America. He read biographies of leaders who had worked hard to improve the lives of their followers. He decided he had wasted his time trying to get rich by helping the syndicate take money from poor people. "I'm tired," he said, "of living in a town where poor people are always being shoved around by everyone else." He felt that it was time for poor people to start speaking up for themselves because, as he said, "there isn't anybody else looking out for us anyway."

When Larry left prison, he came back home and talked five friends into helping form COUP to aid poor people. At first these men and women continued in their regular jobs and only helped with COUP in their spare time. But Larry's ability to talk to the people of his neighborhood, as well as favorable publicity for some of COUP's initial projects, enabled COUP to grow in size and effectiveness. Larry and his friends soon left their old jobs to run the organization full time.

People in the neighborhod depended on COUP to help them apply pressure on public officials to get such services as better garbage

In Somerville, Massachusetts, tenants used a variety of political techniques to persuade the city government to pass a rent-control law. At the left two women demonstrate to keep rent controls.

collection, street repair, recreation facilities, and better police protection. COUP got the unemployed to enter work-training programs and at times helped them find jobs. COUP helped poor people to work with welfare department officials and to get legal aid. Through his leadership of COUP, Larry Mason hopes to convince the people that there is strength in unity and that "clout" can come from a tightly knit and well-led organization.

**COUP Puts Pressure on City Hall.** During the past month Larry Mason has been pressuring the city to do something about the slum tenements. He told the mayor and the council member from his area that he could guarantee a sizable bloc of votes for them in the next election if they would help now. He threatened to cause trouble for the city if the housing problems were not solved.

While the city officials hesitated, trying to decide how to react to the issue about housing standards, Larry Mason and COUP put on more pressure. Picketers parading around City Hall carried signs insisting that the city accept COUP's demands.

At an open meeting of COUP, Larry Mason urged unity:

We must stand up and refuse to cooperate with those who would oppress us. Let the mayor and his cronies see that together we have more power than the landlords. We must convince the mayor that he will lose the next election if he doesn't help us now.

133

Larry's audience cheered as he finished his speech. Joe Johnson was among those attending the meeting. A friend had asked him to come. After listening to Mason's speech, Joe Johnson decided to join COUP. Joe had never heard anyone so much like himself speak so forcefully. "Maybe Mason is right" he said to his friends. "Maybe we can do something about our problems if we stick together and stand up against the big-shots in this city."

1. What are the issues and value conflicts in this story about Miller, Johnson, and Mason?

2. Compare the political behavior of Fred Miller, Joe Johnson, and Larry Mason in terms of these concepts: political resources, political interest, political techniques, and political influence.

3. Try to explain similarities and differences of the three political actors in terms of these concepts: culture, socialization, status, personality, maintenance, and change.

4. Speculate about different possible outcomes of this story. For example, do you think Larry Mason and COUP are likely to achieve their objectives? Why?

5. What are your value judgments about possible outcomes of this story? For example, do you think Larry Mason and COUP ought to achieve their objectives? Why?

## Political Roles of Women: How Much Change?

Women *have been* the real "silent majority" in American politics. Although making up over 52 percent of the population, they have held less than 2 percent of the major public offices.

An important part of the American way *has been* to keep females out of the center ring of the political arena. Thus Congresswoman Bella Abzug and her assistant, Cynthia Edgar, have declared bitterly: "For most of this country's history, women's place has been in the home, in the fields, in the factories, in the sweatshops, or any place except where the power is."[1] And Congresswoman Shirley Chisholm has complained that "I've suffered worse discrimination as a woman than as a black."

In recent years many people have been challenging traditional female roles. The National Women's Political Caucus has been especially prominent in getting females to run for public office and to take part in politics. In addition, several "women's lib" groups have been hard at work for basic reform of woman's place in society.

Have the reformers been effective? Some observers believe so. Gloria Steinem claims that "women are changing more rapidly than

---

1. From "Women and Politics: The Struggle for Representatives" by Bella Abzug and Cynthia Edgar. Reprinted from *The Massachusetts Review,* © 1972 The Massachusetts Review, Inc. Used by permission.

any other group." Pollster Louis Harris contends that "there are many signs that women are playing for keeps in politics more than any time in the past."

What are your views? Following is evidence that can help you decide about the extent of change in the political behavior of women. Does the evidence support your beliefs? Or does it compel you to think new thoughts and to form new conclusions?

## Participation as an Indicator of Change

Participation in various political activities is one chief sign of change in women's political behavior. Americans have tended to believe that women are *not* very active in politics. In the 1920 presidential election, the first after women got the vote through the Nineteenth Amendment, only about one-third of the females of voting age bothered to vote. Twenty-eight years later, in the presidential election of 1948, less than one-half of the females of voting age went to the polls. How about today? How does political activity of women compare with that of men?

*Table 9* shows data about the participation of eligible males and females in the last three presidential elections. What do these data say about change in the political behavior of women?

**Table 9. Participation in Three Presidential Elections**

| Sex | Year | | |
|---|---|---|---|
| | **1964** | **1968** | **1972** |
| Female | 60% | 65% | 62% |
| Male | 65% | 69% | 64% |

*Table 9* shows that the voter turnout rate of females has almost equaled that of males. Among upper-income, well-educated people living in urban or suburban areas, women are as active as men in electoral politics. However, among lower-income, less educated groups, females still tend to be much less involved politically.

According to a nationwide poll taken by Louis Harris and Carolyn Setlow in 1973, three of every five women believed that they should become more active both in electoral politics and in political affairs between elections. However, only one of six women reported that they were involved regularly in political activities.

The Harris-Setlow poll shattered the long-standing belief that women vote as their husbands tell them. Sixty-four percent said that they decide how to vote without depending on their husbands. Sixty percent of the husbands agreed. Louis Harris claims that "women's liberation" in voting is a departure from other times when "it was not uncommon for the poll taker to ring a doorbell and have the woman

*Table 9:* U. S. Department of Commerce, Bureau of the Census.

Left: Congresswoman
Barbara Jordan of Texas
Right: Lieutenant Governor
Mary Ann Krupsak of New
York

of the house say she could not honestly tell whom she was voting
for, because her husband had not yet given her the word."[2]

Using participation as an indicator, what does the preceding
evidence say about change in the political roles of American women?

### Positions in Government as an Indicator of Change

Very few women have held high public office in America. Not
until 1917 was a woman (Jeannette Rankin of Montana) elected to
a seat in Congress. From 1917 to 1974, only ninety more women made
it to Capitol Hill, eleven as senators and eighty as members of the
House of Representatives. Margaret Chase Smith of Maine is counted
twice, since she was the only woman to have served in both the Senate
and the House. There have been no female Presidents or United States
Supreme Court justices.

Women have fared little better in getting top jobs in the federal
bureaucracy. Females in the mid-1970s held over one-third of the

---

2. Reprinted from *The Anguish of Change* by Louis Harris. By permission of W. W.
Norton & Company, Inc. Copyright © 1973 by W. W. Norton & Company, Inc.

federal civil service jobs, but they held only 4 percent of the higher level policy-making positions. By 1975 only three women had ever been cabinet members.

As of 1974 there were few females who had become public officials in state and local governments. There had been only four women state governors, one female lieutenant governor, one woman chief justice of a state supreme court, one woman mayor of a large city, and only a small number of female mayors of small cities.

According to Frances "Sissy" Farenthold, chairperson of the National Women's Political Caucus, 1974 "was the year of the breakthrough for women." In this year Ella Grasso became governor of Connecticut. Janet Gray Hayes became the first woman mayor of a big city—San Jose, California. Susie Sharp became the first female chief justice of a state supreme court—in North Carolina. Mary Anne Krupsak became lieutenant governor of New York. In addition, March Fong was elected secretary of state in California, and eighteen women won seats in the United States House of Representatives.

Few women, past or present, have even been candidates for public office. But this trend may be changing. According to the National

Women's Political Caucus, more than 3000 women have been running for state and national government offices per year since 1974. This is a three-fold increase over the 1028 women who sought offices in state and national government in 1972.

Using positions in government as an indicator, what does the preceding evidence say about the extent of change in the political roles of American women?

## Public Opinion as an Indicator of Change

Public opinion polls are useful indicators of the national mood. They tell what most people think is good or bad, right or wrong. Thus public opinion about women in politics may tell us a great deal about change in the status and power of women.

*Tables 10–11* show the results of several nationwide polls, from 1937 to 1971, about voting for a female candidate for President. *Table 12* shows public opinion about voting for a female congressional candidate.

**Table 10.** Question: If your party nominated a woman for President, would you vote for her if she were qualified for the job?

| Response | Year 1937 | 1945 | 1958 | 1967 | 1971 |
|---|---|---|---|---|---|
| Yes | 34% | 33% | 52% | 57% | 66% |
| No | 66 | 55 | 43 | 39 | 29 |
| No opinion | — | 12 | 5 | 4 | 5 |

**Table 11.** Opinions of Males and Females about Voting for a Woman Presidential Candidate

| | Year 1945 | | 1958 | | 1971 | |
|---|---|---|---|---|---|---|
| Response | Male | Female | Male | Female | Male | Female |
| Yes | 29% | 37% | 51% | 55% | 65% | 67% |
| No or No opinion | 71 | 63 | 49 | 45 | 35 | 33 |

**Table 12.** Question: If your party nominated a woman to run for Congress from your district, would you vote for her if she were qualified for the job? (1970)

| | Sex | |
|---|---|---|
| Response | Male | Female |
| Yes | 83% | 84% |
| No or No opinion | 17 | 16 |

*Tables 10–12:* American Institute of Public Opinion, THE GALLUP POLL, Princeton, New Jersey.

Answer the following questions about *Tables 10–12.*

1. What do these tables tell about changes in opinions about the political roles of women?

2. What are your hypotheses about why these changes in opinion have come about?

3. Note in *Table 12* that 84 percent of the voters were willing in 1970 to cast a ballot for a qualified female congressional candidate. Contrast this with the 66 percent who in 1970 were willing to vote for a woman for President. How would you explain this difference?

4. What do these tables suggest about the future political roles of women?

## The Future of Women in Politics

The preceding evidence about women in politics suggests that major change may be in the air. There have been promising tendencies in public opinion about female political roles and in the voter behavior of women. However, this evidence also shows that few women have reached the top positions of power at the national, state, or local levels of politics. Furthermore, while endorsing the idea of female political activism, only one of six women said that they have done anything other than vote in public elections.

Over the years the protest demonstration has been a political technique often used by women's groups to gain equal rights.

Are there clues in this evidence (and in other data from other sources) about the future of women in American politics? If so, what are they? What predictions might be made about the future political roles of women?

Following are several speculations about the future of women in politics. Which do you agree with and why?

A. Although a majority of men and women say they would vote for a qualified female presidential candidate, most observers doubt that a woman *could be* elected President in the near future. A recent Louis Harris poll revealed that only 37 percent of the female respondents believed that a woman *could* become President within the next ten years.

1. Do you think a woman can become President in the next few years? Should one be elected? Why?
2. Would you vote for a woman candidate for President? Why?

B. In the Harris poll cited above, 50 percent of the men and 57 percent of the women wanted to have a woman on the Supreme Court as soon as possible. Although there are many brilliant women lawyers, few people believe that a woman will be appointed to the Supreme Court in the next ten to fifteen years.

3. Do you agree?
4. Should a woman be appointed to the Supreme Court? Why?

C. A main goal of the National Women's Political Caucus is to elect over 250 women to Congress in the near future. According to Bela Abzug and Cynthia Edgar: "Congress is now dominated by male, white, middle-aged to old, upper middle-class 'representatives'. . . . Rather than replacing a white male elite with a white female elite, the Caucus intends to elect a diversity of women. . . . Such a Congress would be more truly representative, better prepared to deal with the complex problems which beset our society, and unlikely to tolerate laws and procedures which now discriminate against women, the poor, the young, and any underrepresented minority."[3]

5. Do you agree with these objectives of the Women's Caucus?
6. Do you think they can be achieved in the near future—or at any time?
7. Do you think these objective should be achieved? Why?

---

3. Abridged from "Women and Politics: The Struggle for Representatives" by Bella Abzug and Cynthia Edgar. Reprinted from *The Massachusetts Review,* © 1972 The Massachusetts Review, Inc. Used by permission.

D. Many occupations are sex-typed. That is, most people believe that certain jobs are strictly for men and that others are fit only for women. For example, nursing, teaching the primary grades, and household management are thought of as women's jobs. In contrast, law, engineering, and *politics* are supposed to be male occupations.

Sex-typing of occupations can be a barrier to the success of women in politics. For example, when Florence Allen, Chief Justice of the U.S. Court of Appeals (Sixth Circuit), was first appointed a federal judge she encountered strong resistance from her fellow male judges. For a long time they would not speak to her, or even look at her, unless required to by legal business. Judge Allen overcame this resistance, but many less strong-willed people might have quit.

Some observers claim that sex-typing will continue to limit the roles of women in politics. Others argue that basic attitudes about the roles of women and men are changing rapidly and basically and that sex-typing of occupations will not limit the future political roles of women.

**8.** Do you think that the sex-typing of occupations has limited the political behavior of women?

**9.** Do you think that negative attitudes about women will be a big obstacle in the future?

**10.** How can these obstacles be removed? Should they be removed? Why?

The young people of today will have much to say about the political roles of women during many tomorrows. Do you predict a bright future for women in politics? Are you willing to work to achieve this future?

# 7 Political Loyalties

Loyalty is faithfulness or allegiance to a person, group, or set of ideas. Main objects of political loyalty among most people are their nation, its basic ideals, and its system of government.

Each of the following statements provides some clues about the speaker's political loyalty to the nation. Decide which speaker of each pair (1a or 1b, etc.) is the "more loyal" and which is the "less loyal."

*Speaker 1a:* Perhaps the greatest privilege ever offered Americans is the chance to give their life for their country. The quiet courage that enables people to make this noble sacrifice entitles them to join the ranks of those heroes who have made America great.

*Speaker 1b:* I love my country, but I will not kill for it. God's commandment is clear: "Thou shalt not kill." I can kill no person, whatever the risks, however noble the cause, for my first obligation is to obey God. By living a moral life, in agreement with God's will, I can best serve my country.

*Speaker 2a:* A good American supports the President. Once elected, a President is the leader and should be followed.

*Speaker 2b:* The President's policies are bad for our country. They violate our national ideals. If the policies are not changed, our nation will be ruined. All good Americans should join to resist the President's policies.

*Speaker 3a:* Every American should support the law. To those who criticize our nation, I say: "Love it or leave it."

*Speaker 3b:* Every good citizen must be willing to protest unjust laws or acts of public officials. If a law is unfair or immoral, then citizens who truly love their country must strive to change that law. Public demonstrations and passive resistance may be needed to overthrow evil policies or laws and to achieve justice.

## Types of Loyalty

From the preceding lesson it should be clear that it is not easy to decide who is loyal, disloyal, or most loyal. It would be hard to find a person who lacks loyalty. When people are accused of *disloyalty,* it seldom means that they have no loyalty but rather that their loyalties differ from those of the accuser. Let us look at some types of loyalties.

### Loyalty to Other People

One type of loyalty is the feeling people have for their family and friends. For example, Americans expect families and relatives to

142

Loyalty arises from a feeling of belonging to a group. How might an
ethnic-group celebration like this Mexican American festival at Plascentia,
California, and a Girl Scout convention promote feelings of loyalty to a
group? Mrs. Betty Ford spoke to the Girl Scouts.

come to one another's aid in times of trouble. We expect people to defend their families and friends against unfair charges. A young person who told lies about a friend would in a sense be seen as "disloyal."

## Loyalty to Groups

Many groups command our loyalty. Students loyal to their school cheer for their own team, not for the rival's team. School clubs, church groups, civic organizations, perhaps the company we work for, and political parties are other groups which share our loyalty. People hold loyalty to a group either because its goals and beliefs are similar to their own or because of their interest in others who belong.

## Loyalty to Beliefs and Ideas

Another type of loyalty is to strong beliefs. In times of religious persecution, Christians and Jews have been willing to die for their beliefs rather than be "disloyal" to them. Some people are loyal to the idea of private enterprise. Others are attached to socialism.

## National Loyalty

Most people in the world have a sense of national loyalty. This feeling for the nation is learned early in life. In reciting the Pledge of Allegiance and singing the National Anthem, children learn national loyalty. They also learn it by observing national holidays and reading stories about national heroes. Taking part in youth groups (Scouts, 4-H Clubs, and the like) and school clubs helps young people to acquire the political culture and to produce allegiance to the nation.

As a result of political socialization, Americans tend to identify with their nation. They say "we" defeated the Germans in World War II, although they may have been too young to fight. They say "we" were in Vietnam. This sense of identification allows us to feel that we have taken part in the acts of American heroes, such as "our" landing on the moon. (Would you have been as excited if the Russians had landed first?) Feelings of patriotism can also blind us to improper actions by our own citizens, actions we would condemn in other nations.

Even though most Americans have a sense of national loyalty, we can be sure that it does not mean the same thing to everyone. In fact, "national loyalty" seems to be a general term for all of one's group loyalties. Thus when people join the army to defend their nation, they are defending people and groups that mean a lot to them. These friends and groups may not be the same as those being defended by the person who is fighting along side. Thus one person may fight because of a belief that the United States is a nation where one is free to be Jewish, another to be Roman Catholic, another to be Protestant, and still another not to attend church at all. In each case the "nation" stands for their beliefs. Thus the nation's survival is important to the survival of the groups with which they identify.

144

People are loyal to the nation as a result of the satisfactions they get from many groups and because people believe that the nation supports these groups. For example, a Democrat and Republican will disagree on certain domestic policies. Yet Democrats and Republicans can be equally loyal to the nation so long as it continues to be a place in which the beliefs of each are protected or seem to be so.

### Conflicting Loyalties

Any person is able at the same time to be loyal to a variety of groups, including family, friends, club, employer, church, and government. Often these loyalties overlap and support each other. Sally Thompson is a member of a Girl Scout troop sponsored by her church. These two groups lend support to one another. Moreover, both teach national loyalty, as do Sally's family and her school.

In other cases a person's loyalties may conflict. Jane Atwood lives on the same block as Sally and goes to the same school. As youngsters they played together a great deal. Jane and her family are members of a religious sect which believes that the flag-salute ceremony is contrary to the teaching of the Bible. Jane's family and church provide her with one view of the meaning of national loyalty. Her school and community give her a different meaning of the concept.

Some societies try to suppress any expression of loyalty which differs from that of the leaders of the government. The family, church, school, labor unions, news media, and other groups support the goals and policies of the governmental leaders. Dissent and criticism are branded as disloyalty. A free society, on the other hand, can put up with quite a large number of points of view. It makes some provision for people who, for example, object on religious grounds to fighting in a war or saluting the flag.

Once in a while, conflicting loyalties force a person to make basic choices between groups and beliefs. A young man, for example, may have been taught that it is honorable to serve one's country in the armed services. But he has come to believe that his country is engaged in an immoral war. He feels that service in the army would be an act of disloyalty to his new beliefs. If he chooses to be loyal to his new beliefs, he may cut himself off from his family and former associates. He feels a sense of *alienation.*

## What Is Political Alienation?

Loyalty to one group may keep a person out of other groups. For example, people who joined hippie clans during the 1960s felt apart from other groups with whom they once associated. They had feelings of *alienation.*

*Aliens* are foreigners living outside their own country. We say that people are alienated when they feel like a stranger even in familiar surroundings. Alienated persons reject, or feel rejected by, social groups with which they once had close ties—family, friends, school, church, and the like.

Politically alienated persons are ones who reject, or feel rejected by, their society and its political system. They have serious gripes about the government. They do not think their complaints can be met through the usual machinery of government. They have lost faith in their government and the laws, customs, and beliefs which support it.

Some politically alienated people become *political activists* who seek to overthrow the existing political system. These radical political activists tend to have a high sense of power. Alienated political activists may be willing to engage in conspiracy or violence to bring about changes they seek.

Other politically alienated people are *political apathetics* who seek to withdraw from the political system. These political dropouts tend to have a low sense of power. They avoid activities that would show support for the established political system. But they are not interested in revolutionary political activity.

(1) Decide which of the following speakers are alienated from the political system or culture of the United States. (2) Then group the alienated speakers into two categories: (a) the alienated activist and (b) the alienated apathetic. Be prepared to defend your choices.

*Speaker 1:* Someone told me that the city government wants to add fluoride to our water. I think it has something to do with teeth. I don't know much about it. They'll probably do what is best, and I'll accept their decision.

*Speaker 2:* My friends and I are tired of this phoney society and the phoney politicians who run it. We're forming our own commune on some wilderness land that my uncle left to me in his will. This will give us a chance to be free from the corruption and insincerity of the straight world. Why don't you join us?

A commune is a small social unit of families and individuals who share possessions and work duties.

*Speaker 3:* I don't really care who gets elected to public office. I'm satisfied with my life. Whatever happens, it's not likely to affect me very much. I'll still have my job, my family, and my home.

*Speaker 4:* The whole society is sick. It has to be torn apart and rebuilt. Burn, baby, burn—that's the only political slogan that's worth anything.

*Speaker 5:* Some of my friends have tried to get me involved in politics, but I have resisted. I enjoy the 4-H group I work with. I like to think I am making a contribution to our society in that way. Four-H and my family take up just about all my free time.

*Speaker 6:* The government and the political big-shots in this country have always cheated people like me. But what can we do about it? We have to sit back and take their abuse. There's no sense in trying to overthrow the government, but don't expect me to cooperate with the public officials or obey the law if I can get away with it.

*Speaker 7:* Most public officials in this country are socialist traitors who have forgotten the true American heritage. No peaceful efforts can make these public officials change their ways. Therefore, I have started an underground organization of true patriots who will save this country from socialism. If necessary, we will violently overthrow the government in order to preserve the true American way of life.

*Speaker 8:* My friends and I have been working hard to elect Jones as governor of our state. We believe that he is a very able man who will begin to solve the serious problems that afflict our state. It appears that he has a good chance to win this election.

## The Extent of Political Alienation

Polls show that a low percentage of Americans express political alienation. Pollster Daniel Yankelovich estimated that only about 10 percent of young adults in the United States could be called politically alienated during the 1960s.[1] This was a period of unrest with its civil rights demonstrations and an unpopular war in Vietnam.

By 1974, however, Yankelovich found that most young adults considered themselves "middle-of-the-roaders." Only 5 percent said they were radicals.[2] A radical is so alienated that he or she wants to make basic changes in the political system or overthrow it. A Louis Harris poll in 1974 reported that only 3 percent of American adults considered themselves to be political radicals.[3]

## Sources of Political Alienation

Why are most people loyal to a nation or political system? Why does political alienation develop among others? These questions are hard to answer precisely, since people may have many reasons for expressing political loyalty or alienation. However, in every case the social groups such as family, friends, and work groups to which people belong play a large part in shaping their attitudes toward their country.

Through the socialization process most Americans remain loyal. Yet some become alienated. Other Americans shift back and forth between political loyalty and alienation. The following four cases provide some clues about sources of political alienation in the United States.

1. Daniel Yankelovich, *Generations Apart* (Columbia Broadcasting System, 1967).
2. From *The New Morality: A Profile of American Youth in the 70's* by Daniel Yankelovich. Copyright © 1974 by the JDR 3rd Fund, Inc. Used with permission of McGraw-Hill Book Company.
3. Louis Harris, "Harris Survey," *Chicago Tribune* (December 26, 1974), p. 20, section 1. Reprinted by permission of the *Chicago Tribune*. All Rights Reserved.

147

Young protestors staged a counter-demonstration in April 1975 at Concord, Massachusetts, where President Ford took part in Bicentennial observances.

### Case 1. The Bomb Makers

Mary B. was raised in a white, Protestant, middle-class home in a small midwestern town. Her father, an insurance salesman, was earning about $25,000 per year. Mary was an only child.

Mary was popular in high school, earned academic honors, and then went to a small eastern women's college. After graduation Mary and one of her friends traveled in Europe for nearly six months, talking to many kinds of people.

Not sure what career to begin, Mary decided to attend graduate school at a nearby state university in 1968. There Mary made new friends who took part in community action programs to help poor people. These students tutored children to help them improve their reading and writing skills. They helped adults find jobs. They tried to instruct poor people in political protest tactics, to help them organize rent strikes in slum housing, and to provide legal aid.

As Mary became involved in these activities, her political attitudes began to change. She saw that she had led a sheltered life and had been unaware of the problems of poor people. She became more and more disgusted with people who seemed to be ignoring the poor.

At a party she met Jim, a student much different from other men she had known in her home town. Jim had been in many protest activities and was a leader of a radical political group. Soon they were dating regularly. Mary wrote to her parents about Jim and his ideas and was hurt when they disapproved. Mary also began to see less and less of her former friends. And she found excuses to avoid going home to visit her parents because she disliked arguing with them about her new friends and her new ideas.

Gradually Mary began to feel like an outsider. Since she and Jim dressed differently than many of the students on campus, they were often treated rudely. Their own friends were active in radical student groups. Soon Mary began joining them in protest marches to dramatize their stand against American foreign policy and the treatment of the poor. She and Jim dropped out of school and took jobs in a factory.

After taking part in many protest marches, sit-ins, and rallies, Mary and her friends lost hope about changing the system through peaceful protest. They started to discuss the use of violence as a way to bring about change. These talks led to fixing up a basement apartment into an underground bomb factory. Here Mary and her friends began to make firebombs to use in future acts of political violence.

Mary became an angry young woman. She saw the United States as a hostile place for herself and her friends.

### Case 2. The Underground Soldier

John M. is a dentist in a West Coast city and a veteran of the Korean War. Until recently he was a law-abiding citizen.

A few months ago John was discussing politics with one of his patients. They agreed that something should be done to stop the nation's drift into socialism. His patient suggested that John attend a meeting with him where a few others who had the same point of view would discuss what could be done to save the country.

John went to the meeting and made some new friends. He also learned some new ways of thinking about the United States. The speakers and their pamphlets said that many public policies were part of a Communist conspiracy. The pamphlets said that the colleges and universities were run by Communists. He was told that even the federal government was controlled by Communists. The effort to pass firearms legislation in Congress was nothing more than a plot to disarm patriots like himself, thereby letting the Communists take over easily. He was told that civil rights legislation was designed by Communists to weaken the United States.

At first John doubted much of what he was told. But gradually it all began to make sense. He now distrusts most government officials, believing they are either working for the Communists or are subtly influenced by Communist ideas. As a result he has joined an organization of "underground soldiers" who are committed to saving the "true" American heritage. They take part in a number of illegal activities in order to fight for their version of "truth and justice." John and his friends managed to smuggle some guns from Mexico so that the weapons would not be registered and traced to them. They are stockpiling the weapons to be ready to defend their homes against any attempted Communist takeover. These "underground soldiers" take part in secret military training. They send threats by letters and phone calls to public officials who favor policies that John and his friends think are sponsored by the Communists.

John has become alienated from the "mainstream" of American life and from his government. He is afraid the nation may collapse. But he thinks that if he and his friends stand firm, they can root out the traitors.

### Case 3. The Betrayed

During World War II more than six thousand Americans formally declared that they were not loyal to the United States. These were Americans of Japanese ancestry. Why did they renounce their loyalty to the United States?

For nearly a century Japanese had migrated to the United States. They settled mainly on the West Coast, especially in California. The

Scenes at the relocation camps in 1942 are shown—along with a notice of the evacuation orders.

Japanese were not always welcome. Particularly in California they met discrimination in obtaining housing, buying land, and finding jobs. Still, by 1941, second-generation Japanese Americans were beginning to be accepted. They had good reason to think that Japanese Americans in the future would have the same opportunities as other people.

December 7, 1941, dramatically changed the lives of American citizens of Japanese ancestry. On that day Japanese airplanes bombed Pearl Harbor, and the old hostilities against people of Japanese ancestry reappeared. Many Americans feared that the Japanese Americans were a dangerous threat to the nation's security, more loyal to Japan than to the United States. Therefore, it became official national policy in 1942 to evacuate to detention camps all Japanese aliens and American citizens of Japanese ancestry living in Washington, Oregon, California, and Arizona. Even those with as little as one-sixteenth Japanese ancestry and who were even unaware of their Japanese background were forced to relocate. These people had to give up jobs, homes, and possessions to move to one of ten evacuation centers. Most of the camps were in the arid regions of the western states.[4]

---

4. Based on an account, including four quotations, in *The Loyal and the Disloyal* by Morton Grodzins. © 1956 by the University of Chicago. Used by permission of the publisher, The University of Chicago.

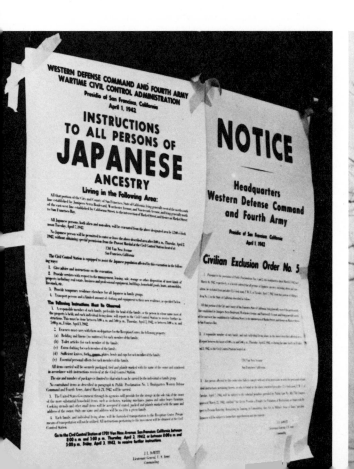

The sudden move brought severe financial hardship. The evacuees got little chance to sell their belongings. When they could sell, it was at a price far below real value. The relocation camps had barracks, barbed wire, guards, and searchlights. Originally the Japanese Americans were to be locked up in these camps for the duration of the war.

In less than a year some government officials had decided that the policy had been a mistake and were trying to change it. Some thought the entire scheme was unjust. Others argued that the plan treated recent Japanese immigrants who might be loyal to Japan the same as Japanese-American citizens who had been born in the United States and who had spent their entire lives here. Others were shocked at the living conditions in the camps. Still others felt that the policy was too costly in money and human resources.

In January 1943 the government announced that it would accept volunteers for an all-Nisei (pronounced nee-say) combat unit. To find these volunteers, a general registration of all the adults seventeen years of age and older was ordered for all ten camps.

A Nisei is a native-born citizen of the United States having Japanese immigrant parents.

Each adult in the camp was asked to fill out a questionnaire. The most crucial question was: "Will you swear unqualified allegiance to the United States of America. . . and forswear any form of allegiance or obedience to the Japanese emperor?" When the registration was completed, nearly 31,000 people had answered "yes" to the loyalty question; more than 6000 "no," and 3000 others either answered "no" or qualified their answers. Here are some typical "no" replies:

"I am loyal to this country, it's the only one I know, but my husband is an alien and I want to be where he is. The only place we know is Sacramento, and if we can't go there we might as well go to Japan."

"My loyalty is now more to Japan than to the United States. That's what my conscience tells me to say. Before evacuation it was different. We were making a pretty good living. Then this thing came and took our property. A country that wants you or wants your loyalty doesn't treat you this way."

"You people say a Jap's a Jap. You've ruined our future. We had something to look forward to, now it is all ruined."

"My dad is fifty-eight years old now. He has been here thirty years at least. He came to this country with nothing but a bed roll. He worked on the railroads and in the beet fields. If I told you the hardships he had, you wouldn't believe me. I owe a lot to my father. All through his life he was working for me. During these last years he was happy because he thought he was coming to the place where his son would have a good life. I am the only son. I have to carry on the family name. My mind is made up. I know my father is planning to return to Japan. I know he expects me to say 'no' so that there will be no possibility that the family will be separated. There isn't much I can do for my father anymore; I can't work for him the way I used to. But I can at least quiet his mind on this."

## Case 4. The Rioters

During the 1960s many civil disorders took place in the black neighborhoods of major American cities. These riots were expressions of severe alienation. However, only a minority of urban blacks took part in or supported these riots. A study of the political attitudes of black Americans shows that most blacks "though they speak in terms that would seem to justify the riots, reject violence both as a general strategy and as an approach they would be willing to take part in themselves."[5] Only 8 percent of a sample of blacks from fifteen major cities said that they would join in a riot, and only an additional 15 percent of this sample said that they would "be ready to use violence" to try to gain their rights.

A study of a riot on April 4, 1968, in Washington, D.C., gives information about why people rioted. Following are conclusions about social and economic factors linked with the Washington riot.[6]

5. *Supplemental Studies for the National Advisory Commission* (Washington: Government Printing Office, 1968), p. 51.
6. Based on material in the Prologue to *Ten Blocks From the White House: Anatomy of the Washington Riots of 1968* by Ben W. Gilbert and the Staff of The Washington Post. Reprinted by permission of The Washington Post Writers Group.

A lone soldier guards a deserted Washington street shortly before a curfew went into effect as an aftermath of the riot.

1. Housing in the riot areas was in bad condition and extremely crowded. Inhabited almost completely by blacks, the areas had been expected to explode when racial riots occurred in other big cities during previous years.

2. While a great many blacks had government jobs or decent jobs in private industry, there were complaints that promotion was infrequent and pay inadequate. Unemployment and underemployment were big problems, and the majority of blacks still held menial jobs at low pay.

3. In some areas blacks and whites lived side by side. But large areas of the city were completely poor and black. Many whites had left Washington to live in the suburbs, leaving a black majority within the city.

4. At least 90 percent of the public school pupils in the District were black. Many whites sent their children to private schools. There were charges that the public schools offered students an inferior education.

5. In 1967 the old three-member board of commissioners which governed Washington under the watchful eye of Congress was replaced by a single commissioner (popularly called "mayor"), an assistant commissioner, and a nine-member council—all appointed by the President. The President appointed a black man, Walter Washington, to be the first "mayor." The city council was given limited power to enact ordinances and to review the budget. But this was not really the "home rule" which many black citizens in Washington demanded.

6. Blacks believed that too many ghetto stores were white-owned and operated. Too few blacks had responsible positions in these stores. There were complaints against merchants for unfair pricing, high credit

154

rates, shoddy merchandise, and other discriminatory actions against slum residents. Citizens were beginning to demand more black ownership and management in business.

**1.** This chapter suggests several factors that help explain why some people become alienated and others do not. Show by example how each of the following factors may be connected with the development of political alienation:
  **a.** group identification
  **b.** political decisions of public officials
  **c.** socioeconomic status
  **d.** feelings of political effectiveness and personal power
  **e.** culture conflict within a country.

**2.** What general statements can you make about the sources of political alienation and national loyalty in our society?

## Political Cynicism

*Political cynicism* means lack of trust in government and politicians. Political cynics are upset about the actions of leading public officials, and they have many criticisms of their government. Below are some typical expressions of political cynicism:
  • Government officials don't really care about people like me.
  • Most of the people running the government are a little crooked.
  • People in government waste a lot of the money we pay in taxes.

Few Americans are extremely alienated from their government (page *147*). But many have become more cynical in recent years. There was a sharp rise in political cynicism during the early 1970s. *Tables 13-17* show a drop in political trust and a rise in cynicism by a national sample of Americans.

**Table 13. Question: Do you feel that the people running the country don't really care what happens to you?**

| Year | Percent Saying "Yes" |
|------|------|
| 1966 | 26% |
| 1972 | 50 |
| 1973 | 55 |
| 1974 | 63 |

**Table 14. Americans saying that they feel disaffected or alienated about the government and political leaders.**

| Year | Percent |
|------|------|
| 1966 | 29% |
| 1968 | 36 |
| 1969 | 36 |
| 1971 | 42 |
| 1972 | 49 |
| 1973 | 55 |
| 1974 | 59 |

*Tables 13–14:* Louis Harris, "Harris Survey," in *Chicago Tribune*, June 27, 1974.
Tables 13–17 reprinted by permission of the *Chicago Tribune*. All Rights Reserved.

**Table 15.** Question: Compared to ten years ago, do you feel that you can trust more men in public office more, less, or about the same as you did then?

| | Percent Responding | |
|---|---|---|
| Responses | 1973 | 1971 |
| Trust more | 3% | 8% |
| Trust less | 54 | 30 |
| About the same | 39 | 54 |
| Not sure | 4 | 8 |

**Table 16.** Question: Compared to ten years ago, do you feel politics is more corrupt than it was then, less corrupt, or not much different?

| | Percent Responding | | |
|---|---|---|---|
| Responses | 1973 | 1971 | 1967 |
| More corrupt | 50% | 35% | 35% |
| Less corrupt | 4 | 8 | 9 |
| Not much difference | 42 | 49 | 49 |
| Not sure | 4 | 8 | 7 |

1. What do the tables reveal about the increase of political cynicism from 1966 to 1974?
2. What does *Table 17* show about how blacks and whites compare in cynicism?
3. What are your hypotheses about (a) why there was a rise in political cynicism? (b) why there are differences in cynicism between blacks and whites?
4. To what extent do you think political cynicism is expressed today? Why?

Expressions of political cynicism are linked to current events. During the early 1970s several political events shocked the American public:

• Vice President Spiro Agnew resigned his office when accused of tax evasion and of accepting payoffs when he had been a county official in Maryland.

• Facing certain impeachment for taking part in a cover-up in the Watergate incident, Richard M. Nixon resigned the Presidency.

• Several other members of the Nixon administration, including Attorney General John Mitchell, were convicted of obstructing justice and other violations.

• Senator Daniel Brewster was convicted in 1972 of accepting a bribe from a lobbyist.

• Officers of a number of business firms were charged with making illegal political contributions.

*Tables 15–16:* Louis Harris, "Harris Survey," in *Chicago Tribune,* Oct. 18, 1973.
*Table 17: Confidence and Concern: Citizens View American Government,* p. 216.
Reprinted by permission of the *Chicago Tribune.* All Rights Reserved.

**Table 17. Responses of Blacks and Whites to Questions about Political Cynicism, 1973**

| Question | Percent Responding "Yes" | |
| --- | --- | --- |
| | Blacks | Whites |
| 1. Do you believe that most elected officials are in politics for all they can get out of it for themselves? | 74% | 58% |
| 2. Do you believe that the people running the country don't really care what happens to you? | 65 | 53 |
| 3. Do you believe that most people with power try to take advantage of people like yourself? | 74 | 52 |
| 4. Do you believe that special interests get more from the government than the people do? | 75 | 73 |

When public officials do first-rate jobs, there is little political cynicism among the public. Clearly then, the way to prevent widespread political cynicism is for officials to make an honest effort to serve all citizens fairly and effectively.

## National Loyalty and the Right to Dissent

Most Americans share some basic beliefs about their country. One is a belief in rule by law. Law establishes order and provides protection and freedom. American law is supposed to be applied equally to all. No one is supposed to be above the law.

News stories with headlines like these helped to give rise to the political cynicism of the 1970s.

Cook County Clerk Found Guilty of Bribery, Fraud

OKLAHOMA TREASURER AND 13 OTHERS INDICTED FOR GETTING FAVORS FROM BANKS

Common Cause Accuses 91 House Candidates of Failure to File Reports on Campaign Spending

JUDGE IS ON TRIAL IN TEXAS SENATE

Ex-Mayor Sentenced in Extortion Case

GRAND JURY INDICTS CONGRESSMAN FOR BRIBERY IN HELPING AIRLINE

Secret GOP Campaign Funds Are Revealed

Nearly all Americans also believe in the principle of majority rule and the protection of the rights of minorities. According to this principle, differences of opinion should be settled by debate and by vote. The losers in a political debate agree to abide by the decisions of the majority. By law, the majority must not infringe on the rights of the minority. These rights include allowing the minority to continue to argue for its views in the hope that today's minority might become the majority in a future election.

## Right to Dissent Is Fundamental to Democracy

The First Amendment to the Constitution guarantees American citizens protection of their rights of free speech and assembly. The rights of the minority would have no meaning without this protection. The right to say what one thinks, to petition the government, and to assemble peaceably with others to discuss public issues is essential for a healthy democratic system. How can public leaders know whether their policies are sound if they do not have the chance to hear what citizens honestly believe about government policies? Thus, *dissent,* the right to disagree openly with policies one believes are bad, is also basic to democracy.

Political dissent is a long and honorable American tradition. Indeed, many who came as original settlers to the colonies were dissenters. They were men and women who disliked the official Church of England and came seeking to practice their own religious beliefs. Throughout our history there have been many great dissenters, including Abraham Lincoln. As a United States Congressman he spoke out against American foreign policy during the Mexican War in the belief that President Polk's reasons for fighting the Mexicans were wrong.

## Dissent and National Security

Almost everyone agrees that freedom of speech and dissent are basic to the American way of life. But many disagree about how much dissent should be allowed. Many Americans agree with the naval hero of the 1790s, Stephen Decatur, who said, "Our country, may she always be right, but our country right or wrong." They say that during a national crisis, such as a war, all Americans must line up solidly even if they do not agree with government policy.

Other Americans agree with Carl Schurz's change in Decatur's famous words, "When right, to be kept right; when wrong to be put right." They say that it is the duty of loyal Americans to protest government actions which they think are wrong. They believe that freedom of speech or the right to dissent should not be limited even during a national crisis.

Both of these views raise hard questions. For example, can a society remain democratic if the people blindly follow their leaders, "right or wrong"? But can a society remain stable, can it be kept in order, if everyone is "free" to decide how to "put right" the affairs of the nation?

Every democratic society faces the problem of balancing the right to dissent with the need for conformity to existing rules. Every democratic society must find answers to the questions of what should be the link between liberty and loyalty, and when does dissent become disloyalty?

These questions are also complicated by the fact that people disagree about the meaning of loyalty. For example, one group of people may take part in a peace march to dramatize their belief that the government's foreign policies are harmful to the United States. Other Americans march to show their support for the President's policies. Both groups think they are loyal Americans—and both groups are likely to remain loyal Americans so long as the nation is free and open enough to accommodate a broad range of beliefs.

## Comparing Loyalty in Dictatorships and Democracies

There are basic differences between the way democratic and autocratic leaders treat questions of loyalty. In a dictatorship any means available is used to make citizens conform totally to the goals and policies of the leaders. Dictators do not allow people to take part in groups which do not give full support to the national leaders and their policies. If the churches oppose the political leaders, the clergy will be arrested and the churches will be forced to conform. The state tries to destroy or weaken existing groups and to replace them with new groups which will promote acceptance of the leader's policies.

In Nazi Germany here was the "ideal" family: The father was a Nazi. The mother was a member of the Association of Nazi Women. The daughter was in the Association of German Girls, and the son in Hitler Youth. They all met once a year at the Nazi Congress in Nuremberg. In this way, the Nazi leaders tried to make sure that there were no competing loyalties in the state. All loyalties in Nazi Germany were directed toward the nation and its leader.

While no dictatorship has ever been able to root out all rival group loyalties, that is the goal. The end result—so dictators believe—is a people who are completely loyal to the national leaders and their policies.

Democracy has an opposite set of beliefs. In the United States people are supposed to be free to believe what they wish, to do what they want, and to associate with whomever they choose. The only major exception to these practices is to limit the activities of those whose policies would prevent others from exercising their freedom. Thus, atheists are not free to burn churches just because they think churches are no good. Yet someone who believes that churches are given unfair privileges may say so and try to convince others to support this view.

159

The question of when one person's freedom harms others is at times hard to decide. It has led to much legislation and is often argued in the courts. Yet the principle is clear. In a democracy one is free to organize a group and to advocate policies that are opposite to those promoted by the national leaders. Indeed, a good citizen is often viewed as one who seeks to convince others that a current policy should be changed.

Following are two cases which raise major questions about the right to dissent, the meaning of loyalty, and the need to balance conformity to tradition with criticism of tradition.

### Case 1. The Civil Rights Protestors

In the 1960s civil disobedience was a tactic used by some black people to overturn laws that supported segregation. For example, in some cities black people were prohibited by state and local law from being served at lunch counters in department stores. Black youth would at times occupy all the counter stools and refuse to leave when asked to do so. They insisted on staying until they were served, thereby violating the local law. These youth were trained to be nonviolent. They were trained to avoid striking back when hit or insulted and to go peaceably when arrested.

Martin Luther King, Jr., was a major leader of the protestors. He said that civil disobedience was a proper reaction to "unjust laws," which he defined as laws that a minority is forced to obey but which are not applied to the majority. According to King, segregation laws were "unjust laws."

Segregation means to keep apart. In Birmingham, and throughout the South, there were segregation laws which kept blacks and whites apart. For example, it was against the law for a white person and a black person to ride in a taxi together. They could not sit together in the buses. Rather, the front portions of the bus were reserved for whites and the back of the bus was set aside for blacks. Blacks were to give up their seats to incoming white passengers if necessary. Blacks and whites attended separate schools and separate churches. There were "white" cemeteries and "black" cemeteries, "white" parks and "black" parks. This was the law.

One of the most dramatic applications of Dr. King's ideas about civil disobedience as a tool of black protestors came in Birmingham, Alabama, in the spring of 1963.

At the the head of the Southern Christian Leadership Conference (SCLC), a civil rights organization, Dr. King marched into Birmingham in April 1963. He called Birmingham the most "segregated city in America."

During the next two months Dr. King and his followers daily protested on the streets of Birmingham. King said that his purpose was to draw the attention of the nation to the problems of black people. He wanted to show that they had neither the freedom of other people

160

guaranteed by the Constitution nor equal chances to make a decent living.

King and his followers believed that segregation laws and customs were wrong. They intended to change these laws. They decided to break the segregation laws and go to jail, if necessary, to draw nationwide attention to their cause.

By contrast, the law-enforcement officials of Birmingham, led by the police commissioner, believed it was their duty to stand behind their state and city laws and to arrest law violators. When blacks, led by King, marched through the streets of Birmingham without legal march permits, the police believed that it was their duty to break up the march. The police commissioner said that King and his followers had no legal right to march in the streets. He said that the marchers were a threat to public order and safety. He said that if they did not disperse peaceably, they would be arrested.

Dr. King and his followers refused to obey the police chief's orders to stop their public demonstrations. They sang songs such as "We Shall Overcome," and they carried signs saying "freedom now" and "end segregation." The Birmingham police reacted to the peaceful, but illegal, protest with force. They used police dogs and powerful streams of water from fire hoses to stop the demonstrators. Many black protestors were arrested, including Dr. King, until the jails were overflowing. But the protest marches continued.

The Rev. Ralph Abernathy (left) and Dr. Martin Luther King lead a long line of chanting black demonstrators in their attempt to march on city hall in Birmingham. Police stopped them short of their goal.

161

The protest marches in Birmingham finally ended when the city officials gave in to some of the demands. They announced an agreement to provide for the desegregation of lunch counters, public restrooms, and other public facilities; the release from jail of arrested demonstrators; the hiring of more black workers for city jobs; and the establishment of a biracial committee to discuss problems of race relations in Birmingham.

Dr. King defended his tactics of civil disobedience in his "Letter from Birmingham Jail." He said:

> . . . One may well ask, "How can you advocate breaking some laws and obeying others?" The answer lies in the fact that there are two types of laws: just and unjust. I would be the first to advocate obeying just laws. One has not only a legal but a moral responsibility to obey just laws. Conversely, one has a moral responsibility to disobey unjust laws. . . .
>
> . . . One who breaks an unjust law must do so openly, lovingly, and with a willingness to accept the penalty. I submit that an individual who breaks a law that conscience tells him is unjust, and who willingly accepts the penalty of imprisonment in order to arouse the conscience of the community over its injustice, is in reality expressing the highest respect for law.[7]

The tactics of civil disobedience used by Dr. King and his followers in Birmingham spread throughout the nation in the 1960s to protest unfair treatment of blacks. During the 1960s, segregation laws were abolished in response to the protests of Dr. King and others across the nation.

That Dr. King's tactics were effective are shown by the results of two opinion polls taken in 1973. Big majorities of a national sample of political leaders (76 percent) and of American adults (67 percent) believed that Dr. King's political tactics "speeded up" the civil rights legislation.

### Case 2. The Fish-In

In 1854, representatives of the federal government and of several Northwest tribes of Native Americans (Indians) signed the Treaty of Medicine Creek. It was ratified by the Senate and became law. This treaty took away several million acres of land from the natives. In return, it guaranteed their fishing rights in their usual and customary places. However, in 1964, descendents of the natives who signed the treaty were being arrested, fined, and jailed for fishing where they had customarily fished.

---

7. Abridged from pp. 84, 86 in "Letter from Birmingham Jail"—April 16, 1963—in *Why We Can't Wait* by Martin Luther King, Jr. Copyright © 1963 by Martin Luther King, Jr. By permission of Harper & Row, Publishers, Inc.

In December 1963, over a century after the signing of the Treaty of Medicine Creek, the supreme court of the state of Washington declared the treaty illegal. The judges argued that the native Americans had begun to use modern fishing methods which the treaty signers had never dreamed of. The Indians were catching too many salmon that were on their way to their spawning grounds. Thus, to conserve the fish supply, the judges decided to restrict gill net fishing by Indians to their reservations. But these lands had few good fishing grounds.

**Indian Reactions to the Decision.** The Indians were angered. They pointed out that conservation of natural resources was part of their culture. While whites gave "lip service" to saving the environment, conservation had always been part of the Native American's way of life. Tribal leaders said that the Indians have their own tribal customs and laws for preserving the salmon runs.

Tribal leaders also saw the court decision as an effort to protect commercial fisheries. Before entering the rivers of Washington, the salmon had to pass through the commercial fishing fleets. The surviving salmon were left to the Indians. In the past, working with spears, long poles, and crude-twined nets, the Indians had caught few fish. Thus no one had made a fuss. But then they began to increase their haul greatly by using gill netting. With this modern method they were catching more than 30 percent of all the fish taken in the rivers. They were starting to make big profits and to compete with the fishing companies. Thus, the Indians argued, the big fishing companies wanted to put them out of business.

Loss of fishing rights was a blow to the Indians' ability to earn a living. Most of them who lived along the coastal rivers and Puget Sound depended on fishing for support. For example, more than 25 percent of the income of the Yakima tribe came from fishing. Thus the tribal leaders decided they had to resist.

**Indian Resistance Begins.** The resistance began at a meeting of the Makah tribal council. The council decided to try to unite all the tribes in Washington to protest the denial of their fishing rights. They asked Mel Thom, Hank Adams, Patrick Hamilton, Bruce Wilkie, Robert Satiacum, Janet McCloud, and others of the National Indian Youth Council to organize protest activities. Most of these young Native Americans had been to college. They had the political knowledge and skills needed to put up a fight.

The Youth Council leaders decided on a special kind of protest, "a fish-in." They would bring hundreds of Indians to "the usual and accustomed grounds" to fish in violation of the state supreme court ruling. At first most of the tribal elders were opposed. Some said that such an activity was beneath their dignity. Others said it was against tribal traditions to take part in public protests or to break the law. Youth Council leaders defended the "fish-in" tactic as the only way to correct an injustice.

There are 26 tribes of native Americans in the state of Washington. The largest tribes are the Colville, Makah, Nisqually, Puyallup, Quinault, Spokane, Swinomish, Tulalip, and Yakima.

163

The first "fish-in" was held in March 1964. Indians rowed their boats to fishing grounds on the Quillayute River. Hundreds of others stood on the river banks in support. Everyone was tense. The Indians had never taken part in a protest demonstration. Furthermore, their fish-in was an act of civil disobedience to the state game laws and to the state supreme court ruling.

State game wardens and police moved in to make arrests. The fishermen fought the police with their fists. Men, women, and children on the riverbanks threw sticks and rocks at the authorities. Many Indians were jailed and fined.

**Spread of the Protest.** The "fish-in" tactic spread to other rivers. The demonstrators got a big boost when the large Yakima tribe decided to take part. At first the Yakimas were against the "fish-ins." They lived on the richest reservation in the state. And government officials had offered special privileges to keep them from joining the public protests. However, Youth Council leaders told the Yakimas that the Indians could not hope to protect their rights unless they worked together. The leaders claimed that enemies always had tried to weaken them through "divide and conquer" tactics. They argued that in this case loyalty to the cause of all Indians should be more important than narrow tribal loyalty. Finally the Yakima tribe agreed and joined the "fish-in."

Left: Indians take part in a protest march in the state capital. Right: An attorney advises the Quinault Indians of their treaty rights in a meeting in Taholah, Washington.

The Youth Council's next move was a protest march to the state capital in Olympia. They performed a war dance on the steps of the state capital. They made speeches. Marlon Brando, the famous actor, was there to support the protestors. The governor met with the protest leaders and publicly turned down their demands.

The Indians' next tactic was to hire lawyers to defend fishermen who had been arrested and to petition officials to restore tribal fishing rights. Fish-ins continued in order to keep the Indian cause before the public and to keep pressure on public officials.

**The Protest Succeeds.** Finally, in 1965, an unexpected political prize was gained. The United States Department of Justice said it would uphold its obligations in defense of the fishing rights of the Indians.

Since 1965, there have been other acts of civil disobedience and public protest by Indians. More and more Native Americans have seemed determined to protect their rights and to win new opportunities and justice through direct political action.

The federal government has responded more and more with court decisions and law-enforcement activities that have protected the legal rights of Indians. In particular, the United States Supreme Court ruled on February 19, 1975, that the Washington state government cannot take away the hunting and fishing treaty rights of Indians.

Use information from this chapter, particularly from the preceding two cases, to assist your discussion of these questions.
1. What is the main issue or value conflict in each of the cases?
2. Why did the blacks and the Indians decide to use public protest tactics rather than other political techniques?
3. In your judgment, were the protestors wise to use public protest tactics? Or should they have chosen to use other political techniques? Explain.
4. Some people say that it is all right to break the law for a "just cause." Do you agree? Explain.
5. What limits should be placed on dissent in our society? Explain.
6. When discussing loyalty or patriotism, some people stress the duty to conform to authority. Others stress the responsibility to dissent constructively, when necessary, from authority.
   **a.** Would you stress either conformity or dissent in a discussion of the meaning of loyalty and patriotism?
   **b.** Are there different views of loyalty and patriotism among your classmates?
7. What are the relationships of culture, socialization, socio-economic status, role, and group identifications to the political behavior of the "protestors" and the "law enforcers" in the preceding cases?
8. What are your value judgments about the political behavior of the "protestors" and the "law enforcers" in the preceding cases?

# UNIT THREE

## Elections and
## the Behavior of Voters

# 8
# Selecting Leaders of Government

Every society selects leaders and gives them power to settle conflicts and to hand out rewards. Every society faces the problems of deciding how to choose its rulers and how to shift ruling power from one group to another.

A society's method of choosing governmental leaders affects the extent to which the people enjoy political stability, peace, order, and justice. The surest way to tell whether a society is more or less democratic is to look at its method of selecting rulers. A democratic society chooses them through majority vote of the people and protects the rights of those in the minority. A democratic society offers regular chances to vote new persons to ruling positions.

## Different Ways of Selecting Governmental Leaders

How should rulers be chosen? How long should they stay in power? How should they be replaced when their period of rule comes to an end? Answers to these questions have varied greatly from society to society throughout history. Following are five examples of reactions to the common problem of how to select rulers and transfer power.

### Example 1. Long Live the King

The young man stood proudly before the Assembly of Nobles that crowded the church to witness his coronation. He was solemn but happy. A few days before, he had been very sad. His father, the king for thirty years, had died. He had loved his father; it had been hard to hide his emotions on that terrible day. But today, as his father's oldest son and heir, he would be crowned king. Could he match his father in war and peace? Could he defend his nation and rule his people? Would he make wise and just laws? Thoughts of happiness and pride, mingled with sadness and worry, ran through his mind as he waited for the crown to be placed on his head by the bishop.

After the ceremony, the new king rode through the main street of his city. The people cheered for their new ruler. Happy shouts of "Long live the king" filled the air.

### Example 2. The People's Choice

The *Daily Times,* the largest paper in the capital city, carried a bold headline proclaiming the election of a new President of the nation. The election had been very close. Fifty-five percent of those

168

who had voted had chosen her to be the new President. Her chief opponent had received 42 percent of the vote.

The paper carried a victory message from the new President. She congratulated her opponents for conducting a fair and hard, if losing, campaign. She thanked the people for giving her majority support. She pledged that during her four-year term she would try to live up to the great record of the former President.

### Example 3. Power Struggle

The radio commentator broke into the scheduled program to broadcast this startling news to his nation.

"Citizens, our beloved leader has died. He suffered a heart attack and died before a doctor could reach him. His body will be displayed publicly tomorrow. All loyal citizens are asked to pay tribute to our fallen leader. Please remain calm."

In spite of the plea to stay calm, the nation was thrown into turmoil. The leader had ruled for twenty years with an iron hand. He had seemed to be healthy. No thought had been given to the selection of a new leader to take his place. He had completely dominated the political life of the nation. Suddenly he was gone. The power that he had controlled for so long was available. Who would claim it?

Two leaders who had worked under the fallen leader claimed the right to succeed him. Each man began to line up support for his claims.

Election scenes on a South Pacific island (right) and in Vietnam (left).

169

People openly talked of the chance of civil war. The people of this great nation waited nervously for the power struggle from which would come their new leader.

### Example 4. The Elders Choose a Leader

The council of elders had been secluded for three days and nights. During this time they faced the problem of choosing a new ruler from among the eligible men of the tribe. They were allowed to choose only from among a select group of warriors, men who had won special honor in battle. Thus, at the start of the talks, the council went over the merits of only twenty-four men. By the end of the third day the list was down to two men. Each elder then voted for one of the two. When the new leader's name was called out to the tribe, the people gave a roar of approval.

### Example 5. The Party's Choice

The voters stood in long lines to cast their votes. For several weeks through radio, TV, and newspapers the leaders of the country's only political party had reminded all citizens of their duty to vote. Now the time had come for the people to approve the candidates whom the leaders of the party had selected.

Each voter got a ballot which listed one candidate for each office. The voters had the right to approve or reject the candidates. However, the leaders of the party expected the voters to approve the official list of candidates. They were not disappointed.

1. What is the method for selecting leaders in each example?
2. Why are different societies likely to have different selection methods?
3. Why do all societies develop a set way of selecting leaders?
4. Which of the methods of selecting rulers are likely to contribute greatly to political stability and orderly behavior? Explain.
5. Which of the methods are likely to contribute to the practice of democracy? Explain.
6. Which of the methods of selecting leaders do you prefer? Why?
7. Which of the preceding questions (a) can be answered exactly with facts? (b) Which must be answered with hypotheses? (c) Which one requires a value judgment? (d) What are the differences between questions that are answered exactly with facts, hypotheses, and value judgments?

## Political Parties and Public Elections

A public election is a method of selecting or approving rulers by popular vote. Public elections are held according to rules. Thus, power to govern shifts from person to person and from group to group in an orderly way.

170

The main effect of choosing leaders of government under a set of rules is political and social stability. Leaders who have been chosen according to the rules of their society are accepted as *legitimate.* In other words, the society accepts their right to govern because they have been chosen according to the rules of the society. People in the society have been socialized to accept these rules.

Public elections give most citizens a chance to take part in politics. Only a few citizens become political leaders or activists. But through elections masses of citizens have the chance to influence the choice and direction of political leadership and to feel involved in the political life of their country.

A society's method of choosing its rulers is a clue to whether or not the society supports democratic values. In a democratic society, leaders have the chance to compete for the support of the people. Rulers are chosen through popular vote in open, competitive elections. Losers have the chance to criticize the victors and to try again to win power in a future election.

In a nondemocratic society, open competition between two or more political parties is not allowed. People with unapproved political ideas are not allowed to work openly to win control of the government.

## The Two-Party System Compared with Others

Two political parties—the Democratic and Republican—dominate electoral politics in the United States. These two major parties pick rival candidates, manage election campaigns, and conduct election-day activities according to state and federal laws. Each party's goal is to elect candidates so that the winning party can reap the rewards of controlling the government.

The Constitution makes no provision for political parties. The Framers feared that political parties would create divisions within the country which might tear it apart. Yet parties emerged, almost inevitably. Political scientists today suspect that almost every political system has some kind of organization that does the job that American parties have come to do.

**"Well, that's democracy for you. My vote nullifies your vote."**

### The One-Party System

In some countries a single party, run by a small group, controls the government. These countries conduct noncompetitive, one-party public elections. For example, in the Soviet Union the rulers allow only the Communist party to function. Prior to an election the Communist party picks one candidate for each public office. The people can vote either for or against the official list of candidates, who usually get almost 100 percent approval.

Since there is only one party and only one candidate for each office, there is no open competition or conflict in Soviet elections. An election campaign serves chiefly as a show of support for the leaders and ideas of the Communist party. Competition for positions of leadership in the Communist party and Soviet government takes place within party circles. The masses of Soviet people are not able to influence the choice of leaders through voting.

### The Multiparty System

Many countries hold elections in which voters choose from among candidates of six to a dozen or more parties. This system is typical in Western Europe. Each party tends to have a fairly specific program to offer. Often some of the parties claim to speak for particular groups, such as shopkeepers, farmers, or factory workers. Voters have the chance to judge many competing viewpoints and candidates under this system.

In multiparty systems usually no one party has enough support among the voters to win a majority by itself. Thus, two or more parties must form a coalition—an agreement to work together—in order to win control of the government. Since each party stands for very different ideas, making compromises to form a coalition can be a hard job.

### The Two-Party System

The United States has a two-party system. Most adult citizens vote for candidates nominated by either the Democratic or Republican parties. Minor parties, often called "third parties," exist. They choose candidates but have little hope of winning control of a state or the nation. In the biggest recent third-party movement George Wallace ran for President in 1968 as the candidate of the American Independent party. He got more than 10 million votes, about 13.5 percent of the total votes cast.

As in other countries, American parties focus on choosing and then electing their candidates to public office. Unlike a one-party system, however, once the candidates are elected, the party has little control over them.

In both two-party and multiparty systems, persons from different parties will almost always win seats in the legislature (Congress or Parliament). And at times members of different parties have high posts in the executive branch. The losing parties are willing to accept

172

temporarily the right of the winners to rule so long as the winners have played by the rules. The winners must allow the losing parties to criticize the winners and to try to win control in future elections.

## Nominating Candidates

In the United States the Democratic and Republican parties choose their candidates through formal nomination procedures. The direct primary is a preliminary election in which the public votes to select candidates to represent each party in a general election to public office.

Most states use the *closed primary.* Voters (a) show in some way their party choice and then (b) get only the ballot of that party. Generally voters must be registered in advance as a Republican or Democrat in order to vote in the primary. And they get only the ballot of the party for which they are registered. A few states allow voters registered as "Independent" to ask for the ballot of either party. In some states voters can ask for the ballot of *either* party; but if they are switching from their choice in the last primary, an election official may issue a "challenge." Then voters must take an oath that they supported their new party in the previous general election or intend to do so in the coming election. Of course, there is no way of proving this.

An *open primary,* used in a few states, is a nominating election open to any eligible voter. In most of these states the voter gets one Democratic and one Republican ballot, both the same size and color. In the privacy of the voting booth, the voter marks one ballot and discards the other. Where voting machines are used, the voter moves the levers of only one party—and the other is automatically locked.

In Alaska and Washington the primary election is so "open" that voters are allowed to vote for candidates from any party taking part in the election. Thus voters who may think of themselves as Democrats may nonetheless vote to nominate some Republican candidates in the very open primaries of these two states.

People who favor the closed primary argue that the direct primary is a party election. They say that voters who are not willing to identify with a party have no business taking part. The closed primary, they say, cuts down "outside interference" in the party's choice of its candidates.

In most states using primary elections the candidate who wins the most votes (a plurality) for an office wins the nomination. However, in a few states, all located in the South, a candidate must win a majority of the votes cast in the party's primary in order to win the nomination. If no one receives a majority of the votes, then the two candidates with the highest number of votes must compete in a "run-off" election to pick the party's nominee.

In some areas one party tends to control political affairs. For example, in some rural areas of Kansas the Republican candidates tend to prevail. The Democratic party offers little real competition.

Likewise, in some urban areas, such as Brooklyn or Gary, the Democratic nominee usually wins the general election. In these areas of one-party domination, the primary election usually determines the winner for public office, since the opposing party tends to offer little or no challenge in the general election.

A party convention is used to nominate candidates for Congress or for state offices in a very few states. A nominating convention is a meeting of party members who have been picked as delegates to nominate party candidates. The delegates represent party members throughout the state. In some direct-primary states the party convention is used to endorse a list of candidates. The endorsed candidates presumably have an advantage in the ensuing primary election, since the ballot will show that they are the convention's choices.

### Other Election Activities of Political Parties

Political parties organize and manage the election campaigns of candidates who have been nominated to represent the party. Through election campaigns a party tries to advertise its candidates and their ideas in order to attract support for the party. Thus, campaigns are likely to feature hard-hitting clashes of candidates and ideas.

Officials of the local government organize and manage the general election. However, "watchers" from each party are present at the polls (voting places) to guard their party's interests and to see that the votes are counted fairly. Party members near the polls pass out campaign literature as "last minute" appeals to the voters.

Political parties limit and channel conflict between individuals and their ideas which must be part of any free and open public election. By holding periodic elections, according to rules, the parties regulate conflict between rivals for governmental leadership. The winning party is a temporary holder of power. It must continue to seek public support to remain in control. The losing party is a temporary "loyal opposition."

What does this cartoon show about basic values shared by Democrats and Republicans?

**The Morning After**

Kuekes in the
*Cleveland Plain Dealer*

174

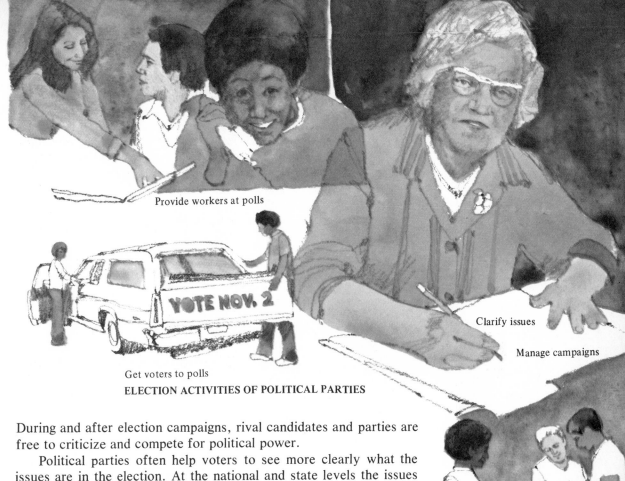

Provide workers at polls

VOTE NOV. 2

Get voters to polls

Clarify issues

Manage campaigns

**ELECTION ACTIVITIES OF POLITICAL PARTIES**

REGISTER

Get voters to register

Nominate candidates

During and after election campaigns, rival candidates and parties are free to criticize and compete for political power.

Political parties often help voters to see more clearly what the issues are in the election. At the national and state levels the issues are set forth in party platforms.

Which of the following statements are correct?

**1.** All countries which hold public elections are examples of democracy.

**2.** The United States has a multiparty system for selecting leaders of government.

**3.** The purpose of a primary election is to nominate candidates for public office.

**4.** A closed primary election prevents voters from voting for candidates of both parties.

**5.** An open primary election requires voters to declare publicly their party preference.

**6.** More states use closed primaries than open primaries.

**7.** More states use some kind of primary election than conventions as a means for nominating candidates.

**8.** Public elections tend to contribute to the legitimacy of leaders.

**9.** Public elections tend to contribute to political stability.

## Leadership Roles in Political Parties

Millions of Americans say they are Republicans or Democrats, but their party activity seldom goes beyond casting an occasional vote. Only a very small percentage of American citizens take an active part in party affairs. Many of these will be in positions of party leadership.

### Kinds of Party Leaders

"Party leader" can mean anything from National Chairman to a precinct captain responsible for a few city blocks of voters. The formal organization of our two major parties differs in many details. It varies from one state to the next or even from city to city. However, there are some nationwide similarities. Let us look briefly at several of these party leadership positions, or statuses.

**The National Committee and Its Head**

One man and one woman from each state and territory serve on the national committee of each major party. They usually win this

The national and state committees have relatively little control over the local party organizations in American politics.

POLITICAL PARTY ORGANIZATION

Democratic        Republican

THE NATIONAL COMMITTEE
A man and a woman from each state and territory

CONGRESSIONAL CAMPAIGN COMMITTEES
Organized by each party to help congressional candidates

STATE CENTRAL COMMITTEES
Members chosen by county committees, by state party conventions, or in primary elections

COUNTY AND CITY COMMITTEES
Elected by a county or city convention, or composed of ward or precinct captains

WARD COMMITTEES
Chairpersons chosen by the captains of the various precincts in the ward

PRECINCT OR DISTRICT CAPTAINS
Usually elected by voters in the primary elections

post in return for past services to the party. And they tend to be strong party leaders in their own states. The committee's chief function is to arrange for the national convention held every four years.

Heading the national committee is the National Chairman. This party leader is officially chosen by the committee, but in practice is picked by the party's presidential nominee. This person's major job is to help manage the presidential campaign. This involves fund-raising and overseeing a staff which prepares campaign literature and maintains a speakers' bureau. At times the role calls for settling arguments among party candidates or other leaders. As official spokesperson for the party, this political leader is often a target for criticism from within and outside the party. This leader has little influence in selecting the party's candidates or setting policy. He or she has little control over party leaders at other levels.

Each of the two major parties also has a *Congressional Campaign Committee.* It is a relatively independent body which aids members of Congress as they battle for reelection.

### State Committees and Chairpersons

Each party has *State Central Committee* in each state. It is made up of county or other district leaders chosen in a variety of ways from state to state. State chairpersons try to build a year-round organization at the state level. They must find able candidates, get them elected, and keep up the image of the party.

### County Committees and Chairpersons

Typically made up of ward or precinct captains, the county committee elects a chairperson who often is the real power in local politics. In large counties this leader may wield great influence in state and national politics as well.

There will be a city committee for each party in most cities. Its job is to see that party candidates for city offices win the election.

### Precinct Captains

These are the party leaders in the voting districts, or precincts. They work with city or county chairpersons in recruiting candidates and getting out the vote. At the precinct level much of the real work of politics is carried on. The precinct is the smallest electoral unit, usually made up of a few hundred voters. Yet, in highly competitive areas, precinct captains are important cogs in the party machine. They organize a small band of volunteer party workers to register voters for the party, hand out campaign literature, canvass the district to make personal contact with the voters, and hold social gatherings where neighbors can meet the current crop of candidates.

From the diagram of party organization on page 176, you may get the impression that a party is like an army with commands flowing down from the generals at the top and with foot soldiers waiting at the bottom to carry the orders out. Nothing could be further from the truth. In actual fact, there is little coordination among the various

Eventually party chairmen may come to be titled chairpersons, but in the mid-1970s neither party had yet changed the title.

177

levels of the party. Leaders at each level guard their own freedom of action. The head of a county committee has local issues and candidates to worry about. She or he may be more concerned with them than about who the state's next senator will be. Friction among leaders at the various levels occurs in both parties. Also the national committee has almost no power over state, county, and city leaders.

How can one call this kind of party an organization at all? Europeans with their more tightly knit, disciplined parties ask this question often. The American political party is a real organization in at least three respects: (a) Party members at all levels share the goal of seeing their party win. (b) National, state, and local leaders do talk and deal with one another. (c) Most Americans begin to identify with a party at an early age.

### What Do Party Leaders Do?

Key decisions are made within political parties, and party leaders have a big say in these decisions.

• Leaders help select candidates. The voter chooses between the Republican and Democratic candidate, but these two nominees were picked from a larger group of possible candidates by their political parties. Leaders are on the lookout for strong candidates. Leaders give more help to some persons running for office than to others.

• Leaders help shape campaign strategy. For example, they help decide what issues to stress. Later if the leader's candidate wins, he or she may help make public policies in line with the campaign issues.

• Leaders help decide which people get "patronage" jobs. Some officeholders have the power to appoint people to government jobs. When these jobs are handed out in return for political support, the practice is called patronage. People who win election with the key support of a party leader may heed the leader's advice in filling jobs. Many government jobs today are under civil service with appointments made on merit instead of politics. But patronage jobs still exist.

Most of what party leaders do has one aim—winning elections. For the head of the national committee this may mean month after month of travel around the country, meeting new candidates and leaders. It means keeping the party machine well oiled, spotting trouble, and trying to patch up the worst problems. There will be high-level conferences to discuss campaign strategy, work out schedules, and sooth offended politicians.

For precinct captains, winning elections may mean knowing the voters in their precinct personally. The captain may keep a set of cards—one for each household in the precinct. A card will have the name of a family, whether adults are registered and with which party, and how they have voted in the past—if this can be learned. The card will tell whether family members can be counted on for party work or campaign contributions. It will list other useful information.

Precinct captains conduct registration drives to make sure that new families in the precinct (especially those of the captain's party) are eligible to vote. Later a captain may follow up by going from house to house to hand out leaflets on the candidates and to make a personal appeal for support of the party. The captain may also be called upon to arrange social gatherings, to conduct telephone campaigns, or to make mailings to voters in the precinct.

Local party leaders also provide certain services for people of their community, such as the following:

- Help unemployed get work.
- Help people get public jobs on a highway crew, the fire department, or police force.
- Show people how to get their Social Security benefits, welfare payments, and unemployment compensation.
- Help citizens with problems like rent gouging, unfair labor practices, zoning, or unfair assessments.
- Help a neighborhood to get a needed traffic light, more parking space, or more policemen.
- Run clambakes and other get-togethers for interested people, even though no political campaign is involved.
- Help citizens who are having difficulties with the law.
- Help newcomers to the community get adjusted and find places to live and work.
- Work with some of the other party's leaders to reduce friction and keep the campaign from getting too rough.
- Help young men with military service problems.[1]

In return for services such as these, party leaders expect support for their candidates in local elections.

Precinct leaders and workers are the link between the small group of higher party leaders and the people. State and county chairpersons know that an effective party must be well organized at the grass roots. Precincts must have able and energetic leaders if a party hopes to get a good turnout on election day.

At higher party levels, leadership is a full-time job. Of course, elected public officials have a great stake in keeping a strong party organization and will devote part of their time to party matters. A governor may be the formal head of the party in the state and will have influence in making party policy and selecting nominees. But the governor will depend heavily upon city, county, and state party leaders who are not burdened by duties of public office and can devote all of their time to party matters.

Mary Louise Smith was National Chairman of the Republican party in the mid-1970s.

1. R. T. Frost, "Stability and Change in Local Party Politics," *The Public Opinion Quarterly*, Vol. 25 (Summer, 1961). Used by permission of the publisher and Mrs. Richard T. Frost.

The activities of party leaders at all levels, then, are directed toward winning elections. But this may mean different things for leaders in different positions. Precinct leaders must make contact with the voters in their neighborhood. They must perform small services where possible with an eye to getting supporters of the party to the polls. County, state, and national party leaders will be concerned with questions of campaign strategy, party finances, and recruiting likely candidates to run for office.

As with any organization, friction will arise as to who should be nominated, where the money should go, where candidates should make personal appearances, and what campaign tactics will be most effective. There is very little effort made to maintain the loyalty of party workers. However, those who are loyal to the party and who work hard are often rewarded by the party for their efforts.

Judging by our account of party leaders thus far, they do not seem as concerned about how public issues should be decided as do interest-group leaders. This does not mean that party leaders do not have strong opinions about public policy. However, at times these opinions must take a back seat to the job of getting the party's nominee elected. By helping choose the candidates and the campaign strategy, the leaders may influence policy in the years ahead.

### Why Do People Work for Political Parties?

To do the many jobs needed to win elections, a political party must have a group of devoted workers who come to the aid of their party year after year. How does it attract these people?

#### Major Incentives for Party Activists

*Patronage* is a major incentive for some party leaders to devote their time to party matters. The hope for a job in government if their candidates win, or the desire to keep the job they already have, spurs some men and women to work loyally for their party in elections. Patronage is not so important as it once was. Still, American parties reward their most faithful leaders with jobs more often than does any other party system in the world.

Closely related to patronage is the notion of *preferments*. These are concrete rewards that can be handed out by some public officials to members of their own party. The owner of a small printing firm who is also a party leader may find juicy government or party printing contracts coming to his company. Officers of a construction firm may take great interest in party politics in hope that their firm will get preference when the time comes to decide what company will pave the city streets or build the new courthouse. An active member of the party in power may also get preferential treatment when government agencies are deciding where to build new sidewalks or sewers. It is not unusual for the party in power to take special care of neighborhoods where party leaders live.

Many people become active in party life because they are hoping for a *political career.* They must show that they are loyal party workers before they can expect help from the party in getting the nomination. Even after election to public office, the ambitious person may stay active in party operations in order not to be forgotten when chances to run for higher office arise.

Party leaders may find that their political activity results in certain *economic rewards* in their own business or job. Contacts made through the party may be very helpful to lawyers, insurance agents, real-estate brokers, or storekeepers in attracting more clients or customers.

Those who are cynical about politics assume that most party leaders are active because they want the kinds of rewards we have named. While incentives of this kind may be important for some, they are by no means the only reasons people become party leaders. Let us look now at some other things the political party has to offer its leaders and workers.

### Other Rewards of Party Participation

Some people may be attracted to positions of party leadership because of the psychological rewards the party can supply. The party may represent a chance for a person to mix with people a little higher on the social ladder. This gives a person more social status. For the lonely or the bored the party offers friends and a way of keeping busy. Some may find the chance to meet with powerful officials attractive in itself. Others will enjoy the excitement of the political battle and relish getting the "inside dope" about what is taking place in the political world. Still others may see party service as a way of meeting their civic duty.

Some party leaders want these positions in order to influence *policy-making.* We have seen that most unofficial political specialists are interested in policy questions. And if American parties are not the most effective way for people to get specific policies passed, they do at least provide a means by which people can work indirectly for the kinds of decisions they consider important.

Personal beliefs and values may also be a factor in attracting party workers. The two American parties differ to some degree on the things that their members (and especially their leaders) think are important and valuable.

Liberals may see the Democratic party as a place where they can work toward handing out social services more equally. Conservatives may see the Republican party as a help in halting governmental inroads on individual freedom.

Finally, once party leaders have strong ties with their party and have worked hard for it, just serving it loyally and seeing it prosper may give them satisfaction. The *welfare of the party* becomes an important end in itself, and its victories may seem personal victories for the party leader.

Some political bosses have been both party leader and public official. "Boss" Frank Hague (below) served as mayor of Jersey City for thirty years, retiring in 1947. For many years he was a member of the Democratic National Committee. Boss Crump of Tennessee held political power in Memphis and eastern Tennessee for forty years but served as mayor only about ten years.

Chicago's Mayor Richard Daley (center) takes part in a parade. For years he has been a powerful leader in Chicago and Cook County.

Of course, no political party can provide all of these rewards to each leader, even if it wanted to. At certain times a party will have to rely heavily upon the psychological incentives. In other situations it may offer the promise of jobs or other economic benefits. People are attracted to the role of party leader for many reasons, and no two leaders will be interested for exactly the same reason. The variety of incentives that a party may offer assures it a leadership of men and women of various skills, personal goals, and viewpoints working together on behalf of their party.

Some party leaders, of course, prove to be more effective than others. A precinct captain who does not turn out the expected vote for the party year after year will not be in a strong position when it comes time for the party to hand out rewards. Likewise, leaders who show good judgment in spotting able candidates, who have a gift for picking the right campaign strategy, or who work hard at getting money for the party will almost certainly advance. At some time they may run for office themselves. Parties have a job to do, and one way their leaders can make sure it is done well is by giving most of the rewards to the workers who helped the most to win elections.

182

## The Impact of Party Leaders on Government

Leaders who help find candidates for public office and then play such a big part in the election will, of course, have an impact on government. But interested as party leaders may be in political issues, their influence on major decisions in government is probably not strong.

Perhaps the chief reason party leaders do not exercise strong direct influence on public policy is that they put other matters first. Few

### CAN THE LAW REACH HIM?—THE DWARF AND THE GIANT THIEF.
by Th. Nast

*Harper's Weekly*, January 6, 1872

Local party leadership, especially as city chairman or county chairman, offered relatively greater opportunities for economic rewards in the past than today. Civil service exams have reduced job patronage in many localities, and laws now generally require competitive bidding on public contracts. Perhaps the most notorious political boss in American history was Boss Tweed of New York City. Nast's attacks on the Tweed Ring helped bring several indictments —and Tweed's eventual imprisonment.

issues are big enough to risk losing an election. Party leaders develop an intense loyalty to their party. One of the surest ways to lose the respect of other leaders in the party is to fail to support candidates because of their stand on a certain issue. Governor Rockefeller's failure to back Barry Goldwater strongly in 1964 may well have cost Nelson Rockefeller the presidential nomination four years later. Party leaders do not quickly forget those who place their own beliefs above the welfare of the party.

There may be big differences among leaders in the same party on current issues. A party is not like an interest group, such as the National Rifle Association, whose leaders agree quite closely on the policy they are working for. The Democratic party in 1968 found itself badly split between those leaders who supported the Johnson administration's war effort in Vietnam and those leaders who did not. In 1972 different groups in the Democratic party disagreed strongly about several issues. This split cost the Democratic presidential candidate, George McGovern, much support.

Even when party leaders agree on an issue, they are not often in a good position to put pressure on elected officials. Party organization is strong just before elections. But in the periods between elections only a skeleton of the organization remains. Yet public officials have to deal with issues all year long. It is very hard, therefore, for party leaders to keep up any kind of steady influence.

From the party's point of view, it is not always wise to play up the issues anyway, at least in very specific terms. It is easy to offend some voters by taking a clear-cut stand on an issue. It is less easy to attract votes by taking clear-cut stands. As a result, parties and their candidates tend to say just enough about the issues so that the voters will think them informed and responsible in meeting the problems of the day.

Platforms and candidates may be intentionally vague. It is safer to favor "lower prices and full employment" (which is, after all, what everyone wants) than to try to spell out exactly *how* one would try to reach these goals. Each definite solution invites criticism from someone. But candidates cannot overdo this, or they may be branded by the mass media as indecisive, insincere, or unwilling to take a stand. The task is trying to *appear* to take wise and strong positions on the issues without really committing oneself too far. The party leaders behind a candidate realize the dilemma and will try to leave freedom to maneuver. It is not surprising, then, that party leaders have little systematic effect upon decisions of elected public officials.

The main way that party leaders affect policy is through their effect on elections. Party leaders help select and nominate candidates and to manage and carry out election campaigns. Through these activities they indirectly influence government decisions. By helping to put Candidate A rather than Candidate B into public office, they

184

contribute support to certain policy decisions that Candidate A will make in office.

Following are three cases about political party leaders. As you read the cases, think about these questions: (1) What do party leaders do? (2) Why do people become party leaders? (3) What are the likely effects of party leaders on election outcomes and decisions of public officials?

**Case 1. Leo Trask Calls the Shots**

Leo Trask paced the kitchen of his large farmhouse, deep in thought. His political future might well be at stake. He had to move with the sure instinct developed over forty-five years of dabbling in Democratic party politics. This was not a normal year. Some Democrats on the slate might have a chance for election in this solidly Republican county. But with this ray of hope came problems. The county Democratic party, which Trask had guided for the last nineteen years, was split. His leadership was being challenged.

How different it seemed from former times. Trask smiled as he thought back to his first years as county chairman of the Democratic party. He got the job because no one else wanted it. There were, after all, only a handful of Democrats in the county. Most of them saw little point in voting, much less running for office. But through the years of the county seat had grown, bringing hundreds of outsiders to work in the new and expanding factories. And, one by one, Trask's Republican farm neighbors had sold their land and moved to the city.

It all had to make a difference in the politics of the county, and the last election showed just how much. Democrats had won the office of county coroner and tax assessor. They even came close to winning a seat on the city council of the largest town. Things looked just as good this year. Or at least they did until the reform movement started up.

It all began with a young teacher who decided Trask had not been doing as much as he should to promote the Democratic party in Scottston. "What does he know about it?" mused Leo. "Why, he only moved to Douglas County three years ago. Did he see the days when the Democrats were lucky to win even one vote in some precincts? You bet your sweet life he didn't—but now that things are looking up, here he is, saying that he can run things better. Complaining because ol' man Trask doesn't hold regular meetings of the party leaders and wasn't able to find candidates for a couple of offices this year. I've half a mind to let him try it. Would do him good to call a hundred people trying to find one who's willing to run for dog catcher and probably get clobbered at that."

But it was the other end of the ticket that troubled Trask tonight. The reform Democrats had picked their own candidate for the state legislature. It was a bold attempt to take control of the party away from Leo. Trask's own choice was a young druggist, well known in town, but a newcomer to politics. In the county Democratic convention last month, precinct workers had seen quite a fight between the two camps. Leo's candidate, Wes Miller, got just enough votes to win the nomination.

The reformers said a newcomer to politics could not win the general election. Now Leo had to prove them wrong. A defeat for Miller would make it even harder for Trask to hold on as county leader the next time around. But Miller seemed intent on beating himself. Leo reached for the phone.

"Hello, Wes," growled Trask, "I'd like for you to stop by my place first thing in the morning."

"Well," Miller hesitated, "I'm supposed to be out at the shopping center shaking hands."

"Wes, my boy," said Leo, "you can shake hands 'till the cows come home, and it ain't going to do you no good unless you and I have a little talk. Try to be here around seven, and I'll have the coffeepot on."

The next morning Wes Miller sipped his coffee uneasily as the old pro spread out the precinct maps on the kitchen table. They chatted about which areas looked good and where there might be trouble in the county. They went over their schedule for newspaper ads and their plans to stretch the thin party finances to buy a few spots on local television. But this was old stuff, and Wes knew this was not why Trask had asked him over. Finally Trask got to the point.

**Wes Miller Gets a Political Education.** "Wes," he said, "you've got a great political future ahead of you. You have a good business, good looks, sensible head, you're young, and you don't rub people the wrong way. I'm getting old, even uglier than I used to be, and probably couldn't pull a hundred votes in this county for state legislator. But I've got one thing you haven't got. I know the politics of this county like the back of my hand. I know the people—who they are, where they live, how they think, what they want. And, Wes, when you got up in front of that dinner club the other day and told them you favored tighter gun-control legislation in this state, I could just hear the votes switching away from you. We've still got more Republicans than Democrats in this county. And we've still got more farmers than big-city types. Most of them got their first rifle on their eighth birthday, and their pappy showed them how to shoot it by plunkin' hedge apples out in the pasture. They been hunting ever since. Now you're coming along and telling them they're going to have to get a license for that rifle or have the state register it with a lot of fancy paperwork. It ain't going to sit well at all."

"But, Leo, it just so happens that I believe we *do* have to have tighter gun control in this country. Look at the crime figures, the accidental deaths by guns, the assassinations of national figures over the past few years. Surely you can see that our society is at a point now where it just can't go on selling guns to any Tom, Dick, or Harry who wants one."

"What I see," countered Trask, "is that you're going to lose this election if you make an issue out of this. And I'm not given to spending the party's money and my time backing losers. You'd better decide right now if you want to win this election so you can do something up there in the state capital. Or do you want to spend the rest of your life counting out pills. If you want to win, you don't go around saying every fool thing that comes into your head."

Wes thought for some time, then spoke up, "What can I do? I'm already on record on the gun-control issue."

"My boy," Trask said with the air of a father who had just scolded his son and was now preparing to guide him back on the path of truth and wisdom, "you don't have to lead the charge *against* gun control. Just play the issue down. Better yet, muddy the water a little. Next time the question comes up, tell them you are only concerned about crime in the big cities and only meant that *pistols* should be registered. Tell them you believe in the right of every law-abiding man to own a gun. Leave yourself a little room to maneuver if you do get elected. You can do what you darn please, once you walk through the door that says 'State Assembly'; but my job is to get you that far."

**The Election.** Late into election night a few weeks later, Trask sat in a wooden chair in the county courthouse where the votes were

being counted. The room was full of familiar faces he had seen on election days over the years. But there were new faces too, including some of the reformers in his own party. It had been a hard week. Decisions had to be made about how to spend remaining party funds. Last-minute literature had to be distributed in the right places. Precinct captains had to be urged to get their workers out ringing doorbells. Jittery candidates who felt they weren't getting enough support from the party had to be soothed.

Today he had to organize a car pool to get Democratic voters to the polls and provide babysitters for others. There had been the usual last-minute drive to get the late voters to the polls. But this was the one day of the year that Leo Trask enjoyed most.

As the returns came in, Trask noted that things were going pretty much according to plan. It was still a Republican county, although the Democrats picked up a local office here and there and finally won a seat on the Scottston city council. But Miller's race for the state legislature was close. According to the figures Trask had scrawled on the pad in front of him, Miller had a chance. As the vote from the outlying areas came in, it seemed that Miller might make it.

A party worker handed him the returns from the small town of Ogden. Trask knew before anyone else in the room what they meant. Ogden had delivered 40 percent of its vote to Miller, better than the Democrats had ever done there before. Miller was in, and Trask flashed the victory sign to Wes across the room. He leaned back in his chair and chuckled to himself. That would take the steam out of those young rebels. It looked like they were going to have to put up with Leo Trask as Democratic county chairman for a while longer.

### Case 2. Joseph Scarpito's Power

What does the head of a state political party do? Why does he or she do it? We can find answers by looking at the role of Joseph Scarpito, state Democratic chairman of a northeastern state.

Joseph Scarpito got his position in 1973. He won it through clever use of patronage. For example, many important people in this state owe political debts to Scarpito. And he has always known how to collect on these debts. Candidates for office feel they need his nod of approval. When his party controls the State House, he has the final word about who is or is not appointed a judge. Jobs at all levels of the state government are granted only with his approval.

Joseph Scarpito holds his position of political power through hard work. He is at his job seven days a week and twelve to fifteen hours a day. He likes his job. He enjoys the power and the prominence it brings him.

Though Scarpito is very powerful, he is no dictator. He must bargain to hold his position and to settle conflicts. But he brings vast political resources to the bargaining table. And he seldom fails to get something from his political deals.

188

Scarpito's job varies, depending on whether the Democratic party is in or out of power. When his party is out of power, then Scarpito has the final say on all party disputes. He is the highest authority in the party organization. However, when a Democrat is governor, then Scarpito plays the role of adviser and servant. He assists the governor in carrying out policies. Sometimes this role is difficult because it may force Scarpito to do things that he disagrees with.

Scarpito is in politics because he loves to exercise power and he loves competition. He has no burning desire to remedy all the social ills. His main political goal is to remain in his state post. This means he must manage the party so that it can win elections and control patronage.

### Case 3. Theodore Williamson—Loyal Republican

"Theodore Williamson, Attorney at Law," read the small gold plaque on the door. The name was widely known in Dalton. For twenty years Ted Williamson had practiced law in his third-floor suite in the First National Bank building. When a business faced bankruptcy, when a real-estate developer wanted a zoning change, when a person considered divorce, the word went out: "Better see Ted Williamson. He'll know what to do."

Williamson usually did know what to do. There were not many problems that he had not faced before with one of his clients. He knew the leaders of Dalton well. The business people, lawyers, and doctors of Dalton were all among his friends. He had been urged several times to run for mayor but chose not to, though he would almost certainly have been elected. He would rather move behind the scenes. If not everyone knew how many strings he could pull, so much the better.

Dalton is a city with more Republicans than Democrats, and Williamson has been a life-long, loyal member of the Republican party. As a lawyer he could set his own schedule and devote some of his working day to party matters. His wide range of acquaintances and the respect city officials had for him were valuable to the party. He could always be counted upon to come up with a list of well-known people who might back an unknown candidate or give money for the campaign.

Williamson was so valuable to the Republican party in Dalton that strong pressure arose for him to run for city chairman of the party. "It is his duty to the party," said friend after friend. "There is no one else who can do as well." Williamson finally agreed to serve, and won the position easily.

This last year had been a busy one. With general elections coming up, Williamson searched for able and appealing candidates. He quietly sought pledges of campaign contributions. Party contacts throughout the state had to be renewed. And he carefully went through the local party organization checking on the past and present performance of precinct captains and other workers—gauging their strengths and weaknesses in an effort to make the best possible use of each person's talents.

Issues also received his attention. His sense of what would concern the voters in the weeks before the election would be crucial in deciding how to fill the ticket. He saw this as a "bread and butter" year in which the public would like candidates who had plans for ending the country's economic problems. There would be local issues, such as urban renewal. He wanted to find a way of presenting the urban renewal issue that would put local blacks, the churches, and the Chamber of Commerce all on his side.

Tonight, however, Ted Williamson's thoughts were on the 1976 Republican National Convention. He had almost turned down the chance to be a delegate to the convention because of the press of party business in Dalton and his own law practice. But something—perhaps the promise of excitement—led him to accept. Some delegates in his state were elected, but most were named by the party caucus as he had been.

Williamson looked at the clock. Then he neatly stacked the papers on his desk and locked the office door behind him. He had worked later than usual tonight, clearing his desk for the trip. Tomorrow his junior law partners could take over the routine office work. He would be helping to select his party's next nominee for President of the United States.

Use information from the previous cases and other parts of this chapter to answer the following questions.
1. What is the role of a political party leader?
2. What are the typical traits of individuals who become party leaders?
3. Why do certain people want to play the role of party leader?
4. How can party leaders influence election outcomes and political decisions in government?

## Electing a President

The Presidency is the leading position in the government of the United States. As the chief executive, the President is responsible for carrying out the nation's laws. As head of the government, the President has the power to make decisions that affect the lives of all American citizens. As chief representative of the people, the President is a symbol of the United States to the peoples of the world.

Since the Presidency is the foremost position in the American government, it is vitally important to the life of the country to select capable Presidents. How is the American President selected? Does this method of selection contribute to, or detract from, the possibility of selecting a capable President?

190

## National Party Conventions Nominate Candidates

The first part of the presidential election process is the nomination of candidates to compete for the Presidency. Every four years the political parties hold nominating conventions. The convention is a meeting of select party members from throughout the country. The nominating conventions are the creations and responsibilities of the political parties. Neither the Constitution nor federal laws tell how candidates for President of the United States must be nominated.

Prior to the national party conventions, persons seeking the nomination of their party announce their intentions and begin to campaign. For example, in 1972, contestants for the Democratic nomination included George McGovern, Edmund Muskie, Hubert Humphrey, John Lindsey, Wilbur Mills, and Shirley Chisholm. Two Republicans—Paul McCloskey and John Ashbrook—put up a token challenge to President Nixon. Each candidate for nomination tried to gain the support of delegates to the party's convention, since the delegates would select the party's presidential candidate. The chart below shows how convention delegates are chosen.

### HOW PARTIES CHOOSE NATIONAL CONVENTION DELEGATES

PARTY PRIMARY ELECTIONS

Thirty states (in 1976) elected all or part of the delegates in the party primary elections. Practices vary:
- In some states, candidates for delegate are *pledged* to vote for a certain presidential candidate at the convention.
- In other states, candidates are *unpledged*, free to vote for the candidate of their own choice.
- In some states the voters indicate which presidential "hopeful" they prefer.

DISTRICT AND STATE CONVENTIONS

Some states (in 1976) chose all or part of the delegates in party conventions. Voters in local party meetings choose delegates to a district or state convention. Generally most of the national convention delegates are chosen in the district convention. The rest are chosen in the party's state convention.

DISTRICT AND STATE COMMITTEES

Members of congressional district and/or state party committees choose all or part of the delegates.

Some combination of the above methods is used by certain states. Part of the delegates are elected in primaries, others by conventions and/or committees.

The size of the delegations from each state varies according to the population of the state and the support that the state has given to party candidates in recent elections. For example, states with large populations and states where the voters supported Republican candidates for national office in 1972 would have more delegates, and more votes, at the 1976 Republican National Convention than would small states and states where voters supported Democrats in 1972.

All the persons seeking to be the party's "standard bearer" in the coming presidential election will have their names presented to the convention. A majority of delegate votes is needed to nominate a candidate. In 1972 a majority of the 3016 delegates to the Democratic National Convention voted for George McGovern as their presidential candidate. A majority of the 1346 delegates to the 1972 Republican National Convention voted for Richard Nixon to represent their party. The delegates usually endorse the presidential candidate's choice as the party's candidate for Vice-President of the United States.

## Other Convention Activities

In addition to picking the party candidates for President and Vice-President, delegates approve a party platform. A platform is a statement of political ideals and policy positions. A platform is really a "bundle of compromises" between different groups within the party who have conflicting ideas. As such, it is a very general statement that is aimed at holding together diverse groups in the party so that they can cooperate to elect the party's presidential candidate.

The competition of candidates to win the party's nomination is likely to create divisions and bitterness among party members. A chief purpose of the party convention is to "bind the wounds" of recent conflict so that the party can present a united front in the upcoming election. Thus the winner of the nomination usually makes complimentary remarks about the losers and asks for party unity.

A major reason for the massive defeats of the Republicans in the presidential election of 1964 and of the Democrats in 1972 was the failure to unify the party after bitter pre-convention conflict.

Following the conventions, which are held in July or August of the election year, the rival candidates campaign to present their ideas and to attract voter support. On the Tuesday following the first Monday in November, the voters across the country indicate their preferences among the rival candidates.

## The Electoral College System

Unlike the nomination process, the election system is defined by state and federal laws. The Constitution of the United States requires that an Electoral College, or group of electors, select the President and Vice-President. (See Article II and Amendment XII of the Constitution.) However, as we shall see, the Electoral College functions much differently than its designers intended.

Some delegates at the Constitutional Convention in 1787 favored direct election of the President by the people. Others believed that

192

Nixon won renomination easily at the 1972 Republican National Convention.

Humphrey delegates whoop it up at the 1972 Democratic National Convention.

In 1968 the delegates favoring Senator Eugene McCarthy displayed the peace sign. McCarthy made peace in Vietnam his chief issue in seeking the Democratic nomination for President.

the President should be elected by the national legislature (Congress). The idea of election by an Electoral College was really a compromise. The states would choose electors, who in turn would elect the President. Along with changes made by the Twelfth Amendment, the plan would work as follows:

1. Each state would choose as many presidential electors as its total of Senators and Representatives in Congress.

2. State legislatures would decide how to choose electors.

3. Each elector would cast a separate ballot for President and for Vice-President.

4. The ballots would be opened and counted at a meeting of the Congress.

5. The person receiving a majority of the votes cast for President would become the President. The person receiving a majority of the votes cast for Vice-President would be elected the Vice-President.

6. If no candidate obtained a majority of the votes cast for President or for Vice-President, the House of Representatives would choose the President and the Senate the Vice-President.

The writers of the Constitution expected that the presidential electors in each state would study, discuss, and carefully vote for a highly capable President from among the country's leaders. The system worked as the "Founding Fathers" intended only during the first and second presidential elections, when George Washington was chosen, without opposition, as the Chief Executive.

With the retirement of George Washington from public life, competition for the Presidency developed between newly organized political parties. The growth of rival political parties led to changes in the election system. The Electoral College remained in the Constitution, but it was made to function in ways that the writers of the Constitution had not intended or foreseen. The major change was the emergence of a popular vote to control the selection and behavior of the presidential electors.

Today, the members of the Electoral College go through the formalities required by the Constitution. However, the voters across the country have the real power to select the President. The members of the Electoral College from each state are expected to vote for the candidate who receives a majority of the popular votes in their state.

### The Electoral College System in the 1972 Election

The 1972 presidential election shows the Electoral College system as it developed over the years. On November 7, 1972, over 77 million Americans voted in a public election to choose a President and Vice-President. The Republican candidate, Richard M. Nixon, received

194

## THE POPULAR VOTE FOR PRESIDENT IN 1972
### (State vote in thousands)

| | Nixon | McGovern | | Nixon | McGovern | | Nixon | McGovern |
|---|---|---|---|---|---|---|---|---|
| Alabama | 729 | 257 | Louisiana | 687 | 298 | Oklahoma | 759 | 247 |
| Alaska | 55 | 33 | Maine | 256 | 161 | Oregon | 487 | 393 |
| Arizona | 403 | 199 | Maryland | 829 | 506 | Pennsylvania | 2,715 | 1,797 |
| Arkansas | 449 | 200 | Massachusetts | 1,112 | 1,333 | Rhode Island | 220 | 195 |
| California | 4,602 | 3,476 | Michigan | 1,962 | 1,459 | South Carolina | 477 | 187 |
| Colorado | 597 | 330 | Minnesota | 898 | 802 | South Dakota | 166 | 140 |
| Connecticut | 811 | 555 | Mississippi | 505 | 127 | Tennessee | 813 | 357 |
| Delaware | 140 | 92 | Missouri | 1,154 | 697 | Texas | 2,299 | 1,154 |
| Dist. of Columbia | 35 | 128 | Montana | 184 | 120 | Utah | 324 | 126 |
| Florida | 1,858 | 718 | Nebraska | 406 | 170 | Vermont | 117 | 68 |
| Georgia | 881 | 290 | Nevada | 116 | 66 | Virginia | 988 | 439 |
| Hawaii | 169 | 101 | New Hampshire | 214 | 116 | Washington | 837 | 568 |
| Idaho | 199 | 81 | New Jersey | 1,846 | 1,102 | West Virginia | 485 | 277 |
| Illinois | 2,788 | 1,913 | New Mexico | 236 | 141 | Wisconsin | 989 | 810 |
| Indiana | 1,405 | 709 | New York | 4,193 | 2,951 | Wyoming | 100 | 44 |
| Iowa | 706 | 496 | North Carolina | 1,055 | 439 | | | |
| Kansas | 620 | 270 | North Dakota | 174 | 100 | | | |
| Kentucky | 676 | 371 | Ohio | 2,442 | 1,559 | Total | 47,169 | 29,170 |

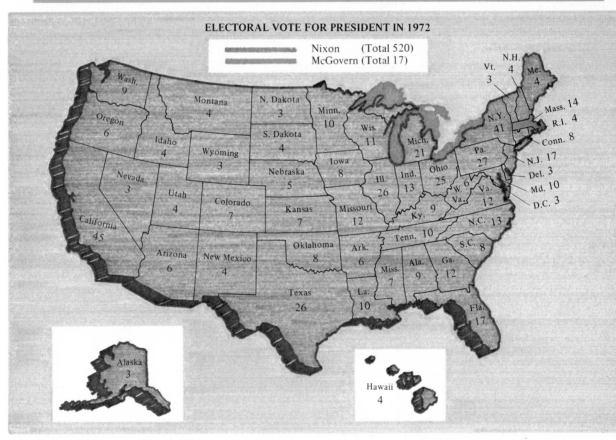

ELECTORAL VOTE FOR PRESIDENT IN 1972

Nixon (Total 520)
McGovern (Total 17)

around 47,169,000 votes, or 61 percent of the total popular vote. The Democratic candidate, George S. McGovern, got around 29,170,000 votes, or 38 percent of the total popular vote. Various minor party candidates received a total of around 1,378,000 votes.

Although Richard Nixon was the winner of the popular vote, the masses of people could not formally elect him to the Presidency. Rather, in each state people were technically choosing between competing lists of Republican, Democratic, and minor party electors. For example, the state of Wisconsin had the right to select eleven electors, since it had two Senators and nine members of the House of Representatives. Richard Nixon, the Republican candidate, won a majority of the popular votes in Wisconsin. According to the "winner-take-all" system practiced in every state, the eleven electors chosen to represent Wisconsin in the Electoral College were those of the Republican party. These presidential electors met in Madison, the state capital, in December to cast their ballots for the Republican candidates, Richard Nixon and Spiro Agnew. These ballots were sealed and sent to Washington, D.C.

On January 6, 1972, the President of the Senate opened the sealed ballots from each of the fifty states and the District of Columbia. The votes were counted before the members of both houses of Congress. Richard Nixon got 520 electoral votes and was officially declared the President.* He needed at least 270 of the 538 electoral votes to gain a majority. His running-mate, Spiro Agnew, got 521 electoral votes and was officially declared the Vice-President. Democrat George McGovern and his running-mate, Sargent Shriver, won 17 electoral votes. Although everyone had known on November 7 that Nixon and Agnew had won the election, their victory did not become official until the electoral votes were counted on January 6.

*One Republican elector from Virginia did not cast his electoral vote for Nixon.

The members of the Electoral College are expected to vote for the candidate that gets a majority of the popular vote in their state. But the Constitution allows them to vote as they please. Thus, it is legally possible for the electors to vote for candidates other than those selected in their states by the popular vote. For example, in 1960 an elector from Oklahoma voted for Senator Harry Byrd of Virginia even though a majority of Oklahoma's popular vote had gone to Richard Nixon. In 1968 one North Carolina man who ran as a Nixon elector actually cast his electoral vote for Wallace. In 1972 a Republican elector from Virginia broke his pledge to vote for Nixon and voted for the candidate of the Libertarian party. However, electors rarely have broken their pledges to follow the popular vote.

In the event that no candidate gets a majority of the electoral votes, the Constitution requires that the House of Representatives choose the President. In this special election, each of the fifty state delegations in the House would have one vote; and it would require a majority of twenty-six votes to elect a President. The House would

196

select a President from among the three candidates with the most electoral votes. In 1800 and in 1824 the House of Representatives chose the President in this manner.

## Should We Change Our Method of Nominating Presidential Candidates?

Although our system for nominating presidential candidates has worked quite well, critics have urged reform. Following are arguments for and against the current method.

### Arguments against the Convention Method of Nomination

The main argument against the convention is that the voters take little part. In many of the states, party leaders, rather than popular votes, select delegates to the party conventions. Thus, the critics argue, many of the delegates are under the influence of their party leaders rather than the masses of people. According to the critics, the convention system is open to selection of a presidential candidate through political deals rather than by the will of the people.

People urging a change call for some type of nationwide primary election as the best means for selecting presidential candidates. Estes Kefauver, the late Democratic senator from Tennessee, was a strong supporter of nomination through primary elections. Following is an excerpt from a statement by Kefauver, before the Senate Judiciary Committee in 1961, in favor of electoral reform:

> The primary method of nomination works well in selecting Governors and Members of Congress in many states. It should be extended to the choice of candidates for President and Vice-President. . . . The more the people have a chance to speak their minds, the closer we get to grassroots opinions and desires, the better our democracy works.
>
> Presidential primary elections in all the states would require candidates to discuss the issues publicly. Such public debate will help to inform and enlighten public opinion via press, radio, and television, and it would pave the way for broadening and strengthening the democratic process.
>
> It will also result, I believe, in better government and government more responsible to the people. A candidate for President who has been nominated by the people instead of the conventions will be, if elected, more responsive to the will of the people and more obligated to the people than to politicians.
>
> Experience shows that presidential primaries arouse public interest and stimulate discussions of public issues, as well as of the character, convictions, and abilities of those who aspire to the highest offices in the land. . . .
>
> . . . The archaic convention system does not necessarily register the preferences of the people.

Engelhardt in the *St. Louis Post-Dispatch*

**"Without me, where'd be all the excitement?"**

**There's got to be a better way for us to travel.**

What is Mauldin's view on the national nominating conventions?

## Arguments for the Convention Method of Nomination

The main arguments in support of national nominating conventions are (1) that they serve to maintain political party unity, (2) that they involve less expense than nationwide primary elections, and (3) that they have produced able candidates. Furthermore, supporters of the convention system believe that the conventions do reflect the popular will in selecting candidates.

Many of the supporters of the convention system believe that some minor changes should be made. But they are united in the belief that this method of nominating presidential candidates is superior to any alternative. Following is an excerpt from a *Chicago Tribune* editorial in defense of the convention system.[2]

Gov. George Wallace has proposed that the Democratic presidential nomination be decided with a single, winner-take-all national primary. This . . . is a very bad idea.

The present hodge podge of individual state primaries constitutes a system that needs improvement. But a single national primary is the worst possible alternative.

It would mean two national elections—with all the waste, excess, and banality that would entail. Worse, it would involve

2. *Chicago Tribune,* December 14, 1974. Reprinted, courtesy of the *Chicago Tribune.*

198

a carnival of candidates—dozens, even hundreds—running all over the country for months.

Instead of testing the waters, finding them frigid, and dropping out—as the present system permits them to do—minor candidates would stay in the running because that one primary would offer them their only chance of winning. Special interest groups might enter blocs of candidates to diffuse a political enemy's vote.

A national primary would serve to destroy both parties as national entities. . . .

**1.** What are the main arguments in opposition to the convention system for nominating presidential candidates?
**2.** What are the main arguments in favor of the convention?
**3.** What are your judgments about arguments for and against the convention system?

## Should We Alter or Abolish the Electoral College?

The Electoral College system has been under attack. Critics have said that the system suffers from several weaknesses and have urged that it be changed or abolished.

### The Case against the Electoral College

The most serious criticism is that under the Electoral College system a candidate with more popular votes than any opponent may fail to win the Presidency. For example, in the elections of 1876 and 1888, candidates with the most popular votes failed to get a majority of the electoral votes. See *Table 1* below.

*Table 1.* **Popular Votes and Electoral Votes in 1876 and 1888**

| Year | Candidates | Popular Vote | Electoral Vote |
|------|-----------|--------------|----------------|
| 1876 | Hayes | 4,033,950 | 185 |
|      | Tilden | 4,284,757 | 184 |
| 1888 | Cleveland | 5,540,050 | 168 |
|      | Harrison | 5,444,337 | 233 |

The "winner-take-all" method of choosing electors in each state is the major reason for the chance of electing a President with minority popular support. For example, a candidate needs only to win the popular vote in a state by one vote in order to gain all the electoral votes of the state. Thus, a candidate could win 270 electoral votes, enough to be elected, by winning the popular vote in several states by a very small margin of victory. At the same time this candidate could lose the popular vote in several states by a very large margin and lose the nationwide popular vote to a rival while winning the Presidency.

A second major criticism of the Electoral College system is that the law does not require the presidential electors to vote for the candidate who has received a majority of the popular votes in their state. Although electors pledge to vote for the winning candidates in their states, and most electors have honored their pledges, there is the chance for electors to violate the public trust and disregard the popular vote in selecting a President.

A third criticism is that the states with less population are favored over the states with more population in the distribution of electoral votes. For example, the population of California is roughly 66 times more than the population of Alaska. Yet California's total of electoral votes is only 14 times that of Alaska.

A fourth criticism is that the present system encourages candidates to focus attention on a few heavily populated states and to neglect the voters in other states. Under the "winner-take-all" system of gaining electoral votes, it was possible to win the Presidency in 1976 by winning the popular vote in the eleven largest states, which had a total of 272 electoral votes. However, these eleven states also had over half the nation's total population.

## A Proposal for Abolishing the Electoral College

Many political leaders have urged the abolition of the Electoral College in favor of direct popular election of the President and Vice-President. Senator Birch Bayh of Indiana was the major spokesman in 1970 for an amendment to the Constitution to abolish the Electoral College and allow the people to elect the President directly. In the event that no candidate got at least 40 percent of the popular vote, a "run-off" election between the top two vote-getters would determine the winner.

Following is an excerpt from one of Senator Bayh's arguments in favor of direct popular election of the President:

Unless we accept the argument that the people should not be trusted to choose their President and Vice-President, there is absolutely no valid argument against the direct popular election amendment now being debated. . . .

Any system that retains the electoral vote, no matter what scheme is devised to divide the vote, can elect a President who is not the first choice of the people.

If our political system is ever to be truly democratic and truly responsive to the will of the people, it must let the people elect their President.[3]

---

3. Birch Bayh, "U.S. Hasn't Corrected Election Inadequacies." Bloomington, Indiana: *Daily Herald-Telephone.* September 12, 1970. (From syndicated column of John P. Roche.)

## Proposals for Altering the Electoral College

Many political leaders want the Electoral College system to be reformed rather than abolished. One widely discussed plan would divide the electoral vote of each state in proportion to the popular vote cast in the state. For example, Vermont has three electoral votes. A candidate winning two-thirds of the popular vote in Vermont would get two of the three electoral votes. The loser, who received one-third of the popular vote in the state, would receive one of the state's three electoral votes. This proportional system of dividing electoral votes would do away with the electors to insure that the electoral votes would reflect the popular vote. The supporters of the proportional system say that their plan keeps the strengths of the Electoral College system while doing away with its main weaknesses.

Many leaders wish to keep the chief features of the present electoral system. Abolishing the electors is the only change they would make. They would have the electoral vote tied directly to the popular vote without electors casting ballots in a ceremony.

## Reasons for Supporting the Electoral College

Since 1880 over five hundred proposals have been heard in Congress to change or do away with the Electoral College. None of these resolutions to amend the Constitution has been able to win the necessary two-thirds vote in each house of Congress to become a "proposed amendment" for the states to ratify. The present system clearly has some support. Those in favor of it tend to use some of the following arguments.

- "No urgent necessity for immediate change has been proven." This is what John F. Kennedy said while defending the current system as a member of the United States Senate.

- The winner usually gets a much higher proportion of electoral votes than of popular votes. This high electoral total gives a desirable appearance of nationwide backing for the winner.

- It strengthens the two-party system. Some proposed changes in the current Electoral College system would encourage minor parties to enter the race even more so than in the past.

- The present arrangement helps preserve the federal system of government by giving each state two electoral votes (carrying on the idea of state equality in the Senate) and additional electoral votes on the basis of population.

1. What are the main arguments against the Electoral College?
2. What are the main arguments in favor of retaining the essential features of the Electoral College system?
3. What is your evaluation of the arguments presented here for changing or abolishing the Electoral College?

# 9 Participating in Electoral Politics

The citizen's right to vote is basic to American politics. Through voting, ordinary people have a chance to choose public officials and to influence public policy. From childhood on, Americans hear that they should show interest in politics and vote in public elections. To what extent do they take part? Are some groups more active than others? If so, why? Finally, does it really matter if people are active in politics nor not? Read on to find evidence on these questions.

## Who Participates in Electoral Politics?

The chart on this page shows different levels at which people take part in electoral politics. The chart gives a name to people operating at each of four levels.

### Levels of Participation in Electoral Politics

**Level 1    Activists**
- a. Holding public and party office
- b. Being a candidate for public or party office
- c. Raising funds for an election campaign
- d. Participating in strategy meetings of a political organization
- e. Participating actively in a political party or other political organization
- f. Giving time to an election campaign through canvassing, passing handbills, etc.

**Level 2    Occasional Participants**
- g. Attending a public meeting or rally of a political party or other political organization
- h. Giving money to a party or candidate
- i. Contacting a public official or party leader to make a request

**Level 3    Spectators**
- j. Supporting a candidate or party by wearing a button, putting a sticker on the car, etc.
- k. Trying to persuade someone to vote
- l. Starting a political discussion
- m. Voting in a public election
- n. Following politics in newspapers and on television

**Level 4    Apathetics**
- o. Nonvoting and no participating in electoral politics

- *Activists* are most involved. Politics takes a big part of their time and energy. We assume that those who take part in activities **a-f** (at the highest level of involvement) also take part in the lower-level activities, **g-n**.

- *Occasional participants* play the game of politics on more of a part-time basis. In addition to doing the kinds of things listed for their level (**g-i**), they will do those listed in items **j-n**.

- *Spectators* enjoy the game of politics but take part mostly on the sidelines. They observe and support the political activities of others.

- *Apathetics* are simply not involved in electoral politics.

1. Where do you fit in the chart? your parents? most of your friends?
2. On a slip of paper write the names of the four levels (activists, occasional participants, spectators, apathetics). After each one write what percentage of American citizens of voting age you think fit in each category.

*Tables 1 and 2* provide some evidence about how much voting-age Americans really do take part in electoral politics. Use the data in these tables to support or reject the speculations you made in question 2 above.

1. Use evidence in *Tables 1 and 2* to support or reject the following hypotheses.
   **a.** Less than 10 percent of American citizens of voting age can be called "apathetics" in electoral politics.
   **b.** More than 25 percent of American citizens of voting age can be called "activists" in electoral politics.
   **c.** There are more "apathetics" than "occasional participants" in American electoral politics.
   **d.** There are more "occasional participants" than "spectators" in American electoral politics.
2. Rewrite each hypothesis that you reject to make it fit the available evidence.
3. The data in *Tables 1 and 2* pertain to the recent past. Look for evidence that will help you answer these questions:
   **a.** At present what proportion of American citizens are involved in electoral politics?
   **b.** To what extent are they involved?

---

Table 1: U.S. Bureau of the Census, *Statistical Abstract of the United States.*
Tables 2–3: H. T. Reynolds, *Politics and the Common Man* (Homewood, Ill.: Dorsey Press, 1974), pp. 123, 127–131. Data from 1970 and 1972 CPS National Election Studies. Data supplied by the Inter-university Consortium for Political Research.

**Table 1. Percentage of the Electorate Voting in National Elections, 1940–72**

| | Civilians of Voting Age | |
|---|---|---|
| | Percent Voting for President | Percent Voting for U.S. Rep. |
| 1940 | 58.9% | 55.4% |
| 1942 | | 32.5 |
| 1944 | 56.0 | 52.7 |
| 1946 | | 37.1 |
| 1948 | 51.1 | 48.1 |
| 1950 | | 41.6 |
| 1952 | 61.6 | 57.6 |
| 1954 | | 41.7 |
| 1956 | 59.3 | 55.9 |
| 1958 | | 43.4 |
| 1960 | 62.8 | 58.5 |
| 1962 | | 46.1 |
| 1964 | 61.8 | 58.1 |
| 1966 | | 45.4 |
| 1968 | 60.9 | 55.2 |
| 1970 | | 43.5 |
| 1972 | 55.7 | 51.0 |

**Table 2. Participation in Electoral Politics, 1970**

| Type of Activity | Percent Who Took Part |
|---|---|
| 1. Worked in an election campaign | 7% |
| 2. Belong to a political group | 5 |
| 3. Attended a political meeting or rally | 9 |
| 4. Tried to persuade someone to vote for one of the candidates or parties | 27 |

203

### Differences in Participation among Groups

Are some groups more likely than others to take part in electoral politics? Studies conducted in the 1950s and 1960s support the following hypotheses.

1. People with higher income are more likely than those with lower income to participate.

2. People with more education are more likely than people with less education to participate.

3. People who work in high-status occupations (professionals, business owners and managers) are more likely than those in low-status occupations to participate.

4. White people are more likely than black people to participate.

*Table 3* shows evidence about participation in electoral politics in 1970–1972 by various groups. Study the table to see if the evidence supports or rejects the hypotheses above.

1. Use evidence in *Table 3* to answer these questions.
   a. Does the table support or reject hypothesis 1? Explain.
   b. Does the table support the following statement? Explain. Mike Woodward earns more than $15,000 a year and Horace Ackerman earns less than $5000 per year. Therefore, we know for sure that Mr. Woodward takes more part in electoral politics than Mr. Ackerman does.
   c. What level of participation do most upper-income people fit: activist, occasional participant, spectator, or apathetic?
   d. What level do lower-income people tend to fit: activist, occasional participant, spectator, or apathetic?
2. Use evidence in *Table 3* to answer these questions.
   a. Does the table support or reject hypothesis 2 on this page? Explain.
   b. Does the table support the following statement? Explain. In the year 1990, college graduates will be more likely than noncollege people to take part in electoral politics.
   c. What level of participation (activist, occasional participant, spectator, or apathetic) do most college graduates fit?
   d. What level do most noncollege persons fit?
3. Use evidence in *Table 3* to answer these questions.
   a. Does the table support or reject hypothesis 3 on this page? Explain.
   b. Does the table support the following statement? Explain. In Mexico, professionals are more likely than laborers to take part in electoral politics.
   c. About what percentage of professionals seem to be activists? occasional participants? spectators? apathetics?
   d. About what percentage of laborers and unskilled workers seem to fit each of the four levels of participation?

**Table 3. Participation in Electoral Politics by Income, Education, Occupation, and Race**

Percent Who:

| Respondent's Family Income | Voted in Last Presidential Election | Voted in Last Congressional Election | Tried to Persuade Someone* | Attended a Political Meeting or Rally | Worked in a Campaign | Belong to Political Group |
|---|---|---|---|---|---|---|
| Less than $1999 | 55% | 39% | 11% | 3% | 2% | 2% |
| $2000–3999 | 63 | 50 | 15 | 4 | 3 | 3 |
| $4000–7499 | 64 | 53 | 19 | 5 | 6 | 4 |
| $7500–14,999 | 76 | 65 | 31 | 10 | 7 | 6 |
| $15,000 and over | 89 | 77 | 46 | 22 | 16 | 11 |
| **Education** | | | | | | |
| 8 grades | 63% | 57% | 12% | 5% | 2% | 1% |
| High school graduate | 75 | 59 | 28 | 7 | 7 | 4 |
| College | 90 | 83 | 53 | 28 | 18 | 16 |
| **Occupation** | | | | | | |
| Laborers and unskilled workers | 52% | 33% | 15% | 0% | 2% | 5% |
| Service and household workers | 62 | 60 | 15 | 5 | 5 | 2 |
| Operatives and semiskilled workers | 68 | 47 | 14 | 5 | 3 | 2 |
| Craftsmen and foremen | 77 | 63 | 32 | 11 | 5 | 7 |
| Farmers | 88 | 57 | 22 | 4 | 4 | 4 |
| Clerical and sales workers | 78 | 67 | 32 | 11 | 10 | 5 |
| Managers and officials | 82 | 71 | 35 | 10 | 10 | 6 |
| Professionals | 87 | 74 | 45 | 24 | 16 | 14 |
| **Race** | | | | | | |
| Nonwhite | 65% | 48% | 20% | 8% | 7% | 4% |
| White | 74 | 61 | 27 | 10 | 7 | 6 |

*Tried to persuade someone to vote for one of the candidates or parties.

4. Use evidence in *Table 3* to answer these questions.

a. Does the table support or reject hypothesis 4 on page 204? Explain.

b. Is the difference in participation between blacks and whites as great as the difference between people of upper and lower socio-economic status? (Use the income levels in *Table 3* as a measure of socioeconomic status.)

c. Which of these two factors—race or socioeconomic status— seems to be more strongly related to differences in participation in electoral politics? Why?

See pages 124–127 in chapter 6 for discussion of the effect of socioeconomic status on political behavior.

Elections that occur in the
years between presidential
elections are called off-year
elections.

Most Americans have the right to vote in public elections, but
a large number of eligible Americans do not vote. *Table 1* shows that
more than a third of the electorate fail to vote in presidential elections.
Less than half take part in off-year congressional elections. *Table
3* shows that some groups are more likely to take part than others.
Why? *Table 4* provides some clues. This table shows reasons given
by nonvoters for not taking part in the 1972 election.

**Table 4. Reasons for Not Voting in the 1972 Presidential Election**

| Reason | Percent Responding |
|---|---|
| 1. Didn't bother to register or prevented from registering by residence requirements | 38% |
| 2. Not interested in politics | 28 |
| 3. Didn't like either candidate | 10 |
| 4. Sick or disabled | 10 |
| 5. Could not leave job, or working two shifts | 7 |
| 6. Away from home/traveling | 7 |
| TOTAL | 100% |

**5.** What are the two most frequently mentioned reasons for not
voting shown in *Table 4?*
**6.** Which of the reasons for not voting are associated with voter
eligibility laws?
**7.** Which of the reasons for not voting pertain to attitudes or opinions about politics?
**8.** How might those who responded to this poll be motivated to
take part in electoral politics?
**9.** The data in *Tables 3-4* pertain to the early 1970s. Look for
evidence that describes the situation today.

## The Influence of Laws on Voter Turnout

Several factors can help us see why people operate at different
levels of political participation. Election laws, or the legal factor, can
account for some of the nonparticipation.

### Legal Qualifications for Voting

Every society that allows citizens to vote for political leaders also
has legal qualifications for voting. Their main purpose is to prevent
the unfit from voting. Persons are judged unfit as voters in terms
of the political culture—the main political values and attitudes in the
society. In times past in American history, black people, women, men
without property, and men who did not believe in God were judged
unfit as voters. However, changes in our political culture are reflected

*Table 4:* American Institute of Public Opinion, THE GALLUP POLL, Princeton, New Jersey.

by changes in voting laws. Today women, black people, people without property, and nonbelievers have the legal right to vote in all states.

In line with our present political culture, aliens, nonresidents, and children are the main groups that are denied the right to vote because they seem in some way to be unfit. Most states also take away the voting right from persons convicted of a felony. Some states restore the right after a person "serves his time."

The Constitution of the United States gives the state governments chief responsibility over voting and elections. But it puts some limits on the power of the states to determine the right to vote. The Fifteenth Amendment declares that no state may prevent a person from voting "on account of race, color, or previous condition of servitude." The Nineteenth Amendment provides that no state may prevent women from voting. The Twenty-fourth Amendment says that the states may not require the payment of a poll tax as a qualification for voting. The Twenty-sixth Amendment lowered the voting age to eighteen.

In order to vote in each of the fifty states a person must be an American citizen, at least age 18, and a resident of the state. We shall look at each of these requirements, and then look at other barriers which have existed in recent years.

## Citizenship and Age as Barriers to Voting

A person who is neither a "natural-born" nor a "naturalized" citizen of the United States can neither vote nor run for office. These restrictions on aliens, or non-citizens, are law in all fifty states.

A person is a natural-born citizen if (a) born within the boundaries of the United States, or (b) born anywhere in the world to parents who are United States citizens.

A citizen of another country may become a naturalized citizen of the United States by satisfying certain legal requirements:

1. *Petition for naturalization:* Any alien who has lived in the United States for five years or more, who is at least 18 years old, who has been permitted to establish a home in the United States, and who can speak, read, and write English may make a petition to become an American citizen.

2. *Examination:* The applicant for citizenship must prove that he or she can meet the English language requirement, has good moral character, and has established legal residence in the United States.

3. *Final court hearing:* The person seeking citizenship appears in court and takes the oath of allegiance to the United States of America. He or she then becomes a naturalized citizen and is entitled to the same rights and duties as any other American citizen.

All the states now limit voting to citizens who are age 18 or older. This voting age became uniform in the nation when the Twenty-sixth Amendment was ratified in 1971. Until 1943, when Georgia dropped

A group of new citizens take the oath of allegiance in a federal court.

the age to 18, the minimum age had always been 21. Later several other states dropped the voting age to 18, 19, or 20. Now, however, it is age 18 in all states.

## Mobility as a Barrier to Voting

Before 1972 all states required that a voter must have lived in the state for a certain period of time, generally six months to two years. Most states also had a local residence requirement (ranging from one month to six months) in the county and/or voting district. Residency limits on the right to vote presumed that a newcomer to a state or county would be unfit to vote for lack of time to know the candidates and issues in the state or local election.

Mobile people—those who changed their place of residence—were victims of these rules. It is estimated that from six to eight million people lost their vote in the 1968 presidential election because they had not lived long enough in their new homes to satisfy the residency rules. These people had moved from one state to another or from one part of a state to another part.

Many of America's better educated people—doctors, lawyers, educators, engineers, and business managers—are among the more mobile elements of the population. The residency laws worked against them when they had to move for business reasons.

208

While some few months of residence may increase the fitness of a person to vote in a state or local election, this argument does not apply to presidential elections. Moving from Ohio to Colorado two months before the election does not make a person unfit to choose among candidates for President.

To remedy this unfairness, Congress in 1970 added a new provision to the law extending the Voting Rights Act of 1965. It set a uniform residency requirement of 30 days in the state or political subdivision for voting in presidential elections.

On March 21, 1972, the United States Supreme Court declared unconstitutional lengthy residency rules for state and local elections. In *Dunn* v. *Blumstein* the Supreme Court struck down Tennessee's one-year state and three-month county residency law. The Court suggested that one month is a fair residency for eligibility to vote in state and local elections. In later court cases, somewhat longer periods have been judged fair.

As of 1976, seven states had laws requiring more than 30 days residency. Georgia's 50-day rule was the strictest. Twenty-five states required less than 30 days. Eighteen states had no minimum number of days of residency to qualify to vote.

## The Decline of Other Legal Requirements for Voting

Throughout American history legal barriers to voting have slowly broken down. During America's colonial period only white males could vote. Seven colonies said that a man had to own land in order to vote. The other six colonies required evidence of personal property or a tax payment of all voters. A few colonies required a person to profess some kind of orthodox religious belief in order to vote.

Property and tax-paying rules stayed in force after the thirteen colonies gained independence. Several states kept property rules for voting until the 1840s and 1850s. New Western states that came into the Union during the nineteenth century usually did not have property qualifications for voting.

Amendments to the Constitution removed some other limitations on the right to vote (page 207).

### Literacy Tests

Literacy tests have also been a barrier to voting until very recently. It is estimated that such tests kept around one million people from voting in the early 1960s. Such tests were used for many years to hinder the registration of black voters in certain Southern states. The Voting Rights Act of 1965, mentioned earlier, suspended the use of literacy tests in states where there was clear evidence of racial discrimination in voting. Then when that law was extended in 1970, Congress added another major provision: a permanent ban against any literacy test as a qualification for voting in any public elections throughout the country.

This 1962 cartoon leveled criticism at the uneven standards used in administration of literacy tests in some states.

Copyright © 1962 *St. Louis Post-Dispatch*,
reproduced by courtesy of Bill Mauldin

**"By th' way, what's that big word?"**

Literacy tests were based on the belief that a person cannot vote intelligently without at least a low level of reading ability. (Today, of course, even nonreaders can get considerable "voter education" by means of radio and television.) The state literacy test in New York was typical of several. It consisted of reading a paragraph and answering eight simple questions about it.

Other states, especially in the South, required a prospective voter to read a section of the state constitution and to interpret its meaning to the satisfaction of the voting registrar. Time after time blacks, even those with college degrees, "failed" such tests. On the other hand, the Civil Rights Commission found in one state where few blacks were registered that thousands of white voters who were unable even to write their name on the election register had "passed" the literacy test.

## Registration and Voting

People who meet all the conditions for voting still must register to vote. To register, a person must tell his or her name, address, place of birth, and age. Proof of residency for the required period of time must be given.

The handling of voter registration varies widely from state to state. In some states it is very easy to register and stay registered to vote. In these states, citizens other than public officials may go from house to house or set up neighborhood offices to register voters. Also people can register by mail. And the deadline for registration is not until a few days before an election—or even the election day itself as in Maine.

In other states, the process is more difficult. In these states only public officials can register voters. It can take place only at some central office—not by mail, not house to house, and not at neighborhood centers. Also the central registration office is closed evenings and weekends.

In states where it is easy to register, and to stay registered, the voter turnout tends to be high. For example, it is easy to register and stay registered in Utah, Minnesota, South Dakota, and Idaho, and these states usually have a high voter turnout.

In recent years there has been a tendency to pass new election laws to make it easier for people to register and vote. Below are some provisions of such laws. Compare your state's laws about registration,

This record of voter registration is used in Kentucky? How does it compare with the form used in your state? Why are there questions about physical characteristics?

| SERIAL NUMBER | SEX | COLOR | MR. MRS. MISS | | | PRECINCT |
|---|---|---|---|---|---|---|
| | | | | LAST NAME | FIRST NAME | MIDDLE NAME |

| PARTY AFFILIATION | | | | STREET NUMBER | RURAL ROUTE AND ROAD OR LOCALITY | PRECINCT |
|---|---|---|---|---|---|---|
| PARTY CHANGE | | | ADDRESS | | | |
| OCCUPATION | | | ADDRESS | | | PRECINCT |
| | | | ADDRESS | | | |
| | | | NEAREST NEIGHBOR IF NOT IN CITY OR TOWN | | | |

| TERM OF RESIDENCE | YEARS | MONTHS | DAYS | APPARENT WEIGHT | APPARENT HEIGHT | | AGE | OTHER MEANS OF IDENTIFICATION |
|---|---|---|---|---|---|---|---|---|
| | | | | | FEET | INCHES | | |
| STATE | | | | | | | | |
| COUNTY | | | | | | | | |
| PRECINCT | | | | | | | | |

DATE OF REGISTRATION

IF REGISTRATION CANCELLED GIVE REASON AND DATE AND RETAIN CANCELLED CARDS IN ALPHABETICAL FILE FOR TWO YEARS.

REMARKS: CHANGE OF ADDRESS OR PRECINCT BOUNDARY

SUBSCRIBED AND SWORN TO BEFORE ME _____19___

PRECINCT_____ DAY OF_____ 19___

COUNTY COURT CLERK | HIS OR HER MARK | SIGNATURE OF VOTER

BY_____

DEPUTY CLERK

| VOTING RECORD | | | | | | | | | | | | | | | | | | | | | | | | | | | | | | |
|---|---|---|---|---|---|---|---|---|---|---|---|---|---|---|---|---|---|---|---|---|---|---|---|---|---|---|---|---|---|---|
| VOTED | 1955 | 56 | 57 | 58 | 59 | 60 | 61 | 62 | 63 | 64 | 65 | 66 | 67 | 68 | 69 | 70 | 71 | 72 | 73 | 74 | 75 | 76 | 77 | 78 | 79 | 80 | 81 | 82 | 83 | 84 |
| PRIMARY ELECTION | | | | | | | | | | | | | | | | | | | | | | | | | | | | | | |
| GENERAL ELECTION | | | | | | | | | | | | | | | | | | | | | | | | | | | | | | |
| CITY ELECTION | | | | | | | | | | | | | | | | | | | | | | | | | | | | | | |
| SPECIAL ELECTION | | | | | | | | | | | | | | | | | | | | | | | | | | | | | | |

residency, absentee voting, and time for voting with the items on this list.[1]

*Registration Systems*

1. Permanent registration (instead of periodic re-registration).
2. Passing of a literacy test not required for registration.
3. Registration by mail permitted.
4. Registration closes no more than one month before the election.
5. Registration conducted in precinct rather than county office.

*Residence Requirements*

6. No more than 30 days residence in state required for voting.
7. New residents (who otherwise have not met voting residence requirements) may vote for President.
8. Former residents (who have not established a new voting residence) may vote for President.
9. People who have moved within the state may vote by absentee ballot in their former precinct.

*Absentee Provisions*

10. Civilians as well as military personnel may vote by absentee ballot if absent from precinct on election day.
11. Handicapped, ill, or incapacitated people may vote by absentee ballot.
12. Absentee ballots may be obtained by mail.

*Election Day Provisions*

13. Polls must be open 12 hours or longer.
14. Polls must remain open until all in line have voted.
15. There must be enough polling places, voting booths, and so on to handle the number of registered voters.

Pretend that the following people want to register to vote in your community. Answer these questions about each person.

A. Does the law in your state permit the person to vote?
B. Can this person vote in any other state?
C. Should this person be permitted to vote?

*Example 1.* Mike is unemployed. He was born and raised in your community. He spends most of his time hanging around pool rooms and bars. He is a high school dropout and reads very poorly. He knows nothing about government and politics and is not concerned about public issues and elections.

*Example 2.* Hector was born and raised in your community. He is in the Navy and is stationed at an island in the Pacific. He wants to vote in the next election in your community.

---

1. Adapted with permission of Macmillan Publishing Co., Inc. from *The Psychology of Politics* by William F. Stone. Copyright © 1974 by The Free Press, a Division of Macmillan Publishing Co., Inc.

*Example 3.* Carolyn is serving the ninth year of a twenty-year sentence in a prison in your state. She grew up in your community and is very interested in politics. She has been a model prisoner.

*Example 4.* Barbara, age 18, moved to your community two weeks ago. She is very interested in politics and wants to vote in the next election, which takes place in one week.

*Example 5.* Aurelia, age 25, moved from Romania to your community five years ago. She intends to become a citizen of the United States. She is regularly employed, speaks English fluently, and is well-educated. She is very interested in politics and wants to vote in the next election, which takes place in three months.

*Example 6.* Charles, age 90, is a lifelong resident of your community. For the last three years he has lived in a home for the elderly located in your community. Although he likes to read and talk politics, he cannot make the trip to the polls.

*Example 7.* Mary, age 17, is a lifelong resident of your community. She wants to vote in the next election two weeks from now.

*Example 8.* Susan, age 50, was a registered voter in your community for many years. However, she has not voted in an election in the past seven years.

## The Voting Rights of Black People: Using the Law to Change the Law

In spite of the fact that large groups of people have been denied the ballot in the past, a belief in "government by the people" has been an important part of the American political culture. Compared with most other countries, the United States was a leader in giving the vote to more and more people.

A major exception to this general trend was the erection of barriers to black voters in the South at the end of the Reconstruction period in the 1870s. The Fifteenth Amendment had barred the states from making race or color a condition for voting. Nevertheless, Southern states devised other means of keeping blacks away from the polls:

*Literacy tests,* as we have seen, could be "scored" to pass illiterate whites and to reject even educated blacks.

*Poll taxes* required that individuals pay a fee, usually one or two dollars, to be eligible to vote. In a few states the prospective voter had to pay any unpaid back poll tax as well as the current tax. Moreover, the individual could escape the tax by not voting. The poll tax, of course, stopped many poor blacks, as well as whites, from voting.

*Economic and social pressures* besides the poll tax included dismissal from a job if a black person asked for the ballot. Threats and actual beatings, house burnings, and even murders were used to terrorize the black community.

*White-primary laws* provided that only enrolled party members could vote in a primary election. The Democratic party would then refuse to enroll any black members, claiming that the party was sort of a private club and not an arm of the government. In states with white-primary laws the winners in the Democratic party election almost always won in the general election. Thus blacks had little or no chance to influence the elections.

*The Grandfather Clause* was first used in Louisiana in 1898. It gave permanent voter registration to anyone whose father or grandfather was qualified to vote as of January 1, 1867. All other people had to pass a literacy test to qualify to vote. Since the only fathers and grandfathers who were registered voters in 1867 were white, the only voters who were allowed permanent voter registration were white. Most blacks had to pass the unfair literacy test described earlier. The Grandfather Clause worked so well in restricting black voting that it spread to several other Southern states.

Most of the devices to keep blacks from voting took the form of state laws which were passed to get around the Fifteenth Amendment. How could blacks knock down these legal barriers? Some black leaders decided to use the courts to win political rights.

A citizen who believes that a law harms him in some special way or deprives him of his constitutional rights may start a case in court. Eventually the case may reach the United States Supreme Court. The Court may decide that the citizen's claim is valid—that the law is unconstitutional and therefore may not be enforced.

The National Association for the Advancement of Colored People (NAACP) led the fight. The first breakthrough came in 1915, when NAACP lawyers presented their case against the Grandfather Clause in the Oklahoma state constitution. The Supreme Court declared the clause unconstitutional, or null and void. Other victories by means of lawsuits came slowly. Then in 1944 the white-primary laws were set aside by the United States Supreme Court in the case of *Smith* v. *Allbright*.

In addition to seeking changes in the law by means of court action, the NAACP and other organizations worked for new federal laws to broaden voting rights. The Civil Rights Acts of 1957 and 1960 gave the United States Attorney General the right to bring suits against election officials practicing racial discrimination. The Civil Rights Act of 1964 required that literacy tests must be given in writing and that anyone with at least a sixth-grade education is presumed literate.

We have seen that the Voting Rights Act of 1965 suspended the use of literacy tests in certain areas. That law also permitted federal officials to register black voters in areas where local officials were blocking black voter registration. The Voting Rights Act was extended in 1970 with an outright ban on literacy tests (page 209).

214

Federal intervention in voter registration has led to a big increase in election participation by blacks. In 1900 Louisiana had only 5320 blacks registered to vote, and Alabama only about 3000. As late as 1940 in eleven Southern states only 250,000 blacks, or 5 percent of the black population, were registered to vote. By 1970 over three million Southern blacks were registered. Since that time, increases in the registration and participation of Southern blacks in electoral politics has continued.

Taking advantage of rights gained under the Voting Rights Act of 1965, blacks in rural Alabama flocked to the polls in 1966. This is a polling place near Peachtree, Alabama.

The chart on this page shows the dramatic impact of legal change upon the right to vote. Federal law has forced state and local governments in several states to relax their restrictions on the voter registration of black people.

Social pressures and traditional apathy still limit the participation of black people in public elections. Some white leaders still try to influence black people to stay out of political affairs. Some older black people have grown used to staying out of politics. However, many younger blacks have accepted the challenge of using political action to improve their lot in life.

It takes more than changes in the law to get people to register and then vote. Many people fail to vote when there are no legal hurdles to jump. We next look at some personal factors associated with voter turnout. Then in chapter 10 we look further at blacks stirring people to political action and winning elections.

**1.** How do voting laws influence popular participation in public elections?
**2.** What reasons are used to defend the various legal restrictions on voting?
**3.** How have black people used the law to change their role in public elections?
**4.** What does culture have to do with the making of legal requirements for voting?

**EFFECT OF VOTING RIGHTS ACT ON REGISTRATION OF BLACKS**

*PERCENT OF VOTING-AGE POPULATION REGISTERED IN 1965 AND 1967*

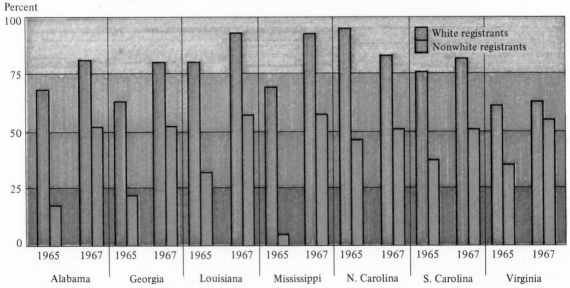

# Non-Legal Factors Associated with Voter Turnout

Failure to satisfy legal requirements explains why some people do not vote. However, the legal factor does not explain why several million American citizens choose not to register or often fail to vote if registered.

## Personal Factors and Voter Turnout

Political scientists have found that personal factors can help explain nonvoting in public elections. Among these factors are sense of political efficacy, political interest, sense of civic duty, and concern with election outcome.

*Sense of political efficacy* is a feeling of having power over what public officials do. For example, people with a high sense of political efficacy feel that they can and should influence governmental decisions. People with a low sense of political efficacy feel that they can do little or nothing about what government does. They feel that they have little or no political influence.

*Political interest* refers to the amount of interest a person has in the election campaign. People with a high degree of political interest are very concerned about campaign issues and the candidates for public office.

*Concern about the election outcome* means caring about who wins an election and about the results that might stem from the election outcome. A person with a low degree of concern about the election outcome cares little or nothing about which candidates win or what these candidates might do once they assume public office after the election.

*Sense of civic duty* is the feeling of responsibility to take part in a public election. A person with a high sense of civic duty believes that he or she should take part in a public election and that those who fail to take part are not very good citizens.

Political scientists sometimes combine the four personal factors just studied under the concept *personal involvement in politics.* Hence, a *high sense of personal involvement in politics* is indicated by a high sense of political efficacy, a high degree of political interest, a high sense of civic duty, and a high degree of concern about the election outcome. A *low sense of personal involvement in politics* is indicated by a low ranking in each of the four personal factors.

As one might expect, studies show that persons with a high sense of personal involvement in politics have higher tendencies (a) to vote in public elections and (b) to identify with one of the major political parties than do those with a low sense of personal involvement in politics.

Studies also show that persons of higher socioeconomic status (SES) tend to have a higher sense of personal involvement in politics than do those of lower socioeconomic status.

**1.** Why might you expect higher SES persons to have a higher sense of personal involvement in politics than lower SES persons have?

**2.** Which personal factor does each of the following statements best illustrate?

> **a.** I'm going to vote because I worry about the country if Candidate X wins.
>
> **b.** This election campaign really turns me on. I want to take part.
>
> **c.** We can win this election and get this city back on the right track.
>
> **d.** I can't get excited about this election, but I'd feel guilty if I didn't vote.

### The Impact of Situations on Participation in Public Elections

The statement that low socioeconomic status is related to a low rate of political participation is a *tendency statement.* Some poor people are quite active in politics. How can one account for such exceptions to this and other generalizations about political behavior?

Differences in situation, from one time or place to another, can account for some of the exceptions to our generalization about socioeconomic status and political participation. For example, black people throughout our country have tended to have less socioeconomic advantages than whites. And, reflecting our generalization, blacks have tended to take part in public elections to a lesser degree than whites. However, in New Haven, Connecticut, the situation was different.

In a case study of political behavior in New Haven in the late 1950s, Robert A. Dahl reported that black people there were active in political affairs, even though they tended to be of lower socioeconomic status. Dahl rated a sample of whites and blacks on their degree of political participation. Among those rated "high" in election campaign participation, and participation in local political affairs generally, Dahl found a larger percentage of blacks than of whites.

Political activity held rewards for black people in New Haven. The political parties provided blacks with chances to get good jobs in the city government and to play important roles in the community. Thus many black people, though of lower socioeconomic status, were motivated to take an active part in politics as a means to getting ahead.

The United Mine Workers (UMW) of West Virginia are another exception to the tendency of upper socioeconomic people to be more active in electoral politics than lower status people are. In West Virginia, members of the UMW are very involved as voters and boosters of pro-union candidates. The leaders of the UMW have motivated members to take part for the past forty years. During this time their political involvement has resulted in actions by public officials that have been helpful to the UMW.

The New Haven and West Virginia examples remind us that explanations and descriptions of political behavior that apply to a particular group at a particular time may not apply to different groups at different times and places. Keep in mind that one can usually find exceptions to generalizations about political behavior.

1. Which of the following factors could be used to construct an explanation about the political participation of black people in New Haven and UMW workers in West Virginia? Justify your choice of factors.
   a. sense of political efficacy
   b. sense of civic duty
   c. political interest
   d. concern with election outcome
   e. lower socioeconomic status

2. Evaluate the following statement, about motivating people to vote, in terms of the personal factors you have studied.

The best way to motivate people to vote is to advertise, through all the communications media, that to be considered a good citizen a person must vote on election day.

3. In some countries, citizens are fined for not voting. In Australia the fine is $10. Should citizens in the United States be fined for not voting?

## Is Participation Worth It?

Everything of value has its price. It costs time, energy, effort, and money to take an active part in politics. Is it worth this high price?

If the costs of voting are clearly greater than the costs of not voting, then one might with good reason decide not to take part in electoral politics. However, if the reverse is true, then one is foolish to decide not to take part. For example, some people know they can have an impact on government which is very favorable to them. They probably ought to assume the costs of taking part as much as possible.

In contrast, those who know that they can have little or no influence on government might believe it makes little sense to spend time, energy, and money on political activity. These people might choose not to take part because they believe that, no matter who wins or loses, an election will change nothing for the better. They are not pleased with the way things are but tend to "drop out" of the political system rather than to try to change it.

Some people choose not to take part, or to do so only casually, because they are basically satisfied with the way things are. They see no sense in trying to change things. These people tend to trust government and to prefer to let others manage public affairs for them.

Before you decide to join the nonparticipants—or those who take part without much thought—you should consider this basic truth about political life: In a political system where public elections count for something, those who don't vote—or who vote carelessly—cannot expect to have their interests represented and to gain special benefits from government.

What are your views about the value of taking part in electoral politics? Can you and others have an effect? Do the benefits of taking part outweight the costs? Following are three cases which can help you think about answers to these questions.

### Case 1. Black Clout in California's Seventh District

The Representative to Congress from California's Eighth District (formerly the Seventh) is Ronald V. Dellums, an outspoken, hard-driving black man. Since his election to the House of Representatives in 1970, he has been a blunt and forceful voice for the interests of blacks, Chicanos, and poor people of all types. Congressman Dellums has been a symbol of clout for the black activists who have supported him.

Dellum's election to Congress was very unusual in at least *three* ways.

1. Dellums was the first black to be elected to the House of Representatives from a district with a large white majority. In 1970 less than 30 percent of his district were blacks.

2. Young voters, black and white, played a major part in Dellum's long campaign.

3. Dellums aroused the interest and active support of a large majority of black voters. In all national elections, and in most local contests, black voters have been less likely than whites to take part. Often black voters have felt, with good reason, that it was all a waste of time. They felt that—no matter what the outcome—little or no benefit would go to them. Yet, Ronald Dellums stirred the black people of his district to gain and use clout through disciplined group action.

At the start of his campaign, Dellums seemed an unlikely winner. His only success had come three years earlier when he had won a seat on the Berkeley City Council. As a young (age 34) political newcomer, he had to challenge incumbent Congressman Jeffrey Cohelan to win the Democratic nomination.

Cohelan seemed unbeatable. He was a highly able veteran of twelve years in Congress. In the last three elections Cohelan had won landslide victories. And most important, he had the solid support of the regular Democratic party organizations.

The party regulars viewed Dellums as an annoying amateur who was too closely tied up with the local black militants and with student activists at the University of California. This complacency led to Dellum's chance for victory. While Cohelan and his followers hardly campaigned against this upstart, Dellums was very busy.

220

Well-organized and highly active black voters provided a key to victory. Dellums's campaign slogan was "Let's Get Organized." And this he and his workers did. They stressed voter registration and get-out-the-vote drives. Many blacks and others who favored Dellums were not registered to vote. The organization first registered these people and then, on the day of the primary election, made certain that they voted. Young people played a big part in getting out these previous nonvoters, most of whom cast their first ballots for Dellums.

The result was a big upset victory for Dellums. He beat Cohelan by 42,619 votes to 35,137. Believing Cohelan to be a certain winner, around 54,000 registered Democrats of the Seventh District did not bother to vote in the primary election. Had most of them voted, Cohelan probably would have won.

Dellums next had to defeat the Republican candidate, John Healy, in order to win election to Congress. Once more, most people saw Dellums as the underdog. And again, through effective organization and active help of black supporters, an upset victory was won. This time the outcome was 88,737 votes (57.3 percent of the total) for Dellums to 63,819 votes (41.3 percent) for Healy.

Dellums won again in 1972 and 1974 and seemed to be a rising political star. His campaigns are examples of what motivated, ably led voters can achieve.

Congressman Dellums discusses strategy with his campaign workers.

### Case 2. Young Canvassers: Are They Effective?

In recent election campaigns, young people have worked prominently as canvassers. A political canvass is a way of getting information about voters that may be vital to a campaign's success.

Briefly, this is how canvassers work. They visit the homes of voters and say that they are supporting a certain candidate. Then they ask the residents whether they are registered to vote and for whom they intend to vote. If residents show interest, the canvassers talk briefly about their candidate's merits and hand out leaflets or posters which tell their story.

A good canvass identifies the people who are likely to give support, those who are unsure, and those who are opposed. An effort is then made to register the likely supporters and to ask them to vote on election day. Finally, on election day, known supporters are contacted and asked if they have voted. If they have not, they are urged to vote. They are offered a ride to the polling place and even baby-sitting service, if needed.

Two political scientists studied the canvassing efforts of college students in seven congressional elections in 1970. The elections were in six states of the East Coast and Midwest. The student canvassers in each election supported the Democratic party candidate. In six of the seven contests, the student-supported candidates were winners. The student canvassers were definite, if moderate, contributors to the successful campaigns.[2]

How effective are young voters' canvassing efforts? Is this a way to wield clout, or is it just political busy-work?

2. Sidney Hyman, *Youth in Politics* (New York: Basic Books, Inc., 1972), pp. 394-397.

222

**Tennessee Senatorial Election.** The 1970 senatorial election in Tennessee shows how young voters can get results by canvassing.

Albert Gore, the Democratic incumbent, had represented Tennessee in the United States Senate since 1952. Many thought of him as a fine example of the best in American politics. However, the Nixon Administration had marked Gore as a man to defeat in the 1970 elections. Gore had led efforts to block several Nixon programs.

The Republicans picked William Brock, a 31-year-old Congressman, to challenge Gore.

Young people actively supported both candidates. A Young Voters for Brock (YVB) group was set up to hand out campaign literature and to help with canvassing. Young people were even more active in the Gore campaign, mostly as door-to-door canvassers.

For the most part, Brock's YVB groups were white and from middle- or upper-income families. The Gore youth group was a mixture of blacks and whites. It included many college student activists who had taken part in other campaigns.

When the hard fight was over, Brock had 562,645 votes; Gore had 518,858. What did the young workers contribute to the result?

Two political scientists who studied this campaign concluded that Brock would have won by a landslide if Gore's young canvassers had not been active.[3] Those workers influenced about 25,000 voters—or about 4 percent of the total.

Brock's canvassers, while not as active as Gore's, made a modest impact on voter decisions in upper-income precincts.

The major finding of the study: Canvassing was the single most effective technique used in either campaign.

Canvassing is far from political busy-work. In a close election, it may mean the difference between victory and defeat.

**Case 3. Tipping the Balance**

The more than nine million Americans of Spanish heritage represent 4.5 percent of our total population. More than five million are of Mexican ancestry and almost two million of Puerto Rican origin.

These people could be a strong force in politics in certain parts of the country. For example, there are more than one million Puerto Ricans in New York City and more than 2.5 million Mexican Americans, or Chicanos, in California. Also Texas, New Mexico, Arizona, and Colorado have large Chicano populations. In close elections these Puerto Ricans and Chicanos could "tip the balance" in favor of candidates who have pledged to help them. However, they have tended not to translate their numbers into vote power. In 1972, for example, only 46 percent of Mexican Americans were registered to vote and only 37.5 percent did vote in the presidential election. Of the Puerto Ricans, 53 percent were registered and 45 percent voted in 1972.

---

3. Martin Lupfer and David Price, "On the Merits of Face-to-Face Campaigning," *Social Science Quarterly* (December, 1972), pp. 535-543.

Those who do take part tend to support the Democrats. In each of the presidential elections from 1960 to 1972, more than 80 percent of the voters of Spanish heritage voted for the Democrat.

Two state-wide elections in the southwest in the 1970s show how these voters could "tip the balance" in close elections. In 1970, Democrat Joseph M. Montoya of New Mexico was the only Mexican American in the United States Senate. His bid for reelection was opposed by Anderson Carter, the Republican challenger.

Carter waged a hard, well-financed campaign against Montoya. Both President Richard Nixon and Vice-President Spiro Agnew gave strong support to Carter, since Montoya had been a leader against many of Nixon's policies.

Mexican Americans were aroused by Carter's challenge to Montoya. They backed Montoya solidly and "tipped the balance" in his favor. Montoya won by only 16,000 votes (52 percent of the total) with 77 percent of Chicano voters supporting him as compared to 47 percent of the "Anglo" voters. Thus, Montoya gained his slim margin of victory from his fellow Mexican Americans.

However, in 1970 in Arizona, Chicano voters let down Raul Castro, the Democrat running for governor. Castro hoped to beat the two-term Republican governor, Jack Williams. Castro needed strong support from Arizona's Chicanos, who make up 15 percent of the

Governor Raul Castro of Arizona takes part in the taping of a TV program in 1975.

state's population. He urged them to help Arizona get its first Mexican American as governor. Over 90 percent of the Chicanos who did vote supported Castro. But less than half of the eligible Chicano voters turned out, and Castro lost to Williams by less than 7000 votes. If a large majority of them had gone to the polls, Castro could have won.

Raul Castro vowed to try again in 1974. He worked hard to build a large base of support among Mexican Americans. This time he won by a narrow margin with the solid support of a large majority of eligible Chicano voters. Helping them "tip the balance" for Castro was a get-out-the-vote drive by Navajo Indians. They joined the winning coalition that made Raul Castro the first Chicano governor of Arizona.

1. What do these three cases suggest about how particular groups might have an impact on electoral politics?
2. In these cases what were some costs and benefits of participation?
3. In your opinion, was participation in electoral politics in these cases worth the costs?
4. To what extent should you, and people like you, become involved in electoral politics? Why?

## Who Ought to Participate in Public Elections?

A main theme of democracy is the belief that people ought to take part in elections. Yet many Americans do so little or not at all. In many elections less than half of the citizens eligible to vote actually bother to cast their ballots. Many, perhaps most, of the voters seem to know little about major public issues and are unfamiliar with most of the candidates on the ballot.

The gap between the "ideal" and the "real" political participation of Americans has led some people to be disappointed about American politics. However, one could respond by saying: "Well, I think our ideals are too unrealistic. When one considers how complex the issues have become and how much pressure Americans have on them to do other things, I believe we are quite active in politics." Or another could respond: "It is true that we fall short of our ideals. We should look for new and better ways to bring Americans into the election process." While people might agree about the facts of political participation in the United States, they might react to the evidence quite differently. There would be differences in value judgments.

In this lesson you are asked to judge conflicting statements about popular participation in public elections and to justify your judgments.

*Speaker 1:* Every citizen should vote in public elections, because one vote can make a difference. In 1839 Marcus Morton was elected governor of Massachusetts by a margin of one vote out of 102,066. In the 1916 presidential election Woodrow Wilson defeated Charles

Evans Hughes in California by a margin of 4000 votes out of the nearly one million cast. Less than one additional vote per precinct for Hughes would have won California for him, and with the addition of California's electoral votes he would have won the election. John F. Kennedy defeated Richard Nixon in 1960 by 112,803 popular votes out of 68.8 million total votes. This was a margin of less than one vote per precinct. In the 1968 election, Nixon's margin was very thin in Illinois and California. If Humphrey had won those two states, he would have become the new President rather than Nixon. One vote can make a difference!

*Speaker 2.* Some people do not vote because they are against all of the candidates. People who do not like any of the candidates have a perfect right to sit out the election.

*Speaker 3:* Even if one were to conclude that all the choices are unsatisfactory, it would be necessary to choose among them. Those who do not vote because they dislike all the candidates probably dislike some candidates less than others. The nonvoter helps the worst candidate's cause as much as the others. Edmund Burke said it best: "The only thing necessary for the triumph of evil is for good men to do nothing."

*Speaker 4:* Perhaps we should not be overly concerned that less than two-thirds of the electorate take part in public elections. Maybe this is a sign of general satisfaction with the political situation. We would have more reason to be concerned if suddenly all Americans were to become eager to take part and were making all sorts of demands on the government. Intense political activity by large numbers of people could result in severe conflict and disorder.

**"I'd like to have voted, but the line was too long."**

*Speaker 5:* Most of the people who fail to vote should not vote. They do not know the candidates. They are ignorant of the issues. We might be better off if we did not encourage people who lack education to vote. Maybe our democracy is better off because many lower-status citizens are apathetic about politics.

*Speaker 6:* You do not have to have a lot of money or a lot of education to know whether the government is doing a good job. If you're living in a ghetto, you know very well if the services you receive from the city are adequate. Someone once compared democracy to buying shoes. Making a shoe, like running the government, requires special knowledge and skill. But when you go to buy a pair of shoes, you know better than the shoemaker whether the shoes fit you or not. Citizens can judge whether the government is pinching them or whether the policies of the government "fit," or satisfy, them. I think many Americans, expecially poor Americans and members of oppressed minority groups, are sick of having decisions made for them by upper-class and middle-class elites. We have a right to participate in making the rules that affect us. That's what "Black Power" is all about. Black people want to gain control over the institutions that affect them. They want black police, black businesses, black-controlled schools, and so on. But to gain power and influence in the government, people have to take part in public elections.

*Speaker 7:* People should have some say in the decisions that affect their lives. People who don't take part in elections, or other forms of political activity, give up their most basic human rights. Since political participation is the essence of a democracy, no country where 40 percent of the people regularly fail to vote can call itself a true democracy.

*Speaker 8:* Many people don't take part because they are too busy with their own affairs. Many working people are too busy caring for a family and making a living to get too excited about politics. Working people generally get little out of giving precious time and energy to helping in an election campaign. Furthermore, it seems to make little difference who gets elected. Working people get little or no benefit from taking the time to vote.

*Speaker 9:* I believe that every citizen has the duty to vote in a public election. Therefore, I would propose that the government make a law that requires every citizen to vote or be subject to payment of a fine. This is the only way to make certain that our public officials will be elected according to the democratic principle of majority rule.

**1.** Identify the speakers with whom you agree or disagree.
**2.** Explain why you agree or disagree with each of the speakers. Do you find any statement with which you agree in part?

# 10 The Voting Decision

In the privacy of the voting booth, Americans influence their country's future through their choice of public officials. What factors lead a voter to prefer one candidate over another? To what extent do family, friends, co-workers, and other social groups influence choices? Are election campaigns a big factor? This chapter looks at these questions. Then we take up the question of whether or not the voting decision really does have a major impact on government policies.

## Voting Tendencies of Various Groups in Recent Presidential Elections

Do certain groups of American voters tend to support Democratic candidates? Do other groups tend to support the Republicans? *Table 5* shows that in several recent elections certain groups tended to prefer either the Democratic or Republican candidates for President.

On the basis of the data in *Table 5*, what factual judgments can you make about the relationship of the following factors to voter choices in presidential elections?

a. educational attainment
b. occupation
c. racial identity
d. age group

e. sex identity
f. religious identity
g. political party preference

Following are descriptions of three types of Americans. Use evidence from *Table 5* and previous discussions and tables to support your answers to the questions that follow these descriptions.

### Descriptions of Individuals

*Mr. Pietrowski* is a steelworker holding a semi-skilled job that pays about $10,000 a year. He is an officer of his local labor union. He attends the Catholic Church, is a member of the Elks Club, and takes part in social activities. He is a high school graduate. He is forty-six years old and has lived in a large eastern seaboard city all his life. His father came to this country from Poland in 1920.

*Mr. Young* owns a large store on the main street of a small midwestern city, population about 45,000. He is the president of the local Chamber of Commerce and is a leader in the city's civic and social activities. He earns over $70,000 a year and lives in a plush home on the edge of the city. He attends the Presbyterian Church. He graduated from his state university with a degree in business administration. He is forty-five years old.

228

**Table 5.** Percentage of Vote by Groups in Presidential Elections since 1960

| | 1960 | | 1964 | | 1968 | | | 1972 | |
|---|---|---|---|---|---|---|---|---|---|
| | **D** | **R** | **D** | **R** | **D** | **R** | **Wallace** | **D** | **R** |
| | **%** | **%** | **%** | **%** | **%** | **%** | **%** | **%** | **%** |
| NATIONAL | 50.1 | 49.9 | 61.3 | 38.7 | 43.0 | 43.4 | 13.6 | 38 | 62 |
| Men | 52 | 48 | 60 | 40 | 41 | 43 | 16 | 37 | 63 |
| Women | 49 | 51 | 62 | 38 | 45 | 43 | 12 | 38 | 62 |
| White | 49 | 51 | 59 | 41 | 38 | 47 | 15 | 32 | 68 |
| Nonwhite | 68 | 32 | 94 | 6 | 85 | 12 | 3 | 87 | 13 |
| College | 39 | 61 | 52 | 48 | 37 | 54 | 9 | 37 | 63 |
| High school | 52 | 48 | 62 | 38 | 42 | 43 | 15 | 34 | 66 |
| Grade school | 55 | 45 | 66 | 34 | 52 | 33 | 15 | 49 | 51 |
| Prof. & bus. | 42 | 58 | 54 | 46 | 34 | 56 | 10 | 31 | 69 |
| White collar | 48 | 52 | 57 | 43 | 41 | 47 | 12 | 36 | 64 |
| Manual | 60 | 40 | 71 | 29 | 50 | 35 | 15 | 43 | 57 |
| Farmers | 48 | 52 | 53 | 47 | 29 | 51 | 20 | — | — |
| Under 30 | 54 | 46 | 64 | 36 | 47 | 38 | 15 | 48 | 52 |
| 30–49 | 54 | 46 | 63 | 37 | 44 | 41 | 15 | 33 | 67 |
| 50 & older | 46 | 54 | 59 | 41 | 41 | 47 | 12 | 36 | 64 |
| Protestant | 38 | 62 | 55 | 45 | 35 | 49 | 16 | 30 | 70 |
| Catholic | 78 | 22 | 76 | 24 | 59 | 33 | 8 | 48 | 52 |
| Republicans | 5 | 95 | 20 | 80 | 9 | 86 | 5 | 5 | 95 |
| Democrats | 84 | 16 | 87 | 13 | 74 | 12 | 14 | 67 | 33 |
| Independents | 43 | 57 | 56 | 44 | 31 | 44 | 25 | 31 | 69 |

*Mr. Jameson* works at odd jobs on farms or in small rural towns. Every summer and fall he works as a migrant fruit picker. He travels from town to town looking for work. Often he is unemployed. He earns about $6000 a year. He is a member of the Baptist Church, but rarely attends. He does not belong to a labor union or to any social clubs. He dropped out of school as soon as he had finished the eighth grade.

**1.** In a presidential election which of the three types of persons described above is most likely to vote (a) for the Democratic candidates? (b) for the Republican candidates?
**2.** In a presidential election which of the three types of persons is (a) most likely to vote? (b) least likely to vote?
**3.** What are some weaknesses of trying to predict party preference, candidate choice, and likelihood of voting solely on the basis of social characteristics?

*Table 5:* Estimates from a national survey by American Institute of Public Opinion, THE GALLUP POLL, Princeton, New Jersey.

## Social-Group Influence on Voting

*Table 5* on page *229* shows that we can put any voter into a number of slots, or *social categories:* male or female; white or nonwhite; college, high school, or grade school education; job categories; young, middle-age, or elderly; and others. Some of these social characteristics can give us clues to how people are likely to vote.

In addition to these social identities, or categories, all of us belong to a number of *social groups.* The family is a social group. So are the students in your government class. All the students and teachers in your school make up a social group. Other social groups exist at work places, at church, and in the neighborhood. Some groups are very informal—a group of close friends. Others are quite formal with officers and membership rules.

Do the social groups that people belong to have an influence on their voting behavior? Let us see what political science has to say.

### Primary Groups and Voting

Primary groups have a direct and far-reaching influence on a person's beliefs and behavior. Primary groups are those in which people have a close, "face-to-face" relationship. The family, friendship groups, and small groups of fellow workers are examples of primary groups. What does *Table 6* show about the link between primary-group membership and voting?

### Secondary Groups and Voting

Secondary groups have an indirect, and usually smaller, influence on a person's beliefs and behavior. Examples of such groups include schools, churches, labor unions, political parties, the Chamber of Commerce, civic groups, the PTA, and so on. One may identify with several secondary groups, but contact with them tends to be impersonal.

Several million Americans belong to a labor union. This is one kind of secondary group. We often hear about how unions influence the voting behavior of their members. National union leaders often come out for one of the candidates for President. They back certain men and women for Congress. People from both major parties get

**Table 6. Relationship of Primary-Group Membership to Voting**

| Respondent Voted | Spouse Voted | | Family Voted | | Friends Voted | | Work Associates Voted | |
|---|---|---|---|---|---|---|---|---|
| | Dem. | Rep. | Dem. | Rep. | Dem. | Rep. | Dem. | Rep. |
| Democrat | 89% | 7% | 80% | 8% | 83% | 15% | 79% | 24% |
| Republican | 11 | 93 | 20 | 92 | 17 | 85 | 21 | 76 |

*Table 6:* Angus Campbell and others, *The American Voter* (New York: John Wiley & Sons, Inc., 1960). Used by permission.

A UAW canvasser seeks to drum up votes for union-supported candidates.

the union "seal of approval." But the record shows that far more Democrats than Republicans do so. Just how much influence does a labor union—and its leaders—have on the vote of union members?

Studies of how members of the United Auto Workers (UAW) voted in the 1952 and 1956 presidential elections help to answer this question. But as you read the evidence, keep in mind that it relates to only *one* union in *two* elections. Some unions—and some union leaders—work harder than do others to get members to vote a certain way. The UAW has a long record of strong political activity

In his book *When Labor Votes,* Arthur Kornhauser reports that in the 1952 presidential election two-thirds of the members of the UAW voted for the Democratic candidate, Adlai Stevenson. However, nearly 75 percent of UAW members strongly attached to the UAW and its leaders voted for Stevenson. Slightly more than 50 percent of UAW members who had a weak identification with the UAW and its leaders voted for Stevenson.

Two political scientists studied the voting behavior of UAW members in Detroit in the 1956 election. In Detroit—and elsewhere—the UAW leaders have been strong supporters of the Democratic party. Also it has been UAW policy to try to get members to take part in politics. Over 75 percent of UAW members in Detroit in 1956 said they were Democrats. Only 10 percent said they were Republicans, and about 15 percent said "independent." Of those auto workers who voted in the 1956 election, 72 percent cast ballots for Democrat Adlai Stevenson. Thus strong auto-worker support came for Stevenson in a year when he got only 42.2 percent of the vote in the nation.

The 1956 study of UAW members also showed that 65 percent favored more influence for labor unions in government. More than 65 percent said "it was all right" for unions to campaign for Stevenson. The study also showed that members who strongly identified with the UAW were more likely to follow the political advice of union leaders than were members who did not identify with the union.

### Cross-pressures and Voting

Social cross-pressures tend to limit or undercut the influence of social groups on voting behavior. Most people belong to, and identify with, several primary and secondary groups. When two or more groups pull a person in opposite directions, a cross-pressure exists. For example, Sally Smith grew up in a family with fairly strong Republican leanings. She now lives a few miles from her parents' home and sees them often. Her husband, a machinist and shop steward for his labor union, is a Democrat. Sally is caught between two opposing influences; she is in a cross-pressure situation. Sally may react (1) by not voting, or (2) by splitting her vote between Republican and Democratic candidates, or (3) by favoring the stronger of the conflicting influences. In our open society such opposing influences are commonplace. Note in the following examples how a person can be subject to social cross-pressures or to consistent social pressures on voter behavior.

Mr. Jankowski heads a big corporation. He is a Roman Catholic of Polish descent. His parents are pro-Democratic. Some of his personal friends support the Democratic party. Most of his business associates are pro-Republican. Mrs. Jankowski and her parents are Republicans. Clearly, Mr. Jankowski is caught in a social cross-pressure situation.

Mr. Brown is a business associate of Mr. Jankowski. Mr. Brown is a Protestant. His parents, wife, and close friends are pro-Republican. He is *not* caught in a cross-pressure situation. Rather, the social forces around him move him all the time in the direction of preference for Republican party candidates.

People faced by nonconflicting social pressures, such as Mr. Brown, tend to have consistent political attitudes. Such people tend to vote for candidates of one party and to decide for whom to vote early in a campaign or before it begins. They tend to have strong views about politics.

By contrast, people faced with social cross-pressures, such as Mr. Jankowski, tend to have conflicting political attitudes. Such people tend to vote a split ticket. They tend to decide for whom to vote

232

late in a campaign. They tend to have weak and shifting views about politics. Often a cross-pressure can only be settled by not voting or by showing little political interest.

Large numbers of Americans are faced by social cross-pressures. And these people tend to be *political independents*. How does this affect American politics? Experts think that it may help to keep the system stable. If most Americans were strongly partisan, political conflicts might become too heated. This could lead to violence. Political independents tend to shift their votes from party to party. Both major parties must compete for the "independent" vote at every election. To do so, both parties are forced to modify and moderate their views instead of taking very strong stands on some issues.

## Political Party Policies, Group Identification, and Voting

*Tables 5* and *7* (pages *229, 233*) show that certain groups tend to favor one of our major parties over the other. For example, both tables show that black people are likely to prefer Democrats.

*Caution.* Before going on, let us stress the limitations of the data in the tables. They show what people *tend* to do. When we say that blacks are highly likely to favor the Democratic party, we are making a tendency statement. And because it is a tendency statement, there are always exceptions. For example, manual workers *have tended to* vote for Democrats. Yet, 57 percent of manual workers voted for Republican Richard Nixon in 1972.

**Table 7. Political Party Identification by Groups**

|  | Republican | Democrat | Independent | Other | Not Sure |
|---|---|---|---|---|---|
| TOTAL | 22% | 45% | 27% | 3% | 3% |
| 18 to 29 years | 16 | 39 | 38 | 3 | 4 |
| 30 to 49 years | 21 | 46 | 27 | 3 | 3 |
| 50 years and over | 27 | 49 | 19 | 2 | 3 |
| White Protestant | 30 | 38 | 27 | 2 | 3 |
| White Catholic | 16 | 46 | 32 | 4 | 2 |
| Jewish | 21 | 56 | 20 | 3 | – |
| 8th grade | 21 | 53 | 15 | 3 | 8 |
| High school | 20 | 50 | 25 | 2 | 3 |
| College | 26 | 35 | 34 | 3 | 2 |
| White | 25 | 42 | 29 | 2 | 2 |
| Black | 6 | 72 | 11 | 2 | 9 |
| Voted in 1972 | 25 | 44 | 27 | 3 | 1 |
| Active citizenship | 27 | 30 | 29 | 2 | 2 |

*Table 7: Confidence and Concern: Citizens View American Government*, p. 320.
Reprinted by permission of the *Chicago Tribune*. All Rights Reserved.

233

Another limitation is that the data tell us about tendencies of the past. They show trends that may continue into the future, but we can't be certain. In order to detect new trends in American voter behavior, we cannot rely entirely on data about the past.

A third limitation is that the data disregard the personality factor. Everyone has a unique personality. Thus, people are not likely to respond in the exact same way to the same influences. For example, some unskilled, Roman Catholic workers always vote Republican, even though most of this group vote Democratic. And some well-to-do corporation executives vote Democratic, while most such people vote Republican.

**Republican Platform**

"A Better Future for All"

Proposed by the Committee on Resolutions to the
**Republican National Convention**
August 21, 1972 Miami Beach Florida

### Examining Political Party Differences

A study of the major party platforms over the past twenty to thirty years shows that both major parties try to appeal to as many voters as possible. Many planks in the opposing platforms say almost the same thing. Both parties have called for keeping up the fight against Communist aggression, support of the United Nations, strong national defense, higher Social Security benefits, farm price supports, and so on. The party in power "points with pride" to what it has done. The party out of power "views with alarm." It blames the ruling party for the sad state of affairs. It promises to set things straight when its candidates win.

The party platforms, however, do reveal differences in ideas and programs. Each party sets forth policies that appeal to different groups in our society. Gerald M. Pomper has reported, in *Elections in America,* his study of Democratic and Republican platforms from 1944 to 1964. He said that Republicans have put more emphasis than Democrats on national defense, on federal-state relations, and on holding down federal spending. Democrats have put more emphasis than Republicans on social-welfare programs and policies to aid labor unions. Pomper concluded:

> Republicans have tended to be regarded as better managers of the government and to be more trusted on issues of war and peace. Democrats have been regarded more highly in terms of domestic policy and group benefits.[1]

Notice that Pomper has made *tendency statements* about the differences between the two parties. One party tends to emphasize some issues more than the other does. But both parties have supported programs to aid black people, the needy, the farmers, and labor unions. Both parties have backed efforts to keep private business strong. Also both parties share many important goals. Their differences often are in how to reach goals, rather than in the goals themselves.

---

1. Gerald M. Pomper, *Elections in America* (New York: Dodd, Mead & Company, 1968).

234

Below are sketches of five persons who may or may not vote in an upcoming election. Read about each person, and consider how he or she is likely to vote.

*Steve Smith* in 1976 worked in a steel mill. He was in a carpool with a group of fellow workers who were all close friends. They would hunt, fish, play cards, and in general have good times together very often during off-work hours. Steve's friends backed the Republican candidate for governor. But Steve was a strong supporter of the steel-workers union. He felt that the union leaders watched out for the best interests of the union members. He had always followed the political advice of the union leaders. They were campaigning for the Democratic candidate for governor. Furthermore, Steve's wife and parents were life-long Democrats who were backing the Democratic candidate. Steve went to church regularly. He looked up to the minister and often followed his advice. The minister was going to vote for the Republican candidate for governor.

*Emma Jones* has lived in Centerville all her life. Her parents, four brothers and a sister, and six aunts and uncles all live in Centerville. Next month the town will be voting for mayor. Two strong candidates are running. Brown, the Democratic candidate, has been a long-time friend of the Jones family. Emma's parents and relatives are all campaigning for Brown against the Republican candidate, Mr. Green.

*George Johnson* is a black man living in Chicago. The year is 1976. Mr. Johnson is a manual worker. His wife and two brothers prefer the Democratic party. He belongs to a labor union. The union leader has urged all members to back the Democrats in the upcoming election. Mr. Johnson also admires several black leaders. He read in the newspaper that they were urging all blacks to support the Democrats. He also knows that members of black organizations around the country are supporting the Democrats. He identifies strongly with these organizations. Mr. Johnson is deciding for whom to vote.

*Harold Murphy* has just moved to Centerville. He is not familiar with local political issues. Mrs. Murphy takes no interest in politics and seldom bothers to vote. Harold belongs to no social organizations. He spends most of his off-work time watching TV or drinking beer at the corner tavern. He is a manual worker. His three close friends care little or nothing about politics.

*Sylvia Bender* is an upper-income, college-educated business-woman. She is white, a Protestant, and a member of the Women's Business and Professional Club. Her firm has a membership in the United States Chamber of Commerce. She employs nonunion workers, and wants to keep it that way.

**1.** Which candidate or party is each of these people likely to favor?
**2.** Support your answers in item 1 by applying these concepts: social categories, primary group, secondary group, cross-pressures.
**3.** What are some problems of predicting how these people will vote or which party they will support?

## The Impact of Campaigns on Voting

Victory on election day is the main purpose of a political campaign. For example, through an election campaign, a Republican candidate tries to keep the votes of loyal Republicans and get as many of them as possible to turn out on election day. He or she also tries to win the support of political independents and of other voters not known to be strong Democrats. Other purposes of a political campaign are to publicize the ideas and the name of a political party, to raise money for the party, and to recruit party workers.

Campaigns are a chief means of communication between political leaders and followers. Candidates supply the voter with information about themselves, their party, and their stand on public issues. This information may help the voter decide on whom to support. At the same time, voters tell the candidate how they stand on public issues and what they want from government. This information may influence the decisions of elected public officials.

One way to see if campaigns have a big impact on voter choices is to find out if voters make up their minds before or during a campaign. What does *Table 8* suggest about the impact of election campaigns on voting?

*Table 8* shows that about a third of the voters have decided how to vote for President prior to the party conventions. These must be loyal Democrats and Republicans. It doesn't seem to matter who will be the party nominee or what the specific issues will be in the campaign.

The party loyalists, or partisans, tend to follow "the party line" on issues. Partisans tend not to study the pros and cons. Rather they use their view of their party's position as a guide to their own position about an issue. Campaigns tend to have little influence on the voting decisions of this kind of person.

**Table 8. Time of Decision on Voter Choice for President**

| Time Decided | 1948 | 1952 | 1956 | 1960 | 1964 | 1968 | 1972 |
|---|---|---|---|---|---|---|---|
| Before Conventions | 37% | 34% | 57% | 30% | 40% | 33% | 43% |
| During Conventions | 28 | 31 | 18 | 30 | 25 | 22 | 17 |
| During Campaign | 25 | 31 | 21 | 36 | 33 | 38 | 35 |
| Don't Remember | 10 | 4 | 4 | 4 | 3 | 7 | 4 |

*Table 8:* © Copyright by Institute for Social Research, The University of Michigan. Reprinted with permission of the Center for Political Studies, Institute for Social Research.

As shown in *Table 8*, a minority of voters decided how to vote during the campaign. These are political independents and people with only weak ties to a party. The campaign issues and the appeal of candidates—not their party ties—determine their voting choices. In a close election these "undecided" voters hold the balance of power. The candidate waging the best campaign is most likely to win their votes.

### The Impact of Social Unrest, Exciting Issues, and Appealing Candidates on Election Campaigns and Voting

Many an election is won by means of a well-run campaign. One candidate simply works harder than another to create a good image and get out the vote. In other elections there are other things that seem to matter more than how well the campaign is run. (1) At times there is unrest in a city, a state, or the nation. Before a campaign starts, the voters may have decided that it is "time for a change." (2) Some serious issue—inflation, high taxes, crime, or war—may dominate a campaign. (3) At times, one candidate or another will simply outshine the opponent no matter how well each runs the campaign.

The Great Depression of the 1930s was a severe social upheaval. In the election of 1932 the voters were ready for a change. For seventy years the Republicans had held the Presidency except for Cleveland and Wilson. More people identified with the Republican party than with the Democrats. But in 1932 and after, many people switched parties. In the minds of many people the depression was linked with Republican policies. Since the 1930s, the Democrats have been the majority party. In election after election the Democrats have had the support of a majority of black people and manual workers—as well as other broad support. Of course, other events, issues, and appealing candidates have helped put the Republicans back in power from time to time.

The 1960s was a period of severe social unrest related to race relations, the war in Vietnam, and radical student protest. Some political scientists think this unrest had a big impact on party identification and voting. George Wallace and his American Independent party in the 1968 presidential election won over many voters in areas of Democratic party strength. The Republicans, before the Watergate scandal of 1973, had gained support among all groups, except blacks, that had supported the Democrats strongly for many years.

The personal appeal of a candidate shows up clearly in the 1952 and 1956 elections for President. Many typical Democratic voters cast their ballots for Dwight D. Eisenhower while at the same time voting Democrats into Congress. Also independent voters were mostly for Eisenhower, which is another sign of his great personal appeal.

Major issues have had a big impact on other recent campaigns. In 1960 a major issue was Democrat John Kennedy's Roman Catholic religion. Many usual Democratic voters switched to Republican Richard Nixon because they didn't want a Catholic as President. Some Roman Catholics who usually voted Republican backed Kennedy in this election.

In 1972 many typical backers of the Democratic party voted for Nixon while supporting Democrats for other offices. These "ticket splitters" disagreed with the political beliefs and style of Democrat George McGovern. In this election, 33 percent of those who identified with the Democratic party said they voted for Nixon. (Four years earlier only about 12 percent of those who identified with the Democratic party voted for Nixon, but another 14 percent did vote for George Wallace.) McGovern seems to have turned off many Democrats with his liberal views. His opponents said he favored abortion, income redistribution through welfare and tax reform, and big cutbacks in defense spending. Meanwhile President Nixon had won some Democratic support by setting up price and wage controls and by improving relations with Russia and China. In 1972, for the first time since the start of scientific polling of voters in 1936, a majority of the nation's manual workers said they voted for the Republican presidential candidate.

Breadlines like this one on Fifth Avenue in New York City in the early days of the Great Depression moved the country to seek a change in government. Franklin D. Roosevelt won the election in 1932.

*Top:* John F. Kennedy speaks with Boston's Cardinal Cushing. Kennedy's religion was an issue in the 1960 campaign. *Bottom:* F. D. Roosevelt was elected to a fourth term in the wartime election of 1944.

*Top:* Welcome signs at the 1956 Convention suggest the warm personality of Eisenhower that helped him win two elections. *Bottom:* Senator Barry Goldwater was seen as ''too extremist'' by many voters in 1964, and Johnson won in a landslide.

DEWEY DEFEATS TRUMAN

President Harry Truman holds up a newspaper which declared Thomas E. Dewey the winner in 1948 on the basis of early returns. By morning, however, Truman took the lead and won the hard-fought race.

**1.** Which of the following two types of people is more likely to decide for whom to vote as a result of the events of an election campaign? Why?

Aurelia Compean, a lawyer, is very active in the Republican party in Zenith City. Her husband, her associates at work, and her closest friends also are active supporters of the Republican party.

Lucy Gonzalez is a professor of economics at Zenith City College. Her husband, a successful accountant, is a strong supporter of the Republican party. Most of Lucy's colleagues at the city college either support the Democrats or are political independents. Unlike her husband, who is a political activist, Lucy is mildly interested in political affairs. She tends to split her vote between Democrats and Republicans but tends to favor candidates of the local Democratic party a bit more than the Republicans.

**2.** Think back to a very recent local, state, or national election campaign. Was social unrest a key factor in the election outcome? How about issues and appealing candidates? Explain.

240

## The Impact of Voting on Government

Upon signing the Voting Rights Act of 1965, President Lyndon Johnson said, "The vote is the most powerful instrument ever devised by man for breaking down injustice and destroying the terrible walls that imprison men because they are different from other men." He was saying that voting is a major political resource, that through the ballot common people can influence the government.

People who believe in democracy stress that voting is a way to influence public officials. Through the vote citizens can defeat unfit officials and support those who are suitable. Abraham Lincoln's famous phrase, "government of the people, by the people, and for the people" only has meaning in our country if the vote is an important political resource.

Some people believe that voting has little or no impact on the making of public policy. These people view voting as merely a political ritual (ceremony) which gives citizens the feeling that they can influence policies.

Does voting really pay off? What is the impact of voting on the decisions of public officials? Are individuals and groups really better off because of using the right to vote?

Evidence on the following pages suggests answers to these questions. However, realize that this evidence, though useful, is limited in scope.

Newark mayor, Kenneth Gibson, and Congresswoman Shirley Chisholm were among the blacks who won public office in the late 1960s.

241

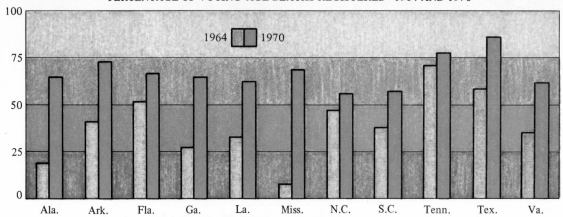

### Black Votes and Black Power

Prior to the 1960s a majority of black adults were not registered and did not take part in public elections. During the 1960s rising political awareness among blacks, along with the new laws to protect and extend voting rights, led to a big rise in participation of black people in public elections.

In 1940 only 5 percent of voting-age blacks were registered to vote. In 1970, five years after passage of the Voting Rights Act, the number rose to 67 percent. The graph on this page compares voter registration in eleven southern states before and after the Voting Rights Act of 1965. The big rise in black voters is one sign of potential black power. What have these new voters achieved?

One way to see how effective the vote is as a political resource is to look at the status of blacks before and after their wide use of the ballot. If, indeed, voting has a real impact, then there must be a link between black votes and the ability of blacks to influence government.

In the 1960s the Congress passed major civil rights laws. These laws boosted the opportunities of black people in education, jobs, housing, and use of public facilities. These new laws did not come about simply by the rise in voting by blacks. The 1960s were years of unusual concern for the rights of minorities and the poor. Also to win equal rights many blacks used other tactics besides the ballot. They took part in picketing, boycotts, sit-ins, and protest marches. Black voting along with these other activities helped get the new laws.

Black voters have a good chance to help swing a close election for President. Many blacks live in the large cities of the big states having the most electoral votes. Suppose these blacks vote as a bloc, backing the candidate who seems ready to help them the most. They may swing a close election to that person. Both parties know about

Graph: Southern Regional Council. Used by permission.

this black power. In recent years the party platforms and campaign promises of presidential candidates have paid attention to the hopes of black voters. In states with many black voters the persons running for Congress also paid more and more attention to the views of black voters.

Large groups of blacks in fifteen states and several big cities also have the chance to swing many local and state elections by voting as a bloc. Notice in *Tables 9–10* that blacks make up over 25 percent of the population of five states and 40 percent in eleven major cities.

*Table 11* shows that blacks have used their new voting power to elect many blacks to public office. In 1960 there were less than

**Table 9. States Where Most Blacks Live**

| State | Black Population | Percent of Total |
|---|---|---|
| New York | 2,166,933 | 11.9 |
| Illinois | 1,425,674 | 12.8 |
| Texas | 1,419,677 | 12.7 |
| California | 1,400,143 | 7.0 |
| Georgia | 1,190,779 | 25.9 |
| N. Carolina | 1,137,664 | 22.4 |
| Louisiana | 1,088,734 | 29.9 |
| Florida | 1,049,578 | 15.5 |
| Pennsylvania | 1,016,514 | 8.6 |
| Michigan | 991,066 | 11.2 |
| Ohio | 970,477 | 9.1 |
| Alabama | 908,247 | 26.4 |
| Virginia | 865,388 | 18.6 |
| Mississippi | 815,770 | 36.8 |
| S. Carolina | 789,041 | 30.5 |

**Table 10. Blacks in Cities**

| City | Black Percent of Total Population |
|---|---|
| Washington, D.C. | 71 |
| Newark | 54 |
| Gary, Indiana | 53 |
| Atlanta | 51 |
| Baltimore | 46 |
| New Orleans | 45 |
| Detroit | 44 |
| Wilmington, Delaware | 44 |
| Birmingham, Alabama | 42 |
| Richmond | 42 |
| St. Louis | 41 |
| Memphis | 39 |

**Table 11. Increase in Black Elected Public Officials**

| Black Elected Officeholders | 1970 | 1975 |
|---|---|---|
| U.S. Senators and Representatives | 10 | 18 |
| State legislators, executives | 168 | 281 |
| Mayors | 40 | 135 |
| Other local officials | 559 | 1,743 |
| Judges, magistrates | 114 | 204 |
| Police chiefs, law-enforcement officials | 47 | 134 |
| Members of local school boards | 362 | 894 |

*Tables 9–10:* 1970 Census, Bureau of the Census.
*Table 11:* Figures from the National Roster of Black Elected Officials, Volume 5, published by The Joint Center for Political Studies, Washington, D.C., 1975. Used by permission.

200 black officials; in 1975 there were 3503. Most (1237) were members of town and city councils. There also were 276 state legislators and 135 black mayors. Nine major cities had black mayors: Los Angeles, Atlanta, Detroit, Cincinnati, Newark, Dayton, Gary, Raleigh, and Washington, D. C..

The increase of blacks in office has been very notable in the South. With 598 blacks winning in 1972, the number of black officials rose to 1307 in eleven southern states by 1974. This was five times as many in office as in 1968.

These states are Alabama, Arkansas, Florida, Georgia, Louisiana, Mississippi, North and South Carolina, Tennessee, Texas, Virginia.

The biggest jump came in Alabama, where 117 won local offices. Greene County became the first county in the nation to have all black officials. Blacks in Selma won five of the ten city council seats. In 1965 only 2.3 percent of eligible blacks were registered in Selma. By 1972 the number rose to 67 percent. *Table 12* shows five southern states among the ten states with the most black officials.

In spite of big gains from 1965 to 1974, blacks held less than 1 percent of the 521,760 elective offices in the United States. But a steady rise in black registration and voting should lead to larger numbers of black officeholders in the near future.

What have blacks gained by taking a bigger part in state and local elections? They have got some better schools. They have won improved legal protection and police services. Such public services as garbage collection, street upkeep, and parks and playgrounds have improved.

Such gains haven't been won by all blacks in every part of the United States. And black people have more of these things in some places than in others. But there does seem to be a link between political activity by blacks and their gains in schooling, legal protection, and other public services. However, we should note that the ballot has not been a powerful political resource in helping blacks win social equality or big gains in income.

The next case, about black voting in Tuskegee, Alabama, shows both the power and the limits of the vote as a political resource.

### Black Power in Tuskegee

Tuskegee is a small town in Macon County in Alabama. It is the home of Tuskegee Institute, the famous school for black students founded by Booker T. Washington. Tuskegee is in the heart of the deep South's "black belt." A majority of the residents are black.

### Table 12. Ten States with Most Black Officials, 1974

| | | | |
|---|---|---|---|
| Michigan | 194 | New Jersey | 152 |
| Mississippi | 191 | Arkansas | 150 |
| New York | 174 | Alabama | 149 |
| North Carolina | 159 | Louisiana | 149 |
| Illinois | 152 | Ohio | 139 |

*Table 12: Statistical Abstract*

244

## TUSKEGEE BLACK VOTER REGISTRATION, 1952–1966

Percent of registered voters who were black

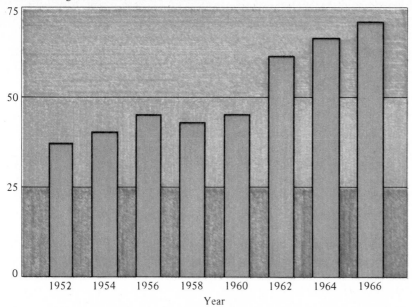

Year

But until 1962 a majority of the registered voters there were whites, as the graph shows.

Until recently, black voter registration and voter turnout had been low in Tuskegee, as elsewhere in the South. Legal and social barriers had been set up to keep most blacks from voting, as we have seen.

The white minority of Tuskegee ran the city government. Whites got the better services. For example, streets in white neighborhoods were paved while those in black areas were not. Whites had their garbage picked up three times a week, and blacks once a week. City housing laws kept blacks out of certain sections of the city. Recreation facilities were segregated.

The Macon County Democratic Club (MCDC) tried to organize blacks in Tuskegee in order to influence the local government. It worked hard to register black voters. Before every election, the MCDC met to choose candidates likely to favor the interests of the black community. Then the MCDC would urge all blacks in Tuskegee to vote for the MCDC slate.

For the most part the attempts of the MCDC to influence public officials failed. Up to 1964, black voters were a minority. They couldn't

*Chart Data:* From William R. Keech, *The Impact of Negro Voting: The Role of the Vote in the Quest for Equality,* © 1968 by Rand McNally & Company, Chicago, Table III-1, p. 26. Adapted in graph form by permission of Rand McNally College Publishing Company.

245

elect a black to public office. Even white candidates having black support felt that they had to follow the traditions of the white community. This meant that the blacks would be shortchanged.

**Blacks Become the Voting Majority.** Finally tradition was shattered in 1964. Tuskegee blacks became a voting majority. The MCDC got some blacks to run for office. Some white candidates promised to support black interests if elected. The MCDC agreed to back such white candidates.

In the 1964 election the MCDC got out enough black votes to elect every candidate on the MCDC slate. The new mayor was a white man who had promised to support black interests. Four whites who had made such promises won seats on the city council. For the first time since Reconstruction days, two blacks got on the city council. Two blacks were elected to the school board and two as justices of the peace. In 1966 a black won the contest for county sheriff. Black power had worked.

The MCDC could have picked an all-black slate. It chose not to do so. It wanted to show that it was willing and able to work with whites. Such an example might get whites in other parts of Alabama to work with blacks. The MCDC wanted to use black power to help black people, not to hurt whites.

Black voting power helped to change some public policies in Tuskegee. But more than the vote was needed. The MCDC kept reminding officials that they had been elected with black votes and that some favors were in order.

One of the first rewards was the paving of streets in black neighborhoods. Garbage service for blacks and whites was equalized. The new city council got rid of the housing laws that discriminated against blacks. Public parks and swimming pools were integrated. Before 1964 no blacks were appointed to serve on any city boards. After the election blacks got seats on every appointive board.

Voting power didn't win social equality for blacks. Nor did it raise their incomes as a group. But it did win big legal and political gains. These changes came about when blacks became a voting majority. Bloc voting helped them get results. But it wasn't the vote alone that turned the tide. A strong organization—the MCDC—had to organize the voters and then put pressure on officials to carry out their election promises.

**A Black Man Runs for Mayor.** In 1972 Tuskegee's black leaders took another big step to add to their political power. They got Johnny Ford to become the first black candidate for mayor in Tuskegee. He ran against C. M. Keever, who had won in 1964 with MCDC support and had been serving since then.

Most of the city's blacks, plus a few whites, supported Ford, who won by only 124 votes. Five blacks and only one white won city council seats.

246

Mayor Ford tried to help the poorer people of his town. He tried to attract new industries and investment money to create more jobs and higher pay. To reach his goals, Mayor Ford was willing to deal with anyone who could help. In particular he sought the help of Alabama Governor George Wallace, who at one time had been a strong supporter of racial segregation. In 1974 Mayor Ford described his relationship with Governor Wallace in practical political terms.

> I don't know if he's really changed the way they're all saying he has, but we've sure arrived at a good rapport. I just seem to get along with him. I think I understand him, and he understands me. Whatever, it's been [good] as far as Tuskegee is concerned. We've had about $9 million in industry steered in here so far. [Of course] associating with him like I have has cost me in terms of criticism, but it's been worth it. My hopes for building up this town are . . . a lot more important to me than any amount of carping.[2]

As shown by the political success of the MCDC and Mayor Ford, the vote can be used—along with other techniques—to get changes.

---

2. Quotation from *New Times,* March 8, 1974, p. 57. Copyright © 1974 by Marshall Frady. Reprinted by permission of The Sterling Lord Agency, Inc.

**1.** How effective was voting as a political resource in Tuskegee? Discuss the limitations as well as the power of the vote as a way to influence government and social change.

**2.** What is your value judgment of the political tactics of the MCDC and Mayor Ford? Do you approve or disapprove of the way the MCDC and Mayor Ford used political power to help their cause?

### Three Views of the Impact of Voting on Government

Following are three views of the impact of voting on government. On the basis of evidence given in Unit Three (pages 168–257), decide which of the views is the more accurate. You should think in terms of more-or-less rather than either-or. Each of the three views tells us something about the election process in the United States. You should decide which is the more accurate picture of reality as shown in evidence presented previously.

#### Elections as Mandates

Some people view elections as providing mandates for public policy. A *mandate* tells an official how to act in behalf of the people he or she represents. The "mandate view" holds that public elections are great debates over issues between rival candidates. The voters show what they want the government to do (or not do) by voting for the candidate who represents their ideas about the issues debated in the campaign. Thus the winning candidate is given a mandate by the voters to carry out certain public policies.

The "mandate view" suggests that voters hold the power to control the policy decisions of officials. Government is a direct reflection of the wishes of the people. Officials who violate their "mandates" are turned out of office by the voters.

#### Elections as Indirect Influencers of Government

Some people view elections as indirectly influencing, not directly controlling, the decisions of officials. The "indirect influence view" holds that voters control the jobs of elected officials, who must therefore pay attention to what the voters want. But the masses of voters can't give specific policy directions to the winning candidates. There are just too many issues raised in a campaign, and different groups of voters support the winners for different reasons.

The voters can't dictate exactly what the elected official must do. Yet he or she must always consider the reactions of the voters when making policy decisions. The official must do this because the voters can put someone else in the office at the next election. The need to win public approval in an election serves to influence the actions of the elected official.

#### Elections as Rituals

Another view of elections is that they are rituals, or ceremonies. Their main function is to give officials the lawful right to make policy. Elections make people feel that they have helped to choose officials.

Shanks in the *Buffalo Evening News*

**It's the Other Side of the Mountain That Counts**

Shanks suggests that it is performance after the election that counts more than campaign promises.

Elections give people the feeling of political participation so that they will readily accept the authority of public officials.

The "ritual view" of elections holds that the voters don't have the chance to make meaningful choices between candidates with conflicting ideas about policies. Rather, the rival candidates try to blur any real differences in beliefs. Thus the voter must choose candidates on the basis of personality, campaign advertising, or party loyalty.

The "ritual view" suggests that the voter has little or no influence on the making of public policy, since candidates are elected without meaningful debate about policy questions. Officials are relatively free from the influence of the voter so long as they avoid blunders that could bring a loss of public confidence.

**1.** On the basis of evidence presented in this unit, which of these views (mandate, indirect influence, or ritual) is the more accurate account of the impact of voting on government? Explain.
**2.** Which view of elections is most desirable? Explain.

## Should You Be a Political Partisan?

A *political independent* refuses to identify with a major political party. In the United States that means either the Republican or Democratic party. A *partisan,* by contrast, is a loyal party supporter. Which should you be—independent or partisan?

### Rising Political Independence

More and more Americans say they are political independents. The number rose from 23 percent of those eligible to vote in 1964, to 30 percent in 1968, to more than 35 percent in 1974. The graph shows changes since 1952. Notice that by 1966 the independents outnumbered the Republicans. Both major parties seem to have had less appeal in the early 1970s than in the preceding twenty years.

In recent years both major parties have lost ground to the independents.

Some political scientists view this increase in political independents as part of a trend toward the gradual disappearance of the political party in the United States. Others think that much of the recent discontent with the major parties is strictly short-term and will pass

### PARTY IDENTIFICATION OF THE AMERICAN ELECTORATE SINCE 1952

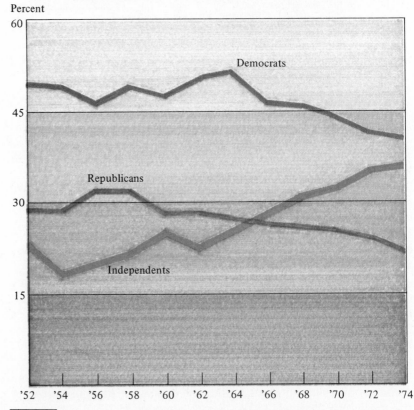

Graph: Based on data gathered by the Center for Political Studies of the Institute for Social Research, The University of Michigan. Used by permission

with changes in leaders and policies. But even if the major parties have a future, they predict, voters will become "ever more independent" than in the past.

State government workers look on as Governor James Longley of Maine signs an executive order. Longley campaigned as an independent in 1974 and won in a big upset over the major party candidates.

### Young Independents

Many young people have decided not to identify with either the Democratic or Republican party. A 1972 nationwide poll of high school students showed that 31 percent favored the Republicans, 29 percent the Democrats.[3] About 38 percent said they were political independents. In a 1974 national survey of college students by the Gallup Poll, 49 percent said they preferred neither major party. About 37 percent said they were Democrats, and only 14 percent said Republicans.

Young adults always have been more likely to be political independents than their elders. What is new is (1) the very large number of independents among young people and (2) the growing number of independents among all age-groups.

## Two Types of Independents

There are two distinct types of political independent—and they cut across all age-groups: the apathetic and the activist. The two types reject party affiliation for different reasons.

The *apathetic independents* have little or no interest in politics. They seldom, if ever, bother to vote. They tend to have little political knowledge and do not care much about issues and elections. For one reason or another, they have tuned out public affairs and politics.

3. The Purdue Opinion Panel, *The Development of Political Attitudes.* Poll Number 96. West Lafayette, Indiana, Purdue University, December 1972, p. 3

251

Most of them in our society are found among less-educated and lower-income groups. These people feel apart from the main course of American life.

The *activist independents,* on the other hand, have a strong interest in politics and many ideas about how to improve government. They are very much tuned in to public affairs and politics. But they believe that needed reforms can't be won through the Democratic or Republican parties. Thus, these people choose to work outside the party system to achieve political change. Most are well-educated, upper-income people with high status jobs. They make up a very small part of the independent group.

### The In-betweeners

More and more American voters occupy the middle ground between obvious independents and strong partisans. These "in-betweeners" take part to some extent in elections and tend to show a moderate interest in public affairs. But they have not given up on political parties. In this group are people who shift their allegiance from one party to the other with changing circumstances.

The in-between people are "ticket-splitters." For instance, a ticket-splitter in 1972 might have voted for Republican Richard Nixon for President, for a Democratic candidate for the United States Senate, and for a mixture of Democrats and Republicans for state and local offices.

"Straight-ticket" voters choose the candidates of one party only. They are the truly devoted partisans.

During the 1940s and 1950s a majority of American voters were loyal partisans. Rarely did they cross lines and vote for a candidate of the *other* party. During the 1960s the number of straight-ticket voters slowly dropped. In the 1968 election only 43 percent of the voters said they voted the straight ticket. In the 1972 election the number fell to less than 40 percent.

Most ticket-splitters tend to support the candidates of one party more than the other. But they still reserve their right to choose "the best person for the job." As a group, they tend to be better educated, more informed, and more interested in politics and public issues than the strong partisans are.

According to two experts on ticket-splitters, "These are the most discriminating voters . . . and offer the best hope for [bringing new life to our democratic system]. They will be the third force in the politics of the 1970s—they are the new independent electorate."[4]

Most ticket-splitters vote on the basis of issues and candidates rather than party. But even though they are independent voters, most

---

4. Walter De Vries and Lance Tarrance, Jr., *The Ticket-Splitter: A New Force in American Politics* (Grand Rapids: William B. Eerdmans Publishing Company, 1972).

are not quite ready to give up on the party system. A key political question for the near future is: Will the ticket-splitters become *more* or *less* independent from the major political parties?

## Cynicism, Independence, and Partisanship

*Political cynicism* is a lack of trust in government and politicians (page 155). Those who strongly identify with a major political party are less likely than independents to express political cynicism. Thus one might expect that a drop in partisanship would be linked with a rise in political cynicism.

Just so. Recent nationwide surveys show a remarkable rise in political cynicism in the past few years (pages 155–156). One sign is the growing tendency to believe that the government favors special interests at the expense of the public. In 1964 only 28 percent of American adults said that the government unfairly favored particular groups or individuals. In 1972, however, 58 percent said that the government gives favors to a few privileged special interest groups.[5]

The rising tide of cynicism can be seen especially among young people. It is in this group that we find the most political independents. In the mid-1960s the young were much less cynical about politics than the middle-aged group was. Ten years later the younger adults are at least as cynical about politics as other age-groups. Many young people distrust especially the major political parties. In a national sample of high school seniors, 58 percent said that the major parties should be either "fundamentally reformed" or "done away with."[6]

Is the rise in political cynicism a sign of massive political change linked with the long-run decline of our two-party system? Do you share the feelings of discontent with political parties expressed by a growing number of Americans? What are your speculations about the long-run significance of this political cynicism for the future of our two-party system?

## The Case for Partisanship

Some people say that taking part in either Democratic or Republican party affairs is the best way for most people to influence government. Two political scientists who have also been political activists say:

> American political parties, whatever their current limitations, offer the best potential means for achieving broad citizen participation in politics and continuing citizen influence in the direction of gov-

5. Figures from Arthur H. Miller, et. al., *A Majority Party in Disarray.* Paper read at the Annual Meeting of the American Political Science Association, 1973, p. 45.
6. From *The New Morality: A Profile of American Youth in the 70's* by Daniel Yankelovich. Copyright © 1974 by the JDR 3rd Fund, Inc. Used with permission of McGraw-Hill Book Company.

ernment . . . . They occupy too strategic a position in American politics to be bypassed or ignored.[7]

Many people argue for partisanship because they believe you can't win any other way. Through custom and law the major parties have such a foothold that it is very hard to work around them. The rules of the political game in America give the two major parties a virtual monopoly of the election process. In most states the law makes it difficult for a political independent or a minor party to get on the ballot.

Independent and third-party candidates face other handicaps. (1) They get little exposure from the mass media. (2) They are usually supported by weak political organizations with very limited experience, skills, and financial resources. (3) Most serious, government in the United States, on all levels, reflects the dominance of the two major parties. For example, Congress is organized on party lines. Leaders are chosen according to which major party holds the most seats. Committee assignments are made on a basis of major party affiliation.

The two parties have a similar lock on state and local government. Even if political independents win election to public office, they are often hamstrung in trying to accomplish their aims.

Rogers C. B. Morton, a prominent Republican leader and cabinet member in the early 1970s, suggests:

> If you want to be effective politically, you ought to be a Republican or Democrat. . . .
>
> Independent voters deny themselves the right to participate in the nominating processes, as well as such other important party functions as candidate recruitment, platform writing and fund raising. . . .[8]

### The Case for Nonpartisanship

In spite of the many strong arguments for partisanship, some political scientists and politicians advocate political independence. They admit that the "rules of the game" favor the partisans. Yet they would rather focus on what should be or could be rather than on what is. They argue and work for ways to loosen the grip of the two-party system on the political process.

---

7. John S. Saloma, III, and Frederick H. Sontag, *Parties: The Real Opportunity for Effective Citizen Politics* (New York: Vintage Books, A Division of Random House, Copyright © 1972 by The Twentieth Century Fund). Used by permission of Random House, Inc.

8. Rogers C. B. Morton, "Why You Should Be a Republican." Copyright © 1972 by Quadrangle/The New York Times Book Co. Reprinted by permission of Quadrangle/The New York Times Book Co. from *The New York Times Guide for New Voters,* pp. 41–42. Edited by Harold Faber.

The case for becoming an independent is stated by Dick Simpson, a political science professor and an independent member of the Chicago City Council:

> The argument for working within the regular parties is not as strong as proponents would pretend; the record of those who would reform parties from within is not as good as it should be. . . .
>
> Parties are difficult to reform—particularly those as fossilized and entrenched as the Republican and Democratic parties—so *competition,* not exhortation, is the best way to move them. If the parties know that whenever they nominate second-rate candidates they will have to run against independents with volunteer armies working for their election, as well as against opponents from the other party, they may learn the necessity for internal change. Should parties nominate good candidates and begin to take progressive stands on the new cleavages of our time, independents are free to join them and the independent movement will disappear.[9]

Young campaigners work for the reelection of President Nixon in 1972.

---

9. Reprinted from *Winning Elections* © 1972 by Dick Simpson, with permission of The Swallow Press, Inc., Chicago.

## Which Way?

Most independent candidates do not succeed. Nor, having got elected, do independents usually have the organization to put their objectives across. Independence—almost by definition—rules out such organization.

On the other hand, there is no guarantee that reformers working *within* the party structure will be any better off than the independent. In some ways they are worse off. They, too, need organizational machinery to reach their goals. And this machinery may well be controlled by a party faction opposed to their views. Furthermore, reformers must present an appearance of loyalty to party aims even when these aims conflict with their own.

So a strong case can be made for going either way.

Republican leader Rogers C. B. Morton urges young people with complaints against the system to seek their reforms within the framework of a political party:

> The political party is the locomotive that puts the government in motion. In its cars are the people who will establish government and maintain it until the next election. Perhaps, like the railroads, we major parties need to modernize a bit. What better time for the new, young voter to get into the act?[10]

But independent Chicago alderman Dick Simpson says:

> If parties fail to reform, independent political organizations, not other parties, may well emerge as the potential framework for a new politics. . . . In effect, independents are saying to existing parties, "Send us the oppressed, the citizens fed up with the political process, the belligerent, the alienated, the ones for whom you can find no use; with their idealism and their labor we will create a more humane political system."[11]

Which way should you go? The following questions may help you decide.

• Do either the Republicans or the Democrats tend to believe in and work to achieve objectives that you can support?

• Do either the Republicans or the Democrats tend to nominate candidates for public office that appeal to you?

• Do either of the two major parties seem flexible enough to permit changes that you, and others like you, might think necessary?

If your answer to all of these questions is yes, then you belong in the ranks of the partisans. If no, then independence is for you—we hope not apathetic independence.

---

10. Morton, *op. cit.,* p. 42
11. Simpson, *op. cit.,* p. 17

# UNIT FOUR

## Political Decision–Makers

# 11 Introduction to the Study of Political Decision-Makers

Units Four and Five are about government in the United States, mainly about some of the people in government who make important political decisions. These units provide some answers to questions like these: What types of people become government leaders? How do they become leaders? Why do the leaders behave as they do? What kinds of decisions do they make and what are the factors that influence their decisions?

Nancy Jefferson's assignment in American Government for today is related to one of the above questions: "What kinds of decisions do political leaders make?" Her specific assignment is to list twenty ways in which government has an impact on her personal life. Before leaving class yesterday, Nancy jotted down half a dozen items. "The others won't come easy," she thought to herself. Let's follow Nancy through the morning to see how easy or difficult the assignment really is.

## In the Presence of Government

Nancy Jefferson, an attractive, friendly high school student in Chicago, was awakened at 7:00 A.M. Daylight Saving Time by her electric alarm clock. Federal law says that clocks are to be moved up an hour in the spring—and back an hour in the fall. Nancy lives in the Central Time Zone, an area set by the federal government. The power for Nancy's alarm clock is provided by a private company whose service is regulated by the state of Illinois. In some cities the power would have been provided by a government-owned utility.

Stretching and yawning, Nancy heads for the bathroom, where she brushes her teeth with water that is stored, purified, tested, and transported by the city of Chicago and with toothpaste containing fluoride, a substance found helpful in fighting tooth decay. Research in dental health is supported by the government. Another agency, the Food and Drug Administration, approved the use of fluoride in Nancy's toothpaste.

Nancy returns to her bedroom where she begins to dress. She chooses a cotton blouse that was made in the United States. The cotton in the blouse was part of a crop subsidized by the federal government. The blouse manufacturer also received a kind of subsidy, since the federal government has put a tax on blouses produced in other countries and sold in the United States in order to give some protection to the American firm from foreign competition. (Laws that provide subsidies to cotton farmers and manufacturers mean that Nancy had to pay a bit more for the blouse than if the subsidies did not exist.) She

also slips on a pair of fake alligator shoes. Nancy had wanted real alligator shoes but could not find any at a price she could afford. The shoe clerk told her that the government has decided to protect alligators from hunters. So very few alligator hides are now available, driving up the price on the few that are made.

Neither the shoes nor the blouse were made in Chicago. The blouse was part of a truck shipment from a New England textile mill. The shoes came by railroad. Both railroad and trucking companies are regulated by the Interstate Commerce Commission, a government agency. (If the shoes and blouse had arrived by plane, they would have landed at O'Hare Field, a government supported and operated airport, under conditions approved by the Federal Aviation Administration.)

Nancy goes into the kitchen, greets her father, and kisses her mother, leaving a slight smudge of lipstick which is judged to be suitable for sale by public health authorities. She sits down at the table to drink a glass of milk (inspected and approved by government inspectors), shakes cereal out of a box clearly labeled as required by the government, and starts to munch on government-inspected bacon.

As she eats her breakfast, she watches the weather report on television. The weather report was based upon data provided by the government weather bureau, and the TV program was broadcast at a frequency assigned by the Federal Communications Commission.

What government activities do the above items represent?

Although the TV set itself was made and sold by a private company, some of its parts were invented or perfected in laboratories supported by government funds.

Finishing her meal, Nancy picks up her books (selected by a textbook adoption committee and paid for by the state of Illinois), walks down the stairs of her apartment house (financed with a low interest mortgage guaranteed by the Federal Housing Administration), and runs out to the sidewalk built with tax money.

Soon she is at school, a publicly owned and managed agency, where she meets her friends, including those who arrived on buses operated by the city of Chicago. She goes to class where she meets her teacher, a government employee whose education was supported in part by public funds. At noon she hurries to the cafeteria where she buys her lunch. She uses money that was printed and minted by the government. The cost of lunch is a bit less than would otherwise be the case because some of the food is provided at reduced cost by the government. Lunch is interrupted by a fire drill. (The state requires at least one fire drill each month.)

Before going to her next class, Nancy has a chance to visit briefly with her friend John (Social Security number 514-24-6215). She asks him to mail a letter, which for the small price of an airmail stamp she assumes the government will deliver to her brother at a military base overseas. Her parting words are "I must run now and finish my Government assignment. I'll never think of twenty ways that government has an effect on my personal life."

**1.** List four examples of government *regulation* in the story.

**2.** List four examples in which government provides *goods* or *services* to citizens.

**3.** Describe briefly one instance from the story in which a different policy decision by a government leader would make a difference in Nancy's life.

**4.** Make a list of activities in which you engage each day that are not affected by government in any way.

## Some Important Rules That Influence Government in the United States

Suppose you were asked to describe professional football for a person who knew nothing about the game. It probably would not help very much to begin by describing the key plays from the last championship game or by listing your favorite players. One can't be expected to appreciate the players' skills until knowing something about the rules that influence their play.

You would need to explain how many players there are on each side and the purpose of the game. The person should know how many tries a team has to advance the football ten yards, the number of points allowed for a touchdown, a safety, a field goal, and an "extra point." It might be important to know the penalities for violations of the rules. And you may have to define such terms as punt, forward pass, huddle, lateral, block, and tackle. In short, full appreciation of a coach's defensive strategy or a quarterback's passing skill begins with knowledge of the rules of the game.

This is also true of government. A full appreciation of the strategy used to change an important policy or of the way a President performs depends on a knowledge of the rules of American politics and government. But while the rules and procedures for playing football are fairly simple, the rules and procedures for the conduct of government are very complex. In a single course we can study only the most basic ones. Still, an understanding of even a few basic rules will help one better understand the American political system.

### Basic Features of American Government

Throughout your study of Units Four and Five you will learn about specific rules and procedures that influence the political behavior of the President, members of Congress, governors, mayors, and other political leaders. However, there are some general features of the American political system you should understand before examining any of its parts.

### The United States Has a Constitutional Government

A constitutional government is one in which officials get their authority to make, implement, and enforce their decisions from a written constitution. They may not legally take on responsibilities beyond the authority either stated or implied by the constitution.

Since 1789 the Constitution of the United States has been a major influence on the behavior of American political leaders. Whenever the top officials enter office, they are asked to pledge loyalty to the Constitution and swear to abide by its terms.

While the Constitution has been changed by amendments and some clauses may be interpreted differently today than they were in the past, the existence of the Constitution assures that affairs will be conducted in similar ways by all public officials.

The Constitution is the foundation of the American legal system. It is a written plan for government. It tells how the government is to be set up and how it is to work. It describes how laws are to be made and enforced. It tells what the government can and cannot do. It describes the powers of government officials.

As the chart shows, all laws made by governments in the United States must agree with the Constitution.

### A Democratic-Republican Form of Government

The American government is *democratic* in that ultimate decision-making power lies with the people. By their votes Americans can change policies by changing political leaders. It is a *republican* form of

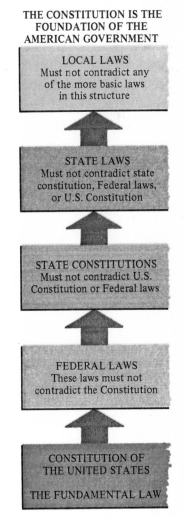

**THE CONSTITUTION IS THE FOUNDATION OF THE AMERICAN GOVERNMENT**

LOCAL LAWS
Must not contradict any of the more basic laws in this structure

STATE LAWS
Must not contradict state constitution, Federal laws, or U.S. Constitution

STATE CONSTITUTIONS
Must not contradict U.S. Constitution or Federal laws

FEDERAL LAWS
These laws must not contradict the Constitution

CONSTITUTION OF THE UNITED STATES

THE FUNDAMENTAL LAW

263

government because most policy decisions are made by representatives, not by the citizens themselves. As compared to direct democracy in which all citizens gather to discuss and to decide policy, Americans elect officials to represent their views and to choose policies that are in their best interests.

The fact that we have a "democratic-republican" form of government has been a major influence on political activity in the United States. It has led, for example, to the emergence of strong political parties to choose candidates, to suggest policy alternatives, and to conduct campaigns.

**ELEMENTS OF DEMOCRATIC-REPUBLICAN GOVERNMENT**

People choose decision-makers in regular competitive elections

Political parties offer candidates and policy alternatives

Elected leaders must be responsive to the voters or risk defeat at the polls

### A Federal System of Government

A federal system is one that has a *division of powers* between the central government and its chief subdivisions—in our country, the fifty states. The United States is a federation of states with a strong central government. Both the states and the national government get their authority from the people by means of the Constitution.

A *federal* system may be contrasted with a *unitary* system in which all political subdivisions draw their authority from the central government. In the United States neither the state governments nor the national government are dependent upon the other for their power. And local governments get their authority from the state rather than from the national government. The Constitution clearly assigns some duties to the national government only (for example, coining money); other powers are reserved to the states (for example, setting up local governments); while still other powers are shared by the national and state governments (for example, ability to tax).

264

The federal system has been a major influence on political activity in the United States. For example, each state has much freedom to write its own laws governing elections. This means that each state decides what residency requirements must be met in order for its citizens to be eligible to vote. The federal system provides that in some matters, such as recruiting men and women for the armed services or delivering mail, the national government may reach people directly. In other matters, such as education, health, and safety, when the national government wishes to provide services for all Americans, it may have to rely upon the state governments to administer its programs. The chart below illustrates the division of powers.

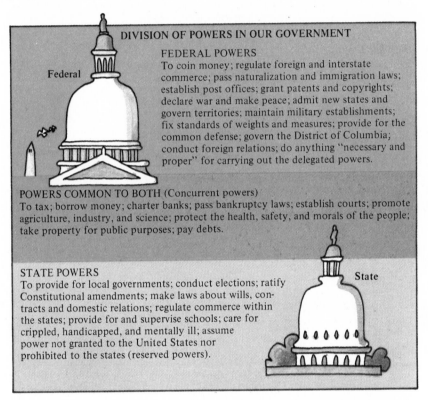

**DIVISION OF POWERS IN OUR GOVERNMENT**

Federal

FEDERAL POWERS
To coin money; regulate foreign and interstate commerce; pass naturalization and immigration laws; establish post offices; grant patents and copyrights; declare war and make peace; admit new states and govern territories; maintain military establishments; fix standards of weights and measures; provide for the common defense; govern the District of Columbia; conduct foreign relations; do anything "necessary and proper" for carrying out the delegated powers.

POWERS COMMON TO BOTH (Concurrent powers)
To tax; borrow money; charter banks; pass bankruptcy laws; establish courts; promote agriculture, industry, and science; protect the health, safety, and morals of the people; take property for public purposes; pay debts.

STATE POWERS
To provide for local governments; conduct elections; ratify Constitutional amendments; make laws about wills, contracts and domestic relations; regulate commerce within the states; provide for and supervise schools; care for crippled, handicapped, and mentally ill; assume power not granted to the United States nor prohibited to the states (reserved powers).

State

**Power Is Separated among Various Branches of Government**

The Constitution provides for a separation of powers at the national level among three major branches of government: the executive, legislative, and judicial. These branches are said to be separated partly because each has a different function. The Congress primarily passes laws; the President mainly administers laws; and the Supreme Court decides disputes growing out of law. This separation is not so neat and clearcut as generally believed and as described above. Still, the Constitution assigns different tasks to the three branches.

265

## The Three Branches Check and Balance One Another

The Constitution does not provide for *absolute* separation of the lawmaking, executive, and judicial powers. Each branch has some power to check the other two. And in practice there is some mutual sharing of responsibility, especially by Congress and the President. This tends to create something of a balance of political power among the three branches, and none can easily gain control over the others.

The main checks are shown in the chart. Notice that the Senate must give consent to treaties and approve many appointments made by the President. The President may veto bills passed by Congress, but Congress can override a veto by a two-thirds vote in each house. The Supreme Court may set aside (declare unconstitutional) a law passed by Congress and signed by the President. Thus, while we have the principle of separation of powers, we also have close links among the three departments through the check-and-balance system.

Most of the checks and balances are listed in the Constitution. But some have developed over the years with custom and usage. For example, the President as leader of a party exerts strong influence over its members in Congress.

*Constitutionalism, the democratic-republican form of government, federalism* and the *separation of powers* among the three branches of the national government have the combined effect of preventing the total, uncontrolled use of political power by a single person or group of people. Since political power is spread throughout the political system and since public officials are subject to restraints by citizens, public officials must bargain with others in order to govern. The American form of government makes politics a fact of life.

### THE SYSTEM OF CHECKS AND BALANCES

**PRESIDENT**

**EXECUTIVE**

CONGRESS checks on EXECUTIVE:
1. Overrides veto by two-thirds vote
2. May impeach officials
3. Controls appropriations
4. May reorganize executive departments
5. Can investigate executive departments
6. Senate approves treaties
7. Senate confirms appointments

**CONGRESS**

**LEGISLATIVE**

EXECUTIVE checks on LEGISLATIVE:
1. Vetoes laws
2. Calls special sessions
3. Sends messages to Congress
4. Leader of party
5. Appeals to the people

EXECUTIVE checks on JUDICIAL:
1. Nominates judges
2. Grants pardons or reprieves for Federal offenses
3. May refuse to enforce court order

JUDICIAL checks on EXECUTIVE:
1. Interprets laws and treaties
2. May rule that the President or other executive officer has acted illegally or misapplied the law

**SUPREME COURT**
**(and lower courts)**

**JUDICIAL**

JUDICIAL checks on LEGISLATIVE:
1. Interprets laws   2. Interprets treaties   3. Decides on constitutionality of laws

LEGISLATIVE checks on JUDICIAL:
1. May impeach judges   2. Senate approves appointments   3. May change size of Supreme Court   4. Sets up new inferior courts and abolishes old ones   5. Regulates the jurisdiction of courts   6. Can propose Constitutional amendments to get around a Court decision

## Three Key Concepts for Studying American Government

In previous units the focus of our study was typical American citizens, how they behave politically, and the factors that cause them to act as they do. Our primary concern was not for people who are full-time politicians or those who hold public office. Rather, we looked mainly at ordinary people who observe politics, follow it as a hobby, and once in a while take part by voting, attending rallies, writing letters to public officials, and so on.

Units Four and Five are mainly about full-time, professional politicians. Most of the people we shall study hold public office. They are members of Congress, governors, mayors, judges, bureaucrats, and state legislators. These are the people we are most eager to influence.

We will give some attention to the institutions in which these people work. But this will be done mainly to show some limits on their behavior. We will be trying to learn: Who are the people who fill public offices? How did they get their positions? What kinds of people are they? What are they expected to do in their positions? How do they make their decisions? What factors, people, and conditions affect the kinds of decisions they will make?

### Role, Recruitment, and Decision-Making

While other concepts are used from time to time, the key concepts are *role, recruitment,* and *decision-making.* These concepts will help us answer the questions stated above and others as well.

Before starting the study of government institutions more removed from us, it might be helpful to examine each of the three concepts in a familiar setting. Let's see how they might be applied to the principal of a high school.

### Role

In analysing the principal's role, we should first note that in any situation the *role* a person plays depends on the status, or position, held. In other words, people who are principals are able to act in certain ways because of the position they hold, rather than because of their personal traits. Any person who holds the position of principal has the authority to behave as a principal. The expectations that people have about the way principals should behave—the rules and customs that go with the status of principal—make up what is called the principal's *role.*

At one time the principal was the "principal teacher" (first or most important teacher). In large high schools today the principal rarely teaches at all. Principals spend most of their time managing the school. They plan schedules, supervise teachers, hold meetings with parents, plan new programs, punish or supervise those who punish students for violations of school rules, and so on.

The principal's role is shaped by many rules, customs, and procedures. For instance, principals in most cases can't change the curriculum very much because it must meet state regulations, school board policy, and the wishes of faculty, parents, and students. Principals on their own can't wipe out sports and clubs. The money they have to spend is set in school budgets. Various rules and pressures can even keep a principal from getting rid of "weak" teachers.

Principals are expected to be "good" persons. Their moral behavior must be in line with community standards. They are expected to be fair and honest. When angry, they are expected to avoid profanity in front of students. They are expected to dress and behave in ways that will set an example for the faculty and student body.

## Recruitment

What kinds of people become senior high school principals? A study published in 1965 of approximately 16,000 high school principals produced the following generalizations:

(1) Almost nine out of ten high school principals are men.

(2) Most have small-town and working-class origins. Therefore, becoming a high school principal is for many of these men a move upward in socioeconomic status.

(3) They tend to be appointed to their first principalship at a relatively early age (early to mid-thirties).

(4) About 90 percent of the principals have earned a master's degree. Only 10 percent had a bachelor's degree or less; only 3 percent had a doctorate.

(5) Nearly all principals have had some teaching experience prior to becoming principals. About 60 percent of the principals had between 4 and 14 years of teaching experience prior to becoming principals.

(6) Over one-third of the principals moved to their first principalship directly from the high school classroom. About one-fifth became principals after serving as assistant principals or vice principals. About 14 percent became principals directly from the position of fulltime coach or athletic director.

(7) About three-fifths of the principals expressed satisfaction with educational administration as a career, but only one-fourth indicated they had no desire to move to another position. Many wanted to become superintendents; others wished to move to larger high schools.

What consequences might follow from having these kinds of people become principals as compared to other kinds of people? Do the principals appear to be trained for their roles?

## Decision-Making

High school principals are called upon daily to make policy decisions for their schools. Therefore, in each high school, the principal is a chief decision-maker. Policy issues can usually be decided in a number of ways. Still, principals are not entirely free to choose from among the possible choices. They are limited in part by their role.

The principal of Julia Richmond High School in New York City talks with a student, discusses a problem with her administrative assistant and a teacher, and motions for a parent to come in.

The customs, rules, and procedures which shape the role and the ties that principals have with other people—faculty, students, school officials, parents—all have a part in determining decisions. A principal's personal beliefs and traits are also important. Also decisions made last week or last year will affect those made today and in the future. By studying decision-making we learn not only about how a role is played but also how the role is linked to other parts of the system.

The following case study provides a chance to study the principal's role. It also provides some examples of the basic elements of decision-making.

### Crisis at Webster Senior High

The buzzer on the telephone brought Principal George Baxter of Webster Senior High School to attention. He picked up the receiver and heard his secretary say, "Willie Smith and Julia Lincoln are here for their appointment. Shall I send them in?"

"Give me two or three more minutes." Mr. Baxter replied. "I'll call you when I am ready."

He returned the phone to its cradle and swung around in his chair to face the window in his office. "Two or three minutes!" he thought. "I won't be ready in two or three years to solve this problem!"

Two weeks ago, when the new school year began, it had not occurred to him that he would face this kind of problem. Most students seemed happy to be back. He had assembled what he believed to be the best faculty ever at Webster Senior High.

And the coaches were predicting a fine football season. Then, last Monday, his troubles began.

Webster Senior High is the only high school in a small midwestern town. The school has 1540 students in grades nine to twelve. Approximately 20 percent of the students are black. Mr. Baxter's trouble arose from a growing tension between white and black students and the coming elections for cheerleaders.

**Cheerleader Selection at Webster High.** Cheerleader elections are held each fall at Webster Senior High on the Friday prior to the first football game. On that day each high school student who wishes to try out for cheerleader leads one cheer at a school-wide pep assembly. Following the assembly all the students vote for the five students they consider to be the best cheerleaders. The five who receive the greatest number of votes are elected.

Traditionally, only whites have been elected. While one or two blacks have entered the competition each year, none has ever been elected.

On Monday, a group of black students charged that no black cheerleaders had ever been elected because of prejudice on the part of white students. They announced that this year at least one black would have to be elected or there would be trouble. Willie Smith,

270

a halfback on the varsity football team, said that neither he nor any of the other fifteen black football players would compete this year unless there was at least one black cheerleader.

Since the announcement by the black students on Monday, Mr. Baxter had been able to think of little else. First of all, he did not doubt that if the election were permitted to run as usual, no black would be chosen cheerleader. This was not because there were no capable black candidates. But a series of small fights between black and white students had created ill-feeling, and many angry white students seemed certain to vote only for white candidates. Secondly, cheerleader try-outs and elections were conducted by the student council. Mr. Baxter tried to avoid interfering in matters that were the student council's responsibility. In the past whenever he tried to influence a student council decision, it had caused a student uproar. The student council had met on Tuesday following the announcement by the black students and decided that the present system of electing cheerleaders was the most democratic process imaginable and that the elections should go on as planned.

**Consultation with the Faculty.** Mr. Baxter discussed the entire issue in a faculty meeting on Wednesday. The faculty was badly divided. (1) Some were angry that the blacks had threatened trouble and were against giving in to their demands. (2) Others were sympathetic to the black demands and argued that if the elections could not be held without discrimination against blacks, there should be no elections at all. The school could simply do without cheerleaders. (3) The coaches, fearful of what a black walkout would do to chances for a winning season, urged that one of the five positions be saved for a black. The black students could compete for that slot while the white candidates competed for the other four positions.

In the meantime Mr. Baxter was getting advice from other sources. The newspaper ran a story on the problem at Webster High and noted that racial harmony in Webster City depended on how the problem was resolved. A group of black parents called on Mr. Baxter and pleaded for a fair election in which blacks would have the same chance to be elected as whites. Many white parents also visited Mr. Baxter and urged him not to interfere in a student council matter but to be prepared to keep order in the school if trouble broke out.

Mr. Baxter called the superintendent of schools for advice. Superintendent Henderson was out of town, but the secretary said that the whole affair and Mr. Baxter's handling of the incident would be reviewed by the school board at its next meeting.

**Mr. Baxter's Dilemma.** To summarize, here is Mr. Baxter's problem: More than anything else he wants a happy, peaceful school. He knows that cheerleader elections in the past have been unfair to black candidates. But since no one had complained, he had not interfered. This time, if he stands by and does nothing, there will surely be trouble.

If he orders the student council to change its procedures, he will be under fire by many white students—and many parents and perhaps the school board as well. And what is a fair decision after all? Would it be best to have no cheerleaders this year, as some faculty members believe? Would it be better to recognize race and apply a quota system? Or would it be better to let the majority of Webster High students decide the issue for themselves in the election?

Mr. Baxter picked up his telephone and rang his secretary. "Send Willie and Julia in. I'm ready to give them my decision."

1. What decision do you think would be best? What decision do you think Mr. Baxter made?
2. What are some of the factors that Mr. Baxter must consider in making a decision?
3. Can Mr. Baxter predict the consequences that will follow from any of the decisions available to him?
4. Would all principals make the same decision that Mr. Baxter will make? What factors might lead other people to make the same decision or different decisions if they were the principal?

## Political Decision-Makers and Unofficial Political Specialists

Unlike typical American citizens who devote only a small part of their time to political affairs, some Americans take part in politics daily. Some of these people work for the government. They include the President of the United States, members of Congress, Supreme Court justices, bureaucrats, governors, state legislators, and mayors. We shall call these people *political decision-makers*. Other persons do not hold official positions in the government, but they try to influence policy decisions. These people include lobbyists, political party leaders, and media representatives. We sometimes call these people *unofficial political specialists*.

### Political Decision-Makers

In Units Four and Five you will study about political decision-makers. A decision-maker is one who holds a position which enables the person to make policy decisions that are binding on other people. There are decision-makers in families, churches, schools, clubs, and corporations. But we shall be concerned with government decision-makers only. Sometimes public policy decisions are made by one person, or in the name of one person, as when the President decides. Other decisions are made by a group. For example, while Supreme Court justices first decide each case for themselves, they take part in a final group decision that is binding. Each senator must decide whether to support a bill or not, but this decision by itself is not as significant as the decision made by the Senate as a whole.

272

When studying political decision-makers, we shall depend chiefly on three major concepts: *role, recruitment,* and *decision-making.* We are less concerned with how specific individuals have behaved in a role as we are concerned with the norms, values, rules, customs, and procedures that make up the role. *Recruitment* will help us to see what kinds of people become political decision-makers, how they are selected, and how they are trained for their positions.

While the norms, customs, and procedures for arriving at decisions vary from role to role, all of the decision-makers do make *political decisions.* A central purpose of government is to produce such decisions. Political decisions often differ from other decisions in one chief way. They tend to be *accommodational* decisions. Political decisions seek to find a point at which the contending parties can be satisfied.

Political decisions do not have to "make sense" or be fully consistent with other political decisions. Political decisions, rather, are ones which tend to make the greatest number of most interested people satisfied with the outcome. For example, studies show that smoking cigarettes can be damaging to one's health. In light of this finding the federal government has taken a number of steps to discourage the use of cigarettes. Cigarette packages now contain a health warning to users. TV and radio may not broadcast cigarette commercials. These actions represent policy decisions to discourage smoking. On the other hand, the government did not ban cigarettes. (This would make cigarette smokers unhappy.) And the government continues to provide various forms of support to tobacco growers, thereby keeping them partially happy in spite of the war on cigarette smoking.

### Unofficial Political Specialists
In Units Four and Five you will also meet people who are deeply engaged in politics but who do not hold positions in government. They are very important in the political process, for they often influence which people will be elected to office and what their decisions will be. Some of these people may be top leaders in political parties at the state and national level. Others work for special interest groups and try to promote policies by the government that are favorable to their groups. Business, labor, and professional associations are only three of the kinds of groups that employ full-time lobbyists to promote their interests in Washington and the state capitals. The news media employ another type of specialist who may devote much time to political matters. Cartoonists, feature writers, reporters, editors, and TV commentators all make politics their business. They try to influence public opinion and government officials. They have more influence than an ordinary citizen.

The most important characteristic of such people is that they devote far more time to political affairs than do typical citizens. In addition, most have access to political resources not available to typical citizens.

The photos show some
unofficial political specialists.
An expert on sonic booms
urges defeat of a program to
subsidize the SST, a
supersonic transport plane.
A newspaper editor and
reporter confer. Lobbyists
for a bankers' association
hold a dinner for state
legislators.

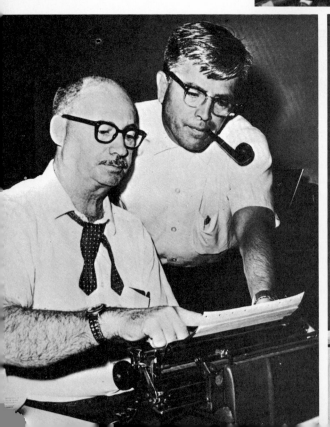

Among these resources are the leadership of a large organization, access to the communications media, and possession of important knowledge that government leaders need.

Throughout Units Four and Five we shall refer to the roles that the unofficial political specialists play. Through case studies and in other ways you will learn in what ways political decision-makers are influenced by such individuals and groups when making decisions.

To show your understanding of the material in this chapter, complete the following exercises

**1.** The President wants to keep taxes at the current rate. Some members of Congress want to lower taxes immediately, especially for low-income individuals. Finally, a law is passed that keeps taxes the same for the current year and lowers taxes on low-income people for the following year. Why is this an example of a *political decision?*

**2.** Following are five statements about government in the United States:

    **A.** The United States has a constitutional government.

    **B.** The United States has a democratic-republican form of government.

    **C.** The United States has a federal system of government.

    **D.** In the American system of government, power is separated among various branches of the government.

    **E.** The three branches check and balance one another.

Below are a series of statements which illustrate the statements above. Match each statement below with one of the statements in the list above.

**(1)** The Congress passes laws; the President administers laws; and the Supreme Court interprets the law.

**(2)** While the Congress passes laws, the President can veto legislation preventing bills from becoming law.

**(3)** Each of the fifty states has its own regulations regarding health, safety, and education. Nevertheless, the Congress has appropriated money to help states increase the quality of health, safety, and education in their states.

**(4)** The government has limits to what it is legally able to do. Moreover, Congress is not free to pass any kind of law it wishes.

**(5)** Voters in the United States make very few policy decisions directly, but voters have regular opportunites to elect government policy-makers.

# 12 The Presidential Role

For Americans, the position of President of the United States is the most important one in the world. The President is the best-known political actor. Most Americans feel that the President more than any other person has the power to affect their lives for good or ill. For many, the President serves also as the symbol of the nation itself, binding us together in times of national danger and representing to others our national values and hopes. Because the United States is so powerful, people in other countries also follow the President's actions with keen interest.

The awesome job may seem to call for a genius. Yet every four years we elect a person to the office who in many ways is like other Americans who hold major positions in society. What kind of person becomes President? How do we choose such a person from the many who are qualified? What does a President do once elected? And how does a President make decisions on public policy issues? These questions relating to *recruitment, role,* and *decision-making* are the focus of this chapter.

## Formal and Informal Rules on Presidential Recruitment

At the time of a presidential election, very few people are viewed as "serious" candidates. That is, few people are thought to have any real chance of being picked by one of the major parties and then winning the election. The process of cutting down the pool of possible candidates is managed through a number of formal and informal rules. *Formal rules* are rules that exist in a formal or legal manner for all to see, as in the Constitution. *Informal rules,* on the other hand, are customs and traditions. Such rules are not required by law, but they operate with nearly as much power.

### Formal Rules

Certain formal rules tell who can and who cannot be President of the United States. These rules are found in the Constitution in Article II, section 1; Amendment XXII; and Amendment XXV (see Appendix).

According to Article II, the President must be (1) a natural-born citizen, (2) at least thirty-five years old, and (3) a resident of the United States for at least fourteen years.

These rules exclude many Americans. More than half of all Americans are less than thirty-five years old. Of the more than 215 million Americans in 1976, only about 90 million could meet the age

President Gerald Ford opens the American Bicentennial celebration with an address at Old North Church in Boston on the eve of Patriots Day (April 19) in 1975. The next day he visited Lexington and Concord.

rule. In addition, any foreign-born person is ineligible. The 1970 census showed nearly ten million foreign-born Americans. Finally, any natural-born citizen must have lived at least fourteen years within the borders of the United States.

The Twenty-second Amendment adds another formal rule. It limits the President to two terms—or to only one additional term if the person has served more than two years of a predecessor's term. In other words, no President may serve more than ten years in office.

Franklin Roosevelt is the only President to have served over two terms. He died a few months after the start of his fourth term in 1945.

## Formal Rules on Election and Succession to Office

Other formal rules outline some of the steps to be taken by a person wishing to become President. The Constitution lays down some rules for electing a President and for filling the office if it is vacant. Let's first look at the formal rules on election, which are chiefly found in Article II and Amendment XII of the Constitution.

• The President and Vice-President are formally chosen by an Electoral College made up of electors from each state and the District of Columbia. Each state has as many electors as it has members of Congress. The District of Columbia has three electors.

• Each state has its own formal rules on how the electors are to be chosen. But all of the states follow a common practice of allowing any qualified party to put up a set of electors to be voted on by the people. The set of party electors getting the most popular votes gets all the electoral votes of that state. About a third of the states *require* the winning electors to vote for their party's candidates for President and Vice-President. In the other states the electors are honor-bound to do so, but in a very few cases an elector has not backed the party's candidate for President. No federal official may serve as an elector. And Congress may set the time when electors are to be chosen (the first Tuesday after the first Monday in November) every four years.

• The electors meet in their state capitals on the first Monday after the second Wednesday in December to cast their ballots. A set of ballots goes to the President of the Senate, who conducts a count of all electoral ballots on January 6 in the presence of both houses of Congress. The candidates receiving a majority of the electoral votes are chosen President and Vice-President.

• If no candidates get a majority of the electoral votes, decisions are made in Congress. The House of Representatives—with one vote per state—chooses the President from among the three candidates who got the most electoral votes. The Senate chooses between the two highest candidates for Vice-President. In 1800 and 1824 the House of Representatives chose the President in this way.

Since we can be sure that nearly every elector will vote for the candidates of his or her party, we know the winners a few hours after the polls close on election day in November.

Another set of formal rules tells who shall be President or Vice-President if either of these two offices should become vacant.

• If the President dies, resigns, or is removed from office, the Vice-President becomes President.

• Under the Twenty-fifth Amendment, ratified in 1967, there is now a way to fill a vacancy in the Vice-Presidency. The President names a person, who takes office if and when confirmed by a majority vote of both houses of Congress. Under this rule, Gerald Ford became Vice-President in December 1973. And when he became President the

next year after Richard Nixon resigned, Ford picked and Congress confirmed Nelson Rockefeller as Vice-President.

- If the offices of President and Vice-President should be vacant at the same time, the Presidential Succession Act would take effect. It provides a line of succession (after the Vice-President) of Speaker of the House, President pro tem of the Senate, and the cabinet officers ranked by the age of their departments.

- If the President is unable to discharge the duties, there is a way for the Vice-President to become Acting President (see Amendment XXV, page 591).

Vice-President Nelson Rockefeller receives congratulations after taking the oath of office in 1974. At his side are President Ford and Chief Justice Burger, who delivered the oath of office.

### Informal Rules on Recruitment

While the Constitution provides the legal framework within which we choose our Presidents, knowing the formal rules is not enough. Informal rules and procedures that have developed over the years play a very big part. For example, the Constitution does not mention political parties, but they are vital to our process of electing a President. No person can hope to be elected without being named by one of the two major parties.

From the point of view of the party, the name of the game is winning. It costs a great deal of money to run an election campaign. In 1968 twenty-one Republican campaign committees reported spending more than $20 million to elect Richard Nixon. The losing campaign of Hubert Humphrey cost about the same.

'ACTUALLY, WE WON'T KNOW WHAT IT'S LIKE TILL WE'VE BEEN THERE'

' WILL YOU CONTINUE TO RUN ? '

Both cartoons by Jack McLeod in the *Buffalo Evening News*

Public opinion polls help identify some possible candidates for President. Then early in the election year most of the "hopefuls" enter the state presidential primaries to win convention delegates—and additional popularity. Defeats in early primaries will lead some to drop out of the race.

It costs a great deal of money to wage a winning campaign, but political leaders think it is worth the price. When Nixon was elected in 1968, he had the chance to appoint around 6500 people to federal jobs. If a popular candidate can also sweep other members of the party into office at national, state, and local levels, other jobs for party members result. Another part of the prize of winning is the chance to carry out programs favored by the people who supported the winner. One person has written: "Win the election—never mind the expense; defeat is the most expensive of all contests."

To win the prize, the parties follow a number of informal rules. These rules guide party leaders in their choice of the person to run for President.

### Popularity

Each party must keep in mind that choosing a nominee requires balancing two factors: (a) who will be a good President? (b) who will be a good campaigner? It would be foolish for a party to pick the best prospect for President if the person had little voter appeal.

How does a party decide who would be the best candidate? Public appeal as judged by major opinion polls is one measure. Months before the nominations are made, the pollsters start their surveys. They ask voters to name their favorite candidates. In most cases in the past forty years, the person in each party judged to be the "leading candidate" early in the election year won the nomination. A recent exception to this rule was George McGovern. He trailed Edmund Muskie as the preferred Democratic candidate early in 1972, but he won after the polls showed a drop in Muskie's popularity. In 1940 the Republicans chose Wendell Willkie and in 1964 picked Barry Goldwater when no clear leader showed up in the polls early in the year.

This means that to win the nomination one must become well known long before the parties begin choosing delegates to the national conventions. Television and the press play a big part in building up the public appeal of some "hopefuls."

If the media fail to take notice of "hopefuls" and report on their actions, they are likely to pass unmentioned in public polls and be overlooked as candidates. But to get good press and TV coverage, the "hopefuls" must usually hold positions that put them in the spotlight. The road to the White House begins with public notice.

Becoming recognized as a public figure and a good prospect for President helps attract campaign funds. Then comes greater visibility and, in time, higher standing in the opinion polls.

### Experience

Some positions are better launching platforms than others. Study the chart and decide which positions provide the best stepping stones to the Presidency.

**PUBLIC OFFICE-HOLDING BY PRESIDENTIAL NOMINEES, 1936-1976**

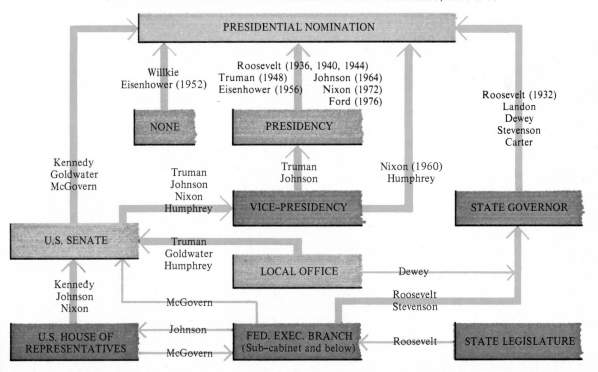

Clearly the Presidency itself is the best spot to be in if the person is eligible to remain in office. Only a few Presidents seeking the nomination have failed to get it.

Notice the importance of the United States Senate as a launching pad. Between 1948 and 1972 out of the ten persons whom the major parties ran for President, seven had served in the Senate. Four of them served as Vice-President before running for President. Another chief stepping stone is a state governorship, mainly of a big state. These positions—senator, governor, Vice-President—get more press and TV coverage than do many other offices. Politicians thrive on publicity. Capable persons in business often try to stay out of the limelight—and thus have little chance to be seen as contestants.

Many army generals won the presidential nomination in the nineteenth century. Winning candidates included Jackson, both Harrisons, Taylor, Grant, and Garfield. In this century only Dwight D. Eisenhower rose to the Presidency from a high military post.

**Geography**

A person has a somewhat better chance to be picked by a major party if from a pivotal state. This is one which could go either to the Republicans or the Democrats and which controls a large number of electoral votes. California is a major example today.

By choosing a person from such a pivotal state, it may be possible to swing that state's vote to the party, thereby winning all its electoral votes. Over half of the presidential candidates of the two major parties from 1868 to 1972 were from New York, Ohio, and Illinois. These three states control a large number of electoral votes. In the 1970s New York had 41 electoral votes; Ohio, 25; and Illinois, 26. These are truly pivotal states. Sometimes they have voted Republican; in other cases Democratic. So the party leaders of these states have much to say about whom the two major parties run for President.

**Sex, Race, and Ethnic Background**

There are no legal barriers to the choice of Presidents based on sex, race, or ethnic background. Yet party leaders know that many Americans hold a number of biases and that these must be considered. By 1972 no woman had ever been picked as a major party's candidate for President or Vice-President. Still, the number of Americans who claim that they would vote for a woman to be President has been growing steadily. It thus seems likely that one of the two parties will break this custom in the near future, probably by first naming a woman to be Vice-President.

To date, all the major-party candidates for President have been white. Some minor parties have chosen blacks, as in 1968 when Dick Gregory was chosen by the Peace and Freedom party. However, since blacks make up only around 12 percent of the population, no major party has been thus far willing to risk losing an election by choosing a person who would be rejected at once by prejudiced white voters.

But this custom too may be eroding. At this time it would be hard to guess which group—blacks or white females—is most likely to break the barrier first. Presidential candidates have been chosen mainly from families that have northern European backgrounds, chiefly English. No President has been elected whose family came from southern or eastern Europe, the Middle East, Asia, Latin America, or Africa.

### Religion and Morality

Americans expect their Presidents to be religious—more specifically, Christian. Until very recently they were expected to be Protestant. John F. Kennedy was the first Roman Catholic to be elected President. Jews, Moslems, Hindus, and Buddhists stand little chance. Even persons with weak religious commitments are expected to act interested in religion when they run for President.

Americans also expect their leaders to be moral. Known violations of widely accepted standards of morality would cost a person the candidacy. Even divorce is an obstacle. Since attitudes on divorce seem to be changing, this factor may be less critical in the future.

### Socioeconomic Status

There are stories about poor persons rising to the Presidency. The fact is that less than a half dozen Presidents have risen from the ranks of the very poor. Most have grown up in the upper-middle class. Several, such as George Washington, Franklin D. Roosevelt, and John F. Kennedy, were very wealthy. Most Presidents have come from families that could pay for a good education.

Presidential candidates have tended to specialize in the law rather than in business. The major parties fear having a candidate who is closely tied to some particular economic interest. The president of United States Steel Corporation, for example, would not likely be chosen because he would be seen as favoring "big business" against the interests of labor. Although Nelson Rockefeller came to the Vice-Presidency from his former position as governor of New York, the congressional hearings on his nomination in 1974 focused largely on his family's business interests and their effect on his ability to serve without conflict of interest. Nor is a major party likely to choose a union leader, who would be seen as likely to represent the interests of labor against business. Perhaps this helps to explain why candidates tend to be chosen from a background of law and politics rather than either business or labor.

### Miscellaneous

Much more might be said about the factors that parties keep in mind when choosing candidates for President. While active in politics, candidates should not be tied to extreme positions that might turn off a big part of the voters. They should have few enemies either in the party or in the public at large. All things being equal, they should have a record of party loyalty. And they should have had some direct experience with foreign as well as domestic affairs.

# Background Characteristics of Twentieth-Century Presidents

| President | Home State When Elected | Age on Taking Office | Ancestry | Religion | Family Background | Education | Occupation | Political Experience |
|-----------|-------------------------|----------------------|----------|----------|-------------------|-----------|------------|----------------------|
| Theodore Roosevelt | New York | 42 | Dutch | Dutch Reform | Wealthy, urban | Harvard | Rancher, soldier, politican | Vice-President, Governor |
| William H. Taft | Ohio | 51 | English | Unitarian | Wealthy, professional | Yale | Lawyer | Cabinet officer |
| Woodrow Wilson | New Jersey | 56 | Scotch-Irish | Presbyterian | Ministry | Princeton | University professor | Governor |
| Warren G. Harding | Ohio | 55 | English | Baptist | Farm | Ohio Central College | Newspaper publisher | Senator |
| Calvin Coolidge | Massachusetts | 51 | English | Congregational | Small merchant | Amherst | Lawyer Politics | Governor |
| Herbert Hoover | California | 54 | Swiss-German | Quaker | Farmer, small merchant | Stanford | Engineer | Cabinet officer |
| Franklin D. Roosevelt | New York | 51 | Dutch | Episcopalian | Wealthy, small town | Harvard | Politics | Governor |
| Harry Truman | Missouri | 60 | Scotch-Irish, English | Baptist | Small town, poor | Kansas City School of Law | Politics | Vice-President, Senator |
| Dwight D. Eisenhower | New York | 62 | Swiss-German | Presbyterian | Small town, poor | West Point | Soldier | None |
| John F. Kennedy | Massachusetts | 43 | Irish | Roman Catholic | Wealthy, business | Harvard | Politics | Senator |
| Lyndon B. Johnson | Texas | 55 | English, French, German | Christian Church | Small town, modest means | Southwest Texas State Teachers College | Politics | Vice-President, Senator |
| Richard M. Nixon | New York | 56 | Irish | Quaker | Small town, merchant | Whittier College, Duke | Lawyer Politics | Vice-President, Senator |
| Gerald R. Ford | Michigan | 61 | English | Episcopalian | Small business | Michigan | Lawyer Politics | Vice-President, Congress |
| Jimmy Carter | Georgia | 52 | English | Baptist | Farmer | Annapolis | Farmer, Business | Legislator Governor |

Source: Adapted from *The Presidency: A Modern Perspective*, by Francis H. Heller, Copyright © 1960 by Random House, Inc. Reprinted by permission of Random House, Inc.

If all of these factors are considered, who stands a chance of becoming President of the United States from the 80 to 90 million people who are legally eligible? It is likely that less than a hundred persons are "available" at the time of any given election. From these few people who are able to meet each of the criteria stated above, the party chooses the one it thinks will have the best chance of being elected. In short, the question for American voters is not who among all the people in the United States is most qualified to be President. Rather, the question is who in the estimate of a group of political leaders stands the best chance on a given day every four years to capture a majority of the electoral votes.

### Applying What You Have Learned about Presidential Recruitment

The chart opposite provides information about eight characteristics of American Presidents who have served during this century. Study it carefully; then answer each of these questions:

**1.** Which of the formal rules and which of the informal rules seem to have been followed in the selection of each President?

**2.** Which of the rules were violated in specific cases?

**3.** Explain, if possible, any exceptions to the rules that you find.

## An Overview of the Presidential Role

*Truman Upsets Dewey.   Ike Beats Stevenson.   Kennedy Squeaks by Nixon.   Nixon Wins in Landslide.*   What an exciting but sobering moment it must be to win the Presidency of the United States. It is exciting because the office is the highest honor this nation can give any of its citizens. A President has joined a small club that in 1975 listed only thirty-eight members, tracing back to George Washington. From the Tuesday in November when elected, to the twentieth of January when leaving office, the eyes of the world will be on the new President. What this person says and does will be heard and seen around the world. The face will be known by millions of people. No matter how successful as President, a place in history is assured.

It must also be a sobering moment for the President-elect, because with the office comes a heavy burden. It is one of the most powerful offices in the world because the United States is such a strong nation. Decisions made by the President affect not only Americans but also other millions of people around the world. Very few people could fail to be sobered by this thought.

The President's power stems from the Constitution. The President may act in ways permitted no other American because the Constitution says so, and Americans accept the Constitution as the supreme law of the land. It is the chief rule book which tells how the "game" will be played in the United States. Moreover, while the framers of

Former President
Eisenhower joined the
new President, John F.
Kennedy, in the reviewing
stand to watch the
Inaugural Parade in
January 1961.

the Constitution divided federal power among three branches of government—the President, Congress, and the courts—no one person dominates a branch of the government as the President does the executive branch. And no other branch is so free to act so swiftly and decisively as the President can in areas of defense policy, foreign affairs, and in many cases domestic affairs.

The power of the Presidency also stems from the fact that Americans expect the President to act. Studies show that while few Americans have a good grasp of many of the issues facing their country, most will support the President in whatever action taken. Most Americans seem to assume that the President will know best.

### The Constitution Provides Guidelines

The Constitution gives the basic rules within which the President can act. Article II outlines the powers and duties.

1. Serves as Commander in Chief of the armed forces: Army, Navy, and Air Force—and the National Guard when it is called into federal service.

2. Appoints—with Senate consent—the heads of the various executive departments, such as the Department of State and the Department of Labor. They provide advice and information. There also are a large number of assistants who make up the White House staff and report directly to the President.

286

3. Makes treaties with the consent of two-thirds of the Senate.

4. Appoints ambassadors and consuls, judges of the federal courts, and many other officials—also with the approval of the Senate. Also appoints officials to fill vacancies without Senate consent if they occur during a Senate recess. But such appointments are limited to a single session of Congress.

5. Delivers an annual "State of the Union" message to Congress and sends special messages from time to time.

6. Can convene Congress when it is not in session, if necessary.

7. Meets with heads of state, ambassadors, and other public officials from foreign countries, and commissions officers of the United States.

## The President and the Executive Branch

The American system of government is often described in terms of three branches: legislative, judicial, and executive. The executive branch, headed by the President, is to make certain that laws passed by Congress are carried out. All but a tiny fraction of the nearly three million federal employees and officials are members of the executive branch. They work in around two thousand departments, bureaus, agencies, and commissions. While Washington, D.C., has the largest concentration of federal employees, members of the executive branch are scattered all over the nation and the world.

### Cabinet Departments

More than a third of all federal employees are in the Defense Department. About another one-fourth work in the other executive departments (see list in margin). Each of the departments is headed by a presidential appointee. Thus, the Secretary of Defense heads the Department of Defense; the Attorney General, the Department of Justice; and so on. The heads of these departments make up the President's cabinet.

At an earlier time in our history, Presidents used to meet often with their cabinets and plan executive policy for the government. In recent years, however, the cabinet as a policy-making vehicle has fallen into disuse.

### Executive Office of the President

The decline in the influence of the cabinet contrasts with the growth in size and influence of the White House staff. Early in our history Presidents had only a clerk or two to help them. Often these had to be borrowed from other departments of the government, such as the Army. Not until 1857 did Congress vote funds to hire a private secretary, a White House steward, and a manager for the President. Grover Cleveland answered most of his mail in longhand. Woodrow Wilson wrote out many of the state documents himself. Herbert Hoover was the first President for whom Congress provided three secretaries.

*Cabinet Departments*

State
Treasury
Defense
Justice
Interior
Agriculture
Commerce
Labor
Health, Education, and Welfare
Housing and Urban Development
Transportation

287

# EXECUTIVE OFFICE OF THE PRESIDENT

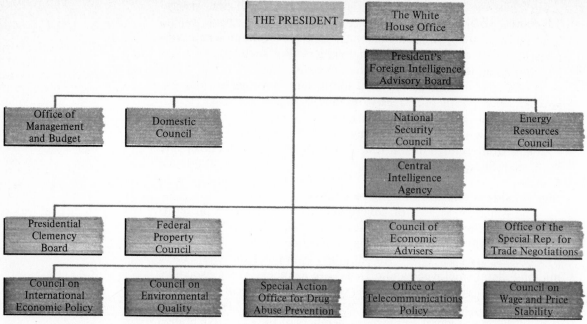

Source: *United States Government Manual 1975/76.*

The Executive Office of the President was created in 1939 when Franklin Roosevelt was President. It was made up of his personal staff of secretaries and administrative aides (called the White House Office), the Bureau of the Budget, and a few other agencies. At one time all of the President's staff could work in the offices in the White House. After World War II the Executive Office agencies took over what came to be known as the Executive Office Building next to the White House. In recent years new buildings have been added to house the Executive Office staff. The chart shows the major offices and councils that recently have comprised the Executive Office.

A number of the agencies serve an advisory and/or coordinating function. Some of them exist mainly to help the President make policy in particular areas. Part of this job is to reduce policy conflicts in the executive branch. The Secretaries of State and Defense are both members of the National Security Council. Part of this Council's job is to see that diplomatic and military policies are in step with each other. The Domestic Council includes the heads of all the cabinet departments except State and Defense. Its purpose is to make and coordinate domestic policy recommendations to the President.

Sometimes an agency is put into the Executive Office because it doesn't fit neatly into one of the cabinet departments. The Office of Economic Opportunity has been an example. It advised the Pres-

288

ident on antipoverty programs, tried to coordinate programs placed in cabinet departments (Labor and HEW, for example), and administered some programs directly. The Office of Management and Budget is in the Executive Office partly because it serves the entire executive branch.

### The White House Office

This Office is made up of the President's personal staff and closest advisers, along with their clerks, secretaries, and assistants. It has become a little bureaucracy of its own. Recent Presidents have felt the need to meet regularly with close advisers who could take prompt action. For example, before Henry Kissinger became Secretary of State, he served President Nixon as Special Assistant for National Security Affairs. His office was in the White House, not in the State Department. He is said to have had more power over the direction of foreign policy than did the Secretary of State. Even after taking over that post, Dr. Kissinger kept an office in the White House, presumably to keep this close link to the President.

As the White House Office has grown, the staff at times has been tempted to meddle in the day-to-day operations of various bureaus. The tragedy of Nixon's fall from office may have begun when some members of his staff formed a special undercover group called the "Plumbers." It took on some tasks that should not have been undertaken at all; other tasks were more properly the business of an agency like the FBI.

The Nixon staff may have carried to an extreme what had become a growing tendency: trying to see that the President's policies were really carried out. Even some appointed officials will drag their feet in carrying out the President's policies. And there will always be in the executive branch some civil servants who don't like the President's policies and try to sidetrack them.

The response of recent Presidents has been to put together a team of bright, loyal people on the White House staff to see that the programs are carried out. Presidents try to organize the staff so that they are free to focus on the most critical issues and leave other matters to the staff.

### Salary and Fringe Benefits

While the pressures on a President are surely intense, taxpayers do a great deal to make the rewards equal to the effort. Americans at the Constitutional Convention might be shocked to learn how closely the privileges given to the President compare with those of the kings in their own time.

We provide the President with a salary of $200,000 per year, plus a $50,000 tax-free expense allowance, the use of the White House, and use of many other facilities. The President is free from most of the bothersome details that take up much of the typical American's life. The President has a physician to give regular, even daily, checkups, and a personal barber to serve at the President's own convenience. The President has use of a movie theater and a private swimming pool. When new clothes are needed, someone buys them. When hungry, the President merely tells a cook what to prepare. A staff of gardeners takes care of the White House grounds.

When the President prepares to travel, the arrangments will be made by others. Perhaps it will be in a limousine with a police escort—no traffic jams, no wait for stop lights. Many trips will be by plane with Air Force pilots ready to take off in modern jets. Presidents who wish to leave the pressures of the White House and have a brief vacation may travel quickly to Camp David in Maryland, a mountain retreat kept for their exclusive use.

Presidents have instant access to the best communications system in the world. In addition to getting the news from the press, TV, and radio, there are outlets for each of the major wire services in the White House. Presidents can talk by phone or wireless radio to points all around the globe. By special hookup they can talk almost instantly to the leaders in the Soviet Union. Whenever they travel, this vast communications network goes along. In short, no other person in the world has as many conveniences to make it possible to focus all energies on the job.

## The Multiple Roles of the President

What does a President actually do? You will learn that there are many aspects of the role. It can be divided into at least eight parts. They are *head of state, chief diplomat, commander in chief, chief executive, chief legislator, chief economic planner, party chief,* and *representative of all the people.* In addition to these official roles, the President also fulfills roles as parent, spouse, grandparent, and citizen as do many other Americans.

### Head of State

The President of the United States is our nation's official host to visiting royalty and heads of governments. When foreign ambassadors present their credentials to our government, they do so to the President of the United States. The President is expected to bestow medals on American heroes, unveil monuments, light the annual Christmas tree, hunt Easter eggs on the White House lawn with Washington children, throw out the first ball to start the baseball season, and buy the first Christmas seals. As *head of state,* the President receives important civic and business leaders of our country and has pictures taken with them to symbolize their visits. The President meets with visiting Girl Scouts, movie stars, and sports champions. When astronauts return from outer space, the President is the first one to call and offer congratulations.

The President proclaims the Fourth of July, Labor Day, and Thanksgiving, and announces American Education Week and other special "weeks" throughout the year. When the nation has lost a hero, the President leads the nation in mourning. To millions of people in other nations, the President of the United States *is* the United States, speaking for all Americans.

Some Americans think that the ceremonial activities interfere with more pressing duties. Yet they are one part of the President's job. The President fulfills duties performed by kings in other countries. The President is as much a symbol of the United States as are the flag and the Statue of Liberty.

### Chief Diplomat

Much stays the same in foreign policy from one President to another. Yet each one faces new issues that require new policies. And while most foreign policy decisions need not demand personal attention and can be resolved by others, the President must approve the general direction of American foreign policy. The President will often make the really big decisions after hearing the advice of others. The Constitution gives the President the sole power to make treaties,

President and Mrs. Nixon visit the Great Wall during Nixon's historic trip to China in 1972.

291

although the Senate must finally approve them. The President receives foreign ambassadors, can ask a country to recall its ambassador, and appoints ambassadors and ministers to other countries with the advice and consent of the Senate.

The Constitution provides some checks on the President's diplomatic powers. Treaties must be approved by the Senate before they can be put into effect. The Senate must also confirm the appointment of ambassadors and ministers to foreign countries. Many treaties cannot be carried out until the Senate and House agree to authorize the funds needed to make the treaty effective. Still, foreign policy is in the hands of the President who chooses to take control of it.

The President may make Executive Agreements without submitting them to the Senate. Under these arrangements President Franklin Roosevelt recognized the USSR in 1933, swapped some American destroyers for naval bases with England in 1940, and arranged with England and the Soviet Union in 1945 for the end of the war with Germany and Japan. Only the President can "recognize" a country. Since 1959, Presidents Eisenhower, Kennedy, Johnson, Nixon, and Ford have refused to extend diplomatic recognition to the government of Cuba.

The President, more than any other official in the country, has access to information upon which diplomatic decisions can be made. The Central Intelligence Agency, the National Security Council, as well as the intelligence divisions of the various armed services and the State Department report directly to the President. This highly secret information need not be shared with others. Congress and the courts may be in the dark about the specific policies we are following and why. Thus the President can influence for many years the ties of our nation to others in the world.

## Commander in Chief

Closely related to the role of chief diplomat is the President's role of Commander in Chief of the armed services. The President is "super-general" and "super-admiral" for the United States. More than any other person, the President can decide whether we shall have war or peace.

The Constitution assigns some war-making powers to Congress. It has authority to declare war, to tax for the common defense, to raise and support armies, to provide and maintain a navy, to make rules governing the army and navy, and so on. Still, Congress has never declared war except at the request of the President. And the President can and often has sent troops to trouble spots around the world without asking the permission of Congress.

The President may take action that starts a war and thereafter wage it. The last time that Congress declared war, in 1941, Japan had already attacked the United States. Since that time, the United

President Roosevelt discusses Pacific war strategy with two of his naval commanders.

States has fought in Korea and Vietnam. In neither case did the President ask for, nor did Congress grant, a declaration of war. Moreover, Presidents have intervened in a number of situations that might have led to violent conflict. For example, Eisenhower sent troops to Lebanon in 1957. Johnson intervened in the Dominican Republic in 1965. Kennedy supported an attempt to invade Cuba in 1961. And Ford sent armed forces to rescue a ship and crew held by Cambodia in 1975.

In the hands of the President we have placed the greatest military power the world has ever known. The enormity of this power should be the most sobering aspect of choosing a President. According to their own accounts, it is the most sobering responsibility that a President assumes.

The President can also use the military to put down revolt within our own nation. The President is not only "super-general" and "super-admiral" but also "super-sheriff." When local police and state militia are unable to control rioting and civil disorder within an American city, the President can use, and on occasion has used, federal troops to bring an end to violence. During such national disasters as a flood or earthquake, the President can arrange to airlift supplies or send troops to prevent looting.

293

## Chief Executive

The Constitution says, "The executive power shall be vested in a President of the United States." As *chief executive,* the President sees that the laws of Congress are carried out, or put into operation. The laws provide for many services. The mail must be delivered, meat inspected, the stock market supervised, air traffic regulated, crime investigated, new dams built, and so on. These and thousands of other activities require federal employees. Most of them are civil servants. They spend their lives working for the government, just as other people work for private business. The President may appoint leaders of each of these activities.

Although there are many workers to help, it is finally the President's duty to make sure that the business of government is carried out. It is not unusual to hear the President blamed for poor postal service, inflation, an energy crisis, a lack of housing, and scores of other things. It is clear that the President cannot begin to know all the people who are working for the government and cannot supervise all of its activities. The President can only hope that the men and women appointed to supervise those activities do so honestly and efficiently and that the government meets its duties to its citizens. It is easy to see why the role of chief executive is perhaps the most frustrating one.

## Chief Legislator

The Constitution clearly says that the function of Congress is to pass laws. But the President is given certain legislative duties. The President can, for example, veto bills that have been passed by Congress and thereby prevent them from becoming law.

The President may also ask for new laws and changes in old ones. This is done in the form of messages and reports to Congress on many topics. The President gives a State of the Union address at the start of each new session of Congress, and sends special messages from time to time.

However, the President's legislative power goes beyond merely proposing laws to Congress. In actual fact, many of the bills in Congress each year have started in the executive branch. The ideas for new laws often begin in executive agencies. In many cases the bills are drafted by executive officials. The bills are then introduced in the House and Senate by members of the President's political party.

Bills are then taken up by committees. At committee hearings members of the administration defend the bills which they drafted. The President holds "breakfasts" and other meetings for House and Senate leaders to get them moving on the measures. The President holds press conferences and at times speaks directly to the American public to explain the legislation and to urge pressure on members of Congress to vote for it. In many cases, therefore, the bills that come from Congress were planned and engineered by the President.

The hands of President Lyndon Johnson rest on the Civil Rights Act of 1964 after he signed the historic measure into law.

Many early Presidents felt that the legislative role should be quite small. They thought that the President should not interfere with the right of Congress to make law. Some Presidents would not even speak up in defense of a bill that they wanted passed. Recent Presidents have not been that timid. Most of them have seen one of their chief roles to be making sure that laws believed vital to the American public make their way through Congress. Therefore, Presidents spend much time meeting with leaders of Congress and with their own aides in working out ways to influence Congress.

**Chief Economic Planner**

Americans have taken much pride in their system of "free enterprise." For many years the role of government in the American economy was to ensure stable conditions within which business could operate freely. But more and more in modern times the role has grown. Particularly since Franklin Roosevelt, the President's job has included the devising of programs to help the economy run smoothly.

Prior to 1921 the business of deciding how much money the government would need each year was left to Congress. But by the end of World War I it was clear that this was not a good way to do business. Therefore, in 1921 the Bureau of the Budget was set up within the executive branch. The Bureau's job was to create a national budget to be sent to Congress each year. This shifted the job of planning the national budget from Congress to the Presidency.

At first the Bureau of the Budget was in the Department of the Treasury. Later it was moved to the Executive Office of the President.

Today all federal programs must be cleared by the Office of Management and Budget (OMB) before they can be sent to Congress. The director of OMB is one of the President's chief aides. OMB must coordinate all the requests of the federal agencies into a single budget to be sent to Congress for approval. To prepare the budget, the President must decide programs and policies for the coming year. The opinions of Congress about the President's policies and programs are largely expressed through their treatment of the budget. Items may be added, reduced, or deleted. Thus Congress decides which of the President's programs will be put into operation.

The passage of the Employment Act of 1946 gave new duties to the President. This act requires the President to send to Congress an annual report on the state of the nation's economy. The Council of Economic Advisers, which prepares the report, looks at various aspects of the national economy and suggests what ought to be done about such problems as recession and inflation. The Employment Act of 1946 set forth the principle that the government should promote high employment, production, and purchasing power. Since that time, the national government's policies on taxing, spending, and many other issues have greatly influenced the economic life of the nation.

### Party Chief

The Constitution does not require the President to be the leader of a political party. But except for George Washington, every President has been recognized as the leader of a party.

As *party chief* the President must at times face the problem of *role conflict*. For example, while acting as *head of state,* representing all American citizens, the President is at the same time the head of the Democratic or Republican party. When choosing people to hold key positions in the government, the President is likely to pick members of his or her own political party. Such people, the President may believe, are more committed to the administration's policies than would be members of the other party. But also the President must reward party members for their faithful activity during the election campaign.

As party chief the President will try to strengthen the party to improve the chances for reelection—or the election of a successor of the President's own party. As party chief the President often assists party members who are running for office, lending support to make certain that they will be elected.

On the other hand, as *chief legislator* the President must have the support of both parties in Congress. There must not be too much favoritism for one party. Otherwise the President will not have the support needed to get bills passed. One way Presidents have sometimes resolved the conflict between the *head of state* role and *party chief* role is to assign much of the strictly party political activity to the Vice-President.

The President often must walk a very narrow path, trying to appear to represent all Americans while providing strong leadership for a party. As *party chief* the President picks the party's national chairperson and helps plan strategies for future elections. The President gives speeches that help the party pay for the election campaign. A President's Club may be set up with a fee of $1000 entitling the member to attend a White House dinner. The fee will go into the party treasury.

## Representative of All the People

President Truman once referred to the President as "lobbyist for all the people." The President and Vice-President are the only persons elected by all the voters. According to this view the President has, in effect, a national constituency. On the other hand, a Senator or Representative has a constituency that is limited to a state or district. Therefore, the President more than any other person has a chance and a duty to think about the needs of the whole nation.

At times, Senators and Representatives may face conflicts between what they believe to be best for the nation as a whole and what their constituency wants. For example, it may be very costly to build ships in an old shipyard. The President may think that we could spend our

Constituency: the body of citizens whom a public official represents; an electoral district.

President Ford plays his role of party chief by speaking at a Republican gathering in Greenville, North Carolina.

money better in other ways. But it is very hard for the Representative from the district that has the shipyard to vote in favor of its closing. This would mean the loss of jobs in that district. It is, therefore, one of the main roles of the President to try to identify "the national interest" and try to promote it.

### The President Depends on Many Other People

While only one person can be President at any single moment, the office of the President requires the time, energy, and loyalty of thousands of men and women. While the President has treaty-making power in the role of *chief diplomat,* the actual work in drafting and negotiating a treaty is done by many other people. In some cases the President may know only the general purposes, not the details, of the treaty.

The vast majority of the President's legislative program does not start in the White House, but rather in the various federal agencies. If not on record as opposed to a program desired by an agency and unless its cost exceeds the agency's budget, the President is likely to recommend the program to Congress. But the President may have only a vague idea of how the program would actually work.

In short, the President is the best-known and final decision-maker in the United States. Yet the decisions depend upon the work and prior decisions of many other people.

## A Typical Day in the Life of a President

In the previous lesson you learned that the President has at least eight roles to fulfill. During any typical day the President may engage in each of these eight roles. In the following exercise you will have a chance to apply what you have learned. Below is a schedule that might be "typical" for a President of the United States. This schedule is based on actual schedules of recent Presidents. Of course, any actual day's schedule can rarely be typical, for on some days the President may be engaged in a single crisis or activity that will call for all one's time and energy. This means that other roles are likely to be passed by. However, this schedule allows one to see things a President might do in all the roles.

Your task is to decide which of the President's activities during the day represents one of the eight roles in action. Note that an additional role—spouse and parent—has been added, since during any day the President is likely also to act in that role. Some of the items on the schedule may be of more than one role type.

| | |
|---|---|
| Head of State (HS) | Chief Economic Planner (CEP) |
| Chief Diplomat (CD) | Party Chief (PC) |
| Commander-in-Chief (CC) | Representative of All the |
| Chief Executive (CE) | People (RP) |
| Chief Legislator (CL) | Spouse and Parent (SP) |

6:30—Awakened by guard; showers and dresses.

7:00—Watches television news in the bedroom and glances through three morning newspapers.

7:30—Two assistants enter the bedroom. One hands the President the *Congressional Record* for the preceding day. A few pages have been clipped to indicate references to be read. The second assistant, the appointments secretary, briefs the President on the schedule for the day and hands over a folder containing notes which explain why each person wants an appointment.

7:50—Meeting completed, assistants leave; and President joins spouse for breakfast. They talk about personal matters, especially the forthcoming marriage of their daughter.

8:15—President arrives at the office and finds on the desk a notebook of clippings containing current news items and commentary. This notebook, about thirty pages long, is put together daily by three assistants drawing upon newspapers and journals from across the nation. President scans through the articles rapidly, making marginal notes by some articles.

8:25—President telephones the Secretary of Defense, expressing concern about press reports that a new bomber is proving far more costly and less efficient than had been planned and asking what can be done to solve the problem.

8:35—Personal secretary enters room, bringing a number of documents for the President to sign and a few selected letters from the early morning mail which the President might like to read personally. Reads the letters, dictates directions for answering them, and signs documents.

8:53—Meets with four congressional leaders of own party to discuss strategy for passing a bill that is of great interest to the President. Reminds leaders how important this bill is to the nation and to their own party.

9:20—President steps from office to an adjoining room to receive an award by the National Audubon Society for efforts to preserve nesting grounds for wild birds. President thanks members of the Society. Photographers snap pictures.

9:35—President returns to office and places three telephone calls:
  —(1) to Senator Smith, a long-time friend who is recovering from an illness. President urges her to get well soon.
  —(2) to Murphy, a labor leader whose union is on strike. President inquires about state of negotiations and expresses hope that strike can be settled quickly as it is having a bad effect on the economy.
  —(3) to Jones, the Director of the Office of Management and Budget, who is asked a specific question about the budget that has been brought to the President's attention.

10:00—Two defeated Representatives, members of the President's political party, arrive to learn whether the President has any jobs for them.

10:20—Calls the Commissioner of Education to ask about the status of an education bill that interests the President.

10:30—The new American ambassador to Sweden drops in to say good-bye and to ask whether there are any special instructions. The President has none, but they chat for a few minutes about political conditions in Sweden.

10:45—President leaves office for an adjoining room where the relatives of five men killed in military action are waiting. President gives a short speech and presents the Purple Heart award to the families of the five men. Photos are taken.

11:15—Returns to office to find Special Assistant for National Security Affairs waiting. Assistant gives rundown on the present status of four international crises that have been occupying the attention of the President. President listens carefully, asks a few questions, but finds no new situation that would require a policy decision at that moment.

11:50—President leaves office and returns to room on the second floor of the White House. Has a quick lunch, talks briefly by telephone with daughter in New York, and lies down for a short nap.

2:00—Returns to the office to find a group that will watch the signing of a new gun-control law. While cameras record the event, the President uses many pens to sign name, giving the pens away to those who aided in passing the bill. President makes a brief speech.

2:40—President steps to the Cabinet Room, where the Council of Economic Advisers is waiting. They discuss plans to slow down the inflation that is affecting the country. President agrees to move quickly on one of their recommendations.

3:15—Returns to office and greets a young Iowa girl who presents a valentine. It is recorded by the cameras; pictures will appear in most daily newspapers on Valentine's Day.

3:25—President invites White House reporters into office and agrees to answer their questions for fifteen minutes. Uses first five minutes to announce plans for overseas travel in the near future. Some persons can't crowd in, and the time is much too short to answer all the questions they have. Still, this brief meeting will get the President on the front page the next day.

3:45—Aide rushes in with a top-secret CIA report on a Latin American nation, one of the four foreign policy crisis areas that the President has been working on. President scans the report and places a call to the CIA Director to send over other needed facts.

The President's White House office is known as the Oval Office.

4:15—President receives the Foreign Minister from an Asian country. The Foreign Minister has spent several days meeting with the Secretary of State. This meeting with the President is more formal and official than for the purpose of conducting business, but the two visit for a time.

4:45—A congresswoman enters the President's office. She has been trying to have an Army base reopened in her district. The President agrees to think carefully about the matter and let her know the decision soon.

5:00—Secretary brings in more mail and documents requiring the President's signature.

5:15—President's personal physician enters. The doctor concludes, after a brief examination, that the President has fully recovered from a cold.

5:30—President leaves to change for a Lincoln Day dinner in a Washington hotel that evening. Goes over the speech to be given at the dinner.

6:30—Arrives at the hotel, eats dinner, and presents the Lincoln Day speech.

10:00—President returns to White House and, feeling the need for some exercise, bowls for forty-five minutes.

10:45—Returns to bedroom with a folder of "night-time" reading of memoranda and brief reports. Reads for one hour, marking questions and writing marginal notes that will suggest actions to be taken in the near future.

11:45—Turns out light and falls asleep.

## The President as Decision-Maker

The significance of presidential decision-making was understood well by John F. Kennedy, who once observed:

A President must choose among men, among measures, among methods. His choice helps determine the issues of his Presidency, their priority in the national life, and the mode and success of their execution. The heart of the Presidency is therefore informed, prudent, and resolute choice—and the secret of the presidential enterprise is to be found in an examination of the way presidential choices are made.[1]

Theodore C. Sorensen, a top-level assistant to President Kennedy, noted that decision-making is central to the presidential role:

The President's entire existence is a continuous process of decision—including decisions not to decide and decisions not to take action—decisions on what to say, whom to see, what to sign, whom to name, and what to do, as Commander-in-Chief and diplomatic chief, as legislative leader and political leader, as a moral leader and a Free World leader, and in taking care that the laws be faithfully executed. Every policy announced is the sum of many decisions, each made in a different mold and manner.[2]

### Types of Presidential Decisions

The scope of presidential decision-making is enormous. A President makes decisions about laws, about the appointment of men and women to office, about our ties with other nations, about how to finance government programs, about national defense, about the space program, about the solution of farm problems and city problems, and so on. These decisions may range from the rather trivial to the great, from deciding whom to invite to a White House luncheon to deciding whether to send troops to a trouble spot. While most small decisions can be handled by assistants, decisions in which the stakes are high usually reach the President. As President Eisenhower told John F. Kennedy, upon introducing him to the White House, "There are no easy matters that will come to you as President. If they are easy, they will be settled at a lower level."

The great importance of many presidential decisions is a burden to any officeholder. As we shall see later, during the Cuban missile crisis of 1962 President Kennedy had to make decisions about "life or death" affecting whole nations, or even the world. President Truman's decision to provide large economic aid to Western Europe through the Marshall Plan was the first step in a rapid rise out of the rubble of World War II. Some observers believe that the Marshall Plan saved both France and Italy from Communist control.

---

1-2. T. C. Sorensen, *Decision-Making in the White House* (New York: Columbia University Press, 1963). Used by permission.

## Factors That Influence Presidential Decision-Making

Decision-making means choosing among possible courses of action. It also refers to the search for alternatives, to setting priorities for which problems will be given attention, and to how policy decisions will be put into effect. Each President goes about the process of decision-making in a different way. However, there are several factors which influence the decisions of all Presidents and are common to decision-making in general. These factors may be grouped as follows: (a) the circumstances of the decision, (b) the individual characteristics of the decision-makers, and (c) other limitations.

## Circumstances of the Decision

In some cases the President knows for several days or weeks that a decision will have to be made, and can thus prepare for it. For example, the President learns that Congress wants to add $200 million to the education budget. A decision may be made to warn Congress that the bill faces a veto. Expecting that the bill will pass Congress in spite of the warning, the President may have several weeks to explore what the political effects of a veto might be. A veto message can be written before it is needed. This decision can be carefully planned.

Some decisions are made after years of study. Special task forces and congressional committees may have studied and shaped a proposal before it needs a final decision by the President. The bill to change the Post Office from a cabinet department into a public corporation came after years of study.

Secretary of Housing and Urban Development Carla Hill meets with President Ford in the Oval Office.

Unfortunately the President and the advisers do not always have the luxury of much time to pick the problems they wish to deal with and to search for solutions. Many decisions are made in a crisis situation. In September 1970 the Palestine Liberation Front "sky-jacked" three jet planes and held the passengers hostage. President Nixon had an unexpected problem. Plans to rescue the hostages and to prevent further such incidents had to be worked out rapidly.

Decisions are clearly affected by the time available to make decisions. When a crisis is unexpected, when the stakes are high, and when time is short, one can't study all the possible angles in detail nor consult with many people. The President must make a decision under poor conditions.

The kind of decision that is made depends also on the importance the decision-maker assigns to the situation. Let's look at the Vietnam war. President Johnson and Secretary of State Dean Rusk believed that the defense of South Vietnam was vital to American interests. They saw the war in Vietnam as part of a general effort to extend Communist control throughout Southeast Asia and to drive American influence out of the area. Moreover, they believed their policy to be in keeping with the policies of Presidents Eisenhower and Kennedy. Critics of their policy argued that no major American interest was at stake, that the fight was chiefly a civil war, and that we should stay out of it. However, the fact that President Johnson and his principal advisers saw the Vietnamese struggle as crucial to American interests greatly influenced American military and diplomatic policies.

### Individual Characteristics of Decision-Makers

Very little is known for certain about the influence of personality on the behavior of decision-makers. Still, it seems likely that certain traits are important. Is the President decisive and willing to take risks? Does the President show a need for power? Is the President intelligent? creative? Does the President have a feeling of self-esteem? Or feel threatened when people disagree? Is the President's outlook on life generally positive or negative?

President X is creative and intelligent and picks people with these traits to come up with new policy alternatives. President Y tends to carry forward policies from the past. Which of these Presidents would seem to have the greater number of solutions to choose from when problems arise? A President who wants to be surrounded by "yes-men" will likely produce different decisions than one who wants debate.

Decisions are likely influenced by the social background and experience of the decision-maker. President Eisenhower set up his White House staff along lines he had used as a general. Also he had no experience in party politics prior to becoming President and preferred to delegate partisan matters to others while he dealt with issues he viewed as more important.

President Nixon appeared on television in 1970 to rally public support of an Administration decision to send American and South Vietnam troops into Cambodia.

Other Presidents, arriving in office after a lifetime of politics, may take a quite different view of the office. Upon taking office after President Kennedy's death, Lyndon Johnson concentrated on domestic problems: civil rights, education, poverty. At first, he showed rather little interest in foreign affairs. Only after his election in 1964 did he begin to shift his attention to foreign affairs.

President Nixon, on the other hand, was more interested in foreign policy than in domestic affairs. He set up the White House staff in such a way that he could center his attention on diplomatic concerns.

Decisions may also be influenced by personal beliefs. A President who sees communism as the greatest threat facing the United States may view many problems as part of a Communist conspiracy and treat them as such. One President may feel the best way to prevent war is to seek areas of compromise, while another may believe that firmness is the best way to deal with an enemy. Some Presidents may have real concern for the plight of minority groups in the United States, while others merely pretend to have concern. Because of their attitudes it is likely that these two types of Presidents would have quite different policies toward minority groups.

President Hoover believed firmly in American values of individualism and private initiative. He felt that government should stay out of economic affairs as much as possible. His personal beliefs may

305

Industrialists Harvey Firestone and Henry Ford and inventor Thomas Edison chat with President and Mrs. Coolidge as they examine a 125-year-old sap bucket. Coolidge and his successor Herbert Hoover generally opposed government interference with business.

have kept him from making decisions that could have reduced the impact of the economic depression in 1930. Other Presidents have felt that the federal government should try to help solve economic and social problems. Their beliefs have helped to expand the role of government in economic affairs.

### Other Limitations on Decision-Makers

No person, least of all the President of the United States, is totally free to decide what to do. Like any other person, the President is influenced by forces in the environment. These forces include rules, status relationships, public opinion, available resources, and external decision-makers.

### Rules

The rules—laws and customs—that define the rights and duties of the Chief Executive put major limits on the President's decision-making power. Both the Constitution and laws passed by Congress set limits. Customs developed over almost two hundred years are also an influence.

American political leaders are expected to play politics according to the "rules of the game." Thus, no President may appoint someone to a major office, such as a federal judge, without the consent of the Senate. This limit is stated in the Constitution. President Lyndon Johnson wanted to appoint Francis X. Morrissey to the position of federal judge. Morrissey was a personal friend of Senators Edward Kennedy and Robert Kennedy, who had recommended him. But after studying Morrissey, a Senate majority believed that he would make a poor judge. Then President Johnson withdrew Morrissey's name and chose another person for the job. In this case the President's decision-making power was limited by the Senate's right to confirm or reject his appointments.

Customs, as well as laws, are a major influence. For example, the custom of "senatorial courtesy" has been followed faithfully over the years. "Senatorial courtesy" refers to an unspoken pledge among the Senators not to consent to a nomination of a person disapproved by the Senator of the President's party from the state affected. For example, if Iowa has a Republican Senator and the President is a Republican, the President must consult with that Senator about whom to nominate, say, as a federal judge or marshal in Iowa. This is a custom, not a law. But Presidents tend to abide by this rule.

**Status Relationships**

Every status, or position, in a society involves relationships with people in other statuses, or positions. The status of father involves relationships with wife and mother and with children. The President is head of the executive branch. This status gives authority over other executive officials. Assistants in the White House Office—the personal staff—have very close ties with the President. How the President gets along with the staff—and how staff members get along with each other—is bound to affect the President's decision-making. The President is also limited by the attitudes and skills of subordinates. Are they skillful in analyzing crucial issues? Do they present all the facts needed, or do they hide some unpleasant things?

With time limited, the President can focus on only the most pressing problems which arise. Aides must identify those issues and try to settle less important ones. Moreover, the aides must assemble the facts needed to make a decision and present them in a form that can be easily and rapidly understood. No President has the time to read long reports. In selecting problems, in helping decide who will see the President, in determining the facts the President will hear, the staff clearly influences presidential decisions.

Moreover, the various executive bureaus and departments often have their own policies, their own view on what the President's decision should be. Often these are policies inherited from a previous administration. In theory, the President can command an agency or department to carry out the President's own policies. But in practice its advice must be heard. Many of the agencies have strong supporters in Congress. At times this makes it unwise for the President to meddle with them for fear of making congressional leaders angry. And the President can remove only the top bureaucrats. Others are protected by civil service rules. Thus the President depends on the departments to provide facts and to carry out policies. In the process the President must at times negotiate with subordinates.

President Franklin D. Roosevelt expressed the frustration he felt from time to time when trying to influence those who served under him.

> The Treasury is so large and far-flung and ingrained in its practices that I find it is almost impossible to get the action and results I want—even with Henry [Morgenthau] there. But the Treasury is not to be compared with the State Department. You should go through the experience of trying to get any changes in the thinking, policy and action of the career diplomats and then you'd know what a real problem was. But the Treasury and State Department put together are nothing compared with the Na-a-vy. The admirals are really something to cope with—and I should know. To change anything in the Na-a-vy is like punching a feather bed. You punch it with your right and you punch it with your left until you are finally exhausted, and you find [it] just as it was before you started punching.[3]

Many observers think that the main skill demanded of a President is the ability to persuade others to act. Presidential power is the power to persuade others to help make and carry out decisions. These "others" include members of the President's personal staff and the big federal bureaucracy.

**Public Opinion**

Public opinion is an ever-present social force influencing presidential decisions about crucial issues. Abraham Lincoln is reported to have said that with public opinion on his side he could do anything. But in the face of public opposition he could do nothing.

Public opinion is a complex matter. On some issues it can almost be said that the public has *no* opinion. The public seems to know and care little about the issue or is simply willing to follow the President's leadership. An example of such an issue might be whether to keep up cultural exchanges with the Soviet Union. It may be that most Americans would support the President in whatever choice made. In other cases a decision seems to be forced on the President by the power of public opinion. For example, a shift in public opinion on America's role in Southeast Asia had a powerful effect on American foreign policy in that area during the 1970s.

In addition to general public opinion, there are special groups whose opinions matter a great deal. These groups have strong views on certain issues. They also have enough influence in Congress to cause political problems for a President who ignores them. One example is the "veterans lobby." It consists of ex-servicemen and women.

---

3. Clinton Rossiter, *The American Presidency*. (New York: Harcourt Brace Jovanovich, Inc., 1960), pp. 60-61. Used by permission.

Most are members of the American Legion or the Veterans of Foreign Wars. They have a special interest in pensions, hospital care, housing loans, and other benefits for vets. They also tend to favor a big defense budget and a firm policy toward Communist nations. Any effort by the President to curtail benefits or to weaken the Defense Department will arouse the veterans lobby.

Thus, public opinion is a major force, and Presidents take steps to be informed of it and to create it. President Lyndon Johnson was a "poll watcher." He gauged the public view of his decisions by reading the results of national opinion surveys. Most Presidents have been avid newspaper and magazine readers in order to assess public opinion. Moreover, they look to editorial columns for views that support the decisions they want to make.

Through TV press conferences and speeches to the nation, press releases, and public ceremonies, Presidents attempt to shape public opinion. Recent Presidents have appeared on TV to inform the public about any new or bold decision. For example, in November 1969 Nixon addressed Americans on his plans to end the war in Vietnam. President Ford dealt with the energy problem in a TV talk in May

Through public service ads like this one, the advertising industry helps the President and executive agencies influence public opinion.

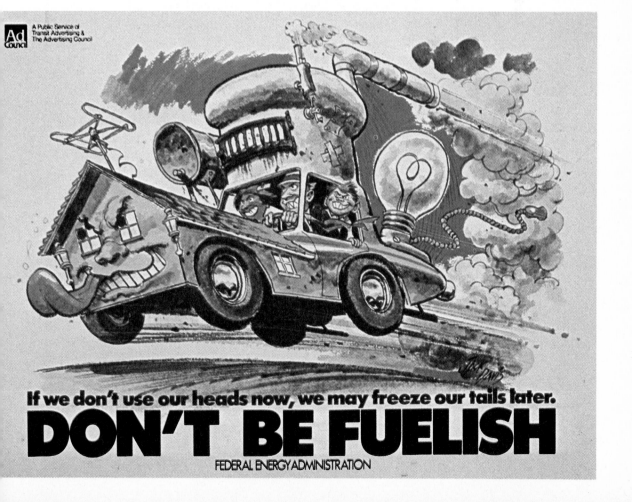

Ad Council — A Public Service of Transit Advertising & The Advertising Council

If we don't use our heads now, we may freeze our tails later.

# DON'T BE FUELISH

FEDERAL ENERGY ADMINISTRATION

1975. Kennedy spoke to the nation to enlist public support for the passage of a civil rights law in 1963. And Franklin Roosevelt, in pre-television days, used the "fireside chat" over radio to influence public opinion behind the bold new economic programs of his "New Deal."

**Available Resources**

Presidential decisions are also limited by available resources. Money, materials, technicians, and highly skilled scientists were all necessary for the decision to "send a man to the moon." Congress has much to say about the availability of resources for such decisions.

The President obtains funds for programs through vote of Congress. The job is to convince Congress of the need. For example, President Truman's skill in getting a hostile Congress to vote funds for the Marshall Plan was the crucial first step in carrying out his decision to aid war-torn Europe. Of course, the President's command of resources depends on a productive nation. Without productive people, the most vigorous President would be doomed to a lack of resources to carry out decisions.

**External Decision-Makers**

In matters of foreign policy the President does not always start the action. A policy decision is often a response to an action by another nation. When choosing a course of action, the President must always think about how foreign decision-makers will react to the decision. Their response will most likely prompt the President to undertake a new round of decisions.

There are also decision-makers within the United States who must be considered. A President is eager to get along with Congress. Thus at times a decision must be made on whether to veto an unwanted bill—and thereby run the risk of alienating some members—or to permit it to become law. Some decisions affect the economic life of the country, but the President cannot always predict how a decision will be greeted and what new problems it will create.

It should be clear that decision-making is a complex problem and involves much more than the President sitting behind a desk answering "yes" or "no" to questions. It involves many people in selecting issues to be resolved, defining the problems, getting facts about the issues, posing alternative solutions, choosing the best ones, carrying out the policies, and judging their effects. In this activity the President is a major but by no means the sole performer.

## Building the Annual Budget

There are two major classes of presidential decisions: those made during a crisis and those that are expected and evolve over time. In the next lesson you will study an example of a crisis decision. This lesson deals with the most predictable, continuing, and complex decision a President faces each year: deciding on the annual budget. Through the budget the President sets program priorities.

Each year the federal government must adopt a budget. Many bills passed by Congress require either the spending of money or the approval of ways for the government to add to its revenues. It is always easier to think of ways to spend money than to get money. Thus much of the business of government is balancing the many activities that the government might undertake and trying to make them fit the expected income.

## Office of Management and Budget

Until 1921 each of the different departments and branches of the federal government prepared separate financial requests, each setting forth its own needs. These requests were assembled in the Treasury Department and forwarded to Congress without comment. Congress thus had the major job of setting up the budget. In 1921 Congress passed the Budget and Accounting Act that set up the Bureau of the Budget as a separate branch of the Treasury Department but reporting directly to the President. The Bureau had the job of putting the budget together. In this way, the initiative for setting priorities passed into the President's hands. In 1939 the Executive Office of the President was established and the Bureau of the Budget shifted from the Treasury Department to the Executive Office. The next major change came in 1970, when its work was expanded and its name changed to the Office of Management and Budget (OMB). It is still a part of the Executive Office.

A study of presidential decision-making in the budgeting process is largely a study of the operations of OMB. This agency, numbering around 700 people, works for the President. The budget is developed within guidelines set by the President. But the task of gathering information, stating policy choices, framing priorities, and weighing alternatives falls mostly on OMB.

## Matching Needs and Resources

The President must try to operate the business of government within the resources available. What these resources will be cannot be predicted with great accuracy. But the Council of Economic Advisers and the Secretary of the Treasury can make some forecasts. The President may, for one or more reasons, elect to spend more money than the government expects to take in. This will lead to a deficit. The government will have to borrow money; the national debt will grow; and interest payments will rise.

Each agency of the government needs funds to operate. In recent years the Department of Defense has had the largest budget of all. Few, if any, agencies ever ask for less money than they have had in the past. Believing in its programs, each can find ways to add to and improve on what it is doing. Without control, the federal budget would become hopelessly out of balance. It is up to the President first—and later Congress—to decide which agencies will get more funds, which will stay the same, and which will take cuts. The President manages this process through OMB.

Let's look at an example. The Department of Health, Education, and Welfare (HEW) is a big department with many programs. It spends part of its resources for research in medicine. Suppose the President thought that a breakthrough in cancer research was needed. Perhaps people in the health agencies thought it would be better to invest more resources on research into mental health and keep up only modest spending in cancer research. Because HEW's budget request must be cleared by the White House, which is to say OMB, before it can go to Congress, the President can insist that the health research funds be shifted to cancer research. Aware of this choice, OMB will talk with HEW about the changes. Later an HEW official will appear at hearings held by committees in Congress to answer questions about the agency's budget. The official will be expected to defend OMB's budget figures.

### Steps in the Budget Process

The major steps in the budget process are shown in the chart on the next page. The federal government operates on a *fiscal,* or financial, *year* (now October 1 to September 30) rather than the calendar year of January 1 to December 31.

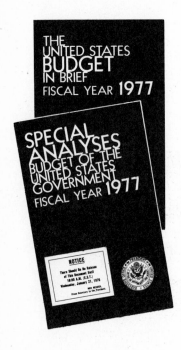

OMB must start work on the budget long before the funds are needed. For example, work on the fiscal 1978 budget (Oct. 1, 1977 to Sept. 30, 1978) began in spring 1976. During March and April, OMB staff worked out forecasts on the national economy—mainly to make guesses on tax revenues. They issued guidelines to the various agencies to help them prepare their budgets. In turn, the agencies made estimates of how much money they would need. They also put together facts and figures to show why certain amounts of money were needed.

During the summer and early fall, OMB staff met with agency heads to try to agree on the amount of funds that would be asked for. At these meetings the people also talked about the level of spending for the various programs: Which programs would need more money than last year? Could any program be cut out? In this exchange between OMB and the agency heads, OMB was acting as a stand-in for the President to make the agencies defend their programs.

### Presidential Action on the Budget

By late fall, early drafts of the budget were ready for the President to look at. Mr. Ford and his close advisers could now order some changes to be made. In December the final budget was put together for printing, and the President's budget message was drafted.

Shortly after Congress convened in 1977, the President presented a budget message to Congress. The message—and the printed budget of around 500 pages—set forth plans for total income and spending.

# STEPS IN THE BUDGET PROCESS

1. March. OMB prepares forecasts and economic studies

2. April–May. OMB calls on government agencies for estimates of needs

3. July–August. OMB examiners help agencies prepare estimates.

4. Sept. Each agency submits request for appropriations

5. Sept–Nov. OMB examines and reviews requests

6. Oct.–Nov. Examiners give OMB Director recommendations for review

7. Nov.–Dec. OMB Director submits recommendations to President for final review

8. January. President transmits Executive Budget, and message, to Congress

9. Joint Budgeting Committee sets spending guidelines

10. Congressional committees hold hearings on various parts of budget

11. Congress considers appropriations

12. OMB checks agencies' performance on previous budget

## Congressional Action

Now the leaders in Congress assign parts of the total budget to specific committees to review. At the same time, the Senate and House Joint Budget Committee begins to meet. Its job is to set overall spending guidelines for Congress. Perhaps the budget calls for spending to exceed revenue by $5.6 billion. Such a *budget deficit* is often planned in order to give the national economy a boost. The Joint Committee may decide that this deficit should rise another half billion to $6.1 billion.

In addition to setting targets for total spending and revenues (with perhaps a deficit), the Joint Committee will set targets for the broad budget areas: national defense, commerce, agriculture, and so on.

Until the passage of the Congressional Budget and Impoundment Act of 1974, Congress had not set overall spending and revenue targets for itself. It merely passed separate bills for various programs and agencies. For example, an education bill would give HEW, say, $8.1 billion to spend on its various education programs. No one could know what the total spending would be until Congress adjourned for the year.

Under the new plan of target-setting by the Joint Committee, Congress can still miss its spending goals. But the plan at least puts some pressure on the committees to think about the overall budget.

## OMB Continues Its Work

While Congress was at work on the fiscal 1978 budget, OMB was busy with start-up work on the 1979 budget. OMB staff members also showed up at committee hearings in Congress to explain the 1978 budget and to answer questions. Another OMB job was also going on: looking at how 1977 funds were being spent. A big OMB task is to check on performance: Are the programs working? Should this program be phased out on the basis of its poor record? Should this one get more money, since it is doing some real good—more than was really expected?

President Ford meets with OMB officials and a member of his personal staff to go over some details of the budget.

### OMB and the President

Drawing up the annual budget is a time-consuming, complex task. The President comes into the process at many stages, but the job lies mainly in OMB's hands acting for the President. It is OMB's job to see that the President's priorities are carried out. In order to do this, OMB must battle with the executive agencies and with Congress.

The crisis decisions that face the President are the ones that get the big headlines. But budget decisions hammered out over long stretches of time are often more important. The federal budget is the chief way that the President can leave a personal stamp on American society.

## The Cuban Missile Crisis

When, if ever, should nuclear weapons be used? This question has haunted every President since Harry S. Truman ordered the atomic bombing of two Japanese cities in 1945. For twelve days in 1962 (October 16-28) President John F. Kennedy faced daily the decision of whether to use nuclear weapons in defense of the national interest. During this time President Kennedy had to decide between war and peace, between life or death for millions of people. The following case shows many aspects of presidential decision-making during a time of crisis.

**Background of the Crisis.** Why was the President forced to consider the awful chance of nuclear war? The answer must begin with a brief look at relations between the United States, Cuba, and the Soviet Union. Since 1959 Cuba had been ruled by Fidel Castro, a Communist dictator. Castro had won power during a revolution in which Fulgencio Batista, a military dictator, had been overthrown.

Soon after Castro took power, relations between Cuba and the United States became strained. Finally, diplomatic relations were broken. The conflict between Cuba and the United States led Castro to cooperate with the Soviet Union. The Soviet Union began to send weapons and military advisers to build up the armed power of Cuba.

American political leaders watched the Cuban arms build-up with grave concern. Rumors circulated that the Soviet Union was sending nuclear missiles to Cuba. However, Soviet leaders assured President Kennedy that Cuba would not receive offensive nuclear weapons.

On Tuesday morning, October 16, President Kennedy found out that Soviet promises not to install nuclear missiles in Cuba were false. The Soviet leaders, including Premier Nikita Khrushchev, had deceived him.

**Aerial Photographs Reveal Missile Sites.** McGeorge Bundy, a special presidential adviser, gave the bad news to Kennedy. The President called a meeting of his chief advisers at 11:45 A.M. in the Cabinet Room. CIA Deputy Director Marshall Carter showed the President

President Kennedy conferred with his brother, Attorney General Robert F. Kennedy, on the missile crisis.

photos of the Cuban missile sites. These photos proved beyond doubt that the Soviet Union had supplied Cuba with powerful offensive weapons to point at the United States. The President asked this group of advisers to meet regularly until a final decision had been made about this crisis. During most of this time they would meet without the President, although he would be kept informed of their progress.

The advisory group was the Executive Committee of the National Security Council, or EXCOM. It consisted of the Secretary of State, the Secretary of Defense, the director of the Central Intelligence Agency, the Secretary of the Treasury, President Kennedy's adviser on national security affairs, and his chief legal adviser on the White House staff. Other members were the Under Secretary of State, the Deputy Under Secretary of State, the chairman of the Joint Chiefs of Staff, the Assistant Secretary of State for Latin America, the President's adviser on Russian Affairs, the Deputy Secretary of Defense, and the Assistant Secretary of Defense. Also meeting with EXCOM from time to time were Vice-President Lyndon Johnson; Adlai Stevenson, Ambassador to the United Nations; Kenneth O'Donnell, Special Assistant to the President; Donald Wilson, Deputy Director of the United States Information Agency; and Attorney General Robert F. Kennedy.

At its first meeting, EXCOM talked about the problem. During the meeting President Kennedy issued the following orders to the group:

1. Take more photos in order to chart progress on construction and expansion of the missile sites. Daily flights over Cuba should be made to get more pictures.

2. Put aside all other tasks so that full attention can be given to the problem.

3. Maintain complete secrecy about this crisis until a final decision is made.

316

Between Tuesday, October 16, and Friday, October 19, the members of EXCOM devoted most of their time to the Cuban missile crisis. They met daily to discuss the problem, and they worked individually and in small groups to clarify their thinking. While EXCOM met, new aerial photos showed some disturbing facts. As of Wednesday, October 17, the Cubans had built 16 missile sites with 32 missiles that could hit targets over 1000 miles away. These missiles were aimed at some major American cities and were able to reach these targets within a very few minutes after being fired. Military experts estimated that the missiles could kill as many as 80 million Americans.

**EXCOM Suggests Six Possible Solutions.** At first EXCOM considered six alternative solutions to the problem:

1. Do nothing.

2. Negotiate with Soviet leaders to work out a deal. For example, agree to remove United States missile bases in Turkey in exchange for Soviet removal of the missiles in Cuba.

3. Try to work out a deal with Castro. Warn him that military force could be used against Cuba.

4. Use ships and aircraft to blockade Cuba—to prevent new shipments of military supplies from being sent there and to put pressure on the Cubans to remove the missile sites.

5. Launch an air strike to destroy the missile sites.

6. Launch a full-scale invasion to destroy the missile sites and overthrow the Castro government.

EXCOM considered the strong and weak points of each of these solutions. From their discussion, four of the six were dropped. Only items 4 and 5 in the above list were kept. Several people in the group favored a blockade. Others favored an air strike. At first the majority of EXCOM favored an air strike. However, by Thursday night, October 18, the majority of the group favored a naval blockade.

At 9:15 o'clock that night, members from EXCOM gave the two solutions to the President. He heard arguments for the two positions and then told the EXCOM to study the two proposals again and report back to him on Friday.

**Two Proposals Are Studied Intensively.** On Friday morning EXCOM members decided to split into two groups—each favoring one of the two proposals. Each group wrote a paper that gave in detail the strong points of its solution. Then the two groups exchanged papers and criticized each other's arguments. Finally the papers were returned to the original groups for rewriting. This work continued all day Friday.

The main arguments of the group favoring an air strike were as follows:

> An air attack against the missile sites would destroy them quickly and completely. The threat to our cities would be removed entirely. The Communists would have warning, from this bold step, not to challenge the United States like this again.

During the Cuban missile crisis in October 1962, President Kennedy met with Army Chief of Staff Earle Wheeler (center) and other officers to discuss the Army's general readiness.

The air strike would be accompanied by a presidential address to the nation in which the action would be explained. At the same time Premier Nikita Khrushchev of the Soviet Union would be notified. Advance notice of the bombing would be given to Cuba through the United Nations. The United States government would call for a high level meeting of leaders from the United States and the Soviet Union to settle the problem and to prevent the air strike from leading to worldwide nuclear warfare.

The naval blockade idea should be rejected. Setting up a ring of warships around Cuba to prevent new arms shipments is like "locking the barn door after the horse has run away." A naval blockade cannot guarantee that the missiles will be removed; an air attack can guarantee this.

Here are the main arguments of those favoring a naval blockade:

The most important arguments for the naval blockade are the arguments against an air attack. An air strike would destroy the nation's moral leadership around the world. It would make the United States appear to be an aggressive, warlike nation picking on a weak neighbor. Thousands of people, including defenseless women and children, would suffer casualties as a result of the attack.

318

The air strike would kill not only Cuban soldiers but also Russians working at the missile sites. This could provoke a Soviet military response that could lead to an exchange of nuclear weapons between the United States and the Soviet Union.

The air strike cannot guarantee destruction of the nuclear weapons and missile sites in Cuba. An air strike would have to be followed with an infantry invasion of Cuba in order to be sure that the missile sites would be removed. This would lead to the death of thousands of American soldiers and the loss of millions of dollars in materials. And it could lead to war with the Soviet Union.

Most of President Kennedy's military advisers favored an air attack. General Curtis LeMay, Air Force Chief of Staff, argued strongly for the air strike. Robert McNamara, Secretary of Defense, was the main speaker for those favoring a naval blockade.

President Kennedy was faced with the decision of choosing between the two alternatives. He called a meeting of the National Security Council, including all members of EXCOM, for 2:30 on Friday, October 19. The meeting continued until 5:10 P.M. The President heard arguments for an air strike and a naval blockade. He was informed that preparations had been made to carry out either decision quickly.

**President Kennedy Makes a Decision.** The majority of those at the National Security Council meeting favored a naval blockade. The President decided in favor of it. He reasoned that the blockade would show that he meant business, that this Soviet challenge to the United States would be met. The blockade would give the United States a point of strength from which to bargain with the Soviets for the removal of the missiles. However, the blockade was a limited response. It gave the Soviets a chance to bargain their way out of the situation without a military response. And it gave the United States a chance to escalate the conflict if the blockade failed. By contrast, the air strike was an unlimited response. The chance that it could lead to total war was too great.

Now the decision had to be carried out. Various assistants to the President took care of actions related to carrying out the decision. A team of writers prepared a presidential address to the nation to be given on Monday. Military chiefs prepared the forces for action. State Department leaders prepared messages to American allies, to American ambassadors in foreign nations, to the United Nations, and to the Soviet Union.

The President met with the National Security Council on Sunday, October 21, at 2:30. He checked the diplomatic messages and the military preparations that had been made during the past day and a half. The Navy Chief of Staff was asked to describe plans for the blockade. The President reviewed the draft of his speech and made several changes in it.

On Monday, October 22, the President met with several key groups to inform them of developments and to gain their support. He met with his cabinet and with twenty top leaders of Congress. At 6:00 P.M. the Soviet Ambassador, Anatoly Dobrynin, was told of the proposed naval blockade.

**Influencing Public Opinion on the Decision.** At 7:00 P.M. the President spoke to the nation. He told the American people that the Soviet Union had built missile sites in Cuba and that missiles were pointed at American cities. He told of his decision to meet the Soviet challenge. He called the proposed blockade a quarantine in order that the decision would sound less warlike. He stressed that all ships carrying offensive weapons to Cuba would be stopped on the high seas and turned away. He declared that the missile sites must be taken from Cuba. President Kennedy hoped to arouse the support and the courage of the American people with words such as these:

> The nineteen thirties taught us a clear lesson. Aggressive conduct, if allowed to go unchecked and unchallenged, ultimately leads to war.
> This nation is opposed to war. We are also true to our word.
> Our unswerving objective, therefore, must be to prevent the use of these missiles against this or any other country; and to secure their withdrawal or elimination from the Western Hemisphere.
> Our policy has been one of patience and restraint, as befits a peaceful and powerful nation which leads a worldwide alliance. . . .
> We will not prematurely or unnecessarily risk the course of worldwide nuclear war in which even the fruits of victory would be ashes in our mouths, but neither will we shrink from that risk at any time it must be faced.[4]

On Tuesday, signs of support for the President's decision appeared both in the nation and around the world. Newspaper editorials and telegrams to the White House were mostly favorable. The main allies of the United States wired support. And, most important, the nations of the Organization of American States voted to support the action of the United States in this crisis.

The Organization of American States (OAS) is a mutual defense treaty organization of the Latin American republics and the United States.

**The Naval Blockade Begins.** The "quarantine" went into effect at 10:00 A.M. on Wednesday, October 24. The world waited tensely as several Soviet cargo ships, accompanied by submarines, moved toward the American naval blockade. Would the Soviet ships turn back? If they refused to turn back, what would the Americans do? Would naval warfare break out? Would nuclear war start? Questions

---

4. *The New York Times,* October 23, 1962, p. 18. © 1962 by The New York Times Company. Reprinted by permission.

320

President Kennedy signs
the proclamation to
quarantine Cuba.

such as these played on the minds of informed people all over the
world as leaders of the two super powers, the United States and the
Soviet Union, braced for the world's first nuclear confrontation.

Throughout this crisis President Kennedy had to consider how
the Soviet leaders would react to his moves. He felt strongly that
he must not put them in a position where they would have to fight
in order to "save face." Yet he knew that he must not back down
from his reasonable demands. Somehow he had to chart a course that
would win his objective of removing the Soviet missile sites from
Cuba without plunging the world into war.

At dawn on Thursday, October 25, a Soviet tanker came into contact with American ships. After identifying itself, it was allowed to
pass. The President, believing that weapons were not aboard the
tanker, was anxious not to provoke the Soviets unnecessarily. At dawn
on Friday, October 26, a Soviet ship was stopped, and Americans
boarded and searched it. It was carrying only trucks and truck parts,
so it was passed on to Cuba. However, the boarding and searching
showed the Soviet leaders that the President was prepared to back
up the blockade with forceful action. Later on Friday, sixteen Soviet
ships turned back from the voyage to Cuba. Since Wednesday, they
had stopped dead in the water, just short of a confrontation with the
American ships. The Soviet decision to send them away seemed to
be a victory for the naval blockade.

A Soviet ship with fifteen bombers pulled out of Cuba is on its way home a few weeks after the end of the missile crisis. The Soviet crew voluntarily opened the fuselage crates for U.S. aerial inspection.

**The Soviet Union Makes a Response.** However, disturbing news was reported from Cuba. The missile sites were still there, and more were being built. Perhaps an air attack or an invasion would be needed to get rid of the missiles. On Friday evening, October 26, a letter from Premier Khrushchev arrived. It said that the Soviet Union would consider removing the missiles from Cuba in return for a promise by the United States that Cuba would not be invaded then or in the future. EXCOM met on Saturday morning to write an encouraging reply to Khrushchev. Before this job was done, another letter came from Khrushchev. It suggested that the United States remove its missiles from Turkey in exchange for Soviet removal of missiles from Cuba. No mention was made of the previous letter.

While EXCOM discussed the latest letter from the Soviet Union, a United States reconnaissance plane (U-2) was shot down while taking photos over Cuba. Military leaders pressured the President to respond with an air strike against a missile site. President Kennedy resisted this pressure. He decided to try, one last time, to reach a peaceful settlement.

The President decided to reply to the first letter from Khrushchev, received on Friday, and to ignore the second letter. In his letter to Premier Khrushchev, President Kennedy agreed to end the naval blockade and to promise not to invade Cuba in return for removal of the missiles from Cuba.

322

On Sunday morning, October 28, Khrushchev's reply to the President's proposal was received. He agreed to accept President Kennedy's terms. The Cuban missile crisis had ended, thirteen days after it had begun. President Kennedy refused to boast publicly of a victory over Khrushchev. An important part of his strategy had been not to put the Soviet leaders into a corner so that they would have to fight to get out. Rather, he tried to use just enough force to achieve a limited objective—removal of the Soviet missiles from Cuba.

**Consequences of the Decision.** President Kennedy's policy achieved its immediate goals—removing the threatening missiles from Cuba while avoiding war. But its long-range effects are harder to judge. Relations between Cuba and the United States stayed unfriendly. The Soviet Union now has a large fleet of nuclear powered, missile-carrying subs that are hard to detect. Perhaps the results in Cuba led to this build-up. The decision may also have led some Americans to think that the way to convince the Soviet Union to back down was to threaten nuclear war.

In short, one can't be sure about what is a "good" decision or a "bad" one because the long-range effects are unknown. A decision-maker can never be certain what might have happened if a different policy had been chosen.

*Circumstances for the decision:*
1. Was this a decision that could be made in advance or was it a crisis decision?
2. How did the amount of time available for making the decision influence the consideration of alternative policies?

*Individual characteristics of the decision-makers:*
3. What clues can you find that reveal how President Kennedy interpreted the build-up of Soviet missiles in Cuba? How might this interpretation have influenced his decision? What other interpretations were possible?
4. What personal values seemed to be held by President Kennedy that may have influenced his decision?
5. To what degree might the approach President Kennedy adopted toward solving the problem have affected the final decision?

*Other limitations on decision-makers:*
6. In what ways did "rules" influence the decision process?
7. What examples can you find that status relationships may have influenced the decision?
8. What evidence can you find that President Kennedy was sensitive to public opinion?
9. In what sense did available resources affect this decision?
10. How was the decision influenced by anticipated reactions of external decision-makers?

## The President and the Media

The links between the President and the media are complex. On the one hand, the President needs the press, radio, and TV and seeks their favor. The media give publicity to the President's programs, plans, goals—and public image. The President needs the media in order to influence public opinion, to sway votes in Congress, and to motivate the bureaucracy.

The media also need the President, for this person is news. Most Americans identify with their government through the President. They want to know about the President's plans, meetings, and trips. They even want details about the President's personal life. In short, the public can rarely be satisfied that they know enough about this public figure.

Since the President needs the media and the media need the President as the subject for daily news, it would appear that their ties should be friendly and warm. But there is more to the matter than this.

The President craves publicity, but wants *favorable publicity*—news that shows a sincere, honest, and fearless leader. The President also often wants to use the news as a way of building public policy. Suppose, for example, that the President wants to learn how Americans might react to a sharp rise in gasoline taxes as a way to deal with an energy problem. An aide could "leak" to the press that such a tax is in the works. If the public reaction is very negative, the President can later say that the idea was not part of the energy plan. "News leaks" give the President a chance to run "trial balloons" on decisions that must be made.

The President also has access to a vast amount of facts and figures. By deciding which data to release and when to do so, the President can influence people. Announcing a major public works project or a breakthrough toward settling a world crisis on the eve of a general election is a tactic that Presidents have used to their own political advantage.

**B.C.**

**by johnny hart**

B.C. by permission of Johnny Hart and Field Enterprises, Inc.

Most Americans give little attention to the day-to-day business of politics. They don't know much about the details of a given policy. They seem to form their judgments as a result of general impressions of what the President gets done. What kinds of things build up a good impression? A TV broadcast of a "State of the Union" address is one. A trip abroad to meet with Chinese or Soviet leaders is another. It is less useful, from the President's point of view, to be watched while answering hostile questions at a press conference. Thus, while seeking publicity, the President also wants to control what the media report.

While the reporters need the President, they often don't want the kind of news that the President wants to hand out. They need news that will sell papers and attract TV sponsors. And "bad news" tends to be better than "good news." Reports on failure are more lively than those on success. Corruption is more exciting than virtue. Back-room deals are more fun than those in the open. In fact, reporters want that part of political news which a President is most eager to hide from public view.

For example, the President may wish to announce that Senator Jones, a leading opponent of the President's policy, has had a change of mind and will now support it. This may build the impression that others will also switch. But such a news release only whets reporters' appetites. They want to know why Senator Jones switched. How did the President do it? What rewards were offered?

Thus a tension builds up between the media and the President. The President wants to use the media to inform and influence the public in order to carry out certain programs. The media don't want to become a tool of the President but do want to report news that the public will buy.

## Nixon and the Media

No President has been very happy with the media. But perhaps Richard Nixon suffered the most from this tension. Over his political career he was both helped and hurt by the media. Nixon first got national attention in the 1940s when he led a congressional investigation of Communist subversion in the government. Then, in 1952 when he was running for Vice-President, the media reported that he had been given an $18,235 "slush fund" by political backers when he was in the Senate. Some Republicans wanted to drop him from the ticket. But Nixon went on TV and radio to defend himself. He claimed no wrong-doing, pleaded poverty, and with great emotion told of a gift to his children of a cocker spaniel named Checkers. His "Checkers speech" swung public sentiment behind him.

In 1960 Nixon faced John F. Kennedy in a series of TV debates in their contest for the Presidency. Many people think that Kennedy had the better image and that this helped him win.

In 1962 at a press conference after losing the race to be governor of California, Nixon made this angry attack: "Now that all of the members of the press are so delighted I lost, I'd like to make a statement—You've had a lot of opportunity to attack me, and I think I've given as good as I've taken. Just think how much you'll be missing. You won't have Nixon to kick around any more. Because this is my last press conference."

It was not Nixon's last press conference, for soon he moved to New York and again became active in politics. In 1968 he ran for President and edged out Hubert Humphrey. In this campaign and later, he proved very adept in using the media. But the battle with the media wasn't over. Tension built up because the President needed to conceal some facts that the media wanted to find and report. In spite of long efforts to cover up the facts, the story became known. The role of the press in the tragic affair of a President's resignation is set forth in the next case study.

**Case: The Watergate Affair**

On August 9, 1974, Richard M. Nixon became the first President to resign. This event brought to a close a two-year ordeal that has become known as the "Watergate Affair."

On June 17, 1972, five men were arrested inside the offices of the Democratic National Committee in a fancy housing and business complex called "Watergate." The men had tools for "bugging" conversations and for taking photos of records.

The break-in came about a month before the Democratic national convention. In June 1972, President Nixon led the top Democratic challenger in public-opinion polls by 19 points. There seemed to be no reason why anyone close to the President would be involved in such a burglary. Yet one of the burglars turned out to be James McCord, the security coordinator for the Committee to Re-elect the President. And the name of Howard Hunt, a White House employee, was found in the address books of two of the burglars.

The first response of the Committee to Re-elect the President and the White House was to deny any connection with the burglary. Two days later, White House press secretary Ron Ziegler dismissed it as a "third-rate burglary attempt." He added that "certain elements may try to stretch this beyond what it is."

**Other Illegal Acts.** But it turned out that the burglary was merely one of many illegal acts that were conducted with the knowledge and support of key officials in the White House. These acts included those of a special security unit, called the "White House Plumbers," set up in 1971 to stop leaks of security information. There was illegal wiretapping of government employees and newspaper people who were thought to be responsible for security leaks. There was the getting of shady campaign gifts from private persons and corporations. The Internal Revenue Service threatened "enemies" with audits.

326

**The Weather**

Today: Sunny and pleasant, high in
60s, low in 60s. Chance of rain near
zero today and 10 per cent tonight.
Wednesday: Variable cloudiness,
high in 80s. Temp. range: Yesterday,
86-60 today; 85-65. Details on C20.

# The Washington Post

**FINAL**

64 Pages—4 Sections

| | | |
|---|---|---|
| Amusements B 6 | Metro | C 1 |
| Classified C 4 | Obituaries | C 3 |
| Comics B 8 | Outdoors | D 3 |
| Crossword B 4 | Sports | D 1 |
| Editorials A18 | Style | B 1 |
| Financial D 6 | Radio-TV | B 5 |

97th Year · · · No. 244 · · · © 1974. The Washington Post Co. · · · TUESDAY, AUGUST 6, 1974 · · · Phone (202) 223-6000 · · · Classified 223-6200 · · · 20c Beyond Washington, Circulation 223-6100 Maryland and Virginia · · · 15c

# President Admits Withholding Data;
# Tapes Show He Approved Cover-up

## The Plan: Use CIA to Block Probe · · · Nixon: Impeachment Not Justified

Such acts would at least be embarrassing if known and could lead to criminal trials for some persons involved. So President Nixon and his aides began an effort to cover up the entire Watergate affair. They denied all charges of involvement. They did not reveal the facts. They misled Department of Justice investigators. They got grand jury witnesses to lie or hold back information. They arranged bribes for the arrested burglars to ensure their silence. And they ordered the CIA to tell the FBI to restrict its investigation for security reasons.

At first, the cover-up seemed to work. Most reporters and TV commentators paid little attention to the Watergate affair at the start. Efforts by George McGovern, the Democratic presidential candidate, to make it an issue were treated lightly.

**The *Washington Post* Was an Exception.** Belief that there was more to the story than appeared on the surface led the paper to make an all-out effort to uncover the facts. Carl Bernstein and Bob Woodward, reporters for the *Washington Post,* filed their first story on the Watergate break-in on the day it took place. In the months that followed, they were to write many stories about Watergate. Getting the facts was not easy. Few people cared to talk to the reporters. Many of those who knew the most had the most to hide and the most to lose. But by following up each lead, by cross-checking every source, by spending hours visiting and phoning people, they were able to piece together the main outlines of the story.

As the paper began to print more and more ugly facts, pressure was put on the *Washington Post.* First, there were public attacks by White House aides for what was termed shoddy journalism. The White House began to prevent the *Post* from covering social events at the White House. Shortly after the 1972 election, challenges against the paper's ownership of two TV stations were filed with the Federal

327

Osrin in *The Cleveland Plain Dealer*

HISTORICAL TWIST!

Lew Harsh in *The Scranton Times*

Communications Commission. Among the challengers were persons with close ties to the President.

**Watergate Gets Increasing Attention.** Other papers, journals, TV, and radio began to devote resources to the Watergate affair. Disclosures followed one on top of another. In time, Watergate crowded other news off the front pages of leading papers. TV networks broadcast the hearings of congressional committees on the case. One by one the President's closest advisers resigned or were fired. Some were tried, found guilty, and served prison sentences.

Finally the story led to the President himself. On August 5, 1974, President Nixon revealed that on June 23, 1972—six days after the break-in—he had ordered the FBI to stop its probe of the affair. Whether he had prior knowledge of the break-in or other misdoings is still unclear. However, in the face of his admission that he had not told the truth about the cover-up, Nixon lost the last bits of political support. Faced with certain impeachment in the House and conviction in the Senate, there was little else for him to do but resign.

Many people played key roles in the events that led to this sad occasion. Judge John Sirica is one. He was the federal judge at the trial of the Watergate burglars. He imposed harsh sentences on them in the hope of forcing confessions. Alexander Butterfield is another. A White House aide, he revealed to a Senate committee that President Nixon tape-recorded conversations in the White House. The tapes provided proof of Nixon's knowledge of the cover-up. But it is hard to say enough about the role of the press as a whole and the reporters who kept the case before the public. By keeping up their probe and making Watergate a topic of general debate, the press prepared the American public for the final shocking conclusion.

## What Are the Limits of Presidential Action?

At one time in our history it was thought that the President's jobs were to handle foreign policy and to carry out laws passed by Congress. Our early Presidents held strictly to the idea of separation of powers and did little to intervene in the work of Congress. But over the years the scope of presidential power has grown. It has grown in part because we have chosen Presidents who have not been content merely to carry out the law. Another factor is that changing times have seemed to call for more activist-minded Presidents.

The depression of the 1930s and World War II were big factors in the growth of presidential power. In times of crisis Americans have tended to expect the President to take forceful action. Over time we have grown used to the President taking some actions in the name of "national security" which could not even be reported to Congress or the American people.

In the last few years, many Americans have begun to question whether too much power has drifted into the President's hands and whether Presidents have always used this power wisely. Because recent Presidents have assumed that they will be held accountable for American successes and failures, they have sometimes been impatient with procedures that seem to limit their capacity to act. Some people believe that recent Presidents have at times violated the Constitution through their actions. It is not enough, they say, that the President has acted "in the national interest," ours is a government of law. Our leaders must live within the rules and be held accountable to the public.

This leads to a basic question. What are the limits of presidential authority? Surely there are times when the President must act swiftly without consulting Congress and the American people, or the chance to act will be lost. (A Congressional debate on whether to go to war with the Soviet Union would be pointless if Soviet missiles were already in flight.) Still, Presidents must face the fact that while democracy may be inefficient at times, certain procedures were instituted to ensure that government would be as just, as fair, and as responsible as possible.

Finally, how "rough" should Presidents be willing to play the game to get their way? Or to put the question in the time-honored way: When do the ends justify the means? Sometimes in the pursuit of a good policy the President may be tempted to use techniques that are immoral or illegal. What are the limits of presidential action?

Below are brief case studies of hypothetical presidential choices. Indicate in each instance what you would do if you were the President.

## Case 1. The Election Campaign

You are in the midst of an election campaign. You are running for reelection against a strong candidate from the other party. A major campaign issue is the threat of war. Your opponent is urging a strengthening of our military effort in Southeast Asia. The polls show that most Americans fear wide involvement by American forces in this region and prefer a candidate who seems to hold out the chance for peace. Your own belief is that your opponent's view is the correct one. Indeed plans are already being drawn up to increase our war effort, once the election is over. What should you do?

**a.** Tell the American people the truth as you know it and let them choose between the two candidates on the basis of which person is most likely to wage war successfully.

**b.** Accept the feelings of Americans as expressed in the polls and avoid any actions which will increase the need to extend our military action in Southeast Asia.

**c.** Tell the American people you will not increase the war effort, denounce your opponent as a militarist, and secretly prepare for war.

## Case 2. The Hostile Columnist

A well-known and highly respected news columnist has begun a campaign to discredit your administration. Some of her charges go too far and are only partly true. But the most serious problem is the truthful but embarrassing information she is getting from someone in the administration. You have tried to cooperate with this reporter in the past, but it is hopeless. She does not like you or your policies. She hopes to help bring about your defeat in the next election. Which of the following actions are reasonable for you to undertake?

**a.** Do nothing.

**b.** Tell your aides that this reporter must not be included in any special press briefings. Try to cut off her sources of news.

**c.** Leak a false story to her. After she publishes it, give the true account to a friendly journalist and make your opponent look silly.

**d.** Order a telephone tap on her telephone and find out who is leaking information. Then fire or otherwise punish the federal employee who is helping her.

**e.** Ask the Internal Revenue Service to give special attention to her income-tax return to see if it is possible to embarrass her through legal action for tax evasion.

## Case 3. The Foreign Revolt

You have learned from the CIA that the leader of a small Southeast Asian nation may be overthrown by a group in the army. You have not liked the behavior of this leader. It seems clear that he supports American policy only so long as it serves his own personal interests. The young officers planning the revolt are likely to provide better government, one that we would prefer. On the other hand, the revolt is not likely to succeed without killing the current leader. The leaders who are planning the revolt want to know your attitude toward their plan. What should you do?

a. Tell the leaders to do what they will. We shall not interfere.
b. Warn the current leader that there is a plot to assassinate him. (This will probably lead to the arrest and execution of the leaders of the revolt and wipe out our sources of information among this group of people.)
c. Agree to support the overthrow of the government only if the current leader will not be harmed.

**Case 4. A Roadblock in Congress**
A bill you want passed in Congress has run into trouble. A leading senator of the opposition party seems to be the chief roadblock. She has threatened to organize a filibuster against the bill when it reaches the Senate floor for debate, and you can't rely on enough votes to end a filibuster. It is an important bill from your point of view. It will be a great political defeat if you fail to secure its passage. You have tried various approaches to the senator to try to reason with her. All have failed. What are some steps you might take next?

a. Call some people in her home state and ask them to bring pressure to drop her opposition to your bill.
b. Order someone in the Department of Defense to leak a story that plans are being considered to close a military base in her state. When people begin to protest, hint that the plans could probably be shelved for a time if the senator were more reasonable on other matters.
c. Try to find out directly whether the senator is willing to do some "trading." For example, would she drop her opposition to your bill if a major federal project were moved from another state to her state?
d. Ask the FBI whether it has any information in its files that would be embarrassing to the senator if revealed. If such information is available, make certain that the senator learns that it will be leaked to a Washington gossip columnist unless she begins to play ball.

# 13 The Congressional Role

More than 215 million people live in the United States. In any given year 535 of these Americans will occupy leadership roles in American politics as members of Congress. One hundred of these will be United States Senators, and 435 will be members of the United States House of Representatives.

## The Recruitment of Members of Congress

Do all Americans have the same chance of becoming a member of Congress? Or are people who have certain characteristics more likely to be elected?

Below are two cases of people hoping to become members of Congress. Decide in each case which of the two is more likely to be elected.

**Case 1. Who Will Succeed Congressman Nelson?**

Representative Robert Nelson is a Republican from Clearwater, Oregon. He is retiring at age 88 from the House of Representatives, where he served as chairman of the House Committee on the Interior for over forty years. He represents a rather conservative Oregon district in which a majority of people live in small towns and on farms. His major concerns in Congress have been conservation of water and forests and internal security against the menace of communism.

Who will replace Representative Nelson? The Republican party has not lost an election in Nelson's district in this century. Getting the GOP nomination in this district almost insures election. Below are sketches of two men who are seeking the GOP nomination.

David Glasgow is 48 years old. His ancestors were among the first settlers in Clearwater. He went to college in Oregon, where he also received his law degree. He has a law firm in Clearwater, but finds time to be active in the American Legion and the Little League. His father is a business executive in Clearwater. David Glasgow has been on the Clearwater town council for six years.

Mathias Beaman is 68 years old. He has been a farmer for his entire life near Clearwater. His father was also a farmer until his death. Beaman, the eldest of eight children, barely managed to complete high school. He believes he would be a real representative of the people. He hasn't had time to belong to any community organizations, but that is only because he works so hard, he says.

*Question:* Which of these men do you think will most likely win the Republican nomination? Why?

### Case 2. Who Will Replace Senator Miles?

Senator Irwin Miles is an 89-year-old Democrat from New York State, a state with a liberal political tradition. Serving for over forty-five years in the Senate, he has always been identified with the liberal wing of the Democratic party. New York State has many small towns and several large cities including, of course, New York City. The people who elected Miles are most often first-, second-, or third-generation Americans who still identify strongly with their Italian, Jewish, or Irish background. Senator Miles has been a strong advocate of civil rights as well as an active member of the labor movement before coming to public life.

Who will be selected to replace Senator Miles? The Democratic party is confident that it will win the Senate seat after Senator Miles retires. Two men who wish to run for the Senate on the Democratic ticket are described below.

Timothy O'Hara is 43 years old, the great-grandson of an Irish immigrant, and the son of a business executive in New York City. O'Hara's family has made much progress in three generations. Timothy O'Hara went to Columbia University in New York for his college education and law degree. He now works in the District Attorney's office in Manhattan. His interest in law led him to organize free legal clinics throughout the ghettos in New York. O'Hara finds time for the Boy Scouts and being a marshall at the St. Patrick's Day Parade. He is a close political and personal friend of Senator Miles and promises to continue Senator Miles's crusades in the Senate.

Matthew Jacobs is 59 years old. He owns a small food processing company in Binghamton, a small city in upstate New York. He is the son of Russian immigrants. His father worked as a clerk in Binghamton. Jacobs finished high school and received two years of college credit through correspondence courses. He has been active in Binghamton's school board for three years. He believes he can best represent the common people.

*Question:* Which of these men do you think will most likely win the Democratic nomination for Senator from New York State? Why?

### Rules Affect the Recruitment of Members of Congress

Most organizations have a set of formal and informal rules that affect which people are likely to become members. Rules also govern who becomes a member of Congress. Because of these rules every citizen does not have the same chance of being elected. Some of these are formal rules in the Constitution. Other rules are informal and are found in tradition and custom. There are still other rules that stem from the requirements of the job.

### Rules on Age, Citizenship, and Residency

The Constitution says that a person must be at least 25 years of age to be a member of the House of Representatives and 30 years of age to be a Senator. In fact, members tend to be older than the minimum age. Typical Senators are in their late fifties and typical Representatives in their late forties or early fifties.

Another rule is that a person must be a citizen for at least nine years to be eligible to serve in the Senate and at least seven years for the House. In a recent ten-year period only a tiny percentage of the members of Congress were naturalized citizens.

The Constitution requires only that a member of Congress be a resident of the state from which elected. Yet custom decrees that candidates for the House must actually have a residence in the congressional district that they want to represent. In the same state, District A may have many qualified people eager to serve in Congress while District B has many fewer potential candidates. Competition for a seat in Congress is less in District B because custom decrees that outstanding men and women in District A can compete in District B only by moving their residence to that district.

### Informal Rules Affecting Recruitment

A majority of adult Americans can meet the age, citizenship, and residency rules set forth in the Constitution for members of Congress. Yet if we look at the kinds of people who actually become members, it is clear that the American voters set other standards for these lawmakers.

334

## Sex Status

Men are more likely to become members of Congress than are women. Over the years, women have not had an equal chance in American politics. Until 1920 most women could not even vote in elections. Today women enjoy the same formal legal status in politics as men. Because of tradition, however, women continue to be "second-class citizens" in many ways. More than 50 percent of Americans are women, but the House and the Senate are heavily male. If women were represented in the House equal to their number in the society, there would be over 215 of them. In fact, in recent years the number of women in the House has averaged around 15, or about 3 percent of the House membership. In 1975 there were 18 female Representatives and no female Senators.

## Race

Whites are more likely to become members than nonwhites. Until recently, when Senator Edward Brooke was elected to the Senate from Massachusetts, there had been no black Senators since the period of Reconstruction following the Civil War. In the House the number has been about five blacks in each Congress (or 1 percent of the House membership), although blacks count for more than 10 percent of the national population. By 1975, however, the number rose to 16.

An exception to the general proposition that whites are more likely to become members than nonwhites is found in the case of the Hawaiian congressional delegation. Since Hawaii became a state, the majority of its members have been, and probably will continue to be, Oriental or of mixed white-Asian heritage.

## Religious Affilation

Protestants are more likely to become members than are Catholics and Jews. In a study made in the 1950s, 59 percent of the American public defined themselves as Protestants, 34 percent as Roman Catholics, 6 percent as Jewish, and 1 percent as "other." A study of the members of Congress in 1975 found that 64 percent were Protestant, 23 percent Catholic, 4.5 percent Jewish, and 8.5 percent "other."

## Education

Highly educated people are more likely to become members than the less educated. In recent years about 90 percent of all Senators and about eight out of ten Representatives have had some college training. Over half of all recent members have either been to law school or have done some other form of post-college work.

## Socioeconomic Status

About 95 percent of the recent Senators and 90 percent of the Representatives have come from middle and upper-middle-class backgrounds. Members of Congress tend to have professional and business backgrounds (high-status occupations). Most members have had incomes in the middle and upper-middle range before coming to Congress. Every Congress, in addition, has some very wealthy members. A study in 1968 found that at least one-fifth of the Senators were millionaires. But very few members are from the working class.

## Occupation

Members are more likely to come from certain occupations than from others. Lawyers lead the field. They have an expert knowledge

A study of House members in 1975 provided the following composite description of a typical Representative: a 49-year-old male, first elected to Congress in 1966, who was either practicing law when elected or was using legal training in a state or local elective office.

of the law, and the main job in Congress is lawmaking. Lawyers who leave their job for a few years to enter Congress may in fact improve their abilities as lawyers. When they return to their job, after a time in Congress, they find they have lost nothing and may have gained in skills and in contacts with important people.

By contrast, many other occupations are not closely related to the job in Congress. And people who spend several years in Congress lose time and opportunity in developing their own careers.

In a recent years lawyers made up 66 percent of the Senate and 57 percent of the House of Representatives. But lawyers made up less than one-tenth of 1 percent of the national labor force. The second largest group in Congress are business people, about 10 to 20 percent of the membership. Education, farming, and journalism each account for about 5 to 15 percent.

**Political Experience**

People with much experience in politics and government are more likely to serve in Congress than are people with little or no experience. Members are not likely to be political amateurs. A study of post-World War II Senators revealed that on the average they had held about three public offices and devoted about ten years of their life to government service before coming to the Senate. Many of them had been law-enforcement officers or state legislators.

**"Joiners"**

Members of Congress, like other political leaders, tend to be "joiners." They are more likely than the average citizen to be members of such voluntary associations as the Masons, Knights of Columbus, Rotary Club, Kiwanis Club, veterans' organizations, and the like.

1. Can you explain why these formal and informal rules regarding recruitment exist? For example, what is there about American society that explains why women are underrepresented in Congress? Why are young people and people from lower socioeconomic classes underrepresented?

2. Do you think these recruitment rules are fair or just? It is estimated that because of these rules only about 5 percent of Americans have a significant chance of becoming members of Congress. Is this good, or do you feel the rules should be changed so as to broaden the range of people who have a good chance to become members of Congress?

3. What effect do you think these recruitment rules have upon American politics and government? Do you think American politics would be different if members were recruited from a broader range of people? For example, would it make any difference if there were more women in Congress? more blacks? more poor people?

## Members of Congress Play Many Roles

How many times have you heard someone say, "There ought to be a law . . . ."? Deciding what federal laws are needed is the main job of members of Congress. Article I of the Constitution granted "all legislative powers" of the central government to a Congress made up of a House of Representatives and a Senate. These "legislative powers" include setting up post offices, levying taxes, regulating interstate commerce, declaring war, providing federal courts below the Supreme Court, and several others.

Members of Congress are often called lawmakers. We are most aware of their duties that relate directly to passing laws: writing and introducing bills, hearing testimony from witnesses, working in committees, debating and voting in the House or Senate. In fact, nearly every official action taken by a member relates in one way or another to the lawmaking job.

At the same time, much of a member's day is spent on activities that are not directly related to current bills. Members may respond to letters from people back home who want a change in some government regulation. They may call on an official in a federal agency to get needed information. Or they may give a speech at a Veterans Day dinner in their home state.

The "congressional role" thus consists of several roles. Before looking at the chief role, that of lawmaker, let us examine three other roles.

## The Member as Ombudsman

For many years the Scandinavian countries have had officials called *ombudsmen.* Their job is to help citizens who are having some kind of trouble with the government. In our country where would the following people turn for help?

Mary Jones, a 72-year-old widow living on Social Security, normally gets her check from the Social Security Administration on the fifth of each month. It is now April 15, and her check has not arrived. Mrs. Jones has called the local Social Security office in her city, and they have informed her that a check of the records shows that her check was prepared at the usual time. The young man in the office tells her he doesn't know what might have happened to her check.

James Black runs a small radio station. At lunch on Tuesday a business friend told him that the Internal Revenue Service had just issued a new tax ruling that may apply to Mr. Black. When Mr. Black returned to his office, he called the local Internal Revenue office to inquire about the matter. The people he spoke to were friendly, but they told him that they have no specialist in their office that could advise him on just how the new ruling would affect his business.

The Zabachi family came from Eastern Europe twenty years ago, and Mr. Zabachi has worked as a janitor in a school since then. One day Mrs. Zabachi suffered a fatal stroke. Their son John is in the army and stationed in Europe. Mr. Zabachi, of course, wants to tell his son of the mother's death and have him come home for the funeral. He knows that his son is in Mannheim, Germany, but the family has only a stateside military postal address.

Our federal government has no officials called ombudsmen to handle such problems. In each of these cases and many thousands like them, it is likely that the people will turn to a member of Congress for advice. Mrs. Jones could ask her Representative to find out about her Social Security check and help her get another one if the first one was lost. Mr. Black can write or call to learn where to get the information he needs. Mr. Zabachi (or perhaps a friend) might call a member's office to learn how John can be contacted and whether a leave can be granted.

About 10 percent of a Representative's time is spent dealing with constituent problems (*Table 1, page 343*). In addition, each member has one or more staff members in Washington who spend nearly all their time dealing with such requests. Most members also have offices in their home districts. The staff member in that office must spend much time with constituent problems.

338

Members of Congress are sort of *ombudsmen.* It is a role which they play with mixed feelings. Requests for help seem excessive, and the help could often be found elsewhere. (For example, students may ask for help in writing term papers.) Still, most members accept such "case work" as a vital part of their job. They know that the chance to perform favors is a chief advantage that they have over challengers in future elections.

## Political Educator and Campaigner

Members of Congress are elected political leaders. To remain leaders, they must keep their backers. At regular intervals (every two years for Representatives and every six years for Senators) they must submit to a new election. No matter how long or how faithful their service, they must stand and be judged by the voters. Few, if any, members can afford to move to Washington and forget the voters back home.

A study of the average Representative revealed that he spent 5.6 days per month in the home district while Congress was in session and made an average of 7.3 radio and 3.5 television appearances per month.[1] Many Representatives and Senators publish a regular newsletter on their activities and points of view on current issues. Finally, members of Congress visit personally with some constituents, either in Washington or in their home district, each month.

Members of Congress look for ways to keep their name and image in the voter's mind. They welcome chances to speak to civic clubs. They are present at the unveiling of statues and the dedication of new buildings. They pose for pictures and prepare press releases for local papers. They appear at county fairs, football games, and Fourth of July picnics. Some send congratulations to high school and college graduates and condolences to members of a family at the time of a death. In every way possible a member of Congress tries to remind voters that he or she is alive, well, and working in Washington with only the voters' best interests at heart.

During an election year the political educator and campaigner role gets more intense. It may even affect the way other roles are played. For example, it may be hard to get a quorum (the number that must be present when a vote is taken) because so many members are in their home districts conducting their political campaigns.

The political campaigner role may lead members to vote differently on bills in the months before an election than they would at other times. For example, some people believe that the Omnibus Crime Control bill of 1970 might not have passed, at least in its present form, had not many members feared that a vote against it would have angered too many voters.

---

1. Donald G. Tacheron and Morris K. Udall, *The Job of the Congressman,* Second Edition. (New York: Bobbs-Merrill, 1970).

# I NEED YOUR VIEWS

Congress of the United States
House of Representatives
Washington, D.C. 20515

Official Business

Phil Sharp
M.C.

POSTAL PATRON
10th Congressional District
Indiana

Dear Friends,

July 31, 1975

As your Congressman it is important that I be kept informed of your views on the many issues I will be voting on in the months ahead. I hope you will take a few minutes of your time to fill out this questionnaire, which is being sent to every household in the 10th Congressional District.

It is difficult to cover all the important issues and to provide for all possible responses in a short questionnaire, but I hope you will select the answer that best expresses your position. If you have additional comments to make on the questions, or on issues not covered in the questionnaire I would be pleased to receive them. I will be able to respond to you personally if you enclose your remarks in a separate letter to me.

Please note that I have provided space for two persons in each family to respond to the questions. I plan to tabulate the results and publish them in a future newsletter. If you would like to receive the newsletter, which discusses key issues currently before the Congress, be sure that you check the appropriate box on the back of the sheet. Also, be sure to write your name and address in the space provided. However, if you wish your response to this questionnaire to be anonymous, just return the questionnaire without your return address and let me know in a separate letter that you would like to be put on the newsletter list.

Sincerely,

Phil Sharp
U.S. Congressman

1. Listed below are a number of proposals which have been suggested as solutions to the country's economic problems. For each, I would like to know if you favor or oppose these recommendations:

|  | Favor 1 | Favor 2 | Oppose 1 | Oppose 2 |
|---|---|---|---|---|
| a. Wage, price and profit controls | ☐ | ☐ | ☐ | ☐ |
| b. Lower interest rates and increase money supply to make credit more available for home mortgages and business investment | ☐ | ☐ | ☐ | ☐ |
| c. Personal income tax cuts to increase purchasing power | ☐ | ☐ | ☐ | ☐ |
| d. Expanded public service job programs to provide more employment opportunities | ☐ | ☐ | ☐ | ☐ |
| e. Raise taxes and lower federal spending in order to reduce the deficit and ultimately achieve a balanced federal budget | ☐ | ☐ | ☐ | ☐ |
| f. Reinstitute a program of Public Works employment to create jobs on such projects as repair of railroad beds, flood control and construction | ☐ | ☐ | ☐ | ☐ |

|  | Yes 1 | Yes 2 | No 1 | No 2 |
|---|---|---|---|---|
| 2. Should Congress approve a 5-year delay on stricter Clean Air standards for automobiles? | ☐ | ☐ | ☐ | ☐ |
| 3. Do you favor allowing the price of natural gas to rise to provide incentives for exploration and development? | ☐ | ☐ | ☐ | ☐ |
| 4. The Supreme Court has ruled that abortions during the first three months of pregnancy cannot be prohibited by law. Which of the following do you favor: |  |  |  |  |
| a. No change in the Court ruling | ☐ | ☐ | ☐ | ☐ |
| b. A constitutional amendment restricting abortion to cases involving the health and safety of a mother | ☐ | ☐ | ☐ | ☐ |
| c. A constitutional amendment banning all abortion | ☐ | ☐ | ☐ | ☐ |
| d. A constitutional amendment allowing states to establish their own laws on the issue | ☐ | ☐ | ☐ | ☐ |
| 5. Should the federal government guarantee farmers a minimum price for farm commodities? | ☐ | ☐ | ☐ | ☐ |
| 6. There is much debate in Congress over the issue of gun control. Please indicate whether or not you would favor any of the following actions: |  |  |  |  |
| a. No federal law | ☐ | ☐ | ☐ | ☐ |
| b. Outlawing the sale of cheap handguns (the so-called "Saturday Night Specials") | ☐ | ☐ | ☐ | ☐ |
| c. Registration of all firearms | ☐ | ☐ | ☐ | ☐ |
| d. Outlawing ownership of all firearms | ☐ | ☐ | ☐ | ☐ |

Members keep in touch with the voters back home mainly as a way of winning reelection. But some self-serving activities also help educate the public. The newsletters, the speeches and tours in the district or state, the pamphlets sent out also serve an educational function.

Members of Congress are political educators. Many consider this service to be a big part of their job. Almost all members feel that they have some duty to inform and educate the people they represent.

### Roles Related to the Executive Branch

When a law is passed, Congress does not lose interest in it. Members care about how the law is administered. When it is done poorly, members are likely to hear complaints. Thus another role is to check on the activities of the executive branch.

#### Investigator Role

Members of Congress have a number of ways to control the executive branch. Congress can create, alter, and abolish agencies. It can grant or withhold funds from agencies. It can prohibit certain agency actions. Even the appointment of cabinet members and some other top bureaucrats must get approval by the Senate before they can serve.

Congress in 1921 set up the General Accounting Office (GAO). It reports directly to Congress on how funds voted by Congress are being spent. At first its job was simply to see that money was spent in ways that Congress intended. In time the GAO got the job of judging how efficiently the money was being used. More recently the GAO has been reporting on program effectiveness: is the money bringing good results? Thus this 4800-member staff serves as a watchdog over the executive branch on behalf of Congress.

#### Consultant Role

Members not only supervise or check on the executive branch but also often act as consultants for it. A member who serves on the same standing committee for many years becomes an expert in the bills handled by it. A long-time member of the House Armed Services Committee may know more about certain aspects of the military than does an Assistant Secretary of Defense testifying before the committee. Also, a few members have even exchanged roles: resigning from Congress to become a cabinet member or winning election to Congress after having served in the executive branch. Congressman Melvin Laird was known as an expert on national defense. He resigned his House seat to become Secretary of Defense when President Nixon took office in 1969. Senator Symington was once Secretary of the Air Force before being elected to the Senate. Thus, upon his election, the Senate got an expert on defense matters.

#### Lobbyist Role

A member may also serve as a kind of lobbyist for some department or bureau. (A lobbyist is a person who is hired by some group—

President Ford meets with Senate Majority Leader Mike Mansfield (right) on the presidential boat, the *Sequoia,* in 1975. The President often needs to consult with the leaders in Congress.

labor union, farm organization, teachers' association, etc.—to get favorable legislation passed and unfavorable bills defeated through contact with legislators.) A member of the House Veterans Affairs Committee, for example, may work extra hard to get other House members to support a bill desired by the Veterans Administration. A member of the House Committee on Agriculture may lobby for measures supported by the United States Department of Agriculture. The Defense Department works hard to get key members of Congress to lobby for its budget.

Once an agency has convinced a key member of a committee that its requests are justified, it may count on the member to rally support in Congress. Moreover, a friendly committee head can help influence the public as well. When people are invited by a committee to testify for and against some bill, the chairperson may arrange for witnesses friendly to the agency's position to have ample time to develop their arguments while critics are given scant attention. Thus the committee head can influence the flow of news that Americans will get about the topic under study.

## The Legislative Role

The roles we have just looked at are important and take up much of the time of members of Congress. But members are first and foremost lawmakers. As such, they are also political decision-makers.

### Time Devoted to the Legislative Role

Most of a member's time is spent on the legislative role. One study found that the average Representative worked almost sixty hours per week while Congress was in session. *Table 1* shows the amount of time given to various activities. Which five or six of the items in *Table 1* seem to be most directly related to the legislative role? Using these five or six items, compute the total percentage of time an average Representative devotes directly to the legislative role.

Members should, of course, spend most of their time on lawmaking. The job is a big one. Members of the First Congress (1789-1791) introduced only 144 bills. Over the years the number grew sharply, reaching a peak of some 44,000 with the 61st Congress (1909-1911). Today each Congress gets about 25,000 measures—public and private bills and resolutions of various types—during its two-year term. The First Congress passed 118 public bills. Today between 600 and 1000 public bills are likely to be passed in the two annual sessions of a Congress. (See *Table 2* for a record of activity of the 93rd Congress.) It is clear that most bills do not become laws. The vast majority die somewhere along the legislative path.

A "public bill" is of concern to the general public. A "private bill" is for the benefit of a specific individual, e.g., a bill to permit the immigration of a person beyond the usual quota.

The legislative role of a member includes the following tasks:

1. Deciding upon a bill to introduce, drafting the bill, and then introducing it.
2. Lining up political support for one's bill.

---

*Table 1.* **Typical Work Week of a United States Representative**

| Hours | Activity | Percent of Work Week |
|---|---|---|
| 15.3 | Attending sessions of the House of Representatives | 25.8% |
| 7.2 | Legislative research and reading | 12.1 |
| 7.1 | Committee work on legislation | 12.0 |
| 7.2 | Answering mail | 12.1 |
| 5.1 | Handling constituent problems | 8.6 |
| 4.4 | Visiting with constituents in Washington | 7.4 |
| 3.5 | Committee work outside of committee meetings | 5.9 |
| 2.4 | Leadership and party functions | 4.0 |
| 2.7 | Writing chores, speeches, magazine articles, etc. | 4.6 |
| 2.3 | Meeting with lobbyists and lobby groups | 3.9 |
| 2.1 | Press work, radio and TV | 3.5 |
| 59.3 | | 99.9% |

343

**Table 2.** Legislative Activity of the Ninety-third Congress

| Activity | First Session January 3–December 22, 1973 | | | | Second Session January 21–December 20, 1974 | | |
|---|---|---|---|---|---|---|---|
| | Senate | House | Total | | Senate | House | Total |
| Measures introduced | 3,334 | 14,194 | 17,528 | | 1,793 | 6,901 | 8,694 |
| Bills | 2,860 | 12,150 | | | 1,400 | 5,540 | |
| Resolutions | 474 | 2,044 | | | 393 | 1,361 | |
| Measures passed | 726 | 717 | 1,443 | | 838 | 807 | 1,645 |
| Senate bills | 280 | 105 | | | 246 | 176 | |
| House bills | 177 | 260 | | | 292 | 288 | |
| Resolutions | 269 | 352 | | | 300 | 343 | |
| Public bills enacted into law | 100 | 145 | 245 | | 168 | 236 | 404 |
| Private bills enacted into law | 7 | 43 | 50 | | 25 | 48 | 73 |
| Bills vetoed | 5 | 5 | 10 | | 6 | 23 | 29 |
| Vetoes overridden | — | 1 | 1 | | — | 4 | 4 |
| Hours in session | 1,084 | 790 | | | 1,068 | 813 | |

Notice that more bills were passed than are finally enacted into law. The reason is that some bills are passed in one house but not in the other.

The line "Bills vetoed" means that, in the First Session, the President vetoed five bills that started in the Senate and five that started in the House. Only one bill—a House bill—was passed over the veto by Congress in the First Session.

3. Studying bills that have been introduced by others, including reading arguments for and against the measure; listening to lobbyists, colleagues, constituents, party leaders, and bureaucrats.
4. Working in committee on legislation, including listening to witnesses, discussing bills with other committee members, testifying before other committees, and drafting amendments to bills.
5. Taking part in and listening to floor debate on bills.
6. Voting on the measure.

A number of formal and informal rules influence how these tasks will be carried out.

### The Influence of Formal Rules on the Legislative Role

A number of formal rules spell out the legislative role. Most of them can be found in the Constitution (Article 1, page 573). Other rules have been made by Congress itself.

#### A Bicameral Legislature

The Constitution called for a two-house (bicameral) legislature made up of a Senate and a House of Representatives. The states were to be represented equally in the Senate (two Senators per state), but in proportion to population in the House. Today a few of the smaller states have only one Representative each, while California—the most populous state—had 43 House members in the 1970s.

With a bicameral rather than a unicameral (one-house) body, both houses must pass the identical bill—down to the commas and periods—before it can be sent to the President to be signed and thereby be-

Table 2: Source of data, *Congressional Record,* January 10, 1975

come law. Thus either the House or the Senate can halt a bill wanted by the other body. (In 1970, for example, the two houses failed to agree on a constitutional amendment providing for the direct election of the President, and the measure therefore failed.) This means that much dealing and compromise must occur between the two houses on many bills before they are ready for final passage.

### Special Duties of Each House

The Constitution also gave special duties to one house that it did not give to the other. For example, all tax bills must start in the House of Representatives. This has led to a very powerful House Ways and Means Committee that deals with all tax measures. The Constitution provides that all treaties must be approved by the Senate. This has meant that the Senate Foreign Relations Committee is more influential than the House Committee on International Relations. The Senate also must approve most officials appointed by the President.

### Terms of Office and Areas Represented

Both Senators and Representatives are chosen by direct election. Representatives are elected for two-year terms from congressional districts created by the state legislature. Senators are elected for six-year terms by the residents of the state as a whole.

The number of Representatives allotted to each state is based on the population of the state. Today, in theory, there should be one Representative for about each 485,000 people. Yet some districts represent much more than this figure and others less. Two Senators are chosen from each state in state-wide elections. As senatorial terms are staggered, voters of a given state are seldom asked to vote for both Senators in any one year.

The fact that Representatives are elected for a two-year term by voters in a specific district influences their role behavior. Members must begin to think about the next election soon after winning the last one. And to stay in office they must heed the wants of people in their district. The district may be a section of a large city, an urban county, or several rural counties. From the same state, one House member may have to think of the wants of city voters while another member represents mainly rural and small-town folk. The Senators from that state, however, must try to represent the entire state.

### Size of the Two Houses

The First Congress consisted of a Senate of 26 members (two for each of the original thirteen states) and a House of 65 members. With the addition of states the Senate has grown to nearly four times its original size. But the House has increased more than six times. Finally, in 1929, Congress ruled that the House should remain at 435 members. Chiefly because of this difference in size, a Senator usually serves on two major committees while a Representative serves on only one. Also debate on the floor of the House is strictly limited, while the Senate has rules that allow more open debate.

Senate reception hall

Both houses of Congress have elaborate rules on lawmaking. In general, because of its greater number of members, the House tends to have more restrictive rules than does the Senate.

### The Influence of Informal Rules

The legislative role is also influenced by a number of informal rules. These represent a series of expectations that new members must learn quickly if they are to get along with others in Congress.

**Courtesy**

Over the years a special system of courtesy has evolved. Members must not direct personal criticism at each other no matter how much they may disagree. In debate, they must always speak politely when referring to their opponent. Moreover, all remarks made on the floor are, technically, addressed to the presiding officer. Therefore, a member of Congress is always addressed in the third person on the floor of the Senate or House. This custom allows members who differ on an issue to attack the arguments put forward by the other side without appearing to be making a personal attack on the person who disagrees.

346

Following is an extract from a discussion that occurred on the floor of the House of Representatives in 1974. The debate was on a bill to set up an American Folklife Center in the Library of Congress. Mr. H. R. Gross (Iowa), one of the speakers, retired in 1974, at the age of 75, after twenty-six years of service in Congress. In those years he became noted for opposing most bills that would raise the size and cost of government.

The Chair recognizes the gentleman from Michigan (Mr. NEDZI).

*Mr. NEDZI.* Mr. Speaker, . . . the United States of America is history's most dramatic example of a progressive society which was begun and has been developed by people from a wide diversity of ethnic and racial origins. . . .

In recent years we have seen a strong upsurge of public interest in folklife and ethnic heritage. This interest is evident in the Congress, as indicated by the fact that over 200 Members of the House and 60 Senators have sponsored bills identical or similar to the bill recommended by the Committee on House Administration. Two days of extensive hearings were held during which testimony was received from the Librarian, Smithsonian, Arts Endowment, and 11 public witnesses who represented a variety of groups prominent in the area of folklife. . . .

Mr. Speaker, this legislation does not compete with other programs or activities. It is meant to be conservatively financed. It seeks to preserve and encourage folk art but not "high art." It is not geared to dry academic analysis but to the grassroots.

The bill recognizes our folk and ethnic traditions as priceless assets which developed naturally in their own regional and historical climates. They should not be allowed to fade away, victims of the pressures to conformity brought on by urbanization and technology.

I urge my colleagues to join the committee in supporting this legislation. . . .

*Mr. GROSS.* Mr. Speaker, I should like to ask the gentleman from Michigan *(Mr. NEDZI),* who pays for these trustees? Does the money come out of the $5 million or nearly $5 million that is authorized for this purpose?

*Mr. NEDZI.* These are unpaid trustees. They get the customary $100 a day expenses that people on boards customarily get.

*Mr. GROSS.* And there are two super grades, a director and a deputy director, both of whom would be super grades; is that correct?

*Mr. NEDZI.* That is correct.

*Mr. GROSS.* You were just adding to the bureaucracy that already exists, plus a retinue. They will have to have some secretaries, will they not?

*Mr. NEDZI.* That is all in the estimated cost that was submitted to us, and which appeared in my opening statement. . . .

*MR. GROSS.* So I take it the gentleman from Michigan considers $5 million to be a limited amount of money for a boondoggle of this kind?

*Mr. NEDZI.* Over a 4-year period, yes.

*Mr. GROSS.* I will not ask the gentleman from Michigan who requested this boondoggle. The report tells us who wants it. Let me read a sentence or two from the report:

> The initial impetus came from individuals and groups concerned primarily with the cultures of the Appalachian region, the South, the West, and native Americans. They were soon joined by proponents of the so-called "ethnic," black, and Hispanic cultures who have rejected the total assimilation of the American "melting pot."

What about the North? The gentleman comes from the North. Do they have any culture up there?

*Mr. NEDZI.* The gentleman from Iowa comes from the North, also.

*Mr. GROSS.* Yes, I do, and I am wondering if there is any culture to be reckoned with there. . . .

*Mr. NEDZI.* The report intended to describe how this bill originated. . . . But as the gentleman from Iowa read, they were subsequently joined by other ethnic groups, and that includes the entire country.

Let me assure the gentleman from Iowa there is no effort to exclude anyone from the provisions of the bill in any particular region of the country. . . .

*Mr. THOMPSON* of New Jersey. Mr. Speaker, as always, my delightful friend, the gentleman from Iowa, amuses me. I would not expect that he would lose an opportunity before his departure to take pot shots at yet another bill affecting the arts.

I might point out, as did the gentleman from Michigan, the distinguished chairman of the subcommittee, that of the 201 sponsors of this legislation 41 States are represented as well as the District of Columbia, Guam, Puerto Rico, and the Virgin Islands.

Mr. Speaker, I rise in support of H. R. 17382, the American Folklife Preservation Act. . . .

Over a period of years, as the sponsor of many bills on the subject of the arts, I have come to be immune from being giggled at and laughed at. The fact of the matter is that those who object would not hesitate to spend a billion dollars on a piece of weaponry and yet would be chintzy about this. The time is not now to balance the budget by defeating this bill. The budget includes the beautiful things in our life and in our society, those which should be preserved. . . . .

348

Ethnic groups often seek to keep their cultures alive by holding parades and festivals.

*MR. NEDZI.* Mr. Speaker, . . . I take this time to pay tribute to the gentleman from New Jersey (MR. THOMPSON) who . . . for several years has diligently worked for it. The fact that some 260 Members of Congress are cosponsors is a tribute to the soundness of his efforts. He more than any single individual is responsible for the guiding of this legislation to its presentation to the House by a unanimous House Administration Committee. And should the Members pass this bill, primary appreciation and congratulations are due the gentleman from New Jersey (MR. THOMPSON). . . .[2]

Senator Alben Barkley once advised a new Senator that if he thought a colleague was stupid, he should refer to him as "the able, learned and distinguished senator." If he *knows* he is stupid, he should call him "the *very* able, learned and distinguished senator."

Such forms of courtesy have a place in Congress. The issues debated there are often ones about which Americans have strong feelings. In order to get laws to cope with these issues, the members must get along with each other.

2. *Congressional Record,* December 16, 1974, H 11954-11956.

## Apprenticeship

Both the House and Senate expect new members to "take a back seat" and let others do most of the talking. Taking a "back seat" is literally true in the Senate, where new members get desks at the back of the chamber.

New members are expected not to take part in debate on the floor. At times, if the debate is about an issue on which a new member has special knowledge, he or she may speak briefly. But usually the debate is carried on by veterans of the House and Senate.

## Specialization

In one sense all members of Congress are specialists in making laws. Still, no member can be fully informed about all the issues that will be covered by bills in any single year. For example, on a single day, June 10, 1975, the following bills and resolutions were introduced.

*H. R. 7749* would require that Memorial Day be observed on May 30 and Veterans Day on November 11 of each year.

*H. R. 7753* would amend the Federal Aviation Act to permit continuation of youth fares and to authorize reduced-rate fares for the elderly.

*H. R. 7756* would amend the Communications Act of 1934 with respect to the renewal of licenses for operating radio stations.

*H. R. 7759* would amend the income-tax law to permit a parent who supports a handicapped child to take a personal exemption for that child even though the child earns more than $750.

*H. R. 7764* would provide that time spent by American civilians in enemy prisoner-of-war camps and similar places shall be creditable (as though it were military service) toward pensions and similar benefits under various federal retirement programs.

*H. R. 7773* would establish a national policy and nationwide machinery for guaranteeing to all adult Americans able and willing to work the availability of equal opportunities for useful and rewarding employment.

*H. R. 7775* would prohibit the Consumer Product Safety Commission from restricting the sale or manufacture of firearms or ammunition.

*S. 1903* would establish a program for the removal of drift and debris from publicly maintained commercial boat harbors and from the land and waters adjacent thereto.

*S. 1908* would direct the Secretary of Commerce to establish and maintain an industrial energy conservation program.

*S. 1910* was a private bill to provide assistance to a constituent of Senator Inouye of Hawaii.

*S. 1912* would provide for the issuance of a special postage stamp in commemoration of Return Day in Georgetown, Delaware.

*S. J. Res. 93* was a joint resolution proposing an amendment to the Constitution to provide that, except in time of war or economic emergency declared by Congress, federal expenditures may not exceed revenues during any fiscal year.

*S. J. Res. 95* would designate September of each year as "National Gospel Music Month."

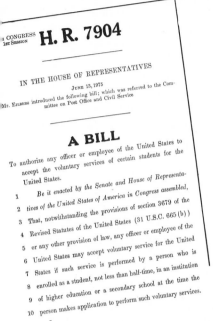

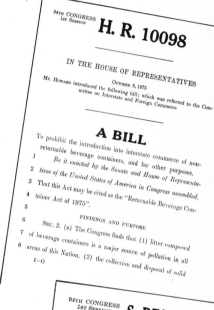

Numerous other bills and resolutions got started in both houses. Throughout the morning various committees met to hear testimony on bills or worked to rewrite bills. On the House floor the members, after extended debate, failed in an attempt to override President Ford's veto of a bill to control strip-mining. They also debated at length a bill to provide for a national energy program to deal with the "oil crisis." The chief Senate debate that day had to do with a bill aimed at cutting red tape in getting food stamps and one that would give Senators additional staff aides. Both Houses received a report from the President on the World Weather Program. He also sent to the Senate the names of five Army officers for promotion to the rank of general.

No member can hope to be fully informed on all the issues coming to Congress. Many of the bills deal with complex issues such as energy policy. The best that members can do is become expert on (a) topics that come before their committees and (b) issues that are of major concern to their own constituents.

In 1975 there were eighteen standing committees in the Senate and twenty-two in the House. The committee system is a method for handling the mass of bills coming before Congress each year. Most

A standing committee is a committee that is permanently provided for by House or Senate rules. A standing committee may be contrasted to special committees created for unusual circumstances.

House members belong to only one standing committee; Senators belong to more than one. Thus a fairly new member of the House from a farming area in Kansas might be a member of the Post Office and Civil Service Committee. As a member of that Committee he would become a specialist in Post Office and civil service matters. Also he would feel a duty to be fully informed about farm legislation.

The custom, therefore, is for members of Congress to become expert on only certain topics. Often members must vote on measures about which they have little knowledge. On such occasions they turn to others for advice on how to vote.

### Seniority

*Apprenticeship* and *specialization* are related to the practice of seniority in Congress. Seniority is the custom of giving privileges on the basis of length of time served in a legislative body. It takes a number of forms. For one, members who have served longest have first choice for committee assignments when vacancies occur. Some committees are more important, hence more desirable, than others. In the House, "Rules," "Ways and Means," and "Appropriations" are seen as choice committees. Since 1946 no first-term member has been assigned to the Rules Committee.

The Rules Committee is very important because it decides the order in which bills will be considered, the amount of time allowed for debate, and whether or not a bill may be amended from the floor.

"Enter and kneel!"

Copyright 1971 by Herblock in the *Washington Post*

"Play ball!"

Copyright © 1960 *St. Louis Post-Dispatch*, reproduced by courtesy of Bill Mauldin

More important, it decides which bills will be brought up for a vote at all. Bills introduced in the House are first screened by the other standing committees. But even after this process there are more bills than the House can properly consider and vote upon. The Rules Committee will ordinarily advance the bills desired by the leadership of the majority party in the House.

Seniority also determines who will head a committee. The committee member of the majority party in the House or Senate who has served longest on the committee usually gets the post. Seniority determines where members sit at the committee table and affects their chances to take part, with new members having the least chance to take part in debate.

The seniority system for committee heads was upset in two cases in 1975. House Democrats replaced the heads of the Agriculture and the Armed Services committees with members who had less seniority but who were seen as more responsive to the wishes of the Democratic majority on each committee.

The customs relating to *seniority, specialization,* and *apprenticeship* tend to center power in the hands of those members who have served the longest. Those who defend these customs say that they assure that Congress will have the advantage of wisdom that comes from experience. Those who oppose these customs claim that they tend to give members with conservative political ideas too much power and that they prevent fresh ideas from being aired.

---

**Standing Committees of Congress in 1975**

**House Committees**

| | | |
|---|---|---|
| Agriculture | House Administration | Post Office and Civil Service |
| Appropriations | Interior and Insular Affairs | Public Works and Transportation |
| Armed Services | International Relations | Rules |
| Banking, Currency, | Interstate and Foreign Commerce | Science and Technology |
| and Housing | Judiciary | Small Business |
| Budget | Merchant Marine and Fisheries | Standards of Official Conduct |
| District of Columbia | | Veterans Affairs |
| Education and Labor | | Ways and Means |
| Government Operations | | |

**Senate Committees**

| | | |
|---|---|---|
| Aeronautical and Space Sciences | Budget | Judiciary |
| Agriculture and Forestry | Commerce | Labor and Public Welfare |
| Appropriations | District of Columbia | Post Office and Civil Service |
| Armed Services | Finance | Public Works |
| Banking, Housing, | Foreign Relations | Rules and Administration |
| and Urban Affairs | Government Operations | Veterans Affairs |
| | Interior and Insular Affairs | |

---

Reciprocity: a giving of
something of equal value in
return for a favor.

## Reciprocity

Often bills are introduced that are of little concern to some members of Congress. They do not really care very much whether the bill passes or not. In such a case a member may be willing to vote the way a colleague wants in hope that the colleague will return the favor at some time in the future. Therefore, I might vote to build a new post office in your district if you will vote for a dam in my district. Such a practice is sometimes referred to as "logrolling." In short, it is a practice of doing favors for others in the hope of getting favors in return.

## Personality Affects Legislative Role Behavior

Formal rules and customs have much influence on the way a member will play the role. Still, the rules and customs affect 535 different personalities in almost as many different ways. It is not surprising, therefore, that no member plays the role in exactly the same way as other members do. Members bring their own personality to Washington, D.C., and this will influence how they interpret the legislative role.

The Legislative
Reorganization Act of 1946
reduced the number of
standing committees,
provided committees with
staff members, required the
registration of lobbyists,
forbade certain kinds of
private bills and raised
congressional salaries.

For example, in 1946 the Legislative Reorganization Act created a Senate Committee on Government Operations, which in turn established a Permanent Subcommittee on Investigations. Little was heard of this subcommittee until 1952, when Wisconsin's Senator Joseph R. McCarthy became its head. Under McCarthy's leadership the subcommittee undertook a series of investigations of alleged Communists in the federal executive branch. Senator McCarthy had attracted public attention in February 1950 as a result of a speech he delivered in Wheeling, West Virginia. In it he claimed that the Department of State was full of Communists and that he and the Secretary of State knew their names. For the next four years he was the object of fear by some, adoration by others. He got much publicity in the press and on radio and television.

In 1954 the Senate censured him—largely because he violated certain informal rules of the Senate, not because of his anti-Communist activities—and his power waned. The subcommittee he had headed went back to its former quiet role. It is clear that the activity of the subcommittee had been influenced strongly by Senator McCarthy. Other persons in his position, with different personalities, behaved quite differently.

Members of Congress are rather free to decide how they will spend their time—which aspects of their role they will emphasize. One member may spend much time dealing with committee affairs while another gives more time to meetings with constituents. Some members may take the lead in speaking up for a certain point of view or cause (for example, civil rights), for a pressure group or lobby (for example, the American Legion), or for the executive branch. Some may become

party leaders in the House or Senate. Some may be seen as skilled strategists who know how to get bills passed. (President Lyndon Johnson had such a reputation when he was majority leader of the Senate.) One may seek a reputation as a statesman who stands above partisan conflict. Others are known as great orators or as writers of books and articles about their work. Still others are seen as "great compromisers" who can get opposing sides to come to some agreement. These and other variations on the role are possible. Rules, custom, and personality all play their part in determining how the legislative role will be played in Congress.

### Summary

What, then, are members of Congress? They are legislators, ombudsmen, political campaigners and educators, and investigators. But they also are father or mother and husband or wife—when they can find time. Whatever else one can say about members of Congress, the vast majority are very busy, *public* men and women. They work in a city where politics is the main business. Meals and parties are used for political purposes. When members of Congress travel, people seek them out, asking for advice and favors. They receive more mail than they can answer personally. They have more to read then they ever have time for. With too little information and depending on the advice of trusted friends, they often must make decisions that will affect the lives of millions of Americans. They must appear to be both the servant of their constituents while remaining their leader. They must often compromise while appearing to stick by principles. They must not lose patience but remain at all times courteous. A successful member of Congress is a political person—a fitting product of a democratic system.

Senator Joseph McCarthy is here giving testimony at a televised hearing held by his Senate subcommittee in the spring of 1954. The hearing dealt with a dispute between McCarthy and the Army. At McCarthy's right is Attorney Joseph N. Welch, counsel for the Army.

355

# A Typical Day in the Life of a Member of Congress

In the previous two lessons you learned about four roles played by members of Congress. Below is a typical day's schedule in the life of a fictional Representative. A Senator's schedule would be similar in many ways.

Your task is to analyze the schedule according to the four roles you have just studied. One other role—spouse and parent—has been added, since some of her activities each day would relate to that role. Some of the items may require more than one role designation. The roles are:

Legislator (L)
Ombudsman (O)
Investigator of, Consultant to, and Lobbyist for the Executive
    Branch of the Government (IC)
Spouse and Parent (SP)
Political Educator and Campaigner (PEC)

### Representative Smith's Calendar—March 10

6:30—Awakened, read the *Congressional Record* and two local newspapers.

7:45—Drove to Capitol for breakfast meeting of Democratic Steering and Policy Committee in the Speaker's dining room.

9:00—Arrived at office. Staff already there; dictated replies to the 25 most urgent messages picked from a stack of telegrams and letters; met with members of staff to go over the day's agenda.

9:45—Called the Veterans Administration about a problem concerning a constituent who had been denied treatment at a Veterans Hospital.

9:55—Talked for five minutes by long-distance telephone to a newspaper editor from one of the major papers in my district. As result of call, the paper has agreed to support a bill I am sponsoring.

10:00—Attended meeting of House Agriculture Committee; listened to and questioned witnesses who came to support the farm bill being studied by the committee.

10:45—Was called from committee room to talk to a constituent who is looking for a job in Washington and who asks if I can help.

11:00—Returned to committee room in time for testimony by the Secretary of Agriculture; questioned him very closely about reports that his present policy was certain to drive food prices upward by next winter.

12:00—Went to House floor for opening of the day's business; gave a five-minute speech pointing out that on this day in 1948 Jan Masaryk, the Foreign Minister of Czechoslovakia, was killed. This marked the rapid takeover of power by the Communists in Czechoslovakia. This speech, suggested by my administra-

# Congressional Record

**United States of America**

PROCEEDINGS AND DEBATES OF THE 94th CONGRESS, FIRST SESSION

| *Vol. 121* | WASHINGTON, TUESDAY, JUNE 10, 1975 | *No. 90* |

# *House of Representatives*

The House met at 11 o'clock a.m.

Rev. Frederick W. Rapp, St. Stephens Church, Port Washington, N.Y., offered the following prayer:

Almighty God, who hast given us this good land for our heritage, grant that we may always be a people mindful of Thy favor and glad to do Thy will. Bless this House with wisdom and nobility of spirit, so that policy decisions will be made, not selfishly, but for the benefit of all Americans. May we possess a proper humility as we confront the problems of our time, and remember the spirit of courtesy and graciousness in dealing with the people of this and every nation. May this House be strong to look for the righteous course, to follow the way of justice, yet never lose the quality of mercy. Save us from hypocrisy and make truth our guiding light. Amen.

votes of the two Houses on the amendments of the Senate to the bill (H.R. 4700) entitled "An act to authorize appropriations to the National Aeronautics and Space Administration for research and development, construction of facilities, and research and program management, and for other purposes."

## REV. FREDERICK W. RAPP

(Mr. WOLFF asked and was given permission to address the House for 1 minute, to revise and extend his remarks, and include extraneous matter.)

Mr. WOLFF. Mr. Speaker, the Reverend Frederick Rapp, a distinguished cleric I am honored to represent in my home district on Long Island, has just delivered an opening invocation as timely as it is inspiring. We in this House today are privileged with the awesome task of weighing policies and making judgments

## PERMISSION FOR COMMITTEE ON RULES TO FILE CERTAIN PRIVILEGED REPORTS

Mr. LONG of Louisiana. Mr. Speaker, I ask unanimous consent that the Committee on Rules may have until midnight tonight to file certain privileged reports.

The SPEAKER. Is there objection to the request of the gentleman from Louisiana?

There was no objection.

## CONGRESS WILL NOT ACCEPT REPUBLICAN FULL UNEMPLOYMENT POLICY

(Mr. O'NEILL asked and was given permission to address the House for 1 minute and to revise and extend his remarks.)

Mr. O'NEILL. Mr. Speaker, I regret the fact that the leadership on the other side of the aisle is not here to hear what

---

tive assistant, will be popular with the many Czechs in my district and get attention in the newspapers and on TV news.

12:30—Left House floor to have lunch with a group of business people from my district who want help in getting a community development grant.

1:45—Returned to House and listened to debate on education bill.

2:00—Spotted a House member who is sponsoring a bill that is opposed by important groups in my district. We left the floor, and I tried to talk him into dropping some of its worst features; had little success, but we agreed to meet again tomorrow.

2:30—Returned to House floor to vote on amendments to education bill.

3:00—Left House floor to talk to a constituent who would like his son to get into West Point; told him to go to my office for application form.

3:20—Returned to House floor to vote on two more amendments to education bill. Voted "nay" to one, and gave in to party leader who asked for a "yes" vote on the other one.

3:45—Left House to have picture taken with Cystic Fibrosis Foundation poster child.

4:05—Returned a telephone call from my son.

4:15—Back to House floor for last vote of the day.

4:30—Returned to office; placed five long-distance phone calls that had come in during the day; signed letters.

5:30—Made phone calls to six federal officials regarding problems facing several of my constituents.

6:45—Returned to House to have an editorial from a paper in my district placed in the appendix of the *Congressional Record*. I try to make certain that at least one editorial from each paper in my district is printed in the *Congressional Record* during the year.

7:30—Arrived at a hotel for dinner with the head of the state university, who is lining up support for a new science lab on the campus.

10:30—Took a briefcase full of committee work home; read and worked on it for more than an hour.

11:45—Had a glass of milk, visited with my husband, and went to bed.

## The 1964 Civil Rights Act: A Case Study in Legislative Role Behavior

On July 2, 1964, President Lyndon B. Johnson signed the Civil Rights Act. This law would have a deep influence on American life, for many of the practices suffered by blacks in America were now judged illegal. Exactly one year before, President John F. Kennedy had urged Congress to pass a strong civil rights law. During the next year much had taken place to influence the passage of civil rights legislation. These events give us a chance to see how the legislative role is played.

Civil rights was not a new issue for lawmakers in 1963. Each year from 1945 to 1957, a bill on civil rights came before Congress; and each time it failed. Through executive action and as a result of Supreme Court decisions, the civil rights of ethnic minorities, especially black people, had come to be more and more accepted. But efforts to pass laws against racial discrimination had failed. Although civil rights bills were finally passed in 1957 and 1961, they were so weakened by compromise that they failed to achieve their purpose.

Apparently President Kennedy had not intended to make civil rights a major part of his legislative program in 1963. The issue was not mentioned in his State of the Union message. He may have been more concerned about getting other bills passed, including a tax-reduc-

Violence in Birmingham aroused nationwide sympathy for the civil rights movement. Marchers in Boston call for action.

tion plan. But he had not foreseen how big the civil rights issue would become that year.

**Public Opinion Becomes Aroused.** In 1963 a storm of "black protest" was sweeping the southern part of the United States. "Freedom rides," "sit-ins," boycotts, "freedom marches," and picketing were focusing the attention of the nation on the complaints of black people and their demands for legal changes. It was one hundred years since Lincoln's Emancipation Proclamation, his famous "Freedom Now" edict. But most blacks in the United States, especially in the South, did not feel free in 1963. They pointed to the segregation system that kept them from using public facilities on equal terms with whites. They pointed to the caste system of the South that kept blacks at the lowest levels of the American society. In 1963, as in 1863, black protesters were shouting "freedom now."

The dominant leader was Baptist minister Dr. Martin Luther King, Jr. At the head of his Southern Christian Leadership Conference (SCLC), Dr. King marched into Birmingham, Alabama, in April 1963. He called it the most "segregated city in America."

For the next two months Americans watched while Birmingham suffered racial turmoil. City officials would not give Dr. King permission to lead his followers on peaceful marches through the city to protest the segregation practices. But he and his followers marched anyway, breaking the law. They were met with fire hoses and police dogs. Many black protesters were arrested, including Dr. King, but the protest marches continued. Violence erupted on May 11 when the home of Dr. King's brother was bombed. In September, the 16th Street Baptist Church in Montgomery was bombed and four black girls killed. A short time later, two black boys were shot and killed by whites in Birmingham. Further, Medgar Evers, a black protest leader in Mississippi, was fatally shot outside his home.

The nation was shocked by this violence. Many whites around the country were angered by the sight of peaceful black demonstrators being clubbed by the white police, water-hosed by the white fire-fighters, and bitten by police dogs. Sympathy for Dr. King's cause began to grow. It was often expressed in letters to members of Congress urging support for a civil rights law that would end segregation. *A climate of public opinion favorable to passage of a civil rights law was starting to develop.*

**A Bill Is Introduced.** On June 11, 1963, President Kennedy appeared on TV to help build public opinion in support of his proposed legislation. He told the American people:

> It ought to be possible for every American to enjoy the privileges of being American without regard to his race or his color. In short, every American ought to have the right to be treated as one would wish his children to be treated. But this is not the case.
>
> The Negro baby born in America today, regardless of the section of the nation in which he is born, has about one-half as much chance of completing high school as a white baby born in the same place on the same day, one-third as much chance of completing college, one-third as much chance of becoming a professional man, twice as much chance of becoming unemployed, about one-seventh as much chance of earning $10,000 a year, a life expectancy which is seven years shorter, and the prospects of earning only half as much.
>
> This is not a sectional issue. Difficulties over segregation and discrimination exist in every city, in every State of the Union, producing in many cities a rising tide of discontent that threatens the public safety. . . .This is not even a legal or legislative issue alone. It is better to settle these matters in the courts than on the streets, and new laws are needed at every level, but law alone cannot make men see right.
>
> We are confronted primarily with a moral issue. It is as old as the scriptures and is as clear as the American Constitution.
>
> The heart of the question is whether all Americans are to be afforded equal rights and opportunities, whether we are going to treat our fellow Americans as we want to be treated. If an American, because his skin is dark, cannot eat lunch in a restaurant open to the public, if he cannot send his children to the best public school available, if he cannot vote for the public officials who

represent him, if, in short, he cannot enjoy the full and free life which all of us want, then who among us would be content to have the color of his skin changed and stand in his place? Who among us would then be content with the counsels of patience and delay?

One hundred years of delay have passed since President Lincoln freed the slaves, yet their heirs, their grandsons, are not fully free. They are not yet freed from the bonds of injustice. They are not yet freed from social and economic oppression, and this Nation for all its hopes and all its boasts, will not be fully free until all its citizens are free. . . .

Within a few days after President Kennedy's address, two identical bills, S. 1731 and H.R. 7152, drafted by the Attorney General's office and carrying the endorsement of President Kennedy, were submitted to the Senate and House of Representatives. Over 150 other civil rights bills were introduced in 1963. But because S. 1731 and H.R. 7152 had the backing of the President, this was the bill Congress would consider, oppose, defend, strengthen, weaken, rewrite, and finally pass.

In the early stages of work on the Civil Rights Bill in Congress, a massive public demonstration was arranged by civil rights leaders. The March on Washington took place in August 1963.

361

**The House of Representatives Acts on the Bill.** House bill 7152 was referred to the Judiciary Committee, which in turn assigned it to a subcommittee for study. Emanuel Celler, head of the subcommittee, was also chairperson of the House Judiciary Committee. Celler, a Democrat from Brooklyn, and William M. McCulloch of Ohio, the senior Republican on the Judiciary Committee, took the lead in the subcommittee hearings.

Celler, an outspoken supporter of civil rights, was from a district populated by ethnic, racial, and religious minority groups. Representative Celler also had a long and close relationship with the Democratic party leadership and could be counted on to support party positions.

McCulloch, a Republican, came from an Ohio district with very few black voters but many whites who seemed to have little interest in civil rights legislation. For Representative McCulloch, civil rights in 1964 had become a matter of personal belief. He was eager to see a strong civil rights law passed because he thought it was the right thing to do.

It was a big surprise, even to Celler and McCulloch, when the subcommittee made the administration bill stronger rather than weaker. In fact it added a section on fair employment which had not been in the original bill.

While the bill would get further changes before it was signed into law, the main provisions of the bill approved by the subcommittee stayed about the same. The five main features of the bill were as follows:

*Voting:* Far more effective enforcement of the right to vote in federal elections. Forbade the misuse of literacy tests and registration forms to disqualify voters on racial grounds.

*Public Accommodations:* Hotels, motels, and other lodging places with more than five rooms must serve all persons regardless of race. Racial discrimination also outlawed in restaurants, lunchrooms, theaters, sports arenas, and other places of entertainment which affect interstate commerce. Private clubs not covered.

*Public Places:* Discrimination and segregation outlawed in public places such as parks, playgrounds, pools, and libraries.

*Schools:* The United States Attorney General could bring to court all complaints of school segregation.

*Employment:* All persons, regardless of race, must have an equal opportunity to get a job. Employers, labor unions, and employment agencies must not discriminate on the basis of racial identity.

The bill was approved in the subcommittee by an interesting coalition of members. Liberal Democrats who had spoken for years, unsuccessfully, for a strong bill were joined by Northern Republicans, who did not wish the Democrats to take full credit for it. In addition, a few anti-civil rights Southern Democrats voted for the strengthened bill in the belief that because it *was* strong it could be more easily defeated later.

Since the Judiciary Committee had a larger number of Southern members, it was more conservative on civil rights issues than either the subcommittee or the House as a whole. Chairman Celler saw that the Committee would try to weaken the bill or defeat it, as they had done with other civil rights bills. Attorney General Robert Kennedy, testifying before the Committee, urged the members to consider a milder form of the bill than the one approved by the subcommittee. He reasoned that a weaker bill would have a chance of passing, while a strong bill would surely be defeated.

Not all civil rights supporters agreed with the Attorney General. The National Association for the Advancement of Colored People (NAACP) continued to press for a strong bill. When, to the surprise of everyone, a strong bill was approved by the Judiciary Committee, Attorney General Kennedy gave much of the credit to two Republicans, McCulloch and House Minority Leader Charles A. Halleck of Indiana. It was important that the Attorney General praise the efforts of the Republicans, since bipartisan support was necessary.

**Death of a President.** Two days after the House Judiciary Committee had approved the bill, a tragic event occurred which would have a great impact on the passage of this bill. On November 22, 1963, President Kennedy was assassinated. Only five days later, President Johnson clearly spelled out his strong support for a civil rights law. In a funeral address to Congress the new President said:

> No memorial oration or eulogy could more eloquently honor President Kennedy's memory than the earliest possible passage of the civil rights bill for which he fought so long. We have talked long enough in this country about equal rights. . . . It is time now to write the next chapter—and to write it in the books of law.

During the first half of 1964, President Johnson used all of his persuasive talents to gain approval of the civil rights bill. In his first State of the Union message the President put passage of a civil rights law at the top of his list of priorities. He said: "Let this session of Congress be known as the session which did more for civil rights than the last hundred sessions combined."

**Challenging the Rules Committee.** In the meantime H.R. 7152 had met opposition in the House Rules Committee. The Rules Committee fixes the order in which bills approved by House committees will be brought to a vote on the floor of the House. It also decides on the "rules" for the debate on each bill. For example, it rules on how much time those favoring and those opposing the bill will get for floor debate. The head of the House Rules Committee was Howard W. Smith of Virginia, a strong opponent of civil rights legislation. In the past he had been able to stop most strong civil rights bills from reaching the House floor for debate.

The cartoon depicts Rules Committee Chairman Howard Smith placing obstacles in the way of passage of the bill by the House.

**"In charge of arrangements."**

Reprinted by permission of the *Philadelphia Evening and Sunday Bulletin* and F. O. Alexander

363

In an attempt to bypass the Rules Committee, Representative Cellar filed a *discharge petition.* It is used to get a bill out of a committee. The petition is placed on the Speaker's desk, where the members of the House can sign it. If more than half of all members sign the petition, a bill can be taken away from a committee and brought directly to the floor. President Johnson made it clear that he favored the discharge petition. He even made personal phone calls to some of the House members who had failed to sign it. Rather than have the bill taken out of the Rules Committee by the discharge petition, Howard Smith finally agreed to hold hearings on the bill. Following other attempts at delay by Smith, the Rules Committee voted to send the bill to the House floor.

Ordinarily the task of managing a bill backed by a Democratic President on the House floor would have fallen to Democratic "party whip" Hale Boggs of Louisiana. But most voters in his district strongly opposed the bill. So responsibility for floor leadership passed to an organization called the Democratic Study Group, comprised of Northern liberals in the Democratic Party. They created a network of monitors to make certain that the bill's supporters would be present when they were needed. During the course of the floor debate almost a hundred amendments designed to weaken the bill were presented without success. Finally, on February 10, 1964, the bill passed the House by a vote of 290-130.

**H.R. 7152 Goes to the Senate.** Senate leaders had decided to try to delay debate on a civil rights bill until one had cleared the House. They feared that the anger certain to arise over the civil rights issue might lead to the defeat of other important legislation. Also the leaders had mapped a strategy that would allow the House bill to bypass the Senate Judiciary Committee, where it would surely be delayed. Usually, when a bill is introduced in either chamber, it is assigned to a committee. However, when a bill has passed the House, it can be intercepted at the door of the Senate chamber and placed directly on the Senate calendar. This is a very rare step, since it bypasses entirely the Senate's committee system. Senate Majority Leader Mike Mansfield of Montana decided that the importance of this bill justified his taking this unusual action. He elected to "meet the bill at the door." Mansfield's decision was challenged by Senator Richard Russell of Georgia, the leader of the Southern bloc. But Mansfield's move was supported by the Senate, and the bill was brought directly to the floor of the Senate for debate. But getting the bill to the Senate floor for debate was only the first skirmish in the battle that lay ahead. Now the civil rights supporters in the Senate had to overcome a filibuster.

**Filibuster and cloture.** A filibuster is an effort by one or more Senators "to talk a bill to death." The Senate has a tradition of permitting debate to continue on a bill until every Senator who wishes to

"Whip" is the name given to the assistant floor leader of each party. The Whip's special duty is to see that members support their party on important issues.

speak has had a chance to do so. As compared to the House, which sharply limits the time set aside for debate, talk can keep up indefinitely in the Senate. In practice few Senators use the chance to extend debate because they do not want to hold up business. But, at times, when an issue means a great deal to a group of Senators who fear the bill will pass if brought to a vote, they will literally hold the floor, dividing the speaking chores, and prevent a vote on the bill from being taken.

The only way a filibuster can be broken is by a vote of *cloture,* or *closure.* In 1964 this required that two-thirds of the Senate vote in favor of ending debate. Later the number was dropped to sixty, but even a vote of this size is hard to get.

Since no other bill can be taken up during a filibuster and since a vote of cloture rarely succeeds, a filibuster, or the threat of a filibuster, can be a powerful bargaining tactic of the opposition. Supporters of a bill may be willing to compromise rather than face a long delay by filibuster. In the past a filibuster had been used successfully to defeat or to weaken each civil rights bill that had reached the Senate floor.

As debate began, most Senators seemed to favor the bill. And most of these members planned to vote for cloture when the time came to do so. A smaller group opposed the bill and would vote against cloture because the filibuster was their best chance to defeat the measure. Most of these Senators were from the South. They were joined by a few Northern and Western conservatives. The leader of this latter group was Senator Barry Goldwater, a candidate for the Republican nomination for President. He argued that the public accommodations and the fair employment sections of the bill were unconstitutional.

**Bipartisan support in the Senate.** Senator Hubert Humphrey (Democrat) and Senator Thomas Kuchel (Republican) were the co-leaders of the pro-civil rights forces. Humphrey had wisely asked Senator Thomas H. Kuchel of California, the Republican Whip, to be co-leader. By this move the bill seemed to be sponsored equally by Republicans and Democrats.

Humphrey and Kuchel assigned each section of the bill to a pair of Senators, a Democrat and a Republican. It was their job to see their section through floor debate as well as to defend it against weakening amendments. Each Senator was given favorable publicity in his hometown newspapers, thereby committing him more completely to the bill.

Cooperation of many kinds was needed. Humphrey later wrote in his book, *Beyond Civil Rights: A New Day of Equality:*

We had to cooperate as Republicans and Democrats. We had to work together as liberals, moderates, and conservatives. We had to maintain close and favorable relations with "the other house"

The record for a single speech was held for many years by Robert La Follette (18 hours in 1908). The record was approached by Huey P. Long (15 hours) in 1935, and finally exceeded by Wayne Morse (22 hours) in 1953. Strom Thurmond held the floor for 24 hours during debate on the Civil Rights Act of 1957, but he got a little relief when colleagues interrupted with questions and comments.

365

(the House of Representatives) lest their rejection of our changes in the bill force a conference, and thus another vote, and thus another filibuster.[3]

Editorial cartoon by Paul Conrad. Copyright,
Los Angeles Times, Reprinted with permission.

**"Stand back, everybody! He's got a bomb!"**

Brooks in *The Birmingham News*

**Awaiting Orders**

On the left, Conrad comments on the use of force against Birmingham blacks. The Brooks cartoon points to a big increase in government interference with business—property rights—under a strong civil rights law. This cartoon appeared in March 1964 during Senate debate on the bill.

Humphrey was careful to keep up courteous relations with the opposition. No personal attacks were permitted. If the debate were not kept on a high level, uncommitted Senators might be offended. Humphrey gave an example of the extent to which he tried to keep on friendly terms with the Southern Senators:

Nearing the point of recess on a day in March, for example, after he had just made a speech ridiculing every title of the bill and I had answered him, he [Sen. Willis Robertson of Virginia] walked over to me . . . and offered me a Confederate flag for my lapel. I accepted the flag as graciously as I could, and I praised Senator Robertson not only for his "eloquence and his great knowledge of history and law, but also for his wonderful . . . gentlemanly qualities and his consideration to us at all times."[4]

The Southerners would not give in easily. For six weeks they refused to allow a vote—even on an amendment to the bill.

3-4. Hubert H. Humphrey, *Beyond Civil Rights: A New Day of Equality*, (New York, Random House). Copyright©1968 by Hubert H. Humphrey. Used by permission of Random House, Inc.

**The role of Senator Dirksen.** A key person in the final success of the bill was Senate Minority Leader Everett Dirksen of Illinois. Dirksen had much influence with conservative Republicans who would provide the swing vote on cloture. Representing a midwestern state with a conservative area in the south and a big city in the north, Dirksen had no record of strong support for civil rights. The black voters of the second and third wards of Chicago regularly opposed his reelection.

During the spring of 1964 the mail from his constituents, around 10,000 letters and cards, ran two to one against the bill. On March 26 he attacked the bill on the Senate floor. Dirksen said he could not vote for the fair employment or public accommodations sections. He suggested that as many as seventy amendments might be necessary before he could support the bill.

Having established himself as a severe critic of the House bill, Senator Dirksen began to play another kind of role. In the weeks following his March 26 speech, he met regularly with Senate leaders, including Humphrey and Kuchel, and Justice Department officials in an effort to reword the bill so that it would win the support of as

Senator Everett Dirksen (right) and House Minority Leader Charles Halleck each had a major role in this case. They are seen here in their weekly news conference, dubbed "The Ev and Charlie Show," which was designed to balance the heavy publicity given to the Democratic President.

many Senators as possible. Each section of the bill was looked at carefully. As the debate went on, it became clear that the chief features of the House bill would be preserved, but new language was found for some of the sections. Finally, two months after his March 26 speech, Senator Dirksen offered a substitute bill in the form of an amendment. The "Dirksen-Mansfield substitute," as it came to be called, was backed by the coalition of civil rights organizations lobbying for the bill, the Justice Department, and conservative Republicans.

The five main provisions of the bill (page 362) had been saved. The main changes were to allow local and state governments that had their own equal-rights agencies time to act before the federal government could step in. Also in cases where federal funds were withheld from a program because of a discriminatory practice, the withholding of funds would apply only to those governmental units directly guilty of the practice and not to the larger units, such as a state, of which they were a part.

**The Senate Passes the Civil Rights Bill.** While the new bill now satisfied most of the uncommitted Senators, Humphrey needed a few more "ayes" before he would risk a vote on cloture. He agreed to put off the cloture vote until a group of conservative Senators could

"The ultimate weapon."

Crook in *Newsday*, Long Island. Reprinted by permission.

present their amendments to the Dirksen substitute. Only one of the amendments (to allow trial by jury in certain contempt cases) passed. But the conservatives were satisfied that their views had been recognized in the bill.

On June 10, with all Senators present, the cloture vote was taken. Seventy-one Senators (four more than necessary) voted for cloture. Senator Clair Engle, Democrat of California, who had just undergone a brain operation was wheeled into the Senate chamber to cast his vote. Although he was unable to speak, he indicated by pointing to his eye, his "aye" vote for the bill.

After the cloture vote passed, the Senators could speak for only one hour on the bill and its amendments. As a delay tactic, the Southerners asked for roll call votes on nearly every amendment. On one day the roll was called thirty-four times, setting a new record. On June 16 the opponents introduced 33 amendments: 14 by Strom Thurmond of South Carolina, 8 by Sam Ervin of North Carolina, and 7 by Russell Long of Louisiana. All were defeated.

On June 20 the civil rights bill passed the Senate. Seventy-three of the one hundred Senators voted for the bill. The debates in the Senate filled 2890 pages of the *Congressional Record* and absorbed 736 hours and 10 minutes—a total of 83 days.

As the Senate had passed a version of the bill that was different from the one passed by the House, it had to be returned to the House for reconsideration. To avoid a conference committee and another possible filibuster in the Senate, the House elected to accept the Senate version by a vote of 289–126.

**The President Signs the Civil Rights Act.** On July 2, 1964, President Johnson spoke to the nation before signing the Civil Rights Act.

> This is a proud triumph. Yet those who founded our country knew that freedom would be secure only if each generation sought to renew and enlarge its meaning. . . .
>
> We believe that all men are created equal—yet many are denied equal treatment. We believe that all men have certain inalienable rights—yet many Americans do not enjoy these rights. We believe that all men are entitled to the blessings of liberty—yet millions are being deprived of those blessings, not because of their own failures, but because of the color of their skins.
>
> The reasons are deeply embedded in history and tradition and the nature of man. We can understand without rancor or hatred how this all happened. But it cannot continue. Our Constitution, the foundation of our Republic, forbids it. The principles of our freedom forbid it. Morality forbids it. And the law I will sign tonight forbids it. . . .

With the President's signature, the Civil Rights Bill became the Civil Rights Act of 1964. From that moment, any state or city law

President Johnson uses
several pens to sign the
civil rights bill as
congressional leaders and
other interested parties
look on.

that conflicted with the Civil Rights Act could not be enforced. Thus, many state and city laws that provided for segregated restaurants, hotels, parks, theaters, and public washrooms were now swept off the law books. Other laws that affected the civil rights of blacks and other minority groups were to follow, including the Voting Rights Act of 1965. However, the Civil Rights Act of 1964 remains landmark legislation.

In a prior lesson you learned about some of the rules and personality factors that influence legislative role behavior. Apply what you have learned to this case study.

**1.** What *formal rules* were important to the outcome of the Civil Rights Act of 1964?

**2.** What *informal rules* were observed in considering this legislation in the House and Senate?

**3.** Give examples in which personality and personal belief were important to the passage of the law.

# Factors That Influence Congressional Decision-Making

Members of Congress must make many decisions each day. They must decide whom to see, what reports to read, what meetings to attend, what requests to honor, and many others. Each decision is part of playing the congressional role. There are many chances for members to take part in policy making. Speeches may help influence public opinion to support or oppose a bill. Committee work may help to shape future laws. But members act most clearly as decision-makers when they vote "aye" or "nay" on a bill brought to the House or Senate floor. So in this lesson we focus mainly on those factors that cause a member to vote for or against a bill.

How do members make up their minds to vote for or against a bill. What factors limit their choices? What factors work to produce a decision?

It would not be possible to find every factor that caused a member to make a certain decision. Not even the member would be fully aware of the forces. Still, we can identify categories of social factors that seem to influence decision-makers. These social factors are (1) rules, (2) status relationships, (3) public opinion, and (4) the social situation. These social factors interact with the personal beliefs of a member of Congress to produce a decision.

## Rules

In a previous lesson we looked at many of the rules that influence how the legislative role will be played. These same formal and informal rules no doubt have some influence on the final decisions a member will make. These rules will not be reviewed here.

There are other rules that are influential. One is that members must vote on specific measures, not abstract ideas. For example, members don't have a chance to decide whether they favor civil rights, aid to education, better health for citizens, as abstract ideas. They must always decide how they stand on the issues in a specific bill that has reached the floor of the House or the Senate.

For example, Senators who favor good schools over poor schools must decide whether they want to have funds for better schools come from the federal government and whether they want to spend as much money as the bill calls for. They must decide if they want to spend money for the types of programs set forth in the bill. They can try to amend the bill: to add, cut out, or change sections they dislike. However, it is very difficult for a single member to gain enough support to amend a bill during debate on the floor. The bill probably represents many compromises that have been worked out in the committee sessions and that have broad support. Supporters of the bill do not like to have others tinker with a bill they believe has enough support to pass in its present form.

371

But amendments can be added to a bill during debate. The addition of a particular kind of amendment, called a "rider," may cause more problems for the decision-maker. Imagine that you are a Senator who favors a bill to set up free hospital care for the elderly. You intend to vote for the bill. But the House version of the bill contains a rider that has no relationship to medical care. The rider calls for a general salary increase of 6 percent for all federal employees. You oppose the rider but are warned that unless the Senate accepts the House version of the bill, the medical-care bill will not pass the House. You must either vote against the bill because you dislike the rider, try to get the rider removed, or vote yes, accepting the pay increase in order to get the medical-care bill you want. You cannot vote for only a part of the bill. In short, the decision that a member makes is influenced in part by the rules that govern the legislative process.

In the illustration on page 373 you can see the progress of the Smith-Jones Education bill from its introduction to its approval by the President. Only the most important legislative steps are shown, but keep in mind that the bill will change in form as it winds its way through the two houses of Congress.

### Status Relationships

Status relationships (page 307) may influence a member's decision-making. A member of Congress has four main types of status relationships that influence his or her decisions: (1) with other members of the Congress, (2) with the executive branch of the government, (3) with political party leaders, and (4) with personal and committee staff members.

Status relationships with other members influence decision-making in a number of ways. (1) There is a strong tendency to accept the report of the committee that was responsible for the bill. Members can't study all of the legislation that comes before Congress. Therefore, they tend to depend upon the committee's view, especially when the bill had heavy support in the committee.

(2) Members take part in "logrolling." This refers to the practice of exchanging support for legislation a colleague wants in return for getting support for a bill you want passed. Thus, Congresswoman Smith might vote for a new airbase in Congressman Jones's state on the understanding that Jones will vote for a shipyard that Smith wants for her state.

(3) A number of Senators and Representatives have won reputations of high integrity and great ability on certain issues. Members who are uncertain which way to vote may ask such persons for advice.

Executive status relationships refer to the give-and-take that members have with the President and others in the federal bureaucracy. Members seek the advice of the heads of federal bureaus when considering a decision. Also, the President or the chiefs of bureaus

THE STORY OF THE SMITH-JONES EDUCATION BILL

in the executive department may try to push a certain point of view on pending bills. For example, President Johnson worked hard to influence members of Congress to support the civil rights bill of 1964.

Party status relationships refer to the ties with leaders of one's political party both in and out of Congress. If state or national leaders of the member's party have taken a strong public stand on some issue before Congress, the member will face pressure from these leaders to support this stand with a vote for or against a bill. These pressures may take the form of refusing to support a bid for reelection unless the member goes along with the stand taken by the party.

Another kind of status relationship is that with members of office and committee staffs. Each member of Congress gets funds to hire aides and other staff for an office in Washington and in the home district or state. These people handle much of the ombudsman work. They also write speeches, handle mail, arrange schedules, and so on. A member of Congress also has access to help from experts employed by the various standing committees. They provide guidance and advice on the technical details of particular bills.

### Public Opinion

Public opinion influences decision-making. Both national public opinion and the public opinion of a member's district or state may influence him or her. But the influence of the home district is strongest. The Senator's state or the Representative's district contains the votes

"Maybe in the next mail we'll find one in favor of your position, Senator."

that can reelect or reject a member of Congress in a bid to retain office. Thus, a member must be responsive to the views of the voters "back home" in order to be reelected.

This does not mean that one bends like a reed in the wind before every pressure from constituents. A state or a congressional district nearly always has conflicting social groups. The member tends to identify with some of these groups rather than others. Hopefully the favored groups can muster enough votes at election time to keep the member in office. Moreover, special-interest groups representing national or local opinion may exert pressure on a member from time to time. But it is easy to overrate the impact of lobbyists. They are likely to have a big impact on the decisions of a member of Congress only when supported by a large segment of the public or by key people in government.

## Social Situation

The social situation at any one time can have a major impact on a member's decision. The "mood" of the nation, issues getting attention in the news, and the actions of national leaders are all important. For example, fear of war has an impact on the amount of funds Congress will vote for the military. In 1970 concern for "law and order" led to the passage of a strong program aimed at fighting crime. In the same year growing concern over air and water pollution led to bills aimed at meeting these problems.

## Personality of Members

The rules and social factors described above do not affect all members the same way. They do not react alike to the same social forces because they differ in their personalities.

Some members are pessimistic about the future while others look on the bright side. Some feel that progress comes through action by government. Others think the "government which governs least governs best." Some may think of themselves as "mavericks," or loners, who are defending the good of the nation against the passions of the mob. They don't want to compromise their principles by bargaining. Yet others may see themselves as "great compromisers" who can be counted on to arrive at a solution to which all can agree. Of course, the "maverick" isn't likely to reach the same decision on an issue as the "great compromiser" will.

## Four Models of Members of Congress

Some political scientists think that members of Congress can be divided into four types, or models: (1) *trustee,* (2) *delegate,* (3) *partisan,* and (4) *politico.*

Representative Edgerly fits the *trustee* model. She follows her own conscience. She thinks that she understands the issues better than do the voters who sent her to Washington. She thinks that they would vote as she does if they knew what she knows. She feels that the voters trust her to make the right decisions.

Representative Widener fits the *delegate* model. He thinks he was sent to represent the views of the people in his district. He thinks he should try to find out their views. He will vote the way the "people back home" want him to vote, even when he disagrees with their judgment.

Senator Brinkman fits the *partisan* model. He is loyal to the party platforms on which he was elected and loyal to the party's line on legislation.

Senator Claudell fits the *politico* model. She combines the other three types. On some occasions she votes her conscience (acting as a trustee). At other times she votes as public opinion in her state seems to direct her (acting as a delegate). At still other times she votes as her party leaders direct her (acting as a partisan). How she votes in any given situation will depend on the circumstances.

Classify each of the four speakers below according to one of the four types described above. In what ways would a member's view of the role influence his or her decisions?

*Congressman Kwong:* I think we have an obligation to represent the people who sent us to Congress. I won't support any legislation that is not supported by at least a majority of the citizens of my district.

*Senator Smith:* The voters in my state elected me to the Senate because of the kind of person I am. They trust me to make wise decisions in their behalf. They expect me to spend six years tending to public business and vote the way I think is best.

*Senator Chavez:* There are some issues about which my constituents know nothing and care even less. I vote in whatever way I please in such cases—hopefully the way I think is best for the whole country. In other matters, mostly domestic issues such as civil rights, my people know exactly how they think I should vote and watch that I vote their way. I would be a fool to go against their wishes.

*Senator Green:* I think one has an obligation to support the party. The President has been trying to stuff a program through Congress to show the American public how great his party is. I think those of us in the other party must stand firm and resist the President. His program would be far too costly, anyway.

Political scientists are not sure which of these types (*trustee, delegate, partisan,* or *politico*) would most accurately describe most members of Congress. Probably, no member always behaves according to only one model. Probably a member sometimes acts as a *trustee,* other times as a *delegate,* and still other times as a *partisan.* Hence, the *politico* model may be the most accurate. In any event, how a member interprets the role surely is one influence on the decision he or she makes.

Now that you understand some of the factors that influence congressional decision-making, you will most likely have an even better understanding of the case study, "The 1964 Civil Rights Act." Reread the case study and complete the following exercises.

**1.** What rules were significant in influencing the passage of the Civil Rights Act of 1964?
**2.** List examples in which status relationships influenced the passage of the bill.
**3.** Which members seemed to be most influenced by public opinion? Did public opinion influence members differently?
**4.** What factors in the social situation influenced the passage of the bill?
**5.** Provide examples in which the personalities of key members were significant.

## What Decision Is Best?

Former Senator Paul Douglas once described congressional decision-making as follows:

> When the committee hearings and the important books and articles on a proposal are read; when the mail has been appraised; when the briefs and arguments have been weighed; when the wise men, living and dead, have been consulted, the Senator still faces that task of moving his own lips to say yes or no. On the clerk's list, his name stands out in all its solitude. And that is the way he must vote.
>
> It is also, I believe, the primary way in which he decides beforehand how he is going to vote. His hour of decision is not seen by the outer world. It can come in the dead of night, in periods of reverie in one's office after the day's work is done, over the breakfast or dinner table with one's family, or in a taxicab ride to or from the Capitol. It is at these times, I believe, that the final decisions which affect the life of the nation are generally made. The tension of the roll-call merely expresses the decision which . . . widely differing men, with different background, have already made in the quiet of their individual consciences.[5]

Members of Congress make many decisions each day. At times they must make decisions when they have had little chance to study the issue and must rely on the advice of others. At times they have little interest in the topic and care little whether the bill is passed

5. *The New York Times Magazine*, April 30, 1950. © 1950 by The New York Times Company. Reprinted by permission.

or defeated. But members also face issues that are vital to the future of the United States, issues in which millions of American lives can be affected by the outcome. Often the "right" decision in such a case is unclear. They cannot predict exactly what will happen if they make one choice rather than another. Often different values are at stake. Passing a military draft law may strengthen national security, but it may also weaken individual freedom and choice. These are the kinds of issues Senator Douglas believes Senators resolve "in the quiet of their individual consciences."

The story that follows is about a mythical Senator who faced such a decision. Your task is to imagine yourself in his place, having to decide the issue he must resolve. How would you vote if you were in his place? Throughout the story you will have opportunities to make up your mind on the basis of what you learned about the issue to that point. You may find that your opinion shifts as you continue through the story. You may change your mind as often as you wish until the end of the story. Then, you must finally choose, and there can be no turning back.

**"Let Your Conscience Be Your Guide."** "What? I'm sorry, dear. I didn't hear what you said," Senator Richard Williams apologized as he became aware that Mrs. Williams was speaking to him. "Excuse me; what were you saying?"

"I said: How do you intend to vote on the Diego Resolution? I assume that's what is on your mind, that's why you rolled and tossed about in bed all night, mumbling in your sleep."

"I really don't know," he replied. "The situation in Ersatz seems certain to get worse before it improves. The Ersatz government acts as though it's paralyzed; it has lost control of the capital city. In the meantime the revolutionaries continue to kidnap Americans and other foreigners and to hold them as hostages. I am afraid that many of the hostages will be killed unless the Ersatz government gives in to the rebels. But would the hostages be any safer then? I don't trust the rebels or the government. We have helped that corrupt government so long that it expects us to come to the rescue in every one of its crises—but at least we can work with it. If the rebels win, they'll probably seek friendly ties with the Soviet Union or China; Americans will be driven out, and American-owned properties in Ersatz will be taken with no payment to the American companies."

**A Newscaster Describes the Situation.** Senator Williams got up from his chair and turned on the morning TV news in time to hear the announcer say: ". . . But the President believes that if the Senate passes the Diego Resolution, it will give him the freedom he needs to deal with the current uprising in Ersatz.

"Very simply the Diego Resolution asks the Senate to endorse the President's plan to move a navy task force to a position ten miles off the shore of Ersatz in order that it will be available if needed.

The resolution does not say what the navy will do after it is there, only that it would be 'ready to take whatever actions are necessary to protect American lives.' Some sources believe that the navy is already on its way to Ersatz. It is unclear this morning how the vote scheduled for 12 noon will be decided.

"Many in the Senate fear that if they approve the resolution, the President will take that as a green light to invade Ersatz, and the United States may find itself involved in a local war that might continue for months or even years. They remember a number of years ago when President Lyndon Johnson viewed the Tonkin Gulf Resolution as a vote in support of policies to widen the war in Vietnam. These Senators are cautious about giving such a blanket endorsement again, because they feel the President abused the power and made many decisions that should have been decided by Congress. These Senators also argue that there are many measures the American government can take to insure the safety of Americans in Ersatz without giving the President the power called for in the Diego Resolution. On the other hand, Senators favoring the resolution argue that the President needs a vote of support to strengthen his hand in dealing with a very delicate problem: how to protect the lives and property of Americans and prevent a Communist takeover without invading Ersatz.

"At this moment the vote looks very close. We may not know the outcome until the very end when Senator Richard Williams makes his decision. At last word Senator Williams was still undecided, despite the fact that he is a member of the President's political party and backed him for the Presidency. It may be that the final vote will be 51-49, with Senator Williams casting the deciding ballot."

"Sounds like a real thriller, doesn't it?" joked Senator Williams as he pulled on his coat and opened the door. "Stay tuned to that station and learn Senator Williams's choice! Well, it's likely to be a hard day. I'll be home for dinner."

*Tonkin Gulf Resolution:* In 1964 Congress gave the President authority to "take all necessary measures" to stop aggression in Southeast Asia. Lyndon Johnson asked for the resolution after reported attacks on U.S. destroyers that were patrolling the Gulf of Tonkin off the coast of North Vietnam.

**Williams Hears Further News.** As he drove to his office, Senator Williams listened to the latest news from Ersatz on his car radio. . . . Five more Americans had been kidnapped, making a total of fifty-three Americans who had been taken from their cars, from their homes, and in a few cases right out of their offices. Thus far, only men had been captured, leaving behind terror-stricken wives and children. . . . Air Force General George Patrick had been quoted as having recommended dropping paratroopers into Ersatz to rescue the Americans, followed by helicopters to airlift all the Americans out. The Department of Defense denied any such plan. . . . Meanwhile the Soviet Union said that it was studying the situation very carefully. Russian diplomats warned that the problem would become very serious if the United States intervened in Ersatz in any way.

"It's not getting any better," Senator Williams thought. "The rebels seem to be moving about the city at random with little opposition from the Ersatz police or government troops. Within a few hours the government may fall. Some—maybe many—Americans will be killed. But what will the President do if we pass the Diego Resolution and give him a blank check to use the navy as he thinks best? If he invades, the rebels will probably kill those Americans being held hostage. We might even have to keep forces there to support the present government. What would the Soviet Union and China do if we took such action? What would other Latin American nations do if we were to invade one of their neighbors? Has the President tried all possible channels of communication between American diplomats and the rebel leaders? Don't we have any allies who might try to negotiate in our behalf?

• On the basis of what you know now, how would you vote—for or against the Diego Resolution?

As he slipped through the side door of his office, Senator Williams was met by his secretary. "Hi boss. Glad you're here. The office is a madhouse. People are stacked up in the outer office waiting to see you, and the phone is ringing constantly. I think everyone in the nation wants to tell you how to vote or be the first to learn what you are going to do."

"How do people want me to vote?" Senator Williams asked.

"I would estimate that opinion is about 2-1 in favor of your voting for the Diego Resolution and supporting the President. But it is hard to tell. You got a long telegram from the faculty of Sinclair College urging you to vote in such a way that (1) no American lives will be lost, (2) there will be no risk of war, (3) American honor will be preserved, and (4) the President is supported. I'll let you figure out how they want you to vote."

"I wish I had a choice like that. What I fear is that if we don't act, someone will be killed. But I'm also afraid that if we do intervene

380

even more people might die. And would American honor be enhanced or tarnished if we sent an invasion force into such a small country? Who is waiting to see me?"

"About twenty reporters and one television crew!"

"Tell them I will have no statement to make until after I vote. Who else is waiting?"

"Probably fifteen other people, including Mrs. Fletcher, whose husband is one of the hostages in Ersatz, and Joe Flynn, a representative from Allied Electrical Corporation. As you know, Mr. Flynn's company not only gave heavily to your last campaign but also owns a lot of property in Ersatz. By the way, Mark Jones, the editor of the *Globe* in your home town, wants you to call."

**Williams Grants Some Interviews.** For the next two hours Senator Williams met with fourteen people and placed or received eight telephone calls. The most difficult interview was with Mrs. Fletcher, who began to weep as soon as she entered the office, pleading with the Senator not to support the Diego Resolution for fear that her husband would be murdered. She urged a policy that would give the rebels what they wanted if they would free the hostages. Joe Flynn, on the other hand, argued that the Senator should back the President and vote for the Diego Resolution. He pointed out that the captured Americans were in serious danger regardless of what action was taken.

No one could predict what the rebels might do. What was certain was that property in Ersatz owned by Americans would be taken over by the new government if the rebels won.

Between interviews Senator Williams called Mark Jones. The *Globe* editor wanted to know how the Senator intended to vote so that the paper could carry the story on the front page that evening. Editor Jones also gave his own opinion that the chief factor to consider was that the United States should take a firm stand and make it clear that it would not stand by quietly when its citizens were threatened.

• On the basis of what you have learned thus far, how would you vote—for or against the Diego Resolution?

As his last visitor was leaving, Senator Williams's secretary rushed into the office and said: "The President is calling. He's on line 9."

Senator Williams picked up the phone, punched line 9, and said: "Good morning, Mr. President."

"Hi, Dick. Sorry to bother you. I know you're very busy. But I thought I'd call before you went over to the Senate. Can I count on your vote today?

"I really don't know, Mr. President. I think it is a very messy situation. I'd like to support you, but I am not sure that the Diego Resolution is good for you or the country. The present government of Ersatz lacks strong popular support. I despise the rebels' terrorist tactics, but I'm not sure the United States should intervene in just this way."

"Look, Dick, I need your vote. It's going to be close. Let me give you some facts that haven't been made public. We think we have found where the rebels are holding the hostages. It's in the countryside, a few miles outside the capital city. Ersatz troops can't free them because the rebels would surely have advance warning of the attack hours before it came off. But I think we have a good chance of dropping our own paratroopers in at night, freeing the hostages, and capturing the revolutionary leaders before they know what hit them.

"It's risky, but doing nothing is risky too. We have a message from the rebels that starting today they will execute one American every six hours until the government agrees to free all of the political prisoners it is holding and enters into negotiations.

"Dick, I need your vote. You'll have to trust me in this matter. A lot of people are depending on us to do the right thing. By the way, drop by the White House at 5:00 P.M., and I'll fill you in on the plans to free those Americans. I'll see you later."

"Good-bye." Senator Williams returned the telephone to its stand.

• On the basis of what you have learned thus far, how would you vote—for or against the Diego Resolution?

382

Roll call had begun when Senator Williams left his office to walk to the Senate. Just before leaving, he had a call from the Senate majority leader (his own party leader) urging him to support the President. In the view of the majority leader, the Diego Resolution would become a big political issue. In his view most Americans favored taking some action to save the hostages. A party that seemed to lack the courage to act would risk losing a lot of votes in the next election. Also, if Williams wanted any help from the White House on any of his own projects, he should plan to support the President today.

As Senator Williams strode toward the Senate chamber, he was met in the hallway by one of his assistants.

"It looks close, Senator. I think your vote will tip the balance. Incidentally, I just heard on the radio that one of the hostages—a guy named Fletcher—was found. He had been murdered."

Senator Williams entered the Senate just in time to hear the clerk call his name.

"Senator Williams: Do you vote aye or nay on the resolution before the Senate?"

• How would you vote?

# 14 The Role of Supreme Court Justices

Each year the United States Supreme Court gets about 5000 requests to review court decisions made by judges in other courts. Most are turned down. During any single year the Supreme Court agrees to consider and offer opinions on less than 200 cases. Why are some cases accepted while others are not? What happens when the Supreme Court agrees to hear a case? How do Supreme Court justices arrive at their decisions? Who are the justices? What kind of people are they? How do they become members of the Court? These are among the many questions that we will look at in this chapter. But first we must learn what function is served by the Supreme Court. The following case study provides some clues about the place of the Supreme Court in our political system and the impact its decisions can have on American life.

## Case Study: Banning Prayer in the Schools

Prior to 1960, prayer and Bible reading were a normal part of opening exercises in many public schools. Probably most Americans did not give much thought to the practice. Most of those who did seemed to approve of it.

Madalyn Murray, a 41-year-old divorcee with two sons, lived in Baltimore, Maryland. Her oldest son, 14-year-old William, was a student at Woodbourne Junior High School. One day in September 1960 he returned home from school with a complaint that led to a major and controversial Supreme Court decision on June 17, 1963.

William Murray complained that he was required to say prayers with his ninth-grade classmates at school. This daily compulsory religious exercise offended him. William had been brought up to be a nonbeliever, an atheist. He protested that as a nonbeliever in religion he should not have to take part in the daily prayer. He asked his mother to complain to school authorities. William said to his mother, "They are praying in school. If you don't insist that I protest, you are a hypocrite. Do I have to pray in school or not?"[1]

**The Case Begins.** Mrs. Murray first tried to change the school rule by contacting the school officials. She petitioned the Baltimore Board of Education to ask that William be excused from the room during religious exercises. Dr. George B. Brain, superintendent of schools in Baltimore, answered Madalyn Murray's petition. He said

---

1. Bynum Shaw, "Nevertheless, God Probably Loves Mrs. Murray," *Esquire,* October, 1963.

that Bible reading and prayer in the schools were required by a 1905 school-board rule that stated:

> Each school, either collectively or in classes, shall be opened by the reading, without comment, of a chapter in the Holy Bible and/or the use of the Lord's Prayer.

No one had ever challenged the rule before. The superintendent said that if William Murray did not want to take part, "he could remain in his seat in respectful silence."

Neither Madalyn Murray nor her son were pleased with the decision. To protest it, Mrs. Murray took her son out of school on October 2, 1960. On October 28 William returned to school after the school board agreed to refer the case to the Maryland Attorney General.

The Attorney General ruled that Bible reading and praying in school was legal and that any student leaving a class to avoid it could be accused of truancy. He also ruled that any student who objected to Bible reading and praying could be excused from taking part.

Madalyn Murray was satisfied with the Attorney General's ruling. Her son asked to be excused from the exercises and in line with the ruling did not have to take part. At this point Mrs. Murray and her son thought the matter was settled. But some people felt otherwise, and the conflict started up again.

**Public Reaction Keeps the Case Alive.** The Murray protest against prayer in the schools had become front-page news. The Attorney General's favorable ruling angered some people in Baltimore. William's schoolmates beat him up for daring to protest against prayer in the school. He was jeered and made a social outcast. Vandals threw bricks through the windows of their home. Some people sent obscene letters and made threatening phone calls.

If these angry people had been willing to "live and let live," the Murray protest against prayer in the schools might have ended. But the abuse directed against her family led Mrs. Murray to fight back. She said, "I decided that the whole country was sick, and one relatively sane person had to make a stand." She decided to fight for a court decision that would stop compulsory Bible reading and praying in the public schools.

Mrs. Murray had very few political resources. She had become a social outcast. She had no powerful organization behind her. She decided to turn to the courts.

**The Case Enters the Courts.** Mrs. Murray began by hiring an attorney, Leonard Kerpelman. Because he believed in her cause, he charged very little for his services. Mrs. Murray filed a petition in the Superior Court of Baltimore asking for the ending of "sectarian opening exercises from the Baltimore public schools." She claimed that for a student opposed to prayer to be merely excused from class (as then permitted by the school board) caused the student "to lose

caste with his fellows and to be subjected to reproach and insult."
She argued that prayer exercises in the school violated freedom "by
placing a premium on belief as against non-belief."

Attorney Kerpelman argued before the Superior Court of Baltimore that the 1905 rule was contrary to the First and Fourteenth
Amendments to the United States Constitution. Therefore, the "rule"
should be declared illegal.

Following are the portions of the First and Fourteenth Amendments that the lawyer said were violated.

> *First Amendment:* Congress shall make no law respecting an
> establishment of religion or prohibiting the free exercise
> thereof. . . .

> *Fourteenth Amendment:* No state shall make or enforce any
> law which shall abridge the privileges or immunities of citizens
> of the United States; nor shall any state deprive any person of
> life, liberty, or property, without due process of law; nor deny
> to any person within its jurisdiction the equal protection of the
> laws.

The Superior Court of Baltimore ruled against the Murrays on
April 28, 1961. The judge decided, after reviewing the evidence, that
Bible reading and prayer in the Baltimore public schools was legal
and could continue. William Murray could refuse to take part, but
he would have to respect the right of other students to do so.

Mrs. Murray and her lawyer did not want to accept this decision.
They thought that they could argue successfully that the school-board
rule was unconstitutional. They appealed their case to the Maryland
Appellate Court, the highest court in the state of Maryland. After
long argument and study, the Maryland court voted 4-3 to uphold
the school-board rule. The majority of the judges argued that since
William Murray was not forced to take part, the religious activities
in school did not violate his basic rights under the Constitution of
the United States.

**The Supreme Court Accepts the Case.** Mrs. Murray and her lawyer
refused to quit. They felt that they were right and that they could
get a fair hearing from the highest court in the land. They appealed
the verdict, and the United States Supreme Court agreed to hear their
case.

Through their attorney, the Murrays argued before the Supreme
Court that their rights to freedom of religious choice had been violated
by the 1905 rule that required "reading without comment a chapter
in the Holy Bible and/or the use of the Lord's Prayer." The Murrays
argued that this rule was "in violation of their rights to freedom of
religion under the First and Fourteenth Amendments and in violation
of the principle of separation between church and state contained
therein."

The Supreme Court announced its decision on June 17, 1963. By a vote of 8 to 1, the Supreme Court declared unconstitutional the Maryland rule that the Lord's Prayer or the Bible be required for religious exercises in public schools. The Supreme Court decided that the "Maryland rule" went against both the First and Fourteenth Amendments to the Constitution and was therefore illegal. Bible reading and prayer requirements in the public schools of Maryland—and elsewhere—could no longer be enforced.

Mrs. Murray and son William are photographed at the Supreme Court in February, 1963.

Justice Clark wrote the majority opinion of the Court. It contained the following statements:

Once again we are called upon to consider the scope of the provision of the First Amendment to the Constitution which declares that "Congress shall make no law respecting the establishment of religion or prohibiting the free exercise thereof. . . ." In light of the history of the First Amendment and of our cases interpreting and applying its requirements, we hold that the practices at issue and the laws requiring them are unconstitutional under the Establishment Clause, as applied to the states through the Fourteenth Amendment. . . .

The place of religion in our society is an exalted one achieved through a long tradition of reliance on the home, the church, and the inviolable citadel of the individual heart and mind. We have come to recognize through bitter experience that it is not within the power of the government to invade that citadel, whether its purpose or effect be to aid or oppose, to advance or retard. In the relationship between man and religion, the state is firmly committed to a position of neutrality. The breach of neutrality that is today a trickling stream may all too soon become a raging torrent. . . .

**". . . and if it isn't unconstitutional."**

Shanks in the *Buffalo Evening News*

Concurring with Justice Clark, Justice Douglas said:

The vice of . . . such arrangements under the Establishment Clause [see the First Amendment] is that the state is lending its assistance to a church's efforts to gain and keep adherents. . . .

Such contributions may not be made by the State even in a minor degree without violating the Establishment Clause. . . .

Justice Potter Stewart was the only Supreme Court member who voted to uphold the practice of religious activities in the Baltimore schools. In his dissenting opinion he wrote:

. . . permission of such [religious] exercises for those who want them is necessary if the schools are truly to be neutral in the matter of religion. And a refusal to permit religious exercises thus is seen, not as the realization of state neutrality, but rather as the establishment of a religion of secularism, or at the least, as government support of the beliefs of those who think that religious exercises should be conducted only in private.

### Steps in the Development of a Legal Case: *Murray v. The Board of School Commissioners of Baltimore City*

The Problem: William Murray was required to take part in Bible reading and prayer in school against his wishes.

Steps Taken to Resolve the Problem

1. Madalyn Murray appealed to school authorities.
   Result: She lost the decision. (October, 1960)
2. Madalyn Murray appealed to the Maryland Attorney General.
   Result: Partial but not totally satisfactory decision. (November 2, 1960)
3. Madalyn Murray appealed to the Superior Court of Baltimore.
   Result: She lost the decision. (April 28, 1961)
4. Madalyn Murray appealed to the Maryland Appellate Court.
   Result: She lost the decision. (April 6, 1962)
5. Madalyn Murray appealed to the United States Supreme Court.
   Result: She won the decision. (June 17, 1963)

The net effect was to reverse all previous decisions against Mrs. Murray which required her son to be in classrooms where prayer and Bible reading took place.

**The Impact of the Murray Case.** The Supreme Court had decided in favor of Madalyn Murray. This decision meant that not only was the Baltimore school rule unconstitutional, but in effect all similar rules in other cities and states were also in violation of the Constitution. Following this decision, many schools voluntarily ended Bible reading and prayer in the classroom. In other cases new court suits were begun to test state and local statutes. In still other cases community and school leaders searched for ways to continue religious exercises without violating Supreme Court rulings. For example, some schools used the prayer delivered in Congress each day and printed in the *Congressional Record.* Some political leaders started a movement to overturn the Supreme Court decision by calling for a constitutional amendment which would permit prayer in the public schools.

1. Why did Madalyn Murray appeal to the Supreme Court?
2. What impact did the decision in her case have on other people?
3. Why in the American political system are issues such as this resolved in the courts rather than in other ways?
4. List some ways in which decision-making in the Supreme Court differs from decision-making in Congress or by the President.

## The Primary Function of the Supreme Court: To Interpret the Law

Heading the judicial branch of the federal government is the Supreme Court of the United States. It is made up of a Chief Justice and eight Associate Justices.

The Constitution set up only the Supreme Court and gave Congress power to set up "inferior," or lower, courts.

The Supreme Court is chiefly an *appellate* court. This means that it seldom begins a case (conducts a trial), but rather it reviews cases already tried in some lower court—either a lower federal court or a state court. But before focusing on the Supreme Court, we need to learn some things about the entire system of courts in the United States.

### The Work of Trial Courts

Courts in the United States may be divided into two general classes: (1) trial courts and (2) appellate courts. State trial courts generally serve one or more counties and are known by various names, such as county, district, circuit, and superior courts. Also part of the state trial court system are municipal courts, which handle violations of city ordinances.

Every state also has at least one federal trial court, known as the United States district court. It handles cases involving federal law. The federal district court may also be used to settle disputes between citizens of different states but only when the amount involved is over $10,000. (Mr. A of St. Louis brings a suit in the United States District Court of Eastern Missouri asking $15,000 in damages for injury in an auto accident against Mr. B of Cairo, Illinois.)

#### Criminal and Civil Cases

Trial courts, as the name implies, conduct trials. Cases tried in court are either *criminal* or *civil* cases. In a criminal case government officials acting for society accuse someone of a harmful act (crime) against society. In court the judge, or judge and jury, hear the charge, listen to and examine the evidence, and decide if the prosecution has proved the commission of a crime beyond reasonable doubt. If the jury's verdict is "guilty as charged," the judge passes sentence—says what penalty, within the limits of the law, the defendant must suffer.

Civil cases are disputes between two or more parties, usually over money or property, as in the auto-accident case cited above. In a civil case one party (the plaintiff) charges the other (the defendant) with causing some harm. Each party has his or her own attorney to argue the case in court. The government has no interest except to insure fair play in the settlement of the case.

**JUDICIAL SYSTEM OF THE UNITED STATES**

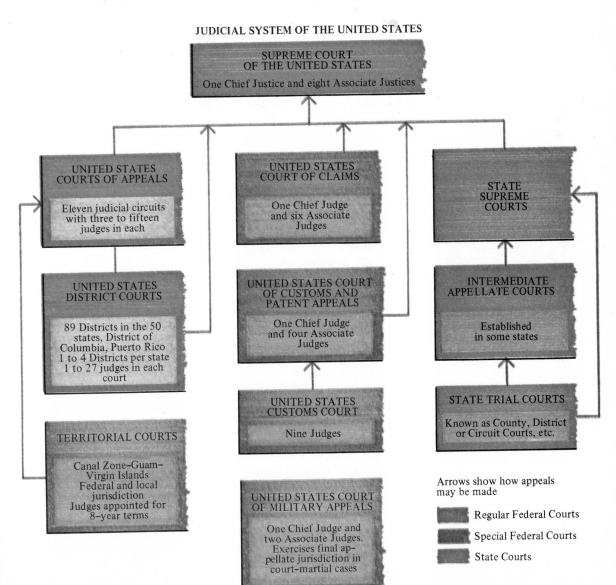

## Determining the Facts and Applying the Law

In the typical court case the plaintiff (the government in criminal cases) charges the defendant with wrongdoing. Much of the trial time is spent in *determining the facts:* Did the accused actually commit some wrongful act? Was the wrong done intentionally or through negligence? Was the defendant sober or drunk, sane or mentally disturbed? How much harm or pain did the plaintiff actually suffer? And so on.

To establish the facts, American courts use the *adversary system.* This is a contest in which lawyers for each side try to present a strong case to support their client's interests. Attorneys will emphasize certain evidence and ignore other facts. They will voice objections when they think they see mistakes in the conduct of the trial which may hurt their client. They will argue how the law should be interpreted to benefit their client most. Supporters of the adversary system believe that this contest between lawyers in the courtroom brings the facts out into the open.

In a jury trial the judge instructs the jury on the law in the case. The judge points out, for example, that if the jury believes the facts to be thus and so, it must return a verdict (judgment in a civil case) against the defendant. In a trial without a jury the judge, of course, determines both the facts and the law in the case.

## The Work of Appellate Courts

The defendant in a criminal case and either party in a civil case may appeal to a higher court if not satisfied with the decision in the trial. Appellate courts—ones that handle appeals from trial courts— exist at both the state and federal levels. The highest appellate court in a state is generally known as the state supreme court. Many states have an *intermediate appellate court* to share the work.

Most cases appealed from the United States district courts go to one of the eleven United States Courts of Appeals. The United States Supreme Court, the highest appellate court in the land, accepts appeals from the United States Courts of Appeals, certain other federal courts, and state supreme courts. But it chooses very carefully the cases it wants to hear and decide.

In an appellate case the court does not hold a new trial. Instead, it looks over the record of the trial and hears arguments of the lawyers on why the decision should stand or be changed. If an error in proceedings is found, the case may go back to the lower court for a new trial.

To show how a case moves from a lower court to the Supreme Court, let us assume that a city has passed an ordinance banning the showing of "X"-rated movies. A theater owner shows such a movie. The police raid the theater, arrest the owner, take the film, and bring the owner before the city judge who levies a $100 fine for breaking the law. The owner appeals this decision to a higher court. In appealing the case, the owner is not likely to dispute the "facts." The appeal will likely claim that the ordinance violates constitutional rights. The owner hopes that a higher court will agree, using prior rulings of the Supreme Court as a guideline to decide in the owner's favor.

If the state appellate court ruled against the defendant, his or her lawyer might then appeal to the United States Supreme Court. If the case were accepted by the Supreme Court, the issue before the Court would not be the specific facts of the case. Rather, the issues would relate to the meaning of obscenity, the rights of a city to pass laws dealing with pornography, the rights of a person to run a business, freedom of speech; in short, the nature of the law that applies to the case. When the Supreme Court decides, it will rule only on the specific case. But afterwards the "opinions" of the justices will join the body of law to be used by other judges to decide similar cases.

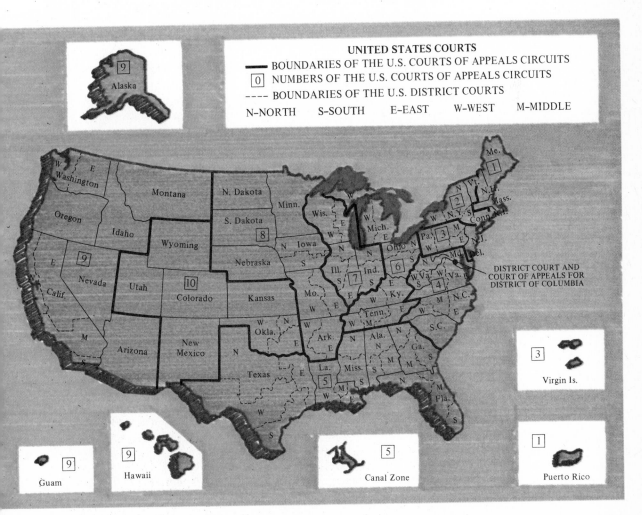

UNITED STATES COURTS

— BOUNDARIES OF THE U.S. COURTS OF APPEALS CIRCUITS
0 NUMBERS OF THE U.S. COURTS OF APPEALS CIRCUITS
---- BOUNDARIES OF THE U.S. DISTRICT COURTS

N—NORTH     S—SOUTH     E—EAST     W—WEST     M—MIDDLE

DISTRICT COURT AND COURT OF APPEALS FOR DISTRICT OF COLUMBIA

Alaska 9

Guam 9

Hawaii 9

Canal Zone 5

Virgin Is. 3

Puerto Rico 1

### Interpreting the Law

The primary function of the Supreme Court is to interpret the law. All laws in the United States must conform to the basic principles of the United States Constitution. Therefore, neither Congress nor state and local governments may make laws that violate the Constitution. And the President must not administer laws in such a way as to violate the Constitution.

What does it mean to "interpret" the law? To answer this question, we need first to see that many words and phrases in the Constitution are somewhat vague and general. For example, the Constitution gives Congress power "to regulate commerce . . . among the several States." For many years the Supreme Court interpreted this phrase to mean that interstate commerce began when goods were loaded for shipment across state boundaries and ended when the goods arrived at their destination. Then in 1937 the Court decided that interstate commerce also included the manufacturing process if the goods were produced for sale across state lines. The Court made this broader

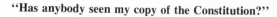

**"Has anybody seen my copy of the Constitution?"**

interpretation of "commerce . . . among the several States" in upholding a federal law regulating labor relations in industry. Through Court interpretation the "commerce power" of Congress is much broader today than it was in the nineteenth century.

Many other phrases in the Constitution can also have various meanings. Does "freedom of speech and press" mean absolute freedom, or are some limits permissible? If the latter, what are the limits and how can they be justified? States may not deny citizens "equal protection of the law." But what is equal protection? The Constitution says, "No person shall be . . . deprived of life, liberty, or property, without due process of law." The Supreme Court has often had to wrestle with the meaning of "due process of law." Chief Justice Charles Evans Hughes once said, "We are under a Constitution, but the Constitution is what the judges say it is." It is clear that interpreting the law is more than reading the Constitution and applying it as a yardstick to a particular case.

Not only is the Constitution subject to differing interpretations, but laws passed by Congress and state legislatures also often have vague language. A law may be clearly constitutional and yet contain a vague clause which needs to be made clear. If a court case hinges on the meaning of this vague clause in the law, the trial judge and the court reviewing the decision on appeal must say what they believe the words mean. To do this kind of interpreting, judges will at times go to the legislative records to try to find out what the legislators actually had in mind. Supreme Court decisions are sprinkled with such expressions as these:

> The history of congressional consideration of this problem leaves little if any room to doubt. . . .
> The history of this legislation emphatically underlines this fact. . . .
> Congress did not intend to. . . .

These are the kinds of complex issues that regularly face Supreme Court justices. The decisions they make are more than interpretations of law. And their "opinions" have far more influence than the opinions of others. Supreme Court justices are important *political decisionmakers* in our society. They often make policy decisions that are as important as laws passed by Congress. Many of their decisions affect American life profoundly.

## Some Rules and Procedures Affecting Judicial Decision-Making

How do Supreme Court justices make their decisions? What factors lead them to make one choice rather than another? Why do they often disagree with each other about the best decision to make in a particular case?

In previous lessons on *official decision-makers* you learned that a number of factors influence decisions. These factors include formal and informal rules and procedures, customs and norms, social forces, and personal beliefs. We shall look at each of these factors in studying decision-making in the United States Supreme Court. We begin with some formal rules set forth in the Constitution and federal laws.

### Size of the Court and Tenure of Justices

One rule is that Congress may determine the number of justices to serve on the Supreme Court. Today the Court is made up of eight Associate Justices and one Chief Justice. The size of the Supreme Court has some influence on its decisions. A one-judge Court or a fifty-judge Court would require different procedures and might lead to different policy choices. The Court is small enough that it can hold

In the 1930s the Supreme Court declared unconstitutional several major laws passed by Congress as a part of President Franklin Roosevelt's New Deal program. Anticipating further difficulties unless he could get new members on the Court, President Roosevelt asked Congress to enlarge the Court. He wanted one new justice for every present one over age 70. Roosevelt's "court-packing" plan failed to pass, but Congress did provide an attractive retirement plan for federal judges. And President Roosevelt soon had a Court more to his liking.

**That's the kind of sailor he is.**

Cartoon by "Ding" Darling. Courtesy of Mr. John M. Henry, secretary of the Ding Foundation, Des Moines, Iowa

396

discussions as a group. Unlike the Congress, major decisions are not delegated to committees. Except when deciding whether to accept a case or not, judicial decisions are made by majority vote. The fact that they can be reached by a simple majority vote rather than by a unanimous vote or even a two-thirds vote influences the decisions that are made. It certainly makes the task of reaching decisions on cases much easier than if all or two-thirds of the justices had to agree.

The Constitution states that federal judges "shall hold their offices during good behavior." This means that a judge can be removed from office only if there is evidence of misbehavior. Once appointed to the Court, a justice has the most secure job in the world. He or she alone decides when to retire, if ever. While subject to impeachment for "bad behavior," over the history of the Supreme Court no justice has ever been removed in this way.

Permitting justices to hold their jobs without competing in elections was intended to make them free and impartial judges. Once selected, they are obligated to no one for their jobs.

No doubt lifetime appointment does influence decision-making by the justices. They are quite free from the kind of political pressures that affect other officeholders. Also lifetime tenure encourages justices to remain active until they are very old. In some cases justices have refused to retire even when it was clear to others that they had lost some capacity to make judgments. In recent years, generous retirement benefits have helped ease some judges "off the bench."

## The Rule on Real Cases

Another formal rule is that the Supreme Court will hear only *real* cases. This means that to test a law in court a person or group must actually violate it or show that they are *directly affected* by it. Merely because one does not like a law is not grounds for testing it in court.

The *spending power* of Congress is very hard to challenge in the courts. Suppose you think that the Constitution gives Congress no right to spend money on urban renewal. The only way that this spending affects you directly is that a small part of the taxes you pay goes for this program. The federal courts would not accept a case brought by you or by any group of taxpayers challenging the urban renewal program, since your interest is not personal but is shared by all citizens generally.

The rule on *real cases* also means that a Supreme Court justice cannot make decisions until presented with a case calling for a decision. It is reported that Justice Felix Frankfurter once wrote a decision and then waited for the "right" case to appear to which he could apply it. The right case did not appear, so after his retirement he published the opinion as an article in a law journal.

The rule on real cases bars the Supreme Court from offering "advisory opinions" on bills in Congress. While the President and

Congress might like to have the Court's advice, its only answer can be: Pass the law if you wish. If it is later brought before the Court, then we will offer our opinion about its validity.

### Rules on the Supreme Court's Jurisdiction

A court is said to have *jurisdiction* over a case when it has the right to hear and decide it. As we have seen, the Supreme Court has broad *appellate jurisdiction* (the right to review a case tried in a lower court). It may review the following kinds of cases:

1. *Disputes involving the Constitution, federal laws, and treaties.* Examples: (a) A citizen claims that a state law (or city ordinance, or school-board ruling) violates the Constitution. (b) A citizen believes that he was deprived of some constitutional right in his trial in state or federal court. (c) A lawyer claims that a state law violated by her client should be voided because it conflicts with a federal statute or a treaty on the same subject.

2. *Admiralty and maritime cases.* Crimes committed on the high seas and disputes between shipowners or between merchant seamen and officers are examples. Maritime cases are handled in federal courts and can be reviewed by the Supreme Court.

3. *Cases in which the United States is a party.* Examples: (a) Jill X sues the Postal Service for injuries suffered in an accident with a postal truck. (b) The government sues a contractor in a dispute over a building contract.

4. *Cases between citizens of different states.* As we saw on page 390, federal district courts handle some cases in this category. The Supreme Court is unlikely to review such a case, however, unless it involves some constitutional issue.

Cases in the above categories would all have been handled in some lower state or federal court. They would be reviewed by the Supreme Court only if the justices felt that an important issue was involved. Besides its appellate jurisdiction, the Supreme Court has *original jurisdiction* over three kinds of cases. That is, the case actually begins in (is tried by) the Supreme Court. (1) Cases affecting diplomatic representatives of other nations may be tried by the Supreme Court. Such cases are very rare. Diplomats enjoy immunity from state and federal criminal prosecution, and a diplomat who breaks the law will be asked to return home. Once in a while, a diplomat may be involved in a civil suit, but effort would be made to settle such a case out of court. The Supreme Court handles (2) *suits between states* and (3) cases involving *a state and the federal government.* In 1963 the Supreme Court settled a dispute between Arizona and California over use of waters from the Colorado River basin. A recent state-federal case involved the ownership of public lands in Hawaii.

398

Over the entrance of the beautiful Supreme Court Building is the motto "Equal Justice under Law."

### "Legal" Questions versus "Political" Questions

The Supreme Court decides only "legal" questions; it will not decide "political" questions. The difference between a legal question and a political question is not always easy to determine. For example, in 1946 in the case *Colegrove* v. *Green*, the plaintiffs charged that they were being discriminated against by the State of Illinois because some Illinois congressional districts had much larger populations than did others. Thus, one member of Congress might represent twice as many people as the member from another district.

The Constitution leaves the task of determining the size and shape of the electoral districts to the states. Over time the districts that included large cities increased greatly in size when compared to the rural districts. State legislatures, often dominated by rural legislators, were slow to change the congressional districts. Those who were able to control the size and shape of the electoral districts could greatly influence the outcome of elections. In *Colegrove* v. *Green*, the Supreme Court decided it could not interfere in this matter because it was a *political question.*

In the case *Baker* v. *Carr* (1962) the Supreme Court reversed the decision of a three-man district court in Tennessee that had based its ruling on the Supreme Court's own prior decision in *Colegrove*

v. *Green*. In *Baker* v. *Carr* the plaintiffs protested that a 1901 Tennessee law which apportioned the members of the General Assembly among the state's 95 counties had the effect of depriving them of their rights, since their vote counted less than the votes of citizens in other districts. The majority on the Supreme Court ruled in their favor, claiming that the issue was not a political question. The plaintiffs were being denied "equal protection" guaranteed by the Constitution. Justice Frankfurter and Justice Harlan dissented, accusing the Court of entering into matters beyond its proper responsibility.

In brief, a "political question" is any question the Court chooses not to decide for that reason. A question becomes "legal" when the Court decides it does have jurisdiction. A political question at one point in time may become a legal question at a later time. In general the Court will avoid deciding such political issues as whether a current war is "legal," questions of foreign policy, and so on.

### Informal Rules

In addition to the formal rules described above, informal rules or customs also influence judicial decision-making. One such rule says that persons who wish to influence a court's policy choices must use lawyers. The judicial process is largely a private domain for lawyers. Only lawyers are recruited for the Supreme Court. The candidates are suggested to the President by the United States Attorney General (a lawyer), sometimes after consultation with a committee of the American Bar Association (the major professional association of lawyers). The President's nominee must be approved by the Senate Judiciary Committee (the one committee in Congress restricted to lawyers). Except for the litigants (plaintiffs and defendants) themselves, who may not even be present when their case is being argued, only lawyers may address the Court. The Court's decisions are written in a technical manner intended mainly for other lawyers.

If an ordinary citizen tries to influence the Court's decision by writing a letter or by petitioning the Court, he or she may be found to be in "contempt of court." At least, the Court does not consider such efforts to be proper. Still, the Court may accept *amicus curiae* ("friend of the court") briefs that are aimed at influencing decisions. Such briefs, written by lawyers on behalf of groups that favor one side or another in a case before the Court, are an accepted part of the judicial process. An article in a legal journal is another proper way to call a judge's attention to how a decision in a certain kind of case might be made. In the past a few organizations with cases pending before the Court have paid for law-review articles that supported their side. It is clear that ordinary people do not have the same access to the justices as do lawyers.

Another informal rule is that Supreme Court justices should not engage in party politics. This does not mean that justices never take

400

part in political discussions. The justices have many friends in Congress and in the federal agencies. Also it is common for justices to dine at the White House. One can't avoid all political talk in Washington. Still, Supreme Court justices are expected not to give active support to one political party against another, to campaign on behalf of candidates, or to take sides in a political issue in Congress.

## Some Important Procedures

Formal and informal rules play a major part in how judicial decision-making takes place. Within this framework the Court itself has set up certain procedures which influence the decisions of the members. These procedures tell how a case will be handled by the Court. We look at them under the following headings: (1) initiation, (2) oral argument, (3) conference, (4) opinion writing, and (5) post-decision alternatives.

### Initiation

Few cases begin in the Supreme Court, as we have seen. The usual way that a case gets to the Court is called *certiorari.* To illustrate, an attorney thinks that a client's rights were violated by the police and therefore the person did not get a fair trial. The attorney applies for a *writ of certiorari.* This is an order from a higher court to a lower one asking that the record of a case be sent up from the lower court. Copies go to all members. They may review each case or, more likely, share this task with one or more of the three law clerks assigned each justice. Each member wants to find out whether the case presents a major federal question that deserves the Court's time. If any one justice thinks that a case should be taken up, it will go on the "conference" list (page 403) for discussion.

Most cases are seen as trivial and are never discussed. If a case is taken up in conference, four members must then agree that it is important before it is granted a formal hearing. Many cases are weeded out at this stage. But if at least four justices agree to review the case, a *writ of certiorari* is granted. Then the case is scheduled for a hearing. Petitions for certiorari make up more than 90 percent of the cases the Court will consider.

Some cases reach the Court by means of a *certificate.* This is used when the judges of a lower court are equally split on a decision. It is also used when the lower court judges feel that the case is so important that the Supreme Court should make the first judgment. In all cases in today's Court, "certificates" are acted upon.

"I'll take it to the Supreme Court" is a common saying. But very few cases get that far. Each year more than 250,000 cases are filed in federal courts, and more than a million in state and local courts. Out of this nearly 1.3 million total, the Supreme Court will get about 5000 requests for review. Most are denied. The Court heard arguments on 170 cases in 1974.

An official prepares the conference room where the justices meet to decide what cases to review and what decisions to hand down.

Time and money are factors in court cases. It may take from two to five years for a case to go from a trial court to a decision by the Supreme Court. And the cost of a case begun in a federal district court with appeal to the United States Court of Appeals and a bid for review by the Supreme Court has been estimated to be no less than $15,000. The case of *Brown* v. *Board of Education* (page 420) is said to have cost the NAACP at least $200,000.

### Oral Argument

Once a case is accepted, it is scheduled for argument some months later. In the meantime, lawyers for each side file a lengthy summary, or *brief*, of their views of the case. In addition, as many as twenty other "friend of the court" briefs may be filed by other parties who claim to have an interest in the outcome of the case. The justices also have the records of the case from any lower courts that handled it. These sometimes run to several volumes. Finally, the lawyer for each party usually gets a half hour for oral argument before the Court. During this time the justices direct questions to the lawyers about points in the case.

402

## Conference Decision

When the Supreme Court is in session, it has a schedule of two weeks of oral arguments followed by two weeks of "recess" to write opinions and study appeals. Argument sessions are held from Monday through Thursday. On Wednesday afternoon and on Friday the justices meet in conference.

Conferences are held in an oak-paneled chamber around a large table. Each chair bears the nameplate of a member of the Court. Only the justices are present—no secretaries or law clerks—in order to prevent "news leaks" about decisions. Such leaks could harm the decision-making process.

The Chief Justice begins the conference by calling the first case and discussing it. After the Chief Justice, each associate justice gets the chance to speak in turn, moving from the one who has served the longest to the one who is newest.

Then a vote is taken. Each member has a large docket book that is kept locked when not in use. Members record their own vote in their docket book. Since the time of Chief Justice Marshall, the formal vote begins with the newest associate justice and goes up the line. The Chief Justice votes last. This is just the reverse of the discussion procedure. Five votes are needed to decide a case and four votes to grant a *writ of certiorari.*

One of the notable features is that the justices as a group take part in each decision of the Court. This means that the time allowed for the talk on some matters has to be very short. If some cases need an hour's discussion, others may get only a few minutes. However, each of the items on the day's agenda has been studied in private by the justices before the conference.

## Opinion Writing

Decisions of the Court come to the public as "opinions." Once a decision has been voted, someone must write the "opinion" of the Court. A Chief Justice voting with the majority will decide which justice shall write the majority opinion—or at times will take on the job personally. If the Chief Justice did not vote with the majority, the most senior associate justice who voted with the majority will decide who shall write the majority opinion.

Deciding who will write the majority opinion involves more than simply dividing up the work load. The way it is written may determine the final outcome of the case. The writer realizes that the statement will be used as a precedent for other cases. Also the writer must try to make the decision as acceptable to the public as possible. Finally, the writer will use the opinion to try to hold the majority of the justices together and to win the support of one or more dissenting members, if possible. A well-written opinion may pick up support from members who had at first voted the other way. A poorly written one may lead some members to drop their support.

The task of writing opinions may be the hardest one a justice has. In some cases months are used researching a case, writing the opinion, and having it read and criticized by the other members. Justices who agree with the decision but disagree with the statement written for the majority may write their own opinion (called a concurring opinion). Often those who oppose the majority will write *dissenting opinions.*

At times members of the Court change sides after reading early drafts of a majority opinion. Once in a while, what was to be the majority opinion turns out to be a dissent. Each time a new draft of a majority opinion is finished, it is passed around to get the reaction and advice of the other justices. Often new ideas have to be added or old ones dropped to keep the vote of a member. By the time a decision is finally made public, the majority opinion may have gone through as many as ten drafts in the writer's chamber. Then it may go through a dozen more to satisfy other justices. Each member writes thirteen to eighteen separate opinions each year.

**Post-decision Alternatives**

What happens after the Supreme Court has announced its opinion on a case? At least five alternatives are available to the disappointed parties to a case:

1. They can apply for a rehearing. If the decision was close (5–4), a change in personnel on the Court or a change in the social situation might alter the view of the Court in the future.

2. Congress may get around the Court by passing new legislation that has the same purposes as the original legislation but is constitutional.

3. Since the Court does not make final dispositions on cases, an individual may be able, in some cases, to return to the lower court for a hearing.

4. The decision of the Court might be ignored. If the decision is unpopular (for example, rulings on school desegregation), some people—even public officials—may choose to ignore it.

5. The Constitution can be amended. In the late 1960s some members of Congress sponsored a proposed constitutional amendment to permit prayer and Bible reading in public schools in order to upset the Court's ban on such activity (pp. 384-390).

## Application of the Law to Specific Cases: A Judicial Norm

Carved on the front of the Supreme Court building in Washington are the words "Equal Justice under Law." This phrase sums up a basic standard, or norm, of judicial behavior. American judges are not expected simply to decide a case by asking, "What would be best for everyone concerned?" Rather, they are expected to ask,

There are times when the Supreme Court may order a lower court to take a certain action. More commonly, the Supreme Court asks the lower court to review its decision, taking the Supreme Court's *opinion* into consideration.

404

"What does the law say about a case like this?" Then if the meaning of the law is not clear, the judges have the duty to say what they think the words of the law mean.

Let us see how this norm, or informal rule, applies to the Baltimore school-prayer case. When the Supreme Court agreed to review this case, its concern was not with such questions as these: Are some children emotionally upset by religious exercises in the schools? Do more children benefit than are hurt by such practices? Would striking down this law have any good or bad results? These would be useful questions for lawmakers to ask when deciding whether to require or forbid religious exercises in the public schools. But the question facing the Supreme Court was simply whether the Baltimore school-board rule was consistent with the highest law of the land, the Constitution of the United States.

## What Is "the Law"?

Justices of the Supreme Court are expected to base their decisions on the law. The highest law in the United States is the Constitution. All other laws—federal, state, and local—must be in substantial agreement with the Constitution. Very many of the cases reaching the Supreme Court involve disputes over whether a law passed by Congress, a state legislature, or a local governing body agrees with the Constitution. Other cases reaching the Court have to do with the behavior of officials. For example, did the police make a legal arrest, or did the judge conduct the trial according to the rules.

In following the judicial norm of basing decisions on the law, justices of the Supreme Court look at the Constitution and any other *written laws* (statutes and ordinances) which apply to the case. But "the law" consists of more than constitutions and laws passed by legislative bodies. *The law also includes prior court decisions.* When

the justices studied the Baltimore school-prayer case, they looked at various earlier rulings by the Supreme Court on the religion clause of the First Amendment. These earlier decisions on related cases are called *precedents.* When the Court made its decision in the Murray case, its ruling became a new precedent for settling other similar cases.

Following is a case which illustrates how judges look at the written law (in this case certain sections of the Constitution) and at precedents in arriving at a decision. You are to play the role of judge in the case. Following a brief summary of the facts, you will find excerpts from the Constitution that apply to the case. You will also read some precedents which the lawyers arguing the case want you as judge to consider. You should write a statement telling how you think the case should be resolved. Your decision must be based on how you think the law (the portions of the Constitution and the precedents) applies to the specific case.

### Case: Applying the Due Process Clause of the Constitution

Henry is arrested and charged with breaking into a poolroom. Henry states that he is innocent. He also claims that he is too poor to pay for a lawyer to defend him in court. He asks the state government to provide a lawyer for him. The government refuses. Henry is tried in court, without a lawyer to help him, and is found guilty.

Henry complains that his trial was unfair because he did not have the help of a lawyer. He declares that poor people cannot get equal treatment before the law because they cannot afford to hire lawyers. He says that American law courts favor the rich and that American law is the rich person's law. He asks that his conviction be overturned. The state government refuses to listen to him, but the United States Supreme Court decides to hear his case.

As one of the Supreme Court justices you must consult a number of laws. Pay close attention to these parts of the Constitution:

> In all criminal prosecutions, the accused shall enjoy the right to a speedy and public trial, by an impartial jury of the State and district wherein the crime shall have been committed, which district shall have been previously ascertained by law, and to be informed of the nature and cause of the accusation; to be confronted with the witnesses against him; to have compulsory process for obtaining witnesses in his favor, and to have the assistance of counsel for his defense.—*Sixth Amendment*

> All persons born or naturalized in the United States and subject thereof are citizens of the United States and of the State wherein they reside. No State shall make or enforce any law which shall abridge the privileges or immunities of citizens of the United States; nor shall any State deprive any person of life, liberty, or property, without due process of law; nor deny to any person within its jurisdiction the equal protection of the laws.—*Fourteenth Amendment*

When Henry's case reached the Supreme Court, he was represented by a lawyer. The state government also had its lawyers. In arguing the case, the lawyers on each side cited the following precedents—previous rulings.

*Powell* v. *Alabama* (1932): Seven black youths were accused of assaulting two white girls aboard a freight train in Alabama. They were found guilty and sentenced to death. They were not advised of their right of counsel, nor were they offered court-appointed counsel, or the opportunity to communicate with their relatives. It was only after they had been convicted that they were offered adequate legal counsel. The Supreme Court reversed the conviction, saying that the due process clause of the Fourteenth Amendment had been violated.

*Johnson* v. *Zerbst* (1938): In this federal court case the government had failed to provide a lawyer for a defendant accused of counterfeiting. Up until 1938 it was generally understood that where a person desired assistance of counsel, but for lack of funds or any other reason was not able to obtain a lawyer, the court was not obligated to furnish him with an attorney unless it was a *capital* case (one punishable by death). In this case the Supreme Court said that the defendant had the right to have a lawyer in *any criminal case in federal court.*

*Betts* v. *Brady* (1942): Betts was accused of robbery in Maryland, and he asked the state court to provide him with a lawyer, since he was unable to pay for an attorney. The judge refused, on the ground that it was not the practice to appoint counsel for poor defendants except in murder and rape prosecutions. The Supreme Court upheld the conviction, concluding that "appointment of counsel is not a fundamental right, essential to a fair trial."

Do you agree with Henry that his trial was unfair? Should his conviction be overturned? Explain your reasons.

**Checking Your Decision.** Henry was tried in court for a criminal offense, without a lawyer, and was found guilty. He complains that his rights under the Constitution have been violated because he did not have the help of a lawyer at his trial.

According to a recent Supreme Court interpretation of the Sixth and Fourteenth amendments to the Constitution, Henry was deprived of his constitutional rights. The Sixth Amendment declares that persons accused of crimes have the right to obtain the help of a lawyer to defend them in court. The Fourteenth Amendment says that no state can deprive a person of his liberty "without due process of law." One aspect of "due process" is the right to have an attorney.

The Sixth Amendment names several requirements for criminal trials *in federal courts.* They must be (a) speedy, (b) public, and (c) by an impartial jury. Persons on trial must (d) be told what they are accused of, (e) have the right to see the witnesses against them, (f) have the right to obtain witnesses in their favor, and (g) have the right to have a lawyer. Without certain of these features it would be difficult to have a fair trial—to have "due process of law." The question in the preceding case is whether all of these requirements are essential to a fair trial. If any of the Sixth Amendment's requirements are basic rights essential to a fair trial, they are covered by the Fourteenth Amendment's due process clause. And the Fourteenth Amendment requires state and local governments to give citizens protection of basic rights.

Since Henry was too poor to hire a lawyer, and the state government would not provide him with a lawyer's services at its expense, Henry was convicted "without due process of law," without "the equal protection of the laws," and in violation of the Sixth Amendment provision that "the accused shall enjoy the right to assistance of counsel for his defense."

### Gideon v. Wainwright

The case *Gideon* v. *Wainwright* was very much like the one above. Clarence Earl Gideon was arrested and charged with breaking into a poolroom in Panama City, Florida, on August 4, 1961. He said that he was innocent. During his trial this dialogue took place:

*The Court:* What says the Defendant? Are you ready to go to trial?

*The Defendant:* I am not ready, your Honor.

*The Court:* Did you plead not guilty to this charge by reason of insanity?

*The Defendant:* No, sir.

*The Court:* Why aren't you ready?

*The Defendant:* I have no Counsel.

*The Court:* Why do you not have Counsel? Did you not know that your case was set for trial today?

*The Defendant:* Yes, sir, I knew that it was set for trial today.

*The Court:* Why, then, did you not secure Counsel and be prepared to go to trial?

*The Defendant:* Your Honor, . . . I request this Court to appoint Counsel to represent me in this trial.

*The Court:* Mr. Gideon, I am sorry, but I cannot appoint . . . Counsel to represent you in this case. Under the laws of the State of Florida, the only time the Court can appoint Counsel to represent a Defendant is when that person is charged with a capital offense. I am sorry, but I will have to deny your request to appoint Counsel to defend you in this case.

*The Defendant:* The United States Supreme Court says I am entitled to be represented by Counsel.

*The Court:* (Addressing the Reporter) Let the records show that the Defendant has asked the Court to appoint Counsel to represent him in this trial and the Court denied the request, and informed

Capital offense: a crime punishable by death.

408

In The Supreme Court of The United States
Washington D.C.
clarence Earl Gideon
    Petitioner    | Petition for a writ
    VS.    | of Certiorari Directed
H.G. Cochran, Jr, as | to The Supreme Court
Director, Divisions | State of Florida.
of corrections state |
of Florida      No. 890 Misc.

OCT. TERM 1961
U.S. Supreme Court

To: The Honorable Earl Warren, Chief
    Justice of the United States
    Comes now the petitioner, Clarence
Earl Gideon, a citizen of The United states
of America, in proper person, and appearing
as his own counsel. Who petitions this
Honorable Court for a Writ of Certiorari
directed to The Supreme Court of The State
of Florida. To review the order and Judge-
ment of the court below denying The
petitioner a writ of Habeus Corpus.
    Petitioner submits That The Supreme
Court of The United States has The authority
and jurisdiction to review The final Judge-
ment of The Supreme Court of The State
of Florida The highest court of The State
Under sec. 344 (B) Title 28 U.S.C.A. and
Because The "Due process clause" of the

Gideon spent hours in the state prison library consulting law books.
Then he penciled this petition asking the Supreme Court to hear his case.

the Defendant that the only time the Court could appoint Counsel to represent a Defendant was in cases where the Defendant was charged with a capital offense. The Defendant stated to the Court that the United States Supreme Court said he was entitled to it. (Addressing the Defendant) Are you now ready to go to trial?

*The Defendant:* Yes, sir.[2]

In this manner, at the start of his trial, Clarence Gideon raised the question of whether his trial was legal. He claimed that his constitutional rights were being violated. He was too poor to hire a lawyer, and the state would not appoint one for him. The trial judge ruled that his rights were being respected. The state, he said, did not have to provide a lawyer.

The jury found Gideon guilty, and he was sentenced to five years in the Florida State Prison. However, Gideon kept up his efforts to win his freedom. On October 11, 1961, he appealed to the Florida Supreme Court, but was refused a hearing.

Gideon next appealed to the United States Supreme Court. The Supreme Court granted Gideon a hearing and appointed Abe Fortas, a famous attorney appointed to the Supreme Court in 1965, to argue Gideon's case. Fortas argued:

> An accused person cannot effectively defend himself. The assistance of counsel is necessary to "due process" and to a fair trial . . . . To convict the poor without counsel while we guarantee the right to counsel to those who can afford it is also a denial of equal protection of the laws.[3]

The Supreme Court agreed with Fortas. Justice Hugo Black read the opinion of the Court. He said that the "due process" clause of the Fourteenth Amendment protects a person from being sent to jail in disregard of his basic rights. Justice Black devoted most of his remarks in the majority opinion to the *Powell* and *Betts* cases (page 407). He said, "We think the Court in *Betts* was wrong . . . in concluding that the Sixth Amendment's guarantee of counsel is not [one of the] fundamental rights" covered by the Fourteenth Amendment's due process clause.

After the Supreme Court decision, the state of Florida gave Clarence Gideon another trial. This time, W. Fred Turner, a local attorney, was named by the court to defend him. This time the jury returned a verdict of "not guilty."

You should note in the *Gideon* case that the Supreme Court sought to *apply* and to *interpret* the law. The justices are not free to make any kind of decision they want. Their decisions must be logically related to the Constitution, to statutes, or to precedents.

---

2-3. Lucius J. Barker and Twiley W. Barker, Jr., *Freedoms, Courts, Politics: Studies in Civil Liberties,* ©1965, pp. 284–285. Reprinted by permission of Prentice-Hall, Inc., Englewood Cliffs, New Jersey.

## Stare Decisis: Another Judicial Norm

As you have learned, judges are expected to look both at statutory law and at precedent (earlier decisions on similar or related cases) in reaching a decision. We now focus on the use of precedent in reaching court decisions. A second major judicial norm (informal rule) is *stare decisis*, which means "let the decision stand." In effect, this rule tells the judge to be consistent, to pay close attention to earlier decisions on related cases.

The Florida judge who told Clarence Gideon that the state was not obliged to provide him with a lawyer was following the *stare decisis* norm. In 1961 the precedent which most nearly fit Gideon's case was *Betts* v. *Brady* (page 407). In that case the Supreme Court said that a state judge was not obliged to offer a defendant in a noncapital criminal case a court-appointed lawyer.

The *stare decisis* norm is more binding on lower courts than on the Supreme Court. The practice of following precedents gives stability to the legal system. Imagine the confusion if judges could decide cases any which way. Lawyers would be unable to prepare cases for their clients. Parties in a court case could not be sure of their rights. A legal *system* could really not exist without the following of precedents. But new social conditions at times require new interpretations of the law. Thus most of the really important decisions of the Supreme Court are those which set new precedents or which modify in some way an old precedent.

When the Supreme Court modifies existing precedent, as it did in the *Gideon* case, it does not ignore previous decisions. Justice Black, speaking for the majority in the *Gideon* case, said that the precedent of *Betts* v. *Brady* was mistaken. He said that the Court in 1942 should have ruled in favor of Betts by following the precedent set in 1932 in *Powell* v. *Alabama* (page 407), in which the Court ruled that the seven boys had failed to get a fair trial for lack of legal counsel. In fact, Justice Black in 1942 had written a dissent in the *Betts* case in which he emphasized the *Powell* v. *Alabama* precedent.

In short, while the Supreme Court does give new interpretations to the law—makes new precedents—it tries very hard to find earlier precedents in support of its new decisions.

The norm *stare decisis* is a powerful influence on judicial decision-making. The lawyers appearing before the Court build their cases by finding prior decisions which hopefully the justices will accept. Each Supreme Court justice listens to the arguments presented by the opposing lawyers. One justice may be impressed by a particular set of precedents, and another justice by another set of prior decisions. And a justice who gets the job of writing the Court's decision in a case will be careful to show how the present decision is based on precedent.

From time to time the justices see that gaps in precedents exist. Social conditions change, and old precedents do not really fit. Faced with this situation, some justices will look for cases which involve the issue. Then "precedent" opinions can be written to fill the gap. In the late 1950s and early 1960s civil rights was such an area. In the early 1960s another area was the rights of persons accused of crime. In the late 1960s and early 1970s the issue of capital punishment was another. It is not too much to say that once in a while a justice has an urge to write a certain "opinion" and then looks for a case to fit it.

### You Be the Judge: *Escobedo* v. *Illinois*

When the Supreme Court in 1963 in *Gideon* v. *Wainwright* decided that a criminal defendant in a state court had to be given a lawyer, the Court still did not answer all the questions about assistance of counsel. One unanswered question was this: Just when in the criminal proceedings must the accused have access to a lawyer? This question came before the court in 1964 in the case of *Escobedo* v. *Illinois*.

You are to imagine yourself a member of the Supreme Court in 1964. A brief sketch of the case follows. The pertinent sections of the Constitution and a number of precedent decisions are cited. You are to write an "opinion" explaining how the case should be resolved.

**The Crime and the Arrest.** On the night of January 19, 1960, Danny Escobedo's brother-in-law was fatally shot. At 2:30 the next morning Escobedo, his sister Grace (wife of the deceased), and two friends of Danny's—a Mr. Chan and a Mr. Di Gerlando—were arrested. They were taken to a Chicago police station and questioned by detectives for over fourteen hours. None of those arrested made a statement, and a lawyer they had called managed to secure their release at 5 o'clock in the afternoon of the same day they were arrested.

The police believed that Escobedo and his friends had killed Grace's husband because she hated him. But the police had no proof, only guesses. On January 30 Benedict Di Gerlando, who was again in police custody and who was later indicted (formally accused) for the murder along with Escobedo, told police that Danny had fired the fatal shots. Between 8 and 9 o'clock on the night of January 30, Escobedo and his sister were again arrested and taken to police headquarters. On the way to the police station one of the arresting officers said to Danny that Di Gerlando had told the police that Escobedo had fired the fatal shots. The officer told Danny that he might as well admit to the crime. To this Escobedo replied: "I am sorry but I would like to have advice from my lawyer."

**The Lawyer's Testimony.** Upon arrival at the police headquarters Escobedo was hurried into a questioning room with his hands tied behind his back. Soon Escobedo's lawyer arrived. At the trial, the lawyer described the events in these terms:

On that day . . . I went to the Detective Bureau at 11th and State. The first person I talked to was the sergeant on duty at the Bureau

Desk, Sergeant Pidgeon. I asked Sergeant Pidgeon for permission to speak to my client, Danny Escobedo. . . . Sergeant Pidgeon made a call to the Bureau lockup and informed me that the boy had been taken from the lockup to the Homicide Bureau. This was between 9:30 and 10:00 in the evening. Before I went anywhere, he [Pidgeon] called the Homicide Bureau and told them there was an attorney waiting to see Escobedo. He told me I could not see him. Then I went upstairs to the Homicide Bureau. There were several Homicide Detectives around and I talked to them. I identified myself as Escobedo's attorney and asked permission to see him. They said I could not. . . . The police officer told me to see Chief Flynn, who was on duty. I identified myself to Chief Flynn and asked permission to see my client. He said I couldn't see him because they hadn't completed questioning. . . . I filed an official complaint with Commissioner Phelan of the Chicago Police Department. I had a conversation with every police officer I could find. I was told at Homicide that I couldn't see him and I would have to get a writ of habeas corpus. I left the Homicide Bureau. . . . at approximately 11:00 [Sunday morning]. I had no opportunity to talk to my client that night. I quoted to Captain Flynn the Section of the Criminal Code which allows an attorney the right to see his client.

The Illinois statute then in effect provided in part that:

All public officers . . . having the custody of any person . . . restrained of his liberty for any alleged cause whatever, shall except in cases of imminent danger of escape, admit any practicing attorney. . . whom such person. . . may desire to see or consult. . . .

**Other Testimony.** Escobedo testified that throughout the questioning he repeatedly asked to see his lawyer and that the police replied that his lawyer "didn't want to see" him. The police testified that throughout the questioning Escobedo was handcuffed in a standing position. Moreover, evidence was introduced to show that Escobedo was upset because he had not slept well for more than a week. Other testimony revealed that during the questioning Officer Montejano, who grew up in Escobedo's neighborhood and knew his family and who spoke to Escobedo in Spanish, told him that he and his sister could go home (and they would be held only as witnesses) if Danny pinned the crime on Di Gerlando.

Escobedo testified that he finally accused Di Gerlando of the murder because of the promises made by Montejano. In turn, Montejano denied making any such promises.

Another police officer testified that during the questioning the following occurred:

I informed him of what Di Gerlando told me and when I did, he told me that Di Gerlando was lying and I said, "Would you

413

care to tell Di Gerlando that?" And he said, "Yes, I will." So I brought . . . Escobedo in and he confronted Di Gerlando and he told him that he was lying and said, "I didn't shoot Manuel, you did it."

At this time Escobedo, for the first time, admitted to having *some* knowledge of the crime. Later he made other statements that further showed his connection with the murder plot. An Assistant State's Attorney was summoned to take a statement. This person, an experienced lawyer, took the statement by asking carefully framed questions designed to assure that Escobedo's answers would be accepted as evidence. Escobedo said that he and his friends had planned to kill his brother-in-law because Grace wanted to get rid of him. Escobedo also said that he had offered Di Gerlando $500 to kill Grace's husband. According to his statement, Chan was a lookout for the job.

Escobedo was convicted of murder and sentenced to twenty years in prison. He appealed his conviction to the Supreme Court, saying that any statements made during the time he was not allowed to see his lawyer should not have been used against him.

## Constitutional Provisions and Precedents

This case involved the "assistance of counsel" clause in the Sixth Amendment and the due process clause of the Fourteenth Amendment (page 406) just as the *Gideon* case did. Also involved was a part of the Fifth Amendment which declares that "No person . . . shall be compelled in any criminal case to be a witness against himself. . . ."

This means that persons may not be *forced* to sign a confession or take the witness stand in their own trial. If they give testimony, it must be voluntary. At first this clause in the Fifth Amendment applied only to the federal government. But over the years the Supreme Court decided that the right not to testify against oneself (called *self-incrimination*) was a basic right protected by the due process clause of the Fourteenth Amendment. It thus applied to state governments as well as the national government.

In the *Escobedo* case the Supreme Court justices cited a number of precedent cases—both in the majority opinion and in the dissenting opinions.

*Bram* v. *United States:* On December 13, 1876, while on board ship to Halifax, a sailor named Brown was accused of murder. He implicated a fellow sailor, Bram, in the crime. Bram was put in irons and held prisoner on board ship until arrival at port. At Boston, Bram was charged with the crime. During the testimony at the trial, it was learned that Bram had been taken into a room, stripped of his clothing, and ordered to answer questions. Bram was convicted, but appealed to the Supreme Court. The Court held that the confession made by Bram was not voluntary and thus could not be used as evidence. He was released.

Why might the police sometimes prefer that a call to the arrested person's attorney be postponed? How do you think the cartoonist feels about the issue?

Wallmeyer in Long Beach (Cal.)
*Independent Press-Telegram*

415

*Powell* v. *Alabama* (1932): See page 407.

*Hamilton* v. *Alabama:* Hamilton was refused the right to counsel in an assault case. He was convicted and sentenced to death. The Supreme Court reversed the Alabama decision saying "only the presence of counsel could have enabled this accused to know all the defenses available to him."

*Ward* v. *Texas:* In June 1942, Ward was harassed by the police for a confession. He was taken to several jails in different counties and held for an extended period of time until he finally confessed. The Supreme Court held that the use of the confession at the trial voided the conviction.

*Haley* v. *Ohio:* Haley, a 15-year-old boy, confessed to a murder after five hours of questioning, starting at midnight, by police officers working in relays. The officers did not inform him of his rights. In 1948 the Supreme Court ruled that the confession should be disregarded because it was not voluntary and thus violated the boy's rights under the Fourteenth Amendment.

*Spano* v. *New York* (1957): Vincent Spano was convicted of murdering a former professional boxer after the man had walked out of a bar with some of Spano's money that had been lying on the counter after Spano had paid for a drink. Spano followed the boxer outside; the boxer beat Spano, kicking him in the head. Spano got a gun, killed the boxer, and then turned himself over to the police, bringing his lawyer with him. After the lawyer left, the police questioned Spano for several hours, finally getting a confession that was used in his trial. He was convicted but the Supreme Court overruled the decision, saying the confession was not voluntary.

*Cicenia* v. *Lagay* (1958): The Supreme Court upheld a lower court's decision convicting Cicenia of murder. Cicenia said he was denied his right to consult his lawyer until he had confessed. He also said he had not been permitted to inspect his confession before pleading.

*White* v. *Maryland:* In April 1963, White was arrested on a charge of murder and pleaded guilty without having the advice or help of counsel. Counsel was later appointed, and White pleaded not guilty at his formal "arraignment." However, the guilty plea made at the preliminary hearing was introduced in evidence at his trial, and he was sentenced to death. The Supreme Court held that the absence of counsel when the guilty plea was entered violated White's rights under the due process clause of the Fourteenth Amendment.

*Haynes* v. *Washington:* In May 1963, Haynes was convicted on a robbery charge and sentenced to prison. He objected, in his appeal, to the use as evidence of a written confession obtained

416

after sixteen hours of being held "incommunicado" and after being told he could not call his wife until he signed the confession. The Supreme Court held the evidence was obtained involuntarily and reversed the lower court's decision.

*Gideon* v. *Wainwright* (1963): See pages 408-410.

How would you decide the case? Was Escobedo deprived of his rights? What precedent opinions did you draw upon to reach your decision?

## The Influence of Social Forces and Personal Belief on Judicial Decision-Making

The norms, rules, and procedures described earlier apply to all justices alike. Still, the members do not always agree about what is a good decision. And a decision believed to be "good" at one time may be reversed years later by another group of justices. Why do such "upsets" occur? One reason is that a society's culture changes over the years. A practice that is viewed as "all right" at one time may be seen as "wrong" some years later. Also new justices with different personal beliefs come to the Court. Supreme Court justices, like other men and women, are influenced by values, attitudes, and beliefs widely held during the time in which they live. They are likely to take advantage of knowledge acquired by recent social science research and will be in influenced by current social theories.

The following case study shows the influence of social forces on judicial decision-making. After you have read the case, answer these questions:

**1.** How may the concept "political culture" be used to explain the reversal in decision?
**2.** How would you use the opinions expressed by Justice Brown and Chief Justice Warren to show that social forces influence the decisions of Supreme Court justices?
**3.** If social forces influence judicial opinions, what advice would you offer regarding the recruitment of judges?

### The Segregation Decisions of 1896 and 1954

In the latter part of the nineteenth century, segregation was established firmly in the South. A civil rights law had been passed in 1875. This law said that segregation was illegal. It said that blacks could not be stopped from using public services on equal terms with whites. But this law was declared "null and void" by the United States Supreme Court in 1881. In the South a social and political system based on unequal treatment of the races was a fact of life. Public opinion throughout the nation was either hostile to or indifferent about the problems of black people.

A major case on segregation came to the United States Supreme Court in 1896. It is called *Plessy* v. *Ferguson.* Homer Plessy was a very light-skinned man with a one-eighth black heritage. He lived in Louisiana, where segregation laws existed. One day he bought a train ticket and took a seat in a car having a sign that read, "For Whites Only." This simple act, a man with dark skin sitting in a car reserved for whites, broke one of Louisiana's segregation laws. The train conductor ordered Plessy to leave the seat and to move to a car reserved for black persons. Plessy refused to move and was arrested. He was taken to jail to await trial. At his trial, Plessy was found guilty of breaking a Louisiana law.

Plessy appealed this decision to the United States Supreme Court. He claimed that the segregation laws of Louisiana violated the Fourteenth Amendment of the Constitution. Plessy said that the segregation laws should be declared unconstitutional and that his conviction for breaking these laws should be overturned.

Following is Section 1 of the Fourteenth Amendement:

All persons born or naturalized in the United States, and subject to the jurisdiction thereof, are citizens of the United States and of the State wherein they reside. No State shall make or enforce

418

any law which shall abridge the privileges or immunities of citizens of the United States; nor shall any State deprive any person of life, liberty, or property, without due process of law; nor deny to any person within its jurisdiction the equal protection of the laws.

This amendment says that *all* persons shall have "the equal protection of the laws." Plessy said that blacks were not given the same protection of the laws as were white people. He claimed that the Louisiana segregation laws did not agree with the Constitution, that they kept blacks from enjoying "the equal protection of the laws."

The Supreme Court did not agree with Homer Plessy. It decided that the state laws did not go against the Fourteenth Amendment if the separate facilities for blacks were equal to those for whites. This decision was called the "separate but equal" doctrine. The vote of the Supreme Court was 7 to 1 against the appeal of Homer Plessy. Justice John M. Harlan voted for Plessy's appeal and against the majority opinion of the Court. Justice David J. Brewer did not vote.

Justice Henry Brown, in the majority opinion, declared:

The object of the Fourteenth Amendment was undoubtedly to enforce the absolute equality of two races before the law, but in the nature of things it could not have been intended to abolish distinctions based on color, or to enforce social, as distinguished from political, equality. . . . Laws permitting, and even requiring, [the separation of the two races] in places where they are liable to be brought into contact do not necessarily imply the inferiority of either race to the other. . . . The most common instance of this is connected with the establishment of separate schools for white and colored children. . . .

Gauged by this standard, we cannot say that a law . . . [requiring] the separation of the two races in public conveyances is unreasonable.

Justice Brown's opinion argued that separation of the races did not stamp "the colored race with a badge of inferiority." The majority felt that while the courts must ensure *the civil and political rights* of both races, the Plessy case was an issue of *social* equality. The Court concluded that "If one race be inferior to the other socially, the Constitution of the United States cannot put them upon the same plane."

Justice Brown noted that segregation of blacks was a way of life in the South. He noted that blacks were seen as inferior by whites. He said that the Constitution could not be used to change the beliefs of whites about blacks. He interpreted the Fourteenth Amendment to mean that segregation could be practiced. The Supreme Court decision in the *Plessy* v. *Ferguson* case gave support to the segregation system.

419

In practice the "separate but equal" doctrine meant separate and *unequal*. Separate black schools were not as good as the white schools. For example, in 1940 the Southern state governments spent about twice as much money for the education of white children as for that of black children. As late as 1960–1961, the state of Mississippi was spending $81.86 per white child in average daily attendance compared to $21.77 for a black child. Similar examples could be provided about other supposedly "separate but equal" facilities to show that the *Plessy* v. *Ferguson* case merely served to make the unequal treatment of blacks legal.

In 1954 the *Plessy* v. *Ferguson* decision, as it applied to segregated schools, was overturned in the case known as *Brown* v. *Board of Education of Topeka, Kansas.* In a vote of 9 to 0, the Supreme Court decided that "separate but equal" public schools violated the Fourteenth Amendment. The Court ruled that segregated public schools denied black children "the equal protection of the laws."

Chief Justice Earl Warren wrote the opinion of the Court. In it he said:

> . . . minors of the Negro race, through their legal representatives, seek the aid of the courts in obtaining admission to the public schools of their community on a nonsegregated basis. In each instance, they had been denied admission to schools attended by white children under laws requiring or permitting segregation according to race. This segregation was alleged to deprive the plaintiffs of the equal protection of the laws under the Fourteenth Amendment. . . .
>
> The plaintiffs contend that segregated public schools are not "equal" and cannot be made "equal," and that hence they are deprived of the equal protection of the laws. . . .
>
> In approaching this problem, we cannot turn the clock back to 1868 when the Amendment was adopted, or even to 1896 when *Plessy* v. *Ferguson* was written. We must consider public education in the light of its full development and its present place in American life throughout the Nation. Only in this way can it be determined if segregation in public schools deprives these plaintiffs of the equal protection of the laws.
>
> Today, education is perhaps the most important function of state and local governments. . . . It is required in the performance of our most basic public responsibilities, even service in the armed forces. It is the very foundation of good citizenship. . . . In these days, it is doubtful that any child may reasonably be expected to succeed in life if he is denied the opportunity of an education. Such an opportunity, where the state has undertaken to provide it, is a right which must be made available to all on equal terms.
>
> We come then to the question presented: Does segregation of children in public schools solely on the basis of race, even

though the physical facilities and other "tangible" factors may be equal, deprive the children of the minority group of equal educational opportunities? We believe that it does. . . .

To separate them from others of similar age and qualifications solely because of their race generates a feeling of inferiority as to their status in the community that may affect their hearts and minds in a way unlikely ever to be undone. . . .

We conclude that in the field of public education the doctrine of "separate but equal" has no place. Separate educational facilities are inherently unequal. Therefore, we hold that the plaintiffs . . . are . . . deprived of the equal protection of the laws guaranteed by the Fourteenth Amendment.

Chief Justice Warren said that segregated schools for blacks were not and could not be equal to white schools. Warren pointed to the inequality of educational opportunities in our society today. He said that segregation by race "generates a feeling of inferiority as to their status in the community that may affect their hearts and minds in a way unlikely ever to be undone." This conclusion was based on current theories of psychology and sociology. Warren based his decisions on the Fourteenth Amendment and current ideas about the relationship of a social environment to equality of opportunity.

Cartoonist Wright pictures the desegregation rulings of the Court as bitter medicine that must be swallowed. The cartoon on the left represents the view of groups organized in the South in the 1950s to delay desegregation. They argued that the Court was trimming away states' rights.

"Judicial tyranny."

Citizens' Council, Jackson, Miss.

"Really, now—you can't hold it there forever."

© 1970, Don Wright, *The Miami News*

## The Influence of Personal Beliefs on Judicial Decision-Making

A changing social situation may help explain why a Court will reverse the opinion of a Court fifty years before. But it does not explain why nine persons serving on the same Court have trouble reaching agreement on the case before them. This can best be accounted for by looking at the personal beliefs of the justices.

Each Supreme Court justice or other judge is a unique person, whose personality was shaped by a set of unique personal experiences. The role of Supreme Court justice is the same for the eight associate justices and nearly the same for the Chief Justice. Yet the members play the role in a way that fits their own personal style. And members look at the world through their own perspectives, their own beliefs and values.

Some judges have tended to take the side of personal freedom in civil rights cases. They think that persons need support against attacks by government on their freedom. Others tend to give greater weight to protecting the majority. For example, in a case on the use of evidence gained by wiretapping, some judges may feel that it cannot be used in court because it was gained illegally. They would see wire tapping as a clear violation of personal freedom. So, even though the evidence points to guilt, these judges might decide that the accused must go free. They think that no one should be convicted with illegal evidence. Other judges, concerned about the rise in crime, may feel that a little loss of freedom through the use of electronic "bugging" is all right if it helps curb crime. These judges are more willing to accept wiretap evidence and thus to uphold the verdict of the lower courts.

Some justices think that the Court should actively support policies aimed at ending racial discrimination. Others think that such questions are usually political questions and should be settled by the political processes.

Judges may also differ in how the "facts" are to be interpreted. In recent years the Supreme Court has heard a number of cases dealing with pornography. After looking at alleged indecent films and books, the Court still has a hard time defining "hard-core pornography." The Court's difficulty stems from the fact that justices have trouble both defining pornography for themselves and getting other justices to accept their definition.

In *Jacobellis* v. *Ohio* (1964) the Court found that a certain movie was not obscene as had been found by the lower court. In his concurring opinion, Justice Potter Stewart said, "I shall not attempt to further define the kinds of material I understand to be embraced within that shorthand description [of pornography]; and perhaps I could never succeed in intelligibly doing so. But I know it when I see it." Many decisions are influenced by how a judge "sees it," that is, by his or her personal beliefs.

## Appointment of a Chief Justice: Two Cases

Imagine that you are President of the United States. A Supreme Court justice has written to say that he will retire at the close of the present term of the Court. You have asked your Attorney General to prepare a list of candidates from which you may choose one name to send to the Senate.

Following are four names given to you. Each has been checked with the Committee on the Federal Judiciary of the American Bar Association and has been awarded a high rating. Moreover, each name has been presented informally to members of the Senate Judiciary Committee, and you have been assured that any of the four can win approval. Whom would you appoint and why?

*Candidate A:* Mr. Rizzo is a well-known law school professor and a specialist on the Supreme Court. He has written many distinguished articles and books on the Court. More of his students have been chosen to serve as clerks to Supreme Court justices than those of any other law professor. He is a close personal friend to three of the present justices. Mr. Brown has not campaigned for or held any political office. Moreover, he is not

Members of the Supreme Court in 1976 were, left to right, Byron R. White, William J. Brennan, Jr., Chief Justice Warren E. Burger, Potter Stewart, Thurgood Marshall, Back row, left to right, William H. Rehnquist, Harry A. Blackmun, Lewis F. Powell, and John Paul Stevens.

identified closely with any political party, as he feared partisan political activity would interfere with his scholarship. He is fifty-five years old.

*Candidate B:* Mr. Lavin is your Attorney General. He is a long-time political ally and friend. He has spent most of his life in political office—first as a state legislator, then as a member of Congress, and later as governor. When you were elected President, he left a profitable private practice to become Attorney General. He has always been active in state and national politics, and you think alike on most political matters. He has never been a judge; he is fifty-seven years old.

*Candidate C:* Mrs. Elias is a circuit judge on the United States Court of Appeals. She was appointed to that post by a former President, also of your political party. She had formerly been judge of a county court and of the appellate court of her state. Before appointment to the bench in her state, she had given some service to your party. But since becoming a judge, she has tried to stay out of politics. You have read some of her majority and dissenting opinions and are impressed with her research, reasoning, and command of language. Many groups around the country—including, of course, the women's rights organizations—are urging you to make history by appointing the first female Supreme Court justice.

*Candidate D:* Mr. Jameson is a federal district court judge. You appointed him only two years ago at the urging of his friend, Senator Strongarm. The Senator had reminded you that without his state's electoral votes, you would not be President. Senator Strongarm's support was important in his state; it was easy to pay your debt by appointing Jameson. Now, Strongarm would like to see Jameson appointed to the Supreme Court. While Jameson is a hard-working, competent judge, you have not always liked his decisions, especially those relating to civil rights and the treatment of criminals. He is fifty-six years old.

Whom will you nominate and why?

**President Johnson Nominates a Chief Justice**
In June 1968 Chief Justice Earl Warren sent a letter to President Lyndon B. Johnson, indicating he would like to retire from the Supreme Court at a time "effective at your [the President's] pleasure." President Johnson replied that he would accept Warren's resignation at a time that a suitable successor could be found.

This exchange of letters touched off an intense political battle. Warren knew that Johnson was not planning to run for reelection. Some observers think that Warren timed his retirement so that Johnson, a President with liberal views, could choose a successor. They think

424

that Warren wished to maintain the liberal strength on the Court. Suppose a conservative Republican were to win the 1968 presidential election. If Warren were to wait until February 1969 to retire, someone with more conservative political attitudes might be chosen to succeed him. A judge with such views would be less likely to make decisions favored by Warren.

Warren's letter was sent at a time when the Supreme Court's popularity was very low. A public opinion poll in the summer of 1968 found over half of the respondents giving the Supreme Court an unfavorable rating. Many Americans were unhappy with recent decisions of the Supreme Court and expressed their displeasure to members of Congress.

Acting on Warren's letter, President Johnson decided to nominate Abe Fortas for Chief Justice. Fortas had been appointed Associate Justice by Johnson in 1965. Johnson also decided to nominate Homer Thornberry, a long-time Texas friend, to fill the "vacancy" left by Fortas. Both Fortas and Thornberry had been close associates of the President. It was clear that, if approved by the Senate, these two men would support Johnson's policies and would likely continue the present decisions of the Court.

**Thurmond Leads Opposition.** A number of Senators spoke out against Fortas and Thornberry. But the strongest opposition came from Senator Strom Thurmond of South Carolina. He had been a major critic of the Supreme Court, especially its decisions on civil rights. Moreover, Senator Thurmond, formerly a Democrat, had become a Republican because he disagreed with most of the policies of the national Democratic party. Finally, he was a supporter of Richard Nixon, the Republican candidate for President. Not only did Thurmond dislike Johnson's nominees, he hoped to put off the appointments to the Supreme Court until January 1969, when he hoped Nixon would be the new President.

Throughout the debate on the Fortas nomination, little was said about his ability to handle the job. He was widely admired as an able attorney. The chief criticisms had to do with his political views and his close ties with President Johnson.

On July 18, Fortas came before the Senate Judiciary Committee for an inquiry into his "qualifications" for the job of Chief Justice. For nearly two hours Senator Thurmond attacked the Court and Fortas personally for past Court decisions:

> Thurmond pressed Fortas for his opinion on a 1957 ruling that freed confessed rapist Andrew Mallory of Washington. Fortas was appointed to the Court in 1965.
>
> "Why did he go free? Do you believe in that kind of justice?" the Senator [Thurmond] demanded.
>
> "Mallory! Mallory! I want that name to ring in your ears. Mallory!" he shouted. "A man who confessed a crime and the

Court turned him loose on a technicality. Do you as a Justice of the Supreme Court condone such a decision as that?"[4]

The hearings revealed that Fortas had been asked to advise President Johnson from time to time on "fantastically difficult" decisions concerning Vietnam and the urban crisis. Some Senators worried whether this was a good practice for an associate justice to have such close ties to the President. Fortas replied:

> Since I have been a Justice, the President of the United States has never, directly or indirectly, proximately or remotely, talked to me about a matter before the Court or that might come before the Court. The President has done me the honor on some occasions to ask my help on a few critical matters having nothing whatever to do with a legal situation.[5]

A third criticism aimed at Fortas was his interpretation of the judicial role as related to the Constitution. Senator Sam Ervin (Democrat of North Carolina) expressed his opposition to the Fortas view in a letter to the *Washington Post,* August 9, 1968:

> Let me assure you that I was courteous to Justice Fortas throughout the hearing and treated him just exactly like I would have liked to have been treated had our positions been reversed.

Justice Abe Fortas (left) at the witness table awaiting questions by members of the Senate Judiciary Committee. At the right, Senator Strom Thurmond is shown while making criticisms of Fortas toward the end of the Committee's hearings.

4-5. *The Washington Post.* July 19, 1968. © *The Washington Post.* Used by permission.

In my deliberate judgment, the cases make it plain that in the performance of his work as an Associate Justice, Mr. Fortas has undertaken to carry into effect the words he spoke at American University on March 20, 1968. At that place and time he declared:

"But the words of the Constitution were not written with a meaning that persists for all time. Words are static symbols.

Words may be carved in impervious granite, but the words themselves are as impermanent as the hand that carved them. They reflect light and shadow, they are modified by rain and sun, they are subject to the changes that a restless life brings upon them. So the specific meaning of the words of the Constitution has not been fixed and unchanging. They never will be fixed and unchanging.

The Constitution is not static. But the changes in those words—changes in the meaning of those words—have not, as one might think, been arbitrary or haphazard."

After reading these words of Justice Fortas, I wondered why George Washington, Benjamin Franklin, James Madison, Alexander Hamilton, and the other good and wise men who framed the Constitution put provisions in that document requiring Supreme Court Judges to take oaths to support a Constitution whose words Justice Fortas says have no fixed meaning, and specifying that the Constitution can be amended, i.e., changed only by the joint action of Congress and the States.[6]

**The Review of the Fortas Nomination Continued into September.** The Senate Judiciary Committee requested that Justice Fortas appear a second time for another round of questions, but Fortas sent a polite refusal.

There was concern among the pro-Fortas members of the Senate that enough strength might be mounted by the anti-Fortas Senators to stage a filibuster when the nomination came to the floor of the Senate. The Republican presidential candidate, Richard Nixon, said he opposed the filibuster on the Fortas nomination. But he did not say whether he was for or against the nomination. The Democratic candidate, Hubert Humphrey, attacked Nixon for "making a deal" with Strom Thurmond to block the nomination of Fortas. Senator Thurmond denied such a deal.

On September 17, 1968, by a vote of 11-6, the Senate Judiciary Committee recommended to the Senate that Justice Fortas be confirmed as Chief Justice. Senate Majority Leader Mike Mansfield (D-Mont.), expecting a filibuster, said he would let the debate continue for about a week before attempting to force an end to the filibuster by using the cloture rule (page 365).

---

6. © *The Washington Post.* Used by permission.

**The Filibuster Begins.** On September 27 a Republican-led filibuster began in the Senate against a motion to call up the nomination of Abe Fortas for Chief Justice of the United States. The Republicans were joined by some Southern Democrats.

The pro-Fortas Senators were dealt a blow the next day when Senator Dirksen, the Senate Republican leader, said that he would not vote for cloture and might oppose confirmation of Fortas if debate was halted. To those pro-Fortas Senators who were counting on Dirksen to carry needed Republican votes, this action came as a complete surprise. Earlier, Senator Everett Dirksen had said he would vote to confirm Fortas.

Some people think that Dirksen had political reasons for changing his views. They noted that Dirksen had not liked the Supreme Court decision in the case *Witherspoon* v. *Illinois.* In this case the Court held that a man cannot be sentenced to death by a jury if persons *opposed* to the death penalty have been kept off the jury. Fortas voted with the majority in deciding this case. Under the precedent of this case, Richard Speck, who was sentenced to death for killing eight student nurses in Chicago in 1966, was appealing his death verdict. Some believed Dirksen would be hurt in his campaign to gain reelection as Senator from Illinois if he supported a man for Chief Justice who made it possible for a convicted murderer to appeal his case and perhaps go free.

**Fortas Withdraws.** On Tuesday, October 1, the cloture vote was taken and fell fourteen votes short. Many liberals supporting Fortas now knew that he had no chance. In a letter to President Johnson two days later Fortas asked that his name be withdrawn for the post.

The attempt to choose Abe Fortas as Chief Justice had failed. President Johnson decided not to send another name to the Senate. It seemed best to have Earl Warren stay on as Chief Justice, at least until a new President was in office.

### President Nixon Appoints a Chief Justice

On May 26, 1969, President Nixon announced his choice for Chief Justice. It was Warren Earl Burger. Who was Judge Burger? Why had Nixon picked him?

There had been guesses that Nixon would pick a close associate, such as his Attorney General John Mitchell or the former Attorney General under Eisenhower, Herbert Brownell. Both of these men seemed highly qualified, and their political views seemed to be close to those of Mr. Nixon. Instead, he chose a person he knew only slightly. Some reporters said that criticism of the Johnson-Fortas relationship led Nixon to choose someone whose views were like his own but who was not tied closely to him.

Chief Justice Burger was born on a Minnesota farm of immigrant parents. He worked his way through school, earning highest honors in the process. He graduated from the St. Paul Minnesota Law School

Chief Justice Warren E. Burger administers the oath of office to President Gerald Ford as Betty Ford looks on.

in 1927, began to practice law in Minnesota, and became active in the Republican party.

Burger first met Richard Nixon at the 1948 Republican National Convention. At that time Burger was a strong supporter of Minnesota Governor Harold Stassen for the presidential nomination. At the 1952 convention Burger urged the Minnesota delegation to support Eisenhower. Since Richard Nixon was the nominee for Vice-President with Eisenhower in 1952, Burger's support indirectly helped Nixon gain national prominence.

When Eisenhower was elected in 1952, he rewarded Burger with a post as Assistant Attorney General. Four years later Burger accepted an Eisenhower appointment as a judge on the Washington, D.C., Court of Appeals. He was on the Court of Appeals when Nixon picked him for the post of Chief Justice.

Nixon and Burger had held similar critical views of recent Supreme Court decisions. They both had said that the Court was too protective of the rights of accused persons at the expense of law-abiding citizens. For example, during his 1968 campaign for the Presidency, Richard

Nixon often spoke out against the Supreme Court for its decisions on criminal cases. Nixon charged that Supreme Court decisions, such as in the Escobedo case (pages 412–417), were "seriously hamstringing the peace forces in our society and strengthening the criminal forces." He called for the protection of the "first civil right of every American, the right to protection in his home, business and person from domestic violence. . ."

Meanwhile, Judge Burger had given a commencement address at Ripon College that caught Nixon's attention. In that address Judge Burger said, "Government exists chiefly to foster the rights and interests of its citizens—to protect their homes and property, their persons and their lives."

President Nixon also favored a dissenting opinion Burger wrote in 1957. In that decision the majority reversed a conviction because police delayed taking the defendant before the judge. Judge Burger dissented, arguing that "under the guise of protecting legitimate individual rights, the majority [of the Court] adandons the balance we are charged with maintaining between individual rights and the protection of the public."

It seemed clear that Nixon had found a nominee whose views were very similar to his own. The American Bar Association approved of Judge Burger and said so in a letter to Senator James Eastland, chairman of the Senate Judiciary Committee. The hearing to secure confirmation before the Senate Judiciary Committee went smoothly. Some of the testimony follows:

*Senator Eastland:* Do you think the Supreme Court has the power to amend the Constitution of the United States by judicial interpretation?

*Judge Burger:* No; clearly no. It has no power to amend the Constitution.

*Chairman Eastland:* Does the Supreme Court have the power to legislate judicial interpretation?

*Judge Burger:* I think as you put the question, clearly it has no such power. No court has that power. . . .

*Senator Eastland:* Is it your philosophy that the Constitution of the United States has a fixed, definite meaning, that does not change but stays there until it is amended as the Constitution provides that it be amended?

*Judge Burger:* Well, within the confines of a limited hearing, Senator, Mr. Chairman, it might call for a lecture . . . to meet all points of that, but surely it is the duty of the judges, all judges, to read the Constitution and try to discern its meaning and apply it.

Approval of the Senate Judiciary Committee and the full Senate was won easily. And on June 23, 1969, retiring Chief Justice Earl Warren swore in his own successor.

Answer the following questions on the basis of information presented in the two preceding case studies.

1. Why did President Johnson nominate Abe Fortas to be Chief Justice? Why was his nomination opposed so strongly?

2. Why did President Nixon nominate Warren Burger to be Chief Justice? Why was his nomination approved easily?

3. It is sometimes said that a great judge is one who makes great decisions. How do Presidents and Senators decide whether a particular candidate is likely to produce great decisions?

# 15 The Role of Federal Bureaucrats

Suppose there is a large building which you have never been able to enter. Every half hour the doors open, and a new car is pushed out. This happens day after day, month after month. Without ever going into the building you can be reasonably certain that the building is an auto factory.

Government is a bit like that building. Most of us never get inside. We see only what comes out the doors. But what does come out? What is the "Product" of government? Among other things, money and orders to spend money. Government spends money for many things including aircraft carriers, school books, parks, and hospitals.

Government also issues other kinds of orders. It decides what rates may be charged for certain utilities such as gas, electricity, and telephone. It also may decide whether two companies can combine to make a larger company or whether a railroad can stop its passenger service. Government orders are often directed not to people but to institutions and corporations. Most of what comes from government seems to be (a) orders to act or not to act and (b) money to support these orders.

## What Is the Federal Bureaucracy?

Many of the orders emerge from doors marked with the names of *administrative agencies.* These agencies are what may be called the federal *bureaucracy,* the largest component of government (in terms of number of people). The various executive departments like the Departments of Commerce, Defense, Justice, Interior, and Transportation are examples of administrative agencies. The agencies are not simply messengers for the President—or for the Congress. They play a part in governmental decision-making, a very important part. These agencies touch all our lives, in ways partly visible and in other ways not so visible.

It seems useful, then, to know something about the behavior of people who work in the agencies—to study the "bureaucratic role." But this role is harder to define than the others we have studied. It is fairly easy to study the President's job, since it is handled by one person at a time. Although Congress has 535 members and the Supreme Court has nine, it is fairly easy to describe their roles. A look at bureaucrats is more difficult because there are so many more of them and the range of their activities is more varied.

Today the federal government employs nearly three million civilians. Many are bureaucrats. They differ from each other in many

ways. Some are specialists in agriculture. Some are lawyers dealing in patent and copyright law. Others are medical doctors. The list of jobs seems endless. Hundreds of jobs that exist outside government can find their match within it.

## Who Is a Federal Bureaucrat?

We shall define a federal bureaucrat as a professional civilian employee of the government who carries out or supervises programs authorized by the President and Congress. Bureaucrats include cabinet members. They can be head of a bureau or be a *program officer*, a person who has the direct day-by-day management of a federal program. In short, all of those people who have responsibility for making bureaucratic policy or who influence or carry out such policy are included. We shall not include in our definition everyone who works for the government. Among the people who are federal employees but not bureaucrats are secretaries, clerks, janitors, cooks, and chauffeurs.

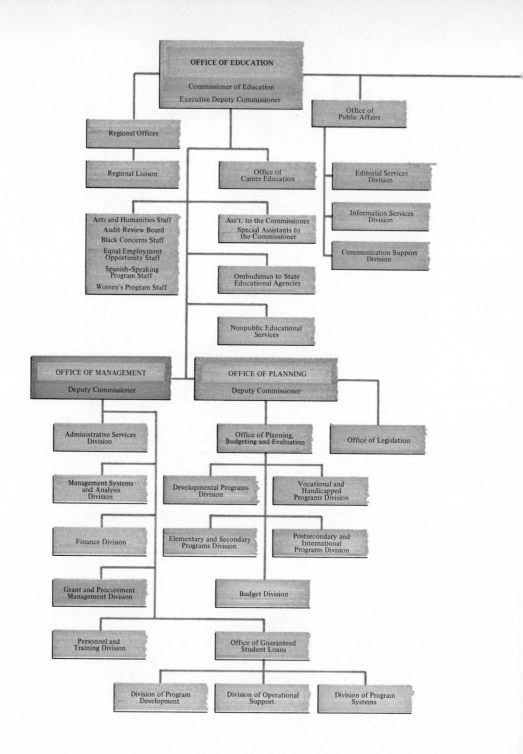

**OFFICE OF EDUCATION**

Commissioner of Education

Executive Deputy Commissioner

Office of
Public Affairs

Regional Offices

Regional Liaison

Office of
Career Education

Editorial Services
Division

Arts and Humanities Staff

Audit Review Board

Black Concerns Staff

Equal Employment
Opportunity Staff

Spanish-Speaking
Program Staff

Women's Program Staff

Ass't. to the Commissioner
Special Assistants to
the Commissioner

Information Services
Division

Communication Support
Division

Ombudsman to State
Educational Agencies

Nonpublic Educational
Services

**OFFICE OF MANAGEMENT**

Deputy Commissioner

**OFFICE OF PLANNING**

Deputy Commissioner

Administrative Services
Division

Office of Planning,
Budgeting and Evaluation

Office of Legislation

Management Systems
and Analysis
Division

Developmental Programs
Division

Vocational and
Handicapped
Programs Division

Finance Division

Elementary and Secondary
Programs Division

Postsecondary and
International
Programs Division

Grant and Procurement
Management Division

Budget Division

Personnel and
Training Division

Office of Guaranteed
Student Loans

Division of Program
Development

Division of Operational
Support

Division of Program
Systems

434

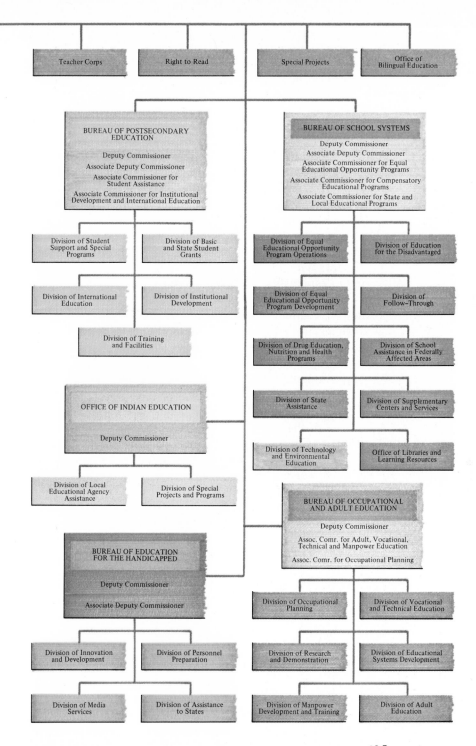

Teacher Corps

Right to Read

Special Projects

Office of
Bilingual Education

BUREAU OF POSTSECONDARY
EDUCATION

Deputy Commissioner

Associate Deputy Commissioner

Associate Commissioner for
Student Assistance

Associate Commissioner for Institutional
Development and International Education

BUREAU OF SCHOOL SYSTEMS

Deputy Commissioner

Associate Deputy Commissioner

Associate Commissioner for Equal
Educational Opportunity Programs

Associate Commissioner for Compensatory
Educational Programs

Associate Commissioner for State and
Local Educational Programs

Division of Student
Support and Special
Programs

Division of Basic
and State Student
Grants

Division of Equal
Educational Opportunity
Program Operations

Division of Education
for the Disadvantaged

Division of International
Education

Division of Institutional
Development

Division of Equal
Educational Opportunity
Program Development

Division of
Follow–Through

Division of Training
and Facilities

Division of Drug Education,
Nutrition and Health
Programs

Division of School
Assistance in Federally
Affected Areas

OFFICE OF INDIAN EDUCATION

Deputy Commissioner

Division of State
Assistance

Division of Supplementary
Centers and Services

Division of Technology
and Environmental
Education

Office of Libraries and
Learning Resources

Division of Local
Educational Agency
Assistance

Division of Special
Projects and Programs

BUREAU OF OCCUPATIONAL
AND ADULT EDUCATION

Deputy Commissioner

Assoc. Comr. for Adult, Vocational,
Technical and Manpower Education

Assoc. Comr. for Occupational Planning

BUREAU OF EDUCATION
FOR THE HANDICAPPED

Deputy Commissioner

Associate Deputy Commissioner

Division of Occupational
Planning

Division of Vocational
and Technical Education

Division of Innovation
and Development

Division of Personnel
Preparation

Division of Research
and Demonstration

Division of Educational
Systems Development

Division of Media
Services

Division of Assistance
to States

Division of Manpower
Development and Training

Division of Adult
Education

435

## The United States Office of Education as a Bureaucracy

Perhaps the best way to begin a study of bureaucracy is to look at one. Since we cannot take you on a trip of Washington to study a federal agency firsthand, we shall do the next best thing: give you a kind of map, an organization chart, of one bureaucratic agency—the United States Office of Education (USOE).

The Office of Education is one of the divisions of the Department of Health, Education, and Welfare (HEW). The chart on pages 434–435 shows USOE as it was in June 1975. It is often reorganized. Still, the chart gives us a glimpse of what a bureaucracy is like.

1. What does USOE do? Make a list.

2. Make a list of adjectives which you think describe USOE.

3. One of the activities administered by USOE in 1975 was a program to encourage instruction in environmental education in the schools. Among other things the Division of Technology and Environmental Education provides grants to school systems seeking to establish environmental education programs. Suppose that you had accepted a job in USOE and had been assigned to work in this program. Your main job is to accept proposals from school systems, to get panels of readers to review proposals in order to recommend which will be supported, and to supervise the grants once they are made. In addition you meet with colleagues to plan improvements in the program and defend it outside the Division.

a. In what bureau do you work? Who directs this bureau?

b. If you had an opportunity to accept a promotion to become head of the "Division of Follow-Through," would you take it? What factors would influence your decision? If you took the job, do you think your feelings about environmental education would change? If so, in what ways?

c. Who do you think has the better access to the Commissioner of Education: the Director of Teacher Corps or the Director of the Division of Adult Education?

d. You have just learned that USOE's budget will be reduced 10 percent next year. What would be your response? What might you do to make sure your program did not suffer?

e. The President of the United States is a Republican. You also are a Republican and voted for the President. In fact, you resigned your job as a college teacher to join the "President's team." You have just learned that in order to save money, the President has decided to abolish a number of USOE programs, including the Division of Technology and Environmental Education. What is your reaction to this information?

4. Suppose a member of Congress wrote a letter to the Commissioner asking what USOE was doing in the field of education for

the handicapped, especially to prepare people to teach the handicapped. Whom would the Commissioner consult for help in drafting a reply?

**5.** What do you think are the functions of the Office of Public Affairs?

## Characteristics of Bureaucracy and Bureaucratic Role

What do you think of when you hear the term *bureaucrat?* It is not a name that you call a friend. Americans often use the term to describe an official whom they see as lazy, inefficient, insensitive, and ignorant. People have referred to bureaucrats as the "pin-headed guideline writers" in Washington. We hear about bureaucratic "red tape." One critic said that they are people who "can't park their bicycles straight but who tell us how to run our schools and businesses."

The term "bureaucrat" is often used in an insulting way. But social scientists use the term bureaucracy simply to refer to a kind of work organization system that has emerged in modern societies. Bureaucracy developed in response to the need in complex societies for skillful, efficient, honest, and fair management. All large organizations, including churches, business firms, labor unions, and professional associations, have bureaucracies. Simply stated, bureaucracy is a way of organizing employees so that they can carry out the programs of the organization in an orderly fashion.

While all large organizations have bureaucrats, we are concerned in this chapter only with the federal bureaucracy and the people who work in it. First we examine some features of the bureaucracy itself; then we look specifically at the bureaucratic role.

### The Federal Bureaucracy Is Large and Complex

In 1792 the federal government had only about 800 civilian employees. Over 600 of these worked in the Treasury Department. Today there are nearly three million civilian employees. If we add military personnel, around five million men and women are on the federal payroll.

In addition, there are 50 state governments, around 3000 county governments, 18,000 municipal units, 17,000 townships, 16,000 public school districts, and 24,000 special districts of various kinds. Most of these units employ bureaucrats. It has been estimated that one of every five American workers (including members of the armed forces) is on a government payroll.

Why has the bureaucracy grown so large? In the United States today, government is expected to do hundreds—even thousands— of different jobs. Most of them are carried out by administrative agencies. As our nation has grown in size, so too has the demand for governmental services. The government delivers our mail, inspects the food we eat

I WONDER IF THE GOVERNMENT CAN SUPPORT ALL OF ITS CITIZENS?

I WONDER IF THE CITIZENS CAN SUPPORT ALL OF ITS GOVERNMENT!

What does this cartoon suggest about the growth of the bureaucracy?

and the homes we live in, regulates our transportation, and licenses our entertainment. It certifies our birth and supervises our burial. There is scarcely a human activity that is not in some way touched by a governmental regulation.

Not only has the size of the bureaucracy grown, but its tasks have become more and more specialized and complex as society has become more industrialized. Federal bureaucrats tend to be highly trained specialists. Among them one can find specialists in African languages in the State Department, marine biologists in the Department of Interior, and space scientists in the National Aeronautics and Space Administration.

### The Bureaucracy Operates Almost Like a Fourth Branch of Government

"Now let me be quite precise in this respect. The Federal Reserve is independent, and the new chairman, who will be sworn in here tomorrow, is one of the most independent men I know."–Pres. Nixon, Jan. 30, 1970.

"However, I hope that independently he will conclude that my views are the ones that should be followed."–Nixon at swearing-in ceremonies the next day (Quoted in TIME, March 2, 1970).

A typical chart of the executive branch, such as the one on page 439, shows the cabinet departments and most other federal agencies as directly responsible to the President. Yet a few years ago, President Johnson is reported to have said that while there are 2,867,356 federal employees, "on a good day maybe 100 are working for the President." How does one account for such a statement? Why is it that the President lacks firm control over the actions and policies of the federal agencies?

In most areas of activity the President has no specific policies—for example, public health, railroad regulation, airports, meat inspection. He does expect the officials in these areas to meet their responsibilities and not to embarrass the administration. In such areas, bureaucrats largely develop their own policies, ones that are carried forward from one administration to the next.

This does not mean that most bureaucrats are free to do whatever they choose. Quite the contrary. The people with whom the agency works most directly must be satisfied. The Office of Education will try to satisfy educators; the Department of Agriculture will try to keep farmers content. And each agency must keep members of

# THE EXECUTIVE BRANCH OF OUR GOVERNMENT

## PRESIDENT

### CABINET DEPARTMENTS

| | |
|---|---|
| State | Labor |
| Treasury | Health, |
| Defense | Education, |
| Justice | and Welfare |
| Interior | Transportation |
| Agriculture | Housing |
| Commerce | and Urban |
| | Development |

### EXECUTIVE OFFICE

The White House Office
Office of Management and Budget
Council of Economic Advisers
National Security Council
Domestic Council
Energy Resources Council
Council on Wage and Price Stability
Council of Environment Quality
and others

### REGULATORY AGENCIES

### CORPORATIONS

### SOME OTHER INDEPENDENT AGENCIES

Federal Communications Commission

Federal Deposit Insurance Corporation

U.S. Civil Service Commission

Veterans Administration

Interstate Commerce Commission

Export–Import Bank

U.S. Tariff Commission

General Services Administration

Federal Power Commission

Tennessee Valley Authority

National Foundation Arts & Humanities

Small Business Administration

Securities and Exchange Commission

Postal Service

U.S. Information Agency

Federal Mediation & Conciliation Service

Federal Reserve Board

St. Lawrence Seaway

National Aeronautics & Space Administration

Selective Service System

Nuclear Regulatory Commission

Panama Canal Company

National Science Foundation

Environmental Protection Agency

Federal Trade Commission

Overseas Private Investment Corp.

National Labor Relations Board

Agencies in the orange boxes tend to have greater independence from presidential control than do the others. Members of regulatory agencies serve for fixed terms (usually seven years). Government corporations have some financial independence.

Congress happy, since Congress can provide generous funds for an agency or abolish it. Some agencies, such as the Federal Bureau of Investigation, are very popular with Congress and are treated generously. Other agencies, such as the Agency for International Development, which handles foreign aid, seem always on the defensive and must constantly prove their worth to Congress.

Sometimes the Army Corps of Engineers, which handles certain flood-control and conservation projects, can get congressional support for programs the President may oppose. When President Eisenhower tried to hold the line on the budget for the Army Corps of Engineers, the Engineers had their funds restored by members of Congress eager to have dams and other projects built in their districts. And Congress at times votes money for military equipment desired by generals and admirals but opposed by the President.

The result is a very complex set of relationships. Most agencies seek the favor of Congress, from whom they get their funds. And many agencies operate with little interference from the President's office. In some areas in which the President has a definite policy, such as foreign relations, he must struggle with department officials—plead, threaten, and persuade—before his policies are carried out.

Nearly every President has spoken at one time or another about the difficulties in getting a policy carried out. This has led to their practice of appointing White House aides whose duties often compete with and overlap the duties of officials who head the regular agencies and departments. For example, recent Presidents have employed a foreign-policy adviser outside the State Department. This person's job is to supply information that the State Department may be holding back and to suggest alternatives to policies presented by the Department. In short, Presidents appoint some persons whose only loyalty is to the President, since bureaucrats may have loyalties to their agencies, the Congress, or many special-interest groups as well.

### The Federal Bureaucracy Makes and Interprets Rules

Federal agencies do more than "administer" laws. Often they "legislate." For example, the Department of Health, Education, and Welfare has created a set of guidelines for school desegregation that are used to decide whether school districts are eligible to receive federal funds. These guidelines have the force of law. In order to receive funds, schools must abide by these agency-created rules.

Agency officials also are involved in lawmaking when they help draft bills, testify before Congress, and provide technical information needed by members who are preparing bills. Members of Congress see that it is very hard to make laws without first seeking the advice—and often the support—of the agency involved.

In some agencies bureaucrats also have a judicial function. A few agencies function almost like courts, settling tax-claim disputes, trade disagreements, and many other matters. Nearly all agencies are engaged in "interpreting the law." While agency decisions often may be appealed in the courts, on a day-to-day basis parties affected by bureau decisions tend to consider them forceful enough to abide by them.

## Some Features of the Bureaucratic Role

While the talents needed to fill one post or another differ greatly, some features of the bureaucratic role are about the same whatever the position.

### Chain of Command

All bureaucracies have a *hierarchy,* a kind of pyramid in which higher status people with greater authority supervise the work of people with lesser status. In the chart for the Office of Education you had a chance to see the chain of command in such a hierarchy.

In a bureaucracy, status, prestige, authority, and responsibility are identified with the office rather than with the person who holds it. In other words, the Commissioner of Education has the right to demand responses from division and bureau heads not because of his or her personal standing but because of the position held.

### Channels of Communication

The formal flow of messages also follows the chain of command. For example, suppose you are a program officer in the Office of Education. You want to tell the Commissioner your feelings about an agency policy. It would be most unusual for you to have a talk with the Commissioner or to write a direct note. Rather, you would send your opinion to your supervisor, who in turn would pass it along to his or her superior, and so on up the line.

In an earlier lesson you were asked to decide whom the Commissioner might consult about a letter that needed to go to a member of Congress about teacher training in USOE's education-for-the-handicapped program. The typical way to handle this would be for the Commissioner to give a memo about the matter to an assistant. This person would then send the memo on to the Deputy Commissioner heading the Bureau of Education for the Handicapped. The memo would pass on to the Associate Deputy Commissioner, who in turn would give direction to the chief of the Division of Personnel Preparation. The Division chief would probably give it to a program officer. The program officer would write the first draft and then forward it to the head of the Division. Thus the letter would finally find its way back to the Commissioner's desk after it had been passed on, and possibly altered, by people in USOE's chain of command.

Such a formal system is vital in a bureaucracy. It keeps all interested parties informed about how an issue is being handled. Also each

# MEMO of the Month

MEMORANDUM    DEPARTMENT OF HEALTH, EDUCATION, AND WELFARE
OFFICE OF THE SECRETARY

TO        :  Assistant Secretaries and Agency Heads

FROM      :  The Secretary

SUBJECT   :  Apologies for Delays in Congressional Responses

Since overdue letters to Members of Congress undermine our efforts to work effectively with the legislative branch, I am requesting your participation in a new effort to repair the badly damaged relationships which result from HEW's negligence in failing to acknowledge or respond promptly to Congressional inquiries.

Hereafter, when your office is responsible for a long overdue letter either because you have failed to prepare the response accurately by the due date or because you have held it up during the clearance process, I will be asking you to call the offended Congressman personally and apologize to him for the wanton disrespect for the legislative branch which occurred in your office.

The following talking points are suggested for such a telephone conversation:

1. Secretary Richardson has reminded me of the fact that I have been negligent in failing to acknowledge your inquiry of __(date)__ about __(subject)__ and, I am calling at the Secretary's request to personally apologize to you for my failure to respond in a timely and ___ manner.

CHIEF OF STAFF
Commander Amphibious Force
U.S. Atlantic Fleet
Norfolk, Virginia 23520

01: jrr
10 September 1971

MEMORANDUM FOR ALL PHIBLANT COMMANDING OFFICERS

Subj: Refreshments in wardroom

1. For your information and action as you see fit, I have personally overheard Admiral Bell say many times that he does not like to see kool aid served in the wardrooms of ships. Over to you.

level of the bureaucracy has a different outlook on the problem. For example, the Commissioner of Education cannot be as familiar with the details of the training program as the officer who runs it. On the other hand, each program officer may be too close to his or her own program to see the big picture. Only the top administrators who have overall responsibility for many programs may be able to see how they all fit together.

In every bureaucracy there are also *informal* communication systems. Some persons have a reputation for making wise decisions and are consulted whether they are exactly in the chain of command or not. Moreover, at lunches, in a car pool, or during golf on Saturday, agency officials share ideas and plans informally.

### The Influence of Rules

Another feature of a bureaucracy is its elaborate system of rules. There are rules for hiring, firing, and promoting people, for vacations, for sick leave, and for travel. There are rules for using consultants, for avoiding conflicts of interests, for managing contracts, and for nearly every other aspect of the job. In the other roles we have studied, formal rules seem to be less important than informal rules. But the bureaucratic role is influenced strongly by many formal rules.

Following are a few real memos that show some aspects of bureaucratic life. Memos are a typical means of sending messages in a large organization. They are often used to announce upcoming events and new rules. The memos don't always deal with big issues. But the examples do show that formal rules cover a wide range of activities. As you read each memo, try to guess what may have prompted it to be written and how you might react if you received it.

### Bureaucrats Are Subject to Cross-pressures

If there is a "military point of view," it is most likely to be found in the Department of Defense. The Department of Agriculture works hard to defend programs for farmers and to oppose efforts by the administration to spend more money on the cities if it means less farm aid.

Any agency expects its members to show full loyalty if they wish to advance their careers. Especially when the agency's and the President's views are at odds, bureaucrats face a cross-pressure situation. For a very high policy-maker, such a conflict may become public knowledge, leading to resignation or dismissal if the person is unable to settle the conflict in any other way.

For example, in 1970, a high-ranking official in the Justice Department did not agree with the desegregation policy of President Nixon and the Attorney General. Appointed by President Johnson, this official's primary loyalty was to his division of the Justice Department rather than to the new President. After failing to convince the Attorney

# EMS

**UNITED STATES DEPARTMENT OF AGRICULTURE
EXPORT MARKETING SERVICE
WASHINGTON, D. C. 20250**

January 7, 1972

SUBJECT: Correspondence

TO: All EMS Secretaries, Stenographers and Typiests

ISSUED BY: General Sales Manager

*Clifford D. Pulvermacher*

The regulations state that between the complimentary close and the title of the sender, you should allow at least five spaces. Some letters and memoranda have been coming through for signature with only four spaces.

In the future any correspondence prepared for my signature should have at least <u>six</u> spaces. This will allow me enough room to sign my name and also have my printed name stamped below my signature.

many of our letters that in correcting
Rec-Type or Kleenertype has
ble for drafts and

OPTIONAL FORM NO. 10
MAY 1962 EDITION
GSA FPMR (41 CFR) 101-11.6

UNITED STATES GOVERNMENT

## Memorandum

TO : ALL MEMBERS OF THE FLOWER FUND

FROM : Nellie Blocker

DATE: DECEMBER 6, 1972

SUBJECT: FLOWER FUND, 1973

Effective January 1, 1973, our flower fund dues will be 50¢ per pay day, to take care of the unusually excessive amount paid out this year, (statement attached).

If any member of the flower fund would like to pay in larger amounts for the year 1973, this would eliminate much collection and book-keeping and your money would be drawing interest in our savings account. This will be strictly voluntary and if you should withdraw anytime during the year, your money will be refunded.

These are the suggested amounts:

| | |
|---|---|
| January 1 to December 31, 1973 (26 pay periods) | $13.00 |
| January 1 to June 30, 1973 (13 pay periods) | 6.50 |
| July 1 to December 31, 1973 (13 pay periods) | 6.50 |
| January 1 to March 31, 1973 (6 pay periods) | 3.00 |
| April 1 to June 30, 1973 (7 pay periods) | 3.50 |
| July 1 to September 30, 1973 (6 pay periods) | 3.00 |
| October 1 to December 31, 1973 (7 pay periods) | 3.50 |

Gifts and Flowers are to be for:

General to change the policy, he called a news conference at which he stated his disagreements with the Administration. He was then asked to resign.

In 1973, Attorney General Elliott Richardson and a chief assistant, William Ruckelshaus, chose to resign rather than carry out President Nixon's order to fire Archibald Cox, who was directing the investigation into the Watergate affair.

Bureaucrats find themselves in other kinds of cross-pressure situations. Some agencies were established "to promote and to regulate" certain activities. Naturally, this means that an agency will have very close ties with the people who are to be helped and regulated. For instance, many of the officials in the Office of Education are former school or college faculty members. Many have been members of education associations and have close friends in education. When these bureaucrats make policies for education, it may be hard to set themselves apart from their own prior experiences and the interests of friends. They may find it difficult to look at a problem without bias.

An agency tends to work out "alliances" with its constituents. The term "military-industrial complex" is used to describe the tie that has developed over the years between the armed services and the major defense industries. For example, military officers at times retire from the armed forces to accept jobs with firms which make military equipment. They return to Washington seeking contracts for their companies from their former co-workers in the government. Bureaucrats are expected to show no favors in assigning defense contracts. But friendships with people in the defense industry make it hard for the bureaucrat to remain unbiased.

This problem takes another form as well. Bureaucracies are supposed to be governed by formal relationships and by formal rules. This presumably avoids favoritism and makes certain that everyone is treated equally. But formal rules also make bureaucracies seem cold and impersonal. At the same time, bureaucrats are expected to take a personal interest in their various constituencies in order to satisfy as many people as possible. But "taking a personal interest" in someone opens the bureaucrat to charges of playing favorites. These cross-pressures often make the job very difficult.

## Recruitment of Federal Bureaucrats

Who are the people who become bureaucrats in the federal government? What are their backgrounds? How are they similar to, or different from, people who do not work for the government?

We can separate them into two general categories. One consists of career officials who have entered government service through one of the career systems: (a) the federal civil service, (b) the foreign service, or (c) the military service. The second category consists of political appointees.

Federal civil service jobs are open to those who can demonstrate their fitness by competitive examination. The exam may be a written test, including skill demonstration; or it may be an evaluation of education and work experience.

## The Career Services

The foreign service consists of a rather small number of people who belong to a special career system in the Department of State. Young people tend to be recruited into the lowest levels of this service and, in time, work their way up to higher positions—even the rank of ambassador.

The military service is a well-known career system in the United States. For about thirty years after World War II, many men and some women spent some time in the military service. Some were drafted; others enlisted. Except for those who had special training or skills (for example, doctors), most people entered the military service at the lowest ranks and through experience and further training won promotions to higher ranks. This system still operates but without the draft.

The federal civil service takes in about 93 percent of the civilian employees in the government. Of course, many of the people covered by civil service do not fit our definition of bureaucrat. The civil service includes guards, cooks, clerks, and postal workers. In this chapter we deal mainly with those people who are in the federal civil service, not with the foreign service and the military service.

Civil service employees tend to make a lifetime career of their jobs. Those in high positions have usually earned them through years of experience in their departments. These persons continue to hold their jobs from one presidential administration to another regardless of who wins an election.

446

## Political Appointees

The second category of federal employment consists of *political appointees*. They are only a small part of all federal employees. An estimate in 1968 put the number of posts filled by presidential appointment at 2150. A majority of these require the approval of the Senate. They include cabinet officers, assistant secretaries in the various departments, ambassadors, and special advisers to the President.

Political appointees, unlike civil service bureaucrats, are often picked because their political views are like those of the President. They tend to get the top policy-making positions in order to ensure that agency policies conform as much as possible to what the President wants. Political appointees rarely are experts in the technical aspects of the agencies they head. They lean on their career civil service advisers in technical matters. Rather, one of their chief jobs is to think about the political effects of agency decisions.

For example, the Secretary of Defense and the chief aides are political appointees. They are not expected to be experts in military strategy. They can rely upon career military officers, including the Chiefs of Staff, for this kind of advice. However, to make sure that decisions by military career officers conform to the policies of the President, it is thought wise to have civilians directing the Defense Department. The President would thus appoint civilians who are able to put the military advice they receive into a general policy-making strategy that both civilian and military leaders can accept.

Political appointees rarely spend many years in any one post. Most resign and are replaced when a new President takes office. This is very much the case when the new President is not from the same political party as the outgoing President. Once in a while, a political appointee may serve in several posts over a period of years. Robert Finch began as Secretary of Health, Education, and Welfare in the Nixon Administration but was later shifted to special assistant in the White House. Elliott Richardson was moved from a political appointee post in the State Department to the position vacated by Finch at the Department of Health, Education, and Welfare. Later he served as Secretary of Defense and then as Attorney General. President Ford later picked him for Secretary of Commerce.

The diagram at the right shows us roughly how the federal bureaucracy is divided. As you can see, political appointees make up a very small part of the total. But their placement at the top of the pyramid emphasizes their influence on policy-making. They tend to wield far greater power in terms of their total number than do the career service employees.

Nevertheless, we shall see later that top career service administrators are important decision-makers and often have as much influence on policy within an agency as does the politically appointed agency head.

**A DIAGRAM OF FEDERAL EMPLOYMENT**

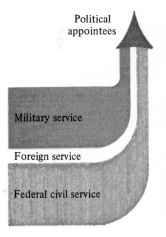

Political appointees

Military service

Foreign service

Federal civil service

## Some Characteristics of Bureaucratic Decision-Makers

The range of activities and the large number of people working in the federal bureaucracy limit the generalizations we can make about federal bureaucrats. Moreover, we do not have data on the ethnic identity, religious affiliation, and political party preference of federal employees. But in spite of these handicaps, some useful generalizations can be made.

Both men and women are employed as federal bureaucrats. However, men occupy the highest ranks far out of proportion to their number in the total adult population. A 1959 study found that 10,851 men and 145 women held appointments in the highest ranks of the civilian bureaucracy. Recent efforts to recruit more women into executive positions in government have altered this ratio to some degree. But it remains true that a high-ranking federal bureaucrat is much more likely to be a man than a woman.

Federal bureaucrats come from all regions of the nation. A 1959 study found that the region of birth of federal executives was nearly identical to that of the population as a whole. Contrary to some popular belief, most federal bureaucrats are not born in Washington, D.C.

Federal bureaucrats tend to be well-educated. A study that compared their education to that of adult males and business leaders revealed the following data:

| Educational Level | Adult Males (1957 data) | Bureaucrats (1959 data) | Businessmen (1952 data) |
|---|---|---|---|
| Less than high school | 46% | * | 4% |
| Some high school | 17 | 1% | 9 |
| High school graduation | 21 | 4 | 11 |
| Some college | 7 | 14 | 19 |
| College graduation | 9 | 81 | 57 |

*Less than 0.5 percent.

Bureaucratic decision-makers tend to be well-educated persons who through much training and experience have become experts in certain fields.

## Bureaucrats as Decision-Makers

Most Americans know that the President, members of Congress, and Supreme Court justices make many key decisions. But people are less aware that federal bureaucrats do the same. In fact, they make more decisions than do the other decision-makers combined.

*Table:* W. L. Warner, P. P. Van Riper, N. H. Martin, and O. F. Collins, *The American Federal Executive* (New Haven: Yale University Press, 1963). Used by permission.

## The Nature of Bureaucratic Decisions

The chief reason that bureaucrats make so many decisions is that the President and Congress can't make all those that are needed. Congress, for example, can make a law that sets guidelines for dealing with air pollution. Another law will provide money for this activity. But the laws will name some agency to carry on from there. The Environmental Protection Agency (EPA) may get the job of making detailed rules and deciding who will get the money to fight air pollution. The pollution law passed by Congress will be a package of decisions. One of these may be that within a certain time span the auto makers must equip new cars with devices that will cut their exhaust emissions to a certain level. This decision by Congress will trigger a large number to be made by the EPA.

A decision by the President will also often trigger other decisions by bureaucrats. For example, Kennedy's decision in the Cuban missile crisis (pages 315–323) forced the Defense Department to make a number of decisions on just how to handle the blockade.

Thus very many bureaucratic decisions are *supplemental.* They add details to more general decisions made by other decision-makers.

### Bureaucrats Also Take the Lead

Bureaucrats, then, respond to decisions made by others. But bureaucrats also at times take the lead. People in a bureau may see the need for a new program or a change in an old one. How can they get the President or Congress to make the needed decision? This is done in a number of ways. We saw earlier that many bills in Congress are really drawn up in the executive branch—by bureaucrats. Many details of a tax law, for example, will be worked out by experts in

In 1969 the United States Surgeon General, William Stewart, appeared before the House Commerce Committee to urge for strong health warnings on cigarette packages and advertising.

449

the Treasury Department. Also bureaucrats may ask for more—or less—money for some program when making up the department's budget. The President and/or Congress will have to respond.

At times the bureaucrats can take the lead with a decision to *supply information* that might get other decision-makers to respond. A few years ago the Office of Education supported a study on how racial segregation in schools could affect learning. The findings of this study, known as the "Coleman Report," gave evidence in support of laws, court decisions, and bureaucratic policies aimed at integrating public schools. Studies by the Public Health Service on the effects of smoking have led to laws and regulations aimed at cutting down on the use of cigarettes.

Bureaucrats can at times use a broad power granted by Congress to move in a direction that Congress did not intend, or even think about, when it passed the law. For example, a law gave the Federal Trade Commission (FTC) the power to deal with unfair competition in part by making rules against unfair and misleading advertising. In 1964 the FTC decided that the tobacco industry was misleading the public in cigarette ads. The FTC issued a rule that the ads must carry this warning: "Cigarette smoking is dangerous to health and may cause death from cancer and other diseases." Congress later overturned the rule, but did provide for a health warning on cigarette packages.

Even when clearly staying within guidelines set by Congress, bureaucrats make decisions on which programs to support and who will get the money to carry them out. Say that Congress votes $10 billion for research in new energy resources. Bureaucrats may have much leeway in picking the various avenues to pursue and the people who get the research funds.

### Decisions that Frustrate

Bureaucrats don't always like a decision that they are supposed to carry out. And they may set up roadblocks. An agency may ask for less money than is needed to carry out a program. This is one way to see that it will fail. An agency may drag its feet by deciding to give a matter "further study." In many ways the agency may fail to use its resources to carry out the program.

### Accommodational Decisions

A chief feature of bureaucratic decisions is that they are often accommodational. The decision-maker seeks a solution that will accommodate, or please, the greatest number of people concerned. Let's say that a law permits the EPA to regulate the discharge of pollutants from industrial plants. The EPA might make such tough rules that some plants would have to shut down. A decision to cut the pollution level drastically and quickly would please some groups but anger others. A decision to do nothing would have a similar effect. Thus the EPA might make an accommodational decision. It might issue rules to reduce—not eliminate—pollution over a period of time—not all at once.

450

**The Patchwork Quilt**

This decision will give some comfort to both the health groups and the industries. Bureaucrats are indeed political decision-makers.

### Who Are the Decision-Makers?

Not everyone who works in a government agency makes policy decisions. On the other hand, policy-making is not limited to the people at the very top. In some cases many people may take part in the decision process. The idea for a new program may begin with a program officer who seeks the branch chief's approval and so on upward through the agency until it is approved as agency policy.

On some questions the top leaders of an agency merely approve what has already been worked out by others down the line. In other cases the decision may be viewed as having serious political angles and may need much thought by top leaders before it is approved, changed, or turned down. For example, decisions made in the Department of Health, Education, and Welfare concern such hot issues as welfare and school desegregation. These issues are often closely watched by politicians, the news media, and the public. HEW decisions on such issues often get much public attention. In some cases the decision on a policy may be made at the top and handed down for others to administer.

451

There seems to be a simple rule on who makes decisions. A decision that doesn't "make waves," is in keeping with agency policy, and deals mainly with carrying out current programs is most likely to be made by people in the middle ranks of the bureau without much review by higher-ups. A policy which is very "political," which departs from the agency's ordinary practices, and which may be criticized by the President or the Congress is more likely to be made by the top people in the agency after listening to the advice of subordinates.

### Factors That Influence Bureaucratic Decision-Making

The factors that influence decision-making in a bureaucracy may be grouped into three general categories: the circumstances leading to a decision, the characteristics of the decision-maker, and other factors.

#### Circumstances Leading to a Decision

Among the circumstances that influence a decision are (1) the time available to make the decision, (2) the seriousness of the problem, and (3) the competing values that are part of the problem.

A sudden crisis may call for a quick decision. An American consul in a foreign city has been kidnapped and is being held for ransom by a group of rebels. A flurry of plane hijackings calls for new security measures. The Arab countries impose a boycott on the shipment of oil to the United States.

In other cases an agency may have months or even years to work on a problem. Deciding how to spend research funds to find new sources of energy has some urgency. But some time can be taken because quick results cannot be expected.

The day-to-day "decisions" of federal agencies are another matter. Ann Jones, a bureaucrat, has a stack of applications to handle. If everything is in order on the one that she takes from the pile, she stamps it "Approved." She doesn't really have to make a decision because the filled-in form fits the guidelines. But the next one doesn't quite fit. What should she do? There is probably a routine for handling this one as well. For most bureaucrats, each day is much like another. They will find their day devoted to "paperwork," responding to questions they can handle easily, delaying on questions that pose problems, and routing to other people the problems that they should handle.

The seriousness of the problem is also a factor in the decisions that are made. Up until around 1950 the United States exported more oil and petroleum products than it imported. In the 1960s it was clear that the nation was becoming very dependent on foreign oil. But the problem didn't seem critical until 1973 when the Arab oil-rich nations cut off oil imports to the United States for a time and then made big price boosts. A wide range of decisions had to be made to deal with the energy problem.

The energy crisis of 1973–1974 led to more than long lines at service stations. Federal bureaucrats had to make many decisions.

Competing social values also influence decisions. Decisions on pollution bring into focus the competing values of economic growth and quality of life. A decision to ban the sale of some harmful product involves the value that society has a duty to promote health and safety. But some people hold a competing value of personal freedom to take risks with one's health.

### Personal Characteristics of Decision-Makers

Decisions are also influenced a great deal by the decision-maker's personal beliefs, social background and prior experience, and personality. A decision-maker with strong views on what is right and wrong is likely to behave in one way. It will differ from what we might expect from a person who is less sure about having the "right" answers. Some decision-makers are aggressive and like to act decisively. Others are content with existing policies and take new action only when it cannot be avoided. Some people are happiest when caught up in fights over new programs. Others prefer to avoid publicity and to apply pressure behind the scenes.

A decision-maker's understanding of a problem is also influenced by social background and prior experience. Imagine three bureaucrats faced with the same general question: How can we best spend public money to improve the schools? One is a male Chicano raised in the barrio of Los Angeles. The second is a woman who used to teach in suburban high schools. The third is a former male college professor who taught Latin and Greek at an Eastern college. Each of these people may propose somewhat different policies.

## Other Factors

These include rules, status relationships, public opinion, available resources, and external decision-makers.

Bureaucratic decision-making is influenced by rules. Federal programs must be authorized and funded by Congress. A bureaucrat can't simply see a need and then make a decision on it.

Still, the authority granted to an agency by Congress is at times a bit vague. This is done on purpose because Congress cannot foresee every circumstance that will arise. Therefore, it passes laws with broad guidelines which leave many of the specific decisions to the bureaucrats. For example, the Federal Aviation Administration is charged by law with the "promotion, regulation, and safety of civil aviation . . . ." This makes it clear that the FAA does not deal with autos and trains. Laws administered by the FAA do outline specific tasks but leave many details to the agency.

Bureaucrats are also bound by rules and procedures for reaching decisions. For example, there are rules requiring that hearings be held on decisions reached by regulatory agencies. There are rules that tell how and in what form policy decisions must be announced. There are rules on choosing and paying outside experts. Rules on how to do this and that abound in the bureaucracy. For decisions to stand up, they must be made under the right procedures and within the authority of the agency.

## Status Relationships

Bureaucrats have important status relationships with five groups: the President, members of Congress, members of the agency itself, bureaucrats in other agencies, and constituencies outside of the government.

On many issues the President has no stated policy. The bureaucrat, then, has much freedom of action. In other cases a general presidential directive—for example, a freeze on hiring or an order to cut spending by 10 percent—will surely affect decisions. In some cases the President will announce a policy decision, and all bureaus must in some way try to bring their programs into line. A notice by the President that energy use must stop rising could trigger a number of actions by federal agencies. Some agency might begin to prepare legislation on this matter. The General Services Administration might order fuel savings in federal buildings and a shift to smaller cars for federal agencies.

Each bureau has to worry about its links with Congress. There must be very good ties with the committees that hold hearings on the bills desired by the agencies. Certain members of Congress may be key people to get along with because their support is vital. The heads of Senate and House committees wield great power. Of course, agency heads want to keep on good terms with all members of Congress. Notice again the memo at the top of page 442 in which a department head orders better relations with members of Congress.

Agencies also try to have good relations with each other. This is not always easy because federal programs are not always in tune with one another. For example, we saw that the Federal Trade Commission tried to get cigarette ads to carry a warning about the harm of smoking (page 450). This got the FTC in bad with the Department of Agriculture, since it had programs aimed at helping tobacco growers. The Federal Communications Commission (FCC) also objected. The FCC tries to help—as well as regulate—radio and TV companies. These firms would lose income if tobacco advertising dropped as a result of the FTC rule. This means that major decisions often have to be talked over with the heads of several agencies in the executive branch.

There are also status relationships with other people in one's own agency. A bureaucrat may have to change a decision in some way to get support within the bureau or department. A bureaucrat must plan a decision so that it will satisfy the boss. And it is often wise to consult people at a lower level. If persons below the decision-maker have to carry out the decision, they want to feel that they have been consulted and have had their views taken seriously.

Still, there are many times in an agency when a decision that one or more people very much oppose becomes policy anyway. The bureaucrat then has only two choices: (1) Accept the policy and try to carry it through. (2) If it is a matter of deep moral principle, resign and seek a job elsewhere. Trying to live with the policy is the usual response.

Finally, bureaucrats have status relationships with certain "constituents." In a sense each of us is a constituent of the Attorney General, Secretary of Defense, or member of the Federal Reserve Board. We have to live under their decisions. But some people and some groups

Bureaucrats are often called to testify at hearings held by committees of Congress.

455

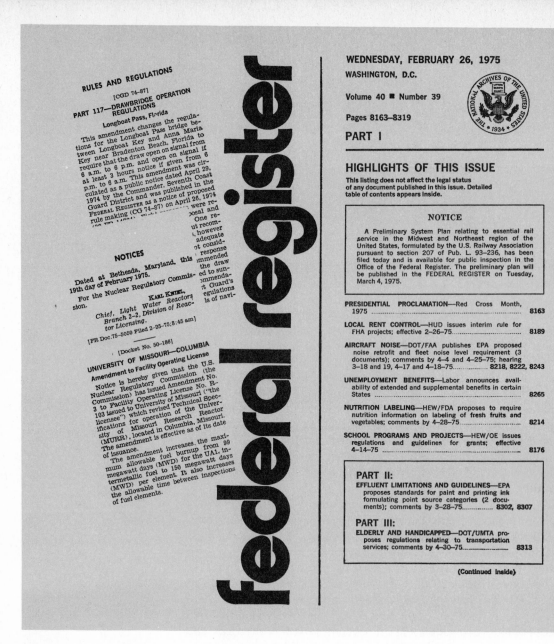

The wide range of federal bureaucratic activity can be sensed by browsing through a few issues of the *Federal Register.* In it are published proposed and final rules and regulations.

are more directly affected than are others. These "most concerned" people make up the bureaucrat's constituency.

The Department of Labor is sensitive to the views of organized labor. The Office of Education consults with the National Education Association and other education groups. The Department of Commerce is alert to the interests of business. The Federal Aviation Administration wants to get along with airplane builders, airport managers, and the airlines. And so on. When making a decision, the bureaucrat must take into account the reactions of "constituents."

## Public Opinion

Decision-making is influenced by public opinion. Problems of pollution have existed for many years, but public opinion was not much aroused until the late 1960s. Bureaucrats now make decisions on problems of air and water pollution that were not even considered twenty years ago. The publicity that Ralph Nader and others have given to consumer protection has helped to get rules on such wide-ranging issues as auto seat belts, the flammability of clothing, and the disclosure of true credit costs.

## Available Resources

Every decision is influenced by available resources, including time, money, and people. A bureaucrat may have a great idea for solving a problem. But lacking the resources to carry it through, it will die. Many people regret the passing of good passenger train service in the United States. Perhaps there are bureaucrats in the Department of Transportation who have fine plans for fast, low-fare, and comfortable train service. But without large sums of money from Congress the plans will not be carried out.

## External Decision-Makers

Each bureaucratic decision-maker must remain alert to other decision-makers over whom he or she has no control. Some of these were referred to in the topic on status relationships above. But there are others. They include state and local officials, business executives, even foreign leaders. Suppose that a bureau wants a rise in the tariff on foreign cars. It needs to consider the probable response of officials in the countries affected by this change in tariff policy. For example, will these countries strike back by raising their tariffs?

We have looked at many of the factors which bureaucrats must consider in reaching their decisions. The following case provides a chance to apply some of these factors.

## When Is a Ham a Ham?

The national government makes many decisions each day on many kinds of issues. A few years ago it had to make a policy decision on such a common item as ham, the kind you might buy at the store. This case is about the making—and remaking—of a policy decision about ham. The key decision-maker was the head of the Agricultural Research Service of the United States Department of Agriculture (USDA).

Years ago Congress passed a meat inspection law to protect against the sale of unfit and mislabeled meat. The law applied to *interstate* commerce (goods moving across state lines), and the major packers of meat were engaged in interstate business.

If meat is to be inspected and judged, there must be standards. Some of these are easy to state. Spoiled meat, for example, should

At work in a packing plant is a meat inspector for the United States Department of Agriculture.

not be approved, or meat from diseased animals, or meat prepared in filthy places. Congress could have written such standards into the Meat Inspection Act. But there are other possible standards. Congress can say that "adulterated meat shall not be approved for sale in interstate commerce." But what, specifically, is adulterated meat?

Because it could not anticipate all the questions of this kind, Congress gave the Department of Agriculture power to *issue regulations* defining such things as adulterated meat. These regulations are actually laws, and violators can be punished. Within the USDA the administrator of the Agricultural Research Service was given power to make these rules. In other words, this person is a decision-maker. In reaching decisions on rules, certain procedures must be used. They are set forth in another law, the Administrative Procedures Act of 1946.

**A Bureaucratic Ruling on Ham.** On December 30, 1960, the administrator issued a new rule that changed the definition of ham. Before that date, a ham was defined as a cured-pork product that could not have any added water (that is, the ham could not weigh any more than it did before it was cured). After December 30, 1960, under the new policy, a ham could be "watered." Enough water could be added to make it weigh as much as 14 percent more than before curing.

Why was this new policy adopted? And what were the effects of this decision?

458

One factor that led to the new policy was that new technology made it possible to pump extra water into a ham.[1] A second factor was that a lot of watered hams were now being sold in intrastate commerce (not moving across state lines) by the end of the 1950s. Some of these hams, not subject to federal control, were less than 80 percent meat and more than 20 percent water. Water is cheaper than ham, and these intrastate hams could be sold for less than hams prepared under the federal meat inspection rules. This led to a third reason for the new federal policy: pressure by meatpackers for the USDA to change the rule. Their business was being hurt by intrastate ham sales. Some of the big packers even went into the watered-ham business, using local branch plants to cure hams so they would not enter interstate commerce. This was an effort to avoid federal control.

In response to a request from the meatpackers, the head of the Agricultural Research Service set up a task force to review the existing meat inspection rules. Starting in September 1960, the group was told to consider the rule, or standard, regulating the water-content of a ham "from the viewpoint of consumer protection and current production and marketing practices."

This group seems to have looked at a "consumer survey" made by the American Meat Institute, the trade association of the industry. The survey claimed that there was a consumer demand "for juicier smoked meats." So USDA—or specifically M. R. Clarkson, the acting administrator of the Agricultural Research Service—changed the standard defining a ham.

We can't know the precise reason behind the change. Clarkson and his advisers may have felt that they should listen to the American Meat Institute because it was a powerful voice for the meatpackers. Or they may have decided that a failure to change the rule would only drive more ham into the intrastate market, where there would be no federal control. They may have really felt sure that the consumer wanted a juicier product. In any event, a policy was made, by a bureaucratic decision-maker, in response to a problem that had to be faced.

But the policy did not stick. The December 30 decision stirred up a storm, and on October 18, 1961, it was reversed. A new rule was issued, and a ham moving in interstate commerce was once again defined as a pork product whose weight "shall not exceed the weight of the fresh uncured article."

---

1. Until the 1930s hams were cured by soaking them in brine for up to two months. Later, someone invented a pump that would inject the curing liquid into the blood vessels of a fresh ham, making possible a quick cure. Then, in the 1950s, it was discovered that by adding certain phosphates to the curing liquid, hams could be made to absorb a lot of water without dripping or looking wet. Now a ham could be pumped, or watered, to bring its weight up to as much as 125 percent of its uncured weight.

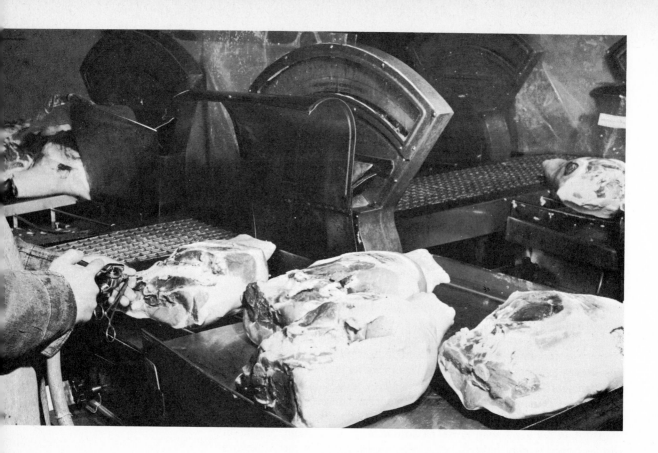

A packing-plant worker
pumps curing liquid into
fresh hams.

Why did Clarkson change his policy? The chief answer is "countervailing political pressure," pressure that was stronger than the force exerted by the meatpackers.

**Opposition Forms.** Even before the December 30 ruling, an interest group speaking for hog farmers was attacking the watering of ham. The October 1960 issue of the *National Hog Farmer* urged, "Let's Not Sell Water at the Ham Counter." It pointed out that "every dollar that the housewife spends for water at the ham counter is a dollar that she won't buy pork with." And pork use in the United States was slowly dropping, as consumers spent more and more of their money for beef instead. By the 1960s Americans were buying less pork—about five pounds per person less each year than in 1930.

Soon after the December 30 rule was issued, it was criticized in the journal of a farm cooperative in the corn-hog country of the Midwest. Within a couple of months the matter had also come to the attention of Consumers Union, a product-rating organization that sends out information about the quality of consumer goods. A feature article in the Union's magazine, *Consumer Reports,* described "The Great Ham Robbery."

460

Meanwhile, complaints were coming to the USDA from other sources, including chain stores, restaurants, and hotels. And citizens were writing to members of Congress to complain. City dwellers had read the *Consumer Reports* article, and hog farmers had read about the ruling in the farm journals.

Thus, the matter came to the attention of the new Secretary of Agriculture, Orville Freeman. Mr. Freeman came to office in January 1961 following the election of President John F. Kennedy. Freeman, a Democrat, replaced a Republican Secretary of Agriculture. Sometime during the winter of 1961 he told the press he was looking into the matter.

On March 28, 1961, Clarkson issued a notice that hearings would be held on the revised meat regulation. "Any interested person" was invited to "present any views, facts, or arguments—orally at one or more of the hearings, or . . . [by sending] . . . a written statement of comments to the Administrator, Agricultural Research Service," not later than May 22, 1961.

During April and May, hearings were held in Philadelphia, Atlanta, Chicago, Denver, Portland, Minneapolis, Los Angeles, and Washington. The December 30 rule was sharply criticized. It became quite clear that many more people—and a lot more interest groups—were opposed to watered ham than were in favor of "juicier" pork products.

The result was almost inevitable. On August 31, Clarkson issued a notice that the December 30 rule was being cancelled. As of November 17, 1961, a ham moving in interstate commerce could not weigh more than it had weighed before being cured. The Great Ham Issue had run its course. And a bureaucratic decision-maker, having made a policy in the form of a rule, had also reversed that policy.

**1.** Who was the key decision-maker? Do you think others took part in the decision? If so, who might have been involved?

**2.** Which groups profited most by each decision? In what way does knowing that there was a change in the political party in the White House between the two rulings help explain the change in the decision?

**3.** Is this an example of a decision made during a crisis or was there time to consider other policies?

**4.** How did different opinions on what was good for consumers affect the two different rulings?

**5.** How did rules and procedures influence the decision?

**6.** What status relationships appear to be key ones in this case?

**7.** What effect did public opinion have on the outcome of the case?

**8.** In your view which of the two rulings was the better example of an "accommodational decision"?

**9.** How did the rules supplement a law passed by Congress?

# Aircraft Noise: A Problem for Bureaucratic Decision-Makers

Most policy decisions begin with the need to solve a problem. This case study concerns the problem of aircraft noise and the efforts of the Federal Aviation Administration (FAA) to establish new rules on the amount of aircraft noise that would be allowed. We shall first look at the problem. Then we shall see how the FAA dealt with it.

## The Problem Is Noise

Here are the words of a man living half a mile from Kennedy Airport, one of the major airports in the New York City area. Like millions of others who live near commercial airports, this man is bothered by a very modern problem—aircraft noise.

> They are using the runway tonight! Wish you were here! Ho, man, I wish you could feel the walls. When they take off, it is like they were shooting at us. It's like they were firing guns at us. I really mean it. Everything vibrates. It's vibrating right now. There are cracks in the walls. The beams are giving way in the basement. The floor slants. I am constantly repairing and plastering the place. If you were here, you could smell the fuel. They have been using the northeast runway for two weeks, and . . . we are catching it.[2]

Propeller aircraft are noisy enough. But beginning in 1958 the airlines began changing over to jets, and passengers liked them. By 1970 there were around 2000 commercial jet liners flying the skies over the United States. On short runs of a few hundred miles, the jets fly at altitudes ranging from 20,000 to 30,000 feet. On longer routes they cruise at 30,000 to 40,000 feet. At these altitudes the jets can't be heard on the ground. But you may see a white streak across the sky. It is when they are close to or on the ground that they give out their wild roar

At busy airports the noise for ground crews goes on and on. It is so loud that "ear defenders" must be worn. For people who live near busy airports, the sound goes on with little let-up. For example, at O'Hare field near Chicago, planes take off and land on the average of once every forty seconds. The noise pollution at O'Hare is shown in the map on the next page.

In 1965 the area of serious noise at O'Hare took in a population of 236,000 with 86 schools and four hospitals. By 1975 the affected area had many more people.

By 1970 the United States had 259 airports handling jet aircraft, and the amount of air traffic kept on rising. Millions of people were already affected, and many more millions would be by the 1980s.

---

2. Quotation from Robert Sherrill, "The Jet Noise Is Getting Awful," *The New York Times Magazine* (January 14, 1968), pp. 24–25. © 1968 by The New York Times Company. Reprinted by permission.

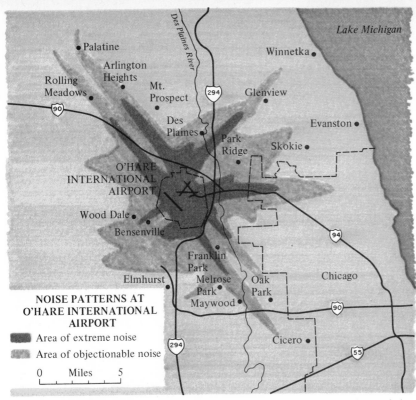

NOISE PATTERNS AT
O'HARE INTERNATIONAL
AIRPORT

■ Area of extreme noise

▨ Area of objectionable noise

0    Miles    5

Adapted from a map by Parios Studios for *Fortune* Magazine. Used by permission

The map shows noise patterns at Chicago's O'Hare Airport in 1969.

## How Much Noise Is Too Much?

There is no single scale for measuring noise. Instruments that measure noise really measure the intensity of the sound in a unit called the *decibel.* But since the human ear and brain do not hear noise in exact proportion to its intensity, various other kinds of scales have been invented that try to approximate the actual annoyance level of noise. Among the scales is one called the *PNdb,* which means perceived noise. Another scale is the "A" scale written *dbA.* This scale emphasizes the sound intensities associated with higher frequency tones, as these are the tones that tend to be most annoying. Following are some sample levels of various kinds of noises as shown on a *dbA* scale: (These are the levels measured at distances from which people would most commonly hear these noises.)

Rustling leaves . . . . . . . . . . . . . . . . . . . . . . .20 dbA
Conversation . . . . . . . . . . . . . . . . . . . . . . . . .60 dbA
Vacuum cleaner . . . . . . . . . . . . . . . . . . . . . . .69 dbA
Heavy diesel truck . . . . . . . . . . . . . . . . . . . . .92 dbA
Power lawnmower . . . . . . . . . . . . . . . . . . . . . .98 dbA
Thunder clap . . . . . . . . . . . . . . . . . . . . . . . 135 dbA
Take-off blast of Saturn Five moon rocket . . . . . 180 dbA

463

There is a strange thing about these scales for measuring noise. According to these scales it appears that a diesel truck (92 dbA) makes only half again as much noise as ordinary conversation (60 dbA). Common sense tells us that this is certainly not the case. In fact, *every increase of 10 decibels means a doubling of intensity of the sound.* Ninety-two dbA (the truck) is over eight times louder than ordinary conversation.

**Too Much Noise**

Eighty decibels is thought to be the top level for comfort. At 85 decibels, hearing damage may occur if there is long exposure. At 95 decibels, serious or even full hearing loss can occur with continuous exposure. Remember that 95 decibels is twice as loud as 85 decibels. Remember, also, that 105 decibels is twice as loud as 95 decibels. A large, four-engine Boeing 707, one of the main jet airliners, produces from 107 to 120 decibels on takeoff. The same plane produces about 120 decibels in its landing approach, or eight times the top level for comfort (80 dbA).

Jet engines can be quieted. Research has shown that a Boeing 707 fitted with sound absorbing material inside the engines will have a landing approach noise level of 105 decibels instead of the usual 120. To do the needed work on airplanes in 1970, however, would have cost about $1 million per plane. Airline officials did not want to invest such sums. They argued that this would lift operating costs about 5 percent.

Even 105 decibels, of course, is more noise than anyone wants. For that matter, 85 decibels is too much noise, and that's how much you would hear if you were a half a mile to the side of a jet runway as the 707 climbs away from the airport.

In 1971 Congress voted to cancel a subsidy for building a supersonic jet transport (SST) which would create even more noise.

### Some Costs of Excessive Noise

What are the costs of all of this noise? Lawsuits give us one measure. In 1968 ten families living near the Los Angeles International Airport sued the city for $400,000 on the grounds that they had suffered permanent hearing damage and emotional disturbance from the noise of jet planes at landing and takeoff.

But the costs are hard to measure in dollars. Open-air concerts along the Potomac near Washington National Airport and concerts in the Hollywood Bowl and in a number of other cities have become almost inaudible. The loss cannot be measured in money. A concert is a priceless thing to some, a worthless thing to others.

Some people argue that modern city people are already adapted to the rising noisiness of their world. After all, such arguments go, electronically amplified music often reaches a level of 120 decibels, and young people pay to hear it!

How much louder is conversation (60) than rustling leaves (20)?

| | |
|---|---|
| 20 dbA | 1 |
| 30 dbA | 2 x |
| 40 dbA | 4 x |
| 50 dbA | 8 x |
| 60 dbA | 16 x |

Conversation is 16 times louder.

464

## The Federal Aviation Administration

Stand on the west steps of the Capitol in Washington and look toward the Washington Monument. Somewhat to the left of your gaze will be a row of bright, modern office buildings along Independence Avenue. One of them, a ten-story building, houses the Department of Transportation. On the upper floors of the building are the offices of the Federal Aviation Administration (FAA).

The FAA licenses pilots, mechanics, and aircraft. It issues rules about the operation of aircraft. It trains and employs more than 20,000 air-traffic controllers. It assigns air space for various types of aircraft. It operates navigation aids, and concerns itself with airport safety.

In this 1969 cartoon Conrad criticizes the federal subsidy to build a supersonic transport (SST) plane. Sonic booms can literally shake buildings. The SST subsidy was cancelled by Congress in 1971.

**Housing Boom**

Editorial cartoon by Paul Conrad. Copyright, *Los Angeles Times*. Reprinted with permission.

The FAA is charged by law with "the promotion, regulation, and safety of civil aviation. . . ." The law under which the FAA operates is the Federal Aviation Act of 1958. At times new problems arise, and the law fails to give the authority needed for the agency to act. This was the case with the aircraft noise problem. Congress then was asked to amend the Federal Aviation Act of 1958 in order to authorize the FAA to issue rules on aircraft noise. This was done, and the new law (Public Law 90-411, page 468) was approved July 1, 1968.

Almost 50,000 people were working for the FAA in 1970. Of these about 2700 worked in the Washington, D.C., offices. The jobs range from that of clerk-typist to top policy-makers. Most of the people who work for the FAA are civil service employees.

The Federal Aviation Administration is a very technical operation. That is, many of the employees have (and need) a high level of technical training. It is hard to think of technicians as "bureaucrats." And most of them probably do not think of themselves that way. The decisions made in the FAA are based largely on technical studies made by FAA experts or by outside consultants. Yet, in spite of their technical nature, many FAA decisions are also *political* in nature. A decision like the aircraft noise rule affects all of us, and it was made by those "bureaucrats in Washington."

The FAA trains and employes thousands of air-traffic controllers to direct takeoffs and landings at the nation's commercial airports.

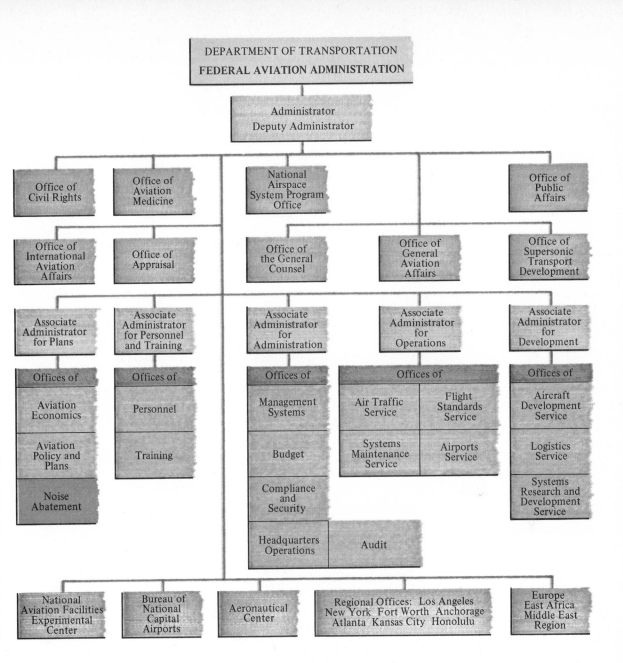

DEPARTMENT OF TRANSPORTATION
FEDERAL AVIATION ADMINISTRATION

Administrator
Deputy Administrator

Office of Civil Rights

Office of Aviation Medicine

National Airspace System Program Office

Office of Public Affairs

Office of International Aviation Affairs

Office of Appraisal

Office of the General Counsel

Office of General Aviation Affairs

Office of Supersonic Transport Development

Associate Administrator for Plans

Associate Administrator for Personnel and Training

Associate Administrator for Administration

Associate Administrator for Operations

Associate Administrator for Development

Offices of

Aviation Economics

Aviation Policy and Plans

Noise Abatement

Offices of

Personnel

Training

Offices of

Management Systems

Budget

Compliance and Security

Headquarters Operations

Offices of

Air Traffic Service

Flight Standards Service

Systems Maintenance Service

Airports Service

Audit

Offices of

Aircraft Development Service

Logistics Service

Systems Research and Development Service

National Aviation Facilities Experimental Center

Bureau of National Capital Airports

Aeronautical Center

Regional Offices: Los Angeles New York Fort Worth Anchorage Atlanta Kansas City Honolulu

Europe East Africa Middle East Region

**The FAA Makes a Decision on Aircraft Noise.** The data for studying this example of decision-making include some documents that trace the development of the decision that led to a new rule on aircraft noise. There is also an excerpt from an interview with an official in the Noise Abatement office in the FAA. The interview gives us a chance to see how the problem was viewed by someone inside the agency. The documents tell us something about the constituencies to

Public Law 90-411
90th Congress, H. R. 3400
July 21, 1968

# An Act

82 STAT. 395

To amend the Federal Aviation Act of 1958 to require aircraft noise abatement regulation, and for other purposes.

*Be it enacted by the Senate and House of Representatives of the United States of America in Congress assembled,* That title VI of the Federal Aviation Act of 1958 (49 U.S.C. 1421–1430) is amended by adding at the end thereof the following new section:

Aircraft noise control.
72 Stat. 775.

"CONTROL AND ABATEMENT OF AIRCRAFT NOISE AND SONIC BOOM

"SEC. 611. (a) In order to afford present and future relief and protection to the public from unnecessary aircraft noise and sonic boom, the Administrator of the Federal Aviation Administration, after consultation with the Secretary of Transportation, shall prescribe and amend standards for the measurement of aircraft noise and sonic boom and shall prescribe and amend such rules and regulations as he may find necessary to provide for the control and abatement of aircraft noise and sonic boom, including the application of such standards, rules, and regulations in the issuance, amendment, modification, suspension, or revocation of any certificate authorized by this title.

"(b) In prescribing and amending standards, rules, and regulations under this section, the Administrator shall—

Administrative provisions.

"(1) consider relevant available data relating to aircraft noise and sonic boom, including the results of research, development, testing, and evaluation activities conducted pursuant to this Act and the Department of Transportation Act;

80 Stat. 931.
49 USC 1651 note.

"(2) consult with such Federal, State, and interstate agencies as he deems appropriate;

"(3) consider whether any proposed standard, rule, or regulation is consistent with the highest degree of safety in air commerce or air transportation in the public interest;

"(4) consider whether any proposed standard, rule, or regulation is economically reasonable, technologically practicable, and appropriate for the particular type of aircraft, aircraft engine, appliance, or certificate to which it will apply; and

"(5) consider the extent to which such standard, rule, or regulation will contribute to carrying out the purposes of this section.

"(c) In any action to amend, modify, suspend, or revoke a certificate in which violation of aircraft noise or sonic boom standards, rules, or regulations is at issue, the certificate holder shall have the same notice and appeal rights as are contained in section 609, and in any appeal to the National Transportation Safety Board, the Board may amend, modify, or reverse the order of the Administrator if it finds that control or abatement of aircraft noise or sonic boom and the public interest do not require the affirmation of such order, or that such order is not consistent with safety in air commerce or air transportation."

72 Stat. 779.
49 USC 1429.

SEC. 2. That portion of the table of contents contained in the first section of the Federal Aviation Act of 1958 which appears under the center heading "TITLE VI—SAFETY REGULATION OF CIVIL AERONAUTICS" is amended by adding at the end thereof the following:

"Sec. 611. Control and abatement of aircraft noise and sonic boom."

Approved July 21, 1968.

which the agency responds and about the relationships between the agency and Congress.

**Public Law 90-411 Amending the Federal Aviation Act of 1958.** The law on page 468 relating to aircraft-noise abatement was passed on July 21, 1968. As you read the law, answer the following questions:

1. If you were an aircraft manufacturer, could you tell from reading P.L. 90-411 the exact amount of noise that will be permitted by the federal government in approving a new aircraft which you are designing?
2. What is the purpose of this law?

**FAA Announces Plans for New Noise Regulations.** Public announcements of new decisions and policies of federal agencies are published in the *Federal Register*. The following announcement appeared in the *Federal Register* on January 11, 1969.

1. What is the relationship between P.L. 90-411 and this announcement?
2. Which of the factors influencing bureaucratic decision-making does this announcement demonstrate?
3. Who would you predict would be most eager to have the information in this announcement?

**Department of Transportation Federal Aviation Administration**

Noise Standards: Aircraft Type Certification
Notice of Proposed Rule Making

The Federal Aviation Administration is considering the adoption of a new Part 36 of the Federal Aviation Regulations prescribing aircraft noise standards for subsonic transport category airplanes, and for subsonic turbojet powered airplanes regardless of category. . . .

Interested persons are invited to participate in the making of the proposed rule by submitting such written data, views or arguments as they may desire. . . . All communications received on or before March 12, 1969, will be considered by the Administrator before taking action upon the proposed rule. The proposals contained in this notice may be changed in the light of comments and will be available . . . for examination by interested persons.

Public Law 90-411 adds new section 611 to the Federal Aviation Act of 1958. This section provides that "the Administrator of the Federal Aviation Administration, after consultation with the Secretary of Transportation, shall prescribe . . . standards for the measurement of aircraft noise and sonic boom and shall prescribe . . . such rules and regulations as he may find necessary to provide for the control and abatement of aircraft noise and sonic boom, including the application of such standards, rules, and regulations in the issuance, amendment, modification, suspension, or revocation of any certificate authorized by this title" (Title VI).

**FAA Issues New Aircraft Noise Standards.** On November 12, 1969, the FAA announced a new rule on the control of aircraft noise. The document on page 471 represents the first page of a news release announcing the new rule. The diagram below indicates the top noise levels permitted by the new rule.

**1.** Which group interested in rules relating to aircraft noise gained the most by this decision?
**2.** Explain the new rule in terms of the concept "accommodational decision."

**FAA Comments on the Noise Abatement Rule.** In a document called "Introduction to the Noise Rule," issued November 13, 1969, the FAA explained further the new aircraft noise abatement rule and published a summary of the comments it had considered in reaching its decision.

*Summary of public comments.* The FAA received a total of 1428 public comments in response to the notice published in the *Federal Register* (page 456). One major group contained around 1000 comments from individuals, citizen groups, and local airport authorities. However, about 960 of these comments were identical form letters from the Los Angeles area. The other major group included comments from aviation trade associations, aircraft manufacturers, and pilots.

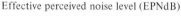

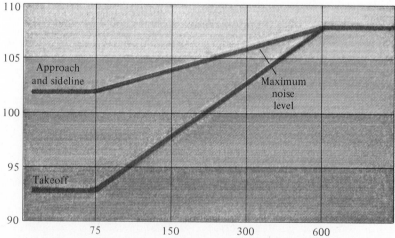

Allowable noise limits, shown on chart, are based on aircraft's certificated gross takeoff weight. Maximum for 600,000-lb. aircraft is 108 EPNdB. The chart is based on a drawing from *Aviation Week & Space Technology*, November 17, 1969, page 35. Used by permission.

Both groups agreed that the standards in the notice should be changed, but for directly opposite reasons. The first group argued that Congress intended greater reductions in noise levels than those proposed by the FAA. The second group said that the law told the FAA to prescribe "technologically practicable and economically reasonable" noise standards. This group felt that such standards could only be met at noise levels higher than those proposed.

*Comments from private citizens and FAA replies.* The document "Introduction to the Noise Rule" summarized the various comments received. It also told how the FAA had replied to the issues that were raised. Excerpts from the document follow on the next page.

## DEPARTMENT OF TRANSPORTATION | NEWS

### FEDERAL AVIATION ADMINISTRATION
#### WASHINGTON, D.C. 20590

In this news release the FAA announced its new regulations on aircraft noise.

69-124

FOR IMMEDIATE RELEASE                    Area Code 202--962-6461

12 November 1969

NOISE CERTIFICATION STANDARDS FOR NEW AIRCRAFT
ADOPTED BY FAA

"We have taken the important first step in reversing the escalation of aircraft noise around airports," Secretary of Transportation John A. Volpe said today, as he announced a new Federal Aviation Administration regulation that establishes noise standards and maximum noise levels for all new subsonic transport airplane type designs, including some airplanes already under development.

"The new regulation will result in an approximate halving of the noise around airports," the Secretary added.

The noise limits prescribed in the new rule are as much as 10 EPNdB (effective perceived noise decibels) less than those for the noisiest aircraft presently in service. This represents an approximate halving of perceived noise when measured on a logarithmic scale.

The new rule establishes the top maximum EPNdB to 93 and 108 EPNdB depending on the type and size of the aircraft. Today's largest aircraft are operating at 110 to 120 EPNdB at comparable measuring positions.

(over)

(1) The 960 form letters from the Los Angeles area stated that the noise standards should be "based on the technology *available* instead of that which would be most advantageous to the airlines."

The FAA replied that it agreed "that available technology must be applied in the reduction of aircraft noise. The noise standards in this amendment are intended to accomplish this result [in keeping] with the requirement in Section 611 (b) (4) that the Administrator must consider whether the standards are economically reasonable and technologically practicable."

(2) Several comments requested that protection against sonic boom be assured.

The FAA replied that "while not a part of this rulemaking action, study of the sonic boom problem is continuing so that appropriate action can be taken specifically in that area."

(3) One comment stated that "the FAA should limit the noise levels to those that do not exceed industrial health standards, . . . and the FAA should permit local standards to prevail if they are [stricter] than FAA standards."

The FAA replied that the goal of achieving noise levels not exceeding industrial health standards can be largely achieved by its ruling. But it recognized "that certain locally desired noise levels might not be achievable within the [limitations of the requirement] that economic reasonableness and technological practicability be considered. . . . This being the case, the FAA . . . recognizes the right of state or local public agencies, as the proprietors of airports, to issue . . . restrictions with respect to the permissable level of noise that can be created by aircraft using their airports."

(4) One citizens' association sent the FAA the results of a noise study indicating that the introduction of commercial passenger traffic at their local airport would have large costs for their community and that the published noise limits would not be acceptable. They requested limits of 90 to 95 EPNdb.

The FAA replied that it was convinced after thorough study that the current knowledge in the field of aircraft noise reduction simply does not permit the attainment of 90 to 95 EPNdb noise levels for the larger aircraft within the limits of the requirement that "economic reasonableness and technological practicability be considered by the Administrator in issuing noise abatement regulations."

*Comments from state and local authorities.* The document "Introduction to the Noise Rule" then took up some comments received from the state and local public officials. To each of the issues raised in these comments the FAA gave a reply as summarized on the next page.

472

(1) One airport commission pointed out that the FAA notice represents "no more than the first step toward an ambitious goal." The commission concluded that, in issuing noise standards, the FAA should recognize the views of the airport's neighbors as well as the views of the aviation industry.

The FAA replied that it agreed and had "fully reviewed each of the many comments received from [persons] directly affected by aircraft noise. . . . These public comments have greatly assisted the FAA in determining . . . that the many and substantial costs to be imposed on the air transportation industry by this amendment are reasonable and appropriate."

(2) One commentator stated that the proposed levels are not adequate because they are not socially acceptable.

The FAA replied that under the legal regulations "socially acceptable noise levels can only be required insofar as they [put] economically reasonable burdens on the aircraft industry and are technologically practicable."

(3) One comment from a city manager stated that the FAA should "take a more militant stand in favor of the general public and opposed to the private monetary interests of airlines and aircraft manufacturers."

The FAA's answer was that it "does not intend to 'favor' or 'oppose' any segment of the public in its noise abatement activities. Rather, the FAA intends to impartially administer the language of [the 1968 noise-abatement amendment to the Federal Aviation Act] in the light of the pertinent statements of congressional intent concerning the public law. . . ."

From *The Wall Street Journal*

The FAA concluded the summary with the following remarks: "The FAA intends to ensure that its noise abatement regulatory program requires aircraft manufacturers to achieve the greatest noise reductions that are consistent with the economically reasonable limits of noise reduction technology. . . ."

**1.** What individuals or groups seemed to be most interested in the new FAA regulations? May these be considered FAA "constituencies"?

**2.** What specific concerns and criticisms did each of these groups have?

**3.** What kinds of arguments does the FAA use to justify its position? What clause in P.L.90-411 (page 468) did the FAA cite most frequently?

**An Interview with an FAA Official.** After the publication of the new regulation on aircraft noise, some FAA officials were interviewed. As you read the brief excerpt from one of these interviews, keep the following questions in mind.

*Circumstances for the decision*
1. Was the noise-regulation decision a crisis decision?
2. Identify the competing values that had to be resolved successfully by the decision.

*Individual characteristics of the decision-makers*
3. What kinds of people work in the Office of Noise Abatement and how did this affect the kind of decision that was reached?

*Other factors in decision-making*
4. What *rules* or *procedures* are referred to in the interview?
5. What *status relationships* are discussed in the interview and what effect did they seem to have on the FAA decision?
6. What influence did *public opinion* have on the outcome?
7. In what sense were *available resources* a factor in the decision?
8. What *external decision-makers* were taken into consideration.

*Interviewer:* Give me some idea of how this office fits into the Federal Aviation Administration.

*FAA Official:* Well, the FAA's Office of Noise Abatement is an element of the Office of Plans under the Administrator for Plans, who in turn reports directly to the administrator of the FAA, Mr. Schaffer. Our office has to do primarily with the establishment of aircraft noise regulations, including both the problems of aircraft noise and sonic boom. In addition . . . we conduct research and development programs which we hope will assist in implementing our regulations. . . . We hope to do the best job we can on lowering aircraft noise levels.

*Interviewer:* Tell us how the noise-abatement rule came about.

*FAA Official:* . . . Around the latter part of 1966, the FAA was aware of the considerable concern that the public had and the industry was also beginning to share this concern about ever increasing aircraft noise. To get legal authority to make any improvements or to pass any rules . . . in this area, we had to go to the Congress. . . . The Congress, of course, had pressures brought on them by various citizen groups, by airport owners, by interested parties in creating aircraft noise legislation.

In July 1968, after [a lengthy period] of committee hearings, the Congress enacted Public Law 90-411, which is the law which gives the administrator of the FAA the legal authority to prescribe rules and standards for aircraft with respect to both noise and sonic boom. O.K., so then in its response to this public law we have just . . . issued our first rule. . . .

What this means is that we have, . . . using the information from our research programs, working with the local government groups, the airport operators, citizen groups, with the aircraft industry, the transport association, . . . we have in this office developed what we believe to be the "technologically reasonable" and "economically viable" upper levels for future aircraft. These levels are prescribed in the rule. This rule, which consists of about 150 pages, describes methods for measuring aircraft noise, methods for evaluating aircraft noise, and then finally the permissible upper bounds and maximum levels for new aircraft.

Implementation of the rule is the responsibility of Federal Aviation Administration regional offices. The call that I was on just before you came in was to our western region which is now in the process of reviewing the certification procedures for the Boeing 747 aircraft. Now this rule has an effective date of 1 December 1969. The Boeing 747 aircraft is attempting to get a type certificate by 15 December.

*Interviewer:* They will not be bound by this rule?

*FAA Official:* They *will* be bound by this. In other words, our rule becomes effective before their type certificate becomes effective. The Boeing Company has actually been put on notice that they will be bound, but the manner in which they are bound will be somewhat different than aircraft which were put on notice after 1 January 1967. You see, the Boeing 747 was well into its design cycle before January 1967. That was roughly the date when the industry was put on notice that the FAA was seeking this rule-making authority. So, what this means is that they started their design, and they didn't have available to them the latest acoustic techniques. So they didn't have the opportunity to include these latest advances into their early design phase. As a result, the Boeing Company may initially not meet our levels. O.K., so the 747 may not come under those limits right now, but they will be required to work with the FAA administrator and to establish a date or a time at which they will meet those levels in the near future.

*Interviewer:* Are most of the people who work in this office basically aeronautical engineers?

*FAA Official:* Well, we have a kind of interesting mixture. We have aeronautical, electrical, physicists, and acousticians. And then we have . . . well old flying pilots, . . . and all of these different disciplines are sort of necessary to be responsive to the many factors. . . .

*Interviewer:* How many professional level people are there now?

*FAA Official:* Let's see, the total staff is thirteen and that's ten professional.

*Interviewer:* Are these the people who handled the development of the rule?

*FAA Official:* Basically, these are the people. Now the rule is not just the product of this staff, but it is truly the product of this staff working together with the public. And the way we have done this in the Noise Office is we have actually set up task forces. These are members of civic groups, of airport communities, Airline

Pilot Association, Aircraft Industry Association. . . . And we have worked with these groups in task force meetings over the past, oh, year and a half, two years. I would say those meetings occurred only every other month roughly on an average. These groups have prepared their recommendations, which we have digested . . .

*Interviewer:* . . . I know there was a lot of community citizen complaint in the Los Angeles airport area. Would someone representing that complaint be on a task force?

*FAA Official:* . . . the airport operators are there, so they are the ones that, of course, receive the complaints. Right now we have had in the present task force the lawyers of the city of Chicago, . . . the ones that are . . . putting the pressure on the airport operators.

*Interviewer:* That's the only representative of the public?

*FAA Official:* . . . The New York, Hempstead area has been a very active group . . . these groups run in the order of 35 people. We have people from all over the country . . . but the groups that are most involved are from New York, Chicago, and Los Angeles. The public obviously gets its word in very strongly through the congressional mails. The congressmen that have the most active citizen groups are the ones that are, well, obviously most responsive to it, and they are the ones that are insuring that the FAA is in fact responsive to the needs of the citizen groups.

*Interviewer:* Well, what's happening right now? I heard you say that you are hearing from people?

*FAA Official:* Well, most of the response so far has been through the press. I have had about three or four congressional inquiries. I think there was one press release that said the Aircraft Industries Association was going to sue the Federal Aviation Administration . . . and then on the other side I think there has been, I'm not sure it's the Hempstead group . . . that suggested that the FAA has sold out to the Boeing Company. So, from our point of view, if we can get about equal complaints from all sides, we feel we might have done a good job on rule making. Because in the noise business . . . we are not going to make anybody happy. . . . So, if you do make one group happy . . . say you make the aircraft manufacturers completely happy . . . then that means that you haven't put enough burden on them. And so if the responses are just about equally squeezing on us, then we have a feeling we might have done a good job.

*Interviewer:* Is that a consideration while the rules are being devised?

*FAA Official:* Well, from a realistic standpoint the considerations are first technological . . .; then this public law . . . this 90-411 was a little bit unique in that they cautioned us to be absolutely sure that everything that we were doing was "economically reasonable." Now that is very vague. . . .

*Interviewer:* That's support of the industry.

*FAA Official:* Yes, but it is more than that, because it supported the gross national product of the United States, because the industry is part of that gross national product. So, if we do something that wrecks the industry, we are also wrecking the United States. So, we've got to be realistic from that standpoint. I mean, obviously, you could evade noise by keeping the aircraft on the ground; that would be about the most extreme thing that one could do.

*Interviewer:* . . . there must be occasions when the technical people find themselves not quite totally in agreement with the policy decision.

*FAA Official:* Well, we could imagine a situation where the technicians say, "Boy, I could squeeze an extra five decibels out of that aircraft, if you let me increase the direct operating cost by 50 percent." And this would be an economically unrealistic burden. Now, this kind of a situation could occur, but I can't think of any specific examples right off hand. Obviously rule-making must necessarily be a compromise. . . .

**1.** Was the decision leading to new noise regulations primarily a "technical decision" or a "political decision"?

**2.** As an agency in the executive branch of the government, the FAA administers laws passed by Congress. Can you find any evidence in this case that the FAA "legislates" and "interprets laws" as well as administers laws?

**3.** Do you approve of the decision reached by the Federal Aviation Administration? Explain your answer in terms of the factors that influence bureaucratic decision-making.

## Some Value Conflicts in the Bureaucratic Role

The federal bureaucracy was set up to carry out programs that people want. Thus, it would seem that we employ bureaucrats to carry out tasks in the public interest. There should not be any moral confusion in this, but life is not so simple.

Because there are money and people to support only a limited number of "public interest" activities, agencies compete with each other. Suppose that Congress votes a $20 billion increase for the Department of Defense in a year when it is trying to "hold the line" on total spending. Then some other departments may get less than they "need." It is easy for bureaucrats to tell themselves that what is good for my agency and program is good for the country.

Furthermore, it is not always easy to define the "public interest." Surely, all Americans expect the government to defend them against foreign attack. But the Defense Department looks at other factors in building its budget. Should an old shipyard be kept open to provide jobs even though new ships are not needed at present? Should the Department ask Congress for military aid funds to give to a dictator so that he can stay in power because some American firms want to keep on doing business with his country? What is the public interest?

For these and other reasons, bureaucrats are often faced with value conflicts. In the examples that follow, indicate the choice you would make in each situation.

### Case 1. Is It Worth the Cost?

You are the head of a teacher education program in the Office of Education. Several million dollars have been spent on this program in the past five years. Recently a team of scholars has sent you its report on the program's overall effectiveness. In general, the report shows the program did not reach its main goals and, though popular, is clearly not worth its cost. The Office of Education budget for next year is now up for study in Congress. Funds to continue the program are called for in the budget. You think it is not likely that anyone in Congress knows about this study. It has not even been passed around in the Office of Education. What should you do?

**a.** Send a copy of the report to each member of the education committees in Congress, calling attention to the findings and showing how you intend to improve the program in the future.

**b.** Thank the evaluation team for its work, keep one copy of its report for your own reference, and burn the rest.

**c.** Send a copy of the report to the Commissioner of Education, saying that the program needs to be changed. Suggest that no public attention be given to the report until the budget has passed Congress, but that efforts be started soon to improve or revise the program totally for the next year.

**d.** Resign and take the blame for the program's failure.

### Case 2. What to Tell Congress?

You are an Air Force management expert in the Department of Defense. One of the major Air Force projects is to develop and produce a huge new cargo plane. Plans for it have been underway for a long time. Congress approved funds for developing it and for making a small number of the planes. In studying the Air Force budget, Congress now must decide whether to extend further support for this project. Costs for the cargo plane are turning out to be nearly double the original figure. In your opinion, part of the cost ''overrun'' stems from wasteful management on the part of both the Air Force and the company making the plane. You have been invited to testify on the Air Force budget to the Appropriations Committee in Congress. You know that some members of Congress would like to kill the costly project. You think that the plane is needed but that the country is paying too much. What should you do?

**a.** Testify to the very best of your knowledge. Show where wasteful practices exist and how savings could be made.

**b.** Tell the Secretary of the Air Force that you would prefer not to testify because you can't do so truthfully without damaging the Air Force case before Congress.

**c.** Try to avoid a direct lie, but avoid as best you can giving Congress any facts about the true state of affairs and try to improve

the management of the project by using your influence internally.
**d.** Resign, then tell Congress exactly what you know.
**e.** Resign and remain silent.

### Case 3. Stop Enforcing the Law?

You are a bureaucrat in the Department of Justice. For many years you have worked on antitrust cases. The recent election brought in a new administration, including a new President and a new Attorney General. You have been ordered to stop your work on certain cases that were nearly ready to go to trial. In your opinion the present administration does not wish these antitrust actions to reach court because of promises made to certain business firms in return for gifts made during the election campaign. What do you do?

**a.** Drop the cases and carry on as if nothing has happened.
**b.** Take no further action on the cases but quietly leak the facts to some newspaper friends in the hope that public exposure will embarrass the administration and lead it to reverse its stand.
**c.** Tell the Attorney General that if the policy is not changed, you will hold a press conference on the matter.
**d.** Resign and publicly announce why you had to do so.

### Case 4. Mislead or Inform the Public?

You work in the Department of State. You have been asked to pull together all the relevant documents that give the background to our military activities in Southeast Asia. This is a very secret job, and the final report is only for the President and some close advisers. Most of the documents you are using are classified as "secret."

As you work on the report, you become aware that the American public has been badly misled about our military involvement. Indeed, you decide that the administration has lied to the people about the purpose and extent of our commitment. What should you do?

**a.** Do nothing. The decision about how much Americans can and should know is for the President to decide.
**b.** Find ways to get the facts to the public by leaking documents to the press and members of Congress. (Incidentally, if you are caught, you may well face a criminal trial.)
**c.** Resign.

### Case 5. How Much to Tell Congress?

You work in one of the intelligence agencies. You have taken part in a number of undercover jobs abroad that remain top secret. Recent news stories guessing about some of these overseas activities have led to a public outcry. Now Congress has launched a special inquiry into the operation of your agency. Frankly, several of the

480

projects that you have taken part in can't be aired in public without risking lives and causing embarrassment to our country. You have always assumed that at times national defense requires some actions that can't be easily explained and justified to the public. You have been called as a witness before a committee of Congress. What should you do?

a. Answer all questions as truthfully as you can.

b. Refuse to answer any question that you think would embarrass the government or risk an agent's life.

c. Refuse to appear in a public hearing. Agree to answer questions only in an executive session with people who have taken oaths to maintain secrecy.

d. Assume that any facts given in any kind of session will at some time leak out. Therefore, be frank and candid in answers when you can; refuse to answer tough questions when possible; lie when it is necessary.

e. Resign.

# UNIT FIVE

## State and Local Decision–Makers

# 16 The Nature of American State and Local Governments

The American government consists of much more than the national government: the President, members of Congress, federal judges, and the federal bureaucracy. The national government is big and attracts much public attention. But it is only one of our units of government. Most Americans get services from—and pay taxes to support—at least two other units of government (state and local). Indeed, one of the striking features of the American political system is that governmental authority is divided between the national government and the subdivisions, or states. The states in turn share their power with other subdivisions—counties, cities, and other units.

Some scholars believe that this feature of shared power in our political system is one of our special strengths. A state or locality can try out some program on a small scale. If it works, the idea may spread. Also some people want more services from government—and are willing to pay for them—than do people in other places. Shared governmental power makes it possible to take into account regional and local differences. On any given day in the United States, political decisions that will affect your life are being made in a variety of political units.

## Our Constitutions Provide for Shared Authority

Where do these "governments" get their authority? The first place to look is the United States Constitution. As you learned earlier (pages 264–265), ours is a federal system. Some governmental functions are limited to the national government. Others are reserved to the states. Still others are shared by the national and state governments.

The Tenth Amendment to the Constitution gives a general definition of state authority: "The powers not delegated to the United States by the Constitution, nor prohibited by it to the States, are reserved to the States respectively, or to the people." For example, the Constitution gives the national government the power to coin money (Art. I, Sec. 8) and forbids the states to do so (Art. I, Sec. 10). Thus, coining money is a federal power. But the Constitution gives the federal government no specific power to handle education, and does not prohibit the states from doing so. Thus, public education is essentially a state power. In effect, the United States Constitution gives the states broad power to organize their business as they wish. Each has done so by writing its own constitution.

State constitutions vary in detail from one state to another, but they share common features. They provide for key government officials, the method of choosing them, and their duties. State constitutions also set up guidelines for delegating power to local units of government. Thus, state constitutions basically accept the powers reserved to the states by the United States Constitution and decide how the various services and functions will be exercised within their state boundaries. So long as local officials stay within the limits of power granted by state law, they have much freedom to operate as they wish in response to local public support.

## Kinds of Local Units of Government

What are some of the local units of government? *Table 1* shows five types and how they have risen or dropped in number over the decade 1962-1972. Notice that the total number of governmental units in the United States has been falling. This is mainly a result of a decline in the number of school districts as small districts are combining into larger ones.

## Counties and Their Government

Counties are political subdivisions of a state. They were set up chiefly to bring state government to the people. Before the motor car, it made no sense to try to administer all state law from the state capital. Moreover, from colonial days to the present, Americans have liked the idea of local control. They set up county courts with sheriff, prosecuting attorney, and judge to deal with people breaking state laws or having legal disputes. Other county officials handled such state duties as keeping records of property deeds, assessing property for taxes, and collecting taxes.

In some parts of the nation the county is the chief unit—and in some places the only unit—of local government serving people living on farms and in rural villages. The county may handle education, road building and upkeep, public health and safety, and public welfare.

*Table 1.* Governmental Units in the United States, 1962–1972

| Type of government | 1972 | 1967 | 1962 |
|---|---|---|---|
| TOTAL | 78,269 | 81,299 | 91,237 |
| U.S. government | 1 | 1 | 1 |
| State governments | 50 | 50 | 50 |
| Local governments | 78,218 | 81,248 | 91,186 |
| Counties | 3,044 | 3,049 | 3,043 |
| Municipalities | 18,517 | 18,048 | 18,000 |
| Townships | 16,991 | 17,105 | 17,142 |
| School districts | 15,781 | 21,782 | 34,678 |
| Special districts | 23,885 | 21,264 | 18,323 |

*Table 1:* The Book of the States, 1974–1975. Used by permission of The Council of State Governments.

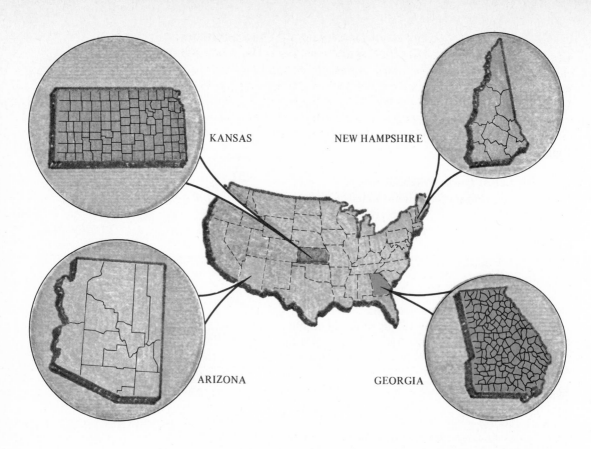

KANSAS

NEW HAMPSHIRE

ARIZONA

GEORGIA

In Louisiana this unit of government is known as a *parish,* and in Alaska as a *borough.* Rhode Island and Connecticut do not have any organized county government, and in the other New England states the county has very limited duties—chiefly judicial.

Counties vary greatly in shape, area, and population. Notice some differences in area and shape on the map on this page. The number of counties per state ranges from three in Delaware to 254 in Texas. New York County, one of the five boroughs of New York City, is only 22 square miles in area. The largest county—San Bernardino in California—measures over 20,000 square miles. Some twenty counties have less than a thousand people, while the largest—Los Angeles County—has over seven million; Cook County, Illinois, has almost 5.5 million.

Clearly, such a wide array of counties means that there must be big differences in county government from place to place. A fairly typical plan is shown in the next chart. A chief feature of this plan is that the voters elect six to a dozen or more officials who operate pretty much on their own. The elected county board appoints and supervises other officials. Decision-making is scattered under such a plan.

486

In order to make county government more unified and efficient, a few counties have adopted the county manager plan. The voters elect fewer officials. The elected county board hires a manager to supervise—and sometimes to appoint—other officers and employees. The county board makes policies, and the manager's job is to carry them out. A little different plan in a few places is to have one member of the county board serve as president or supervisor to act much like a mayor in city government.

If possible, find a chart of your county government. How does it compare with this one?

**TYPICAL PLAN OF RURAL COUNTY GOVERNMENT**

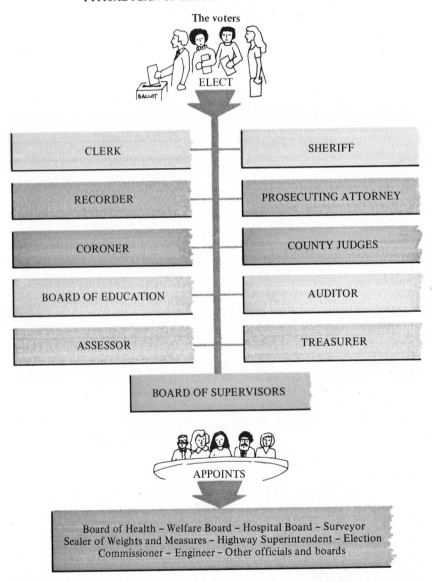

The voters

ELECT

| | |
|---|---|
| CLERK | SHERIFF |
| RECORDER | PROSECUTING ATTORNEY |
| CORONER | COUNTY JUDGES |
| BOARD OF EDUCATION | AUDITOR |
| ASSESSOR | TREASURER |

BOARD OF SUPERVISORS

APPOINTS

Board of Health – Welfare Board – Hospital Board – Surveyor
Sealer of Weights and Measures – Highway Superintendent – Election
Commissioner – Engineer – Other officials and boards

487

Counties were organized in the first place to serve a largely rural population. With the growth of cities, much overlap of city and county government began to show up. Why have separate police departments, health offices, and so on? One response in a few places is to combine local units into one city-county government. Such consolidation exists in Hawaii where the island of Oahu with its city of Honolulu is organized as one unit of local government. Among others, consolidations exist at Denver; San Francisco; Indianapolis; Nashville, Tennessee; Jacksonville, Florida; and at least two in Virginia.

### Decision-Making in County Government

We see, then, that a few counties really have a city government with decision-making largely in the hands of an elected council and a chief administrator (mayor or manager). More usual, however, is the scattered authority shown in the diagram on page 487. Each elected official tends to go his or her own way. This system often works well enough because the officials are mainly just carrying out state law—the decisions made in the state capital. Even the county board, which votes on budgets, has limited decision-making power.

However, in administering state law, county officials, like federal bureaucrats, do have decisions to make from day to day. The sheriff and county prosecutor can decide whether to be strict or lenient in law enforcement. Shall we set up a trap to catch speeders? move against gambling or other vice? protect or harass civil rights activists? and so on. County judges have some leeway in how they decide cases. Officials decide who will get welfare payments, where roads and bridges will be built or fixed, how property will be assessed for taxes, etc.

## Municipalities and Municipal Government

*Table 1* shows that the United States has over 18,000 municipalities. These are mainly cities and towns. They range in size from New York City with almost eight million people to small towns of one or two thousand people. A municipality is a government corporation. Somewhat like a business corporation, it operates under a *charter* granted by the state. The charter is kind of a constitution telling what kind of government the city will have: what officials, how they are to be chosen, their duties, and so on.

Both municipalities and counties are political subdivisions of the state—as are all local governments. But a municipality differs from a county in that (1) it is incorporated and (2) it is nearly always created upon application of the people of the area involved. A further distinction is that a municipality doesn't just administer state laws and programs but may make some laws for local use and provide services beyond those required by the state.

In the next chapter we look at three main types of municipal (city) government with special attention to the role of mayor as decision-maker.

## Townships and Township Government

A township is a political subdivision of a county (as well as of the state, of course). It exists in only parts of the nation, mainly the Northeast and Middle West. In New York and Wisconsin this political unit is called "town."

The township typically has constables and justices of the peace for local law enforcement. Other officials include tax assessors and road commissioners. A township board has limited policy-making power including the approving of the budget. Some units have a trustee or supervisor to administer township business. Where townships have become highly urban but people have not applied for a city charter, the township government may carry on regular municipal functions. In some places the voters in a *township meeting* make general policies and act on the budgets.

It's town meeting time in Peterborough, New Hampshire.

## New England Town Government

The New England states were originally subdivided into towns for local government purposes. Some of these towns later incorporated as cities. So in New England you live in either a town or a city even if you are in a rural area.

A chief feature of government is that the citizens are major decision-makers. Residents may attend *town meeting* to make local laws, make changes in zoning, approve the transfer of town property, and act on town budgets. Some large towns have a *representative town meeting* where only elected members may vote but any citizen may attend and be heard. An elected *moderator* chairs the town meeting. One annual meeting—sometimes lasting two or three evenings—is devoted chiefly to the budget. Special meetings may be called.

Day-to-day policy is made by other elected officials: clerk, treasurer, assessor, school committee, finance committee, planning board, and especially a board of selectmen. The selectmen appoint other officials and hire workers. Some towns have a manager who administers town business under the direction of the selectmen.

Many New England towns are really municipal governments with a distinctive type of legislative body—the town meeting.

### Table 2. Kinds of Special Districts

| Function | Number | Percent |
|---|---|---|
| TOTAL | 23,885 | 100.0 |
| Natural resources | 6,639 | 27.9 |
|   Soil conservation | 2,561 | 10.7 |
|   Drainage | 2,192 | 9.2 |
|   Irrigation, water conservation | 971 | 4.1 |
|   Flood control | 684 | 2.9 |
|   Other and composite resource purposes | 231 | 1.0 |
| Fire protection | 3,872 | 16.2 |
| Urban water supply | 2,333 | 9.8 |
| Housing | 2,271 | 9.5 |
| Cemeteries | 1,494 | 6.3 |
| Sewerage | 1,411 | 5.9 |
| School buildings | 1,085 | 4.5 |
| Parks and recreation | 750 | 3.1 |
| Highways | 698 | 2.9 |
| Hospitals | 657 | 2.7 |
| Libraries | 498 | 2.1 |
| Other single-function districts | 1,273 | 5.3 |
| Multiple-function districts | 904 | 3.8 |

*Table 2:* The Book of the States, 1974–1975. Used by permission of The Council of State Governments.

## School Districts and Special Districts

Most public school systems operate as a separate governmental unit. In four New England states the school board is part of the town or city government, but it has some independence in making policy. In five other states (see *Table 3*) and the District of Columbia all public schools are part of some other unit of government. One reason for setting up schools as a separate unit was to remove them somewhat from local party politics. School districts may cover a whole county, a town or city, two or more adjacent townships, or some other area.

Much school policy is dictated by state law. Other policy, including approval of a school budget, rests with a school board. A board hires a superintendent to carry out policy and administer the school system. The superintendent and other administrators, of course, are also decision-makers. They make rules and other decisions within the guidelines set down by state law, the state education bureaucracy, and the local school board.

A *special district* is a unit of government set up to do a particular job, or sometimes two or three jobs. (A school district is really a special district but is treated separately.) *Table 2* shows the broad range of services provided by special districts.

Some special districts have the same boundaries as a township, county, or city: for example, the Adams Township Fire District. Other districts take in two or more townships or counties. Still others may cover only one city neighborhood or part of a township. One reason for setting up special districts is that they can serve only an area that wants the service and is willing to pay for it. Another chief reason for their growth is that state law often puts limits on the taxing and borrowing power of local units. If a city or county is near its debt limit, it may be able to get around this obstacle by creating a special district.

Decision-making for a special district is usually in the hands of a board of three or five members. They decide policy, set the tax rate needed to support the service, borrow money, and sometimes hire a manager to administer the program.

1. You are served by several units of government, each with definite political boundaries. Starting with the one largest in area and going to the smallest, list these governmental units. Do any of the separate units have identical boundaries?

2. State law (including the state constitution) generally tells in some detail the form and the powers and duties of local governments. Does federal law put the same kind of limits on state governments? Explain.

3. In small groups (or as individual projects) draw up charts of the various typical units of local government in your state: county, township, city, school district, special district, etc.

**Table 3.** Organized Local Governments in the United States

| | Total | Counties | Munici-palities | Town-ships | Special districts | School districts |
|---|---|---|---|---|---|---|
| Alabama | 875 | 67 | 396 | — | 286 | 126 |
| Alaska | 120 | 8 | 112 | — | — | — |
| Arizona | 406 | 14 | 65 | — | 90 | 237 |
| Arkansas | 1,283 | 75 | 454 | — | 366 | 388 |
| California | 3,819 | 57 | 407 | — | 2,223 | 1,132 |
| Colorado | 1,319 | 62 | 258 | — | 812 | 187 |
| Connecticut | 428 | — | 34 | 149 | 231 | 14 |
| Delaware | 158 | 3 | 52 | — | 78 | 25 |
| District of Columbia | 3 | — | 1 | — | 2 | — |
| Florida | 865 | 66 | 390 | — | 315 | 94 |
| Georgia | 1,243 | 158 | 530 | — | 366 | 189 |
| Hawaii | 19 | 3 | 1 | — | 15 | — |
| Idaho | 901 | 44 | 197 | — | 543 | 117 |
| Illinois | 6,385 | 102 | 1,267 | 1,432 | 2,407 | 1,177 |
| Indiana | 2,792 | 91 | 546 | 1,008 | 832 | 315 |
| Iowa | 1,818 | 99 | 951 | — | 305 | 463 |
| Kansas | 3,715 | 105 | 626 | 1,517 | 1,136 | 331 |
| Kentucky | 1,135 | 120 | 378 | — | 446 | 191 |
| Louisiana | 834 | 62 | 287 | — | 419 | 66 |
| Maine | 714 | 16 | 22 | 472 | 126 | 78 |
| Maryland | 403 | 23 | 151 | — | 229 | — |
| Massachusetts | 682 | 12 | 39 | 312 | 268 | 51 |
| Michigan | 2,649 | 83 | 532 | 1,248 | 139 | 647 |
| Minnesota | 3,395 | 87 | 854 | 1,798 | 211 | 445 |
| Mississippi | 796 | 82 | 270 | — | 282 | 162 |
| Missouri | 2,807 | 114 | 894 | 343 | 820 | 636 |
| Montana | 992 | 56 | 126 | — | 258 | 552 |
| Nebraska | 3,561 | 93 | 537 | 476 | 1,081 | 1,374 |
| Nevada | 184 | 16 | 17 | — | 134 | 17 |
| New Hampshire | 499 | 10 | 13 | 224 | 94 | 158 |
| New Jersey | 1,456 | 21 | 335 | 232 | 341 | 527 |
| New Mexico | 309 | 32 | 89 | — | 99 | 89 |
| New York | 3,306 | 57 | 618 | 931 | 954 | 746 |
| North Carolina | 802 | 100 | 454 | — | 248 | — |
| North Dakota | 2,726 | 53 | 358 | 1,368 | 561 | 386 |
| Ohio | 3,259 | 88 | 936 | 1,320 | 275 | 640 |
| Oklahoma | 1,683 | 77 | 547 | — | 402 | 657 |
| Oregon | 1,446 | 36 | 231 | — | 826 | 353 |
| Pennsylvania | 4,935 | 66 | 1,012 | 1,552 | 1,777 | 528 |
| Rhode Island | 115 | — | 8 | 31 | 73 | 3 |
| South Carolina | 583 | 46 | 262 | — | 182 | 93 |
| South Dakota | 1,770 | 64 | 308 | 1,034 | 136 | 228 |
| Tennessee | 881 | 94 | 316 | — | 457 | 14 |
| Texas | 3,624 | 254 | 981 | — | 1,215 | 1,174 |
| Utah | 459 | 29 | 214 | — | 176 | 40 |
| Vermont | 658 | 14 | 61 | 237 | 74 | 272 |
| Virginia | 385 | 96 | 231 | — | 58 | — |
| Washington | 1,682 | 39 | 266 | 39 | 1,021 | 317 |
| West Virginia | 508 | 55 | 226 | — | 172 | 55 |
| Wisconsin | 2,448 | 72 | 570 | 1,268 | 121 | 417 |
| Wyoming | 383 | 23 | 87 | — | 203 | 70 |

*Table 3: Statistical Abstract.*

**4.** How does county government in your state differ from the chart on page 487?

**5.** Identify some chief decision-makers in the local governmental units that serve you. Try to find out what kinds of decisions each such official makes.

**6.** Speculate on advantages and disadvantages of having citizens in "town meeting" make major local government decisions.

# 17 Chief Executives in State and Local Government

Like the President, our governors and mayors are the leading political figures in their arenas of activity. If the state or city government is running smoothly, the governor or mayor gets much of the credit. If things seem out of order, they tend to get the blame.

The duties of governor, mayor, and President differ in many details. Yet their roles are much alike. The lessons that follow treat the roles of governor and mayor and give examples of executive decision-making.

## The Role of State Governor

The role of governor can be divided into parts that match rather closely those of the President (pages 290–298). As *head of state* the governor greets official visitors and takes part in a broad range of ceremonial activities. For example, in one month a governor might speak or send greetings to three conventions meeting in the state. He or she might dedicate a bridge or public building, attend a governors' conference, proclaim a state holiday, and congratulate citizens who have brought honor to the state.

Governors are *chief executive* of their states. In seeing that the "laws are faithfully executed," they usually appoint a large number of persons to head departments, boards, and other agencies. But in the next topic we shall see that their power to carry out laws is often much more limited than that of the President.

Most governors have the role of *chief legislator.* In messages to the legislature they outline the need for new laws and changes in old ones. They present the state budget. Many bills are drawn up in agencies under the governor's control, and persons from these agencies appear at committee hearings. A governor may phone or meet with one or more legislators to urge them to vote "yea" or "nay" on a bill.

Except in North Carolina, the governor has the veto power. And in all but a handful of states this power includes the *item veto.* This means that a governor, unlike the President, can strike out parts of a bill instead of having to take all or none. The item veto is used mainly to cut out, or get the legislature to reduce, budget items. The legislature, of course, may be able to override the veto.

Another part of the governor's legislative role is to issue *executive orders.* These are used to "fill in the details" of a general law. Many laws can't take care of all specific details. In issuing an executive order, the governor will cite the law that gives the authority to act.

494

Governor George R. Ariyoshi of Hawaii prepares to sign an official document.

Governor Jerry Apodaca of New Mexico addresses a joint meeting of the state legislature.

Governor Ella Grasso of Connecticut meets a group of young students.

We noted that one part of the President's role is *chief economic planner.* To a much smaller degree, this may also be a part of the governor's role. But it is really just a part of the role of chief legislator. Much of a governor's legislative program is likely to deal with measures aimed at making the state a good place to live and do business.

The governor has a *commander-in-chief role* as civilian head of the state militia (National Guard). Governors may call out the National Guard (when it is not called into federal service) to put down riots or deal with other crises.

Another role is that of *party chief.* It corresponds closely to that of the President (page 296). And, like the President, of course, the governor has the role of *representative of all the people.* As we saw earlier, these two roles can give rise to a good bit of role conflict. While trying to serve all the people, the governor also wants to advance the interests of his or her own political party. As representative (or spokesperson) for all the people, the governor has a related role of *public opinion leader.* A big part of the job is leading the public and their legislators to accept policies that seem needed for the good of the whole state.

The President's role of *chief diplomat* can hardly be said to apply to the governor, since foreign affairs are reserved to the national government. But as *head of state* the governor deals with officials of other states and the federal government.

### Limits on the Governor's Powers

Americans tend to think of the governor as the person who is "running the state." If there are problems, the governor should be able to step in.

How much power do we give the governor to set things right and keep them that way? Simply in carrying out the *chief executive* role—seeing that state laws are carried out and that state programs are working well—can we hold the governor responsible? The answers vary from state to state. But clearly most governors have more limits on their power than does the President. Let's look at a few of the limits.

We elect only two federal executives—President and Vice-President. In many states the voters elect six or more. The elected state officials (see chart, page 501) have their own duties and powers. The governor can't really control them—nor remove them. The appointed Attorney General of the United States and the district attorneys in the Department of Justice must stay in line with the President's policies—or get out. An elected state attorney general can go his or her own way.

The President's executive arm can reach into district offices all across the land to hold federal officials in line. This is less true of the governor's power. Local officials not under the governor's control enforce the state's general laws and carry out many state programs.

496

Also the typical state has scores of semi-independent boards and commissions to regulate business and handle certain other activities. Often the members serve for a fixed term, and the governor's power to remove them is very limited. Such agencies also exist at the federal level (Federal Trade Commission, Federal Reserve Board, etc.), but perhaps to a smaller extent.

Let's see how this system of shared power works in a major state area—public education. Often there is an elected state superintendent of education to see that state school laws are carried out. A state board of education will make rules and policies under the guidelines set forth in the general laws. Today's governor may get to fill some vacancies on the board—but not often a whole new board. And once on the board, the members do not have to take orders from the governor. Often there will be another such board for the state college system. Then the laws and policies made at the state level are interpreted and carried out by other persons at the local level. Thus many state governors have almost no power to see that the state school laws are "faithfully executed." About their only power over education comes with their influence over state spending for the schools and colleges.

The trend today is to give the governor more power—by electing fewer state officials and giving the governor the right to appoint and remove more officials. Also limits on the governor's term of office have changed in some states. Most states now have a four-year term in place of the two-year term that was once common. But some states do not permit a governor to serve two terms in a row; others have a limit of two consecutive terms. In about half the states the governor and lieutenant governor now run for office as a team. In states where they do not do so, the lieutenant governor may feel no need to support the governor.

Much of the governor's power rests on the ability to persuade others. According to Thomas Dye, the governor's power

> depends upon his ability to persuade administrators over whom he has little authority, legislators who are jealous of their own powers, party leaders who are selected by local constituents, federal officials over whom the governor has little authority, and a public that thinks he has more authority than he really has.[1]

## What Do Governors Do?

Fifty state governors will not each play the role in the same way. They have different personalities, and their states differ. Also what a governor does will differ from day to day and month to month. At times the party-chief role will get much effort. When the legislature

---

1. Thomas R. Dye, *Politics in States and Communities,* © 1973, pp. 165–166. Reprinted by permission of Prentice-Hall, Inc., Englewood Cliffs, New Jersey.

Governor Richard Ogilvie inspects an official document of an executive agency before signing his approval.

meets, another role will come center stage. Still, we can get some idea of what governors do by looking at the kinds of things one person did during one month.

*Table 4* shows how a governor of Illinois, Richard B. Ogilvie, used the month of June 1971. He spent twenty-four days on official business and reserved the other six days (all Saturdays and Sundays) for time with his family. He had two offices where he spent most of his time—one in Springfield, the state capital, and one in Chicago. About 5 percent of the time was spent in out-of-state travel. The table shows 251 hours spent on "scheduled time"—an average 10 to 11 hours per day for the twenty-four days.

Looking at the "public relations" category in the table, we may point out that Ogilvie might have asked the lieutenant governor to "pinch hit" at some dinners and ceremonies. But in this case the two officials did not run for election as a team, and they belonged to opposing political parties.

In looking at Ogilvie's "political leadership" in the table, we should not assume that this was the total time his office gave to party matters. His personal aides gave much time to handling requests, listening to gripes and advice, and trying to settle party squabbles. Most of these would reach the governor's desk only if they seemed very important. Also he may have accepted some invitations to private functions because it would be "good politics."

Governor Ogilvie gave rather little time to office matters. His aides had to handle most details. One of his own chief office jobs was scheduling his time: whom to see? where to speak? when to travel? and so on.

**Table 4. Analysis of a Governor's Monthly Schedule**

| Activity | Hours | Percent of Total Scheduled Time |
|---|---|---|
| **Public Relations** | **67** | **27%** |
| Meetings in Illinois communities | 18 | |
| Dinner and luncheon speeches | 17 | |
| Ceremonial appearances (ground-breakings, graduations, etc.) | 11 | |
| Press interviews and conferences | 8 | |
| Photos in office | 5 | |
| Receptions | 4 | |
| Television appearances | 4 | |
| **Managing State Government** | **48** | **19%** |
| Meetings with personal staff | 20 | |
| Meetings with department officials | 14 | |
| Budget meetings—with budget officials and personal staff | 11 | |
| Cabinet meetings | 3 | |
| **Legislative Relations** | **39** | **16%** |
| Meetings with legislators (including 4 hours with leaders) | 19 | |
| Meetings with personal staff on legislative matters | 10 | |
| Bill signings | 6 | |
| House and Senate dinners | 4 | |
| **Political Leadership** | **27** | **11%** |
| Office visits—local or general political problems | 13 | |
| Meetings with staff on political matters | 10 | |
| Group meetings with party officials | 4 | |
| **Personal—Invitations to Private Functions** | **44** | **18%** |
| **Staff and Office Management** | **14** | **6%** |
| **Out-of-State Travel** | **12** | **5%** |

*Table 4:* Adapted from Ronald D. Michaelson, "An Analysis of the Chief Executive: How the Governor Uses His Time," *State Government,* Vol. 45 (Summer, 1972), pp. 153-160. Used by permission of The Council of State Governments.

What can one say about the role of the governor? One thing is clear: governors, like the President, devote many hours to ceremony— to the role of head of state. While voters expect the governor to "manage" the state, they also want to see their leader and be assured that the government is in safe hands. The process of reassuring people means that much of the management must be left to others.

1. Link the activities in *Table 4* to the various roles of a governor. For example, which category shows the role of head of state, chief executive, etc.? In some of the specific activities the governor is performing two or more roles. Point these out.
2. Point out specific activities where the governor may be making decisions on state policy or taking part in decision-making by persuading others.
3. Compare the time spent by the governor with the members of his personal staff with that spent with other executive officials. What seem to be some duties of the personal staff?
4. The Illinois legislature was in session in June 1971. How would you expect the governor's schedule to differ in a month when the legislature was not meeting?
5. How might the governor's "public relations" time have been cut down if the lieutenant governor had not been a political rival? Explain.

## A Governor's Program for Environmental Quality

Of all a governor's roles, clearly the most important are those of chief executive and chief legislator. In this lesson we focus on these two roles as we look at some of the things one governor did in one area of public concern—the quality of the environment.

Our role player is Governor Tom McCall of Oregon. He served two terms (1967-1975) and made the environmental issue his major concern.

### The Environmental Issue in Oregon

A value of many Americans over the years has been that *more* or *bigger* is *better:* more people, bigger cities, more houses, more factories, bigger highways and airports, more industries, etc. But in Oregon that value has been challenged. Indeed, the state has decided that more development and more people should not be invited unless there is proper planning and control.

This attitude has made Oregon a national leader in environmental protection. Other states have copied its laws. The federal government has also borrowed ideas from Oregon. Thus a state is a laboratory for testing a new program, and judging its success, before it is adopted on a big scale. Not all government programs begin in Washington. Indeed, a number of programs later adopted by the federal government

500

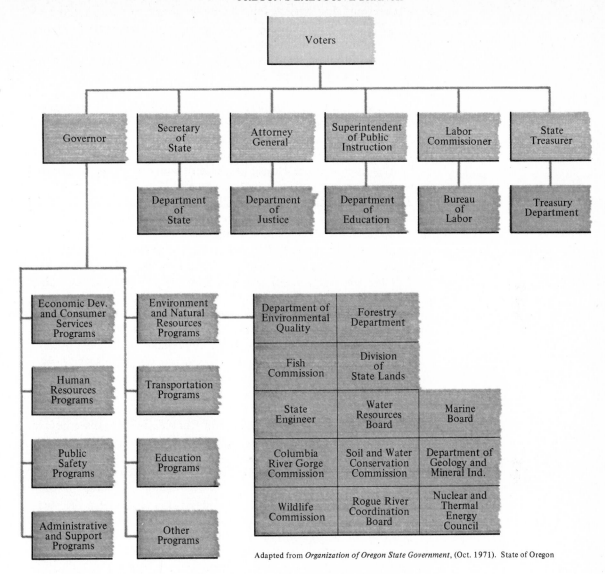

Adapted from *Organization of Oregon State Government*, (Oct. 1971). State of Oregon

first began in the states—minimum wages, for example, and child-labor laws.

Oregon made a decision that big is not necessarily better. In 1970 it had a little over two million people. Its largest city, Portland, had only about 382,000 people. Thus, it is not crowded like many other states. Also Oregon has much natural beauty. Its rugged coast has many fine beaches. Its thick forests make lumbering the chief industry. Many people were drawn to Oregon by its outdoor advantages, and these people want to keep Oregon green and beautiful.

## Oregon's Government and Political Environment

At the start we need to look at the structure in which Governor Tom McCall had to operate. Look at the chart on page 501. Notice that the governor shares executive power with five other elected officials. But the chart also shows that a variety of state programs are at least partly under the governor's control. McCall could appoint key officials in these areas.

The lower part of the chart shows the agencies in the program area concerned with the natural environment. They have played a big role in drafting and enforcing laws dealing with the environment. A key agency is the Department of Environmental Quality. It can even shut down factories until steps are taken to reduce pollutants dumped into streams or allowed into the air.

Tom McCall ran for office as a Republican. In the mid-1960s his party had two main factions, and he was the leader of one of them. This split in the party made his role of party chief less important than it might have been with a united party. Moreover, McCall was able to draw a lot of support from Democrats. Before he left office in 1975, there was even talk that he might try to get the Democratic nomination for United States Senator and run against the Republican incumbent. A former Oregon Senator, Wayne Morse, had made such a successful switch from Republican to Democrat years earlier.

In recent years in Oregon the registered Democrats have outnumbered the Republicans, but Republicans often win. Thus there is a strong independent element in the electorate. Voters in Oregon take government seriously. One sign of this is the high turnout at elections. Another is that voters have the right to propose laws by petition (the initiative). The referendum is also used a good deal. This is a device for getting on the ballot for voter approval or rejection a law passed by the legislature.

In this kind of political climate it was easy for Governor McCall to play the role of representative of all the people, or public opinion leader. One of his key political resources for handling this role was his former experience as a TV newscaster.

### Cleaning up the Willamette

In 1967 an interest group concerned with sport fishing called Oregon's Willamette River a "stinking, slimy mess." For many years it had been used as an open sewer, a place where cities and factories could dump their wastes. Chinook salmon that once had spawned in the Willamette could no longer live there. About 66 percent of the state's people lived in the Willamette Valley.

Efforts to clean up the river had started as early as 1929, when a major study of the problem was made. In 1938 the voters in a referendum approved a law that created a State Sanitary Authority to develop and enforce a program to restore and maintain the natural

502

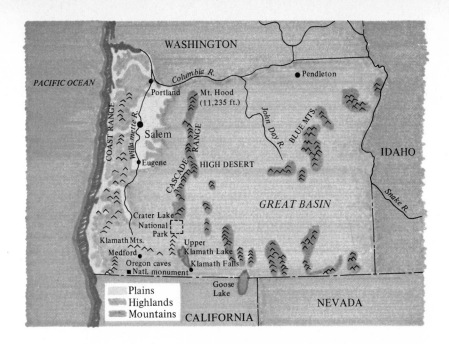

Plains
Highlands
Mountains

purity of all public waters. In the years that followed, much was done in getting cities and industries to build sewage treatment plants. But by 1965 the effort needed another big push. Both candidates for governor in 1966 chose cleanup of the Willamette River as a major theme.

Shortly after taking office the next year, Governor McCall began an attack on the problem. He appointed himself head of the State Sanitary Authority, which later became the Department of Environmental Quality (see chart). He ordered hearings to be held across the state on water quality standards. The state authority issued an enforcement plan covering every city and industry on an Oregon waterway. When he stepped down as chairman of the control board, he appointed a tough control officer to take the job. Cities and industries were put on a faster schedule for upgrading sewage treatment plants.

While engaged in enforcing existing laws, McCall got the legislature to pass a new bill. It set up a system whereby cities and industries would have to get a state permit to dump waste water into a stream— with definite limits on the amount of pollutants. The state could fine offenders or even close their facilities. The new law also directed the control board to set up time limits for meeting the higher water quality standards. And the legislature provided (a) some state aid for city sewage plants and (b) tax credits for industries that were putting in pollution controls. The state effort was linked with federal action going on at the same time.

By 1972 the change in the Willamette River was striking. That autumn it was estimated that 60,000 Chinook salmon spawned in the Willamette, whereas a few years earlier only a small number appeared. The river once again became appealing to swimmers and boaters.

### Tourism and Population Growth

In 1972 around 12 million tourists came to Oregon. This was almost six times as many people as were living in the state. Clearly, tourism is a major industry in Oregon. McCall saw no need to attract more visitors until it could be proved the state had the capacity to care for them. He therefore cut back in 1973 a budget item that called for money to pay for ads to attract tourists. He also urged people not to move to Oregon. In 1971 on a national TV program he said, "Come visit us again and again. But for Heaven's sake don't come here to live." His refrain was picked up by others. A group called the James G. Blaine Society began to publish cards such as the one below. Bumper stickers began to appear: "Oregon for Oregonians" and "Keep Oregon Green, Clean—and Lean."

A group in Oregon favoring a no-growth policy put out these cards.

504

## Land Use Planning

"Balanced growth" was a McCall theme. His thrust was to see that growth took place slowly and orderly. He said, "The population is certain to grow, and housing must be made available, but it must not be allowed to scatter willy-nilly all over the landscape."[2] In the past too much growth had taken place without planning. New housing and shopping centers had sprung up with little concern for waste disposal, noise, traffic, and scenic blight. However, building can take place in ways that protect the natural environment. Such building calls for planning. It calls for comprehensive land use planning and zoning that tells basically how the land in a city or county is to be used.

In 1969 Governor McCall joined with interested legislators to get the legislature to pass a law which required every city and county to adopt a land use plan and zoning law. When a city or county failed to take such action, the governor could take over the job. On several occasions, the McCall administration stopped a county from issuing building permits until a zoning plan was prepared.

Use of land along a scenic coast is a special problem. All too often a shore area becomes cluttered with highways, roadside stands, and billboards. McCall helped push through a state law banning billboards outside of areas zoned for commercial or industrial use. In 1970 he issued an Executive Order which had the effect of stopping road construction in the coastal zone. And he worked to get a beach law that ensures public rights to the use of ocean beaches.

## The Greenway Plan

Almost always one part of a land use plan has to do with parks and other open space. Making the banks of a cleaned-up Willamette River into a parkway caught Tom McCall's interest during the 1966 election campaign. The Dean of Students at the University of Oregon had sent such a proposal to both candidates. Right after the election, McCall appointed a task force of citizens and public officials to work out plans for a river parkway. Within six months a plan was drawn up as a bill and passed by the legislature.

The task force found that an unbroken parkway was not possible because there were towns and cities in the way. Thus the plan changed to a series of parks. The task force also saw that existing farm and marshland fit into the idea of a Greenway—the name given to the project. Thus a big part of the plan had to do with finding ways to keep land along the river and outside the cities in its present use—to stop it from being sold for commercial development. A chief device is for the state to buy scenic easements from property owners. The holder of an *easement* does not own the property but has the right to use it for one or more specific purposes.

---

2. From Tom McCall, "Oregon: Come Visit but Don't Stay," *State Government,* Vol. 46 (Summer, 1973), p. 169. Used by permission of The Council of State Governments.

McCall helped form a Greenway Committee to oversee and promote the program under the central administration of the State Highway Division, which in Oregon is in charge of state parks.

One part of the plan was for cities and counties to buy big chunks of land along the river. When such action lagged, McCall announced a new program to shift the buying of land to the state and federal level. He also supported a project to set up five major state parks bordering the river.

### The Bottle Bill

In 1971 Oregon became the first state to ban the use of "flip-top" beverage cans and to make other beverage containers returnable. McCall urged that such a law be passed. It requires a two-cent deposit and refund on bottles that can be reused by more than one bottler, and five cents on all other beer and carbonated soft-drink bottles and cans.

The chief goal of the law was to reduce litter. And a study showed that can and bottle litter dropped over 60 percent in the winter of 1972-1973 compared to a year earlier. A second benefit is a saving in mineral and energy resources through a drop in use of throwaway containers.

### Energy Conservation

Oregon faced an energy crisis a couple of months before the Arab oil embargo hit the nation in October 1973. For electric power the state depends chiefly on hydroelectric plants, and they need a steady flow of water. Drought had reduced the water flow in the summer of 1973. McCall declared a statewide energy emergency in August. He ordered all state agencies to cut their use of power. When the public failed to follow the example well enough, he dramatized the crisis by ordering that all outdoor display lights be turned off. Questions arose about his legal right to issue such an order, but he went ahead because it was important to bring results, and he believed he had the authority to act. The ban was widely obeyed. But McCall was ready to deal with firms that kept their lights on. He brought court action against violators. But just before the lawsuit was to be tried, the Public Utility Commissioner stepped in and reinforced the order. He told the power companies to shut off the power of customers who ignored the ban after due warning.

McCall tried—without success—to get a month-long Christmas recess for schools to save fuel. But he did proclaim an Energy Crisis Week for early December and got the Superintendent of Public Instruction to organize its observance in the schools.

By the time the energy crisis hit the nation, the people of Oregon had got the message to save on energy. Heavy rainfalls in late autumn eased the power crisis, but now gasoline and fuel oil were in short

supply. McCall ordered the legislature to meet in a special session in January 1974. It granted the governor emergency energy powers. He could order for limited periods changes in the public's use of energy. Earlier one of McCall's energy officials came up with an idea to deal with the long lines of cars waiting to get gas. It was to have motorists with license plates ending in an even number get gas on one day and those with an odd number the next day. The plan was put into effect within twenty-four hours, and was copied widely across the nation.

Governor Tom McCall dramatized the energy crisis by using a kerosene lamp at his desk. He also worked to preserve the beauty of Oregon's beaches.

**1.** Identify several activities that show McCall acting as (a) chief executive and (b) chief legislator.
**2.** Much of a governor's influence rests on the power to persuade others. Show that this was the case with Governor McCall.

## City Government and the Role of the Mayor

Most of the 18,000 municipalities reported in the table on page 485 are cities. The Census Bureau lists a place as *urban* if it has at least 2500 people. But how big an urban place must be to have a city government differs from state to state. Whatever its size, a city is a creature of a state. The state government can create new cities. It can tell cities what form of government they must have. Or it may provide a home-rule charter giving a city broad powers to run its own affairs.

### The Need for City Government

In contrast to rural areas, cities have many people on a rather small area of land. Most American cities of 100,000 or more people have a density of 3000 to 15,000 people per square mile. A rural county with people living on farms and in small villages may have only a few hundred people—or far less—per square mile. Rural people can often manage very well with a volunteer fire department, a small police force, and septic tanks instead of a sewer system. They have less need than their city cousins for trash collection, street cleaning, and public parks.

We saw on page 485 that most states are divided into counties to carry out tasks that are needed throughout the state: peacekeeping through a law-enforcement and court system, keeping records of land ownership, licensing marriages, registering autos, collecting taxes, and so on. But cities need to carry out additional tasks. States meet this need by setting up city governments.

As population density rises, not only does the need for extra services rise, but also the need to *manage conflict.* How people behave and use their property can affect many others where people live close together. Thus cities need special powers to deal with noise, pollution, auto parking, factory and office location, and many other matters. Cities usually have a zoning law and a planning board to say where land may be used for single-family homes, apartments, stores, offices, and factories. Cities have the right to pass ordinances (local laws) on traffic control, trash disposal, noise, upkeep of property, and many other matters. All of these efforts are attempts to get policies that will help people get along with one another in crowded places.

To carry out its jobs, a city must have a plan of government. One part of a city's charter sets forth the type of government. Three main types of city government exist in the United States They are the mayor-council plan, the council-manager plan, and the commission plan. *Table 5* shows how widely each is used.

### Mayor-Council Government

Notice that the very largest and the smallest cities tend to use the mayor-council form of government. It resembles the federal and

508

state governments with the mayor serving as chief executive and with the council serving as the city legislature.

The plan and the way it works differ from place to place. Some cities have a "strong-mayor" type. The mayor is chief executive in fact as well as in name. The mayor appoints department heads and may remove them. He or she also has a strong voice in city council affairs: making policy proposals, presenting the city budget, and having the veto power.

In a "weak-mayor" type the mayor has less power in both executive and legislative matters. Some department heads may be elected, or be appointed by the council, or be appointed by the mayor with the council's consent. The "weak mayor" does not have real control over the city administration nor a strong voice in council decisions.

Most cities are not at either extreme. The mayor is fairly strong but can be "checked" by the council. Even in some cities of the "weak-mayor" type the mayors may be very strong because they control the political party which wins most of the seats on the city council.

In addition to their other duties, mayors take part in many ceremonies and listen to countless complaints and proposals.

The usual city council has from nine to seventeen members, but Chicago's has fifty. The council's three chief duties are to pass ordinances, approve the city budget, and levy city taxes.

### The Council-Manager Plan

The council-manager plan grew rapidly after around 1915. The city is a big public-service corporation. More and more people began to say that it ought to be run like a business—with a trained manager.

**Table 5. Form of Government in Municipalities of 5000 Population and Over**

| Population Group (1970 Census) | Total Number of Cities | Mayor-Council Number | Mayor-Council Percent | Commission Number | Commission Percent | Council-Manager Number | Council-Manager Percent | Town Meeting Number | Town Meeting Percent |
|---|---|---|---|---|---|---|---|---|---|
| Over 500,000 | 26 | 21 | 80% | none | | 5 | 20% | none | |
| 250,000 to 500,000 | 30 | 13 | 43 | 3 | 10% | 14 | 47 | none | |
| 100,000 to 250,000 | 98 | 38 | 39 | 9 | 9 | 51 | 52 | none | |
| 50,000 to 100,000 | 256 | 93 | 36 | 13 | 5 | 145 | 57 | 5 | 2% |
| 25,000 to 50,000 | 520 | 170 | 33 | 39 | 8 | 293 | 56 | 18 | 3 |
| 10,000 to 25,000 | 1,360 | 585 | 43 | 55 | 4 | 620 | 46 | 100 | 7 |
| 5,000 to 10,000 | 1,550 | 881 | 57 | 43 | 3 | 530 | 34 | 96 | 6 |
| All cities over 5,000 | 3,840 | 1,801 | 47% | 162 | 4% | 1,658 | 43% | 219 | 6% |

Table 5: Based on: International City Management Association, *The Municipal Year Book 1975* (Washington, D.C.: International City Management Association, 1975), Table 3, "Inside the Year Book." Copyright © 1975, by the International City Management Association.

509

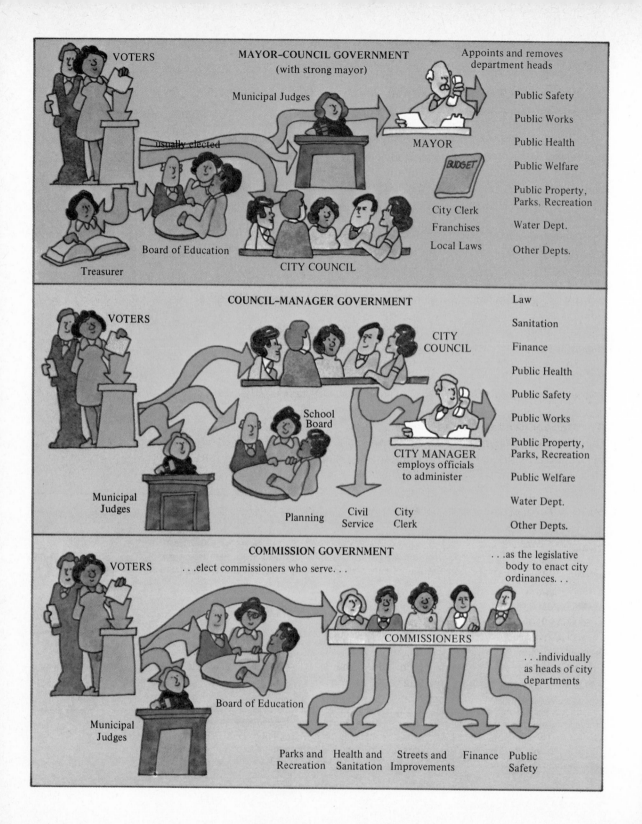

MAYOR–COUNCIL GOVERNMENT
(with strong mayor)

VOTERS

Municipal Judges

usually elected

MAYOR

Appoints and removes
department heads

Public Safety

Public Works

Public Health

Public Welfare

Public Property,
Parks, Recreation

Water Dept.

Other Depts.

BUDGET

City Clerk

Franchises

Local Laws

Board of Education

CITY COUNCIL

Treasurer

COUNCIL–MANAGER GOVERNMENT

VOTERS

CITY
COUNCIL

School
Board

CITY MANAGER
employs officials
to administer

Municipal
Judges

Planning

Civil
Service

City
Clerk

Law

Sanitation

Finance

Public Health

Public Safety

Public Works

Public Property,
Parks, Recreation

Public Welfare

Water Dept.

Other Depts.

COMMISSION GOVERNMENT

VOTERS

. . .elect commissioners who serve. . .

. . .as the legislative
body to enact city
ordinances. . .

COMMISSIONERS

. . .individually
as heads of city
departments

Board of Education

Municipal
Judges

Parks and
Recreation

Health and
Sanitation

Streets and
Improvements

Finance

Public
Safety

Under this plan the city council hires, and may dismiss, a city manager to oversee the entire city administration. When this plan works under its ideal form, the manager picks and may remove department heads, prepares the city budget, and submits other proposals to the council. The manager attends council meetings but has no vote.

The elected city council, usually five to nine members, makes general policies for the manager to carry out. It approves a budget, levies taxes, and passes ordinances. Of course, it reviews the manager's work but is expected not to meddle in it.

Generally in this plan there is a mayor to handle ceremonial tasks, to preside over the city council, and to provide some civic leadership. The mayor is either elected by the voters or chosen by the council.

The manager is supposed to stay out of "politics" and run the city as much as possible like a business. But running a city—especially a big city—is a political as well as a business enterprise. There is the constant need to balance the interests of one group against those of another. A mayor who really runs a city can make some trade-offs. The very weak mayor in the council-manager system doesn't have the tools to provide political leadership. This may be partly the reason that most of our very big cities have stayed with the mayor-council plan. Probably many small cities have kept the mayor-council plan because they need only a part-time mayor and council.

### The Commission Plan

First used in 1901, the commission plan gives both legislative and executive powers to a single body of usually five members. In theory, they share mutual responsibility for all the city's activities. In practice, however, each commissioner acts as a department head, as shown in the chart on page 510. As a legislative body, the members act much as any city council does. One member is picked by the others to serve as mayor to perform ceremonial functions and to preside at the group's legislative meetings.

The plan works quite well when the members are in basic agreement on public policy. A chief drawback is that each member tends to push for his or her own department.

### The Mayor's Role in Modern City Government

In all three types of city government one person almost always serves as mayor. In two of the plans the mayor serves chiefly as "head of state" to perform ceremonial tasks. In the mayor-council system some mayors are "strong" and others "weak." Still, a few general statements can be offered about mayors.

First, the job of mayor is one of the most challenging in America. Many of the problems of the United States seem to be exaggerated in our large cities. Crime rates are high. Costs of caring for poor people on welfare are enormous. Ever since World War II, every major city has had to cope with racial tension, urban blight, transportation problems, and a decline in city services. President Lyndon Johnson is once reported to have said, while facing problems of his own, "Things could be worse, I could be a mayor."

A second general point is that mayors very often do not have the power and resources to meet the problems. In many cases mayors cannot appoint department heads. Mayors must deal with a variety of commissions and boards (for example, school boards) that have been separately elected or appointed. Mayors and city councils usually cannot levy new taxes without the approval of the state legislature and/or the voters. In some cities, even the city budget must be approved by a state or other agency outside the city before it can be put into operation. Mayors also must compete with federal and state agencies operating in the city but not under the mayor's power. For example, decisions about public welfare programs may be largely out of a mayor's control. The city gets some welfare funds from the federal government and the state but must follow federal and state guidelines. But if the poor people in a city fail to get what they feel is due them, the mayor will often get the blame.

In the mayor-council system, mayors are seen chiefly as administrators. But their main work is not managing city agencies. The public, of course, will blame them for corruption and bad management. Yet mayors have full-time department heads to see that the city's work is being done right. The mayor's role is chiefly ceremonial and political. The ceremonial side of the office is the one most often seen on TV and in the press. The mayor gives the "keys to the city" to important visitors, dedicates new public buildings, brings "greetings" to conventions, and rides in parades. Such jobs are a large part of the mayor's schedule, but they are not the key tasks.

### The Mayor as Bargainer and Promoter

The main role of a mayor is that of bargainer and promoter. If cities are to solve their problems, the mayors must be strong leaders. This means, for example, that they must convince business firms to keep offices and stores in the city and to resist the flight to the suburbs. Each time a business moves out of the city, jobs are lost and more people appear on the welfare rolls. The mayor must bargain with city workers so that their wage demands do not boost taxes to the point that people and firms move out. The mayor must convince the leaders of poor people and racial minorities of a serious concern about their problems and of progress toward solving them. The mayor must get funds from state and federal sources to improve transportation, to provide welfare, to run schools, to improve housing, and in general to improve the quality of life in the city. The mayor must decide how strictly certain laws will be enforced. Will there be a drive against gambling? or illegal parking? or jaywalking? How strict should the city be on violations of the building code?

512

Successful mayors are skillful politicians. They balance the interests of one group against another in an effort to line up political support for projects that will move the city forward. To reach long-range goals, mayors must have the support of business in order to get the needed funds. They need the support of the media to build public approval. They must try to help labor and poor people see that the projects serve their interests. And they must hope that upper- and middle-class taxpayers will view the city as a nice place to live.

## Machine Politics

From fifty to a hundred years ago, a number of our big cities were run by political "machines." A city "boss" and his followers handed out favors and provided special services in return for votes. City bosses helped families in distress, gave out public jobs, and solved problems that people were having with the government. Money to "keep the machine oiled" came partly from taking kickbacks from people awarded city contracts. Bosses made a special point of helping recent immigrants who were crowding into the cities. Word got around the ethnic groups about where to seek help—and for whom to vote on election day. The city's political clubs also often provided social mobility to ethnic groups that found it hard to gain a foothold in the business world.

Machine politics has declined sharply in the past fifty years. The growth of the civil service has removed much of the patronage power

**It's a business like anything else—Boss Pendergast**

Fitzpatrick in the *St. Louis Post-Dispatch*

from city bosses. Federal and state welfare and social security programs have replaced handouts from the political machine. Also public reaction to the graft and corruption led to demands for reform. One reform was to put an end to partisan politics in local government, and some cities today use a nonpartisan ballot in city elections. The idea of a nonpolitical city manager was also aimed at lessening party politics in city affairs.

City government is much more honest, efficient, and democratic than it was in 1900. But the hope of the reformers that politics could be removed from city government was unrealistic. If politics is the art of influencing people to lend support to public policy and programs, then cities will continue to need skilled politicians as mayors for many years to come.

**1.** Describe the role of mayor (a) in council-manager and commission forms of city government, (b) in the "weak-mayor" system, and (c) in the "strong-mayor" system.
**2.** What are some limits on the power of even "strong" mayors in mayor-council government?
**3.** Look for examples in the news of mayors performing their role. Part of this role is to provide political leadership. Think of some examples.
**4.** Study the government of your city or a city near you.
   **a.** What form of government does it have?
   **b.** If the form is mayor-council, is the mayor "weak" or "strong"? What criteria did you use to reach your conclusion?
   **c.** Are city elections partisan or nonpartisan? Has a single party or "machine" had control of city hall for many years? If so, how do you account for this long-time control?

## Decision-Making in the Mayor's Office

Politics in the American city is like politics anywhere. People with various interests compete with each other to have the city do things that favor their interests. Some ideas for new programs start in the city agencies as the bureaucrats think of ways their work could be done better or new services could be added. Some ideas begin outside of government. Business groups, labor unions, political parties, the media, environmental groups, and others suggest new programs and changes in old ones. From time to time a taxpayers' group asks the city to start "holding the line" on ever-rising costs.

In one way or another a mayor must deal with a broad range of issues. In some cases a mayor takes the lead in some direction. In a great many cases a mayor must react to proposals put forward by others. In such cases mayors must decide whether to try to kill the idea, delay it, modify it, or promote it. Whatever is done, decision-making lies at the heart of the mayor's role.

514

## Aspects of Decision-Making

The factors that influence a mayor's decision-making are the same as those that influence other officials. As we saw on pages 303–310, these include (a) the circumstances of the decision, (b) the characteristics of the decision-maker, and (c) such other factors as rules, status relationships, public opinion, available resources, and external decision-makers. Let us look briefly at how these factors might affect decision-making in the mayor's office.

### Circumstances of the Decision

The kinds of issues and how they are resolved depend greatly on the circumstances. Prior to 1960 few cities paid a great deal of attention to racial problems. Although the proportion of urban black people to whites had been rising since World War II, blacks tended to have little influence in city government and had a rather small portion of city jobs. Blacks lived in run-down areas of the city, where services were often poorer than in other sections. Some black officials avoided civil rights issues in order to protect the small gains that blacks had made. Following the racial riots in the mid-1960s, American cities had to face up to racial problems. In many places the old ways of doing business changed. Blacks made demands and were heard. A number of blacks were elected as mayors.

Rising costs also affect decision-making. In 1975 New York City was on the edge of bankruptcy. Some other cities faced money problems that were nearly as severe. New York Mayor Abraham Beame and other mayors faced with big budget deficits had to move fast to deal with the crisis.

### Individual Characteristics of the Decision-Makers

The kind of person who is mayor will also affect decisions. Mayors might be typed as promoter, broker, or figurehead. Any mayor may fit each of these types at one time or another. But some mayors tend to be "promoters." Others tend to be "brokers." Still others tend to be "figureheads."

A "promoter" mayor is one who has a clear set of goals and programs to achieve the goals. A promoter takes pride in sponsoring new programs and is usually willing to take risks. Such a mayor has ideas about the nature of the major problems that face the city and tries to mobilize the political and financial support needed to solve them.

A "broker" mayor is content to let others take the lead in starting new programs. The broker sees the mayor's role mainly as finding ways to reduce conflict and to balance competing interests. The broker tries to get compromises that satisfy most of the contending parties. The broker's main task is to solve the political problems that result when new issues appear on the city's agenda.

A "figurehead" mayor is one who presides over the city. Such persons tend to take most interest in the ceremonial side of the mayor's

Mayor Janet Gray Hayes of San Jose is greeted by Chicago's Mayor Richard Daley. Mayor Hayes is the first woman mayor of a big American city.

role. They leave the day-to-day running of the city to department heads. Political disputes arising from issues often are settled in the city council or informally by groups operating on their own. Figureheads are not likely to start any action that might prove unpopular. Often little progress on major problems is made under such a mayor.

Which of the three types is most likely to be elected seems related to what the voters think the situation requires. If things are running smoothly, voters may turn down the candidate who calls for change, who wants "to get the city moving again." Because new programs cost money, a majority of voters may prefer to leave things as they are and choose figureheads or brokers as mayors. But there are times when people sense a crisis. Perhaps there has been a drop in the city's economy, or the crime rate is growing, or there is severe racial unrest.

In such cases doing business in the old way may not be good enough. A promoter with good ideas and the energy to carry out new programs may then win.

### Rules

What a mayor can get done depends in part on the rules that affect the office. Mayors in the mayor-council plan have more authority then those in the council-manager or commission forms of government. And "strong" mayors, of course, have more power than "weak" mayors. The city charter, the state constitution, and state and federal laws are some of the sources of rules that set boundaries within which a mayor must act.

### Status Relationships

The mayor's capacity to make decisions is influenced also by relationships with others. For example, the mayor must seek close working ties with at least a majority of the city council for proposals to win approval. Mayors also need to get along with city employees, especially department heads. Often a mayor's appointive power is limited; many employees are protected by the civil service. Thus the power that a mayor has over city employees may be limited.

### Public Opinion

Favorable public opinion is vital if a mayor's program is to produce results. The newspapers, TV, and radio in a city can help or hurt the mayor. A mayor has to try to stay in the public eye, to show concern for the city's problems, and to show interest in matters that appeal to various people. Much of the ceremonial side of the mayor's role is aimed at building favorable public support. Former New York Mayor Fiorello H. La Guardia used to ride the fire engines to fires. During one newspaper strike he read the Sunday comics to children over the radio.

### Available Resources

Any mayor is limited by available resources. The best idea cannot be put into effect without the money and the skilled people to carry it out. Perhaps the chief problem facing all big-city mayors is where to find the resources to match well-defined needs.

### External Decision-Makers

Mayors have to contend with many people they do not control. What the governor is willing to support in the state budget may make a big difference in what a mayor can get done. As a group, mayors lobby in Washington for more federal funds and the freedom to use the money to meet their city's critical needs.

Each city has powerful people outside of government who can influence a mayor's decisions. These people include bankers, realtors, factory owners, labor leaders, and political party leaders. Each controls resources that can advance or hold back a mayor's program. Their views must be heard when new programs are planned or existing programs are changed.

### It's Your Decision

Imagine that you have been elected mayor. It is your first term in that office. You have served one term on the city council. So you know the city's problems but have no experience as a city administrator. Following are some of your thoughts as you take office.

The city has about 750,000 people. It has been growing only slightly over the past ten years. The urban growth has taken place in the nearby suburbs. The kind of people who live in the city has been changing. Many of the middle class have moved to the suburbs. A growing proportion of the people in the city are black (15 percent) and Chicano (10 percent).

The main industry is steel, and the largest firm is Amalgamated Steel. The steel companies pay a big share of the city property taxes. The steel industry is also the biggest polluter. It dumps chemicals into the city's main river and spews gases into the air.

A major problem has been the decay of the downtown area. Many of the fine shops have moved to the suburbs. Some business firms have also moved their offices there. In spite of efforts to attract suburban shoppers by building expressways into the city, the downtown decay continues.

Many residents are on welfare or have low-paying jobs. Good low-cost housing is scarce. People are crowded into run-down apartments and old homes.

Crime is on the rise—another factor that has driven people out of the city. Hiring more police has not seemed to help.

While there is some evidence that organized crime is behind the drug traffic and gambling, citizens worry more about the rise in armed robbery, assault, and murder. The blacks and Chicanos complain that their people make up less than 2 percent of the police force. They argue that the police harrass blacks and Chicanos while treating whites with respect.

### Government Structure and Political Environment

The mayor in your city is fairly "strong" compared to those in many cities. It's your job to prepare the city budget. You can veto actions taken by the city council. You appoint the chief of police, the fire chief, and other department heads. The city council is made up of fifteen members elected from wards. Three blacks and twelve whites are now on the council.

A number of strong groups outside the government need your attention. One is the media. The major newspaper also owns both a TV and a radio station. The head of this media group tends to take a pro-business position on issues, but often takes a broad point of view on city problems. This media company calls for the city to take steps to reverse its downward slide. The newspaper gave you some support in the campaign and seems ready to give much more if the publisher likes your policies.

There is a growing "Poor People's Organization." It is calling for more city jobs, especially in the police and fire departments, for blacks and Chicanos. It also wants the city to start big programs in low-cost housing and in clinics where poor people can get low-cost health care. A taxpayers' association, made up mostly of white home owners, wants better police protection, cuts in the welfare program, and a drop in property taxes. The Chamber of Commerce favors more public parking garages as part of a plan to revive the downtown area. An environmental group threatens to take the city and Amalgamated Steel to court unless steps are taken to cut down pollution.

Labor unions are strong in your city. The largest is the steelworkers union. The fire and police forces are also organized. The unions tend to be most concerned about job security, good wages, and a fight on crime.

You won a close victory in a three-person race. One candidate was a black person who ran on a "Poor People's" platform. She won most of the black and Chicano votes, but received little support from whites. The third person ran on a tax-reduction, law-and-order platform. You campaigned on the theme that it was time to get the city "moving again." While you were vague about the details, you promised to pursue new programs with vigor. This image was good enough to convince a plurality of whites, blacks, and Chicanos that you were the best person for the job.

### Studying Proposals for Action

Now it is time to take action. You have asked your aides to come up with ideas. After each proposal they have listed "pro" and "con" arguments that will help you decide what you should do.

Before you begin, you should know that the budget for the city is very tight. It will be hard to balance the budget next year even if there are no new programs. Thus you must be cautious on the amount of funds you commit.

Your task is to consider each of the following proposals. Rank them in order of priority and throw out any that you think will not work. For each of the proposals that you keep (1) tell why you have ranked it as you did and (2) mention any obstacles you expect to meet in carrying it out. (3) Next, list the steps you will take to overcome the obstacles. (4) Finally, identify the factors that most influenced your decision. Remember that many of the proposals will require the support of the city council as well as of strong interest groups. You can't anger many groups and expect to succeed.

### Proposal 1

Take steps to hire more blacks and Chicanos in the police and fire departments—to a total of 25 percent of each force.

*Pro:* Blacks and Chicanos do not get a fair share of the city payroll. If something is not done, the city can expect more racial tension. Unemployment is highest among these groups; hiring Chicanos and

Copyright 1966 Herblock in the *Washington Post*

"Help!"

Hesse in the *St. Louis Globe-Democrat*

**"A thousand billion would help"**

In recent years most big cities in the United States have had to plead for money from the state and federal governments to help solve their serious problems.

blacks is one way the city can help. Having black police officers will help reduce crime in the black areas of the city and build more respect for the law.

*Con:* This action will anger the fire and police unions, perhaps leading to strikes. The city can't hire many new workers without getting rid of old ones or spending much more money for fire and police protection. Filling vacancies with blacks and Chicanos will take "too long" to suit them. Many young whites also want these jobs.

**Proposal 2**

Introduce a series of antipollution ordinances in the city council in order to cut air and water pollution by 80 percent over the next five years.

*Pro:* It will be hard to rebuild faith in the city until we do something about the general environment. We can't hold current business firms and attract new ones until the city has been cleaned up.

*Con:* Amalgamated Steel will consider this a direct attack, and it will fight back. It controls jobs. If instead of putting in anti-smoke devices it should close down some furnaces and thus cut back employment, its action would merely worsen conditions in the city. The city should look for ways to help the steel industry expand, not for ways to drive it out of town.

520

## Proposal 3

Start a massive program for low-cost housing in the poorest sections of the city.

*Pro:* Good, low-cost housing is much needed. This will win support of blacks and Chicanos more than any other program. While the program will take some money from the city budget, probably 75 percent of the initial cost can be met through federal funds.

*Con:* This is the wrong place to spend city funds. Jobs are needed first. When people have jobs, they can buy homes without city help. First, efforts should be made to rebuild the downtown area of the city in order to attract and hold business firms.

## Proposal 4

Order a stiff crackdown on crime. Get the city council to pass whatever new laws are needed to control the drug traffic, gambling, and other vice.

*Pro:* This proposal can do no harm and might do some good. It is important to try to wipe out organized crime in the city. The effort will help build your image.

*Con:* Any big effort will require a much bigger police budget. If the effort doesn't succeed, people will become even more cynical. It probably can't succeed without a "shake-up" in the police department, and you will have the police union and police bureaucracy to deal with.

## Proposal 5

Launch a major urban renewal program designed to rebuild the downtown area.

*Pro:* Without a healthy business district the city cannot survive. While the cost of the program will put a strain on the city budget, the city can likely attract some federal funds and private funds from banks and insurance companies.

*Con:* Poor people will view this as merely another rip-off by the well-to-do. City funds should be used to help those who can't help themselves. If business wants to invest in the downtown area, it can find the funds to do so.

# 18 Legislative Bodies in State and Local Government

Each state has a legislature. The name differs from one state to another (*Table 6*, page 523). But in each state this elective body reviews the state budget, appropriates funds for state programs, levies taxes, reviews the work of the executive branch, tries to resolve conflict through legislation, and proposes amendments to the state constitution.

Rule-making bodies exist also at the local level. They are not called legislatures. But a wide range of councils, boards, and commissions have the power to approve budgets, to levy taxes, and to review the activities of administrators. These local bodies also try to settle conflict by passing ordinances and writing guidelines or regulations. While their spheres of influence are quite limited when compared to state legislatures, their decisions do have much impact on our lives.

## An Overview of State Legislatures

State legislatures have much in common. Except for Nebraska, which has a unicameral (one-house) legislature, all are two-house bodies (usually called a Senate and a House of Representatives), patterned after the United States Congress. They deal with similar issues and follow similar procedures.

*Table 6* shows that state legislatures also differ. They differ in *size.* New Hampshire has 400 Representatives while Delaware has only 39 in the House. Minnesota has 67 Senators while Delaware has 19 and Nevada 20. They differ in *pay* for members. In 1972-1973 New Hampshire's lawmakers got $200 for the two-year period. California paid $53,490. They differ in *length of sessions* (nearly year round in some states to merely two months in alternate years in others). They also differ in *number of bills enacted* (California, 3263 bills in 1971-1972; Utah, 226).

### Amateurism vs. Professionalism in the State Legislature

*Table 6* gives clues to some of the issues that surround state legislatures. In the past, while these bodies were seen as important, it was thought that people should serve from a sense of civic duty and not merely to earn a salary. A farmer might serve for two or three winter months when farm work was light. It seemed out of order to pay a large salary, since the person continued to draw income from a farm or business. It was enough to pay expenses and perhaps a bit more. Most legislators did not see themselves as "professionals," as say a member of Congress does. Rather, they were "amateurs," people willing to devote some time to the state's business.

# Table 6. Some Facts about American State Legislatures

| State | Official Name | Years in Which Sessions Are Held | Length of Regular Session | Typical Pay for Two Years[3] | Number of Members H.R. | Number of Members S. | Term in Years H.R. | Term in Years S. |
|---|---|---|---|---|---|---|---|---|
| Alabama | Legislature | Odd | 36 days | $11,670 | 106 | 35 | 4 | 4 |
| Alaska | Legislature | Annual | no limit | 27,835 | 40 | 20 | 2 | 4 |
| Arizona | Legislature | Annual | no limit | 16,980 | 60 | 30 | 2 | 2 |
| Arkansas | General Assembly | Odd | 60 days | 4,380 | 100 | 35 | 2 | 4 |
| California | Legislature | Annual | no limit | 53,490 | 80 | 40 | 2 | 4 |
| Colorado | General Assembly | Annual[1] | no limit | 15,200 | 65 | 35 | 2 | 4 |
| Connecticut | General Assembly | Annual | 120/90 | 13,000 | 151 | 36 | 2 | 2 |
| Delaware | General Assembly | Annual | 6 months | 12,000 | 41 | 21 | 2 | 4 |
| Florida | Legislature | Annual | 60 days | 27,275 | 120 | 40 | 2 | 4 |
| Georgia | General Assembly | Annual | 45/40 | 17,400 | 180 | 56 | 2 | 2 |
| Hawaii | Legislature | Annual | 60 days | 28,940 | 51 | 25 | 2 | 4 |
| Idaho | Legislature | Annual | 60 days[2] | 7,218 | 70 | 35 | 2 | 2 |
| Illinois | General Assembly | Annual | no limit | 40,408 | 177 | 59 | 2 | 4 |
| Indiana | General Assembly | Annual | 61/30 | 20,120 | 100 | 50 | 2 | 4 |
| Iowa | General Assembly | Annual | no limit | 16,000 | 100 | 50 | 2 | 4 |
| Kansas | Legislature | Annual | 90/60[2] | 11,970 | 125 | 40 | 2 | 4 |
| Kentucky | General Assembly | Even | 60 days | 12,350 | 100 | 38 | 2 | 4 |
| Louisiana | Legislature | Annual[1] | 60/30 | 16,500 | 105 | 39 | 4 | 4 |
| Maine | Legislature | Odd | no limit | 4,308 | 151 | 33 | 2 | 2 |
| Maryland | General Assembly | Annual | 90 days | 22,000 | 142 | 43 | 4 | 4 |
| Massachusetts | General Court | Annual | no limit | 36,502 | 240 | 40 | 2 | 2 |
| Michigan | Legislature | Annual | no limit | 34,000 | 110 | 38 | 2 | 4 |
| Minnesota | Legislature | Odd | 120 days | 21,420 | 134 | 67 | 2 | 4 |
| Mississippi | Legislature | Annual | no limit | 14,740 | 122 | 52 | 4 | 4 |
| Missouri | General Assembly | Annual | 6 months | 16,800 | 163 | 34 | 2 | 4 |
| Montana | Legislative Assembly | Annual | 60 days | 11,020 | 100 | 50 | 2 | 4 |
| Nebraska | Legislature | Annual | 90/60 | 9,600 | — | 49 | — | 4 |
| Nevada | Legislature | Odd | 60 days[2] | 6,300 | 40 | 20 | 2 | 4 |
| New Hampshire | General Court | Odd | 6 months[2] | 200 | 400 | 24 | 2 | 2 |
| New Jersey | Legislature | Annual | no limit | 20,000 | 80 | 40 | 2 | 4 |
| New Mexico | Legislature | Annual[1] | 60/30 | 3,240 | 70 | 42 | 2 | 4 |
| New York | Legislature | Annual | no limit | 47,000 | 150 | 60 | 2 | 2 |
| North Carolina | General Assembly | Odd | no limit | 9,525 | 120 | 50 | 2 | 2 |
| North Dakota | Legislative Assembly | Odd | 60 days | 4,150 | 102 | 51 | 2 | 4 |
| Ohio | General Assembly | Annual | no limit | 35,000 | 99 | 33 | 2 | 4 |
| Oklahoma | Legislature | Annual | 90 days | 18,960 | 101 | 48 | 2 | 4 |
| Oregon | Legislative Assembly | Odd | no limit | 15,105 | 60 | 30 | 2 | 4 |
| Pennsylvania | General Assembly | Annual | no limit | 31,200 | 203 | 50 | 2 | 4 |
| Rhode Island | General Assembly | Annual | 60 days[2] | 600 | 100 | 50 | 2 | 2 |
| South Carolina | General Assembly | Annual | no limit | 14,300 | 124 | 46 | 2 | 2 |
| South Dakota | Legislature | Annual | 45/30 | 5,000 | 70 | 35 | 2 | 2 |
| Tennessee | General Assembly | Odd | 90 days[2] | 18,050 | 99 | 33 | 2 | 4 |
| Texas | Legislature | Odd | 140 days | 11,040 | 150 | 31 | 2 | 4 |
| Utah | Legislature | Annual | 60/20 | 3,200 | 75 | 29 | 2 | 4 |
| Vermont | General Assembly | Odd | no limit | 5,500 | 150 | 30 | 2 | 2 |
| Virginia | General Assembly | Annual | 60/30 | 14,190 | 100 | 40 | 2 | 4 |
| Washington | Legislature | Odd | 60 days | 13,200 | 98 | 49 | 2 | 4 |
| West Virginia | Legislature | Annual | 60 days | 7,830 | 100 | 34 | 2 | 4 |
| Wisconsin | Legislature | Annual | no limit | 31,362 | 99 | 33 | 2 | 4 |
| Wyoming | Legislature | Annual | 40/20 | 1,940 | 62 | 30 | 2 | 4 |

[1]One annual session (usually even years) devoted solely to state budget.

[2]Daily expense allowance (or other pay) stops, but session may continue.

[3]Salary and allowances for typical two-year period.

Table 6: *The Book of the States*, 1974–75. Used by permission of The Council of State Governments.

The notion of "citizen-legislators" had an effect on how legislatures were organized and how their business was managed. Since members were not expected to spend much time in the state capital, they wouldn't need an office or staff. Even today, in a majority of cases, members have only a desk on the House or Senate floor to call their own. If they wish to meet a constituent or conduct business, they must do so at this desk, or in the lobby, or in a coffee shop. Space for committee rooms is also in short supply.

Unlike members of Congress, most state legislators lack personal aides to conduct research on bills, to keep them informed of what is taking place in committees, to prepare speeches, and to write bills. Thus the members have to depend very much on bureaucratic agencies and lobbyists for information and help.

While short sessions enable some busy people to serve who might otherwise fail to do so, the short sessions have some bad effects on the legislative process. Much work occurs in committees. When sessions are short, committees are faced with much more work than they can handle responsibly. The result is usually a logjam of bills near the end of the session. This leads to giving bills only slight attention on the floor before passage.

The lack of professionalism also helps to explain the high turnover among state legislators. In 1971-1972 the average turnover for both House and Senate in all of the legislatures combined was about 40 percent. This means that each two years there is a high proportion of people serving their first terms and trying to learn their way.

**Role of the Legislator**

Numerous studies have pointed out the various roles that state legislators assume. One writer divides legislators into leaders, work horses, and spectators. The *leaders* include the presiding officer (typically Speaker of the House and President of the Senate), a majority and a minority floor leader, heads of committees, and often a steering committee made up of the leadership.

The Speaker is elected by a vote of the House, but the person picked in a meeting of members of the majority party is bound to win. The Speaker can usually appoint committee heads, assign members to committees, and decide which bills will go to each committee. Thus the Speaker has power to reward or punish members and to decide which bills will get a favorable hearing. In the Senate, the presiding officer may have similar power.

In each legislature there are *work horses,* people who know the rules and who take on the job of preparing bills. Often they are experts on certain types of bills—taxes, budget, highways, or education. The leaders rely on the work horses very much.

Another group consists of *spectators.* Usually new members, they may not know what to do. They are often passed over by the leaders.

524

They carry little weight with other members. They look and listen, try to find out what is going on, and search for clues on how they should vote.

A number of norms guide the conduct of legislators. Many of these are similar to those we found in Congress: courtesy, getting along with the leaders, and so on (pages 346-354). Old members are likely to give new legislators such advice as the following:

• If all the legislators from a certain city or county support a "local bill" that affects only their area of the state, we go along and don't oppose them.

• If the leaders ask "unanimous consent for the suspension of the rules," don't put up an objection. Once in a while we have to take up a bill that is not on the calendar and pass it without all the formalities.

• Don't make a pest of yourself by talking too much, or fighting too hard, or introducing too many bills or amendments.

• Respect the system: seniority, committee assignments, and so on.

• Be willing to compromise.

• Keep your word, and notify in advance if you can't keep a commitment.

• If the author of a bill wants to make changes, accept the amendments.

A committee of the Massachusetts state legislature holds a public hearing before an overflow crowd in Boston.

Members that stray too far from the norms will be punished in various ways. Their own bills will be bottled up in the committees, or loaded with amendments, or defeated outright. The nonconformists

*Right:* Governor Jimmy
Carter addresses a joint
session of the Georgia
legislature in 1971.
*Below:* Stacks of bills are
on the shelves in a wing of
the New York Assembly in
the capitol at Albany.
*Bottom right:* The
Wisconsin legislature meets
for business.

may get the poorest committee assignments and lose out on other courtesies.

### State Legislatures Are Changing

The kind of amateurism described earlier is giving way to greater professionalism. More and more states are making the job of legislator a full-time one. They are starting to pay the salaries and to provide the office and staff support that will attract full-time professionals.

One reason for the change is that today's problems are more complex than before. Modern legislatures not only have traditional rural concerns but must face complex urban problems as well—and the conflicts that often arise between rural and urban interests.

There are signs that members are growing tired of merely responding to issues presented to them by the governor, by bureaucrats, by the federal government, and by special interests. More and more state legislatures are starting to employ staff. The staff can dig up facts and figures that will enable legislators to take a more critical look at budget requests and to introduce bills of their own without prompting from others.

### How a Bill Becomes a Law: Formal Steps

The formal steps by which a bill becomes a law are much the same from state to state and in Congress.

#### Introduction and Referral

A member files the bill. The clerk assigns it a number and announces the title. This reading of the title gives the bill its *first reading.* The bill then goes to a committee for study.

#### Committee Action

In a few states every bill must be given a public hearing. But the general rule is to hold hearings for only the major bills. Bills are discussed in committee sessions. Changes are made, and at times a bill is rewritten. Bills on the same topic may be combined.

In about a third of the states every bill must be reported back to the floor. In other states a committee may kill a bill (by pigeonholing). Only a bill with a favorable committee report has any real chance.

#### Floor Action

A bill reported by a committee is placed on a *calendar,* a list of bills arranged in the order in which they have been reported. In some states a Rules Committee tells when a bill will come up for debate. But usually bills come up in their calendar order.

When a bill comes up for debate and vote, it is given its *second reading.* If there is to be floor debate, it will occur at this time. Amendments may be allowed from the floor. Sometimes a bill is "stripped." Perhaps a bill failed in committee. Its sponsors then offer their defeated bill as an amendment to a bill that is on the floor for debate. Once in a while, all that is left of the original bill is the number assigned when it was introduced. When debate ends, a vote is taken on whether to advance the bill to *third reading.* This is the crucial vote.

When a bill comes up for third reading, the clerk again reads it by title and a final vote is taken. Usually there must be a full calendar day between the second and third readings.

### Conference Committee

A bill passed by one house is sent to the other chamber, where it goes through the steps listed above. If the second house makes any changes and the first house does not accept them, the differences must be worked out in a *conference committee.* It usually consists of two or three members from each chamber. If the conferees can agree, the amended bill goes to each house for passage.

### Governor's Action

In all but one state an enacted bill goes to the governor to sign into law or to veto. Usually the legislature has the right to override a veto by a two-thirds majority of each house.

### Informal Processes in Legislation

The steps noted above are correct but incomplete. As we learned in studying Congress, to understand the legislative process we need to know more than the formal steps. Pressures from voters, from leaders in and out of the legislature, and from the governor are part of the process but do not appear in the formal steps.

What are some other measures each of these groups might support or oppose? Can you think of other state lobbying groups?

SOME IMPORTANT STATE LOBBYING GROUPS

Very important is the role of lobbies, or interest groups. While their influence is felt in Washington, it may even be greater in state capitals. Crippled by lack of time and staff, legislators often depend on lobbyists for facts and figures on bills. At times, lobbyists even draft bills, and they provide suggestions for amending bills. The following case study shows how the formal rules and the informal processes combine to produce a new law.

## The Medical Malpractice Act: A Case Study in Legislative Action

This case is a dramatic example of the power of lobbies in the state legislature. As you read the case, consider the following questions:

1. Who were the "authors" of the medical malpractice bill?
2. What role did the typical legislator play in drawing up this bill?
3. Which groups seemed to gain the most from the legislation?
4. What key activities occurred outside the "formal steps" of bill passage outlined in the preceding lesson?
5. What are your feelings about the role of lobbyists in the state legislature? What positive contributions can they make? What are the possible negative results of their influence?

**The Malpractice Insurance Issue.** In 1975, Americans became familiar with a new term—medical malpractice insurance. It is carried by doctors and other people or institutions providing health care. The insurance is used to pay persons who claim—usually in court suits—that they were harmed by the mistakes or carelessness of someone in the health-care field. Of course, doctors do sometimes err. And patients should have a right to collect damages for carelessness or simply poor skill. Doctors buy malpractice insurance in order to be protected in the event a court suit is lodged against them.

In the past, few patients sued their doctors, and the amount of damages awarded tended to be small—a few thousand dollars. In the early 1970s, however, the number of suits and the amount of damages awarded began to grow. Insurance companies had to raise their rates. Some companies began to drop this part of their business, leaving doctors with no insurance. In New York City, California, Ohio, and elsewhere doctors went on strike. They refused to perform surgery unless something was done to protect them.

One of government's basic jobs is to see that members of the society can obtain vital goods and services. If such a basic need as medical care is in danger of being shut off, public officials can't afford to stand by and hope the problem will go away.

**The Indiana Legislature Acts on the Problem.** In 1975 the Indiana legislature passed a landmark bill in the field of medical malpractice insurance. The law has several chief provisions. (1) It put a $500,000 ceiling on malpractice awards. While this is a very large amount, it is far below what some juries have awarded. (2) It set a ceiling of $100,000 as the maximum sum that any one insurance company would have to meet on a single claim. (3) It created a state-operated trust fund to handle claims that go over $100,000. (4) It set a limit on lawyers' fees for court suits on medical malpractice. (5) It created a panel of doctors, plus a nonvoting lawyer, to screen out "nuisance suits" in order to cut down on the number of malpractice cases taken to court.

The push by the health-care organizations to get a malpractice law may have been the most expensive and well-run lobbying effort in Indiana's history.[1] Estimates as high as $500,000 have been cited. The Indiana State Medical Association spent the most. But it was joined by the state associations of chiropractors; eye, ear, nose, and throat doctors; and nurses. The lobbyists used well-known methods: (1) Legislators were taken to lunch. (2) Expert witnesses were brought before legislative committees. (3) Heavy phone and mail campaigns were used. (4) Lobbyists for other interests were asked to use their influence.

The lobbying was out in the open with no sign of illegal or unethical methods. What took place is merely an example of a well-run campaign such as occurs in any of the fifty state legislatures.

**Getting the Malpractice Bill Underway.** On February 4, 1975, State Representative Chester Dobis dropped a malpractice insurance bill in the "hopper" on the clerk's desk in the Indiana House of Representatives. But it wasn't his handiwork. It was the thirteenth draft of a bill that had been hammered out by, among others, attorney Fred Stewart, member of an Indianapolis law firm that did legal work for the Indiana State Medical Association.

At least two other members of the same law firm played a big role. Richard Guthrie guided the bill through the legislature. He knew the ropes, for he had once served as Speaker of the House. Fred Garver, who had served as an aide to a former governor, served in many ways. It was Garver who stopped Dobis in the State House lobby in mid-January to find out if he would introduce the bill. It wasn't just a chance meeting. Garver and Dobis, both Democrats, were friends. And Dobis had close ties with a fellow Democratic legislator from Lake County—Phillip Bainbridge, Speaker of the House.

Two other House members—one a Republican and the other a Democrat—agreed to co-sponsor the bill. More co-sponsors joined later. It was part of the Guthrie-Garver plan for the original sponsors to be two members of the majority party in the House and one member of the minority. Bipartisan support was vital.

Editorial cartoon by Don Hesse. Copyright © St. Louis Globe-Democrat. Reprinted with permission of Los Angeles Times Syndicate.

---

1. The account that follows draws heavily on a copyrighted story by L. D. Seits, a reporter for *The Evansville Press*, a Scripps-Howard newspaper. Used by permission.

The next step was to get the bill sent to a friendly committee. The lobbyists heard that Speaker Bainbridge had the Judiciary Committee in mind. But this committee—made up of lawyers—would be a threat to the bill. One of its key provisions was to take malpractice claims out of the courts, and some lawyers earn a good deal of income from handling such lawsuits. Guthrie and Garver were able to get the Speaker to assign the bill to the Committee on Labor and the Economy, headed by another Lake County Democrat.

With the bill in the Labor committee, Guthrie saw the need to line up the support of labor union leaders to get the committee to hold a hearing on the bill. He got in touch with the head of the state AFL-CIO and hinted that organized labor might get blamed if the bill failed to get out of the Labor committee. The union chief talked to the Speaker, and in a few days the committee called for a public hearing on the bill.

**Passage in the House and Trouble in the Senate.** Soon committee members began to hear public testimony from medical and insurance experts on why the law was needed and how it was expected to work. Experts also talked with committee members in private.

On March 5 the committee sent the bill back to the House with a favorable report. Six days later the House passed the bill 81 to 16.

Republicans held a majority in the Senate. When the bill went to the Senate, two Republicans and one Democrat were lined up as sponsors. One Republican sponsor was seen as having close ties with the top GOP leader in the Senate, President pro tem Phillip Gutman. The other Republican sponsor was a key member of the Judiciary Committee to which the bill was assigned. The third sponsor was another Lake County Democrat, attorney Adam Benjamin, Jr. One of his brothers was a physician, and Benjamin said that he had an open mind on the bill.

President pro tem Gutman's support was vital. But he said that he hadn't heard that the malpractice issue was much of a problem. So the lobby went to work. The bill's promoters started a flood of mail and phone calls to the legislators. Mail came from ordinary citizens as well as from doctors. On one day an estimated 5000 pieces of mail on the issue came to the Statehouse. Gutman himself got so many messages that he passed the word to "call 'em off."

One of the marvels of the campaign was the ability of the medical lobby to get the public to respond. Ads were run in newspapers. In their monthly bills to patients, doctors sent letters hinting that they might have to close up shop if the bill didn't pass. Booklets in doctors' offices urged people to write or call their legislators.

The House bill still had the provision that the courts would not handle malpractice claims. This was a signal to Warren Spangle, lobbyist for the Trial Lawyers Association, to go into action to protect the interests of lawyers.

# WHAT NOW?

**INDIANA STATE MEDICAL ASSOCIATION**
3935 NORTH MERIDIAN STREET
INDIANAPOLIS, IND. 46208

The medical profession in Indiana is currently faced with a serious problem which affects its capability of serving you, the patient. The problem is fourfold:

1. More and more physicians in Indiana cannot get liability insurance. This is the insurance which covers medical care lawsuits.

2. Those who are able to get it are compelled to pay premiums which have skyrocketed from $600 annually to as high as $25,000 a year, and no physician can afford the cost to practice without insurance.

3. Even physicians who have not been threatened with a lawsuit are unable to have their insurance policies renewed.

4. New physicians are unable to obtain liability insurance.

Now for you, the patient, this means the following:

1. Some surgeries and emergency rooms in your local hospitals could be closed down since surgeons do not want to operate without this coverage.

2. The cost of the high premiums will be passed on to you from those doctors who can afford the insurance and can get it.

3. The cost of your medical care will increase, additionally, because your physician, to protect himself against suit, will have to ask you to submit to more exhaustive examinations—some of which he would not ordinarily ask for.

4. Your community may lose doctors because they will move to other states where they can get adequate coverage.

5. Some physicians will retire early from practice rather than attempt to continue practice with no insurance.

6. Your community will be unable to attract new physicians because they cannot afford or cannot obtain the insurance.

In short, these and other factors are going to affect you, your care and treatment, and the availability of that care.

As your doctor, I am asking that you call or write to your representatives in the Indiana General Assembly, urging they vote in favor of the "Patient's Compensation Board Bill" which is being introduced to solve the problems mentioned above.

The bill will help guarantee patients deserving of compensation a fair amount and will keep your doctor practicing.

**A Revised Bill Becomes Law.** Eight days after getting the bill, the Senate Judiciary Committee held a five-hour public hearing. This was the start of five days of almost non-stop work by the bill's Democratic sponsor in the Senate, Adam Benjamin. The bill was revised to make it acceptable to lawyers by allowing court handling of malpractice claims and by other changes. Benjamin met with leaders of the two political parties and of interest groups: doctors, nurses, other health-care specialists, hospitals, trial lawyers, and insurance companies.

Other revisions of the bill were made and checked out with the parties concerned. Finally at 4 P.M. on Sunday, March 23, Benjamin began a 12-hour final drafting session with four other key senators. On Monday they took the revised bill to the Senate committee, where it was approved.

The Senate passed the bill, and the House accepted the Senate's changes a week later. Governor Otis Bowen, himself a physician, signed it into law.

## Legislative Bodies in Local Governments

Almost every unit of local government has some policy-making body that acts in a way as a legislature. It may set tax rates and vote on budgets. It may decide where public projects—schools, roads, dams, and the like—will be located. It may have power to pass ordinances (local laws) or make other rules.

The rule-making power of local councils and boards tends to be quite limited, since local units are creatures of the state. A school board makes policy for the schools of its district. But the local board's rules and policies must be in line with those set forth in state law and in the rules made by the state department of education. Counties and townships, we saw in chapter 16, were set up chiefly to carry out state law. Their councils or boards often do little except deal with the annual budget.

On the other hand, city councils tend to have more rule-making power than do other local bodies. Cities are set up to provide people with extra services beyond those set up throughout the state. City councils also have fairly broad power to regulate traffic, parking, land use, building construction, business hours, and a host of other things.

The federal and state constitutions provide for a fairly clear separation of executive and legislative powers. Each branch can check the other, but the lines of authority are pretty clear. Separation of powers does not always exist at the local level. We saw in chapter 17, for example, that in the commission form of city government the same five or seven people both make and carry out the law. In the weak-mayor system the city council tends to exercise quite a lot of power in city administration. It is not uncommon to find other "local legislatures"—policy-making bodies—that spend much time carrying out policy rather than just making it.

Let us look at a few broad classes of local policy-making bodies to see the kinds of decisions they make.

## City Councils

City councils come in a variety of sizes, but five to nine members are most common. In some places each member represents one section of the city (a ward). But the trend today is for at-large elections in which all the voters elect the entire slate.

People who feel that their interests might be overlooked in the council tend to favor the ward plan. They feel that they then have "our representative who will listen to us." Those who support at-large elections say that members chosen by all the voters will be more apt to put citywide interests above those of neighborhoods.

Trying to please voters by doing special favors is seen by many council members as one of the chief parts of their role. This is the *ombudsman* role that we saw members of Congress performing (page 338). It seems to be even more important at the local level. Here are some of the calls for help that council members get:
• Get us a stop light at the corner of James and Lilly streets.
• Do something about the late-night noise and rowdy behavior at Joe's Tavern.
 • The trash collector keeps missing our street.
 • The owner of our building won't make needed repairs.

The list could easily fill two pages. And each complaint could be made directly to a city department. Many compaints do go there first. But when a bureaucrat gives the caller the run-around or makes a promise that isn't kept, why wouldn't a person turn to a council member!

Such complaints and efforts to do something about them tend to get city councils off their chief job of making policy. And there are many policy decisions that have to be made. Many of the very big ones come in dealing with the annual budget. What programs must be cut back in order to make ends meet? What vital new services must the city offer? Can we lift any rates on existing taxes? What new taxes will the state let us levy? The mayor or city manager will give the council some answers to such questions, but the council must make the final decisions.

Another big policy area is land use. The next lesson shows a city council dealing with a request to change part of a "residential zone" to a "business zone." Granting licenses, franchises, and other permits to engage in business is often another council concern.

Many policy decisions are made by passing ordinances, or local laws. They deal with such matters as traffic, parking, littering, no-smoking rules, trash disposal, and many other public health and safety concerns.

## County Boards and Councils

In a few places, like Indianapolis, the city boundaries have been moved out to take in an entire county and the area has a combined city-county government. In some other densely populated counties the state has given the county the right to make many local laws and provide city-like services: fire protection, trash collection, and so on. In such cases the county board or council acts much like a city council.

The government of rural counties differs from state to state, but look again at a typical plan in the diagram on page 487. Our concern here is with the county board. It goes by various names: board of supervisors, county commissioners, fiscal court, and others. Some states have large county boards—fifteen members and up. Others have small boards of three to seven members. The large board often tries to handle its work by splitting up into committees to oversee and recommend policy in a particular area.

Whether large or small, the county board tends to perform both legislative and executive functions. It must handle all the work that is not in the hands of the other elected officials. The board, of course, can set up departments to carry out such duties as upkeep of roads. But the board usually takes an active part in administration.

The legislative part of a board member's role tends to be much more limited than that of a city council member. For the most part, counties simply administer state laws. Of course, there is the job of

drawing up and voting on the county budget. There are decisions on where roads will be built or improved, drainage ditches dug, and the like. As we saw in chapter 17, some states now permit or require counties to work out land use plans. Thus the county board may often have to deal with requests for zoning changes. Often a state law will not go into great detail but rather provide guidelines to local officials. Thus the county board will have some legislative work to do in spelling out the details.

Members of the city council of Pleasantville, New York, discuss business.

### District Boards and Commissions

Chapter 16 describes the government of school districts and other special districts (page 491). The boards and commissions set up to handle the special activity (schools, fire protection, parks, or whatever) often try to limit their role to that of policy-makers. In this case they hire an expert to administer the program. In other cases one or all of the board members try to run the program as well as to make policy.

Like every other local legislature, the district board must approve a budget. Often it must borrow money—to buy land, buildings, and equipment. In some places a state or county agency—or the district voters directly—must approve the financial policies of the district board. Usually a district board will also have power to make rules within the guidelines set down by state law. A school board, for example, may decide whether and where students may smoke on school property. A park board will make rules for use of parks. A district sanitation board may make rules on trash collection.

1. List the local legislatures that represent you and your family.
2. Try to obtain a meeting agenda, or news items about a meeting, of one or more of your local legislative bodies.
   a. What policy issues do the items suggest?
   b. What decisions, if any were made?
   c. A policy, or political, issue involves a conflict that needs to be resolved. Identify some conflicts in the items you collected.
   d. Do any of the items suggest that the legislative body was trying to carry out an executive function? Explain.
3. Below are two conflicting values about the role of local legislators:

   (1) They should be willing and active in helping citizens settle their complaints with administrators.

   (2) They should deal only with broad policies, not individual complaints. And one policy should be to set up a complaint-handling service open to all citizens.

   a. Which value do you tend to favor? Why?
   b. Can you state other values dealing with the issue of legislators as ombudsmen?

## The Case of the Crowded Corral

In at least one respect, city council members have harder decisions to make than do members of Congress and state legislatures. Council members must often come face to face with people who will be closely affected by council decisions. Members may live in the same neighborhood with the people after the decision is made.

The case which follows describes an issue handled by the city council of Beloit, Wisconsin, in 1959.[2] The council was asked to change the zoning of some land from "Residential" to "Business." The kind of issue and the way it was resolved is fairly typical of city councils across the nation.

---

2. This case study draws heavily on one by the same name that appears in Warner E. Mills, Jr. and Harry R. Davis, *Small City Government: Seven Cases in Decision Making* (New York: Random House, © Copyright, 1962, by Random House, Inc.). Used by permission.

536

Beloit, a city of 33,000 people in 1959, is near the Illinois-Wisconsin border. It is a manufacturing town and the home of Beloit College.

Beloit has a manager-council form of government. Voters choose seven council members for two-year terms of office. Three are elected one year and four the next in order always to have some members who know what has been going on. It meets nearly every week.

**A Zoning Issue Faces the Council.** "The Corral" in 1959 was a popular restaurant located in a chiefly residential section of Beloit (see map). Michael Bonafede, the owner, began the restaurant in what had been a small tavern. Over time, Mike made it into the most popular eating place in the city, and therein lay his problem. As the place grew more popular, it became harder for his patrons to find places to park.

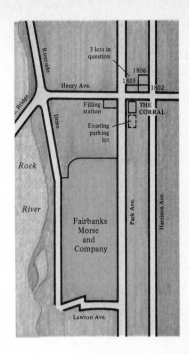

"The Corral" was at the corner of two busy streets, Henry Avenue and Park Avenue. On-street parking near the restaurant was, of course, very limited. But the parking problem worsened in 1958. Concern for the growing number of auto accidents in this area led the city to limit parking to one side of the street within a block of the Park-Henry intersection.

Mike had one parking lot just south of his business. But it was shared with a bowling alley and could not meet his needs. When the city in 1958 cut back the nearby on-street parking space, Mike saw that he would need one or two more parking lots. Some members of the city council had urged him to try this remedy. And the council for some time had been trying to get business people to develop off-street parking lots. Thus Mike had every reason to feel that his effort to arrange off-street parking would have council support.

After some shopping around, Mike was able to get options to buy lots 1802 and 1806 on Harrison Avenue and 1803 on Park Avenue. The lots were not ideal. They were small and expensive. Two lots had houses that would have to be torn down or moved. Still, it seemed to Mike that making these into parking lots would be the best solution to his problem.

All of the property in Beloit is zoned, or classified, according to how it can be used. Since these lots were zoned then as "Residential," they couldn't be used for business parking without a zoning change. A change in zoning had to have the approval of the city council.

Mike hired George Blakely, a lawyer, to draw up a rezoning petition for each of the lots. Blakely suggested that Mike seek a "Business" classification. It would permit him to use the lots for parking, but later he could use or sell them for other business purposes.

**The City Plan Commission Votes on the Issue.** The first step was to submit the petitions to the City Plan Commission. It was an advisory body to the city council. Its members were the city manager, city engineer, one council member, and four citizens chosen by the council and the manager. The Plan Commission receives zoning petitions, holds

The New Orleans City
Planning Commission
listens to a proposal.

hearings, and makes recommendations to the Council; but its decisions
are not binding.

When word of Mike's petitions got out, residents in the area became
worried. Business had been creeping into this residential neighborhood
over several years. It seemed time to call a halt. Some people said
that the parking lots would be noisy at night. As a result, the area
would become a less desirable place to live and the homes would
decline in value.

The Plan Commission held its hearing on May 6. It listened to
both sides of the argument and voted to deny Mike's petition. One
of those voting against it was Herman Schultz, the council member
of the Plan Commission. In its report to the city council, the Plan
Commission recommended that the council restore on-street parking
to both sides of Park and Henry in order to help relieve the problem.

**The City Council Makes a Decision.** On May 18 the city council
received Mike's petition and the Plan Commission's recommendation.
A number of people showed up to speak against the petition. But
the council president told the audience that no action could be taken

538

until a notice of public hearing had been published. The hearing was set for June 1, and the traffic department was asked to look into the question of restoring parking to both sides of Park and Henry streets.

After the official meeting on May 18, the council members stayed late to talk. The zoning issue came up again. All except Schultz felt that they had to help Mike. After all, they had urged him and others to seek off-street parking. Schultz said that he would have to vote against the petition for two reasons: (a) He had already taken a stand in the Plan Commission. (b) A close friend owned 1807 Park Avenue.

Between May 18 and June 1 some steps were taken. One of Blakely's partners was a close friend of one of the council members and took this member on a ride in the neighborhood around "The Corral." He pointed out the crowded parking conditions. In the meantime, a letter protesting the zoning change was signed by home owners in the neighborhood and was sent to the council.

On May 28 the council met as the Board of Public Works. They heard a report from the traffic department advising against a change in the parking rules near the corner of Park and Henry.

On June 1 the council met in regular session. Blakely spoke first and was followed by property owners from the neighborhood. Council members asked Blakely why Mike had asked for a "Business" zone rather than merely "Parking." Lots zoned as "Parking" would go back to residential when parking was no longer needed. Blakely replied that "Parking" would be acceptable, if necessary. But Mike would prefer "Business."

Finally, the time had come to vote. Council President Kevin Keenan moved that Mike's petition to rezone 1806 Harrison be tabled—and thereby defeated. Blakely made a feeble protest, but he seemed to be aware of what had been planned. Keenan's motion passed unanimously. Then Keenan suggested to Blakely that the petitions be amended to ask for a "Parking" classification instead of "Business." Blakely quickly agreed to the change. Council member Joseph Falco then moved that the rezoning petitions for "Parking" for all three lots be approved. All council members exept Schultz voted to approve. Mike was given the right to build the parking lots as he had hoped.

1. What informal processes were involved in influencing the council's decision?
2. Did the council rely on any technical information?
3. What were the contending interests that the council had to weigh?
4. Do you think the council's decision was fair? Was it in the public interest?

# 19 Courts in State and Local Government

Citizen contact with courts differs from that with other agencies. People are usually "taken to court" by the government or by someone seeking to settle a dispute. And the procedures that courts use differ from those used by mayors, governors, legislatures, and city councils. Still, courts provide another avenue for settling disputes. And the decisions that courts make can have profound effects on our lives.

## Organization of Courts within a State

All states have three general levels of courts as shown in the chart on page 541. Court systems vary from state to state. Also courts with similar tasks operate under different names from state to state.

### State Appellate Courts

Each state has one supreme court. It is often called by other names, such as Supreme Court of Errors, Supreme Judicial Court, Supreme Court of Appeals, and Court of Appeals. By whatever name, this is the highest court in each state. Unless a federal law or the United States Constitution is involved, this is the "last court of appeals." Like the United States Supreme Court there is more than one justice— the number varies from three to nine. Mainly it reviews decisions that have been appealed from lower courts. The procedures are similar to those used by the United States Supreme Court. The judges do not hold a trial. They review the record of trial in the lower court, listen to arguments by the attorneys for the two sides, then retire to make their decision. Their decisions provide precedents in the state for similar cases in the future.

The number of cases that are appealed from lower state courts is often very large. Therefore, about half of the states have created one or more intermediate appellate courts. They are called by such names as appellate court, court of appeals, appellate division of supreme court, and superior court. Each court has three or more judges. They act on cases in the same way as supreme court judges do.

What kinds of cases come to the state appellate courts? Some people make an appeal because they think a state or local law is unconstitutional. The *Murray* case on religious exercises in the schools (pages 384-390) was heard by the highest court in Maryland before going to the United States Supreme Court. You recall that Mrs. Murray claimed that the school board rule (a kind of local law) did not agree with the United States Constitution. Other cases have to do with conflicts between state or local laws and the state constitution.

## STATE COURT STRUCTURE

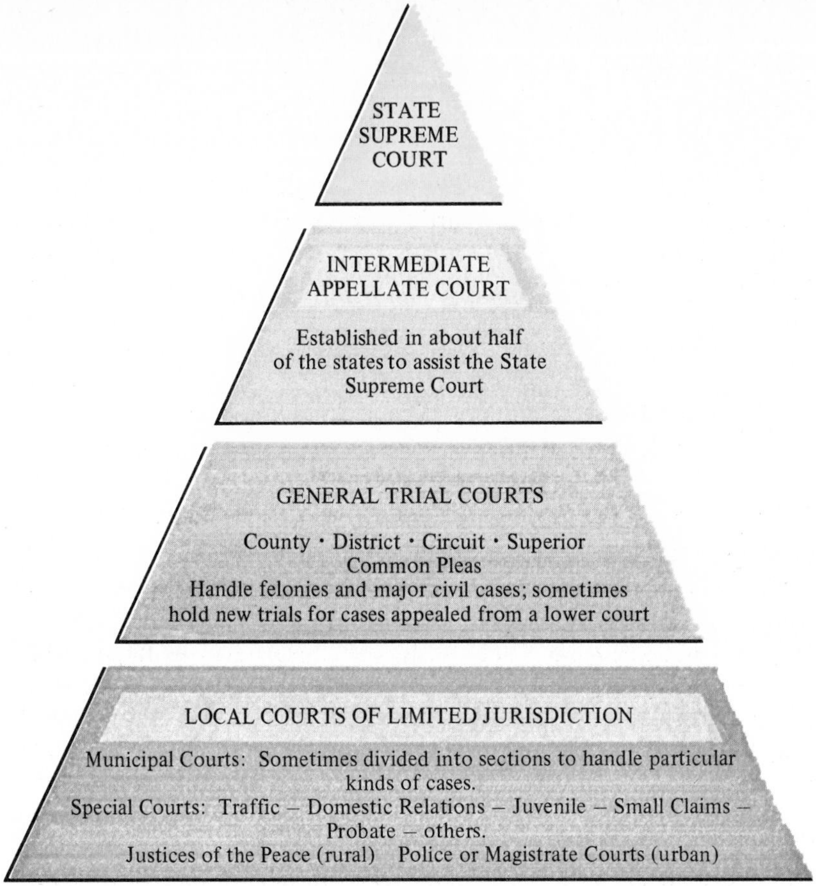

STATE
SUPREME
COURT

INTERMEDIATE
APPELLATE COURT

Established in about half
of the states to assist the State
Supreme Court

GENERAL TRIAL COURTS

County · District · Circuit · Superior
Common Pleas
Handle felonies and major civil cases; sometimes
hold new trials for cases appealed from a lower court

LOCAL COURTS OF LIMITED JURISDICTION

Municipal Courts: Sometimes divided into sections to handle particular
kinds of cases.
Special Courts: Traffic — Domestic Relations — Juvenile — Small Claims —
Probate — others.
Justices of the Peace (rural)   Police or Magistrate Courts (urban)

Other cases go to the state supreme court because the defendants claim that they did not get a fair trial. Clarence Gideon (page 408) appealed to the Florida Supreme Court on the ground that he should have been furnished a lawyer. When the court turned down his appeal, Gideon asked the United States Supreme Court to hear the case because it involved an issue dealt with in the United States Constitution.

## General Trial Courts

There are about 1500 general trial courts in the United States. These courts handle major civil and criminal cases arising from violations of statutes, common law, and constitutions. Felony cases involving murder, robbery, arson, and so on are tried in such courts. Most cases in which one person is suing another for damages are tried at this level. Usually the court serves one or more counties. The names of general trial courts differ from state to state. Among the names used are circuit court, county court, superior court, district court,

A lawyer at a Legal Aid Society provides counsel for a client.

and common pleas court. In New York State the general trial courts are called supreme courts, and the state's highest court is known as the Court of Appeals.

It is in general trial courts that jury trials are held. But at times the parties to a case elect to have the case handled by the judge alone; they waive a jury trial. In addition to such criminal cases as murder, assault, and theft, the general trial court handles a flood of lawsuits. Many of them are auto-accident claims.

Very many criminal and civil cases are settled before actually coming to trial. In a lawsuit the parties may decide to settle out of court, perhaps to save further expense. In a criminal case the prosecutor and the defense attorney may bargain for a guilty plea to a lesser charge. For example, a person charged with first-degree murder may agree to plead guilty to manslaughter in order to get a lighter sentence. Or a person charged with "assault" agrees to plead guilty to "disorderly conduct." The judge in such cases simply ratifies the agreement, and a trial is avoided. Such *plea bargaining,* it is argued, keeps our general trial courts from collapsing with an overload of cases.

### Local Courts of Limited Jurisdiction

Below the general trial courts are various courts that handle minor cases or only one special kind of case. Some have grown up in response to particular needs. For example, traffic courts came into being as the number of autos grew in the United States. Also, some states decided to create juvenile courts in order to handle young people in a special way. Some courts have been set up to handle only "small claims" (pages 554-557). Domestic relations courts handle family problems and seek to prevent divorce. Probate courts oversee the settlement of estates after a person dies.

### Justice and Magistrate Courts

The lowest level of state courts are those presided over by a *justice of the peace* or by a *magistrate.* The justice court is used most in rural places. Magistrate, or police, courts are found in cities.

The justice of the peace in some places has been able to handle traffic cases and other small offenses. But if an accused person wanted a trial, the case would have to go to a trial court. The main jobs of the justice of the peace have been to issue arrest warrants and to hold preliminary hearings for persons accused of crime.

In cities the magistrate has similar duties. The two offices differ in that magistrates tend to have some legal education while justices of the peace usually do not. Also the JP often gets no salary but is paid part of the court fees, while the magistrate usually gets a salary. In some states magistrate courts have been set up in both rural and urban localities to replace the JP.

### Municipal Courts

The special courts named above—traffic, small claims, domestic relations—are usually municipal courts. Sometimes they are divisions of a unified municipal court.

In some places the municipal (city) court is a general trial court. In other places it handles only misdemeanors (small crimes), the smaller civil suits (lawsuits), and the violation of city ordinances. This court also handles appeals from the magistrate courts.

## State Courts Face Heavy Caseloads

"Justice delayed is justice denied" is an old saying that applies in many state courts today. A person trying to collect money for harm done by another party doesn't want to wait two to five years for a settlement. But this often happens. There are also some long delays between the time a person is charged with a crime and the final disposal of the case.

In Philadelphia one study found an average delay of over three years in many civil cases going to trial. In Pittsburgh the average delay was two years, eight months; and some cases waited almost six years. Several factors help to account for such long delays in handling lawsuits: (1) Auto accidents give rise to a flood of cases. (2) Interest groups have been making increasing use of the courts to accomplish their goals. A group may bring a suit to stop the building of a nuclear power plant. Another group may sue to get an employer to give equal pay or employment rights to women. Consumer groups and civil rights groups have also used the courts to advance their causes. (3) Defendants in civil suits often seek delays in the hope that the party seeking payment will give up the fight or settle out of court for a small amount. (4) Most states have no system for moving cases from judges who have a heavy backlog of cases to those who are not very busy. (5) Some trials tie up the court for days or weeks before settlement.

Ever-rising crime rates help to account for the big backlog of cases in some courts. Most regular trial courts handle both civil and criminal cases. (In some places a special criminal court may be set up to relieve the county or district court of such cases. Sometimes other trial courts are set up to handle only civil cases.) Serious delays in handling criminal cases also occur. In a series of jail riots in New York City in 1970 one of the grievances of the rioters was the lack of speedy trials. A survey showed an average delay of three months in jail before trial. One person, charged with murder, had been waiting three years to go to trial.

Problems arise when a court gets more criminal cases than it can handle with reasonable speed and care. (1) Some people will he held in jail too long without a trial. (2) Some persons released on bail will commit other crimes while awaiting trial. (3) In some courts the accused persons, especially those charged with minor crimes, are rushed through the process as if on an assembly line.

LET'S FIX UP THOSE POTHOLES!

### Efforts to Reduce Backlogs
In the long-run the ideal way to reduce case backlogs would seem to be to find ways to reduce social conflict and crime. The common short-run remedy is to add courts and judges. We have already looked at one widely used way to cut down on the number of criminal trials—plea bargaining (page 542).

Some people say that we label too much behavior as criminal. They would reduce the number of criminal cases by changing the law. For example, they would take "public intoxication" and gambling off the list of crimes. These, along with some other offenses, are sometimes called "victimless crimes" because the harm is chiefly to the person committing the offense. "Drunk driving," however, would remain a crime because it clearly endangers other people.

Auto accidents account for a big share of civil cases. Most injury and property-damage claims are settled out of court, but perhaps more of them could be. A few states have adopted "no-fault" auto insurance, and the courts get fewer cases to decide who was at fault and how much payment should be made.

In chapter 18 we saw that Indiana adopted a medical malpractice law that might cut down the number of lawsuits in this legal area.

Another response to the glut of court cases is the *unified state court.* Under this system all courts in a state would be tied into a single system under the direction of the state's chief justice. Judges could be assigned where needed. The ideal plan would have appointed judges, at least some of whom would be specialists in certain fields of law. Where states have tried to streamline their court system, they have usually also taken steps to upgrade the quality of judges.

In 1975–1976 the Maine legislature adopted a new criminal code that took most of the victimless crimes off the books. The chief purpose was to speed up the criminal justice system.

1. List the courts in your state, going from the lowest local court to the highest court of appeals.
2. Try to find out where the following cases would be handled in your city or county:
   a. Parking ticket
   b. $50,000 suit for accident damages
   c. Vandalism by a juvenile
   d. Burglary by an adult
   e. Divorce case
   f. Settlement of an estate
   g. Claim against someone for $50
   h. Dispute by neighbors over the ownership of a valuable tract of land
3. How are judges chosen in your state?
4. Think of arguments for and/or against the following ways of dealing with the heavy caseloads of our state and local courts.
   a. Plea bargaining
   b. Taking "victimless crimes" out of the criminal law code
   c. Adding more courts and judges
   d. No-fault auto insurance
   e. "No-fault divorce" under which neither party would have to state grounds for divorce against the other
   f. Shifting judges to places where they are most needed
5. Can you think of other "remedies"?

## Decision-Making in the Courts

Someday you may be in court. You may be asked to serve on a jury or be called as a witness. Or you may be a party in a lawsuit to collect money that is owed to you or by you. Or, worst of all, you may be accused of committing a crime. Whatever may bring you to the court, you should know something about the legal procedures that have developed to secure justice while protecting innocent people from reckless and wrong charges.

State and local courts deal with both civil and criminal cases. A civil suit arises when a dispute occurs between two or more people, businesses, or governments, or any combinations of these. A civil suit might involve one person suing another for payment of a debt. It could involve a person suing a business for not fulfilling a contract. Or it might involve a group bringing a lawsuit to force the city to close a dump that is causing pollution. In civil suits generally one party seeks (a) to get payment for some loss caused by the other party or (b) to stop the other party from doing something that is harmful or likely to be harmful. Some civil suits seek to break or change legal contracts—divorce cases, for example.

Criminal cases arise when a person violates a specific law that prohibits some action. While a civil suit involves a dispute between one or more persons or groups, a criminal suit pits the government against the presumed violator. In theory, the government represents the public interest. Those who violate laws presumably harm everyone. Therefore, the government seeks to punish lawbreakers on behalf of all of us.

### Kinds of Criminal Offenses

Crimes are generally classified as felonies or misdemeanors. The more serious crimes are called *felonies*. They include murder, arson, rape, robbery, serious assault, kidnapping, and all kinds of major theft. In most states a crime is classified as a felony if it carries a penalty of at least a year in prison.

Law violations of a less serious nature are called *misdemeanors*. They include such offenses as petty theft, vandalism, carrying concealed weapons, traffic violations, public drunkenness, and disorderly conduct. Misdemeanors are punishable by a jail sentence, a fine, or both.

Misdemeanors that are punishable by fine only are called "petty offenses" in some states. Traffic violations are the most common. Parking in a "no parking" zone is an example. In this case there may be no trial at all. Most people don't want to appear in court and would rather just pay the fine. For other "petty offenses" the offender may have to go before a magistrate or justice of the peace (page 543) to hear the charge, perhaps give his or her side of the story, and learn what fine has to be paid.

546

Magistrate or police courts handle most misdemeanor cases. There is no jury trial. The offender may get a lawyer to go along, but usually doesn't. The judge listens to the evidence and then passes sentence. The offender may get off with a warning. If the offender wants a jury trial, the case is passed up to a general trial court.

### The Role of the Court

The role of the court in both civil and criminal cases is mainly a passive one. The courts cannot arrest people; nor do they conduct investigations. They can act on only those cases brought before them. The court cannot punish criminals until they have been arrested by others and charged with a crime by the prosecution agencies of the government. Nor can courts settle disputes until at least one person asks the court's help by filing a formal complaint.

The procedures under which courts operate have developed over hundreds of years and are quite formal. These procedures are assumed to ensure that justice and fair treatment will result. Within these formal procedures, however, judges have a number of chances to make decisions that affect the outcomes of both civil and criminal cases. Some of these decision points will show up as we look at criminal and civil procedures.

### Arrest and Formal Charges in Criminal Cases

Criminal cases begin with the arrest of someone who is accused of committing a crime. Sometimes the police are able to arrest the person at the scene of the crime or trying to escape. In other cases the accused is arrested only after an investigation that points to a certain person as the suspect. Generally, if the police have time to get an arrest warrant, they must do so. The arrest warrant describes the suspect, names the offense, and directs that the person be brought before a magistrate. A magistrate or other judge decides if a warrant should be issued.

The next step is to bring the suspect before a magistrate for a *preliminary hearing.* The magistrate listens to the arresting officer and decides whether the person who was arrested should be released or be "held to answer," that is, held in custody in jail or released "on bail" to await a decision whether formal charges will be made. Every state requires that all persons be given a preliminary hearing shortly after arrest in order to learn the charges being placed against them. If the police lack solid evidence for holding the suspect, the person must be released.

Before anyone can be placed on trial for a crime, he or she must be formally charged with the offense. The *formal charge* is drawn up by the prosecuting attorney. It must inform the accused of a specific crime or crimes, and he or she can be tried in court only on these charges.

## TRIAL JUDGES AS DECISION-MAKERS
### THEY MUST DECIDE

Whether to seat or dismiss prospective jurors

Whether to sustain or overrule objections by attorneys

What are the facts if a jury trial is waived

What facts and personal judgments should be admitted as evidence

Whether criminal charges should be dismissed for lack of evidence

Whether persons should be cited for contempt of court

What law or laws apply to this case

What points to stress in the charge to the jury

In some cases, what penalty or judgment to assess against losing defendants

In some states the formal charge must be in the form of an *indictment* by a grand jury. The prosecutor prepares a bill of indictment and brings it before a grand jury (6 to 23 persons). The prosecutor also presents enough evidence to try to convince the grand jury that the person should stand trial. If the grand jury agrees, it "returns a true bill."

In some states the formal charge may be either an indictment or an *information.* The latter is a written complaint by the prosecutor charging the defendant with one or more specific crimes. It is filed with a judge or magistrate. The "information" type of formal charge is widely used where permitted because it saves time and expense. The United States Constitution requires the grand jury indictment to be used in federal courts. It was seen as a protection against officials wanting to put someone on trial unjustly for personal or political reasons.

In some cases the formal charge is drawn up before any arrest is made. For example, suppose that someone has embezzled funds from a company. The company suspects a certain employee. The police and prosecutor's office investigate the case and gather all the evidence they can. An information or indictment is drawn up, and then an arrest is made.

### Arraignment

Once the procesutor is ready to bring formal charges, the suspect is arraigned before a judge. *Arraignment* consists of reading the substance of the "information" or "indictment" to the accused in open court and asking how the person wishes to plead: "guilty" or "not guilty."

At this stage many criminal cases come to an end. Persons who know they are guilty and that the prosecution can prove it may choose to plead guilty. They may hope that the court will be lenient because of their cooperation. Or defendants or their lawyers may ask for a brief adjournment in order to bargain with the prosecuting attorney on the nature of the charge. For example, an accused person charged with murder might agree to plead guilty to a manslaughter charge. It carries a lighter penalty. If the prosecutor thinks there might be trouble getting a conviction on a murder charge and wants to avoid a long trial, the parties may agree to switch the charge to manslaughter with the accused pleading guilty to the new charge. A big proportion of criminal cases are settled through such *plea bargaining*.

At the arraignment the defendant might ask the judge to dismiss the charges, arguing that the prosecution's case is too flimsy to conduct a trial. If the court denies this request, the defendant must plead innocent or guilty. If the defendant makes no plea, the judge will order a plea of "not guilty." After a plea is recorded, the judge will set a date for a trial.

### Preparing for the Trial

During the period between the arraignment and the trial, both the prosecution and the defense prepare their cases. This is again a time in which the defense can change its plea to "guilty" or, with the permission of the court, to "guilty" for a lesser offense.

A number of tactics may be followed by the defense during this period. It may ask that the indictment be dismissed. It may seek a

549

court order permitting a look at some of the evidence the prosecution intends to use at the trial. Or the defense may ask the court to prohibit the use of certain evidence because it was obtained illegally. Examples include evidence taken by forced confession or by illegal wiretaps.

The defense may also ask for a "change of venue," changing the trial to a court in a different locality or to a different judge. The defense may argue that publicity on the case hurts the chance of the defendant's getting a fair trial in the district or that the judge is prejudiced. Or the lawyer for the accused may argue that the charges really require prosecution in federal court rather than a state court. In each of these cases the defense is seeking to find ways to increase the chances for the accused to win acquittal.

The prosecution may also change its mind between the time of arraignment and the trial. Perhaps new evidence has been uncovered, raising doubt about the guilt of the suspect. Perhaps certain key witnesses are proving uncooperative, and it is no longer possible to rely on their evidence. Or perhaps some hoped-for evidence did not show up. In such cases the prosecutor may tell the court that it is dropping all charges. Or the prosecution may bargain with the defense, promising to drop the more serious charges in return for a plea of guilty to lesser ones.

At times the prosecutor would like to avoid a criminal trial but feels pressure to proceed with it. Perhaps the case involves a prominent citizen. Or maybe the accused has a lot of popular support in the district. While forced to bring charges, the prosecutor may seek ways to duck a politically difficult problem. One way is to agree to drop the more serious charges for pleas of guilty to lesser ones, as described above. A second is to recommend to the judge that for a plea of guilty a very minimal sentence be awarded. A third is to delay taking the case to trial until public interest has died down or until witnesses have moved away. Later the prosecution might ask that the case be dismissed.

While the judge may believe that adequate grounds for a trial exist, there is little a judge can do to force a reluctant prosecutor to conduct a vigorous case.

## The Criminal Trial

Trials in criminal cases may be by a judge alone or by a judge and jury. In about half the states, defendants have a choice. In other states jury trials are required even though the defendant might prefer trial by a judge alone.

The judge's main role is that of refereeing a contest between the prosecuting and defense attorneys. The prosecutor seeks to present facts and reasoning to convince the judge or jury that the accused is guilty as charged. The defense attorney tries to cast doubt on the prosecution's evidence and witnesses. The defense may also present

550

# LEGAL PROCEDURES IN CRIMINAL AND CIVIL SUITS

| CRIMINAL (FELONY)<br>(State vs. Defendant) | CIVIL LAW SUITS<br>(Between persons, including corporations,<br>partnerships, and government agencies) |
|---|---|
| <br>Grand jury votes indictment<br>(or Prosecutor files an "information") | <br>Summons and Complaint served |
| <br>Warrant of arrest served,<br>person is taken into custody | <br>Interchange of pleadings<br>to define issues |
| <br>If person pleads not guilty<br>to charge, trial by jury | <br>Trial by jury<br>(in some cases before Judge alone) |
| <br>If convicted, right to appeal | <br>Jury verdict; judgment<br>and right to appeal |
| <br>Fine and/or imprisonment if guilt upheld<br>(Trial Judge may suspend execution of sentence) | <br>If claimant prevails, defendant<br>must pay damages and costs |

additional evidence to show that the accused is not guilty as charged. This courtroom contest is called the *adversary system.* It operates on the assumption that all major facts will come out, since both sides want to use all the facts that will aid their case. One of the judge's big tasks is to see that facts not relevant to the case are not introduced.

Jury selection is part of the contest between the opposing attorneys. Persons picked for jury duty are questioned about their fitness to serve. It is the judge's task to dismiss any persons who are not suitable. The attorney for each side may also "challenge" a certain number of jurors without giving any cause. This is part of the contest to get a favorable jury.

After the jury is chosen, the prosecution presents its case. From time to time, the defense attorney may object to the tactics used by the prosecutor or to the kinds of evidence being offered. The judge must decide whether to sustain or overrule the objections. When the defense presents its case—if it chooses to do so—the prosecutor may raise objections for the judge to rule on. The defense is likely to ask the judge to dismiss the charges for lack of sufficient evidence, and the judge must make another decision.

After the closing arguments by each side, the judge must "instruct," or "charge," the jury. They hear about the legal aspects of the case and how they should weigh the evidence. They are told to find the defendant guilty if the evidence points to guilt beyond reasonable doubt. In a few states the judge may comment on the evidence. But generally the merits of the testimony and other evidence are left to the jury to decide.

If the jury finds the defendant guilty, the judge usually has some leeway in passing sentence. The criminal laws usually give maximum and minimum penalties to be applied—with the exact penalty to be fixed by the judge. The judge may also suspend the sentence—either permanently or for a given period of time, to see how the person will behave. Often the judge will consult with the prosecutor on the appropriate penalty. And if the case ends before or during the trial with a guilty plea to a lesser charge (plea bargaining), the sentence will almost surely be the one worked out in the bargaining process.

The sentence ends the work of the trial court. But the defense may appeal to a higher court—usually on grounds that the trial was in some way or ways not a fair one. The appeal will generally cite what the defense claims to be wrong decisions by the trial judge. A few appeals will claim that there should be a new trial because new evidence favorable to the defendant has been found.

### The Trial of Civil Cases

Most trial courts handle both criminal and civil cases. General procedures are much the same. In both kinds of cases the trial judge serves chiefly as a referee in the adversary system.

552

A civil suit begins when a person or group claiming some harm (the plaintiff, or one who complains) files a written document called a *complaint* with the court. The party complained against is called the defendant.

The complaint states how the plaintiff has been harmed (or will be harmed if corrective action is not taken). It generally asks for a certain sum of money (a judgment) to be paid by the defendant to the plaintiff. The court then issues a *summons* to the defendant. It notifies that a suit has been filed, by whom, in which court, and for what reasons.

The defendant may merely call the plaintiff and offer to settle out of court. But perhaps the defendant does not believe that the plaintiff is due the sum requested. Then he or she may hire a lawyer and fight the case. The defendant can, of course, simply ignore the summons and do nothing. In this event the court is likely to rule for the plaintiff by default.

If the defendant elects to fight the case, the lawyer will prepare an *answer* to the complaint. It will usually challenge all or part of the statements in the complaint. In addition, the defendant may file a counter complaint against the plaintiff.

Let's assume for a moment that there has been an auto accident. One person in the accident was crippled and is no longer able to work. Such a person might sue the driver of the other car for damages: payment for medical expenses, "pain and suffering," loss of income, car repair, and so on. The second driver, while sorry about the accident, may feel little or no responsibility and thus no obligation to pay damages. Thus, in responding to the complaint, the defendant's lawyer will prepare an answer saying that the defendant was not responsible but that the accident was caused by such factors as ice, bad visibility, or perhaps carelessness on the part of the plaintiff.

Prior to the trial, the two lawyers may meet to narrow down the issues before the trial. If they can agree to certain facts, these need not take time in court. Only the disputed facts need to be presented to the jury. Often such discussions will lead to a settlement before the trial.

If the only dispute between the two parties is an issue concerning the law, the case will usually be settled by a judge after hearing arguments from the two attorneys. If the dispute is over the facts of the case—and this is usually the issue—then the case will likely be tried before a jury.

If the defendant wins the case, the judgment may read as follows: "Adjudged: that the plaintiff receive nothing by this action." If the plaintiff wins, the judgment might appear as follows: "Adjudged: that the plaintiff recover from the defendant ten thousand dollars ($10,000.00) with interest thereon at 6% per annum from this date until paid."

If either party is not satisfied with the decision, it may appeal the case. The appellate court will receive a condensed version of the court proceedings. No testimony is heard by the appellate court. The appellate court hears only arguments by the two attorneys regarding the pros and cons of what the trial court decided. After hearing the oral arguments and reading the written documents, the appellate court decides whether to uphold or to overturn the original verdict.

1. Most criminal cases never go to trial. Name some points where decisions may be made to stop the case short of trial. Who participates in the decisions?
2. Name some kinds of decisions that trial judges need to make.
3. Why do you suppose many civil suits are settled out of court?

## "Go Ahead, Sue Me!"

What should each of the following people do? Four people have been hurt in their business dealings. Each made a complaint but got no good remedy.

### Case 1. Potholes in the Parking Lot

John Jones was driving his car through a shopping center parking lot. Suddenly the left front wheel dropped into a big hole, bending the rim and knocking the front wheels "out of line." John went to the owner of the store nearest the chuck hole and complained about the damage to his car. The store owner said he was sorry but he did not own the property. He gave John the name of the property owner. When John called, the property owner referred him to an insurance company. When John called the insurance company, they told him to get the damage repaired and to file a claim. The total damages were $45, but the insurance company would settle for only $25.

### Case 2. The Defective TV Set

Mary Smith bought a new TV set. Three days after taking it home, the set began to work poorly. She called the dealer, who sent a repair truck. After some brief tinkering, the picture was a little better. But two days later the set just stopped working. Mary called the store to complain. She said the set was defective. She wanted the store to pick it up and return her money. The store owner refused to do anything.

### Case 3. The Rental Deposit Fee

James Brown leased an apartment for one year. Prior to moving in, he had to pay a $200 deposit in case there was breakage. When Jim was ready to move at the end of the year, he asked for the return of his deposit. The owner refused, saying that the deposit was used to pay for some plumbing repair during the year. Jim argued that the repair of plumbing was a normal maintenance duty of the owner. Jim had broken nothing and was entitled to the $200. The owner still refused to pay.

554

### Case 4. The Broken Promise

Nancy Remington, a typist, agreed to type some short stories for a writer. In payment, Nancy would receive tutoring in English or $100 in cash. Nancy quickly decided that the tutoring was useless and asked that she be paid for her typing. The writer refused. The writer claimed that Nancy learned good writing practices from typing the stories.

In each case a person was cheated and is entitled to payment. But where can an ordinary citizen turn for quick, simple, and low-cost justice? More and more people have begun to take advantage of the small claims court for problems such as those described above.

## What Is a Small Claims Court?

Small claims courts exist in all parts of the United States. Often they are divisions of a city or county court, or are run by justices of the peace. However organized, they share a number of features.

1. *They are cheap.* Usually one can file a suit in a small claims court for five dollars or less.

2. *There is no need to have a lawyer.* Indeed, this is one of the their special attractions. Often the amount of money spent on hiring a lawyer is more than the damages you are claiming in your suit. But if it costs only $5 to go to court, it makes sense to sue even if all you are claiming is $35. Some states do not permit lawyers to represent clients in small claims courts. The result is a great deal of informality in how the case is conducted.

3. *Small claims courts are quick.* Usually a case will come to trial within four weeks after the complaint is entered. The conduct of a case is also quick and efficient. A typical hearing takes no more than twenty minutes. Often the judge will give his ruling right after the parties have testified. In other cases the plaintiff and defendant learn the judge's decision by mail within ten days of the trial. If one or the other party dislikes the decision, the judge's ruling can be appealed to a higher court. But when the case is appealed—and few are—then lawyers must usually be hired prior to further trial.

4. *Only small claims can be filed.* Small claims courts were set up to help citizens resolve small issues. Often claims have a top limit of $500. If you wish to sue for more than this, you must file a claim in another court.

5. *Judgments are legally binding.* Although small claims courts are informal and devoid of most of the legal niceties that we have seen on TV trials, the decision of the judge is just as binding as in any court of law. If you win your case and the defendant refuses to pay, the judge could punish with a contempt of court ruling. Or the judge could order the sheriff to sell enough of the defendant's property to pay your claim. Or the judge might get the defendant's employer to pay a portion of the wages to you until the debt is settled.

## How Does One File a Suit in a Small Claims Court?

Suppose that you bought defective merchandise and the seller refused to repair it or to return your money. The first thing to do is to make every effort to convince the seller to do what is right. It is best if at least one of your requests is in writing so that the seller cannot claim later that you never asked for help.

When all of your efforts have failed, you can then file suit in a small claims court. This is usually a simple matter. You should go to the clerk of the court of the district in which you live. The clerk will have you make out a form like the one shown below. On the form you must give the name and address of the person you are suing, tell how much money you are seeking, and what the claim is about. You should take with you any evidence that you have: copies of correspondence, warranties, and so on. One copy will be kept for the court; another will be sent to the defendant.

The clerk will ask for a filing fee (often about $5) and a service charge. The latter charge, usually about $1.50, pays for notifying the defendant of the suit by a registered letter. If you want to hire a process server to deliver the court summons in person, you can do so at an extra cost.

You should consider one thing before "going to court." If you know that the person you are suing can't pay even if you win the case, you might as well forget the whole matter. The court could decide in your favor, but you would not be able to collect unless the person has money or property to settle your claim.

---

Name _____

Street and Number _____

City _____

Telephone _____ Plaintiff

Against

Name _____

Name _____ Defendant(s)

**SMALL CLAIM**

**BLOOMINGTON CITY COURT**
122 S. Walnut Street
Bloomington, Indiana 47401

Case No. _____

TO THE CLERK:

Please summon the defendant(s) to appear in court to answer this claim.

**STATEMENT OF CLAIM**

☐ Account or Note—Attached       ☐ Wages _____

☐ Other _____

_____

_____

_____

Plaintiff asks judgment against defendant for $_____, plus interest from _____, 197__, at the rate of _____% and costs of this proceeding.

**AFFIDAVIT**

_____ state(s) that (he is/she is/they are) the Plaintiff(s) in this proceeding, that the statement of claim is true, that the defendant(s) owe the Plaintiff(s) the amount claimed and (is/are) not now serving in the armed forces of the United States.

_____

Affirmed and signed before me on _____, 197__

_____
Clerk/Deputy Clerk/Notary Public

After you have filed suit, the court will notify the defendant, who usually has three or four weeks to respond. The defendant may settle the case with you outside of court or perhaps may file a counter claim against you. Many cases are settled before the trial because the defendants feel they are likely to lose.

Finally the day of the trial is set. You and the defendant have been notified when to appear. Both have brought records and other kinds of evidence to bolster their claims. One or both may have brought witnesses also.

After swearing all to tell the truth, the judge will call on the plaintiff to tell his or her story. Then the defendant is given time to speak. The judge may ask one or the other questions. Usually the judge acts almost as a lawyer might, trying to get each side to enter all of the facts into the record. Finally after both parties have told their stories, the judge decides. If the decision is for the plaintiff, the judge will tell the defendant how much to pay and when the money is due.

The small claims court is sometimes called the "People's Court" because it deals with the day-to-day conflicts and because people do not have to be a lawyer or to hire one to get their day in court. Small claims courts may be one of the legal remedies to help sustain Americans' faith in the legal system.

# 20 State and Local Bureaucrats

Bureaucracies in state and local governments touch our lives from birth until death. They see that births and deaths are put on public record. They run the public schools. They regulate business. They build and maintain streets and roads. They see that people get the wide range of public services authorized by law. And they collect the taxes to pay for these services.

A state bureaucracy is made up of all the departments, boards, bureaus, and other agencies that carry out state programs. More often, however, we speak of the highway bureaucracy, the education bureaucracy, and so on. At the local level we can identify a number of separate bureaucracies: police, fire, sanitation, public works, schools, etc.

By the mid-1970s over 11 million people worked in state and local bureaucracies. But, as we saw in chapter 15, we don't usually call all of these people *bureaucrats.* We use this term to refer to people who supervise or manage (page 433).

## An Overview of State and Local Bureaucracies

Most of the work of bureaucrats is fairly routine. But news items about them or their agencies can be found in the newspaper almost any day. Below are some samples.

1. What bureaucrats are mentioned? Identify by name or title.
2. What bureaucratic agencies are named?
3. What tasks are the persons or agencies performing?

Chicago—A big shakeup in the Chicago Police Department will take place soon, according to insiders, in order to get a stronger narcotics unit.

Supt. James Rochford is said to be considering shifts in top command posts and a major change in the way the department is set up.

But the changes could leave Mitchell Ware, a black deputy superintendent, without a command. It is said that the plan calls for abolishing the Bureau of Inspectional Services, headed by Ware, and distributing its units to other bureaus.

Marshall, Tex.—Officials of the Texas Water Quality Board and the Texas Parks and Wildlife Department are looking into a massive fish kill on the Sabine River in Gregg and Harrison counties.

558

The stench from the fish kill, which occurred about four days ago, is keeping livestock from going near the water. The kill is along ten miles of the river.

The amount of oxygen in the water was barely enough for the fish, but officials said that might not be the reason for the deaths.

Jim Toole of Marshall, biologist for the parks department, said a crew would go by boat in search of the source of the kill. He said water samples will be taken at various points in the river.

Boston—More than 90 miles of state highway will be treated with little or no salt this winter, Commissioner John J. Carroll, head of the Department of Public Works, announced this plan today. He said that public hearings on the plan will be held in the two areas where a stretch of highway will get no salt or chemical use and in five other areas where there will be reduced use.

The plan is a response to action taken earlier this year by Secretary Evelyn Murphy, head of the Department of Environmental Affairs. A recent state law gives her the right to block the DPW from doing any road salting if a complete environmental impact statement is not turned in at least 60 days prior to any salting. Miss Murphy rejected the DPW impact statement on salting. She said that it failed to show that the DPW had experimented to find out if the amount of road salt to melt snow and ice could be reduced. The DPW impact statement did show that road salt hurts water supplies.

## Who Controls the Bureaucrats?

We saw in chapter 15 that the President has general control over the federal bureaucracy. But Congress shares in the control. Together the President and Congress make decisions on what programs the bureaucrats will carry out and how much money will be spent on the programs.

In most states a big part of the bureaucracy is under the governor's control. And the legislature plays a role similar to that of Congress. But we learned in chapter 17 that the typical governor shares executive power with a number of other elected officials. The chart of Oregon's executive branch (page 501) is typical. For example, the state education bureaucracy is under the control of an elected State Superintendent. What other bureaucracies are under an elected official other than the governor?

We can look at the roles of the governor and legislature in news item 3 above—the one on road salting. The heads of the Public Works and Environmental Affairs departments are appointees of the governor. They are both trying to deal with a state law, the Environmental Policy Act, passed by the legislature.

Bureaucrats represent a wide range of jobs. A chemist measures pollution in water samples. A rent-control official hears a complaint. Various jobholders manage public land.

The diagrams of the mayor-council and council-manager forms of city government on page 510 suggest the kinds of links that exist between city bureaucrats and the chief executive and city council. The "strong" mayor and the typical city manager have general control over the city bureaucracies. In news item 1 above, the Chicago police superintendent reports to the mayor. And the mayor and council lay down general policy for the police department to follow.

Bureaucrats in state and local government can be thought of as *links* between chief executives and legislatures who make decisions and the public for whom the decisions are made. For example, the state legislature—with the governor's support—may pass a law that gives more money to people on welfare. The director of the State Department of Public Welfare, appointed by the governor, is the bureaucrat most responsible for carrying out this law. The director and other members of the department are the *links* between the officials who made the new law and the members of the public who get the benefits.

The importance of these links is highlighted when some public service halts. When garbage piles up on the streets, or schools shut down, or city transit workers strike, we become very aware of jobs that bureaucracies perform.

## The Recruitment of Workers in Bureaucracies

In the past hundred years the means of recruiting state and local employees have changed gradually. In the past—and to some extent today—jobs were given out as *patronage.* In return for services to a public official or political party, a person might get a job in the bureaucracy. Political loyalty, rather than ability, determined who got the jobs.

Today some type of *merit system* guides the recruitment of people for the majority of jobs in state and local bureaucracies.

In 1883 in the Pendleton Act, Congress set up a merit system for the filling of some federal jobs. In that same year the state of New York also created a merit system, and Massachusetts followed the next year. To get a job under the merit system a person must pass a test showing ability to handle the job. In some cases the "test" consists of papers showing that the jobseeker has the training for the job. For example, a public health post might require proof that the person has graduated from a medical school and has a license to practice medicine.

The merit system allows many bureaucrats to see themselves as professionals rather than as political party agents. They are experts who provide some kind of special service. In the civil service ranks one can find skilled accountants, doctors, lawyers, social workers, and engineers. Such professionals belong to state and national associations like the American Bar Association and the American Medical

Association. These people are influenced to perform their roles in line with the standards set by their professional organizations.

We have seen that the top federal bureaucrats are appointed by the President with Senate consent. They include the department heads along with their chief assistants. The same situation exists in state and local government, but practices differ from place to place. Some top bureaucrats expect to be replaced if a new mayor or governor is elected. In other cases a department head or bureau chief may serve year after year under different chief executives.

There is a valid reason for not extending the merit system to some of the top jobs. A mayor or governor wants to have department heads who are loyal and will carry out the chief executive's policies. Civil servants often think in terms of what is good for their department rather than what the governor or mayor wants.

## The Growth of Bureaucracies

The graph on page 563 shows the rise in state-local employees in a recent ten-year period. Nearly all these people work in bureaucracies. In that decade, state-local employment rose around 52 percent while the nation's population grew by only some 11 percent.

*Table 7* shows where the biggest increases are taking place. Notice the fast growth in jobs in the fields of education, health, and welfare.

**Table 7. Number of State and Local Employees**

|  | 1963 | 1973 | Percent Rise |
|---|---|---|---|
| Education | 3,437,000 | 5,901,000 | 72% |
| Through high school | 2,781,000 | 4,371,000 | 57 |
| Higher education | 623,000 | 1,445,000 | 132 |
| Welfare | 151,000 | 311,000 | 106 |
| Health | 89,000 | 180,000 | 102 |
| Correction | 102,000 | 178,000 | 75 |
| Parks and recreation | 113,000 | 191,000 | 69 |
| Police protection | 368,000 | 581,000 | 58 |
| Hospitals | 664,000 | 975,000 | 47 |
| Others | 2,264,000 | 3,036,000 | 34 |

Payrolls have gone up even faster than the number of jobs. In 1963 the *monthly* payroll for state-local workers was around $2.8 billion. By 1973 it had reached $8 billion.

The growth of bureaucracies is linked with a larger population asking for more and more services from government. Expanded services have called for bigger and bigger bureaucracies to administer the programs.

*Table 7:* U.S. Department of Commerce.

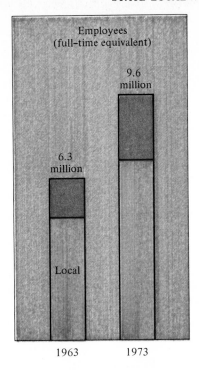

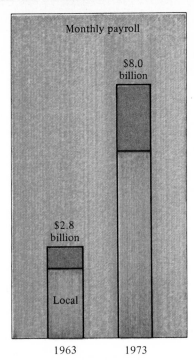

**1.** Who are the bureaucrats in the following list. Explain your choices.

a. County health officer

b. Mayor

c. File clerk in water department

d. Director of Animal Control

e. Member of city council

f. Chief of Detectives

g. Head of city water department

h. City judge

**2.** Below are some needs that people in your community might have. Try to name one or more state or local bureaucracies which try to cope with these needs.

a. Clean air

b. Clean water supply

c. Reading skills

d. Street repair

e. Recreational facilities

f. Property protection

g. Family income support

h. Care of the mentally ill

i. Trash disposal

j. Job hunting

**3.** What local or state bureaucrats have you or your family had dealings with in the past month? Why?

**4.** Can you think of needs in your community that are not attended to by state or local bureaucracies? Why does the government not attend to these needs? Should it do so? Why or why not?

## Making Decisions in Bureaucracies

We have emphasized that bureaucrats are expected to carry out decisions made by chief executives and legislatures. But bureaucrats do not merely receive and carry out orders. They must often make decisions of their own.

In the road salting case on page 559 it is doubtful that the governor told Secretary Murphy to reject the DPW impact statement. And it is likely that Commissioner Carroll himself made the decision to go ahead with the no-salt tests.

Let's look at another example. In 1965 the Massachusetts legislature passed a racial imbalance law. It provided that school boards must try to prevent or eliminate racial imbalance in the schools in drawing school attendance boundaries and in selecting new school sites. Funds from the state could be withheld from school boards which did not follow this law. The Massachusetts Commissioner of Education had major responsibility for enforcing this law. In performing this duty, this bureaucrat had to make decisions about which schools were making good-faith efforts to obey the law and which ones were not. The commissioner also had to make decisions on what penalties to apply.

Bureaucrats must make decisions. But they do not have a free hand. A useful way to look at decision-making by bureaucrats is to focus on the controls. We can examine four types: legislative, judicial, executive, and community.

### Legislative Controls

We have already seen that bureaucrats carry out programs authorized and funded by legislative bodies. Let's look at these controls in more detail.

1. *Laws set forth general policies and guidelines.* The Massachusetts racial imbalance act did not merely direct the Commissioner of Education to end racial imbalance in the schools. The law defined racial imbalance. It set forth procedures. It provided state aid for school boards to get the job done—and penalties for foot-dragging.

Let's look at another example. In 1967 the city council of Bloomington, Indiana, passed a law creating an Air Pollution Control Commission. The law sets forth the major goal of reducing air pollution in the city. The law also provides that the commission shall consist of eight persons including the fire chief and at least one person with a degree in chemistry. The law defines pollutants and the levels of air pollution which are unlawful. The law tells how pollution complaints are to be handled. The commission must investigate, hold a hearing within thirty days, and tell its findings and recommendations to the city engineer, who has the power to order a halt to the violation.

2. *Legislatures vote the money.* Bureaucrats are limited in the tasks they can do by the amount of money available. To satisfy people

who want to cut down on pollution, lawmakers may pass a "strong" antipollution bill. But then they can control enforcement by voting too little money for bureaucrats to do the job. Or an agency that "gets out of line" in the judgment of lawmakers may find its budget slashed the next year. The "power of the purse" can be a powerful force to influence bureaucrats.

3. *Lawmakers approve some appointments.* Many top-level bureaucrats who are named to their posts by the chief executive must get approval from some legislative body: the city council, state senate, or both houses of the legislature. Once a person has been approved, however, the lawmakers have to look for other ways to control the bureaucrat.

4. *Lawmakers can investigate bureaucracies.* Complaints against bureaucrats can lead to legislative investigations. A committee may try to find out if a person or agency has made unfair decisions, or managed a program poorly, or not followed the guidelines set forth in the law. Evidence of poor performance may force the chief executive to remove the bureaucrat. Even the bad publicity that comes with an investigation can help keep bureaucrats in line.

## Judicial Controls

Bureaucrats are subject to both criminal and civil suits for wrong-doing in the line of duty. Misuse of public money and bribery are criminal offenses. Many bureaucrats are in a position to give special favors in return for a bribe. We have no way of knowing, of course, how much influence the criminal law has on preventing bureaucrats from giving improper favors. But without judicial controls on bribery there would surely be much more than now exists.

In a civil case a person who claims unfair treatment from a bureaucrat can go to court to try to get some remedy. For example, a building inspector may order several hundred seats removed from a gym to permit better exit in case of fire. The owner or manager may take the inspector to court on the ground that an error of judgment was made. Or a person or group who thinks that an agency is not providing some legal benefit may go to court to force action.

If a court decides to support a complaint, it can issue a variety of orders. An *injunction* stops an official from taking some action. For example, suppose that a street department says that it is going to cut down a row of shade trees in order to widen a street. The residents may be able to get a temporary injunction to prevent the cutting until a hearing has been held. Or they may be able to get a permanent injunction that orders the department not to cut the trees at all.

The *writ of mandamus* is a court order telling an official to carry out some action. For example, it might be used to get a welfare official to start sending monthly checks to someone who is eligible but has not been getting them. Or an agency might be ordered to put up a traffic light where it has refused to put one.

The *writ of habeas corpus* can be used to order an official to bring a person in custody before a judge to decide whether it is legal to detain the person. It might be used, for example, to get a person out of a state mental hospital or to get a juvenile out of a detention center.

### Executive Controls

Bureaucrats are part of the executive branch of the government. Thus, the chief executive oversees their work. A mayor has to take the blame for a breakdown of city services if he or she appoints and controls the top bureaucrats who are in charge.

Effective control by chief executives in states and big cities is often very difficult. Thousands of employees in hundreds of scattered bureaus are hard to keep track of. An aide to a former mayor of New York City has said, "The administrative machinery of the city has become so complicated . . . that few people know how the government functions."

The civil service (merit system) also limits executive control. Most bureaucrats have strong job protection. Dismissal can be only for serious causes, and then only after drawn-out procedures. Saying that a bureaucrat is "not very effective" would not be enough to get rid of him or her. Often bureaucrats can resist changes ordered by a mayor or governor.

More and more workers in bureaucracies now belong to labor unions. Unions seek to protect members from being pushed around by executives. The strike, or even the threat to strike, is a powerful tool that many workers in government now have to get the wages and working conditions they want. Unions tend to give workers a sense of independence from executive control.

Yet in spite of these limits on the power of executives to control their bureaucracies, some control is possible. Many top bureaucrats owe their jobs to the mayor or governor. Chief executives pass on agency budgets before the assembled budget goes to the legislature. And executives can issue direct orders that many bureaucrats have to obey.

### Community Controls

Bureaucrats can be influenced by those whom they serve. As in other areas of political life, those with the most resources are in the strongest positions of influence. A neighborhood association will have more influence than people who are not organized. Business and professional people often have more influence than do manual workers.

Bureaucrats often have the power to make decisions on who will get certain services or who will get better quality services. The highway

566

department may have a fairly free hand in deciding what roads will be improved this year. The police department makes decisions on where to put police patrols. School bureaucrats decide where to place the best teachers or in what schools to run new programs. Building inspectors have some leeway in deciding which owners to crack down on and which violations will be overlooked. In short, government services are often not handed out equally to all citizens. And people with the most influence may get the edge in government services over other people.

See pages 122-127 for discussion of the links between socioeconomic status, political resources, and political behavior.

This situation has led some citizens to demand broader community involvement in the decisions of bureaucrats. Some people have called for more direct citizen participation. Others focus on the need for creating citizens' advocate roles.

One plan for getting more direct citizen action calls for setting up more elected citizen boards to oversee a particular service. One of the antipoverty programs of the 1960s was the Community Action Programs. Local agencies were set up to provide neighborhood service centers, legal aid for the poor, and other help. The board that controlled each agency had to include representatives of the poor people being served. This was the first time in the history of social welfare programs that poor people were asked to take part in the programs designed to help them.

Some people have called for police review boards to hear complaints against the police bureaucracy. Some people think that big-city school bureaucracies should be broken up by creating neighborhood districts. Each district would have its own local board, elected by the citizens, to run the neighborhood schools. The central bureaucracy would then just provide services to the local districts.

Attempts to get citizens to take a more direct part in the decisions of local bureaucracies has met with only moderate success. Critics point out that most people, and especially poor people, do not have the skills and knowledge—and very often not the interest—to be effective.

Another approach to community control is the *citizens' advocate role*. One type of such role is the *ombudsman* (page 338). Instead of using lawmakers to handle complaints, citizens could get in touch with a public official appointed as complaint-handler. Hawaii and Oregon have created the office of ombudsman as part of their state governments. A number of cities and counties also have such an office.

A second kind of citizens' advocate role is that of the *professional community organizer*. This person offers political skills to the community to help people make demands on officials. The main goal of such a leader is to teach community groups to develop their own skills and resources so that the organizer can get out of the picture. Saul Alinsky was very effective in organizing community groups in Chicago and elsewhere—and in training other community organizers.

In order to bring city government closer to citizens, some mayors have set up "little city halls" in a few neighborhoods.

Answer these questions about limits on the role behavior of bureaucrats.

**1.** How is the power of bureaucrats limited by the legislative and judicial branches of government?

**2.** How can chief executives control bureaucrats? What are often some limits on their control?

**3.** Describe some proposals and current programs for giving citizens more control over bureaucrats.

**4.** Imagine that you are Recreation Director for a medium-sized city. You supervise a staff of twenty people, run summer programs for children, maintain two teen-age drop-in centers and one for the elderly, and carry out a variety of other programs.

    **a.** Suggest three kinds of decisions that you might have to make.

    **b.** Name some controls that would influence your decisions.

## Decision-Making in a State Welfare Department

State welfare departments supervise a variety of programs that give financial aid to the needy. As part of the Social Security Act of 1935 Congress set up a program of *public assistance* to the needy aged and blind. Later, disabled persons were made eligible as well as needy families with dependent children. The program was to be administered by the states with the federal treasury supplying around half of the funds. Another type of aid is called *general assistance.* It covers needy people not eligible for the other programs. Welfare departments also handle the food stamp program, medicaid (health care for the needy), and other programs.

County and city departments of public welfare handle these programs at the local level under the federal and state guidelines. Social workers in the local agencies decide which applicants are eligible and how much aid they should receive.

Federal law and the federal welfare agency set minimum standards that states must meet in order to qualify for federal welfare grants. But the states have much leeway in deciding who may qualify for aid and the amounts of payments. In 1975 one state was paying about $50 per month on the average to a family with dependent children while three states were paying over $300.

The costs of public assistance (including general assistance) rose steadily over the years—in good times as well as in recessions. The total was under $1 billion in 1945. In the early 1950s it had risen to over $3 billion. And by 1971 the figure had jumped to over $10 billion. Such big increases—and stories about welfare "chiselers"—brought cries for reform.

### Governor Reagan Calls for Welfare Reform

The pattern of welfare in California in the late 1960s was typical of the nation. Between 1965 and 1971 the number of people on welfare more than doubled, reaching a peak of nearly 2.3 million.

In response to the rising costs and the rising public outcry for welfare reform, Governor Ronald Reagan in 1970 appointed a task force to study the situation and come up with some answers. They conducted some 700 in-depth interviews, and within four months they reported back to the governor.

One task force member, Robert B. Carleson, said of the system, "It's an administrative nightmare, a multibillion-dollar operation man-

aged by social workers with no managerial skills." Reagan asked him to become state welfare director and told him to "clean up the mess."

### Carleson Goes into Action

One of Carleson's first actions was to appoint a team of assistants to help bring about reforms. Then he focused on two problems that the task force had found. One had to do with the finding that the rules on who was eligible for welfare were being stretched to favor people who were not very needy. Instead of trying to keep costs down, some decision-makers were really helping people to get on the welfare rolls. A second problem was that some people were being allowed to claim big work-related expenses, such as child-care and travel costs. For example, a working woman with three children might claim that child care and car expense took half (or more) of her pay. This expense would be taken into account in deciding how much welfare aid she should get. Carleson said that they found that "a mother of three in the Los Angeles area would be making around $1300 a month before she would have to leave welfare."

In response to these and other problems, Carleson replaced a number of officials. He also got a rewriting of vague and loosely written rules on who should be allowed to get welfare checks. Two months after taking office, Carleson could see a big drop in the rolls. And the decline went on over the next eight months.

But Carleson was still working within the rules set forth in the state welfare laws. It was clear to him and others that much of the problem was in the laws with which he had to work. In his judgment the law had to be changed so that only really needy people could get help. And he also wanted to see that the people in real need got enough to live on. Both Carleson and Governor Reagan made a big issue of a value held by many—probably most—Americans that anyone on welfare who can work should have to take a job if it is available. Thus, another change in the law that Carleson and Reagan wanted was the right to cut employable people off the rolls if they wouldn't work or take job training.

Carleson and his aides drew up a series of changes in the law, and gave them to the governor for his advice and approval. Then Reagan asked the legislature to make the changes. Most of them were passed. One of the items had to do with the "no work, no welfare" issue. If there were no job in private industry or no suitable training program, an employable person on welfare would have to take part in a community work force doing jobs for the local government. As a result, a large number of people worked on a part-time basis in libraries, schools, road work, and other public jobs. Governor Reagan noted, "When given the option of finding regular employment or performing public-service jobs for their welfare check, such persons often leave the welfare rolls entirely."

The graphs on page 572 show what happened to welfare rolls and costs in California. Carleson's work won praise from many people over the nation. He and several of his aides went to Washington to help bring changes in the federal programs. Several other states used his work as a model.

**1.** How did Governor Reagan as chief executive influence the decisions made by Welfare Director Robert Carleson?
**2.** How did legislative controls limit what Carleson could do when he took over as welfare director? What did he do to change this situation?

**3.** Another action taken by Carleson was to use computers to check up on income reported by people on welfare. A number of lawsuits were started to stop this action on the ground that it was an "invasion of privacy." A state judge issued an injunction to stop the check-ups, but three months later a state court of appeals threw out the injunction. How does this action show judicial control of bureaucrats?

**4.** How do you suppose public opinion and community pressures may have influenced decision-making in this case?

**5.** What conflicting values can you identify in this case? What are your values about the reforms?

### WELFARE TRENDS IN CALIFORNIA

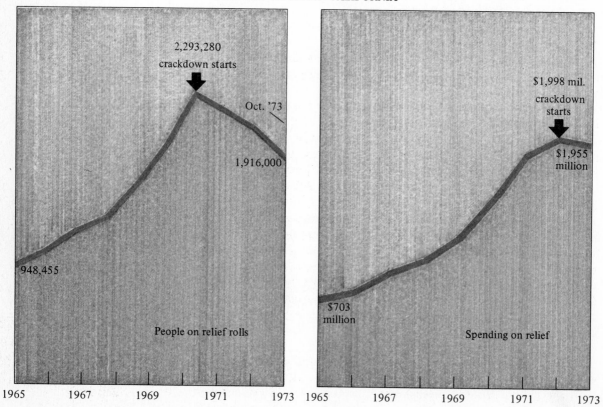

Source: California State Department of Welfare

572

# We the People

of the United States, in order to form a more perfect union, establish justice, insure domestic tranquillity, provide for the common defense, promote the general welfare, and secure the blessings of liberty to ourselves and our posterity, do ordain and establish this CONSTITUTION for the United States of America.

*Six reasons are given here for the establishment of our Constitution.*

## Article I. Legislative Department

### Section 1. Congress

All legislative powers herein granted shall be vested in a Congress of the United States, which shall consist of a Senate and House of Representatives.

*A bicameral legislature.*

### Section 2. House of Representatives

**Election and Term of Members.** The House of Representatives shall be composed of members chosen every second year by the people of the several States, and the electors in each State shall have the qualifications requisite for electors of the most numerous branch of the State Legislature.

*Representatives are to be chosen for two-year terms by the electors (voters) who are permitted to vote for members of the lower house of their own state legislature.*

**Qualifications.** No person shall be a representative who shall not have attained to the age of twenty-five years, and been seven years a citizen of the United States, and who shall not, when elected, be an inhabitant of that State in which he shall be chosen.

**Apportionment.** Representatives and direct taxes shall be apportioned among the several States which may be included within this Union, according to their respective numbers, which shall be determined by adding to the whole number of free persons, including those bound to service for a term of years, and excluding Indians not taxed, three-fifths of all other persons. The actual enumeration shall be made within three years after the first meeting of the Congress of the United States, and within every subsequent term of ten years, in such manner as they shall by law direct. The number of representatives shall not exceed one for every thirty thousand, but each State shall have at least one representative; and until such enumeration shall be made, the State of New Hampshire shall be entitled to choose three; Massachusetts, eight; Rhode Island and Providence Plantations, one; Con-

*The number of representatives per state is determined by its population.*

*"All other persons" refers to slaves. Amendment XIV changed this "three-fifths compromise" provision.*

*A census of the population shall be taken every ten*

The words printed in the margins in this kind of type explain some of the more difficult passages. The parts printed in color are no longer in force.

573

years to determine how many representatives each state shall have.

House vacancies shall be filled by a special election called by the governor of a state.

necticut, five; New York, six; New Jersey, four; Pennsylvania, eight; Delaware, one; Maryland, six; Virginia, ten; North Carolina, five; South Carolina, five; and Georgia, three.

**Vacancies.** When vacancies happen in the representation from any State, the executive authority thereof shall issue writs of election to fill such vacancies.

**Officers; Impeachment.** The House of Representatives shall choose their Speaker[1] and other officers; and shall have the sole power of impeachment.

### Section 3. Senate

Amendment XVII in 1913 provided for *direct* election of senators.

One-third of the senators are elected each two years.

**Number of Senators: Election.** The Senate of the United States shall be composed of two senators from each State, chosen by the legislature thereof, for six years; and each senator shall have one vote.

**Divided into Three Groups.** Immediately after they shall be assembled in consequence of the first election, they shall be divided as equally as may be into three classes. The seats of the senators of the first class shall be vacated at the expiration of the second year; of the second class, at the expiration of the fourth year; of the third class, at the expiration of the sixth year, so that one-third may be chosen every second year; and if vacancies happen by resignation, or otherwise, during the recess of the legislature of any State, the executive thereof may make temporary appointments until the next meeting of the legislature, which shall then fill such vacancies.

Senate vacancies are filled by the governor. Such appointees serve until a new election is held (see Amendment XVII).

**Qualifications.** No person shall be a senator who shall not have attained to the age of thirty years, and been nine years a citizen of the United States, and who shall not, when elected, be an inhabitant of that State for which he shall be chosen.

The Vice-President serves as presiding officer in the Senate but may vote only in case of a tie.

**President of Senate.** The Vice-President of the United States shall be president of the Senate, but shall have no vote, unless they be equally divided.

The Senate elects a temporary president to serve in Vice-President's absence or when there is no Vice-President.

**Officers.** The Senate shall choose their other officers, and also a president *pro tempore,* in the absence of the Vice-President, or when he shall exercise the office of President of the United States.

If impeached persons are found guilty, they are removed from office and not permitted to hold any federal office. If they have broken any laws, they may be tried for these violations in a court.

**Trials of Impeachment.** The Senate shall have the sole power to try all impeachments. When sitting for that purpose, they shall be on oath or affirmation. When the President of the United States is tried, the Chief Justice shall preside; and no person shall be convicted without the concurrence of two-thirds of the members present.

**Judgment in Case of Conviction.** Judgment in cases of impeachment shall not extend further than to removal from office, and disqualification to hold and enjoy any office of honor, trust, or profit under the United States: but the party convicted shall nevertheless be liable and subject to indictment, trial, judgment, and punishment, according to law.

574

## Section 4. Both Houses

**Manner of Electing Members.** The times, places, and manner of holding elections for senators and representatives shall be prescribed in each State by the legislature thereof; but the Congress may at any time by law make or alter such regulations, except as to the places of choosing senators.

**Meetings of Congress.** The Congress shall assemble at least once in every year, and such meeting shall be on the first Monday in December, unless they shall by law appoint a different day.

Today all our states hold elections for Congress on the first Tuesday after the first Monday in November, in the even-numbered years.

The meeting time of Congress was changed in Amendment XX, Section 2.

## Section 5. The Houses Separately

**Organization.** Each house shall be the judge of the elections, returns, and qualifications of its own members, and a majority of each shall constitute a quorum to do business; but a smaller number may adjourn from day to day, and may be authorized to compel the attendance of absent members, in such manner, and under such penalties, as each house may provide.

**Rules.** Each house may determine the rules of its proceedings, punish its members for disorderly behavior, and, with the concurrence of two-thirds, expel a member.

Each house determines if its members are legally qualified and have been elected fairly. A quorum is the number required to conduct business. Absent members may be compelled to attend so that business may be transacted.

**Journal.** Each house shall keep a journal of its proceedings, and from time to time publish the same, excepting such parts as may in their judgment require secrecy; and the yeas and nays of the members of either house on any question shall, at the desire of one-fifth of those present, be entered on the journal.

Recording the yeas and nays on a measure lets us see how a member of Congress has voted.

**Adjournment.** Neither house, during the session of Congress, shall, without the consent of the other, adjourn for more than three days, nor to any other place than that in which the two houses shall be sitting.

## Section 6. Privileges and Disabilities of Members

**Pay and Privileges of Members.** The senators and representatives shall receive a compensation for their services, to be ascertained by law, and paid out of the treasury of the United States. They shall in all cases, except treason, felony, and breach of the peace, be privileged from arrest during their attendance at the session of their respective houses, and in going to and returning from the same; and for any speech or debate in either house they shall not be questioned in any other place.

Members are paid by the federal government, and they have the power to set their own pay.

They may be arrested for law violations but not for civil suits while Congress is in session. They may not be sued for anything they say in Congress.

**Prohibitions on Members.** No senator or representative shall, during the time for which he was elected, be appointed to any civil office under the authority of the United States, which shall have been created, or the emoluments whereof shall have been increased, during such time; and no person holding any office under the United States shall be a member of either house during his continuance in office.

During the term of office a member may not be appointed to any federal job which was created or for which the pay was increased during that term.

---

1. The Speaker, who presides, is one of the representatives; the other officers—clerk, sergeant-at-arms, postmaster, chaplain, doorkeeper, etc.—are not.

## Section 7. Method of Passing Laws

Tax bills must begin in the House but the Senate may propose changes.

**Revenue Bills.** All bills for raising revenue shall originate in the House of Representatives; but the Senate may propose or concur with amendments as on other bills.

A bill passed by Congress must be sent to the President for his approval and signature. If he disapproves, he returns it with his objections to the house where it started (veto). Congress may pass a bill over his veto by a two-thirds vote of each house.

**How Bills Become Laws.** Every bill which shall have passed the House of Representatives and the Senate shall, before it become a law, be presented to the President of the United States; if he approve, he shall sign it, but if not, he shall return it, with his objections, to that house in which it shall have originated, who shall enter the objections at large on their journal, and proceed to reconsider it. If after such reconsideration two-thirds of that house shall agree to pass the bill, it shall be sent, together with the objections, to the other house, by which it shall likewise be reconsidered, and if approved by two-thirds of that house, it shall become a law. But in all such cases the votes of both houses shall be determined by yeas and nays, and the names of the persons voting for and against the bill shall be entered on the journal of each house respectively. If any bill shall not be returned by the President within ten days (Sundays excepted) after it shall have been presented to him, the same shall be a law, in like manner as if he had signed it, unless the Congress by their adjournment prevent its return, in which case it shall not be a law.

The President can let a bill become a law without his signature. But a bill sent to the President in the last ten days of a session of Congress is dead (by "pocket veto") if the President does not sign it.

The President's approval is likewise required on resolutions and other matters (except adjournment) passed by both houses.

**Resolutions, etc.** Every order, resolution, or vote to which the concurrence of the Senate and House of Representatives may be necessary (except on a question of adjournment) shall be presented to the President of the United States; and before the same shall take effect, shall be approved by him, or being disapproved by him, shall be repassed by two-thirds of the Senate and House of Representatives, according to the rules and limitations prescribed in the case of a bill.

## Section 8. Powers Granted to Congress

These are the "enumerated powers" of Congress.

**Powers of Congress.** The Congress shall have power:

To lay and collect taxes, duties, imposts, and excises, to pay the debts and provide for the common defense and general welfare of the United States; but all duties, imposts, and excises shall be uniform throughout the United States;

Federal tax rates must be the same in all states.

To borrow money on the credit of the United States;

This is the "interstate commerce clause."

To regulate commerce with foreign nations, and among the several States, and with the Indian tribes;

Naturalization and bankruptcy laws.

To establish a uniform rule of naturalization, and uniform laws on the subject of bankruptcies throughout the United States;

Congress determines our system of measurements.

To coin money, regulate the value thereof, and of foreign coin, and fix the standard of weights and measures;

Securities are government bonds and notes.

To provide for the punishment of counterfeiting the securities and current coin of the United States;

To establish post offices and post roads;

576

To promote the progress of science and useful arts, by securing, for limited times, to authors and inventors the exclusive right to their respective writings and discoveries;

To constitute tribunals inferior to the Supreme Court;

To define and punish piracies and felonies committed on the high seas, and offenses against the law of nations;

To declare war, grant letters of marque and reprisal, and make rules concerning captures on land and water;

To raise and support armies, but no appropriation of money to that use shall be for a longer term than two years;

To provide and maintain a navy;

To make rules for the government and regulation of the land and naval forces;

To provide for calling forth the militia to execute the laws of the Union, suppress insurrections, and repel invasions;

To provide for organizing, arming, and disciplining the militia, and for governing such part of them as may be employed in the service of the United States, reserving to the States respectively the appointment of the officers, and the authority of training the militia according to the discipline prescribed by Congress;

To exercise exclusive legislation in all cases whatsoever over such district (not exceeding ten miles square) as may, by cession of particular States, and the acceptance of Congress, become the seat of the government of the United States, and to exercise like authority over all places, purchased by the consent of the legislature of the State in which the same shall be, for the erection of forts, magazines, arsenals, dockyards, and other needful buildings;—and

**Implied Powers.** To make all laws which shall be necessary and proper for carrying into execution the foregoing powers, and all other powers vested by this Constitution in the government of the United States, or in any department or officer thereof.

Patent and copyright laws.

Congress may set up other federal courts

Congress, rather than the states, has power over crimes committed at sea.

Letters of marque and reprisal are permissions for private vessels to attack enemy shipping.

Armed forces are ruled by regulations passed by Congress.

The federal government helps the states maintain a militia, called the National Guard. It may be called into federal service.

This provides for the establishment and government of the District of Columbia. The federal government is also given complete authority over other federal properties.

This "elastic clause" has been interpreted by the courts as power for Congress to do many things not named specifically in the Constitution.

## Section 9. Powers Forbidden to the United States

**Absolute Prohibitions on Congress.** The migration or importation of such persons as any of the States now existing shall think proper to admit, shall not be prohibited by the Congress prior to the year one thousand eight hundred and eight, but a tax or duty may be imposed on such importation, not exceeding ten dollars for each person.

The privilege of the writ of habeas corpus shall not be suspended, unless when in cases of rebellion or invasion the public safety may require it.

No bill of attainder or ex-post-facto law shall be passed.

No capitation, or other direct, tax shall be laid, unless in proportion to the census or enumeration hereinbefore directed to be taken.

No tax or duty shall be laid on articles exported from any State.

This was to prevent Congress from interfering with the foreign slave trade for 20 years.

Habeas corpus gives a person held in custody a chance to be set free if he is being held illegally.

Export taxes are forbidden.

Commercial regulations and taxes may not favor one region or place over another.

No federal funds may be spent without authorization of Congress. Financial records must be published.

Congress may not grant titles of nobility. Nor may any public official accept a title, office, or pay from a foreign country without the consent of Congress.

Certain powers are forbidden to the states, either because these powers belong to the federal government or because they are things no democratic government should do.

The states may not, without the consent of Congress, tax goods entering or leaving the state except for small fees to cover the expense of inspection.

The states may not tax the cargo of ships, keep troops or warships, make compacts with other states or with foreign countries, or engage in war, unless invaded, without the consent of Congress.

Federal officials may not serve as presidential electors.

No preference shall be given by any regulation of commerce or revenue to the ports of one State over those of another; nor shall vessels bound to, or from, one State, be obliged to enter, clear, or pay duties in another.

No money shall be drawn from the treasury, but in consequence of appropriations made by law; and a regular statement and account of the receipts and expenditures of all public money shall be published from time to time.

No title of nobility shall be granted by the United States: And no person holding any office of profit or trust under them, shall, without the consent of the Congress, accept of any present, emolument, office, or title, of any kind whatever, from any king, prince, or foreign state.

### Section 10. Powers Forbidden to the States

**Absolute Prohibitions on the States.** No State shall enter into any treaty, alliance, or confederation; grant letters of marque and reprisal; coin money; emit bills of credit; make anything but gold and silver coin a tender in payment of debts; pass any bill of attainder, ex-post-facto law, or law impairing the obligation of contracts, or grant any title of nobility.

**Conditional Prohibitions on the States.** No State shall, without the consent of the Congress, lay any imposts or duties on imports or exports, except what may be absolutely necessary for executing its inspection laws; and the net produce of all duties and imposts, laid by any State on imports or exports, shall be for the use of the treasury of the United States; and all such laws shall be subject to the revision and control of the Congress.

No State shall, without the consent of Congress, lay any duty of tonnage, keep troops, or ships of war, in time of peace, enter into any agreement or compact with another State, or with a foreign power, or engage in war, unless actually invaded, or in such imminent danger as will not admit of delay.

## Article II. Executive Department

### Section 1. President and Vice-President

**Term.** The executive power shall be vested in a President of the United States of America. He shall hold his office during the term of four years, and together with the Vice-President, chosen for the same term, be elected, as follows:

**Electors.** Each State shall appoint, in such manner as the legislature thereof may direct, a number of electors, equal to the whole number of senators and representatives to which the State may be entitled in the Congress: but no senator or representative, or person holding an office of trust or profit under the United States, shall be appointed an elector.

578

**Proceedings of Electors and of Congress.** The electors shall meet in their respective States, and vote by ballot for two persons, of whom one at least shall not be an inhabitant of the same State with themselves. And they shall make a list of all the persons voted for, and of the number of votes for each; which list they shall sign and certify and transmit sealed to the seat of the government of the United States, directed to the president of the Senate. The president of the Senate shall, in the presence of the Senate and House of Representatives, open all the certificates, and the votes shall then be counted. The person having the greatest number of votes shall be the President, if such number be a majority of the whole number of electors appointed; and if there be more than one who have such majority, and have an equal number of votes, then the House of Representatives shall immediately choose by ballot one of them for President; and if no person have a majority, then from the five highest on the list the said house shall, in like manner, choose the President. But in choosing the President, the votes shall be taken by States, the representation from each State having one vote; a quorum for this purpose shall consist of a member or members from two-thirds of the States, and a majority of all the States shall be necessary to a choice. In every case, after the choice of the President, the person having the greatest number of votes of the electors shall be the Vice-President. But if there should remain two or more who have equal votes, the Senate shall choose from them by ballot the Vice-President.

**Time of Choosing Electors.** The Congress may determine the time of choosing the electors, and the day on which they shall give their votes; which day shall be the same throughout the United States.

**Qualifications of President.** No person except a natural born citizen, or a citizen of the United States at the time of the adoption of this Constitution, shall be eligible to the office of President; neither shall any person be eligible to that office who shall not have attained to the age of thirty-five years, and been fourteen years a resident within the United States.

**Vacancy.** In case of the removal of the President from office, or of his death, resignation, or inability to discharge the powers and duties of the said office, the same shall devolve on the Vice-President, and the Congress may by law provide for the case of removal, death, resignation, or inability, both of the President and Vice-President, declaring what officer shall then act as President; and such officer shall act accordingly until the disability be removed, or a President shall be elected.

**Salary.** The President shall, at stated times, receive for his services a compensation which shall neither be increased nor diminished during the period for which he shall have been elected, and he shall not receive within that period any other emolument from the United States, or any of them.

The manner of electing the President and Vice-President was changed by Amendment XII. The change was made because in 1800 Thomas Jefferson and Aaron Burr both received the same number of electoral votes, even though the electors wanted Jefferson for President and Burr for Vice-President. The Twelfth Amendment required the electors to cast *separate* ballots for President and Vice-President.

The date of presidential elections is the first Tuesday after the first Monday in November. Electoral votes are cast on the first Monday after the second Wednesday in December.

The President must be a citizen by birth rather than by naturalization.

The 25th Amendment provides for the election of a new Vice-President by Congress (on nomination by the President) when the office is vacant.

The President's salary may be neither increased nor decreased during the term of office. The President may not receive other pay from the government.

The oath of office is prescribed.

**Oath.** Before he enter on the execution of his office, he shall take the following oath or affirmation:—"I do solemnly swear (or affirm) that I will faithfully execute the office of President of the United States, and will, to the best of my ability, preserve, protect, and defend the Constitution of the United States."

## Section 2. Powers of the President

This implies that the President will correspond with the heads of departments, but in practice they also serve as the Cabinet.

**Military Powers; Reprieves and Pardons.** The President shall be commander in chief of the army and navy of the United States, and of the militia of the several States, when called into the actual service of the United States; he may require the opinion, in writing, of the principal officer in each of the executive departments, upon any subject relating to the duties of their respective offices; and he shall have power to grant reprieves and pardons for offenses against the United States, except in cases of impeachment.

The Senate is given the special powers of approving treaties and presidential appointments.

**Treaties; Appointments.** He shall have power, by and with the advice and consent of the Senate, to make treaties, provided two-thirds of the senators present concur; and he shall nominate, and by and with the advice and consent of the Senate shall appoint ambassadors, other public ministers and consuls, judges of the Supreme Court, and all other officers of the United States, whose appointments are not herein otherwise provided for, and which shall be established by law; but the Congress may by law vest the appointment of such inferior officers, as they think proper, in the President alone, in the courts of law, or in the heads of departments.

This is intended to prevent the President from appointing officials, except temporarily, without the Senate's consent.

**Vacancies.** The President shall have power to fill up all vacancies that may happen during the recess of the Senate, by granting commissions which shall expire at the end of their next session.

## Section 3. Duties of the President

At the opening of each session of Congress the President sends or delivers a "State of the Union" message, and sends special messages from time to time.

**Message; Convening of Congress.** He shall from time to time give to the Congress information of the state of the Union, and recommend to their consideration such measures as he shall judge necessary and expedient; he may, on extraordinary occasions, convene both houses, or either of them, and in case of disagreement between them with respect to the time of adjournment, he may adjourn them to such time as he shall think proper; he shall receive ambassadors and other public ministers; he shall take care that the laws be faithfully executed, and shall commission all the officers of the United States.

## Section 4. Impeachment

**Removal of Officers.** The President, Vice-President, and all civil officers of the United States, shall be removed from office on impeachment for, and conviction of, treason, bribery, or other high crimes and misdemeanors.

580

# Article III. Judicial Department

## Section 1. United States Courts

**Courts Established; Judges.** The judicial power of the United States shall be vested in one Supreme Court, and in such inferior courts as the Congress may from time to time ordain and establish. The judges, both of the Supreme and inferior courts, shall hold their offices during good behavior, and shall, at stated times, receive for their services a compensation which shall not be diminished during their continuance in office.

Federal judges hold indefinite terms, but they may be removed by impeachment.

## Section 2. Jurisdiction of United States Courts

**Federal Courts in General.** The judicial power shall extend to all cases, in law and equity, arising under this Constitution, the laws of the United States, and treaties made, or which shall be made, under their authority;—to all cases affecting ambassadors, other public ministers, and consuls;—to all cases of admiralty and maritime jurisdiction;—to controversies to which the United States shall be a party;—to controversies between two or more States;—between a State and citizens of another State;—between citizens of different States;—between citizens of the same State claiming lands under grants of different States, and between a State, or the citizens thereof, and foreign states, citizens or subjects.

This describes the kind of cases which are to be handled in the federal courts.

Amendment XI took away the right of private citizens to bring a law suit against a state in a federal court.

**Supreme Court.** In all cases affecting ambassadors, other public ministers and consuls, and those in which a State shall be party, the Supreme Court shall have original jurisdiction. In all other cases before mentioned, the Supreme Court shall have appellate jurisdiction, both as to law and fact, with such exceptions and under such regulations as the Congress shall make.

Certain kinds of cases must be handled by the Supreme Court directly. Cases handled by the lower courts may be reviewed by the Supreme Court, but Congress may change the appellate (review) power.

**Trials.** The trial of all crimes, except in cases of impeachment, shall be by jury; and such trial shall be held in the State where the said crimes shall have been committed; but when not committed within any State, the trial shall be at such place or places as the Congress may by law have directed.

This section on how trials shall be held is strengthened by the Bill of Rights, especially Amendment VI.

## Section 3. Treason

**Treason Defined.** Treason against the United States shall consist only in levying war against them, or in adhering to their enemies, giving them aid and comfort.

No person shall be convicted of treason unless on the testimony of two witnesses to the same overt act, or on confession in open court.

Treason is very strictly defined. Conviction requires the testimony of two persons to the same specific act, or confession in court by the accused.

**Punishment.** The Congress shall have power to declare the punishment of treason, but no attainder of treason shall work corruption of blood, or forfeiture, except during the life of the person attainted.

Punishment for treason may not extend to one's descendants.

# Article IV. Relations of the States to Each Other

### Section 1. Official Acts

The states are required to honor each other's laws, records, and legal decisions.

Full faith and credit shall be given in each State to the public acts, records, and judicial proceedings of every other State. And the Congress may by general laws prescribe the manner in which such acts, records, and proceedings shall be proved, and the effect thereof.

### Section 2. Privileges of Citizens

Each state must offer fair treatment to citizens of other states.

The citizens of each State shall be entitled to all privileges and immunities of citizens in the several States.

The process of returning an accused person to a state from which he has fled is called "extradition."

**Fugitives from Justice.** A person charged in any State with treason, felony, or other crime, who shall flee from justice, and be found in another State, shall, on demand of the executive authority of the State from which he fled, be delivered up, to be removed to the State having jurisdiction of the crime.

This was the basis for the fugitive slave laws. This provision became ineffective with the adoption of Amendment XIII.

**Fugitive Slaves.** No person held to service or labor in one State, under the laws thereof, escaping into another, shall, in consequence of any law or regulation therein, be discharged from such service or labor, but shall be delivered up on claim of the party to whom such service or labor may be due.

### Section 3. New States and Territories

New states may not be formed by dividing or joining existing states without the consent of the state legislatures and Congress.

**Admission of States.** New States may be admitted by the Congress into this Union; but no new State shall be formed or erected within the jurisdiction of any other State; nor any State be formed by the junction of two or more States, or parts of States, without the consent of the legislatures of the States concerned as well as of the Congress.

Congress has authority over federal territory and property.

**Territory and Property of United States.** The Congress shall have power to dispose of and make all needful rules and regulations respecting the territory or other property belonging to the United States; and nothing in this Constitution shall be so construed as to prejudice any claims of the United States, or of any particular State.

### Section 4. Protection of the States

A republican form of government is interpreted to mean a representative government governing by will of the people.

The United States shall guarantee to every State in this Union a republican form of government, and shall protect each of them against invasion, and on application of the legislature, or of the executive (when the legislature cannot be convened) against domestic violence.

The federal government is required to protect the states against invasion and, when the states so request, against domestic violence.

## Article V. Amendments

Amendments may be proposed by a two-thirds vote of each house of

**How Proposed; How Ratified.** The Congress, whenever two-thirds of both houses shall deem it necessary, shall propose amendments to this Constitution, or, on the application of the legislatures of two-thirds of the several States, shall call a convention for proposing amendments, which, in either case, shall be valid to all intents and purposes, as part of this Constitution, when ratified by the legislatures of three-fourths of the several States, or by conventions in three-fourths thereof, as the one or the other mode of ratification may be proposed by the Congress; provided that no amendment which may be made prior to the year one thousand eight hundred and eight shall in any manner affect the first and fourth clauses in the ninth section of the first article; and that no State, without its consent, shall be deprived of its equal suffrage in the Senate.

Congress or by a national convention called by Congress at the request of two-thirds of the states. Amendments may be ratified by legislatures of, or by conventions in, three-fourths of the states. No amendment may deprive a state of its equal vote in the Senate.

## Article VI. General Provisions

**Public Debt.** All debts contracted, and engagements entered into, before the adoption of this Constitution, shall be as valid against the United States under this Constitution, as under the Confederation.

Debts and obligations made by the United States before the adoption of the Constitution were to be honored.

**Supremacy of Constitution.** This Constitution, and the laws of the United States which shall be made in pursuance thereof; and all treaties made, or which shall be made, under the authority of the United States, shall be the supreme law of the land; and the judges in every State shall be bound thereby, anything in the Constitution or laws of any State to the contrary notwithstanding.

The Constitution, laws, and treaties of the United States are supreme. Judges in every state are bound by them.

**Official Oath; Religious Test.** The senators and representatives before mentioned, and the members of the several State legislatures, and all executive and judicial officers, both of the United States and of the several States, shall be bound by oath or affirmation to support this Constitutuion; but no religious test shall ever be required as a qualification to any office or public trust under the United States.

All public officials, state as well as national, shall promise to support the U.S. Constitution.

Religion may not be used as a qualification for holding a federal office.

## Article VII. Ratification of the Constitution

**Ratification.** The ratification of the Conventions of nine States shall be sufficient for the establishment of this Constitution between the States so ratifying the same.

The Constitution was to go into effect when approved by nine states.

Done in convention, by the unanimous consent of the States present, the seventeenth day of September, in the year of our Lord one thousand seven hundred and eighty-seven, and of the independence of the United States of America the twelfth.

In witness whereof, we have hereunto subscribed our names.

George Washington, *President, and Deputy from Virginia*

*New Hampshire*
John Langdon
Nicholas Gilman

*Massachusetts*
Nathaniel Gorham
Rufus King

*Connecticut*
William Samuel
Johnson
Roger Sherman

583

| New York | Pennsylvania | Virginia |
|---|---|---|
| Alexander Hamilton | Benjamin Franklin | John Blair |
| | Thomas Mifflin | James Madison, Jr. |
| *New Jersey* | Robert Morris | |
| William Livingston | George Clymer | *North Carolina* |
| David Brearley | Thomas Fitzsimons | William Blount |
| William Paterson | Jared Ingersoll | Richard Dobbs |
| Jonathan Dayton | James Wilson | Spaight |
| | Gouverneur Morris | Hugh Williamson |
| *Maryland* | | |
| James M'Henry | *Delaware* | *South Carolina* |
| Daniel of St. Thomas | George Read | John Rutledge |
| Jenifer | Gunning Bedford, Jr. | Charles C. Pinckney |
| Daniel Carroll | John Dickinson | Charles Pinckney |
| | Richard Bassett | Pierce Butler |
| *Georgia* | Jacob Broom | |
| William Few | | |
| Abraham Baldwin | | |

ATTEST: William Jackson, *Secretary*

# Amendments

The first ten amendments were proposed in 1789 and adopted in 1791.

## Amendment I

Congress may not set up an official church or pass laws limiting worship, speech, the press, assembly, and the right to petition.

**Religion, Speech, Press, Assembly, Petition.** Congress shall make no law respecting an establishment of religion, or prohibiting the free exercise thereof; or abridging the freedom of speech, or of the press; or the right of the people peaceably to assemble, and to petition the government for redress of grievances.

## Amendment II

The right of the states to maintain a citizens' militia is guaranteed.

**Militia.** A well-regulated militia being necessary to the security of a free State, the right of the people to keep and bear arms shall not be infringed.

## Amendment III

Limits the army's right to take over private housing.

**Soldiers.** No soldier shall, in time of peace, be quartered in any house, without the consent of the owner; nor in time of war but in a manner to be prescribed by law.

## Amendment IV

This clause limits the right of the government to search and take custody of

**Unreasonable Searches.** The right of the people to be secure in their persons, houses, papers, and effects, against unreasonable searches and seizures, shall not be violated, and no warrants shall

584

issue, but upon probable cause, supported by oath or affirmation, and particularly describing the place to be searched, and the persons or things to be seized.

*persons and property. Specific warrants for search and arrest are required.*

## Amendment V

**Legal Protection of Accused Persons.** No person shall be held to answer for a capital, or otherwise infamous crime, unless on a presentment or indictment of a grand jury, except in cases arising in the land or naval forces, or in the militia, when in actual service in time of war or public danger; nor shall any person be subject for the same offense to be twice put in jeopardy of life or limb; nor shall be compelled in any criminal case to be a witness against himself, nor to be deprived of life, liberty, or property, without due process of law; nor shall private property be taken for public use, without just compensation.

*Guarantees grand-jury indictment in federal trials (except military trials). Prohibits double jeopardy and self-incrimination. Requires due process of law (fair legal procedures) and fair payment for private property taken for public use.*

## Amendment VI

**Right to Trial.** In all criminal prosecutions, the accused shall enjoy the right to a speedy and public trial, by an impartial jury of the State and district wherein the crime shall have been committed, which district shall have been previously ascertained by law, and to be informed of the nature and cause of the accusation; to be confronted with the witnesses against him; to have compulsory process for obtaining witnesses in his favor, and to have the assistance of counsel for his defense.

*Trials shall be speedy and public, by impartial juries, in the district and state where the crime occurred. The accused shall be told of the charges against him, be allowed to face the witnesses against him and call defense witnesses, and have a lawyer.*

## Amendment VII

**Suits at Common Law.** In suits at common law, where the value in controversy shall exceed twenty dollars, the right of trial by jury shall be preserved, and no fact tried by a jury shall be otherwise re-examined in any court of the United States than according to the rules of common law.

*Jury trial is guaranteed in civil suits when the matter amounts to more than $20.*

## Amendment VIII

**Bail, Punishments.** Excessive bail shall not be required, nor excessive fines imposed, nor cruel and unusual punishments inflicted.

*Bails, fines, and punishment must be fair and humane.*

## Amendment IX

**Reserved Rights.** The enumeration in the Constitution of certain rights shall not be construed to deny or disparage others retained by the people.

*The listing of these rights does not mean that other rights may be disregarded.*

## Amendment X

**Reserved Powers.** The powers not delegated to the United States by the Constitution, nor prohibited by it to the States, are reserved to the States respectively, or to the people.

*Powers not given to Congress are reserved to the states and the people.*

## Amendment XI

This preserves the right of a state not to be sued without its own consent. Proposed in 1794 and adopted in 1798.

**Suits against States.** The judicial power of the United States shall not be construed to extend to any suit in law or equity, commenced or prosecuted against any of the United States by citizens of another State, or by citizens or subjects of any foreign state.

## Amendment XII

The Twelfth Amendment made some changes in the method of electing the President and Vice-President (see Article II, Sec. 1). The major change was that the members of the Electoral College (called "electors") should vote separately for President and Vice-President.

**Method of Electing President and Vice-President.** The electors shall meet in their respective States, and vote by ballot for President and Vice-President, one of whom, at least, shall not be an inhabitant of the same State with themselves; they shall name in their ballots the person voted for as President, and in distinct ballots the person voted for as Vice-President; and they shall make distinct lists of all persons voted for as President, and of all persons voted for as Vice-President, and of the number of votes for each, which list they shall sign and certify, and transmit sealed to the seat of the government of the United States, directed to the president of the Senate;—the president of the Senate shall, in the presence of the Senate and House of Representatives, open all the certificates, and the votes shall then be counted;—the person having the greatest number of votes for President, shall be the President, if such number be a majority of the whole number of electors appointed; and if no person have such majority, then from the persons having the highest numbers not exceeding three on the list of those voted for as President, the House of Representatives shall choose immediately, by ballot, the President. But in choosing the President, the votes shall be taken by States, the representation from each State having one vote; a quorum for this purpose shall consist of a member or members from two-thirds of the States, and a majority of all the States shall be necessary to a choice. And if the House of Representatives shall not choose a President whenever the right of choice shall devolve upon them, before the fourth day of March next following, then the Vice-President shall act as President, as in the case of the death or other constitutional disability of the President. The person having the greatest number of votes as Vice-President, shall be the Vice-President, if such number be a majority of the whole number of electors appointed; and if no person have a majority, then from the two highest numbers on the list, the Senate shall choose the Vice-President; a quorum for the purpose shall consist of two-thirds of the whole number of senators, and a majority of the whole number shall be necessary to a choice. But no person constitutionally ineligible to the office of President shall be eligible to that of Vice-President of the United States.

If no candidate for President wins a majority, the House of Representatives chooses a President from the three highest—with each state having one vote. If no candidate for Vice-President wins a majority, the Senate chooses from the two highest.

The phrase in color was changed by Amendment XX.

Article XII was adopted in 1804.

## Amendment XIII

Adopted in 1865.

**Slavery Abolished.** *Section 1.* Neither slavery nor involuntary servitude, except as a punishment for crime whereof the party shall have

586

been duly convicted, shall exist within the United States, or any place subject to their jurisdiction.

*Section 2.* Congress shall have power to enforce this article by appropriate legislation.

## Amendment XIV

**Blacks Made Citizens; Protection of Citizens.** *Section 1.* All persons born or naturalized in the United States, and subject to the jurisdiction thereof, are citizens of the United States and of the State wherein they reside. No State shall make or enforce any law which shall abridge the privileges or immunities of citizens of the United States; nor shall any State deprive any person of life, liberty, or property, without due process of law, nor deny to any person within its jurisdiction the equal protection of the laws.

*Section 2.* Representatives shall be apportioned among the several States according to their respective numbers, counting the whole number of persons in each State, excluding Indians not taxed. But when the right to vote at any election for the choice of electors for President and Vice-President of the United States, representatives in Congress, the executive or judicial officers of a State, or the members of the legislature thereof, is denied to any of the male inhabitants of such State, being twenty-one years of age, and citizens of the United States, or in any way abridged, except for participation in rebellion or other crime, the basis of representation therein shall be reduced in the proportion which the number of such male citizens shall bear to the whole number of male citizens twenty-one years of age in such State.

*Section 3.* No person shall be a senator or representative in Congress, or elector of President or Vice-President, or hold any office, civil or military, under the United States, or under any State, who, having previously taken an oath, as a member of Congress, or as an officer of the United States, or as a member of any State legislature, or as an executive or judicial officer of any State, to support the Constitution of the United States, shall have engaged in insurrection or rebellion against the same, or given aid or comfort to the enemies thereof. But Congress may, by a vote of two-thirds of each house, remove such disability.

*Section 4.* The validity of the public debt of the United States, authorized by law, including debts incurred for payment of pensions and bounties for services in suppressing insurrection or rebellion, shall not be questioned. But neither the United States nor any State shall assume or pay any debt or obligation incurred in aid of insurrection or rebellion against the United States, or any claim for the loss or emancipation of any slave; but all such debts, obligations, and claims shall be held illegal and void.

Citizenship was conferred on blacks. States were forbidden to deny equal privileges to any citizen. The effect of Section 1 was to apply the basic protections in the Bill of Rights to the states as well as to the federal government.

Section 2 provides that a state's representation in Congress may be cut if it denies the right to vote to any group of adult male citizens. This Section has never been applied.

Section 3 barred from federal office any former federal or state official who served the Confederacy in the Civil War.

Legalized the federal Civil War debt. But voided all debts incurred by the Southern states and the Confederacy in fighting the war.

Adopted in 1868.

*Section 5.* The Congress shall have power to enforce, by appropriate legislation, the provisions of this article.

## Amendment XV

Adopted in 1870.

**Blacks Made Voters.** *Section 1.* The rights of citizens of the United States to vote shall not be denied or abridged by the United States, or by any State, on account of race, color, or previous condition of servitude.

*Section 2.* The Congress shall have power to enforce this article by appropriate legislation.

## Amendment XVI

Permits Congress to levy income taxes. Adopted in 1913.

**Income Tax.** The Congress shall have power to lay and collect taxes on incomes from whatever source derived, without apportionment among the several States, and without regard to any census or enumeration.

## Amendment XVII

United States senators formerly were chosen by the state legislatures (see Article 1, Section 3) Adopted in 1913.

**Direct Election of Senators.** The Senate of the United States shall be composed of two senators from each State, elected by the people thereof for six years; and each senator shall have one vote. The electors in each State shall have the qualifications requisite for electors of the most numerous branch of the State legislature.

When vacancies happen in the representation of any State in the Senate, the executive authority of such State shall issue writs of election to fill such vacancies: Provided, that the legislature of any State may empower the Executive thereof to make temporary appointments until the people fill the vacancies by election as the legislature may direct.

This amendment shall not be so construed as to affect the election or term of any senator chosen before it becomes valid as part of the Constitution.

## Amendment XVIII

Forbade the making, selling, and transporting of intoxicating liquors. Ratified in 1919, it was repealed by the Twenty-first Amendment in 1933.

**National Prohibition.** *Section 1.* After one year from the ratification of this article the manufacture, sale, or transportation of intoxicating liquors within, the importation thereof into, or the exportation thereof from the United States and all territory subject to the jurisdiction thereof for beverage purposes is hereby prohibited.

*Section 2.* The Congress and the several States shall have concurrent power to enforce this article by appropriate legislation.

*Section 3.* This article shall be inoperative unless it shall have been ratified as an amendment to the Constitution by the legislatures of the several States, as provided in the Constitution, within seven years from the date of the submission hereof to the States by the Congress.

## Amendment XIX

**Woman Suffrage.** *Section 1.* The right of citizens of the United States to vote shall not be denied or abridged by the United States or by any State on account of sex.

*Section 2.* Congress shall have power to enforce this article by appropriate legislation.

Ratified in 1920.

## Amendment XX

**"Lame Duck" Amendment.** *Section 1.* The terms of the President and Vice-President shall end at noon on the twentieth day of January, and the terms of senators and representatives at noon on the third day of January, of the years in which such terms would have ended if this article had not been ratified; and the terms of their successors shall then begin.

*Section 2.* The Congress shall assemble at least once in every year, and such meeting shall begin at noon on the third day of January, unless they shall by law appoint a different day.

*Section 3.* If, at the time fixed for the beginning of the term of the President, the President-elect shall have died, the Vice-President-elect shall become President. If a President shall not have been chosen before the time fixed for the beginning of his term, or if the President-elect shall have failed to qualify, then the Vice-President-elect shall act as President until a President shall have qualified; and the Congress may by law provide for the case wherein neither a President-elect nor a Vice-President-elect shall have qualified, declaring who shall then act as President, or the manner in which one who is to act shall be selected, and such person shall act accordingly until a President or Vice-President shall have qualified.

*Section 4.* The Congress may by law provide for the case of the death of any of the persons from whom the House of Representatives may choose a President whenever the right of choice shall have devolved upon them, and for the case of the death of any of the persons from whom the Senate may choose a Vice-President whenever the right of choice shall have devolved upon them.

*Section 5.* Sections 1 and 2 shall take effect upon the fifteenth day of October following the ratification of this article.

*Section 6.* This article shall be inoperative unless it shall have been ratified as an amendment to the Constitution by the legislatures of three-fourths of the several States within seven years from the date of its submission.

Provided for the President to take office on January 20 and members of Congress on January 3 to reduce the time between an election and taking office. A "lame duck" is an official who continues to serve though not reelected.

Congress is to meet once a year.

Provides for succession to the Presidency if the President-elect should die or fail to qualify before January 20.

Ratified in 1933.

## Amendment XXI

**The Repeal of Prohibition** *Section 1.* The Eighteenth article of amendment to the Constitution of the United States is hereby repealed.

*Section 2.* The transportation or importation into any State, Territory, or possession of the United States for delivery or use therein

Section 2 permits state prohibition of alcoholic beverages.

of intoxicating liquors, in violation of the laws thereof, hereby is prohibited.

*Section 3.* This article shall be inoperative unless it shall have been ratified as an amendment to the Constitution by conventions in the several States, as provided in the Constitution, within seven years from the date of the submission hereof to the States by the Congress.

## Amendment XXII

**Presidential Term.** *Section 1.* No person shall be elected to the office of the President more than twice, and no person who has held the office of President, or acted as President, for more than two years of a term to which some other person was elected President shall be elected to the office of the President more than once. But this article shall not apply to any person holding the office of President when this article was proposed by the Congress, and shall not prevent any person who may be holding the office of President, or acting as President, during the term within which this article becomes operative, from holding the office of President or acting as President during the remainder of such term.

*Section 2.* This article shall be inoperative unless it shall have been ratified as an amendment to the Constitution by the legislatures of three-fourths of the several States within seven years from the date of its submission to the States by the Congress.

## Amendment XXIII

**Electors for the District of Columbia.** *Section 1.* The District constituting the seat of Government of the United States shall appoint in such manner as the Congress may direct:

A number of electors of President and Vice-President equal to the whole number of senators and representatives in Congress to which the District would be entitled if it were a State, but in no event more than the least populous State; they shall be in addition to those appointed by the States, but they shall be considered, for the purposes of the election of President and Vice-President, to be electors appointed by a State; and they shall meet in the District and perform such duties as provided by the twelfth article of amendment.

*Section 2.* The Congress shall have power to enforce this article by appropriate legislation.

## Amendment XXIV

**Poll Tax.** *Section 1.* The right of citizens of the United States to vote in any primary or other election for President or Vice-President, for electors for President or Vice-President, or for Senator or Representative in Congress, shall not be denied or abridged by the United States or any State by reason of failure to pay any poll tax or other tax.

*Section 2.* The Congress shall have power to enforce this article by appropriate legislation.

Ratified in 1933 by conventions in the states.

Provides that a President may serve only two full terms plus two years of a previous President's term. If a person fills out more than two years of a previous term, he may be elected only once.

Ratified in 1951.

The District of Columbia is given three electoral votes, and Congress may determine how the three electors are to be chosen. In proposing this amendment, Congress made it clear that qualified residents of the District would get the right to vote for President and Vice-President.

Ratified in 1961.

Forbids use of poll tax as a requirement for voting in election of federal officers.

Ratified in 1964.

590

# Amendment XXV

**Presidential Disability and Vice-Presidential Vacancy.** *Section 1.*
In case of the removal of the President from office or his death or
resignation, the Vice-President shall become President.

*Section 2.* Whenever there is a vacancy in the office of the Vice-
President, the President shall nominate a Vice-President who shall
take the office upon confirmation by a majority vote of both houses
of Congress.

*Section 3.* Whenever the President transmits to the President pro
tempore of the Senate and the Speaker of the House of Representatives his written declaration that he is unable to discharge the
powers and duties of his office, and until he transmits to them a written
declaration to the contrary, such powers and duties shall be discharged
by the Vice-President as Acting President.

*Section 4.* Whenever the Vice-President and a majority of either
the principal officers of the executive department or of such other
body as Congress may by law provide, transmit to the President pro
tempore of the Senate and the Speaker of the House of Representatives their written declaration that the President is unable to discharge the powers and duties of his office, the Vice-President shall
immediately assume the powers and duties of the office of Acting
President.

Thereafter, when the President transmits to the President pro tempore of the Senate and the Speaker of the House of Representatives
his written declaration that no inability exists, he shall resume the
powers and duties of his office unless the Vice-President and a majority
of either the principal officers of the executive department or of such
other body as Congress may by law provide, transmit within four
days to the President pro tempore of the Senate and the Speaker of
the House of Representatives their written declaration that the President is unable to discharge the powers and duties of his office. There-
upon Congress shall decide the issue, assembling within 48 hours for
that purpose if not in session. If the Congress, within 21 days after
receipt of the latter written declaration, or, if Congress is not in session, within 21 days after Congress is required to assemble, determines
by two-thirds vote of both houses that the President is unable to discharge the powers and duties of his office, the Vice-President shall
continue to discharge the same as Acting President; otherwise, the
President shall resume the powers and duties of his office.

Ratification completed in
February 1967.

Clarifies role of
Vice-President when the
President is disabled.

# Amendment XXVI

**Voting Age.** *Section 1.* The right of citizens of the United States
who are eighteen years of age or older, to vote shall not be denied
or abridged by the United States or by any state on account of age.

*Section 2.* The Congress shall have power to enforce this article
by appropriate legislation.

Proposed in March 1971.
Ratification completed in
record time on June 30,
1971.

## Amendment XXVII (Proposed)

Proposed in March 1972. Ratified by 30 states by the end of March 1972, but by only four more by May 1976.

**Equal Rights Amendment.** *Section 1.* The equality of rights under the law shall not be denied or abridged by the United States or any State on account of sex.

*Section 2.* The Congress shall have the power to enforce, by appropriate legislation, the provisions of this Article.

*Section 3.* This amendment shall take effect two years after the date of ratification.

# Index

Conventions, party, 174, 190-192, 197-199
Cook County, Illinois, 486
Coolidge, Calvin, 284; *photo,* 306
Council-manager plan, 87, 509, 511; case on, 536-539; *chart,* 510; *table,* 509
County board, 487, 488, 534-535
County government, 485-488, 508, 534-535; *chart,* 487; *map,* 486
County manager plan, 487
Courtesy: in Congress, 346-349, 366; senatorial, 307
Courts, federal, 384-430; *chart,* 391; *map,* 393
Courts, state-local, 540-557; bureaucracy and, 565-566; *chart,* 541; malpractice law and, 529-532
Courts of Appeals, U.S., 392
Cox, Archibald, 445
Crime, in cities, 511, 518
Criminal cases, 390-392, 541, 542, 544, 546-552
Cronkhite, Walter, *photo,* 22
Cross-pressures: bureaucratic, 443, 445; and voting, 232-233, 235
Crowded Corral, case of, 536-539
Crump, Edward H., 181
Cuba, 292, 293; missile crisis, 315-323
Culture: defined, 94; political behavior and, 94-115; roles and, 116
Cushing, Cardinal, *photo,* 239
Customs, 12; in Amish subculture, 106-112; in Congress, 346, 350-354; in presidential decision-making, 306-307; in principal's role, 268; roles and, 119-120. *See also* Informal rules
Cynicism, political, 155-157, 253

Dahl, Robert A. 218
Daley, Richard, *photos,* 182, 516
Decatur, Stephen, quoted, 158
Decibel, 463-464
Decisions, political, as aspect of political behavior, 10-11
Defense, Department of, 287, 447, 478, 479
Deficit, budget, 311, 314, 515
Delaware, 486, 555
Dellums, Ronald V., 220-221
Democracy: leadership selection in, 168-169, 172-173; right to dissent and, 158-160; United States government as, 263-264; voting and, 225, 227
Democratic party: Chicanos and, 224; in cities, 174; civil rights law and, 362, 364, 365; in election campaigns, 237-239; in 1972

election, 184, 191, 192; in Oregon, 502; policies, 234; in Tuskegee, 244-247; voter preference for, 228-229, 231-234, 235, 250-251; white-primary laws and, 214
Democratic political beliefs, 101-104
Democratic-republican government, 263-264
Demonstrations, political, 30, 359-360; *photos,* 361; in Shoreline case, 18-19; on Vietnam, 41-43; violent, 153-155
Denver, 488
Depression, of the 1930s, 237, 238, 329
DeSimone, Herbert, 64
Detention camps, for Japanese Americans, 150-153
Detroit, union vote in, 231-232
*Detroit Free Press,* 66-67
Dewey, Thomas E., 240
Dictatorship: leadership selection in, 169-170, 172; loyalty in, 159
Diego Resolution, 378-383
Dinaric Serbs, 79-80
Direct democracy, 264
Direct primary, 173-174; in presidential elections, 197-199
Dirksen, Everett, 367-368, 428
Discharge petition, 364
Discrimination, racial: civil rights law and, 358-370; against Japanese Americans, 151; judicial personality and, 422; protests against, 160-162; segregation cases, 417-421; in Tuskegee, 245-246
Disloyalty, *see* Loyalty
Dissent, right to, 157-165
Dissenting opinion, 404
District of Columbia, 491
District Courts, U.S., 390, 391
Division of powers, 264-265, *chart,* 265
Dobis, Chester, 530
Dobrynin, Anatoly, 320
Docket book, 403
Domestic Council, 288
Domestic relations courts, 542
Dominican Republic, 293
Douglas, Paul, quoted, 377
Douglas, William O., quoted, 389
Due process clause, 406-410
*Dun* v. *Blumstein,* 209
Dye, Thomas, quoted, 497

Easement, 505
Eastland, James, quoted, 430
Economic Advisers, Council of, 296, 311
Economic Opportunity, Office of, 288

Economic planning, President and, 295-296
Edgar, Cynthia, 134, 140
Edison, Thomas, *photo,* 306
Editors and editorials, 44, 52, 55
Education: Amish school case, 106-115; of bureaucrats, 448; civil rights law and, 362; governor and, 497, 506; members of Congress and, 335, 339-340; political participation and, 204, 205; racial imbalance law, 564; school districts, 491; school prayer case, 384-390; segregation case, 420-421; socialization and, 97-99; state superintendent of, 497, 506; urban riots and, 154; voting tendencies and, 228-229, *tables,* 229, 233
Education, United States Office of (USOE), 434-437, 438, 441, 445, 450, 456; case on, 478; *chart,* 434-435; Commissioner, 436, 441, 447
Eisenhower, Dwight D., 237, 284, 293; bureaucracy and, 440; *photo,* 286; quoted, 302; Vietnam and, 304; W. E. Burger and, 429
Election outcome, concern about, 217
Elections: examples of, 168-169, 170; of 1972, 191-192, 194-196, *map,* 195; nominating candidates for, 173-174; participating in, 202-227; political parties in, 170-192, 197-199; for President, 190-201, 278; values of, 170
Electoral College, 192-197; 199-201, 278
Employment: civil rights law and, 362; federal, 432-433, 437, 445-447, *chart,* 447; issue in Gary steel case, 58-61; state-local, 558, 568, *chart,* 563; and voting rights of blacks, 213
Employment Act of 1946, 296
Energy crisis, 452; bureaucratic decisions and, 453, 454; in Oregon, 506-507
Engle, Clair, 369
Environmental protection: air pollution law, 564; aircraft noise case, 462-477; in Gary steel case, 58-61; judgments about, 44-46; in Oregon, 500-507; road-salting case, 559, 564
Environmental Protection Agency (EPA), 58-61, 449, 450
Equal protection clause, 400, 419-421
Erickson, Donald, quoted, 111-112
Ervin, Sam, 369; quoted, 426-427

Quillayute River, 164
Quorum, 339

Radical identity: of members of Congress, 335; party preference and, 228-229; political participation and, 204, 205
Racial imbalance law, 564
Radicals, 147
Radio: members of Congress and, 339; President and, 325-326; regulation of, 455
Random samples, 66-71
Rankin, Jeannette, 136
Reagan, Ronald, 569-571
Real cases, rule on, 397-398
Reciprocity, in Congress, 354, 372
Referendum, 502
Registration, voter, 211-212; blacks and, 214, 215-216; parties and, 179; in Tuskegee, 245
Religion: Amish school case, 106-115; freedom of, 95-96; 384-390; groups, 25-26; party preference and, 228-229
Religious identity: of members of Congress, 355; presidential selection and, 283
Republican form of government, 263-264
Republican party: civil rights law and, 362, 365, 368; in election campaigns, 184, 191, 192, 237-239; in Oregon, 502; policies, 234; voter preference for, 228-229; 232-234, 235, 250-251
Reserved powers, 264, 265, 484-485
Residency: for election to Congress, 334; voting rights and, 208-209, 212
Resources: fitting activities to, 29-30; of interest groups, 36-37, 39-40
Rewards: of party participation, 180-182; political behavior and, 14
Rhode Island, 64, 486
Richardson, Elliott, 445 447
Rider, legislative, 372
Rights, individual, 102-104
Riots: President and, 293; urban, in 1960s, 153-155
Rituals, elections as, 248-249
Rizzo, Frank J., 64-65
Road salting, 559
Robertson, Willis, 366
Rockefeller, Nelson, 184, 279, 283
Roles: in Congress, 337-358; in high school, 267-268; of President, 285-301; statuses and, 116-122
Roosevelt, Franklin D., 71, 238, 284, 288,292; photos, 239, 293; quoted; 308; radio and, 310; Supreme Court and, 396

Roosevelt, Theodore, 284
Ruckelshaus, William, 445
Rules: as aspect of political behavior, 11-14; basic governmental, 262-266; bureaucrats and, 440, 443, 454; congressional, 334-337, 344-354, 371-372; formal and informal, 84; mayors and, 517; President and, 276-285, 306-307; in principal's role, 268; in state legislatures, 525-526; for Supreme Court, 395-401
Rules Committee, 352-353
"Run-off" election, 173
Rusk, Dean, 304

Sampling, 47-48, 66-71, 74
San Bernardino County, 486
San Francisco, 488
San Jose, California, 137
Saudi Arabia, government in, 86-87
School board, 491, 533, 536
School districts, 491
School-lunch program, 262
Schools, see Education
Schurz, Carl, quoted, 158
Secondary groups, and voting, 230-232
Security leaks, 326
Segregation: court cases on, 417-421; laws, 160-162
Selectmen, board of, 490
Self-incrimination, 415
Selma, Alabama, 244
Senate, United States: in check-and-balance system, 265, 266; Chief Justice and, 425-430; in presidential elections, 194, 196-197; road to Presidency and, 282; special powers of, 287, 292. See also Congress
Senatorial courtesy, 307
Seniority, in Congress, 352-357, 363-364
Sentencing, in criminal cases, 552
"Separate but equal" doctrine, 419-421
Separation of powers, 265-266, 329; diagrams, 88, 89; in local government, 533
Setlow, Carolyn, 135
Sex identity: of bureaucrats, 448; of members of Congress, 335; party preference and, 228-229
Sex-typing, of occupations, 141
Sharp, Judge Alan, 60-61
Sharp, Judge Susie, 137
Sheriff, county, 488
Sherrill, Robert, quoted, 462
Shoreline Airport Case, 14-19
Shriver, Sargent, 196
Sierra Club, 26, 29, 31, 44, 45, 46

Simpson, Dick, quoted, 255, 257
Sirica, John, 328
Sixth Amendment, 406, 407, 408
Slander, 80
Slums, case on, 128-134
Small claims courts, 555-557
Smith, Alfred E., 65
Smith, Howard W., 363, 364
Smith, Margaret Chase, 136
Smith, Mary Louise, photo, 179
Smith v. Allbright, 214
Social categories, 230
Social forces, courts and, 417-421
Social groups, voting and, 230-233
Social Security Act, 569; party platforms and, 234
Social status, 116-134
Socialization, 97-100, 144
Socioeconomic status, 122-134; characteristics of, 123-124; defined, 122; influence and, 124, 126-134; involvement in politics and, 217, 218; of members of Congress, 335; of presidential candidates, 283
Sorenson, Theodore C., quoted, 302
South: black officials in, 244; voting rights in, 209-210
South Dakota, 211
Southern Christian Leadership Conference, 160, 359
Soviet Union: as autocracy, 102; in Cuban missile crisis, 315-323; elections in, 172
Spano v. New York, 416
Speaker, in legislature, 524
Special districts, 491, 535-536; table, 490
Specialization, in Congress, 350-352
Speech, freedom of, 158
Split ticket, 232, 252-253
Stare decisis, 411
Stassen, Harold, 429
State, Department of, 440, 446, 480; in Cuban crisis, 317-322; Secretary, 289
State government: in Amish school case, 110-115; bureaucracies, 558-571; courts, 390-393, 540-557; election laws, 207-216; in fish-in case, 160-165; governors in, 494-507; gun control case, 33-36; legislatures, 522-532; nature of, 484-492; in school prayer case, 385-390; women in, 137
State of the Union message, 287, 294
Status and role, 116-122
Status relationships: of bureaucrats, 454-457; in Congress, 372, 373; of Presidents, 307-308
Steel production case, 58-61
Steinem, Gloria, 134-135

600

# Picture Credits

Production
Craven & Evans/Creative Graphics

Illustration
Randall McKissick, Jim Stewart,
Vantage Art

Cover Design
Captain Graphics, Inc.

Photography
Unit One
22 *tl*, Russ Adams, Courtesy of U. S.
Tennis Association
*tr*, Courtesy of Mayor Tom Bradley
*bl*, CBS News
*br*, Xerox Corporation
23 *tl*, Courtesy of *The Washington
Post*
*tr*, Cary Hertz
*bl*, AFL-CIO
*br*, Mayor's Office, Los Angeles
30 *tl*, Wide World Photos
*bl*, Carlo Bavagnoli from Time/Life
*r*, Arthur Tress from Magnum
Photos
39 Joseph Muench
42 UPI
45 EPA-DOCUMERICA, Boyd Norton
50 Molly Heron
58 EPA-DOCUMERICA, Paul
Sequeira
59 Courtesy, American Iron and Steel
Institute

Unit Two
79 John Launois from Black Star
86 G. D. Hackett
96 *tl*, Courtesy, Maryknoll Fathers
*r*, Burt Glinn from Magnum Photos
*bl*, Joan Menschenfreund
98 *tl*, Eve Arnold from Magnum
Photos
*tr*, Cary Wolinsky from Stock Boston
*bl*, Dick Raphael
*br*, Cornell Capa from Magnum
Photos
101 *t*, Sovfoto
*b*, Wide World Photos
107 Black Star
108 *tl*,EPA-DOCUMERICA, Frank
Aleksanrowicz
*tr*, Alex Webb from Magnum
Photos
*bl*, John Launois from Black Star
*br*, Black Star
109 *t*, *bl*, John Launois from Black Star
*br*, Black Star
114 *Des Moines Register & Tribune*
129 EPA-DOCUMERICA, Danny Lyon
133 *l*, Richard Balagur from Nancy
Palmer Agency
*r*, William Ives

136 *l*, Wide World Photos
*r*, Cary Herz
137 *l*, Office of the Secretary of State,
California
*r*, Randall Page
139 Wide World Photos
143 *t*, Michal Heron
*b*, Courtesy, Girl Scouts of
America
148 Peter Southwick from Stock Boston
ton
150 UPI
151 National Archives
152 Wide World Photos
154 Wide World Photos
164 Wide World Photos

Unit Three
169 *l*, Dick Swanson from Black Star
*r*, Jack Fields from Photo
Researchers
179 Courtesy, Republican National
Committee
181 Acme
182 Claude Lejeune from Black Star
193 *l*, Wide World Photos
*tr*, Constantine Manos from
Magnum Photos
*br*, Burt Glinn from Magnum
Photos
208 Courtesy, U. S. News & World
Report
215 UPI
221 Courtesy of Ronald V. Dellums
222 Alex Webb from Magnum Photos
224 Ted Rushton, Office of the Governor, Arizona
231 Courtesy, United Auto Workers
234 Courtesy, Republican National
Committee
238 Culver Pictures
239 *tl*, John F. Kennedy Library
*tr*, Wide World Photos
*bl*, Franklin D. Roosevelt Library
*br*, Cornell Capa from Magnum
Photos
241 *l*, Wide World Photos
*r*, Lee Goff from Magnum Photos
247 Mayor's Office, City of Tuskegee,
Alabama
251 Office of the Governor, State of
Maine
255 Hiroji Kubota from Magnum
Photos

Unit Four
261 Molly Heron
269 Joan Menschenfreund
274 *t*, UPI
*bl*, *The New York Times*
*br*, Massachusetts Bankers Assn.
277 Dennis Brack from Black Star
279 Wide World Photos
286 Wide World Photos
291 Wide World Photos
293 F. D. Roosevelt Library
295 UPI
301 UPI

305 Wide World Photos
306 The Bettman Archive
309 The Advertising Council, Inc.
316 Art Rickerby from Black Star
318 UPI
321 John F. Kennedy Library
322 UPI
327 Courtesy, *The Washington Post*
336 U. S. Capitol Historical Society
346 U. S. Capitol Historical Society
349 Sepp Seitz from Magnum Photos
355 UPI
361 Fred Ward from Black Star
367 Wide World Photos
370 The Lyndon Baines Johnson
Library
387 Wide World Photos
399 Paul Conklin from Monkmeyer
Press Photos
402 National Geographic Society
418 Bob Adelman from Magnum
Photos
423 UPI
426 Wide World Photos
429 UPI
446 Tony Jackson, photographer, U. S.
Civil Service Commission
449 UPI
453 Werner Wolff from Black Star
454 Dennis Brack from Black Star
458 U. S. Department of Agriculture
460 "How to Pump Up a Ham." Reprinted with permission from
"The Great Ham Robbery."
*Consumer Reports*, March, 1961.
Copyright 1961 by Consumers
Union of U. S., Inc., a nonprofit
organization.
466 Federal Aviation Administration

Unit Five
489 Stephen Whitney
495 *t*, UPI
*bl*, Mark Nohl
*br*, Doug Bruce from Camera 5
498 Courtesy of Richard B. Ogilvie
504 James Clautier
507 *l*, EPA-DOCUMERICA, David
Falconer
*r*, Joan Menschenfreund
516 Courtesy of Janet Gray Hayes
525 Owen Franken from Stock Boston
526 *l*, Mimi Forsyth from Monkmeyer
Press Photos
*tr*, Ron Sherman from Nancy
Palmer Agency
*br*, Wide World Photos
535 Cary Wolinsky from Stock Boston
538 Courtesy, Office of the Mayor, City
of New Orleans
542 Joan Menschenfreund
560 *tl*,EPA-DOCUMERICA, Dan McCoy
*tr*, Alex Webb from Magnum
Photos
*b*, U. S. Department of Agriculture
568 Burt Glinn from Magnum Photos
570 Sybil Shelton from Monkmeyer
Press Photos

DEFGHIJ   0798